POETRY
for Students

Advisors

Jayne M. Burton is a teacher of secondary English and an adjunct professor for Northwest Vista College in San Antonio, TX.

Klaudia Janek is the school librarian at the International Academy in Bloomfield Hills, Michigan. She holds an MLIS degree from Wayne State University, a teaching degree from Rio Salado College, and a bachelor of arts degree in international relations from Saint Joseph's College. She is the IB Extended Essay Coordinator and NCA AdvancEd co-chair at her school. She is an IB workshop leader for International Baccalaureate North America, leading teacher training for IB school librarians and extended essay coordinators. She has been happy to serve the Michigan Association for Media in Education as a board member and past president at the regional level, advocating for libraries in Michigan schools.

Greg Bartley is an English teacher in Virginia. He holds an M.A.Ed. in English Education from Wake Forest University and a B.S. in Integrated Language Arts Education from Miami University.

Sarah Clancy teaches IB English at the International Academy in Bloomfield Hills, Michigan. She is a member of the National Council of Teachers of English and Michigan Speech Coaches, Inc. Sarah earned her undergraduate degree from Kalamazoo College and her Master's of Education from Florida Southern College. She coaches the high-ranking forensics team and is the staff adviser of the school newspaper, *Overachiever*.

Karen Dobson is a teen/adult librarian at Plymouth District Library in Plymouth, Michigan. She holds a Bachelor of Science degree from Oakland University and an MLIS from Wayne State University and has served on many committees through the Michigan Library Association.

Tom Shilts is the youth librarian at the Okemos branch of Capital Area District Library in Okemos, Michigan. He holds an MSLS degree from Clarion University of Pennsylvania and an MA in U.S. History from the University of North Dakota.

POETRY
for Students

**Presenting Analysis, Context, and Criticism on
Commonly Studied Poetry**

VOLUME 52

Sara Constantakis, Project Editor

Foreword by David J. Kelly

GALE
CENGAGE Learning·

Farmington Hills, Mich • San Francisco • New York • Waterville, Maine
Meriden, Conn • Mason, Ohio • Chicago

Poetry for Students, Volume 52

Project Editor: Sara Constantakis

Rights Acquisition and Management: Moriam Aigoro, Ashley Maynard, Carissa Poweleit

Composition: Evi Abou-El-Seoud

Manufacturing: Rhonda Dover

Imaging: John Watkins

For product information and technology assistance, contact us at
Gale Customer Support, 1-800-877-4253.
For permission to use material from this text or product,
submit all requests online at **www.cengage.com/permissions**.
Further permissions questions can be emailed to
permissionrequest@cengage.com

Gale
27500 Drake Rd.
Farmington Hills, MI, 48331-3535

ISBN-13: 978-1-4103-1448-2
ISSN 1094-7019

This title is also available as an e-book.
ISBN-13: 978-1-4103-1451-2
Contact your Gale, a part of Cengage Learning sales representative for ordering information.

Printed in Mexico
1 2 3 4 5 6 7 20 19 18 17 16

Table of Contents

Just a Few Lines on a Page

I have often thought that poets have the easiest job in the world. A poem, after all, is just a few lines on a page, usually not even extending margin to margin—how long would that take to write, about five minutes? Maybe ten at the most, if you wanted it to rhyme or have a repeating meter. Why, I could start in the morning and produce a book of poetry by dinnertime. But we all know that it isn't that easy. Anyone can come up with enough words, but the poet's job is about writing the *right* ones. The right words will change lives, making people see the world somewhat differently than they saw it just a few minutes earlier. The right words can make a reader who relies on the dictionary for meanings take a greater responsibility for his or her own personal understanding. A poem that is put on the page correctly can bear any amount of analysis, probing, defining, explaining, and interrogating, and something about it will still feel new the next time you read it.

It would be fine with me if I could talk about poetry without using the word "magical," because that word is overused these days to imply "a really good time," often with a certain sweetness about it, and a lot of poetry is neither of these. But if you stop and think about magic—whether it brings to mind sorcery, witchcraft, or bunnies pulled from top hats—it always seems to involve stretching reality to produce a result greater than the sum of its parts and pulling unexpected results out of thin air. This book provides ample cases where a few simple words conjure up whole worlds. We do not actually travel to different times and different cultures, but the poems get into our minds, they find what little we know about the places they are talking about, and then they make that little bit blossom into a bouquet of someone else's life. Poets make us think we are following simple, specific events, but then they leave ideas in our heads that cannot be found on the printed page. Abracadabra.

Sometimes when you finish a poem it doesn't feel as if it has left any supernatural effect on you, like it did not have any more to say beyond the actual words that it used. This happens to everybody, but most often to inexperienced readers: regardless of what is often said about young people's infinite capacity to be amazed, you have to understand what usually does happen, and what could have happened instead, if you are going to be moved by what someone has accomplished. In those cases in which you finish a poem with a "So what?" attitude, the information provided in *Poetry for Students* comes in handy. Readers can feel assured that the poems included here actually are potent magic, not just because a few (or a hundred or ten thousand) professors of literature say they are: they're significant because they can withstand close inspection and still amaze the very same people who have just finished taking them apart and seeing how they work. Turn them inside out, and they will still be able to come alive, again and again. *Poetry for Students* gives readers of any age good practice in feeling the ways poems relate to both the reality of the time and place the poet lived in and the reality of our emotions. Practice is just another word for being a student. The information given here helps you understand the way to read poetry; what to look for, what to expect.

With all of this in mind, I really don't think I would actually like to have a poet's job at all. There are too many skills involved, including precision, honesty, taste, courage, linguistics, passion, compassion, and the ability to keep all sorts of people entertained at once. And that is just what they do with one hand, while the other hand pulls some sort of trick that most of us will never fully understand. I can't even pack all that I need for a weekend into one suitcase, so what would be my chances of stuffing so much life into a few lines? With all that *Poetry for Students* tells us about each poem, I am impressed that any poet can finish three or four poems a year. Read the inside stories of these poems, and you won't be able to approach any poem in the same way you did before.

David J. Kelly
College of Lake County

Introduction

Purpose of the Book

The purpose of *Poetry for Students* (*PfS*) is to provide readers with a guide to understanding, enjoying, and studying poems by giving them easy access to information about the work. Part of Gale's "For Students" Literature line, *PfS* is specifically designed to meet the curricular needs of high school and undergraduate college students and their teachers, as well as the interests of general readers and researchers considering specific poems. While each volume contains entries on "classic" poems frequently studied in classrooms, there are also entries containing hard-to-find information on contemporary poems, including works by multicultural, international, and women poets.

The information covered in each entry includes an introduction to the poem and the poem's author; the actual poem text (if possible); a poem summary, to help readers unravel and understand the meaning of the poem; analysis of important themes in the poem; and an explanation of important literary techniques and movements as they are demonstrated in the poem.

In addition to this material, which helps the readers analyze the poem itself, students are also provided with important information on the literary and historical background informing each work. This includes a historical context essay, a box comparing the time or place the poem was written to modern Western culture, a critical overview essay, and excerpts from critical essays on the poem. A unique feature of *PfS* is a specially commissioned critical essay on each poem, targeted toward the student reader.

To further help today's student in studying and enjoying each poem, information on audio recordings and other media adaptations is provided (if available), as well as reading suggestions for works of fiction and nonfiction on similar themes and topics. Classroom aids include ideas for research papers and lists of critical and reference sources that provide additional material on the poem.

Selection Criteria

The titles for each volume of *PfS* are selected by surveying numerous sources on notable literary works and analyzing course curricula for various schools, school districts, and states. Some of the sources surveyed include: high school and undergraduate literature anthologies and textbooks; lists of award-winners, and recommended titles, including the Young Adult Library Services Association (YALSA) list of best books for young adults.

Input solicited from our expert advisory board—consisting of educators and librarians—guides us to maintain a mix of "classic" and contemporary literary works, a mix of challenging and engaging works (including genre titles that are commonly studied) appropriate for different age levels, and a mix of international, multicultural and women authors. These advisors also consult on each volume's entry list, advising on which titles are most studied, most appropriate, and meet the broadest interests across secondary (grades 7–12) curricula and undergraduate literature studies.

How Each Entry Is Organized

Each entry, or chapter, in *PfS* focuses on one poem. Each entry heading lists the full name of the poem, the author's name, and the date of the poem's publication. The following elements are contained in each entry:

Introduction: a brief overview of the poem which provides information about its first appearance, its literary standing, any controversies surrounding the work, and major conflicts or themes within the work.

Author Biography: this section includes basic facts about the poet's life, and focuses on events and times in the author's life that inspired the poem in question.

Poem Text: when permission has been granted, the poem is reprinted, allowing for quick reference when reading the explication of the following section.

Poem Summary: a description of the major events in the poem. Summaries are broken down with subheads that indicate the lines being discussed.

Themes: a thorough overview of how the major topics, themes, and issues are addressed within the poem. Each theme discussed appears in a separate subhead.

Style: this section addresses important style elements of the poem, such as form, meter, and rhyme scheme; important literary devices used, such as imagery, foreshadowing, and symbolism; and, if applicable, genres to which the work might have belonged, such as Gothicism or Romanticism. Literary terms are explained within the entry, but can also be found in the Glossary.

Historical Context: this section outlines the social, political, and cultural climate in which the author lived and the poem was created. This section may include descriptions of related historical events, pertinent aspects of daily life in the culture, and the artistic and literary sensibilities of the time in which the work was written. If the poem is

a historical work, information regarding the time in which the poem is set is also included. Each section is broken down with helpful subheads.

Critical Overview: this section provides background on the critical reputation of the poem, including bannings or any other public controversies surrounding the work. For older works, this section includes a history of how the poem was first received and how perceptions of it may have changed over the years; for more recent poems, direct quotes from early reviews may also be included.

Criticism: an essay commissioned by *PfS* which specifically deals with the poem and is written specifically for the student audience, as well as excerpts from previously published criticism on the work (if available).

Sources: an alphabetical list of critical material quoted in the entry, with full bibliographical information.

Further Reading: an alphabetical list of other critical sources which may prove useful for the student. Includes full bibliographical information and a brief annotation.

Suggested Search Terms: a list of search terms and phrases to jumpstart students' further information seeking. Terms include not just titles and author names but also terms and topics related to the historical and literary context of the works.

In addition, each entry contains the following highlighted sections, set apart from the main text as sidebars:

Media Adaptations: if available, a list of audio recordings as well as any film or television adaptations of the poem, including source information.

Topics for Further Study: a list of potential study questions or research topics dealing with the poem. This section includes questions related to other disciplines the student may be studying, such as American history, world history, science, math, government, business, geography, economics, psychology, etc.

Compare & Contrast: an "at-a-glance" comparison of the cultural and historical differences between the author's time and culture and late twentieth century or early twenty-first century Western culture. This box includes pertinent parallels between the major scientific, political, and cultural movements of the time or place the poem was written, the time or place the poem was set (if a historical work), and modern Western culture. Works written after 1990 may not have this box.

What Do I Read Next?: a list of works that might give a reader points of entry into a classic work (e.g., YA or multicultural titles) and/or complement the featured poem or serve as a contrast to it. This includes works by the same author and others, works from various genres, YA works, and works from various cultures and eras.

Other Features

PfS includes "Just a Few Lines on a Page," a foreword by David J. Kelly, an adjunct professor of English, College of Lake County, Illinois. This essay provides a straightforward, unpretentious explanation of why poetry should be marveled at and how *PfS* can help teachers show students how to enrich their own reading experiences.

A Cumulative Author/Title Index lists the authors and titles covered in each volume of the *PfS* series.

A Cumulative Nationality/Ethnicity Index breaks down the authors and titles covered in each volume of the *PfS* series by nationality and ethnicity.

A Subject/Theme Index, specific to each volume, provides easy reference for users who may be studying a particular subject or theme rather than a single work. Significant subjects from events to broad themes are included.

A Cumulative Index of First Lines (beginning in Vol. 10) provides easy reference for users who may be familiar with the first line of a poem but may not remember the actual title.

A Cumulative Index of Last Lines (beginning in Vol. 10) provides easy reference for users who may be familiar with the last line of a poem but may not remember the actual title.

Each entry may include illustrations, including photo of the author and other graphics related to the poem.

Citing Poetry for Students

When writing papers, students who quote directly from any volume of *PfS* may use the following general forms. These examples are based on MLA style; teachers may request that students adhere to a different style, so the following examples may be adapted as needed.

When citing text from *PfS* that is not attributed to a particular author (i.e., the Themes, Style, Historical Context sections, etc.), the following format should be used in the bibliography section:

> "Grace." *Poetry for Students.* Ed. Sara Constantakis. Vol. 44. Detroit: Gale, Cengage Learning, 2013. 66–86. Print.

When quoting the specially commissioned essay from *PfS* (usually the first piece under the "Criticism" subhead), the following format should be used:

> Andersen, Susan. Critical Essay on "Grace." *Poetry for Students.* Ed. Sara Constantakis. Vol. 44. Detroit: Gale, Cengage Learning, 2013. 77–80. Print.

When quoting a journal or newspaper essay that is reprinted in a volume of *PfS,* the following form may be used:

> Molesworth, Charles. "Proving Irony by Compassion: The Poetry of Robert Pinsky." *Hollins Critic* 21.5 (1984): 1–18. Rpt. in *Poetry for Students.* Ed. Sara Constantakis. Vol. 44. Detroit: Gale, Cengage Learning, 2013. 189–92. Print.

When quoting material reprinted from a book that appears in a volume of *PfS,* the following form may be used:

> Flora, Joseph M. "W. E. Henley, Poet." *William Ernest Henley.* New York: Twayne, 1970. 119–41. Rpt. in *Poetry for Students.* Ed. Sara Constantakis. Vol. 43. Detroit: Gale, 213. 150–52. Print.

We Welcome Your Suggestions

The editorial staff of *Poetry for Students* welcomes your comments and ideas. Readers who wish to suggest poems to appear in future volumes, or who have other suggestions, are cordially invited to contact the editor. You may contact the editor via E-mail at: **ForStudentsEditors@cengage.com.** Or write to the editor at:

Editor, *Poetry for Students*

Gale

27500 Drake Road

Farmington Hills, MI 48331-3535

Literary Chronology

c. 612 BCE: Sappho is born in Eresos, on the Greek island of Lesbos.

c. 590s–580s BCE: Sappho composes "He seems to be a god."

c. 580 BCE: Sappho dies of unknown causes on the Greek island of Lesbos.

1564: William Shakespeare is born around April 26 in Stratford-upon-Avon, England.

1609: William Shakespeare's Sonnet 60 is published in *Sonnets*.

1616: William Shakespeare dies of unknown causes on April 23 in Stratford-upon-Avon, England.

1788: Lord Byron is born on January 22 in London, England.

1807: Henry Wadsworth Longfellow is born on February 27 in Portland, Maine.

1824: Lord Byron dies of fever on April 19 in Mesolonghi, Greece.

1830: Lord Byron's "So We'll Go No More A Roving" is published in *Letters and Journals of Lord Byron, with Notices of His Life, by Thomas Moore*.

1860: Henry Wadsworth Longfellow's "The Children's Hour" is published in *Atlantic*.

1882: Henry Wadsworth Longfellow dies of peritonitis on March 24 in Cambridge, Massachusetts.

1913: Muriel Rukeyser is born on December 15 in New York City, New York.

1922: Jack Kerouac is born on March 12 in Lowell, Massachusetts.

1926: Ingeborg Bachmann is born on June 26 in Klagenfurt, Austria.

1939: Seamus Heaney is born on April 13 in Castledawson, County Londonderry, Northern Ireland.

1941: Mahmoud Darwish is born on March 13 in al-Birwa, Palestine.

1947: Jane Kenyon is born on May 23 in Ann Arbor, Michigan.

1949: Bei Dao is born on August 2 in Beijing, China.

1952: Gary Soto is born on April 12 in Fresno, California.

1954: Sandra Cisneros is born on December 20 in Chicago, Illinois.

1955: Cathy Song is born on August 20 in Honolulu, Hawaii.

1956: Ingeborg Bachmann's "An die Sonne" is published in *Anrufung des Großen Bären*. It is published in English as "To the Sun" in *Encounter* in 1964.

1960: Katia Kapovich is born in Kishinev, Moldavian Soviet Socialist Republic.

1964: Mahmoud Darwish's "Identity Card" is published in Arabic as "Bitaqat Hawiyyah" in *Awraq Al-Zaytun*. It is published in English in the United States in *Leaves of Olives*.

1966: Seamus Heaney's "Mid-Term Break" is published in *Death of a Naturalist*.

1966: Natasha Trethewey is born on April 26 in Gulfport, Mississippi.

1968: Muriel Rukeyser's "Poem" is published in *The Speed of Darkness*.

1969: Jack Kerouac dies of internal bleeding due to years of heavy drinking on October 21 in St. Petersburg, FL.

1973: Ingeborg Bachmann dies of burns and drug withdrawal on October 17 in Rome, Italy.

1976: Bei Dao's "The Answer" is published in Chinese as "Huida" in *Bei Dao shixuan*. It is published in English in the United States in 1988 in *The August Sleepwalker*.

1980: Muriel Rukeyser dies of a stroke on February 12 in New York City, New York.

1988: Cathy Song's "Heaven" is published in *Frameless Windows, Squares of Light*.

1991: Gary Soto's "Saturday at the Canal" is published in *Home Course in Religion: New Poems*.

1992: Jack Kerouac's "Nebraska;" is published in *Pomes All Sizes*.

1994: Sandra Cisneros's "Loose Woman" is published in *Loose Woman*.

1995: Seamus Heaney is awarded the Nobel Prize in Literature.

1995: Jane Kenyon's "Reading Aloud to My Father" is published in *Poetry*.

1995: Jane Kenyon dies of leukemia on April 22 in Wilmot, New Hampshire.

2003: Katia Kapovich's "They Called Them 'Blue'" is published in *Jacket*.

2007: Natasha Trethewey is awarded the Pulitzer Prize for Poetry for *Native Guard*.

2008: Mahmoud Darwish dies of complications brought on by heart surgery on August 9 in Houston, Texas.

2012: Natasha Trethewey's "Enlightenment" is published in *Thrall*.

2013: Seamus Heaney dies after an illness on August 30 in Dublin, Ireland.

Acknowledgements

The editors wish to thank the copyright holders of the excerpted criticism included in this volume and the permission managers of many book and magazine publishing companies for assisting us in securing reproduction rights. We are also grateful to the staffs of the Detroit Public Library, the Library of Congress, the University of Detroit Mercy Library, Wayne State University Purdy/ Kresge Library Complex, and the University of Michigan Libraries for making their resources available to us. Following is a list of the copyright holders who have granted us permission to reproduce material in this volume of *PfS*. Every effort has been made to trace copyright, but if omissions have been made, please let us know.

COPYRIGHTED EXCERPTS IN PfS, VOLUME 52, WERE REPRODUCED FROM THE FOLLOWING PERIODICALS:

American Conservative, vol. 14, 2, March-April 2015. Copyright © 2015 *American Conservative.—Americas*, vol. 61, 3, May-June 2009. Copyright © 2009 *Americas.—Antioch Review*, vol. 65, 4, Fall 2007. Copyright © 2007 *The Antioch Review.—Atlantic*, August 14, 2012. Copyright © 2012 Alex Hoyt.—*Booklist*, vol. 90, 17, May 1, 1994. Copyright © 1994 *Booklist Online.—Harvard Review*, 30, June 2006. Copyright © 2006 *Harvard Review.—Horn Book*, vol. 85, 2, March-April 2009. Copyright © 2009 The Horn Book, Inc.—*Journal of Beat Studies*, vol. 2, 2013. Copyright © 2013 Cary Nelson.—*Journal of Jewish Women's Studies and Gender Issues*, vol. 19, Spring 2010. Copyright © 2010 Indiana University Press (Books).—*New Criterion*, vol. 19, 4, December, 2000. Copyright © 2000 John Derbyshire.—*New Yorker*, vol. 91, 4, March 16, 2015. Copyright © 2015 Daniel Mendelsohn.—*Prairie Schooner*, vol. 77, 4, Winter 2003. Copyright © 2003 *Prairie Schooner.—Publishers Weekly*, vol. 238, 18, April 19. 1991. Copyright © 1991 *Publishers Weekly.—Publishers Weekly*, vol. 239, 49, November 9, 1992. Copyright © 1992 *Publishers Weekly.—Publishers Weekly*, vol. 249, 8, February 25, 2002. Copyright © 2002 *Publishers Weekly.—Studies in English Literature*, 1500-1900, vol. 34, 4, Fall 1994. Copyright © 1994 John Hopkins University Press.—*Women's Review of Books*, vol. 13, 10-11, July 1996. Copyright © 1996 *Women's Review of Books.—Women's Review of Books*, vol. 23, 5, September-October 2006. Copyright © 2006 *Women's Review of Books.—World Literature Today*, vol. 75, Summer-Autumn 2001. Copyright © 2001 *World Literature Today.—World Literature Today*, vol. 78, 3-4, September-December 2004. Copyright © 2004 *World Literature Today.—World Literature Today*, vol. 83, 3, May-June 2009. Copyright © 2009 *World Literature Today.*

COPYRIGHTED EXCERPTS IN PfS, VOLUME 52, WERE REPRODUCED FROM THE FOLLOWING BOOKS:

Achberger, Karen R. From *Understanding Ingeborg Bachmann*, 1995. © 1995 University of South Carolina Press.—Baker, William. From *William Shakespeare*, 2009. © 2009 Bloomsbury Publishing.—Bei Dao. From *The August Sleepwalker*, 1988. © 1988 New Directions Publishing Corporation.—Lord Byron. From *Byron: Poetical Works*, Frederick Page, ed., 1970. © 1970 Oxford University Press.—Collins, Floyd. From *Seamus Heaney: The Crisis of Identity*, 2003. © 2003 Associated University Presses.—Darwish, Mahmoud. From *Mahmoud Darwish: The Poet's Art and His Nation*, 2014. © 2014 Syracuse University Press.—Foster, Thomas C. From *Seamus Heaney*, 1989. © 1989 Cengage Learning.—Grace, Nancy M. From *Jack Kerouac and the Literary Imagination*, 2007. © 2007 Palgrave Macmillan Ltd.—Heinzelman, Kurt. From *Critical Essays on Lord Byron*, Robert F. Gleckner, ed., 1991. © 1991 Cengage Learning.—Kenyon, Jane. From *Otherwise: New and Selected Poems*, 1997. © 1997 Graywolf Press.—Kerouac, Jack. From *Poems All Sizes*, 1992. © 1992 City Lights Publishers.—Longfellow, Henry Wadsworth. From *Tales of a Wayside Inn*, 1863. © 1863 Ticknor and Fields.—Mattawa, Khalled. From *Mahmoud Darwish: The Poet's Art and His Nation*, 2014. © 2014 Syracuse University Press.—Neuwirth, Angelika. From *Arabic Literature: Postmodern Perspectives*, Angelika Neuwirth, Andreas Pflitsch, and Barbara Winckler, eds., 2010. © 2010 Saqi Books.—Perez-Torres, Rafael. From *Modern American Literature*, 1999. © 1999 Cengage Learning.—Rust, Richard Dilworth. From *Fifteen American Authors before 1900: Bibliographic Essays on Research and Criticism*, Robert A. Rees and Earl N. Harbert eds., The University of Wisconsin Press, 1971. © 1971 The University of Wisconsin Press.—Sappho. From *Seven Greeks*, 1995. © 1995 New Directions Publishing Corporation.—Solberg, S.E. From *The Asian Pacific American Heritage: A Companion to Literature and Arts*, George J. Leonard, 1999. © 1999 Taylor & Francis Group.—Soto, Gary. From *Home Course in Religion: New Poems*, 1991. © 1991 Houghton Mifflin Company.—Sullivan, Nancy and Sandra Cisneros. From *Conversations with Mexican American Writers: Languages and Literatures in the Borderlands*, Elisabeth Mermann-Jozwiak and Nancy Sullivan, eds., 2009. © 2009 University of Mississippi Press.—Trethewey, Natasha. From *Thrall*, 2012. © 2012 Houghton Mifflin Company.—Van Dyne, Susan R. From *Re-placing America: Conversations and Contestations*, Ruth Hsu, Cynthia Franklin, and Suzanne Kosanke, eds., 2001. © 2001 University of Hawaii at Honolulu.

COPYRIGHTED EXCERPTS IN PfS, VOLUME 52, WERE REPRODUCED FROM THE FOLLOWING WEBSITES:

Fresh Air, 2012. Copyright © 2012 National Public Radio Inc. (NPR).—*TeachingBooks.net*, August 29, 2007. Copyright © 2007 TeachingBooks.net.

Contributors

Bryan Aubrey: Aubrey holds a PhD in English. Entry on "Reading Aloud to My Father." Original essay on "Reading Aloud to My Father."

Rita M. Brown: Brown is an English professor. Entries on "The Children's Hour" and "Sonnet 60." Original essays on "The Children's Hour" and "Sonnet 60."

Catherine DiMercurio: DiMercurio is a novelist and freelance writer and editor. Entry on "So, We'll Go No More a Roving." Original essay on "So, We'll Go No More a Roving."

Klay Dyer: Dyer is a freelance writer specializing in topics relating to literature, popular culture, and innovation. Entries on "Nebraska" and "Poem." Original essays on "Nebraska" and "Poem."

Kristen Sarlin Greenberg: Greenberg is a freelance writer and editor with a background in literature and philosophy. Entry on "Heaven." Original essay on "Heaven."

Michael Allen Holmes: Holmes is a writer with existential interests. Entries on "Saturday at the Canal," "They Called Them 'Blue'," and "To the Sun." Original essays on "Saturday at the Canal," "They Called Them 'Blue'," and "To the Sun."

Amy L. Miller: Miller is a graduate of the University of Cincinnati, and she currently resides in New Orleans, Louisiana. Entries on "The Answer" and "Identity Card." Original essays on "The Answer" and "Identity Card."

Michael J. O'Neal: O'Neal holds a PhD in English. Entry on "He Seems to Be a God." Original essay on "He Seems to Be a God."

April Paris: Paris is a freelance writer with a degree in classical literature and a background in academic writing. Entry on "Mid-Term Break." Original essay on "Mid-Term Break."

Bradley Skeen: Skeen is a classicist. Entries on "Enlightenment" and "Loose Woman." Original essays on "Enlightenment" and "Loose Woman."

The Answer

BEI DAO

1976

Bei Dao's poem "The Answer" ("Huida" in Chinese), published in 1976, is remarkable both for its beautiful surrealist imagery and for its immeasurable effect on the 1989 Tiananmen Square protests against Communism in the People's Republic of China. Written after Bei Dao participated in the Tiananmen Square demonstrations of 1976, in which more than one hundred thousand protesters stormed the surrounding government buildings, "The Answer" obliquely critiques the government with strong individualistic rhetoric. It culminates in the speaker's unapologetic declaration that he does not believe. This sentiment became the battle cry of the student protesters of the pro-democracy movement in Tiananmen Square in 1989 that led to Bei Dao's exile from China after the massacre.

Bei Dao begins "The Answer" by describing the nightmarish society in which he lives: the sky is clouded by the shadows of the dead. He does not believe in this corrupt and contradictory society and wishes for a new existence on a high peak. In this new world, where humanity is valued most, the light of the stars will shine down unobstructed, representing both the distant past and the future generations. Despite Bei Dao's brilliant subtlety and careful avoidance of direct political criticism, he was condemned as an enemy of the state, and his work was banned from publication. Its social impact aside, "The Answer" remains a work of undeniable skill and

Bei Dao (© *Alberto Paredes / Alamy*)

complexity as the speaker searches for a light in dark times. The poem appears in *The August Sleepwalker*, published in 1988.

AUTHOR BIOGRAPHY

Bei Dao, born Zhao Zhenkai in Beijing on August 2, 1949, was two months old when the People's Republic of China was formed. He came of age during the Cultural Revolution, a violent purge of perceived nonconformists led by the Communist Party leader Chairman Mao Zedong that plunged Chinese society into chaos. Bei Dao's education was interrupted when the revolution began in 1966. As a teenager, Bei Dao joined the Red Guard movement, enforcing the iron will of the revolution. Later, as a suspected nonconformist, he worked building roads and bridges and as a blacksmith as part of a reeducation program.

In the early 1970s, Bei Dao began to write surrealist poetry at odds with the Communist state–approved style of realism set forth by Mao's 1942 speech in Yan'an. Bei Dao founded the underground literary magazine *Jintian* ("Today") in 1978 with fellow poet Mang Ke. *Jintian* was officially banned by the state after nine issues, and the work collected within was deemed *menglong*, meaning "vague" or "obscure" (translated as "misty"). *Menglong shi ren*—or misty poetry as it was called in the West—became the most popular form of poetry among the student protesters who made up the democracy movement.

Bei Dao's dissident poem "The Answer" was taken up as an anthem by those opposed to Mao's oppressive rule. Written in 1976, after Bei Dao participated in demonstrations on Tiananmen Square, "The Answer" became enormously popular with protesters. It was reprinted on posters and chanted at rallies. Bei Dao became a powerful voice of the counterculture as a result of its popularity. The poem was collected in *The August Sleepwalker*, first published in English in 1988.

In 1989, while he was at a literary conference in Berlin, Germany, Bei Dao learned of the Tiananmen Square massacre, in which the Chinese People's Liberation Army opened fire on unarmed student protesters occupying the square. Exiled for his role as an inspirational figure to the protesters, Bei Dao lived, lectured, and taught throughout Europe and the United States. He was unable to reunite with his wife and daughter until seven years after the massacre.

As an exile, Bei Dao continued to publish poetry, such as the collections *Old Snow*, published in 1991, and *Unlock*, published in 2000; essays, including the collections *Blue House*, published in 1998, and *Midnight's Gate*, 2005; and short fiction, including the collection *Waves* in 1990. He brought *Jintian* back to life in 1990 as a magazine focused on Chinese people living abroad.

An international success, Bei Dao has won the Swedish PEN Tucholsky Award, the Struga Poetry Evenings Golden Wreath, the PEN/Barbara Goldsmith Freedom to Write Award, and the Argana International Poetry Award from the House of Poetry in Morocco. He was named as an honorary member of the American Academy of Arts and Letters and has been nominated for the Nobel Prize in Literature. His poetry has been translated into more than thirty languages. Bei Dao was not permitted to return to China until 2006, after seventeen years of exile.

POEM TEXT

> Debasement is the password of the base,
> Nobility the epitaph of the noble.
> See how the gilded sky is covered
> With the drifting twisted shadows of the dead.
>
> The Ice Age is over now,   5
> Why is there ice everywhere?
> The Cape of Good Hope has been discovered,
> Why do a thousand sails contest the Dead Sea?
>
> I came into this world
> Bringing only paper, rope, a shadow,   10
> To proclaim before the judgement
> The voice that has been judged:
>
> Let me tell you, world,
> I—do—not—believe!
> If a thousand challengers lie beneath your feet,   15
> Count me as number one thousand and one.
>
> I don't believe the sky is blue;
> I don't believe in thunder's echoes;
> I don't believe that dreams are false;
> I don't believe that death has no revenge.   20
>
> If the sea is destined to breach the dikes
> Let all the brackish water pour into my heart;
> If the land is destined to rise
> Let humanity choose a peak for existence again.
>
> A new conjunction and glimmering stars   25
> Adorn the unobstructed sky now:
> They are the pictographs from five thousand years.
> They are the watchful eyes of future generations.

POEM SUMMARY

The text used for this summary is from *The August Sleepwalker*, New Directions, 1988, p. 33. A version of the poem can be found on the following web page: http://www.poetryfoundation.org/poem/ 180413.

"The Answer" begins with a series of contrasts. The speaker notices that debasement is the secret of individuals who are base. Nobility is the particular doom of the nobles. Drifting shadow-memories of the dead mar the beauty of the golden sky. Though the Ice Age is long over, there is ice everywhere the speaker looks. Though the Cape of Good Hope has been discovered, sails blanket the stagnant waters of the Dead Sea. The speaker has entered the world

carrying only paper, rope, and a shadow with which to judge society's judgments. He tells the twisted world that he does not believe in it. If there are a thousand challengers already lying crumbled in defeat beneath the power of this society, he declares himself challenger number one thousand and one. The speaker does not believe the sky is blue. He does not believe that thunder echoes. He does not believe that dreams are not real. He does not believe that death does not seek revenge. If the sea fulfills its destiny and overflows the levees holding it back, let the salty water flow directly into the speaker's heart. If the land would rise, let humankind rebuild on a new, high peak. A new gathering of stars dots the night sky now. The view of the stars is clear from obstruction. The stars are photos of five thousand years past. They are the eyes of future generations, watching history unfold.

THEMES

Disillusionment

The speaker expresses his disillusionment with society through antitheses, negative imagery, and outright denial of commonly held beliefs. He begins by stating that nobles die for their nobility and that base people debase others. In this backward world, the sky rather than the ground is littered with the dead, the Dead Sea is crowded while the Cape of Good Hope is ignored, and the Ice Age has passed, but ice covers everything. These contradictory statements establish the poem's setting: an existential world devoid of sense, where destruction, death, and disconnectedness are favored over life, compassion, and love.

The speaker cannot live in the world he describes and fights its power by refusing to believe it is real. He denies the reality of such a society by claiming to question its rarely questioned facts: that the sky is blue, that dreams are not real, that thunder is not loud. This is his way of disobeying the logic of a society that he finds cruelly illogical. In his deep disillusionment with the way things are, he wishes to start anew—to be washed away in the waters of a breaking dam, to rebuild on a high mountaintop, where the constellations are clear. He seeks a culture that values not facts (blue sky, loud thunder)

TOPICS FOR FURTHER STUDY

- In a small group, choose a stanza from "The Answer" to explore further. What are the main images of the stanza, and what do you think they mean? How is the stanza you choose to examine similar to or different from the rest of the poem stylistically and thematically? Write down your group's thoughts on these questions in preparation for a class discussion.

- Read *Su Dongpo: Chinese Genius* (2006), by Demi, a book of poetry for young adults about the life of the great Chinese humanist Su Dongpo, who served as secretary to the emperor. Between what you know of Su Dongpo and of Bei Dao, how would you define humanism? Compared with Bei Dao, how did Su Dongpo express his humanism? Write a short review of Demi's book; include your thoughts on humanism.

- Create a blog dedicated to a Chinese poet of your choosing from any period in Chinese history. Compose at least five posts on the subject of your poet, including a brief biography, an explication of one of the poems, and background information about the time and place in which the poet lived. After you have completed your blog, visit the blogs of two of your classmates and leave a comment on one post in each blog. Respond thoughtfully to any comments you receive. The site blogspot.com is a source for free blog space.

- Write a poem using metaphor to compare two unlike things. Your poem can be funny or serious, rhymed or free verse, as long as you use your imagination and creativity to express yourself.

- What effect did the massacre in Tiananmen Square have outside China? Research online to learn how other nations responded to the events of 1989. Who is Tank Man, and what effect did he have on the global community's reaction to the massacre? Organize your thoughts into an essay; include citations of your online sources.

---

and death (in the sky, in the sea, and in revenge) but beauty, humanity, the past, and the future.

Hope

Despite the proliferation of negative and contradictory images in "The Answer," Bei Dao infuses the poem with an impressively hopeful conclusion. The speaker, after listing both his grievances against the cold world and his proclamation of defiance against its soulless logic, offers a solution. There is destined to be a new society, rebuilt once the old one meets its fate, destroyed in a flood (a symbol of the disillusioned masses rising against those few in power). Afterward humanity will rise again to a high peak—suggestive of a golden age of compassion among neighbors to replace the ice and death of the old world and its rigid rules.

Perched high on the summit of a mountain, free from obstacles blocking the view, the new society will see and contemplate the stars. Likewise, the stars will more easily observe the society below. The stars, a metaphor for both ancient ancestors and future generations looking back, shine in approval of the citizenry, who look up at them with an unobstructed view, as opposed to those in the old world, who could not see them past the dead cluttering the sky, past their contradictions and harsh lives.

Judgment

As society passes judgment on the speaker, the speaker passes judgment on society. He claims to have been born to sit in judgment of the voice of judgment and finds it wanting—too cold, too hypocritical, too morbid, and too unchanging. He renounces the society by

The poem's stark mood is set in the first stanza with the image of the sky hidden by shadows.
(© basel101658 / Shutterstock.com)

refusing to believe in its facts, joining thousands of others who feel the same disillusionment. The speaker understands that society will judge him whether or not he believes, but he does not recognize society's ability to judge correctly. He believes that members of society are irrational, that they have skewed values that undermine the quality of life.

The speaker is especially troubled by society's obsession with death, which he questions three times: once in the context of the dead who litter the sky, once in wonder at the fascination with the Dead Sea rather than the Cape of Good Hope, and once to deny society's belief that death has no revenge. Meanwhile, the speaker continually returns to the subject of life: his own birth, the cleansing rebirth of humanity, and the future generations waiting eagerly in the stars to take their turn on Earth. Rather than submit to the judgment of a society in whose logic he does not believe, the speaker wishes for humanity to be judged from the higher perspective of the stars—symbols of generations both future and past who look down with hope in their unclouded eyes.

STYLE

Antithesis

An antithesis is a direct opposite. For example, the antithesis of yes is no. In poetry, an antithesis is a figure of speech in which a thesis statement is immediately contrasted by the antithesis statement, creating a balance between the two opposing ideas. Bei Dao uses antithesis throughout "The Answer" to define the nonsensical nature of the world. He asks why ships crowd the Dead Sea when the Cape of Good Hope exists, playing on the names of these geographic entities (Good Hope and Dead) to point out society's macabre fascination with death and its lack of interest in peace and happiness. He asks why, if the Ice Age is over, there is ice everywhere. This is a comment on the cold distance between members of the same society and the emotional disconnection rampant in modern life. By using antithesis, Bei Dao indirectly critiques the absurdity of society by highlighting its hypocrisies.

Metaphor

A metaphor is a figure of speech in which two unrelated objects are compared directly. For example, in "The Answer," the stars are photographs taken five thousand years ago. The stars and the photographs are one and the same through their direct comparison. Bei Dao further complicates the image of the stars by adding a second metaphor: the stars are the eyes of future generations, watching. As a result of this double metaphor, time is expanded in the poem to include not only millennia past but also generations future, so that actions taken today are both the history of the future and the future of the past. Metaphors add symbolic significance to an image, like the stars that shine down on the speaker's statement of disbelief in a world whose rules do not suit him.

Symbol

A symbol in literature is something that stands for something else without losing its original identity. As a strongly political poem that never broaches the subject of politics, "The Answer" is littered with symbols, some easy to define, others more difficult. The ice that covers the land is a symbol of the frozen progress of the society. The Dead Sea is a symbol of stagnation. The flood that bursts the dikes is the flood of rising dissent against the regime, and the high peak on which humanity reestablishes itself is a symbol of an advanced new society free of corruption. The stars are symbols of both the past and the future. In Bei Dao's writing, which is intentionally obscure, symbols are sometimes private or inscrutable and are subject to multiple interpretations. Through assigning a hidden meaning to seemingly unrelated objects in "The Answer," Bei Dao points an accusatory finger at the government while retaining his distance from the subject.

HISTORICAL CONTEXT

Cultural Revolution

The People's Republic of China was formed in 1949 under Communist Party Chairman Mao Zedong. The Cultural Revolution, which lasted from 1966 until Mao's death in 1976, was a plan to consolidate his power through the elimination of dissidents after his disastrous Great Leap Forward social program lost forty-five million Chinese lives to starvation.

The Cultural Revolution sought to destroy all that had come before Mao and established the Red Guard (of which Bei Dao was briefly a member) to do so through violence, intimidation, and fear. A purge of Mao's closest officials and cabinet members began the revolution, followed by propaganda targeting the Four Olds—customs, culture, habits, and ideas—but lacking any specific detail, causing the movement to quickly spiral into chaos. Many historical landmarks, priceless texts, and religious sites were destroyed, anywhere from hundreds of thousands to three million people died as a result of torture, suicide, murder, and starvation.

Notices were posted in May 1966 claiming that bourgeois elements had infiltrated the People's Republic with plans to overthrow the Communist Party. This essentially turned the country's citizens against one another in an attempt to root out the capitalist spies allegedly embedded in their midst. By December 1967, 350 million copies of Mao's *Little Red Book* of quotations had been printed. In the hands of the Red Guard, the book was used to justify brutal actions against those perceived as nonconformists. The authority of the Red Guard trumped that of the police and military. There was no system in place to control their activities, and local governments, schools, and economies were brought to a standstill by the frenzied destructive force of the revolution.

In 1968, the Down to the Countryside movement slowed the pace of death and destruction as young adults from the city were sent to villages to learn from the peasants. In the absence of the Red Guards, the People's Liberation Army regained its military power.

As Mao's health declined, the Gang of Four carried on the Cultural Revolution, though years of chaos had taken its toll at all levels of Chinese society. When the Gang of Four restricted public displays of mourning after the death of Zhou Enlai, a popular political figure, the long-suffering citizenry turned on their leaders in the Tiananmen Square demonstrations of 1976—the inspiration for "The Answer." After the Gang of Four had the square cleared of the memorials left behind by more than two million mourners, violent protesters swarmed the square

COMPARE
&
CONTRAST

- **1976:** The final year of the Cultural Revolution sees Mao Zedong's death and the arrest of the Gang of Four in a political coup that begins a gradual reformation and reconstruction of the Chinese government.

  Today: Still governed by the Communist Party, the People's Republic of China has greatly relinquished control over citizens' everyday lives. The government's focus rests instead on economic development and globalization.

- **1976:** On April 4, 1976, as many as two million people take part in a national day of mourning, laying wreaths and memorials on Tiananmen Square. When, on August 6, the memorials and banners are removed on the orders of the Gang of Four, who deem the mourning inappropriate for the revolution, violent riots break out involving more than one hundred thousand participants, including Bei Dao.

  Today: Tiananmen Square remains the largest open square in Beijing and the fourth largest in the world. Infamous for the 1989 massacre, the square houses the National Museum of China, the Monument to the People's Heroes, the Great Hall of the People, and the Mausoleum of Mao Zedong. It is a popular tourist destination; more than six hundred thousand people can fit inside its borders.

- **1976:** With "The Answer," Bei Dao perfects his misty poetry style, a style soon to be defined in his underground literary magazine, *Jintian*. *Jintian* survives for only two years and nine issues until it is banned by the state as a subversive publication in 1980.

  Today: Bei Dao resurrects *Jintian* in Stockholm, Sweden, in 1990 as a magazine for the Chinese diaspora, meaning Chinese citizens who live outside China. He is allowed to return to China in 2006, after seventeen years of exile.

and broke into nearby government buildings in a leaderless demonstration of their dissent. Mao died five months later, on September 9, 1976. Soon after, the Gang of Four were arrested for their role in the Cultural Revolution. It was in this environment that Bei Dao came of age as an anti-establishment poet.

Misty Poetry

When the Anti–Spiritual Pollution Campaign denounced Bei Dao's underground literary magazine *Jintian* as *menglong* (obscure or vague, but literally translated as "misty"), it unintentionally gave a name to the new poetry movement favored by counterculture revolutionaries. Misty poetry explored existentialism, surrealism, abstraction, and Western modernism—the opposite in every way of the crowd-pleasing, simply written, folkloric poetry approved by the Communist Party. Using baffling images and illogical juxtapositions, Bei Dao and the misty poets voiced their harsh disapproval of the government while avoiding the subject of politics altogether. *Jintian* was banned two years after its first publication, after only nine issues, but the misty poets had already become the favorites of the protesters at Tiananmen Square. Bei Dao was revered as a counterculture icon by the pro-democracy student movement. Distinguishing traits of misty poetry include the use of figurative language, intentionally difficult syntax, experimentation with form and grammar, and indistinct time and setting. State-approved poetry was characterized by realism, concrete imagery, and simplistic language.

The image of sailboats on the Dead Sea suggests futility. (© imagIN.gr photography | Shutterstock.com)

CRITICAL OVERVIEW

"The Answer" is Bei Dao's most famous poem by far, taken up by student protesters during the democracy movement leading up to the massacre in Tiananmen Square and Bei Dao's subsequent exile in 1989. The poem was printed on posters, chanted by demonstrators, and published countless times both inside and outside China. "The Answer" and other misty poetry published in Bei Dao's *Jintian* literary magazine were officially condemned by the Communist Party's Anti–Spiritual Pollution Campaign.

In "Servant of the State" in the *New Yorker*, Jianying Zha writes of Bei Dao's place in Chinese popular culture as a counterculture icon: "Dao is the Allen Ginsberg of my generation, men and women who, born in the decade straddling the fifties and sixties, grew up in the Cultural Revolution."

In her introduction to *The August Sleepwalker*, Bonnie S. McDougall recognized Bei Dao's literary talents and his ability to capture the zeitgeist of his country. She calls him "one of the most gifted and controversial writers to emerge from the massive political and social upheavals of twentieth-century China." She goes on to praise "The Answer," as "a clear expression of his personal challenge to the political leadership . . . it marked his emergence from underground to dissident poet."

In a preview of Bei Dao's Stanford Presidential Lecture in the Humanities and the Arts, Ramon H. Myers considers the humanism apparent in Bei Dao's writing style: "Dao's poetry is marked by the effort to reveal the nature of the self, to identify both public and private wounds, to trust in instinctive perceptions, and to reach out to other afflicted souls."

In his note on the translation of Bei Dao's collection *Unlock*, Eliot Weinberger noted Bei Dao's place as the most widely translated contemporary Chinese poet in the West and admired the unexpected similarities between Bei Dao's radical style of dense, elusive poetry and that of classical Chinese poets. He writes, "Dao's poems, like those of the late T'ang poets . . . cannot be paraphrased; they are mysteries composed of strange and arresting images and snatches of speech."

WHAT DO I READ NEXT?

- In the young-adult memoir *China's Son* (2004), Da Chen recounts navigating the dangerous political atmosphere of China as a teenager during the Cultural Revolution as he sought an education despite his family's status as farmers.

- Louisa Lim's *The People's Republic of Amnesia* (2014) revisits the Tiananmen Square massacre of 1989: the participants on both sides, the long history of the square as a site of protests, and the political atmosphere of the time. Lim also explores the place of the massacre in Chinese history with a focus on how it changed the lives of those who survived.

- In "The Street" from *Early Poems of Octavio Paz* (1973), the Nobel Prize–winning Mexican poet blends identity, memory, and history during the speaker's surreal night spent walking the streets of his city.

- Bei Dao's 1991 poetry collection, *Old Snow*, gathers work written during his long exile from China, including the poems "He Opens Wide His Third Eye," "Exhibition," "A Local Accent," "Restructuring the Galaxy," and "Rebel."

- U.S. Customs confiscated Allen Ginsberg's "Howl" (1956) at its publication, finding the work obscene, and its publisher was placed under arrest. A surrealist poem that captures the bohemian zeitgeist of the Beat generation, "Howl" was defended in court by Ginsberg's colleagues, professors, and poets and launched Ginsberg into fame as a counterculture revolutionary.

- Bei Dao's collection of essays *Midnight's Gate* (2005) gathers his observations from years of travel in exile and his memories of home. Essays in the collection include "Paris Stories," "Empty Mountain," "Death Valley," "Backyard," "Uncle Liu," and "Kafka's Prague."

- *Five T'ang Poets* (1990), translated by David Young, gathers the best of classical Chinese poetry from the T'ang dynasty. These poets' lyrical, imagistic style is reflected strongly in Bei Dao's work, despite his label as an avant-garde poet.

- Wang Meng's short story "A New Arrival at the Organization Department" (1956), caused controversy at its publication for its depiction of an office of state propaganda. Mao Zedong stepped in to defend the work as antibureaucratic, silencing the critics. Meng served as the minister of culture for the People's Republic of China and is one of the country's most famous authors.

- Liu Xiaobo was in prison in Beijing for political subversion when he was awarded the Nobel Peace Prize in 2010. *No Enemies, No Hatred: Selected Essays and Poems* (2012) covers two decades of his remarkable life as a Chinese dissident, including works on the massacre in Tiananmen Square.

CRITICISM

Amy L. Miller

Miller is a graduate of the University of Cincinnati, and she currently resides in New Orleans. In the following essay, she considers the question posed in the text of Bei Dao's "The Answer" and the message hidden beneath the poem's defensive obscurity.

"The Answer" may seem inscrutable, its images impenetrable, and its meaning too subtle to grasp, but a reader who knows the poem's historical context can decipher the lines of poetry to find an elegant protest against an oppressive society. Poets choose each word carefully to express themselves ideally in a small space. In even the most avant-garde poems, a category in which "The Answer" absolutely

> **THE AUDACITY OF A SPEAKER WHO QUESTIONS THE COLOR OF THE SKY REPRESENTS THE POET'S CELEBRATION OF HUMANITY'S RIGHT TO QUESTION, TO WONDER, AND TO NEVER KNOW FOR CERTAIN. IT IS THROUGH EMBRACING THIS SPIRIT OF AMBIGUITY AND OPENNESS THAT 'THE ANSWER' IS REVEALED."**

belongs, the words were not chosen at random. By considering closely the weight of the poem's individual words, a reader can more easily interpret the poem's lines. Once the lines are understood, the poem's images, stanzas, and motifs fall into place, revealing the poem as a whole.

Though it is the nature of Bei Dao's misty poetry style to hide behind a veil of mystery, the poet's dissent is evident on the most superficial level when the speaker proclaims that he does not believe in the perverse world in which he lives. This, the poem's climax, is intentionally the boldest statement among the poem's gossamer imagery. No wonder that it was printed on thousands of flyers and chanted by protesting masses on Tiananmen Square. "The Answer" is a poem of reversals, contradictions, antitheses, and denials. The audacity of a speaker who questions the color of the sky represents the poet's celebration of humanity's right to question, to wonder, and to never know for certain. It is through embracing this spirit of ambiguity and openness that "The Answer" is revealed.

Under Chairman Mao, amid the fever of the Cultural Revolution, the poetry of the people was meant to build the image of a unified, Communist China. Prideful parroting of the Communist Party rhetoric, elevation of the proletariat through socialist folktales, and representing the work of nation building through realism using easily accessible language were the orders of the day for Chinese artists after Mao's 1942 Yan'an speech on the arts, which called for concrete artistic expression with broad appeal. In response, Bei Dao created misty poetry, as Ramon H. Myers describes it: "a hermetic, semi-private language characterized by oblique, oneiric imagery and elliptical syntax . . . in which

subject, tense, and number are elusive and transitions are unclear." Bei Dao's style of poetry could not have been further from the party's intentions for Maoist literature. It seemed intentionally provocative, flouting the government's limited definition of acceptable art.

Weinberger writes, "The poetry these young Chinese poets wrote was imagistic, subjective, and often surreal. Although it had no overt political content, its assertion of individual sentiments and perceptions, of imagination itself, was considered subversive." In a collectivist society, emphasis rests on the group rather than the individual. The People's Republic of China, a Communist nation, values collectivist thought to this day—putting the we before the I. Misty poetry harbors dangerously individualistic traits when viewed from a collectivist perspective. The language is deliberately difficult, at times even inaccessible, limiting those who can understand the poet's meaning. Bei Dao rejected the restrictions that aiming to please a large audience would place on his work, choosing instead to fully express himself without holding back. Outraged by the brutality of a society claiming to be egalitarian, he found a safe haven to express his dissent in vague language. Bonnie S. McDougall writes: "Dao's poetry is not fundamentally an act of political engagement with the system but a statement of personal concerns that he cannot ignore or disguise."

It is challenging to discern Bei Dao's specific concerns about his society from the labyrinthine text of "The Answer." If this poem is the answer, what is the question? Stanzas 1 and 2 set the scene: the spirits of the dead scar the lovely sky, preventing clear sight. This could be a reference to the hundreds of thousands of deaths caused by the Cultural Revolution or the tens of millions of lives lost from the Mao regime's inception. In this world, the noble die of their nobility, and the secret of the base is to debase others. The land is ice and death: a stagnant place like the Dead Sea, stuck in the past as if it were still the Ice Age. Everything is the opposite of how it should be, an example, McDougall writes, of "the self inhabiting two unreal universes: a dream world of love, tranquility and normality, that should exist but does not, and a nightmare of cruelty, terror, and hatred, that should not exist but does."

This twisted world is the speaker's reality. Stanza 3 describes his being born prepared to cast judgment. Bei Dao makes him into a satire of the folk heroes so desired by the party. Immaculately conceived in stanza 3, line 1 and carrying simple tools, he arrives on the scene not to blindly follow orders but to save the corrupt society from itself by pronouncing his decision. Stanzas 1 through 3 quietly pose the question Do you believe in this cold and rigid world? The speaker's unflinching answer would shake the ground in Tiananmen Square and end in Bei Dao's exile from China. He does not believe. This passionate declaration puts the I of selfhood inarguably before the we of a collectivist society, an intentional choice on Bei Dao's part meant to challenge the status quo of a government involved in every aspect of the lives of its people. The speaker will not swallow what this corrupt society feeds him and does not trust its judgment over his own.

Stanza 4 is devoted to a series of shocking contradictions best understood in the context of a collectivist society in which the leader, in this case Mao, is revered as godlike. When Mao said to write realism, writers wrote realistically. When Mao said to destroy the past, the people desecrated the grave of Confucius, chipped the faces off statues of Buddha, and burned ancient texts. By the nature of his power, Mao's logic was not questioned. Thus, when Bei Dao's speaker says he does not believe the sky is blue, he is declaring war on the foundation of this nightmare society, attacking its logic at its most basic.

Bei Dao's signature obliqueness is used to maximum capacity as he denies the simple facts that the sky is blue and thunder echoes. McDougall writes, "His verse is not obscure just because of fear of censorship but because the pain caused by all forms of oppression is so intense that conventional epithets are too shallow to express it." Unable to express the power of his emotion through existing idioms, Bei Dao creates a new language of protest, answering the absurdity of society with an absurdity of his own. He fights against the inflexible rules by showing extreme flexibility of thought, claiming that dreams are real (an encouraging sentiment for the outnumbered protesters) and the dead do seek revenge (a significant threat to a regime responsible for so many deaths). Zha writes of Bei Dao's influence on his contemporaries, those who had experienced the horrors of the Cultural Revolution as young adults, "The themes of his early poetry... struck all the keynotes of our journey from Mao's little red children to bitterly disillusioned

adults." Losing faith in their government, the people found an impressive counterculture icon in Bei Dao, who could utterly disassemble the party in his poetry without ever broaching the subject of politics.

Bei Dao's speaker, the individualistic, skeptical folk hero, predicts the destruction of his bleak society. Appropriately, it will die by a flood of water breaching the levees—symbolic of the growing masses of protesters occupying Tiananmen Square—a flood the speaker welcomes to flow through his heart in all its rough power. When society rebuilds, it will be on a high peak of a mountain, not in the lowlands of their former, polluted world. This is the fantasy world of love and tranquility that McDougall observed—the opposite of the nightmare world in that it does not exist, but should. She writes, "The central force shaping Bei Dao's poetry has been his complex reaction to the pressures of a brutalized, conformist, and corrupt society."

Bei Dao's solution to the unrelenting pressure that turns neighbor on neighbor out of fear is his new world on the symbolic mountaintop of love, hope, and humanity, where society can see the stars and the stars can gaze back in approval. The poem's harsh tone softens as the poetic narrative moves from the depths of nightmare world into the dream of the mountaintop. Unlike the sky in the nightmare world of reality, the sky on the mountain is not clogged by the dead but filled with a gallery of five thousand years of history and the pinprick eyes of generations to come. In this world, free thought is valued over strict obedience, and modern leaders learn from the leaders of the past rather than order their destruction. The poem concludes with the double metaphor of the stars as both past and future, an image as beautiful and comforting as stanza 1 is bleak.

The obscurity of "The Answer" serves to hide its secrets from those who cannot open their minds to the abstract, the mysterious, and the illogical. Yet, using these nonsensical forms of expression, Bei Dao creates a world more habitable than the reality in which the speaker struggles, where rules are strict but backward, unquestioned but harmful. Through his delicately subversive misty poetry, Bei Dao gave a generation of traumatized survivors of the Cultural Revolution their voice of dissent.

Source: Amy L. Miller, Critical Essay on "The Answer," in *Poetry for Students*, Gale, Cengage Learning, 2016.

The sea breaking through the dike represents the power of nature. *(© Zacarias Pereira da Mata | Shutterstock.com)*

Vera Schwarcz

In the following essay, Schwarcz discusses the dark mood of much of Bei Dao's work.

From the first time we met (at the Asia Society's November 1988 forum on the writer's role in contemporary society), Bei Dao has impressed me with the art of understatement. Whereas Gu Cheng came in sporting an eccentric hat and twittering speech filled with quotable aphorisms, Bei Dao stood his ground in darker light. That chilly autumn before the student demonstrations of 1989, he already understood the healing power of wintery speech. A refugee from the enforced, loquacious ardor of the Red Sun, Bei Dao knew that saying less— leaving large gaps between his carefully crafted words and broken lines—allowed him, and his readers, to make room for imagination, for additional historical trauma, and maybe even for the possibility of healing poetic language of its addiction to the oracular.

Now, two decades after the crushing of the Beijing spring of 1989, Bei Dao remains a bard faithful to chilling landscapes. In his poem "Black Map," we find again a poet who intends to "bring the heart of winter / when spring water and horse pills / become the words of night." Brighter seasons such as spring contain cliched recipes for hope, giant horse pills that might weaken the effort needed to hear the words of night.

What is this night? A code word for the History that casts a shadow over all of Bei Dao's work—not only because he is a survivor of the late Mao period, not only because he suffered exile for his sympathy with the victims of June Fourth, not only because tragedy walks with a heavy step in his personal life. It might be that "Northern Island" finds it difficult to unfold himself from what he calls "the fan of history" out of fear that he might fall silent, run out of things to say as his wounded generation finds fewer scabs to pick.

The challenge that Bei Dao faces head on is how to become a poet without that cursedly capital "P." I found his gloomy conclusion at the end of the 2003 interview with Tang Xiaodu especially moving, especially honest: "The history of modern Chinese poetry in the last hundred years ought to make us pause and reflect. I think this has to do with the Chinese nation's collective lack of religious faith...our carpe diem tendencies." What shines through here is the realization that poetry cannot be a substitute for faith, or a cure for materialism. It can, however, map the parameters of wintery perception, as well as the joys of sheer survival.

In this search for a de-capitalized poetics, Bei Dao might find solace in the voice and verses of Yehuda Amichai, the Israeli poet who also struggled with the shadows of history. Living in Jerusalem, he took delight in evoking the quotidian alongside the sacred. His poem called "Tourists" confesses quietly: "Redemption will come only if their guide tells them, 'You see that arch from the Roman period? It is not important: but next to it, left and down a bit, there sits a man who's bought fruit and vegetables for his family.'"

Bei Dao, my friend, the time has come to look beyond the Roman arch of the aching past. The hour has come for poets to go into the market, listen, and record how folks make do with daily grief seasoned by hard-earned fruits and vegetables.

Source: Vera Schwarcz, "Winter's Voice: Bei Dao," in *World Literature Today*, Vol. 83, No. 3, May–June 2009, p. 4.

Jeffrey Twitchell-Waas

In the following review, Twitchell-Waas praises Bei Dao's striking imagery.

The development of Bei Dao's poetry over the past two decades has in a sense lived up to the accusation of "obscure" or "misty" (menglong) with which Chinese officialdom denounced him and his fellow poets in the early 1980s. The label stuck, and the Misty Poets became renowned as marking the first decisive break with Maoist literature. For Western readers, while the early work that provoked the charge hardly appears especially obscure, Bei Dao's recent poetry has become increasingly hermetic. *Unlock* is the fourth collection by Bei Dao to appear since he was forced into permanent exile in 1989—all handsomely produced in bilingual editions by New Directions. (Another volume, *The August Sleepwalker*, translates a comprehensive selection of his early verse.)

As the best-known post-Maoist poet, both inside and outside China, Bei Dao has experienced a reception of his work determined to a considerable degree by his early adoption as a spokesperson for a dissatisfied younger generation in China and his inevitable labeling and marketing as a dissident writer in the West. The hermeticism of his recent poetry is continuous with his earlier work in that it is an assertion of subjectivity against those social pressures that would deny individuality, which presumably now includes the expectations of his Western audience. By his own admission, Bei Dao has been strongly drawn to a number of Western poets of agonized exile and linguistic estrangement, such as Tsvetaeva, Vallejo, and Celan.

For those familiar with Bei Dao's other volumes that have appeared over the course of the 1990s (see e.g. *WLT* 66:3, p. 578, and 72:1, p. 202), *Unlock* does not offer any striking new developments. We find here the usual carefully constructed short lyrical poems that deliberately undermine surface coherence to suggest more oblique meanings. Given the complex of pressures that would attempt to determine the poet's identity, these poems can be understood as efforts to construct a private space, a space that is constantly threatening to collapse into mere characters on the page. As with a number of exiled Chinese poets, Bei Dao's poetry tends toward an elusive fluidity, momentarily coalescing in striking images, for which Bei Dao has always been noted, only to segue surrealistically into non sequiturs. The translators have valiantly attempted to replicate the syntactical looseness whereby a following line can be read simultaneously as both discrete from its preceding line and continuing it in a redirected trajectory.

Bei Dao's poetry has always been relatively disembodied—unsituated in a definite space and time—and this tendency has now reached the point where there are virtually no concrete indicators of the poet's specific culture or setting. Or, more precisely, the siting of his poetry is largely within language itself, the compulsive groping within the traumatized Chinese of the mainland for renewed possibilities, which often depend on subtle shifts and contrasts of tone and register. Inevitably, translation will tend to result in an even more abstract version. Such poetry is likely to strike Western readers as either irritatingly amorphous or as an apt expression of exile and linguistic alienation.

Source: Jeffrey Twitchell-Waas, Review of *Unlock*, in *World Literature Today*, Vol. 75, Summer–Autumn 2001, p. 106.

SOURCES

"Bei Dao," Poetry Foundation website, http://www.poetry foundation.org/bio/bei-dao (accessed May 1, 2015).

Bei Dao, "The Answer," in *The August Sleepwalker*, translated by Bonnie S. McDougall, New Directions, 1988, p. 33.

"Cultural Revolution," History.com, 2009, http://www .history.com/topics/cultural-revolution (accessed May 2, 2015).

Han, Dongping, "Farmers, Mao, and Discontent in China: From the Great Leap Forward to the Present," in *Monthly Review*, Vol. 61, No. 7, http://monthlyreview .org/2009/12/01/farmers-mao-and-discontent-in-china (accessed May 2, 2015).

Hilton, Isabel, "Tiananmen: The Flame Burns On," in *Guardian*, May 2, 2009, http://www.theguardian.com/ world/2009/may/03/tiananmen-square-anniversary-china- protest (accessed May 1, 2015).

McDougall, Bonnie S., Introduction to *The August Sleepwalker*, by Bei Dao, New Directions, 1988, pp. 9–14.

Myers, Ramon H., "Stanford Presidential Lectures in the Humanities and the Arts: Bei Dao," Stanford University website, 1999, https://prelectur.stanford.edu/lecturers/ dao (accessed May 1, 2015).

Weinberger, Eliot, "A Note on the Translation," in *Unlock: Poems by Bei Dao*, New Directions, 2000, 107–11.

Zha, Jianying, "Servant of the State," in *New Yorker*, November 8, 2010, http://www.newyorker.com/magazine/ 2010/11/08/servant-of-the-state (accessed May 1, 2015).

FURTHER READING

Barnstone, Tony, and Chou Ping, *The Anchor Book of Chinese Poetry: From Ancient to Contemporary*, Anchor, 2005.
> This anthology of Chinese poetry covers three thousand years of poetic history, including more than six hundred poems by 130 poets, ranging in style from classical to postmodern, all carefully translated into English.

Bei Dao, *Blue House*, translated by Ted Huters and Feng- Ying Ming, Zephyr Press, 1998.
> Dao's collected essays from his life in exile describe his experiences as a globe-trotting poet and his struggles living as an outsider unwelcome in the country of his birth. Among the essays collected in *Blue House* are "Allen Ginsberg," "God's Chinese Son," "Octavio Paz," "Journey to South Africa," and "A Day in New York."

MacFarquhar, Robert, and Michael Schoenhals, *Mao's Last Revolution*, Belknap Press, 2008.
> *Mao's Last Revolution* chronicles the years of the Cultural Revolution leading up to Mao's death and the arrest of the Gang of Four with a particular focus on the long-lasting effects of Mao's violent cultural purge.

Siu, Helen F., and Zelda Stern, *Mao's Harvest: Voices from China's New Generation*, Oxford University Press, 1983.
> This anthology of works written by the first generation of writers to grow up in Communist China includes Dao's poem "Reply." Like Dao, these writers experienced the terror of the Cultural Revolution as young adults, and their lives were shaped by Maoist doctrine.

SUGGESTED SEARCH TERMS

Bei Dao

Bei Dao AND "The Answer"

Bei Dao AND "Huida"

Bei Dao AND 1976

The Answer AND 1976

Bei Dao AND The August Sleepwalker

The August Sleepwalker AND 1986

Bei Dao AND Tiananmen Square

Bei Dao AND misty poets

"Huida" AND Tiananmen Square

Bei Dao AND Chinese poetry

The Children's Hour

Henry Wadsworth Longfellow's "The Children's Hour" was originally published in the *Atlantic Monthly* in 1860. It was one of a group of poems from his middle period that made Longfellow the most popular and financially successful poet in the United States in the nineteenth century. The sentimental use of his daughters' affection for him in "The Children's Hour" is typical of Longfellow's work, appealing to the new middle-class conception of family life, as in other poems he appealed to their taste for education and moral improvement through poetry. An index of how firmly Longfellow is embedded in American popular culture is that for almost a century after they were written, many of his middle-period narrative poems were so well known to the popular audience that they were given detailed satirical treatments in Warner Brother's cartoons: many lines of Longfellow stay in popular culture through Bugs Bunny. Even today, most people know some lines of Longfellow, even if they have no idea of the source. The phrase *the pitter-patter of little feet*, for instance, comes, with slight alteration, from "The Children's Hour." Familiar figures from American history, such as Paul Revere and Miles Standish, would probably be completely unknown were it not for Longfellow's treatment of them as heroes.

HENRY WADSWORTH LONGFELLOW

1860

AUTHOR BIOGRAPHY

Longfellow was born in Portland (in present-day Maine, then part of Massachusetts) on February

Henry Wadsworth Longfellow (© Everett Historical / Shutterstock.com)

27, 1807. His grandfather, Peleg Wadsworth, had been a general in the Revolutionary War, a member of Congress, and the founder of Bowdoin College. His father, Stephen Longfellow, was a successful lawyer. Longfellow attended prep school at the Portland Academy and published his first poem, "The Battle of Lovell's Pond," in the Portland *Gazette* in 1820, when he was only thirteen years old. The poem commemorated an episode from the Revolutionary War. He enrolled at Bowdoin College at the age of fifteen (not an unusually young age for college entrance at the time). Influenced at college by friends like Nathaniel Hawthorne, Longfellow developed the desire to become a professional writer—he published over forty poems in his senior year—but his father discouraged him, saying such an occupation was too uncertain. Bowdoin agreed to hire him as a professor after he had broadened himself through travel, and Longfellow was sent by his father on a three-year tour of Europe.

He began teaching at Bowdoin in 1829, where he continued publishing short poems and translations of poetry. In 1831, Longfellow married his first wife, Mary Potter. Three years later, Longfellow

was recruited to Harvard, again with the provision that he travel to Europe to learn additional languages (in this case he studied Icelandic and Finnish). His wife died after delivering a stillborn child on the trip. Teaching at Harvard, he lived in what is now known as the Longfellow House, which had been George Washington's headquarters during the early days of the Revolutionary War. Longfellow's popularity as a poet increased with his continuing publications, including "The Village Black Smith" (1840) and "The Wreck of the Hesperus" (1842). In 1843, Longfellow married Fanny Appleton, who bore Longfellow's sons, Charles and Ernest, and Alice, Edith, and Allegra, the three daughters mentioned in "The Children's Hour." (A fourth daughter, Fanny, died in infancy.) In 1847, he published *Evangeline*, a successful epic poem about the experience of the Acadian people in America. By now, his writing was producing twice the income of his teaching (a job he hated, since he considered dealing with immature students to be tedious), and in 1854 he retired from teaching. This brought about an outpouring of new work, including another epic, *The Song of Hiawatha* (1855), a rather confused collection of mythologies from various Indian tribes and Finland and whose eccentric trochaic tetrametric meter immediately inspired satire. In 1858, "The Courtship of Miles Standish" was published, and two years later, Longfellow published two of his best known poems, "The Children's Hour" and "Paul Revere's Ride."

In 1861, Longfellow's wife, Fanny, was carrying out a common middle-class Victorian custom, sealing locks of her daughters' hair in envelopes, when the candle used to melt the sealing wax caught her dress on fire, and she burned to death. Longfellow rushed from his study and tried to put out the flames with a rug. He was burned badly enough that he thereafter wore a beard to cover the scars. He was too devastated to write for a considerable time after that and gradually worked his way out of depression by beginning to translate Dante's *Divine Comedy*, which would be completed and published in 1867. Longfellow's late poetry, such as "*Morituri Salutamus*" (1875), is often considered his best by modern critics but never penetrated into popular culture as the poems of his middle period did. Nevertheless, by the late 1850s, Longfellow's income from writing was close to $50,000 a year (several million dollars in today's money). This kind of popularity was possible only with the new industrial manufacture of books and periodicals and only with the new and growing middle-class audience. In the 1870s, Longfellow generally withdrew from public life. After several weeks of decline in his health, Longfellow died of peritonitis in his Cambridge home on March 24, 1882.

POEM TEXT

Between the dark and the daylight,
When the night is beginning to lower,
Comes a pause in the day's occupations,
That is known as the Children's Hour.

I hear in the chamber above me   5
The patter of little feet,
The sound of a door that is opened,
And voices soft and sweet.

From my study I see in the lamplight,
Descending the broad hall stair,   10
Grave Alice, and laughing Allegra,
And Edith with golden hair.

A whisper, and then a silence:
Yet I know by their merry eyes
They are plotting and planning together   15
To take me by surprise.

A sudden rush from the stairway,
A sudden raid from the hall!
By three doors left unguarded
They enter my castle wall!   20

They climb up into my turret
O'er the arms and back of my chair;
If I try to escape, they surround me;
They seem to be everywhere.

They almost devour me with kisses,   25
Their arms about me entwine,
Till I think of the Bishop of Bingen
In his Mouse-Tower on the Rhine!

Do you think, O blue-eyed banditti,
Because you have scaled the wall,   30
Such an old moustache as I am
Is not a match for you all!

I have you fast in my fortress,
And will not let you depart,
But put you down into the dungeon   35
In the round-tower of my heart.

And there will I keep you forever,
Yes, forever and a day,
Till the walls shall crumble to ruin,
And moulder in dust away!   40

POEM SUMMARY

The text used for this summary is from *Tales of a Wayside Inn*, Ticknor and Fields, 1863, pp. 209–11. A version of the poem can be found on the following web page: http://www.poetry foundation.org/poem/173894.

MEDIA ADAPTATIONS

- The American composer Charles Ives set "The Children's Hour" to music in 1901. There are many commercial recordings of the piece, including the version by Eric Trudel on *Charles Ives: Songs, Vol. I*, released by Naxos in 2008. The running time is two minutes, twenty-eight seconds.

- A reading of "The Children's Hour" by Layne Longfellow can be heard on the 2002 compact disc *Longfellow Reads Longfellow: Dreams That Cannot Die*, published by Lecture Theatre. The running time for the album is fifty minutes, twenty-nine seconds.

The forty lines of Longfellow's "The Children's Hour" are divided into ten unnumbered quatrains (four-line stanzas).

I

The speaker of the poem establishes that it is set at a certain time, the hour of twilight before night. Fathers are often consumed with work during the day, but they can devote this time to their children; hence he gives the time the name of the children's hour. The poem was published in 1860, and there was certainly artificial illumination available, for the most part in the form of whale-oil lamps. But it was not possible to simply turn on a whole array of bright lights and continue any activities one wanted as if during the day. Because people went to bed earlier, they could easily awaken at or before dawn.

II

The father hears the sounds of his daughters running around their room on the floor above him. He further hears the door open and the girls softly talking among themselves.

III

The father mentions that he is in his study. Presumably he has been working there all day in relative isolation from his family. The girl's invasion of his study is in response to the hour when he ceases work. If they had done the same thing they are about to do now earlier, they might have been punished for interrupting him. The marker of the late afternoon hour is the lamplight that illuminates the scene. Through the open door of his study, the father sees his three daughters running down the stairs and names them: Alice, Allegra, and Edith. Alice and Allegra are given the matching characteristics of being serious and frivolous, while the father mentions Edith is blonde.

IV

The father hears the girls whisper to each other and then go stealthily silent. They are plotting together to take their father by surprise. This reads somewhat oddly since the father says he can see their emotions betrayed in the eyes of his daughters. Surely, then, they know he has seen them (if he can see their eyes, they can see his), and so any chance of surprise would already be lost.

V

The three girls run into the father's study. He mentions that each one comes in through a different doorway. In fact, the study in Longfellow's house has four different doors (although it would be impossible to see the staircase through any of them, a reminder that the narrative of the poem cannot be confused with the actual circumstances of Longfellow's life). The father describes his daughters' entry into his study as their breaching the curtain wall around his castle. This metaphor will be extended throughout the rest of the poem. This language reflects the daughters' imaginative play.

VI

As the father describes what is happening, he suggests the confused actions of his daughters climbing all over him in the confused language he employs. In one line, he sticks to the figurative language of the castle-assault metaphor; in another, the girls are directly described climbing up his chair. He cannot escape because he is surrounded: the girls are everywhere. The idea of escape belongs to imaginative play; the garrison of a castle whose curtain wall had been breached might well retreat to an interior fortification (the keep or dungeon).

VII

Now that their assault is successful, the daughters carry out their plan of kissing and hugging their father. The father likens this too to the metaphor of medieval imaginative play. He invokes the image of Bishop Hatto being eaten alive by an army of rats that attack him after he thought he was safe in a castle tower. The story is obscure today but was common in the travel literature known to Longfellow's middle-class audience. Travel handbooks were arranged with an entry for each town on the itinerary, and the story of Hatto was the regular fare printed for the entry on Bingen, an inevitable part of a cruise up the Rhine. Nevertheless, that the father being kissed by his daughters is reminded of a bishop being eaten by rats suggests some ambivalence on the father's part. No doubt the comparison is comic. Mark Twain satirized the middle-class culture of European grand tours of which the story of Hatto is part in his *The Innocents Abroad* (1869).

VIII

The remainder of the poem is a direct address of the father to his daughters. He speaks to them in terms of the medieval role-playing, in the persona of the master of the castle under attack. He calls the girls *banditti*, an Italian word for robber redolent of Gothic literature and already old-fashioned at the time of the poem's composition. He suggests that the girls/knights think they have won because they have breached the outer defenses of the castle, but like a stereotypical villain, he assures them he is still in control and still able to defeat their attack.

IX

This stanza must mean, in the ordinary narrative of the poem, that the father is now hugging his daughters and holding them within his affections. The metaphorical description, again, suggests something more aggressive. Late medieval castles were often designed so that any raiding party that penetrated the outer walls would be directed through the castle's corridors to a dead end and could be caught in the chamber by dropping a heavy iron gate behind them. The ceiling of the chamber would have murder holes, through which things like heavy stones or boiling oil could be dropped. This is the situation into which the girls/knights have blundered and now surrender into a captivity that will see them imprisoned in the rooms under the castle dungeon or main tower, metaphorically referring to the father's heart.

X

Now that the father has the girls/knights in captivity in his heart, he will keep them there forever, until the dungeon holding them collapses into ruin, that is, until he himself dies.

THEMES

Fatherhood

The structure of the family was being swiftly changed in Longfellow's lifetime by the Industrial Revolution and the subsequent rise of the middle class. In traditional households of the working poor (mostly farmers) from which the middle class emerged, families were together all the time as they cooperated in the work necessary to maintain the household. In a middle-class family, however, the father was away at the office for most of the day, leaving the mother alone with the children. Poor families, who began to model themselves on the middle class to the extent leisure time and disposable income allowed, were transformed in a similar way, with the father leaving the house each morning to work in a factory or mine. As Christoph Irmscher explains in *Longfellow Redux*, an entirely new family dynamic came into being: "The new idea of the middle-class family, emerging around 1830, assigned the child a privileged place in the home, where the mother, in the absence of the bread-winning father, assumed the primary function of the child raiser." The father in many respects became a visitor to his own household: "Fathers, once the undisputed heads of the households, the sources of intellectual power and stern administrators of corporal punishment, were relegated to an advisory function." The father in "The Children's Hour" seems to work at home in his study, as Longfellow did, but his position seems typically middle class in terms of his isolation from the family during the workday. The time the poem describes is not so much the children's hour as the father's hour with the children. His daughters seem to have spent some time carefully planning how they will spend their limited time with their father (reflected in the fantasy structure of the castle assault), as one prepares for the visit of a guest. The poem's appeal is its reflection of the new reality of its readers. The rather didactic explanation in the first stanza is meant to explain and routinize the new domestic arrangements.

The speaker hears his children coming down the stairs and knows they are trying to surprise him.
(© Goygel-Sokol Dmitry | Shutterstock.com)

Imagination

In "The Children's Hour," the father/narrator decodes and relates the speech and even the thoughts of his three daughters. In their imaginations, they are knights from a medieval romance storming a castle. They must be saying lines memorized from such literature that convey the idea to their father, although they are never quoted—no doubt much of what the father does say should be taken as paraphrase of his daughter's speech. The image of the assault is carried through the poem, even in the allusion to the rats' assault on the Mouse Tower of Bingen. The father enters into the same imaginative play when he represents himself as the lord of the castle, overcoming his attacking daughters and taking them captive. Imagination in this sense is clearly the ability to think and pursue something similar to a fictional story that is used by the mind to organize play. This is a very modern way of using the word *imagination,* and the display of imagination in children's play will

TOPICS FOR FURTHER STUDY

- A Google Ngram search (https://books.google .com/ngrams) queries the entire Google Books database of millions of books and periodicals published between 1800 and 2000. Searching for a term on this database reveals the change in its absolute frequency over time. Make a presentation to your class based on Ngram searches of unusual words in "The Children's Hour." You may also search related terms that are not directly mentioned in the poem (such as Hatto, the bishop referred to but not named in the poem). Is the language archaic, composed of words that fell out of fashion after Longfellow's time? Or is it modern? What do your results suggest about the language of the poem?

- *The Children's Hour* (sometimes subtitled: *A Magazine for the Little Ones*) was a journal of children's and young-adult literature published in the 1870s and 1880s. Many full issues are available online through Google Books. The title was borrowed from Longfellow's poem and reflects the same sentimental Victorian approach to childhood as in "The Children's Hour." Select a piece of young-adult literature from a volume of *The Children's Hour* and write a paper comparing it with one of your favorite pieces of modern young-adult literature. What do the two pieces suppose about their audience? What attitude do they take toward young people?

- Robert Louis Stevenson's *A Child's Garden of Verses* (1885) is a collection of poetry written with young adults in mind that addresses the new social role of extended childhood conditioned by the growth of the middle class after the Industrial Revolution. Select a poem from the collection and write a paper comparing it with "The Children's Hour."

- *The Father-Daughter Plot: Japanese Literary Women and the Law of the Father* (2001), edited by Rebecca L. Copeland and Esperanza Ramirez-Christensen is a collection of scholarly articles that analyze the relationship between fathers and daughters in both traditional and modern Japanese literature. Much of the material discussed is presented in English translation for the first time. Even contemporary Japanese literature tends to conceive of the father-daughter relationship in traditional terms; resistance to the transformation of society by industrialization and the rise of the middle class has been greater in Japan than in the United States. Write a paper contrasting the type of father-daughter relationship that is valued in Japanese literature with that shown in "The Children's Hour."

---

seem unexceptional to modern readers. It is remarkable, however, that Longfellow's concept of the imagination is completely different from that universally held by the previous generation of romantic poets in England, such as William Wordsworth or John Keats. Poets traditionally used the philosophical conception of the imagination as a tool to probe beneath and beyond everyday reality. Longfellow has abandoned this use because his poetic world had to be comprehensible and engaging without challenging the reader. In "The Children's Hour," the imagination is reduced from a philosophical concept to

children's play that the reader can easily recognize and identify with.

STYLE

Poetics

"The Children's Hour" scrupulously follows traditional poetic conventions. It is composed of ten quatrains, or stanzas of four lines each. The lines follow a regular rhyme scheme with the second and fourth line of each stanza rhyming.

It is composed in a definite meter, trochaic tetrameter, with each line made up of four trochees (a foot consisting of a stressed followed by an unstressed syllable) with a very limited range of substitutions. This meter is extremely unusual in English, or indeed Indo-European, poetry; it is a reversal of the usual iambic character of English verse. In fact, one of the few notable instances of it before Longfellow is in Shakespeare's *A Midsummer Night's Dream*, where it is the meter of many of the lines spoken by the fairies, a device clearly meant to set them apart as otherworldly. Trochaic tetrameter was Longfellow's favorite meter, however, because of the influence of the Finnish epic *Kalevala*, which Longfellow had learned Finnish specifically to read. It should be noted that Finnish is a Uralic rather than an Indo-European language. Longfellow also composed his own epic *The Song of Hiawatha* in trochaic tetrameter.

Metaphor

A metaphor is a description of one object or set of circumstances that the reader is meant to understand as applying to another is a symbolic fashion. In "The Children's Hour" there is an extended metaphor by which the daughters' running into their father's study to smother him with kisses is described in terms of a medieval army attacking and invading a castle. This is drawn from the medieval romance literature that was so popular among the Victorian middle class, as exemplified in novels like Walter Scott's *Ivanhoe* (1820) or Alfred, Lord Tennyson's Arthurian poetry, and in a far greater mass of subliterary work that is not read today. Mark Twain frequently satirized the middle-class taste for the Middle Ages, for example in *A Connecticut Yankee in King Arthur's Court* (1889) and, more pointedly with respect to "The Children's Hour," in the scenes in *Huckleberry Finn* (1884) in which Tom Sawyer becomes dangerously detached from reality through his newly discovered passion for medieval role playing. However, the medieval metaphor in "The Children's Hour" also serves a more serious purpose that may not be so readily apparent. It addresses the role of the father in the new middle class, as a distant, isolated ruler over the family: there is a wall—the wall of work—separating the father from his daughters. The military nature of the metaphor implies a great deal of violence, a factor that seems to be emphasized by the poem's reference to the medieval bishop eaten alive by rats. The

exaggerated comparison is no doubt humorous, but humor is successful only to the degree it is concealed aggression. This military metaphor could suggest unconscious aggression on the part of the father, who might feel under siege by the obligations of family life. However, nothing of this kind is spelled out, but rather is implied for the reader to supply from his or her own understanding of the metaphor and its sources. Since the expression of hostility is at best unconscious, it is perfectly possible to read the poem without any such considerations, and no doubt that was the consensus reading of its Victorian audience.

HISTORICAL CONTEXT

The Bishop and the Mouse Tower

In the sixth stanza of "The Children's Hour," the speaker likens his daughters' affectionate assault on him, giving him kisses like bites, to the Bishop of Bingen in his Mouse Tower. This is a reference to a medieval German legend. The little information that Longfellow provides suggests its meaning even to those unfamiliar with it: namely that the bishop in question must have met his end, overwhelmed in a tower full of hungry mice. (Some versions of the legend refer to mice, others to rats.) The inference is perhaps gruesome, but it is veiled enough not to break through the sentimentality of the poem. The story is recorded by Lilian Grask in her collection of folktales, which was not published until after "The Children's Hour," but as she says, it is told to visitors to Bingen, so Longfellow may have heard it from a tour guide during one of his grand tours of Europe. The story was already recounted by the romantic poet Robert Southey, in his "God's Judgement on a Wicked Bishop" (1799). (This poem has often been retitled.) Southey's poem was a standard in the tourist handbooks that were mass-produced in the nineteenth century, so it would seem that Longfellow encountered the story as part of the tourist industry, another creation of the growing middle class.

The story concerns an historical if obscure tenth-century bishop, not of Bingen, but of the nearby larger city of Mainz, named Hatto. Bishop Hatto had more concern for hoarding wealth than in providing Christian charity to the inhabitants of his diocese. Since his fields were very productive, he had vast stores of grain as well as a considerable fortune in gold. During a famine, the poor came to him seeking relief,

COMPARE
&
CONTRAST

- **1850s:** Lighting in private houses, while not rare, was usually not used to extend the day's activities long after sunset.

  Today: Most Americans' daily schedule has been shifted to later in the day by the ubiquity of electric lights and entertainments such as evening television shows.

- **1850s:** The middle class is newly emerging as the total wealth of society increases with the Industrial Revolution.

  Today: The middle classes and middle-class culture dominate American life, but the size of the middle class as a proportion of the population has been shrinking since its height in the 1970s.

- **1850s:** Because of the lack of practical birth control, the fact that women are not economically required to work outside the home, and the easy availability of servants, middle-class families tend to be large. The fact that the Longfellows have five surviving children is not unusual.

  Today: Few families can sustain their position in the middle class without both spouses working outside the home, while the cost of day care (also outside the home) has dramatically increased as a proportion of middle-class income. This has resulted in middle-class families being typically much smaller than the Longfellows', with one or two children.

pleading that their children would die if the bishop did not feed them. The bishop contemptuously refused them charity, dismissing them as hungry rats. But the peasants persisted, so finally Hatto had the hungry crowd enter one of his granaries, but one that was empty, after which his soldiers locked them in and set the building on fire, killing them. That night, the bishop's sound sleep was disturbed by scrabbling noises in his bedroom; in the morning he found his portrait had been chewed to shreds. He then heard the report that an army of rats was coming from the ashes of the granary toward the palace. Hatto ran for his life and rowed a boat downstream to a tower built on a small island in the Rhine at Bingen. (Historically, the tower was used to collect tolls on river traffic by the archdiocese of Mainz.) The rats swam after him and eventually gnawed their way into the tower and devoured him. That the story is a folktale arising from the class inequalities of the Middle Ages is obvious, and it is told about various remote historical figures in many locales in the Germanic and Slavic language areas, although the nature of the ruler's cruelty varies a great deal between reflexes.

CRITICAL OVERVIEW

In his own lifetime, Longfellow was the most prominent American poet. His poems were frequently republished in every kind of magazine and newspaper and were known to practically any literate person. "The Children's Hour" was reprinted widely in the 1860s, including as a separate pamphlet complete with the reproduction of an oil painting of Longfellow's three daughters. A popular magazine of children's literature in the 1860s and 1870s took the title *The Children's Hour*, much to Longfellow's displeasure, although copyright cannot be enforced on titles. In the nineteenth and early twentieth century, a surprisingly large part of the English curriculum in American grade schools was devoted to memorizing and reciting poetry. "The Children's Hour" was among the most commonly used poems for this purpose (as noted, for example, by Lewis Atherton in *The Elementary School Teacher* in 1914). Perhaps only Longfellow's own "The Ride of Paul Revere" was more prominent. As a result, "The Children's Hour" became well known in popular culture. Two of its lines entered popular speech

The girls have mischievous twinkles in their eyes, but they are clearly happy children. (© art4you / Shutterstock.com)

as common expressions: the slightly altered *pitter-patter of little feet*, and the phrase used in song and film titles such as *Forever and a Day* (1943). Longfellow's reputation could hardly be maintained at that lofty level, however, and by the early twentieth century it was seriously attacked, for example by the Nobel Laureate W. B. Yeats in his essay, "What Is 'Popular Poetry'?"

The final assessment of traditional literary criticism is reflected in the 1963 reassessment of Longfellow by Newton Arvin, in *Longfellow: His Life and Work*, who considers Longfellow an important minor poet: not trivial or talentless, but not a figure to stand beside Shakespeare or Dante, as he was perceived in his lifetime. Arvin describes "The Children's Hour" as "a kind of cheaply manufactured, as it were machine-produced 'poetry'—newspaper verse, domestic doggerel, rhymes about mines and prospectors, and the like—which may conveniently be called masscult [mass culture] poetry."

A new generation of Longfellow studies was sparked by Christoph Irmscher. Modern criticism tends to evaluate literature from various analytical perspectives, and Irmscher in his *Longfellow Redux* (2006) treats "The Children's Hour" in the context of Victorian family history. He writes,

> At least at first sight, Longfellow's "The Children's Hour" encapsulates neatly the mixture of affection and desire for control with which mid-nineteenth-century American parents approached their children, the freedom within carefully prescribed limits that they extended to them.

Similarly, Robert Arbor, in his article "'Not from the Grand Old Masters': The Art of Henry and Ernest Wadsworth Longfellow," seeks to explore the relationship of the poem to Longfellow's actual household. He does so through comparison to a memoir written by Longfellow's daughter Alice in the *Strand* (though obviously as a commercial product that article would have been expected to conform to reader's expectations based on "The Children's Hour" itself). Critics such as Irmscher and Arbor treat the poem as important for cultural history rather than as literature. Today, literary history is generally viewed as a process of limitation, where the literature of the past determines the course of future literature though ever-narrower channels, in part by simply exhausting a given area of literary production and in part by cutting off other potentials. But according to Irmscher, "Longfellow saw it [literature] as progressive, steadily rising enrichment, as the inexorable diversification of subjects and artistic options available to every new writer." Noticeably, Longfellow's work is notorious for lacking the kind of intertextual and other indirect references to earlier literature that is usual in significant work.

CRITICISM

Rita M. Brown

Brown is an English professor. In the following essay, she applies W. B. Yeats's critical assessment of Longfellow to the specific instance of "The Children's Hour."

Longfellow was the most popular American poet of his time, and by many measures of all time. His most popular poems, such as "The Village Blacksmith," "The Ride of Paul Revere," and "The Children's Hour," have left an indelible mark on the English language in the form of lines that almost everyone has in their heads even if they could not immediately say where the lines came from. One could say that the most noteworthy characteristic of Longfellow's poetry is its popularity. Although in his lifetime Longfellow's greatness was inferred from his popularity, his reputation among critics today has decidedly diminished. The most natural question to pursue in relation to Longfellow's poetry, then, is the difference between popularity and greatness. This trial has been blazed before by the Nobel Laureate poet W. B. Yeats, in his essay "What Is 'Popular Poetry'?" (originally published in 1901 and incorporated into his essay collection *Ideas of Good and Evil* in 1903), probably the most important critique of Longfellow yet written.

Yeats is not kind to Longfellow. He speaks of "the triviality of emotion, the poverty of ideas, the imperfect sense of beauty of a poetry whose most typical expression is in Longfellow" and means especially his short, popular middle-period poems like "The Children's Hour." Yeats believed that there are two kinds of great poetry. The first he called the unwritten

WHAT DO I READ NEXT?

- Charles C. Calhoun's *Longfellow: A Rediscovered Life* (2004) is especially useful for the details of Longfellow's biography and gives a conventional reading of the poetry.

- *The Diary of Clara Crowninshield: A European Tour with Longfellow, 1835–1836*, is a transcription of the journal Crowninshield kept when she was a member of Longfellow's tour group on his second trip to Europe. The diary was published for the first time in an edition by Andrew Hilen in 1956 by the University of Washington Press.

- *Folktales from the Japanese Countryside* (2007), is a retelling of traditional Japanese stories for young adults by Hiroko Fujita. The domestication of traditional stories into a form palatable to bourgeois taste was a major concern of Longfellow's, as exemplified by his use of the story of the Mouse Tower of Bingen in "The Children's Hour."

- The Library of America volume *Henry Wadsworth Longfellow: Poems and Other Writings* (2000) is an anthology containing all of Longfellow's major works, including poems like "The Village Blacksmith" and "The Ride of Paul Revere," which are the poems most comparable to "The Children's Hour."

- *Mrs. Longfellow: The Letters and Journals of Fanny Appleton Longfellow* is an edition of the surviving papers of Longfellow's second wife, edited by Edward Wagenknecht in 1956.

- *Evangeline* (1847) is an epic by Longfellow that tells the story of the expulsion of the Acadians (Cajans) from Nova Scotia and their journey to Louisiana. A modern edition was published by Nimbus Publishing in 1995.

tradition. By this he means the folktales and ballads that exist among the great masses of the poor going back to time immemorial as well as the aristocratic traditions of oral epics like the *Iliad*, *Beowulf*, or the various mythological cycles

"THE HONEY-DRIPPING SWEETNESS OF THE
POEM IS THE LITERARY EQUIVALENT OF SOFT-FOCUS,
IN WHICH ANY DISTURBING DETAIL IS EDITED OUT."

of his own Irish tradition. The second is the poetry of the written tradition, which represents an utterly different approach from folk tradition precisely because it produces discrete written works, although these works are informed by the study of folk tradition. This tradition is represented by poets like Shakespeare or Percy Bysshe Shelley. Longfellow is not, in Yeats's view, a poet of either kind. He is instead what Yeats terms a popular poet. This means first that "Longfellow has his popularity, in the main, because he tells his story or his idea so that one needs nothing but his verses to understand it." In other words, he does not interact with either the unwritten or written tradition of English poetry. In contrast, "Poetry that is not popular poetry presupposes, indeed, more than it says." Art can be produced only on a foundation of other art. For Yeats, Longfellow is a poet,

> of the middle class, of people who have unlearned the unwritten tradition which binds the unlettered, so long as they are masters of themselves, to the beginning of time and to the foundation of the world, and who have not learned the written tradition which has been established upon the unwritten.

The middle class has stepped away from an unself-conscious participation in folk tradition but at the same time is not at ease in high literary culture because the middle classes have not received an elite education. In Yeats's view, the middle class is essentially imitative: "Nature, which cannot endure emptiness, has made them gather conventions which cannot disguise their low birth though they copy, as from far off, the dress and manners of the well-bred and the well-born." Although Yeats's language is somewhat archaic, middle-class culture certainly models elite culture. It seems that for Yeats, Longfellow is essentially imitative, an observation that suggests a basis for further investigation.

Art history has something to contribute to understanding imitative literature. Gillo Dorfles,

in his book *Kitsch*, has developed an understanding of the middle-class aesthetic implicit in Yeats's essay that is very helpful in reading Longfellow. The term *kitsch* originated in German artistic circles in the 1860s. It originally referred to cheap, mass-produced copies of art: German tourists who visited Florence would come back with miniature plaster casts (today it would be plastic casts) of Michelangelo's *David*. But Dorfles gave the term new significance. He recognized that kitsch is more useful as a description of an attitude toward art than of art objects themselves. Left to themselves, most people will appreciate the beautiful, no matter how or in what medium it is expressed. But when a person becomes miseducated regarding art or literature; when he thinks it must be improving, or educational; when he thinks that the point of experiencing art is not enjoyment but to build up an image of himself as sophisticated so he can impress others, then the appreciation of art will become kitsch. Kitsch man (as Dorfles terms a person thinking in this way), does not understand a cultivated appreciation of art but believes that he does so; therefore, it is impossible for him to develop true cultivation. Even when kitsch man sees an original masterpiece, his response is imitative; he reacts as he thinks a cultivated person ought to, even though he has no real understanding of what that reaction means. Kitsch man removes the meaning from art. The result is to treat the appreciation of art as a parody of education, as if kitsch man were taking a test and received a point for each work of art he could check off as having seen. The sentiment or feeling in art is reduced to the sentimental. Kitsch man believes that the experience of viewing art should make him feel good about himself; he knows nothing of art that explores troubling, dangerous emotions.

It should be obvious that Dorfles's kitsch man is the same as Yeats's middle class. While Yeats's polemic may be overreaching, it is true that the middle class is peculiarly disposed to fall into kitsch. The middle classes have the leisure and income necessary to devote time to the exploration of art and literature, but too often an education that prepared them only for professional pursuits. Yeats is a believer that, in culture, half an education is worse than none. To mix the language of the two theorists, Yeats views Longfellow's popular poetry as popular with the middle class precisely because it is purposely written to be consumed as kitsch. The features that make this true in the case of "The

Children's Hour" can now be examined against this theoretical background.

The father and daughters in "The Children's Hour" love each other in an ideal and uncomplicated way that any reader, without thinking about the matter too deeply, would want for himself. The honey-dripping sweetness of the poem is the literary equivalent of soft-focus, in which any disturbing detail is edited out. The reader does not encounter real emotion or sentiment, does not have to consider the imperfect emotional character of his own life, but can momentarily bask in the sentimental sweetness and light of the poem. The reader is not called upon to think in order to understand the poem. It is self-contained without reference to other literature and does not call on any special knowledge to be understood. The poem's extended metaphor of the knights' assault on the castle might seem to belie this, but the image is available in popular nineteenth-century romance literature, which is better treated as a commercial product supplied to the middle-class audience than as art. If anything, the overeducated reader, in order to appreciate the poem as Longfellow intended, must keep away from his consciousness the brutality of medieval warfare that supplies the basis of the metaphor. History is used to supply trappings rather than to give meaning. Even the seemingly obscure reference to the fate of Bishop Hatto calls for nothing from the reader. In the first place, those lines are perfectly comprehensible in themselves. It would be perverse to consider them an intertextual reference to Robert Southey's poem on Hatto in the usual sense. Instead, Longfellow is making a reference to the guidebook literature of the grand tour. The very height of middle-class Victorian culture was the grand tour of Europe, by which middle-class kitsch man could come to control and consume not European culture, but a miniature copy of European culture laid out to him in his Baedeker's tour book. Each city on the Rhine cruise has some interesting or educational tidbit associated with it, each one of which must be checked as accomplished once the city is visited. The story of Hatto teaches an important, improving fact about Bingen, so the middle-class traveler has absorbed it and will understand when Longfellow regurgitates it. Yeats insists that Longfellow's poetry contains neither anything original nor anything learned. "The Children's Hour" seems beautiful on its surface, but rather than that image being conditioned by

a deeper meaning below, there is not very much underneath the surface at all. Longfellow intended the poem for a middle-class market and shaped it to appeal to his audience. Hence the poem is better understood as kitsch rather than art. This hardly diminishes the poem's importance as the history of modern culture is often the study of kitsch rather than art or, as Yeats terms it, of popular art.

The recent tendency of criticism of "The Children's Hour" has been to treat it as evidence for the history of culture, of family life, of the middle class, rather than as literature. Henry James, in his short story "The Point of View" (1882), points out that "Longfellow wrote a charming little poem called 'The Children's Hour,' but he ought to have called it 'The Children's Century.'" He means that childhood assumed in the nineteenth century a new importance never before conceived of, a trend that would only increase in later periods as mass culture became dominated by marketing primarily aimed at youth culture. The poem marks a shift toward a new sensibility that today is called Victorian, with a new conception of the family, and a new conception of childhood that marks one of the greatest changes of industrial culture. Bearing witness to that change is the legacy of "The Children's Hour," rather than an inherent greatness in the poem itself.

Source: Rita M. Brown, Critical Essay on "The Children's Hour," in *Poetry for Students*, Gale, Cengage Learning, 2016.

John Derbyshire
In the following excerpt, Derbyshire discusses why some critics feel Longfellow's work is trite.

Strolling around Disneyland this summer, re-acquainting myself with Peter Pan, Winnie the Pooh, Mister Toad, Simba, and so on, the following reflection occurred to me: that these strange imagined characters were originally (at one slight remove, in Simba's case) the creations of some very bourgeois persons. Barrie, Grahame, Milne, and Kipling were conventional, sober, uxorious, well-dressed gentlemen of respectable employment and opinions, yet the fruits of their imaginations have proved far more durable than those of any bohemian counterculture you can name. Not a very original reflection, to be sure, but it is something to be able to reflect at all while heading from

The father's chair is compared to a turret of a castle. (© SergeBertasiusPhotography / Shutterstock.com)

> THOUGH LONGFELLOW WAS AN EXTREMELY INTELLIGENT MAN … AS A CREATOR OF VERSE, HE WAS AN IDIOT SAVANT. THE STUFF JUST BUBBLED UP OUT OF HIM UNPREDICTABLY. HE COULD NOT EXPLAIN IT AND HAD NO REAL THEORY OF POETIC COMPOSITION."

Fantasyland to Adventureland in ninety-degree heat with a first-grader and a preschooler in tow.

Some similar thoughts came to mind as I was reading the new selection of Longfellow's works recently published by the Library of America. Longfellow was as respectable as it is possible for a man to be. Writing and public lecturing apart, his entire paid employment consisted of five-and-a-half years teaching modern languages at Bowdoin and seventeen years teaching the same at Harvard. He had two wives, both of whom he adored, both of whom predeceased him. We know of no other liaisons involving physical intimacy, and on both internal and external evidence, it is extremely unlikely that any such connections existed. He was raised in a happy family and begat another, was a filial son and a loving father. He had only the feeblest interest in politics, and never stood for any office. As best I have been able to determine, Henry Wadsworth Longfellow never broke the law, never got drunk, never discharged a firearm or socked anybody on the jaw in anger, never played at cards for money or speculated on the stock market, never betrayed a friend or made a pass at another man's wife.

Nor is it in the least probable that this outward sobriety was a lid clamped on some raging inner turmoil. I spoke of internal evidence for Longfellow's character—that is, his own writings, letters, recorded talk and private journals. These are plentiful throughout his life, from a letter written at age six to his father to journal entries a few days before his death. There is nothing in them to suggest any quirks of personality more extraordinary than a mild and occasional hypochondria. (Longfellow died of peritonitis at age seventy-five, declining from good health to death in just five days.)

It is therefore not very surprising that literary critics in present-day academia, obsessed as they are with the "transgressive" do not find much of interest in Longfellow's life. There is no scholarly English-language biography of the poet in print, nor has there been for decades. A list of materials one might recommend to a nonspecialist inquirer into Longfellow's life and work would look very much the same now as it did thirty years ago. At its head I should put Professor Edward Wagenknecht's 1966 sketch, *Henry Wadsworth Longfellow: Portrait of an American Humanist*. (For those who are amused by such oddities, I note that the last word in the title is misprinted as "Humorist" in the notes to Mr. Paul Johnson's *A History of the American People*.) Wagenknecht had a gift for encompassing literary personalities in a couple of hundred pages; he did the same service for Poe, Hawthorne, Irving, and other nineteenth-century American authors. Some civic-spirited publisher could do a service to literature by bringing out a uniform edition of Wagenknecht's little handbooks. Newton Arvin's 1962 *Longfellow: His Life and Work* has more critical depth so far as the works are concerned, and the *Life* by Longfellow's youngest brother, Samuel, gives as much as any non-academic would want to read of the poet's journals and correspondence.

As with the life, so with the verse. Drop Longfellow into a literary conversation nowadays and you will get some odd looks. The exchanges that follow will include words and phrases like "mawkish," "shallow," "trite," "mechanical," "unadventurous," "tame, "jingles," "slave to conventional modes and diction," "the innocence of America's literary youth," and so on. When I produced my own CD of readings from American poetry in 1999, I included more pieces from Longfellow than from any other poet. This, a number of people have told me, was a serious error of judgment. "Four poems by Longfellow," scolded one lady indignantly, "and not one from Vachel Lindsay?" A friend who teaches English in an excellent suburban high school tells me that Longfellow is not on the curriculum. So far as the literary authorities of our time are concerned, Longfellow is not merely a dead poet, he is a dead dead poet.

For all that, Longfellow has been a continuous presence in our language since *Voices of the Night* was published in 1839, and his lines are still familiar today, though many who know them could not tell you who wrote them. "I shot an arrow into the air"; "Under a spreading chestnut tree"; "A banner with the strange device"; "Ships that pass in the night"; "One, if by land, and two, if by sea"; "Though the mills of God grind slowly, yet they grind exceeding small." No other American poet has so penetrated the general consciousness of the entire English-speaking world. And, whatever our literary clerisy may feel, he is still with us.

Item: My wife and I arrived early one afternoon for our ballroom dancing lesson. Our instructor, a thoughtful, well-educated man of about thirty-five, was attempting to teach some basic steps to a class of girls from the local high school, who seemed more interested in giggling and shrieking. When it was over he came to sit with us and, with obvious relief, watched the schoolgirls leave. As the door closed behind the last of them he turned to us with an expression of mock desperation and recited through clenched teeth the first stanza of "The Children's Hour":

Between the dark and the daylight, When night is beginning to lower, Comes a pause in the day's occupations, That is known as the children's hour.

Item: Reviewing a book by Amitai Etzioni, guru of the "communitarian" movement, for a political magazine a year or so ago, it occurred to me that many of the author's prescriptions depended on our being able to recapture the social habits and attitudes of an earlier time, and that it was unlikely we could do this because, as we say nowadays, the toothpaste is out of the tube. Seeking for an apt way to phrase the thought in context, I recalled some lines from "The Golden Milestone," which served my purpose very well:

We may build more splendid habitations, Fill our rooms with paintings and with sculptures, But we cannot Buy with gold the old associations!

These items bring to mind a word Samuel Longfellow used somewhere in respect of his brother's verse: serviceable. You can bring out Longfellow's lines and use them in all kinds of circumstances. He had a knack for expressing commonplace thoughts very memorably.

It is an interesting question why poets of our own time cannot do this. It may be that we have a very limited requirement for such "serviceable" lines and that the nineteenth century supplied all we need. Much more likely, in my opinion, it is because modern poets are intellectuals, who are expected to have some well-turned ideas about form, system, method, and, of course, politics, and that this precludes them from having commonplace thoughts, or from being willing to express such thoughts in verse.

Longfellow was the very opposite of an intellectual. This might seem an odd thing to say about a man who spoke numerous languages and served on the faculty of Harvard University for seventeen years, yet it is certainly true. To anyone immersed in the literary culture of the present day, Longfellow's utter lack of interest in criticism-much less "critical theory"!—or in abstract systems of any kind, must be astounding. "What is the use of writing about books?" he asked in 1850, "excepting so far as to give information to those who cannot get the books themselves?" Oh, dear. Nor was this just writer's pique at negative reviews, which he took in his gentlemanly stride. Of Edgar Allan Poe's often scathing remarks about his work, he said only: "The harshness of his criticisms, I have never attributed to anything but the irritation of a sensitive nature, chafed by some indefinite sense of wrong." (Which also happens to wrap up in one sentence an extraordinary amount of insight into Poe.)

Similarly with religion and politics. Longfellow had the typical middle-class American horror of strong opinions. Though deeply religious, he had no patience with theological doctrine, and probably could not understand it. The author of *Poems on Slavery* was, says Wagenknecht, anti-slavery but not abolitionist, when he associated with abolitionists he felt "like Alfred among the Danes." There is an entry in his journal that is pertinent here. On November 27, 1861 he records: "George Sumner and Mr. Bakounin to dinner. Mr. B. is a Russian gentleman of education and ability....An interesting man." This was, of course, the great anarchist and revolutionary Mikhail Bakunin, the familiar of Marx, Proudhon, and Alexander Herzen, but what Longfellow found interesting was Bakunin's narration of his adventures and escapades, not—or, at any rate, not worth recording—anything he might have said about class struggle or the specter haunting Europe.

...Though Longfellow was an extremely intelligent man—he was Bowdoin's Professor of Modern Languages at age twenty-two—as a creator of verse, he was an idiot savant. The stuff just bubbled up out of him unpredictably. He could not explain it and had no real theory of poetic composition. "The Arrow and the Song" was jotted down one Sunday morning before church; "The Wreck of the Hesperus" was written at one sitting. He could not write vers d'occasion and usually begged off requests to do so; the elegantly beautiful "Morituri Salutamus" is almost the lone exception. The history of his life as a poet contains strange pauses and spells of sterility; between the ages of nineteen and thirty, usually a poet's prime years, he seems to have produced no verse at all....

Source: John Derbyshire, "Longfellow & the Fate of Modern Poetry," in *New Criterion*, Vol. 19, No. 4, December 2000, p. 12.

Richard Dilworth Rust

In the following excerpt, Rust provides an overview of critical reception to Longfellow's work.

...Three dominant modes of evaluating Longfellow are found in the early criticisms by

> **LONGFELLOW WAS ONE OF THE FIRST AMERICAN POETS WHO WAS WIDELY READ. HECHT CITES TEN RUSSIAN TRANSLATORS OF LONGFELLOW BEFORE 1900, AND NOTES THAT FROM 1918 TO 1935 THE APPEARANCE OF SEVEN EDITIONS OF HIS POEMS INDICATED LONGFELLOW'S POPULARITY UNDER THE SOVIET REGIME."**

Nathaniel Hawthorne, Edgar Allan Poe, and Margaret Fuller, and have continued to the present. Hawthorne represents those who admire Longfellow the man and comment, sometimes extravagantly, on the virtues they find in his writings. Thus, in his letter of December 26, 1839 (quoted by Samuel Longfellow), Hawthorne says concerning Longfellow's poems, "Nothing equal to some of them was ever written in this world, this western world, I mean; and it would not hurt my conscience much to include the other hemisphere." Again, in his review of *Evangeline*, reprinted by Randall Stewart in "Hawthorne's Contributions to the *Salem Advertiser*" (*AL*, Jan. 1934) and discussed by H. H. Hoeltje in "Hawthorne's Review of *Evangeline*" (*NEQ*, June 1950), Hawthorne praises the poem for the "simplicity of high and exquisite art" with which it is told.

Poe's criticisms of Longfellow are often brilliant and incisive, yet they demonstrate what Longfellow called "the irritation of a sensitive nature chafed by some indefinite sense of wrong." Poe represents critics whose evaluations are negatively biased by their seeing Longfellow as a representative of imitative poetry, superficiality, sentimentality, and the like. Poe's reviews, collected in *The Complete Works of Edgar Allan Poe* (New York, 1902), contain guarded praise for several poems but are in the main disparaging. Reviewing *Hyperion* in 1839, Poe considers Longfellow "singularly deficient in all those important faculties which give artistical power, and without which never was immortality effected. He has no combining or binding force." Reviewing *Ballads and Other Poems*, Poe criticizes the theory of poetry which regards the inculcation of a moral as essential. Then, in reviewing *The Waif* in 1845, Poe started "the Longfellow war" by charging Longfellow with plagiarism—a charge he repeated later that year. (For a summary of Poe's criticisms, see Wagenknecht, *Longfellow: A Full-Length Portrait*, and Perry Miller, *The Raven and the Whale*, New York, 1956.)

Margaret Fuller, like Poe, resented the excessive praise given Longfellow, but neverthe-less demonstrated a kind of balancing of strengths and weaknesses which is found in the most penetrating Longfellow criticism. In *Papers on Literature and Art* (London, 1846) and in *The Writings of Margaret Fuller*, edited by Mason Wade (New York, 1941), she says: "Longfellow is artificial and imitative. He bor-rows incessantly, and...is very faulty in using broken or mixed metaphors. The ethical part of his writing has a hollow, secondhand sound. He has, however, elegance, a love of the beautiful, and a fancy for what is large and manly, if not a full sympathy with it. His verse breathes at times much sweetness; and if not allowed to supersede what is better, may promote a taste for good poetry. Though imitative, he is not mechanical." Again, his work is "of little original poetic power, but of much poetic taste and sensibility."

REPUTATION

Longfellow's readership and popularity during his lifetime was immense in the United States (as indicated by Wagenknecht and by L. E. Hart, "The Beginnings of Longfellow's Fame," *NEQ*, Mar. 1963) and was unequalled by any other writer of the period throughout the world (as noted by Clarence Gohdes in *American Literature in Nineteenth Century England*, New York, 1944). Gohdes says that in England Long-fellow was better known than Tennyson or Browning; critical reviews there mixed harsh criticism with extravagant praise. In Russia, according to David Hecht, "Longfellow in Rus-sia" (*NEQ*, Dec. 1946), Longfellow was one of the first American poets who was widely read. Hecht cites ten Russian translators of Longfel-low before 1900, and notes that from 1918 to 1935 the appearance of seven editions of his poems indicated Longfellow's popularity under the Soviet regime. And in South America, Long-fellow has had the largest number of poems translated by the greatest number of South American translators, although he lost ground in the twentieth century to Poe and Whitman, as J. E. Englekirk tells us in "Notes on Longfellow in South America" (*Hispania* [Stanford], Oct. 1942). (For an overview of Longfellow's reputa-tion in Latin America, see Robert S. Ward's introductory note to Ernest J. Moyne's "The Origin and Development of Longfellow's *Song of Hiawatha*," *Journal of Inter-American Studies*, Jan. 1966.)

Longfellow's position and popularity reached a peak in the 1880s and remained high through the Longfellow centennial in 1907. Expressing a widely held opinion, Charles Eliot Norton in *Tributes to Longfellow and Emerson by The Massachusetts Historical Society* (Bos-ton, 1882) states: "It was not by depth of thought or by original views of nature that he won his place in the world's regard; but it was by sym-pathy with the feelings common to good men and women everywhere, and by the simple, direct, sincere, and delicate expression of them, that he gained the affection of mankind." Long-fellow's appeal to Eric S. Robertson, as shown in his *Life of Henry Wadsworth Longfellow* (Lon-don, 1887), was his ability to embellish the com-mon and to produce "a wealth of tender and beautiful sayings that in every civilized land... became household favorites." And William Dean Howells, in *Literary Friends and Acquaint-ance* (New York, 1900) and in "The Art of Long-fellow" (*NAR*, Mar. 1907), praises Longfellow as a poet who saw beyond his native New England to express the universal in the sense that "the poet has nothing to tell, except from what is actually or potentially common to the race."

A sampling of criticism during or near the Longfellow centennial finds Longfellow lauded for his moral purpose (R. B. Steele, "The Poetry of Longfellow," *SR*, Apr. 1905), his "trustwor-thy and graceful" translations (Leon H. Vincent; *American Literary Masters*, Boston, 1906), his popularizing "our scant store of American tra-ditions" (M. C. Crawford, "Longfellow: Poet of Places," *Putnam's Monthly Magazine*, Feb. 1907), his simplicity, reverence, and grace which appeals to the "intellectual middle class" (Bliss Perry, "The Centenary of Longfellow," *AtM*, Mar. 1907), his interpreting to his gener-ation "the hitherto alien treasures of European culture" (Bliss Perry, *Park-Street Papers*, Bos-ton, 1908), and his mastery of the sonnet (Paul Elmer More in *Shelburne Essays, Fifth Series*, New York, 1908, and H. W. Mabie, "Sonnets from the *Divine Comedy*," *Outlook*, Jan. 1909). Summing up Longfellow's reputation at the turn of the century, Thomas Wentworth Higginson in *Henry Wadsworth Longfellow* affirms that "he is a classic" who "will never be read for the profoundest stirring, or for the unlocking of the deepest mysteries" but "will always be read for invigoration, for comfort, for content."

Paradoxically, it was often the elements praised by Norton, Higginson, Perry, Stedman, and others that were deprecated by later critics. Thus Longfellow's ability to reach all levels of society is dismissed by Gamaliel Bradford as mere commonplace ("Portraits of American Authors," *Bookman*, Nov. 1915) or is considered by John Macy to be an appeal to "simple minds" (*The Spirit of American Literature*, New York, 1913). Instead of Longfellow's being an adaptor of "the beauty and sentiment of other lands to the convictions of his people" (E. C. Stedman, *Poets of America*, Boston, 1913), he is considered a grizzled old man to whom "the world was a German picture-book, never detaching itself from the softly colored pages" (Van Wyck Brooks in *America's Coming-of-Age*, New York, 1915, reprinted in Philip Rahv, *Literature in America*, Cleveland, 1957). And rather than a "storyteller in verse" with "power to transplant to American literature some of the colour and melody and romantic charm of the complex European literature he had studied" (William P. Trent, "Longfellow," *CHAL*), Longfellow is considered "bounded by his books and he cannot see beyond them" (Gorman, *A Victorian American*).

That Longfellow ceased to appeal to certain moderns of the twenties and thirties is illustrated by I. A. Richards's experiment, described in *Practical Criticism* (New York, 1929), in which 92 percent of his students judged Longfellow's "In the Churchyard at Cambridge" unfavorably— "by far the most disliked" of the thirteen poems they criticized. And Ludwig Lewisohn in *Expression in America* (New York, 1932) says: "Who, except wretched schoolchildren, now reads Longfellow? . . . He never touches poetry. He borrows form and accepts content from without. . . . To minds concerned with the imaginative interpretation of man, of nature and of human life, Longfellow has nothing left to say."

Responding to the type of disparagement found in Lewisohn and others (such as V. L. Parrington) who found "little intellect" and "little creative originality" in Longfellow, G. R. Elliot in "Gentle Shades of Longfellow," in *The Cycle of Modern Poetry* (Princeton, N.J., 1929),

argues persuasively that the modern taste is too caught up in aesthetic dogmas to recognize Longfellow's vital place in the mainstream of American poetry. Saying that the academics have "a fatal aversion for American naïveté," Elliott proposes a literary-historical study of American literature which views its past growth "more largely and more organically." Commenting on Longfellow's simplicity, George Saintsbury in *Prefaces and Essays* (London, 1933) asserts that while one never has to question Longfellow's meaning, his meaning is never contemptible and is sometimes very admirable. Saintsbury advocates selectivity in evaluating Longfellow's poetry—which already had been a practice of Longfellow's most discerning critics but which allowed a hasty discounting, in Saintsbury's case, of *Evangeline*, "The Arsenal at Springfield," and the sonnets.

An important contribution to the revaluation of Longfellow during the thirties was Odell Shepard's introduction to *Representative Selections* of Longfellow's writings. Discussing Longfellow's environment, opinions, limitations, and popularity, Shepard notes weaknesses such as Longfellow's uncritical temper, incomprehensive grasp of contemporary fact, self-indulgent romanticism, escape to the past, and flinching "from all violence, satire, and stern denunciation"; yet he balances these by praising Longfellow's success in "saying what all have thought and in singing what all have felt," his "harmony and unity of the whole composition," and his deepening "our sense of the American past," thereby providing a link with what we have been. In the same vein as Shepard, Howard Mumford Jones called for a revaluation of Longfellow, first in "The Longfellow Nobody Knows" (*Outlook*, 8 August 1928) and later in *American Writers on American Literature*, edited by John A. Macy (New York, 1934). While recognizing that Longfellow lacks depth and sharpness of philosophy, Jones esteems his narrative talent, sense of humor, and command of the sonnet, and considers "lucidity, gentleness, musicality" his essential qualities. It was also in the midthirties that Van Wyck Brooks in *The Flowering of New England* (New York, 1936) revised his earlier opinion and asserted that while "Longfellow's flaccidity debarred him from the front rank," his work possessed "a quality, a unity of feeling and tone, that gave him a place apart among popular poets." . . .

Source: Richard Dilworth Rust, "Henry Wadsworth Longfellow," in *Fifteen American Authors before 1900: Bibliographic Essays on Research and Criticism*, edited by Robert A. Rees and Earl N. Harbert, University of Wisconsin Press, 1971, pp. 270–74.

SOURCES

Arbor, Robert, "'Not from the Grand Old Masters': The Art of Henry and Ernest Wadsworth Longfellow," in *Reconsidering Longfellow*, edited by Christopher Irmscher and Robert Arbor, Fairleigh Dickinson University Press, 2014, pp. 159–76.

Arvin, Newton, *Longfellow: His Life and Work*, Little, Brown, 1963, pp. 318–29.

Atherton, Lewis, "Selections Most Frequently Memorized in the Elementary School," in *The Elementary School Teacher*, Vol. 15, No. 5, 1914, pp. 208–20.

Dorfles, Gillo, *Kitsch: The World of Bad Taste*, Universe, 1969, pp. 14–35.

Grask, Lilian, "The Mouse Tower," in *Folktales from Many Lands*, Thomas Y. Crowell, 1910, pp. 186–92.

Irmscher, Christoph, *Longfellow Redux*, University of Illinois Press, 2006, pp. 77–81.

James, Henry, "The Point of View," in *Complete Stories 1874–1884*, Library of America, 1999, pp. 519–64.

Longfellow, Alice, "Longfellow with His Children," in *Strand Magazine*, Vol. 14, No. 81, September 1897, pp. 250–53.

Longfellow, Henry Wadsworth, "The Children's Hour," in *Tales of a Wayside Inn*, Ticknor and Fields, 1863, pp. 209–11.

Southey, Robert, "The Tradition of Bishop Hatto," in *A Handbook for Travelers on the Continent: Being a Guide through Holland, Belgium, Prussia, and Northern Germany, and Along the Rhine from Holland to Switzerland*, John Murray, 1841, pp. 278–79.

Wagenknecht, Edward, *Henry Wadsworth Longfellow: His Poetry and Prose*, Ungar, 1986, pp. 135–37.

Yeats, W. B., "What Is 'Popular Poetry'?," in *Ideas of Good and Evil*, A. H. Bullen, 1903, pp. 1–14.

FURTHER READING

Howe, Daniel Walker, *What Hath God Wrought: The Transformation of America, 1815–1848*, Oxford University Press, 2007.

> Howe presents the history of the rise of the American middle class.

Longfellow, Henry Wadsworth, *The Song of Hiawatha*, Ticknor and Fields, 1855.

> *Hiawatha* is one of Longfellow's best-known and most significant works. It is written in the same trochaic tetrameter as "The Children's Hour." It is a rather confused presentation of Ojibwe mythology layered over with names drawn from Iroquois tradition and further material from the Finnish *Kalevala*.

Skinner, Henrietta Dana, *An Echo from Parnassus, Being Girlhood Memories of Longfellow and His Friends*, J. H. Sears, 1928.

> Skinner was a childhood friend of Longfellow's daughters.

Williams, Cecil B., *Henry Wadsworth Longfellow*, Twayne, 1964.

> Williams's general treatment of Longfellow's life and work is intended as an introduction for students.

SUGGESTED SEARCH TERMS

Henry Wadsworth Longfellow

"The Children's Hour" AND Henry Wadsworth Longfellow

realism

kitsch

middle class

gothic romance

Victorian

Hatto of Mainz

Enlightenment

NATASHA TRETHEWEY

2012

"Enlightenment" (2012), by Natasha Trethewey, poet laureate of the United States from 2012 to 2014, is about the poet's own racial identity and how that reality is conditioned by the history of race in the United States. The poem investigates changing racial attitudes organized around public perception of the affair between Thomas Jefferson and his slave Sally Hemings. That forgotten historical incident flashed into public consciousness in 1998 when DNA testing all but confirmed that Jefferson was the father of Hemings's children. Although this fact has been alleged for nearly two centuries and largely accepted by historians for a generation, the new evidence provoked a vigorous political reaction that denied Jefferson could have fathered children by one of his slaves, implying that if that guilt could be erased, the whole abusive history of race in America could be erased, or at least could go on being repressed. Trethewey has no such illusion, but she does not quite seem able to come to terms with the bewildering mixture of race that centuries of racism have left in America and what it means for her own biracial identity.

AUTHOR BIOGRAPHY

Trethewey was born in Gulfport, Mississippi, on April 26, 1966, on the one hundredth Confederate Memorial Day, as she likes to point out.

Natasha Trethewey (© *Bill O'Leary* | *The Washington Post via Getty Images*)

Events before her birth are unusually important for her life and literary career. Her father, Eric Trethewey, and her mother, Gwendolyn Ann Turnbough, met while they were both attending Kentucky State College. Trethewey was a white Canadian, while Turnbough was black and came from Gulfport. At the time, state law in Kentucky forbade the couple to marry because one was white and the other black, so they had to cross the Ohio River to get married in Cincinnati. Neither Kentucky nor Mississippi, where the couple moved after graduation, recognized the marriage. The Ku Klux Klan burned a cross on their front lawn. The family lived in Canada for two years while Eric Trethewey served in the Canadian navy. The elder Trethewey went to graduate school in New Orleans and would eventually become a professor, spending his career at Hollins University in Virginia, and a well-published poet. During school, he supported himself as a professional boxer. Trethewey's mother became a social worker in Atlanta. The marriage soon dissolved in divorce.

Natasha lived with her mother but frequently visited her father. Her mother had two more marriages, both to abusive husbands, and two divorces, but her third husband eventually murdered her, while Trethewey was studying English at the University of Georgia. Trethewey worked briefly as a social worker but took her father's advice to begin an MA in creative writing from Hollins under his own direction. She later earned an MFA in poetry from the University of Massachusetts Amherst (1995). She was hired as a professor at Emory University in Atlanta, where she still teaches. In 2000, Trethewey published her first book of poetry, *Domestic Work*, and her second, *Bellocq's Ophelia*, in 2002. *Native Guard* (2006) won the Pulitzer Prize for poetry, and her work has earned various other prizes and awards. She also served a term as poet laureate of Mississippi (2011–2012). The unifying theme of Trethewey's work is the recovery of lost black history. In 2012, she began the first of her two terms as poet laureate of the United States. She is unusually young to have received this honor, and she also took the unusual step of moving to Washington, DC, during her appointment. During this time, she published her collection *Thrall* (2012), which includes "Enlightenment." Her father died in 2014.

POEM TEXT

In the portrait of Jefferson that hangs
at Monticello, he is rendered two-toned:
his forehead white with illumination—

a lit bulb—the rest of his face in shadow,
darkened as if the artist meant to contrast   5
his bright knowledge, its dark subtext.

By 1805, when Jefferson sat for the portrait,
he was already linked to an affair
with his slave. Against a backdrop, blue

and ethereal, a wash of paint that seems   10
to hold him in relief, Jefferson gazes out
across the centuries, his lips fixed as if

he's just uttered some final word.
The first time I saw the painting. I listened
as my father explained the contradictions: 15

how Jefferson hated slavery, though—*out
of necessity*, my father said—had to own
slaves; that his moral philosophy meant

he could not have fathered those children:
would have been impossible, my father said.   20
For years we debated the distance between

word and deed. I'd follow my father from book
to book, gathering citations, listen
as he named—like a field guide to Virginia—

each flower and tree and bird as if to prove   25
a man's pursuit of knowledge is greater
than his shortcomings, the limits of his vision.

I did not know then the subtext
of our story, that my father could imagine
Jefferson's words made flesh in my flesh—   30

*the improvement of the blacks in body
and mind, in the first instance of their mixture
with the whites*—or that my father could believe

he'd made me *better*. When I think of this now,
I see how the past holds us captive,   35
its beautiful ruin etched on the mind's eye:

my young father, a rough outline of the old man
he's become, needing to show me
the better measure of his heart, an equation

writ large at Monticello. That was years ago.   40
Now, we take in how much has changed:
talk of Sally Hemings, someone asking,

How white was she?—parsing the fractions
as if to name what made her worthy
of Jefferson's attentions: a near white,   45

quadroon mistress, not a plain black slave.
Imagine stepping back into the past,

our guide tells us then—and I can't resist
whispering to my father: *This is where
we split up. I'll head around to the back.*   50
When he laughs, I know he's grateful

I've made a joke of it, this history
that links us—while father, black daughter—
even as it renders us other to each other.

POEM SUMMARY

The text used for this summary is from *Thrall*, Houghton Mifflin Harcourt, 2012, pp. 68–71. A version of the poem can be found on the following web page: http://www.poetryfoundation.org/poem/249398.

Trethewey's "Enlightenment" was published in her 2012 collection *Thrall* (an archaic term for *slave*). The fifty-four lines of the poem are divided into eighteen unnumbered three-line-long stanzas. The poem is free verse with no discernible meter or rhyme. The overall theme of the poem is a consideration of the speaker's own multicultural status in comparison with the descendants of the slave Sally Hemings (herself multiracial), fathered by her white master, Thomas Jefferson.

Stanza 1
The speaker of the poem (who cannot be simply or carelessly identified with the poet) is visiting Monticello, Thomas Jefferson's mansion on his plantation. The building has been preserved as a museum devoted to Jefferson. She is looking at a painting of Jefferson. There are many portraits of Jefferson at Monticello, but the 1805 painting by Gilbert Stuart is probably the one meant. It hangs in the main entrance hall and so is among the first things a visitor would see. She calls attention to the odd lighting of the picture, showing a very bright light reflecting from Jefferson's forehead while the rest of the face is in shadow.

Stanza 2
The speaker links the qualities of the painting to moral categories. The lightened forehead stands for Jefferson's undoubted genius; she cannot resist the conventional modern image of a light-bulb to suggest genius. The darkened face suggests something more sinister lurking beneath the surface.

Stanza 3

The speaker mentions that the portrait was done in 1805, confirming that it is the one by Gilbert Stuart. She also mentions that in 1805, at the beginning of his second term as president, Jefferson had already been attacked by his political opponents for having an affair with one of his slaves. Then she again turns to the artistic qualities of the painting.

Stanza 4

The background of Stuart's portrait is unusually abstract for its period. It is a bluish-green field with some detailing that does not correspond to any probable background that Jefferson might have been seated in front of. It would be unusual even for wallpaper. In the speaker's estimation, the image therefore resembles a sculptural relief and works to abstract Jefferson from time and space.

Stanza 5

Jefferson in the portrait looks to the speaker as if he has just finished speaking himself. She now recalls a time when she visited Monticello and saw the painting before. This was in the company of her father, probably when she was a good deal younger, very likely not yet an adult. At that time, her father had explained to her the contradictions that she is ruminating over now.

Stanza 6

The contradiction is that Jefferson personally hated slavery but was forced by necessity (the words are italicized for emphasis) to own slaves.

Stanza 7

The speaker's father believed that Jefferson's moral character would have prevented him from keeping a slave mistress (Sally Hemings) and fathering children by her. The impossibility is also emphasized by italics. The speaker must have been of a different opinion, since she debated the proposition with him over the years.

Stanza 8

The issue at hand is the disparity between Jefferson's words, which suggest that he ultimately favored emancipation and an end to slavery, compared with his undeniable actions of keeping slaves, even in the most degrading form—as a sex slave. The speaker and her father would read the scholarly literature on the subject to fuel their debates.

Stanza 9

The speaker describes the research as being like compiling a field guide to the natural history of Virginia. The research proved by example that the polymath Jefferson with all of his achievements rose above his shortcomings. Even Jefferson, however, could see only so far.

Stanza 10

The speaker says she did not then know the story that lay underneath the debate between her and her father. She must mean that she did not realize it, but her father certainly realized it. What her father had done was in part to make Jefferson's words flesh in the flesh of his daughter.

Stanza 11

The poem now quotes Jefferson's own words in a passage from his 1785 book, *Notes on the State of Virginia*. In the quotation, Jefferson suggests that blacks are inherently inferior to whites and that the only way to improve them would be to breed them with whites, producing individuals that are a mixture between the two races. The speaker now asserts that her current understanding (which she did not know before) is that her father believed that he was accomplishing this very thing in fathering her. As a point of reference, Trethewey's father was white, while her mother was black.

Stanza 12

The speaker suggests, based on this understanding, that the past ineluctably shapes the thinking of people alive today, as if they were the past's hostages. The past is both beautiful and ruined and leaves an image that cannot be ignored.

Stanza 13

The speaker suggests that when her father was young and took her to Monticello for the first time, he somehow needed to justify to her the correctness of what he had done, that it was done out of love.

Stanza 14

The speaker makes it clear that the circumstance of the poem is a later visit she and her father made to Monticello. She points out how much has changed in the experience of the tourists there compared with their earlier visit. The visitors now actually ask the guides about Sally Hemings.

Stanza 15

In particular, a visitor is quoted as asking how white Hemings was. The speaker suggests that this reveals an unspoken truth that Jefferson was attracted to her specifically because she was mostly white in her ancestry.

Stanza 16

The speaker, using the antiquated word *quadroon*, points out that Hemings had three white grandparents and was not an ordinary black slave. She then quotes the tour guide inviting the visitors to imagine themselves in Jefferson's time. Naturally this would mean that the speaker would find herself in Hemings's position, if not with Jefferson, then with some other owner. The stanza ends in the middle of the sentence in which the speaker begins to say that she cannot resist, which the reader might take at first to refer to the preceding thought and that she cannot resist that fantasy.

Stanza 17

In fact, what the speaker cannot resist is telling her father that she is abandoning the tour and will wait for him outside.

Stanza 18

Her father is relieved that the speaker can make a joke out of the situation, but the racial divide between them still makes them alien to each other.

THEMES

Enlightenment

The title to Trethewey's poem "Enlightenment" has a double sense. In the first sense, the one that readers will likely assume when they learn the poem deals with Thomas Jefferson, concerns the philosophical movement of the Enlightenment, a vital turning point in European and Western history. Traditional human cultures look to the past for authority. The source of wisdom and knowledge in a traditional culture is the old books and stories that define the culture's heritage and the institutions that mediate traditional wisdom to the culture at large. In the case of medieval Europe, tradition was defined in the first instance by the Christian Bible and then the other surviving writings from classical antiquity. Law came from the Catholic Church's canon law as well as the traditional law codes of the ancient Germanic tribes (common law); information about the natural world came from the Bible and from ancient authors such as the astronomer Ptolemy, who were mostly known from Arabic translations introduced into Europe through Spain, and so on for every other body of knowledge and area of life. Things began to change in Europe in a unique way in the sixteenth century thanks to the Protestant Reformation, which undermined the Church's authority, and the reexamination of ancient writings occasioned by the Renaissance. By the seventeenth century, scientists like Galileo Galilei and Johannes Kepler were proving not only that the old books were in many instances wrong but also that new information that was never dreamed of in antiquity could be obtained by studying nature directly.

By the eighteenth century, the philosophers of what would be called the Enlightenment (often called by the French term *philosophes* because France was the center of the movement) applied the same critical standards to every aspect of life. Their conclusion was that the class-based cultures and governments of Europe were built on false premises of elitism and privilege and that society needed to be reordered along rational lines, based on a foundation of human freedom and equality. The whole foundation of the modern world, built on science and industrialism, together with the ideals of equality between classes, sexes, and races, was laid during the Enlightenment, though they would be realized only in gradual stages over the next several centuries and are still not complete. Benjamin Franklin and Jefferson, especially during their terms as ambassadors to France in the 1780s, were celebrated as heroes of the Enlightenment because of their role in ending monarchical rule in America and founding a new state based on freedom and equality. Jefferson was especially praised as the author of the Declaration of Independence, a document that enshrined the principles of the Enlightenment (as would the later Bill of Rights).

This is not the enlightenment that Trethewey really has in mind in the poem, or at least not entirely. She is referring to her own enlightenment in the discovery that Jefferson's private life as a slave owner, and particularly as the father of children by a slave, conflicts with Jefferson's own ideals, and this disconnect between perception and society still haunts American culture and even her own family.

TOPICS FOR FURTHER STUDY

- *Poetry for Young People: African American Poetry* (2013), edited by Arnold Rampersad and Marcellus Blount, is a collection of poems by leading writers of the Harlem Renaissance (1920s–1940s), including Countee Cullen and James Baldwin. The poems were chosen and introduced with young adults in mind. Write a paper comparing the attitude toward race and the role of race in American consciousness in one of these poems and Trethewey's "Enlightenment."

- Trethewey's *Bellocq's Ophelia* (2002) is a cycle of poems about the title character, who is a mixed-race prostitute working in New Orleans in the early twentieth century, catering to a white clientele. Write a paper comparing this work with "Enlightenment" and focusing on issues of racial identity and Trethewey's interest in history.

- Thanks to her appointment as poet laureate, the Library of Congress maintains a page of links to Trethewey's presence on the web, including videos of her giving interviews and reading her poetry. The page includes links to Trethewey's occasional Public Broadcasting Services series, *Where Poetry Lives*, in which she examines contemporary social issues through poetry, and to important reviews and blog entries about her as well as to large numbers of her poems archived online. Utilizing this material, prepare a video presentation that gives a general introduction to Trethewey and her work.

- Beginning with the American occupation of Japan after World War II, and throughout the continuing occupation of Japan, American servicemen, both white and black and both in and out of marriages (and sometimes by rape), have fathered children with Japanese women. Yet in traditional Japanese culture, racial purity is an important cultural factor, so the children of these unions are often considered transgressive and face discrimination. The issue was recently highlighted with the Miss Japan contestant chosen for the 2015 Miss Universe pageant, Ariana Miyamoto. Miyamoto is biracial, with an African American father and Japanese mother. The controversy concerning the pageant highlights the same kind of racial tensions with Japanese culture as they exist in America. Research the topic and make a class presentation comparing the situation of biracial children in Japan with the place of biracial individuals in American culture with its history of slavery and discrimination.

Race Relations

When the father in "Enlightenment" denies that Jefferson could have had relations with Hemings, he means that he finds it morally repugnant and cannot imagine the venerable Jefferson doing such a thing. The only reason to think this way is that the violation repels his own moral sensibilities. This suggests that the father sees nothing similar to Jefferson and Hemings in his own relationship with his black wife. The daughter, however, is far from certain of this. No doubt Jefferson made justifications to his own moral sense for what he was doing with Hemings. Trethewey quotes this passage from Jefferson's *Notes on The State of Virginia*: "The improvement of the blacks in body and mind, in the first instance of their mixture with the whites." The narrative voice of the poem suggests that this is what her father believes: that he has made his own daughter better by giving her white ancestry. In other words, she says, he is as much trapped in racist American culture as Jefferson was, with no way out. With respect to her own father, Eric Trethewey, this proposition seems hard to sustain. He is Canadian and married a black woman in 1966 in defiance of the racist Jim Crow laws in place in Kentucky, their place of residence at the time. (Her parents had to travel to Ohio to be married.) Yet, Trethewey has spoken out, evaluating her father's relationship to her in racist terms.

In an interview with Marc McKee in the *Missouri Review*, Trethewey recalls her father's picking her up for his visitation after her parent's divorce:

> He would grab my hand and turn it over and look at my fingernails. You know, it's a kind of thing all parents do, I suppose . . . but because I am my white father's black daughter and I know about things in history, I could never completely escape feeling that there was something problematic about that inspection.

When she incorporated this memory into her work, she says, "I place[d] it within a context of chattel slavery, when people purchasing slaves in Louisiana would inspect them the way you inspect livestock." Yet the relationship between the father and daughter in "Enlightenment" never becomes hostile, any more (apparently) than did that between Natasha and Eric Trethewey before his death in 2014. Nevertheless, Trethewey seems to feel that the difference in their races has placed a barrier between her and her father. At the end of the poem, she says that the father must view the daughter as an *other* and vice versa. *Other*, in this case, derives from the work of Edward Said. According to Said, orientalism is a constructed way of viewing dominated, colonized cultures outside Europe or the United States. The colonizers view the colonized as an exotic other, something to be controlled and exploited and above all something that does not have a real human identity as an African or Asian. The identity of the *other* is that he or she does not belong to your own group and so can be molded into anything desired. Trethewey seems to feel that, after four centuries of slavery and racism in America, blacks and whites, even if they are father and daughter, can view each other only across this divide. Alexander O. Boulton, in his thoughtful review of several works on Hemings and Jefferson published in the years after the 1998 DNA findings, asks that question about America that Trethewey has in mind:

> The story of the Jefferson-Hemings relationship is part of an ongoing national conversation on issues of race, sexuality, and American culture. . . . Have we consistently ignored these issues in an effort to "whitewash" our national history? Have we excluded discussions of race

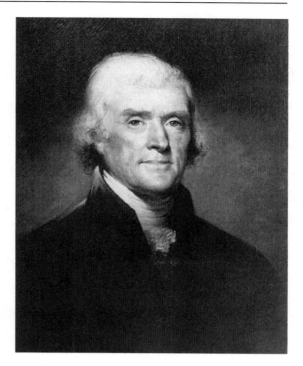

Trethewey's poem captures Jefferson's contradictions: he was the author of the Declaration of Independence but owned slaves. (© Everett Historical / Shutterstock.com)

and sexuality in an effort to make our historical memory conform to a Jeffersonian rhetoric of equality?

But indeed, as Trethewey recalls at the beginning of "Enlightenment," Jefferson has, as it were, two faces. The face of the slaveholder seems to suggest that race must forever be an unbridgeable divide. The Jefferson of the Enlightenment offers, in the Declaration of Independence, as much as Friedrich Schiller does in the "Ode to Joy," the hope of the brotherhood of man, in which race plays no part.

STYLE

Free Verse

What is poetry? A very conventional answer will look at such traditional poetry as Shakespeare's sonnets and point out that they are written in a specific meter (iambic pentameter) and a given rhyme scheme. Those superficial characteristics are not the essence of poetry. There are many thousands of sonnets written in conformity with the metrical rules but which are ignored because they are deficient in the real qualities of poetry. In the nineteenth century, as English poetry became more the product of culture rather than nature, poets began to realize this and began to write in free verse, which compared with a sonnet has no more metrical stereotyping than prose. What sets a sonnet apart from an essay is, at a minimum, figurative language; this is the vital part of poetry that is preserved in free verse. When Trethewey wants to convey the idea of her intensive research into the history of Sally Hemings and Thomas Jefferson, she does not describe sitting in a library reading through stacks of books. She describes looking for flowers and birds in the Virginia countryside. And yet the reader understands what she means in a far more precise and a far more important sense than a literal description could have provided. That use of language, rather than an arrangement of iambs with the occasional dactyl or trochee, is what makes "Enlightenment" a poem.

Intertextuality

Quotation is the direct transcription of an existing text into a new one. Trethewey does this when she prints the exact words that Jefferson wrote in *Notes on the State of Virginia* (though even then she leaves it to the reader to discover the source of the quotation). In line 36 of the poem, however, Trethewey, does something different. It is first evident that she presents an interesting idea: the ruins of the past are beautiful, and it is because humans are attracted to their beauty that the past determines the future. The idea that the past is a pile of ruins comes from the Renaissance. Europeans during the Middle Ages certainly knew that their world was full of ruined Roman buildings, but they had no conception that civilization had once come to a halt and fallen down. (Why should they? In 1300 Europe was more populous, richer, and more technologically advanced than it had been in the year 200.) The Renaissance was as much as anything else the imposition of this view on the past. In the romantic era, ruins were held to be more beautiful per se than the buildings of the modern world for the first time out of a sense of nostalgia and longing for an ideal past that existed only in the romantic's incredibly fertile imaginations. (One can see this, for instance, in the paintings of Caspar David Friedrich or Hubert Robert.) So far, Trethewey seems to be

evoking these ideas. Perhaps she had some more specific text in mind when she wrote this line?

The sense that the modern world is the ruin of some older, greater era that has been lost gained new currency after the disaster of World War I. Even in America, untouched by the destruction of the conflict, it became a dominant theme of the writers that are even called the Lost Generation. It is certainly true of William Faulkner, the most prominent southern writer. Reading Faulkner is like taking part in an archaeological excavation, digging down from the trivial, meaningless, absurd world of the present into the meaning of a perfect past. Even closer to the very language of Trethewey's line is the poetry of T. S. Eliot, with his description of the modern world as a pile of ruined statues. Although Trethewey does not quote any other piece of literature, when she wrote that line, all of this or something like this must have been in her mind, and reading the line calls the same into the mind of her audience. Trethewey refers to all of these texts, whether poetry, novels, or paintings, and the thought worlds in which they are embedded without naming or quoting them—all in a single line. This technique is called intertextuality.

HISTORICAL CONTEXT

Jefferson and Slavery

At the most personal level of connection between Jefferson and slavery, he owned a slave plantation, the basis of the New World economy inherited from Arab and Roman civilization. It was fueled by the capture of slaves in Africa and their transportation to the Americas. Throughout his life, Jefferson owned almost 700 slaves but never more than 140 at any one time. It must be admitted that his slaves had better lives than most. He did not interfere with slave families, and when he had to sell slaves, he would sell them only in family units so that husbands and wives or parents and children would not be forcibly separated. He preferred to sell rather than to punish unruly slaves. Nevertheless, his slaves suffered the proscription of liberty and the control of their own labor inherent in the institution. His overseers were empowered to use violence to keep order and frequently did so. Runaways from Monticello were hunted down by slave catchers. It must be noted that Jefferson was especially benevolent to the Hemings family, whom he owned. He trained them in skilled labor and freed them either in his lifetime or in his will. Jefferson inherited his plantation and most of his slaves from his father-in-law. They came with a large debt for which the slaves were collateral and which grew throughout Jefferson's life, making it impossible for him to free his own slaves without facing bankruptcy.

In his *Notes on the State of Virginia*, Jefferson deals with the larger issues of slavery. He takes it for granted that slavery should be ended as quickly as possible. He does not think it would be practical to simply free the existing slaves and expect them to function in American society. This would be impossible not only because the slaves would have a justified grievance against their former masters but also because of, as he put it, "deep rooted prejudices entertained by the whites." This would suggest that Jefferson considers that he is viewing the matter dispassionately, but he is hardly free from such prejudices himself. He considers another impediment to black freedom to be the fact that blacks are "in reason much inferior, as I think one could scarcely be found capable of tracing and comprehending the investigations of Euclid." Of all the choices available to end slavery, Jefferson thinks the best, or the least bad, is to free the blacks and transport them overseas (he had Liberia in Africa in mind), supplying them with the means to feed and house themselves. He thought that an equal number of white colonists should go with them, to oversee and safeguard the intellectually stunted, animalistic blacks. Once Jefferson, as governor of Virginia and as president, took up the task of actually dealing with slavery, he found that politics always forced him into a compromise position. Before the Constitution went into effect, Jefferson tried and failed to have slavery outlawed in the western territories gained from the British in the Revolution. According to the Constitution, the importation of slaves from abroad could not be ended before 1808, but given the opposition of slaveholders to such a prohibition, that any ban would ever be enforced was much in doubt. Still, Jefferson, as president, managed to pass the necessary legislation. As secretary of state and president, Jefferson was anxious to assist the French with large loans to help them suppress the slave revolt in their Caribbean colony of Haiti. He certainly did not want American society to suffer the disruptions that would follow blacks fighting against their owners for their own freedom as white Americans had against the British.

Passing from the merely personal to Jefferson's private relationship with his slaves, which is the subject of "Enlightenment," especially his relationship with Sally Hemings, the reader will encounter a complicated and controversial body of scholarship that deserves attention. The historiographical tradition had tended to reject Jefferson as the father of his slave/sister-in-law Sally Hemings's six children and accept Jefferson family tradition, which argued that Jefferson's cousins were the father or fathers. Fawn M. Brodie, however, in her 1974 biography of Jefferson, pointed out that if the matter were considered like any other historical fact, there was overwhelming evidence to support Jefferson's fatherhood, so that the matter ought to be settled. By 1997, Annette Gordon-Reed was able to produce a special monograph on the subject, *Thomas Jefferson and Sally Hemings*, and not only reinforce Brodie's conclusion but also report that in the intervening twenty years scholarly opinion had reversed itself to accept Jefferson as the father of Hemings's children. In 1998, a genetic test was performed comparing the DNA of descendants of two of Sally Heming's sons with descendents of Jefferson's brother Randolph. This showed that the Jefferson and Hemings families were related and ruled out Jefferson's cousins, the Carrs, who had been the only candidates ever proposed as fathers of Hemings's children other than Jefferson himself.

The matter appeared so settled that in 2000 the Thomas Jefferson Foundation, the historical trust that owns Monticello, issued the *Report of the Research Committee on Thomas Jefferson and Sally Hemings*, supporting Jefferson's paternity. Nevertheless, a group of wealthy southern businessmen quickly created the Thomas Jefferson Heritage Society for the sole purpose of publishing a rival report. The committee of scholars they assembled were not Jefferson specialists, and their head, Robert F. Turner, was a political scientist with expertise in the role of constitutional law and executive war powers in the post-Vietnam era. They saw it as their duty to present the best case in defense of Jefferson's not being the father, as though he were on trial, rather than to conduct an ordinary historical investigation. In a report issued in 2001 (and updated in 2011 as *The Jefferson-Hemings Controversy: Report of the Scholars Commission*), they quickly declared Jefferson not guilty.

The huge amount of labor needed to maintain a plantation like Jefferson's Monticello was used as a justification for owning slaves. (© *Daniel M. Silva | Shutterstock.com*)

They proposed something that no one had ever suggested, that either Randolph Jefferson or his sons were the father or fathers of Hemings' children. Nonetheless, if the case were tried in a modern court, whether Jefferson was himself the father or merely supplied Hemings to his relatives, he would be guilty of rape. Nevertheless, the Thomas Jefferson Heritage Society proved adept at propagating their proclamation of Jefferson's innocence to the popular press. Alexander O. Boulton's review of the 2001 *Report of the Scholars Commission* pointed out that it was inconsistent for Turner and his colleagues to claim that they were both conducting an impartial investigation and defending Jefferson from politically correct criticism. Like a defense attorney, its "authors frequently make the point that we lack the critical information necessary to reach a conclusive opinion; they then seize on that lack as proof of their own position." He also observes:

> The largest onus that the Heritage Society has to bear is the long and tainted history of its case. For many years, those who denied the charges of Jefferson's paternity of slave children dismissed issues of race and slavery as important elements

of his life and, by inference, of American history as a whole; discounted or impugned black testimony in favor of white testimony; and used their influence to discredit opposing views. These charges . . . have not been rebutted by the members of the Heritage Society.

Boulton points out that because Turner and his colleagues argue that Hemings slept with several of Jefferson's relatives, they dismiss her testimony (reported by her sons) on the ground that she was promiscuous. This is a standard element of racist belief, despite the fact that, as a slave, she would have been compelled by force to accept each sexual encounter. The erasure made by the *Report of the Scholars Commission*, coming on top of centuries of earlier erasures, has helped to make the palimpsest of the text of black history in the South that "Enlightenment" seeks to reveal.

CRITICAL OVERVIEW

Trethewey's rise to prominence is still recent and a critical consensus has not yet been fully developed. One fruitful approach to Trethewey, however, is suggested by Charles Henry Rowell in his 2004 interview with Trethewey. He tells her, "When I read your poetry, the first word that comes to my mind is *restoration*. Your project seems to be the restoration of what is not seen or is forgotten as a result of erasure from local and national memory." This certainly holds true for "Enlightenment," first published in *Thrall* in 2012. The poem deals with an attempt to make a very deep and thorough erasure from American history. Elizabeth Lund, in her *Washington Post* review of the book, finds that its main theme is that Trethewey, in her mixed race identity, cannot transcend her black heritage. Lund notes the unreconciled relationship with her father and their racial difference that Trethewey explores in "Enlightenment" and several other poems in the collection.

The themes of slavery and marriage between races are not new for Trethewey in "Enlightenment" but are also important, for example, in her Pulitzer Prize–winning collection *Native Guard*. Daniel C. Littlefield, in his 2013 article "Reflections on the History behind the Poetry of Natasha Trethewey," commenting mainly on that earlier collection, gives a historical survey of the relationship spectrum between white men and black women in the nineteenth and twentieth centuries. He notes the ubiquity among slaveholders of black mistresses and mulatto families consisting of the owner's own enslaved children. Often these children were sold so as to not antagonize the white wife, and he cites examples of white women taking violent revenge on their husband's black mistresses. In the Jim Crow South, Littlefield points out, conditions did not change much, since a black woman who refused a white man was still liable to be punished with violence. It was illegal, but in practice a crime of this kind would never have been prosecuted. During the civil rights era, rape was a more common weapon of white supremacy than lynching. Black mistresses of powerful white men with white wives and families of mixed race children did not disappear either. U.S. Senator Strom Thurmond, who fathered a child with a household servant of his parents, is an example from the second half of the twentieth century.

William M. Ramsey, in his 2012 article in *Southern Literary Journal*, reads Trethewey's work against the overhanging edifice of William Faulkner's imagined South. According to Ramsey, "Faulkner, conflicted and ghost-haunted by memories of the past, saw himself in the grip of a concrete reality so palpable that it could not be wiped away with time. But multiple communities, genders, and races lived in that past, and they stimulate divergent takes on it." Trethewey, he thinks, sees her job as telling the story of the black South forgotten by Faulkner. One of the main things about the South forgotten from southern memory is the South's history of miscegenation, the mixing of the races that produced Sally Hemings's children.

CRITICISM

Bradley A. Skeen

Skeen is a classicist. In the following essay, he explores the historical background of Trethewey's "Enlightenment" in the Sally Hemings controversy.

The narrative of Trethewey's "Enlightenment" depends upon the research that the speaker and her father do into the historical controversy over Sally Hemings and Thomas Jefferson and how their opinions change on the matter over time and through discussion with each other. Within the poem, the same process goes on at Monticello, reflected in the interactions between the tour guides and visitors. These developments are, of course, informed by the parallel and more fundamental investigations carried out by professional historians over the last generation. Trethewey assumes a great deal of knowledge on this subject from the reader, so it will be worthwhile to give an overview of this larger process.

Thomas Jefferson was the third president of the United States, the author of the Declaration of Independence, and the inspiration for the Bill of Rights. He was an early champion of the abolition of slavery, a polymath of fantastic accomplishment, and the very essence in America of the Enlightenment and its program of political reform and progress leading to liberty and freedom. In popular consciousness, he is an American hero, although the discipline of history can have no concern for popular beliefs. He was also a slave owner. The same applies to many of the other founding fathers, including George Washington and James Madison, and to many other historical figures. Almost every

WHAT DO I READ NEXT?

- Chandra Prasad's *Mixed: An Anthology of Short Fiction on the Multicultural Experience* (2006) is a collection of short stories by and intended for young adults grappling with establishing an identity based on their multiracial identities. Writers have parents of races and nationalities from around the world. Unions between individuals from the Indian subcontinent or East Asia face particular difficulties, as their parents' marriages break ancient taboos of caste and race.

- *Sally Hemings* (1979) is the first novel by the poet Barbara Chase-Riboud. Inspired by Fawn Brodie's challenge to Jefferson historiography, Chase-Riboud presents Hemings as a vivid character, fitted to be Jefferson's companion. It was the basis of the 2000 network television miniseries, *Sally Hemings: An American Scandal.*

- *Native Guard* (2006) is Trethewey's Pulitzer Prize collection of poems that tells the story of a black regiment raised by the Union during the Civil War from black freedmen in Louisiana to guard Confederate prisoners of war. The collection also contains themes inspired by the life and murder of Trethewey's mother.

- *Jefferson's Children: The Story of One American Family* (2000), by Shannon Lanier, with photographs by Jane Feldman, is a historical investigation for young adults not only of the controversy concerning Jefferson and Sally Hemings but also of the connections made between the two families descended from Jefferson after the 1998 DNA analysis. The book grew out of the 1999 Jefferson family reunion (a reunion held each year at Monticello), to which the descendants of Eston Hemings (the son of Sally) were invited for the first time.

- *Mongrel Nation: The America Begotten by Thomas Jefferson and Sally Hemings* (2010), by Clarence E. Walker, examines the Hemings controversy within the context of the American slaveholding society of the early nineteenth century, since it was typical in its own era. The real interest of the book is in American culture's historic denial of the facts of the frequent interbreeding of masters with their slaves.

- *Langston Hughes* (2013) is an anthology (in the "Poetry for Young People" series) of Hughes's verse selected and introduced for young-adult readers by the distinguished literary critic Arnold Rampersad. Hughes's poems deal with black identity in America before the civil rights movement.

famous person known from classical antiquity, for instance, owned slaves, including great ethical thinkers like Plato, Aristotle, and Saint Augustine. (Socrates and Jesus are exceptions, owing to their poverty.) Today, slavery is considered an abominable crime and has been done away with. (This is true in name at least, but many millions of people, especially in the developing world, still live in economic conditions very similar to chattel slavery, usually some form of debt bondage.) Yet for much of human history, slavery was considered an ordinary part of life.

Slavery damaged everyone involved in it, both master and slave. The damage done to the slaves is more obvious, since the institution involved kidnapping them, holding them in the equivalent of prison against their will for their entire lives, stealing from them the entire product of their labor, denying them any advantage of civilization or society, and giving them only the bare minimum of food and shelter necessary to keep them alive and productive. It is relevant to the discussion that masters also had absolute control over the bodies of their slaves and could beat and torture them as punishment. (In Virginia, the

> **THIS TRANSFORMATION FROM BEING BLACK IN VIRGINIA TO BEING WHITE IN OHIO, RATHER THAN BEING AN EXAMPLE OF *PASSING*, AS RACIST JIM CROW CULTURE WOULD TERM IT, IS RATHER PROOF THAT RACE HAS NO REAL EXISTENCE AND IS A SOCIAL CONSTRUCT."**

law forbade only mutilation and death as punishments.) They could also rape them at any time they wished. (Note that, given the disparity of power involved, there is no possibility of meaningful consent in any sexual encounter between master and slave.) Jefferson refers, in *Notes on the State of Virginia*, to all of these factors, which even at the time would have been crimes if conducted against anyone else except black slaves. He explains that in his view it would be impossible to simply emancipate all the black slaves in the United States and incorporate them into society. The blacks, he says, could never be peacefully integrated because of the "ten thousand recollections, by the blacks, of the injuries they have sustained." He adds, "Among the blacks is misery enough, God knows." The damage done to the master is no less real: he had to become the kind of degraded individual who is capable of performing everything required by slavery.

The former slave Frederick Douglass, in his 1845 memoir, *A Narrative of the Life of Frederick Douglass, an American Slave*, describes the process with respect to his master's wife. He observed that at the beginning of her marriage she was kind, generous, and sympathetic, exhibiting natural moral instincts. After a few years as head of a household dependent on slave labor, she was possessed of an animal-like fierceness toward her slaves that far exceeded even what was necessary to control them. One can clearly see the effects of slave owning on Jefferson in the vituperative racism he displays in *Notes on the State of Virginia*. His brilliant mind somehow keeps itself from investigating the almost childish suppositions that slavery depended on—that blacks are stupid, ugly, and smell bad. More chillingly he voiced the opinion that "they are

more ardent after their female: but love seems with them to be more an eager desire, than a tender delicate mixture of sentiment and sensation." How did Jefferson reconcile this statement with his treatment of Hemings? The institution of slavery and its effect on historical figures from Andrew Jackson to Cicero are a fact that has to be considered by historians. The discipline of history does not make moral judgments about the past based on the morality of the present. Jefferson is more forward looking than his contemporaries in realizing that the slave system was destructive and had to be ended, even if he was unable to extract himself from it.

Sally Hemings was born as a slave on the plantation of Jefferson's father-in-law, John Wayles. Hemings was also Wayles' daughter, by Betty Hemings, a slave he kept as his mistress. This made Sally the half-sister of Jefferson's wife, Martha. When Wayles died, Sally came into the Jefferson household as inherited property. Hemings had three white grandparents and one black, making her, as Trethewey notes, a quadroon in the Franco-Spanish pidgin that supplied the technical language of slavery in America. Her children, with seven of eight white great-grandparents, were octoroons. Hemings's role in the Jefferson plantation is discussed later, but it is certain that she and her children were comparatively well treated by Jefferson and freed in his lifetime or in his will. After Jefferson's death, the family moved to the Midwest and were accepted as white (in that they were allowed to vote and were enrolled in the federal census as white and so on), as much, no doubt, because they were free as because of their skin color. This transformation from being black in Virginia to being white in Ohio, rather than being an example of *passing*, as racist Jim Crow culture would term it, is rather proof that race has no real existence and is a social construct.

In the 1802 presidential election, a political opponent of Jefferson—James T. Callender—published the report that after his wife's death, Jefferson took her half-sister Sally as his mistress and had a number of children with her. This was meant to be a scandalous disclosure because, although many if not most plantation owners had children by their slaves (there is no question, for example, that Wayles was Hemings's father), it was not a matter that was generally discussed. That Hemings had children by Jefferson was later confirmed by the children themselves, who openly maintained to census takers, newspaper reporters, and anyone else who inquired that they were Jefferson's children. Moreover, the situation was obvious to any visitor to Monticello. Elijah Fletcher, the headmaster of New Glasgow Academy, visited Jefferson in 1811 and wrote afterward in a letter: "The story of black Sal is no farce—That he cohabits with her and has a number of children by her is a sacred truth—and the worst of it is, he keeps the same children slaves—an unnatural crime which is very common in these parts."

Long before there was any possibility of appealing to DNA evidence to link Jefferson and Hemings, Fawn M. Brodie, in her *Thomas Jefferson: An Intimate History*, observed that Jefferson's wife, Martha, died in 1782 when Jefferson was thirty and that he neither remarried nor remained celibate for the rest of his life. He is known to have had several affairs with women of his own class, all of them adulterous or otherwise transgressive. An affair with Hemings would, according to Brodie, also have the lure of the forbidden, which seemed to attract Jefferson. She concludes that "the liaison with Sally Hemings [is] passionately denied [by many historians] as libelous. One wonders why." Jefferson's use of Hemings is in keeping with the condition and circumstances of his own culture. There seems little point in denying it except to preserve an image of Jefferson incompatible with his raping one of his slaves.

The genetic testing reported by Eugene A. Foster in *Nature* in 1998 determined the relationship between Jefferson and the living descendants of two of Hemings's sons: her first child, Thomas, who was conceived in Paris and her last child, Eston. The test confirmed that Eston was related to Jefferson and ruled out two of Jefferson's cousins, the Carrs (who apologists going back to Jefferson's own daughter Martha, who was Sally Hemings's niece and half-sister, had held to be the father). Eston had to have been fathered either by Jefferson or by his brother Randolph (his only brother to survive infancy) or one of his sons. Thomas's descendants are not related to Jefferson, though it is not certain that the Woodson family that supplied the DNA is, in fact, descended from Hemings. Moreover, in a test of this kind, a positive result is far weightier than a negative, since a single instance of illegitimacy anywhere in the genealogy would also produce a negative result.

The question is, why would the fact that Jefferson had children by one of his slaves be scandalous? Why was the well-known fact that many slave owners routinely raped their slaves and had children with them and kept their own children as slaves something that was not discussed in polite society? Historical investigation provides the answer that it threatened the whole economic and class structure of America. It is common for facts that a society considers immoral to be suppressed if their exposure would discomfit the powerful. Robert F. Turner and the other authors of the Thomas Jefferson Heritage Society report (who are virtually alone in denying Jefferson's paternity) imagine that they are defending Jefferson from a charge, as if in a criminal court. If they can deny that he was the father of Hemings's children, they will find him innocent. What is the true nature of that charge? If one admits and openly discusses the practices that Jefferson engaged in with Hemings, then anyone, in the eighteenth century or today, would have to admit that they are morally wrong by the standards of either era. The condemnation of slavery could not end there: the whole thing would have to be eliminated root and branch, because no part of it is less morally repellent than the worst part. The men who hold the power in society would be exposed as hopelessly corrupt and, if emancipation actually followed, they would lose the greater part of their wealth, which was invested in the bodies of their slaves. When slavery was finally ended, it took not mere moral enlightenment but a civil war of the nation against the slave owners that killed over half a million Americans.

Even today, the purpose of the denial of Jefferson's particular exploitation of Hemings is to protect his reputation. Turner and his colleagues, in the publication of *The Jefferson-Hemings Controversy*, insist they are finding Jefferson not guilty (a concept completely alien to historical investigation). It is as if by declaring him innocent on this one count, they can draw attention away from the whole network of crime on which American slaveholding society was based and again make it something not to be publicly acknowledged. They offer the unspoken inference from their proclamation of Jefferson's innocence that slavery and its aftermath in America was not a moral wrong. It is certainly impossible to make out that case, but even in the most limited case (as they term it) of Jefferson's raping Hemings, their efforts fail. Even if one grants all of their conclusions, then Jefferson did not father Hemings's children; they are still left

The father turns to books and cites facts at his daughter, as if looking for information that will somehow prove Jefferson's worth. (© Stocksnapper / Shutterstock.com)

with the conclusion that he supplied his sister-in-law's body to his nephews as part of the hospitality of Monticello along with their meals and rooms. It is hard to see what moral distinction they are drawing between the two acts.

Once Trethewey was enlightened by her investigation of Hemings and its inevitable conclusion, she had to come to terms with the impact it must have on every American and also with the particular meaning it must have for her as the daughter of a white father and black mother. In "Enlightenment" and in *Thrall* as a whole, she seems convinced that she can never escape history, that there is still something that cannot be spoken in public about her identity, that her father is complicit in Jefferson's guilt.

Source: Bradley A. Skeen, Critical Essay on "Enlightenment," in *Poetry for Students*, Gale, Cengage Learning, 2016.

Dave Davies and Natasha Trethewey
In the following interview excerpt, Trethewey explains how her biracial heritage has influenced her work.

. . . *Before we talk about what it was like to grow up mixed-race, I'd like you to read a poem called "Miscegenation," and this again is Natasha Trethewey from her latest collection of poems called* Native Guard.

(*Reading*) Miscegenation. In 1965 my parents broke two laws of Mississippi; they went to Ohio to marry, returned to Mississippi. They crossed the river into Cincinnati, a city whose name begins with a sound like sin, the sound of wrong—mis in Mississippi. A year later they moved to Canada, followed a route the same as slaves, the train slicing the white glaze of winter, leaving Mississippi.

(*Reading*) Faulkner's Joe Christmas was born in winter, like Jesus, given his name for the day he was left at the orphanage, his race unknown in Mississippi. My father was reading *War and Peace* when he gave me my name. I was born near Easter, 1966, in Mississippi.

(*Reading*) When I turned 33 my father said, It's your Jesus year—you're the same age he was when he died. It was spring, the hills green in

Mississippi. I know more than Joe Christmas did. Natasha is a Russian name—though I'm not; it means Christmas child, even in Mississippi.

You know, in that poem "Miscegenation," you mention that when your parents got married, they broke two laws. One was the law of miscegenation, black people and white people were not allowed to marry, and that law was still on the books in Mississippi, which is why they got married out of state. What was the second law of Mississippi that they broke?

Going out of state to get married and returning to Mississippi.

(LAUGHTER)

Oh, a catch-22.

Right, they get you either way.

When you were growing up, did you get different reactions when you were out with your white father as opposed to when you were out with your black mother?

I did. At an early age, I could detect subtle differences in how we were treated if I was with my father or with my mother and together, what it meant when we were out together. And that's the way that I learned a little bit about how it was possible for me to pass for white when I was with my father and be treated better than if I was downtown with my mother in a store.

Was there ever a part of your life in which you wanted to pass for white or even tried to?

Oh yes, as an adolescent. I think that it's hard enough being an adolescent and wanting so much to fit in with your peers, your schoolmates, and to erase any sign of difference, to be part of the group. And being biracial but also being black in a predominately white school marked me as different. And so upon arriving at a new school, it was quite possible for me to pass by not saying anything at all.

Often people would mistake me for white when I was younger, and I didn't correct them, there would be a period of time that they just thought I was.

Were there consequences your parents faced living in Mississippi and being an interracial couple? And were there consequences that you faced as a child of mixed race?

Well, I think that the difficulties really weighed on my parents and their marriage, but I think that beyond the kind of problems that

people who are in that kind of relationship, any kind of marriage would have—my parents also these external forces that were quite scary.

And for example when I was a baby, the Klan burned a cross in the driveway of my grandmother's house, where we were all living briefly. And I think that there was always that threat somewhere looming behind us.

How scary was that for you when you saw a cross burning on your lawn? And did you even understand, were you old enough to understand yet what the Klan was and what the intention was of burning the cross?

No, I really was too young to understand any of that, and my parents, of course, were keeping me from seeing what was going on. And so a lot of it has returned to me as stories that they told in recollecting what happened. And even now, we wonder what the intention of the cross burning was because my grandmother lived across the street, in Gulfport, Mississippi, from the Mount Olive Baptist Church, which in the late '60s was doing voter registration drives for black voters.

And so my grandmother had a driveway, the church did not have a driveway, and so on Sunday, she let the church park its bus in her driveway. And so it's quite possible that people thought that the driveway belonged to the church and that the cross was burned as a threat to the people who were doing voter registration.

It might have also been a threat to this interracial couple who was living inside the house, or it might have been a way to threaten both.

How old were you when your parents divorced?

I was six.

And then you went to live with your mother.

That's right. My mother and my father divorced during the time that my father was getting his Ph.D. at Tulane. And we had been commuting back and forth from Gulfport to New Orleans, which was about an hour's drive. We had an apartment in Gulfport, and my father had a roommate in New Orleans that he would go and stay with during the week for class, and sometimes we'd go and visit him on the weekends, or he'd come to Gulfport.

And so it seemed like a very gentle transition, strangely, for me when they actually divorced, and my mother and I moved to Atlanta for my mother to start graduate school.

Did it change your racial identity when there was no longer, like, a white father in your home?

Well, I can't say that it changed my racial identity because though I was a biracial child, and my parents talked to me about what they thought that meant, I also understood that I was a black child. And that didn't change.

Now, your father is a poet and a professor of literature at Hollins University in Virginia, which is where you got your master's degree, and I believe he was teaching there at the time.

That's right.

At the risk of sounding obvious, he must be awfully proud you won the Pulitzer Prize this year.

Indeed he is. He is a proud papa right now.

Were there poems you remember him reading to you as a kid?

Oh yes. From the time that I knew, I understood that he was a poet, which was probably about the time that I was in the seventh grade, that's when I really got it and knew what it meant, his first book had come out. And I had read all those poems myself, but he also read them to me, talked about them because a lot of them were—well, they're very autobiographical about his own family and growing up in Canada.

And so it was great to hear those poems because they were the first poems that I really felt that I could enter into not as simply a kind of distant reader, the way you might read a poem in class at school, but as an intimate reader who knew the stories and found my own place in the language....

Source: Dave Davies and Natasha Trethewey, "Poet Laureate: 'Poetry's Always a Kind of Faith,'" in *Fresh Air*, 2012.

Alex Hoyt and Natasha Trethewey
In the following excerpt, Trethewey discusses her writing process.

Six or seven years ago, my father and I were fishing the Miramichi River in New Brunswick. It's a great salmon river. We met a writer friend of his named Dave Richards, a novelist, and Dave hired a guide for us. This was a famous guide who'd taken people like Bill Clinton fishing on the Miramichi. Once we got out there into the river the guide gave us a quick lesson about

how to fly-fish, how to cast. We practiced the motions, then we got our rods and started fishing. There was this almost mystical look to the river. It seemed reverent just to be quiet, going through the mist.

I've talked to my father about the trip many times. His memory's kind of bad these days. He doesn't remember, or doesn't want to remember, that I caught these two trout. He's really bothered that I present him in the poem, as he sees it, as someone who's not a very good fisherman. He tried to tell me on the phone the other day that the fish I caught were guppies, and I told him, "Daddy, I've caught a few trout in my life. I know what a trout looks like."

Though he wants to look like an expert fisherman, my father thinks it's a beautiful poem. He says he feels kind of lucky, because most people are not lucky enough to hear an elegy by their child while they're still living. I think it's also a way to be slightly in denial about what else the poem is mourning. Even though this poem is called "Elegy," what's being elegized is not my father's life—he's not dead—but a kind of loss between a father and a daughter, a kind of estrangement. He's casting his invisible lines, slicing the sky between us, and I mean that image to suggest a kind of division.

As much as we love each other, there is some growing difficulty in my adult relationship with my father. Because we're both writers, we're having a very intimate conversation in a very public forum. Before I was ever a poet, my father was writing poems about me, so it was a turning of the tables when I became a poet and started answering, speaking back to his poems in ways that I had not before. My whole life as a child going out with my father, I'd be mid-sentence and my father would take his notebook out of his pocket and jot something down. And I remember, as I got older, wondering, "Was it something I said? What is it that he's recording right now?"

Clearly, this poem represents me now being the voice who's telling the story. At this point in my life, my father's very proud of me, and some of that pride can be difficult for me, because it means that he'd love to able to take as much credit for who I've become as I'm entitled to take. Certainly, he encouraged me and gave me some genes, that kind of thing. But he'd love to imagine that I was like Athena, sprung fully-formed from his imagination. I've tried to use that line in another poem. It still hasn't worked out. It felt like I was branching off into too many directions. But it is about, again, my father's perception of me.

Now, the reader seeing the final draft doesn't know that I have my own secret journal in which I feel "silenced" by my father. The work of the poem is following certain paths and not others. I have to decide whether or not I'm going to reveal to an audience this side of my relationship with my father. When I write notes in my journal, I'm just trying to scribble down as much as possible. Later on I decide whether to follow some of those first impressions or whether to abandon them.

Writing [by hand] frees up a mode of thinking that allows me to consider more things without censorship, the way I would censor if I were typing. If I start writing on a computer, I feel that it's official. When I'm actually writing by hand, I get more of a sense of the rhythm of sentences, of syntax. The switch to the computer is when I actually start thinking about lines. That's the workhorse part. At that point, I'm being more mathematical about putting the poem on the page and less intuitive about the rhythm of the syntax.

I like to write in the morning. I developed that habit at Hollins. I'd get up, make my coffee, and write from nine until noon, or until I made a poem, whichever came first. These days, my life is so busy, with teaching and everything else, I have to make the time and find it when I can. When I wrote these drafts, I was on a fellowship at Yale. I can remember sitting in my apartment at my desk reading Claudia Emerson's Pulitzer Prize-winning volume, *Late Wife*. I remember turning the page and reading, "I think by now it is time for the second cutting." It was at that moment that the notes I had written in the journal turned into an actual draft of the poem in its couplets. Her poem was in couplets like that. I opened my notebook. It began, "I think by now the fields must be . . . ".

I wanted the poem to feel sinewy, like a fishing line, which is why there's a stepdown second line that moves away from the first line. Something felt right about it, so the poem never went through any other stanza patterns. That may be an influence from the Claudia Emerson poem. Once I'd filtered the material into that form, it clicked. It was like putting the key in the right lock.

I let a friend of mine read it, a novelist. She made one suggestion, which I did not take. It concerned these lines that are important for the atmosphere of the poem: "drizzle needling / the surface, mist at the banks like a net / settling around us—everything damp / and shining." She didn't think that on a misty, overcast day you could also have things that were shining. And I had to go and find out. I want to be factual about natural details, about science. Once I figured out it was true—as long as there's light, things will shine, even on a grey and overcast day—those lines had to be there. In fact, we're driving through New Orleans in a rainstorm right now, and all the sidewalks are shining. . . .

Source: Alex Hoyt and Natasha Trethewey, "How Poet Laureate Natasha Trethewey Wrote Her Father's Elegy," in *Atlantic*, August 14, 2012.

Rafael Campo

In the following excerpt, Campo praises Trethewey's creative use of traditional poetic forms.

In her recent book *Wonder and Science*, a brilliant reading of European early Renaissance texts describing encounters with the many worlds (both real and imagined) that humankind has tried to occupy, the literary historian Mary Baine Campbell writes, "What is human, and how various? . . . A question once central to the task of poetry became the property of a science opposed to the indeterminate and the inspired." She is referring to a tension she astutely identifies between the ancient art of poetry, and the nascent 16th- and 17th-century "science" of anthropology: the recording of details of human cultures, full of astonishment and terror and joy, and long the province of the poem, was being encroached on by a novel literature that sought to comprehend humanness by examining New World peoples much as a botanist might coolly dissect exotic orchids. In the trajectory formed by these stunning new volumes of poetry under review—from Natasha Trethewey's post-Reconstruction Deep South to Grace Schulman's modern New York—one has a sense of how contemporary American poetry continues to be shaped by these forces of natural beauty versus conquest, of intuition against definition. Ultimately, through powers of insight that transcend mere observation, each of these books supports Campbell's conclusion (she herself is a poet) that poetry yet retains its unique capacity for expressing wonder—which perhaps is only heightened by science's attempts to supercede it.

Selected by Rita Dove for the Cave Canem Poetry Award, Natasha Trethewey's first book *Domestic Work* is profoundly concerned with this fundamental question of what it means to be human; she teaches us her appropriately elusive definition, by example after patient example. This precocious book is full of quiet portraits of dignity and duty, brimming with the unobvious yet gleaming details of daily life. If she yields perhaps a bit more to the anthropological approach of such concern to Campbell, she does so like a young Zora Neale Hurston, with such great empathy for her subjects that she can't help but sing her soulful lyrics. She begins with a series of poems that examine antique photographs, breathing life effortlessly back into their subjects; elsewhere, she chillingly documents Jim Crow disenfranchisement with an almost reverent accuracy.

Restraint perhaps, but not detachment, is what most characterizes her art; in her poem "Hot Combs," for example, she unearths not just a significant artifact, but catalogues an emotional find of utterly heartbreaking import:

> At the junk shop, I find an old pair,
> black with grease, the teeth still pungent
> as burning hair. One is small,
> fine-toothed as if for a child. Holding it,
> I think of my mother's slender wrist,
> the curve of her neck as she leaned
>
> over the stove, her eyes shut as she pulled
> the wooden handle and laid flat the wisps
> at her temples. The heat in our kitchen
> made her glow that morning I watched her
> wincing, the hot comb singeing her brow,
> sweat glistening above her lips,
> her face made strangely beautiful
> as only suffering can do.

Trethewey, true to the gifted poet within herself, does not merely describe with precision the terrible comb; her word choice is laden with connotations that insist she is a participant, an implicated witness, and not just an observer. She shows us what is in fact a kind of instrument of torture, a device fashioned by human hands made to serve a racist ideal of beauty, its blackness and grease seemingly emblematic of what it was employed so painfully to "correct." So Trethewey not only depicts the damage a cultural construct can inflict (as the reader must ask, does the little girl see herself as ugly, as deserving of this kind of punishment?); what makes the poem even more remarkable is how the figure of her mother, even as she toils under such a cruel brand of oppression, transcends the disgrace of it in her so very human suffering. Thus ennobled and exalted, "sweat glistening above her lips," by the poem's conclusion it is her own genuine beauty that shines through, and endures.

Trethewey also exerts interesting pressures on traditional forms; she herself identifies as a particular hybrid, an African American woman who can "pass" as white. This internal duality helps produce entirely unique sonnets shot through with bluesy inflections, and occasionally-rhymed quatrains that resonate with a kind of call-and-response undercurrent. It is poems like "Flounder," "Saturday Matinee," and "White Lies," in which she courageously places herself at the crossroads of two oft-opposing narratives, that most fully reveal her mettle as a poet. It is at these moments, when she is speaking her own complicated language of beauty tempered by loss, that she is making something at once new and yet as ancient as our heartbeat, a labor of love worthy of the Black laundresses and barbers and elevator operators whose hardworking fellowship she embraces. Like them, she knows what she produces is more than just the nourishing stock from "neck bones/ bumping in the pot," or the sheer joy of "a choir/ of clothes clapping on the line;" more than mere knowledge, more that what we can see and taste and touch, what she gives us is a glorious and ineffable wisdom.

Trethewey's exploration of racial identity takes on a more explicitly narrative but no less trenchant form in her new book, *Bellocq's Ophelia*, a novella-in-verse imagined in the voice of an octoroon prostitute living in turn-of-the-century New Orleans. The trademark lyrical beauty of her poems is never sacrificed to her equally compelling plot here, a story in which beauty is itself never quite subjugated, even as her protagonist confronts the racism that forces her from one form of slavery, "the white oblivion of cotton," into another, that of imposed male sexual desire. Even the gripping photographs to which some of the poems allude (and upon which she bases her title, subtly emphasizing her central theme of possession) fail to capture the true essence of our heroine. "Now I face the camera, wait/ for the photograph to show me who I am," says Ophelia, oracular, her pale image trapped forever in the gaze of the beholder—to some, nothing more than a common black woman laborer, to others, an almost-white woman save for an imagined exotic animal appetite for sex, and to all, it might seem, merely an object of one sort or another—yet her spirit, as articulated in these memorable poems, remains forever elusive and, indeed, indomitable....

...We are indebted to poets like Schulman and Trethewey, who continue to transport us to these mythic places "beyond the skyline," to "the world...that we aspire to but never own." Let us be grateful for tiptoeing white pear trees, that can seem to us like brides; let us rejoice in all that which we cannot understand. Such is the irreplaceable, unsurpassable gift of great poetry: to remind us of our souls, of the inexplicable yet universal substance from which each one of us is made.

Source: Rafael Campo, Review of *Domestic Work* and *Bellocq's Ophelia*, in *Prairie Schooner*, Vol. 77, No. 4, Winter 2003, pp. 181–87.

Publishers Weekly

In the following review, the anonymous reviewer describes the collection as "quiet" but significant.

Following up her debut, *Domestic Work* (2000), which included a number of historical monologues, Trethewey's short sophomore effort is a quiet collection of poems in the persona of a "very white-skinned black woman mulatto, quadroon, or octoroon," a prostitute in New Orleans just before WWI. *The Bellocq* of the title is E.J., the Toulouse-Lautrec–like photographer whose *Storyville* prostitute portraits, brought out from oblivion by Lee Friedlander, inspired Louis Malle's 1978 film *Pretty Baby*— and now this sequence. A stanza that begins "There are indeed all sorts of men! who visit here" predictably yet elegantly ends "And then there are those,! of course, whose desires I cannot commit! to paper." Yet this is not generally a sentimentalized account of a conventional subject. Much more like Bellocq's artless, sympathetic and gorgeous portraits are lines like these, describing the "girls": "They like best, as I do, the regular meals, warm! from the cooks in our own kitchen, the clean! indoor toilet and hot-water bath." While the trend of the first-person historical novel (think Wittgenstein's Nephew as much as Corelli's Mandolin) has passed, the best poems here fulfill the genre's mandate to spice up the period piece with intellectual frisson; Trethewey goes two-for-two by successfully taking

on the poetically dubious task of working from art and making it signify anew.

Forecast: Despite the hook's brevity, expect review attention, as well as short items in glossies profiling Trethewey with the requisite provocative *Bellocq* reproductions. National Poetry Month reviewers wanting to take stock of recent poetry by African-American women might place this book alongside Harryette Mullen's *Sleeping with the Dictionary* (*Forecasts*, Dec. 17, 2001) and Elizabeth Alexander's *Antebellum Dream Book* (published last year).

Source: Review of *Bellocq's Ophelia*, in *Publishers Weekly*, Vol. 249, No. 8, February 25, 2002, p. 57.

SOURCES

Boulton, Alexander O., "The Monticello Mystery—Case Continued," in *William and Mary Quarterly*, 3rd Series, Vol. 58, No. 4, 2001, pp. 1039–46.

Brodie, Fawn M., *Thomas Jefferson: An Intimate History*, W. W. Norton, 1974, p. 29.

Douglass, Frederick, *A Narrative of the Life of Frederick Douglass, an American Slave*, Anti-Slavery Office, 1845, pp. 40–41.

Foster, Eugene A., "Jefferson Fathered Slave's Last Child," in *Nature*, Vol. 396, November 5, 1998, pp. 27–28.

Gordon-Reed, Annette, *The Hemingses of Monticello: An American Family*, W. W. Norton, 2008, p. 617.

———, *Thomas Jefferson and Sally Hemings: An American Controversy*, University Press of Virginia, 1997, pp, 210–38.

Jefferson, Thomas, *Notes on the State of Virginia*, Wells and Lilly, 1829, pp. 143–48, https://archive.org/details/notesonstateofvi00jeff (accessed May 1, 2015).

Littlefield, Daniel C., "Reflections on the History behind the Poetry of Natasha Trethewey," in *Historically Speaking*, Vol. 14, No. 1, 2013, pp. 15–18.

Lund, Elizabeth, Review of *Thrall*, in *Washington Post*, September 13, 2012, http://www.washingtonpost.com/entertainment/books/thrall-by-natasha-trethewey-the-poet-laureate-of-the-united-states/2012/09/13/35dfe932-fb59-11e1-b2af-1f7d12fe907a_story.html (accessed May 1, 2015).

McKee, Marc, "A Conversation with Natasha Trethewey," in *Missouri Review*, Vol. 33, No. 2, 2010, pp. 144–59.

Ramsey, William M., "Terrance Hayes and Natasha Trethewey: Contemporary Black Chroniclers of the Imagined South," in *Southern Literary Journal*, Vol. 44, No. 2, 2012, pp. 122–35.

Rowell, Charles Henry, "Inscriptive Restorations: An Interview with Natasha Trethewey," in *Callaloo*, Vol. 27, No. 4, Fall 2004, p. 1021.

Said, Edward, *Orientalism*, Vintage Books, 1979, pp. 1–28.

Thomas Jefferson Foundation, *Report of the Research Committee on Thomas Jefferson and Sally Hemings*, 2000, http://www.monticello.org/site/plantation-and-slavery/report-research-committee-thomas-jefferson-and-sally-hemings (accessed May 2, 2015).

Trethewey, Natasha, "Enlightenment," in *Thrall*, Houghton Mifflin Harcourt, 2012, pp. 68–71.

Turner, Robert F., ed., *The Jefferson-Hemings Controversy: Report of the Scholars Commission*, Carolina Academic Press, 2011, pp. 43–45.

FURTHER READING

Chase-Riboud, Barbara, *The President's Daughter*, Crown, 1994.
This volume is the sequel to Chase-Riboud's *Sally Hemings* (1979). It tells the story of Jefferson and Sally Hemings's daughter Harriet in the Civil War era. It was reprinted in 2009 with a study guide for student use.

Ishida, Yoriko, *Modern and Postmodern Narratives of Race, Gender, and Identity: The Descendants of Thomas Jefferson and Sally Hemings*, Peer Lang, 2010.
Ishida presents a rhetorical analysis of literary as well as historical treatments of the Jefferson-Hemings controversy.

Shuffelton, Frank, ed., *The Cambridge Companion to Thomas Jefferson*, Cambridge University Press, 2009.
This introductory volume covers every aspect of Jefferson's life, with chapters on his role in the Enlightenment, on his relations with his own slaves at Monticello, and on slavery in America in the age of Jefferson.

Trethewey, Natasha, *Domestic Work*, Graywolf, 2000.
Trethewey's first volume of verse focuses on the lives of black maids and other domestic workers.

SUGGESTED SEARCH TERMS

Natasha Trethewey

"Enlightenment" AND Trethewey

Trethewey AND poet

free verse

Sally Hemings

Thomas Jefferson

Gilbert Stuart

Monticello

slavery

Heaven

CATHY SONG
1988

Although poet Cathy Song describes herself as "a poet who happens to be Asian American," as the Poetry Foundation reports, preferring not to be categorized based on her race or background, the influences of her mixed Chinese and Korean family are undeniable, being intricately threaded throughout her work. Her poem "Heaven," which is included in the collection *Frameless Windows, Squares of Light* (1988), is a prime example, focusing on Song's Chinese grandfather, who immigrated to the United States to work on the railroads in the West. Like many of Song's poems, "Heaven" examines themes of family and the importance of place and reflects the poet's awareness of her own history.

AUTHOR BIOGRAPHY

Song was born on August 20, 1955, in Honolulu, Hawaii. Her mother was a second-generation Chinese American, while her father's parents immigrated from Korea to work in Hawaii's sugarcane fields. Song has an older sister and a younger brother. After spending her early childhood in Wahiawa, on the island of Oahu, Song moved with her family to Waialae-Kahala, a suburb of Honolulu, when she was seven.

Song's father was a pilot, and the family traveled a lot. Song credits these travels with inspiring her to write. When she was about nine years old,

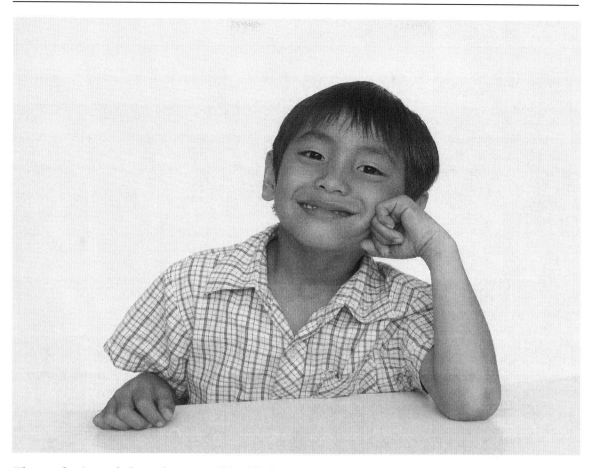

The speaker's son believes heaven will be filled with people who look like him. *(© naluwan | Shutterstock.com)*

she made up her mind to be the "family chronicler," as Gayle K. Sato records in a profile, and wrote pages upon pages—so much that her father, who always encouraged her writing, began to buy surplus target paper. Sato cites Song as relating, "I wrote on the backs of bull's-eyes."

After starting college at the University of Hawaii, Song transferred to Wellesley College. She graduated in 1977 with a bachelor's degree in English and then continued her education at Boston College. She finished her master of fine arts degree in 1981. While in Boston, Song met and married Douglas Davenport, who was a medical student at Tufts University. The couple had a son there before moving to Denver for Davenport's residency. While in Colorado, they had a daughter. In 1987, the family moved to Hawaii, where Song's third child was born.

Song's first book, *Picture Bride*, was published in 1983. The collection brought Song much critical acclaim, having won the prestigious Yale Younger Poets Competition in 1982 before its publication and being nominated for the National Book Critics Circle Award. Her other collections, *Frameless Windows, Squares of Light* (1988)—which contains "Heaven"—*School Figures* (1994), *The Land of Bliss*, (2001), and *Cloud Moving Hands* (2007), also proved popular with both critics and readers. Many of Song's poems feature exploration of family themes, the experiences of women, and Song's Asian American heritage.

In 1993 Song was awarded the Hawaii Award for Literature, and she has also won the Poetry Society of America's Shelley Memorial Award. As of 2015, she continues to live and work in Hawaii. In addition to writing poetry, Song teaches creative writing at the University of Hawaii and conducts creative writing workshops for Hawaii's Poets in the Schools program.

POEM SUMMARY

The text used for this summary is from *Frameless Windows, Squares of Light: Poems*, W. W. Norton, 1988, pp. 77–79. A version of the poem can be found on the following web page: http://www.poetryfoundation.org/poem/172142.

"Heaven" is written in free verse, which means it has no regular meter (*meter* being the pattern of stressed and unstressed syllables in poetry) or rhyme scheme. Indeed, the poem has practically no rhyme at all. "Heaven" also lacks a regular structure: Each of the five stanzas has a different number of lines, varying from ten to fifteen.

Lines 1–10

The first word in the poem is a pronoun. There is no way for the reader to know it immediately, but the speaker is referring to her son, who believes that in the afterlife they will travel to China. In line 2, the speaker asks the reader to imagine such a thing: a heaven where people's faces will look like her son's, who shares her own Asian features, though he has his father's fair hair.

The latter part of the first stanza describes China on a map. It is compared to a blue blossom with more intense color than the water of the ocean. China is far away from where the narrator and her family live, so far that her young son's hand must stretch far across the map's ocean to touch it, as if he is straining to reach keys an octave apart on a piano keyboard.

Lines 11–25

The speaker has not visited China. In line 12, Song uses the unexpected verb "sing" instead of a word that would fit the sentence more conventionally, like *see* or *think*, perhaps to lend a creative connotation to the idea that she is unable to imagine traveling to such a distant place, though it is important to her family.

The narrator invites the reader in line 13 to again examine the imaginary map and see the mark indicating the city where her family lives. Although Song does not specify the city by name, it seems likely to be Denver, Colorado. This city perfectly fits the description in the poem, being situated on the flat plains to the east of the Rocky Mountains. Line 19 also alludes to Denver's nickname, the Mile-High City, which derives from the altitude across the city, ranging from just below to just above a mile. Although readers must be careful not to

assume that the speaker of a poem necessarily represents the poet, many of Song's poems are drawn from her life, and she was indeed living in Denver when her son was young and her daughter was born.

In line 20, Song uses another unexpected word *starve*, which usually refers to a lack of food rather than a lack of air. However, the word quickly communicates the drastic conditions of Denver, where the air is low in oxygen because of the high altitude. Lines 21–23 connect the speaker's home with China, where in place of bamboo, Colorado has tall, thin aspen trees.

In the final two lines of the second stanza, the speaker introduces her grandfather, who spent his boyhood in Guangzhou, a Chinese city about seventy miles northwest of Hong Kong. The poem asks a question, wondering whether the grandfather could have imagined that his life would end in a place like Denver.

Lines 26–38

The narrator describes the area in which her family lives, where trains rattle by during the night and dogs bark behind neglected fences. The speaker compares the region to the old Wild West. The place still has a kind of wildness to it. Although the alley fights described in the poem probably refer to modern crime, the reader may be reminded of cowboys and gunslingers.

As she sits in her yard with her infant daughter and young son, whom she calls a dreamer, the speaker wonders what brought her to this place. By extension, she is asking what brought her grandfather all the way from China. Although this question has a literal aspect—asking, why this specific city and this specific body of water?—there is a more philosophical element as well, questioning how the choices made by one's ancestors as well as by oneself influence the direction one's life takes.

Lines 39–49

The speaker explains that her grandfather had not intended to stay in America. He was one of the thousands of Chinese workers who helped to build the western railroads, some of whom did indeed earn about a dollar per day for their labor. As a young man, the grandfather planned to someday go back to China, and the narrator wonders when he fully realized that he would never return and that he would spend the rest of his life in America.

Line 47 refers to the name given by Chinese immigrants to California after the discovery of gold in 1848: Gum San, which translates as "Gold Mountain." The phrase usually has a positive connotation, representing the western United States as a land of opportunity. Song, however, describes it as a cold, seemingly unfeeling place in lines 48–49, with cold wind and abandoned frontier towns.

Lines 50–63

The final stanza ties the speaker's son to his great-grandfather. The speaker suggests that her grandfather's wish to someday return home to China has somehow survived in the very blood of his descendants, lying dormant through the lives of his child and then his granddaughter, only to awaken in his great-grandson.

Line 54 brings the poem back to the speaker and the present. It is an average day for the family: a cool day in spring, with the mother calling to her son and daughter and laundry drying on the clothesline. However, the day is unique in that the speaker feels that her grandfather's memory is with them.

The narrator and her children can see the Rocky Mountains; they are far in the distance and cannot be seen clearly, appearing to flicker in and out of focus and having a blue cast. The speaker's son imagines that just as he can see the distant mountains, he can also see all the way to heaven if he tries hard enough.

THEMES

Family

Family is a major theme in "Heaven," as it is in many of Song's poems. Each stanza mentions at least one of the speaker's relatives, and moving through the poem, the reader sees how each person is tied to the others by the bonds of family. The poem begins with a pronoun; although the reader might not realize it immediately, the narrator is referring to her son. Right away, the son is tied to another family member when the speaker mentions his fair hair, which he inherited from his father. The narrator's son, along with her infant daughter, is also mentioned in stanza 3.

Although the second and third stanzas are mostly devoted to the setting, the last two lines of stanza 2 introduce the idea of the speaker's grandfather, who is the main focus of stanza 4. The grandfather never intended to stay in America,

likely hoping to earn money by working on the railroad and then return home. Neither the narrator nor her mother (presuming her parent of Chinese descent is, like Song's, her mother) ever had a strong desire to go to China, but at the beginning of stanza 5, the speaker suggests that her grandfather's hopes of returning home have somehow passed on to her son, who sees the mountains in the distance and imagines he can see all the way to China, or even all the way to heaven. Just like his ancestor, who might have had a *dream*, as per line 24, of his life in America, the speaker refers to her son as a *dreamer* both in line 33 and in line 60. The use of the same root word ties the two together more firmly in the reader's mind. The idea that an affinity for a distant, never-seen homeland can be carried on through generations of a family instills the poem with a sense of history, highlighting the fact that relatives and their experiences are part of who one is as a person.

History

In "Heaven," Song speaks about her individual family history, but in doing so, she provides insight into American history. The fact that Song's grandfather came to America to work on the railroad is specific to her family. However, the story of this lone man and his family contains elements central to national history: he was one of the thousands of Chinese laborers who were integral to building the transcontinental railroad, which in turn was vital to communication, shipping, and travel throughout the country and of central importance in the movement of the population in settling the western United States. This unique family story is one example of the many immigrant stories that could be told by the millions of people who came to America hoping for a better life.

American Identity

The first few lines of the poem address the appearance of the narrator's son. She is contemplating how her ancestor's choices have brought her to where she is, and as a mother, she wonders how those choices, as well as her own, will affect her young children. As she sees her son's heritage reflected in his appearance, she thinks about how his heritage might influence his choices in life.

America is a nation of immigrants. Many Americans have a mixture of races and ethnicities in their backgrounds, and their appearances can reflect that. This poem portrays the experience of one immigrant, as seen through the eyes of his granddaughter, and how this experience

TOPICS FOR FURTHER STUDY

- Song's poetry often draws from her own life experiences and those of her family members. Think about your own family history. Consider the choices your ancestors made that resulted in the circumstances of your life, such as where you live, what family and ethnic traditions you practice, and how you think about the world. Write a poem like "Heaven" that hints at your family's history and how it has influenced you.

- Read a young-adult novel that features a protagonist of mixed heritage. One choice is Nancy Osa's *Cuba 15* (2003), which centers on Violet Paz, a half-Polish, half-Cuban American teenager learning about her heritage before celebrating her quinceañera. Younger students might enjoy *Rain Is Not My Indian Name* (2001), by Cynthia Leitich Smith, in which a teenage girl with both white and Native American blood struggles to hold her own in a small, mostly white midwestern town. Write a letter from the perspective of your chosen novel's protagonist to the children of the narrator in "Heaven," who are likely too young at the time of the poem to be aware of prejudice they might face based on their appearance and their mixed heritage. Consider what advice your protagonist might give the children about finding their own identity.

- Using print and online resources, research Chinese immigration and Chinese railroad workers in the late nineteenth and early twentieth centuries. Prepare a PowerPoint presentation that explains the circumstances these immigrants left behind in China, what life was like for them in their new home, prejudice they faced from white Americans, laws passed to regulate immigration, and how that legislation affected relations between the United States and China. Share your presentation with your class.

- Read Marilyn Chin's poem "How I Got That Name" (available at Poets.org), which has the subtitle "An Essay on Assimilation." Think about how Chin addresses issues of heritage, assimilation, and family and write an essay that compares this poem with Song's "Heaven."

---

has directed the lives of his family long after his death. "Heaven" reflects the familiar story of someone coming to America to start a new life, but Song seems to want to remind readers that Americans, as people and as a nation, should not forget their collective history when forging personal identities.

STYLE

Everyday Language
Rather than the formal, at times artificial-sounding language of some poems, Song uses everyday language in "Heaven." It seems almost as if the narrator is just talking to the reader or even thinking out loud. The effect of the speaker's simply speaking to share her thoughts is reinforced by the structure of the lines and the poem as a whole. In most lines, Song uses standard punctuation, with periods or question marks at the end of each idea. Sentence-ending punctuation usually comes at the end of a line, and commas indicate pauses, just as in prose. Also, the poem's stanzas are like paragraphs, with each stanza focusing on a cohesive idea rather than having the subject matter run from one stanza into the next.

Line Breaks
Although Song uses free verse and everyday language, this does not suggest that she does not use

Though the family lives on the plains, they can see the Rocky Mountains in the distance. *(© Ann Cantelow / Shutterstock.com)*

any poetic devices. One device that appears in "Heaven" is the strategic use of line breaks. Song places many line breaks at natural pauses after phrases or between sentences, as shown by the fact that punctuation often appears at the ends of lines. However, there are places where the line break interrupts a phrase, and the reader must consider why Song placed the words as they appear on the page. One strategic use of a poetic line break is to amplify the meaning of the lines it bridges. For example, at the end of stanza 1, a line break appears in the middle of a phrase between lines 8 and 9. By adding a pause in thought as the reader's eye moves to the next line, the line break reflects the idea of reaching for something far away.

Poets can also use line breaks to draw attention to a word or phrase to stress its importance. Song does this in line 13 of "Heaven." By placing the words "But look" on a line of their own and ending with a dash, Song focuses the reader's attention and provides a sense of anticipation regarding what will come next. Song uses a similar technique in line 46. It is the only line in the poem that consists of only one word, which highlights its importance. This single word strikes a melancholy note in the poem, as if providing a moment of mourning for the death of the narrator's grandfather, or more specifically to mourn the fact that he died far away from his homeland.

HISTORICAL CONTEXT

Chinese Railroad Workers

The gold rush of 1849 brought many people to California from all over the country and around the world seeking a better future. Among those flocking to California were laborers from China who found work in mines, agriculture, and the railroads. These workers called their new home Gum San, which Song translates in "Heaven" as "Gold Mountain."

The work of Chinese immigrants was vital to the completion of the transcontinental railroad in the United States. There are no exact records of how many Chinese workers contributed to the railroads in total, but there are some details that give an idea of the vast numbers. In July 1865, Central Pacific Railroad employed almost four thousand Chinese workers, and that number grew almost threefold by 1867, with approximately eight thousand Chinese workers laboring in tunnels and three thousand laying track. As the demand for workers grew and deadlines for government contracts loomed, Central Pacific had contractors arrange the transport of hundreds of additional workers directly from China. Some historians estimate that ten to fifteen thousand Chinese workers were employed by Central Pacific at the height of the project.

COMPARE
&
CONTRAST

- **1980s:** After the early wave of Chinese immigration to the United States from the 1850s to the 1880s, the Chinese Exclusion Act of 1882 brings about a long lull. Immigration reform in both China and the United States in the 1960s and 1970s leads to a second wave of immigration beginning in the 1970s and continuing into the 1980s.

  Today: A review of 2013 immigration data indicates that China has surpassed Mexico and India as the country sending the most immigrants to the United States. Asian Americans are the most quickly growing racial group in the country, at a rate of annual increase of 2.9 percent, with immigration causing most of that growth. In 2012, 74 percent of Asian American adults were foreign born.

- **1980s:** In 1980, the US Census Bureau attempts to better reflect the country's population and identity in terms of race and ethnicity by adding a question about Spanish/Hispanic heritage.

  Today: More than 6 percent of respondents in the 2010 census select "some other race" in regard to their ethnic identity, which means a lack of information about millions of citizens. As census official Nicholas Jones, cited by the Pew Research Center, explains, "increasingly, Americans are saying they cannot find themselves" on census forms. In anticipation of the 2020 census, the US Census Bureau is conducting research to refine its race and ethnicity categories.

- **1980s:** China's adoption of an open-door policy to spark economic growth in the late 1970s leads to an increase in travel to the country, both for business and for pleasure. There are more foreign visitors to China in 1980 than in the preceding twenty-five years altogether. However, Chinese airlines have only eighteen regularly scheduled flights to fourteen countries. Throughout the decade, China works to increase both domestic and international airline travel networks to be more globally competitive, though safety regulations are poorly enforced, leading to an appalling safety record well into the 1990s.

  Today: By the end of the twentieth century, there were regular international flights from China to more than sixty cities in thirty-three countries. The US Federal Aviation Administration has determined that the Chinese Civil Aviation Authority, which regulates China's airlines, meets all requirements of international safety standards. Today, the number of flights traveling between the United States and China is limited by political treaties.

Most workers brought over from China by labor contractors came from Guangdong Province, which was plagued by poverty and civil unrest. Going to America gave workers hope that they could send money home to their families. Song's narrator mentions that her grandfather earned a dollar a day, and, indeed, some early Chinese workers earned only twenty-five to thirty dollars per month. Later, the rate increased to thirty-five dollars per month, which was close to what was paid to workers of European heritage. Chinese workers were expected to work longer hours, however, and many had to reimburse their employers for food and lodging, which were provided to white laborers at no charge. In June 1867, five thousand Chinese workers went on strike, demanding better working conditions and fair wages.

Building the railroad entailed hazardous work: crossing mountains by using blasting

When the speaker hears trains, she is reminded of her great grandfather, who came to America from China for a job building the railroads. (© IxMaster | Shutterstock.com)

powder to carve out ledges for level roadbeds, carving tunnels, clearing trees and rocks, and laying tracks. Avalanches and bad weather, among other catastrophes, claimed lives. Central Pacific kept no records of worker deaths, but historians estimate that anywhere from 50 to 150 Chinese workers were killed by explosions, falls, avalanches, snow slides, and other accidents during the construction of the transcontinental railroad. Disease such as smallpox was a threat, and there are unconfirmed contemporary reports of Chinese railroad workers being killed in a raid by Native Americans in Nevada.

After the Central Pacific Railroad was built, some Chinese workers returned to China. Many, however, decided to make the United States their new home. A large percentage of workers went on to work with other railroad companies, such as the Southern Pacific and Northern Pacific. Others chose different lines of work, finding jobs in mines and factories, on farms, or as domestic servants.

The railroad facilitated travel from the more heavily populated eastern part of the United

States to the West. More workers moving to the area made jobs scarce. Racial prejudice and resentment from white workers about Chinese immigrants holding steady jobs led to the passage of the Chinese Exclusion Act in 1882, which completely suspended immigration of Chinese laborers and denied citizenship to any Chinese immigrants already living in the United States. It was the first time the US federal government passed legislation to limit immigration based on race. The Chinese Exclusion Act was repealed in 1943, largely because China was an American ally during World War II.

CRITICAL OVERVIEW

Song's work has received largely positive critical attention. Her first collection, *Picture Bride* (1983), won the Yale Younger Poets Competition and earned a nomination for the National Book Critics Circle Award. She has also won the Shelley Memorial Award and the Hawaii Award for Literature. In a review of the collection *The*

Land of Bliss in *Library Journal*, Rochelle Ratner praises both Song's subject matter and her technical skill: "Song writes culturally fascinating work that at its best displays a superb mastery of craft." Alison Townsend, writing in the *Women's Review of Books*, also praises Song's style and craftsmanship, calling *School Figures* "an intensely lyrical, elegantly modulated collection."

Several critics point to Song's perceptiveness as making her poems particularly noteworthy. *Southern Review*'s Leslie Chang describes *Cloud Moving Hands* as "clear-eyed" and highlights the fact that Song's "gaze is unwavering," even when exploring difficult issues, such as grief and loss. Townsend marvels at how "Song's careful, painterly eye makes her the mistress of small moments of perception that, strung together, expand into a larger, frequently numinous understanding."

Critics do not shy away from mentioning the minor flaws in Song's work but still highly recommend her collections to libraries and readers. Chang feels that in her efforts to communicate lessons to her readers, Song sometimes "struggles too hard for instruction." Ratner points out that the poems in *The Land of Bliss* are "uneven" and feels that "when Song strays too far from autobiography, . . . the speaker is lost to us, and the poems become shrouded in mystery." Ratner nevertheless characterizes the volume as "containing some of the finest long poems this reviewer has read in recent memory," and Townsend particularly highlights how "Song's poems freeze the moment like a photograph." Grace Bauer, in her review of *Frameless Windows, Squares of Light* in *Library Journal*, agrees, pointing out how the poems capture "poignant visions of childhood, the family, and moments of perception . . . to be recalled and savored."

CRITICISM

Kristen Sarlin Greenberg

Greenberg is a freelance writer and editor with a background in literature and philosophy. In the following essay, she examines the importance of place in Song's "Heaven" as it reflects the theme of family history.

Many of Song's poems are autobiographical, focusing on stories of her parents and grandparents as well as her own experience, including being a daughter, wife, and mother. The subject

> HALFWAY THROUGH THE POEM, THE SPEAKER FINDS THE WORDS FOR THE FUNDAMENTAL QUESTION 'WHY HERE?'"

matter of each of her poetry collections reflects where she was living and what she was doing at the time. Her first book, *Picture Bride* (1983), was written while she was in graduate school, when she met and married her husband. The bride of the title is Song's Korean grandmother, who came to America for an arranged marriage. It is understandable that Song would be thinking about such a meeting when she was beginning her own marriage. While writing the collection *Frameless Windows, Squares of Light* (1988), Song was living in Colorado, where her husband was completing his medical residency at Denver General Hospital. By this time, the couple had two young children, and Song's interest in exploring her family's stories with her poems extended to her role as a mother. Some of the poems in Song's later collections, which were written and published after she moved back to her home state of Hawaii, close to her parents, reflect the difficulties of helping them as they aged.

Clearly, family history and a sense of place are both central to Song's work. Both themes are woven tightly into her poems. "Heaven," which is included in *Frameless Windows, Squares of Light*, is a perfect example. Halfway through the poem, the speaker finds the words for the fundamental question "why here?" As a young mother, she is examining her family history and wondering what the future will bring for her children. She begins to recognize how past choices her ancestors made as well as those she herself has made, including where she and her family have lived, have led to her life in the present.

The first place mentioned, in the very first line of the poem, is China. At first, it is an abstraction of the place—a little boy's conception of heaven as a place where everyone shares his Asian features. To him, heaven and China are equally distant and unreachable. Song makes the idea a bit more concrete by introducing a map, but China is still a remote, almost imaginary place. The boy has trouble reaching across the map's ocean to the blue mass of China.

WHAT DO I READ NEXT?

- With the poems included in her first collection, *Picture Bride* (1983), Song won the Yale Younger Poets Competition. The title is based on the practice in the early part of the twentieth century of immigrant workers from Japan, Korea, and China being matched with brides in their homelands based on photographs and recommendations from family or friends. Song's poems are often semiautobiographical, and her Korean grandmother came to Hawaii as a picture bride.

- Sandra Cisneros's book *The House on Mango Street* (1984) is told in a series of poetic scenes rather than the prose chapters of a traditional novel. Esperanza, Cisneros's protagonist, is an American teenager who struggles to find her own identity under the weight of her Mexican heritage.

- In *To the Golden Mountain: The Story of the Chinese Who Built the Transcontinental Railroad* (2002), Lila Perl provides an overview for student readers about the Chinese immigrant laborers who were instrumental in the completion of the American transcontinental railroad.

- Like Song, poet Marilyn Chin often focuses on themes of identity, her Asian heritage, and women's issues. Chin's collection *The Phoenix Gone, the Terrace Empty* (1994) was written for young adults.

- In *American Dragons: Twenty-Five Asian American Voices* (1993), editor Laurence Yep has gathered poems, short stories, and excerpts from longer works. All of the selections focus on issues central to Asian American teens.

- In Rainbow Rowell's *Eleanor & Park* (2013), both of the title characters feel like outsiders. Park is half Korean and tries to avoid attention from everyone except his father, who is difficult to please. Eleanor struggles with her weight but dresses in daring clothes almost in defiance of those who would say that she should hide her generous figure. In each other, they find love, acceptance, and self-confidence.

The next place described, however, is more exact and less abstract. Rather than being a lovely "flower," as China is described, the city where the speaker and her family live (most likely Denver, Colorado, which fits the poem's description and is also where Song was living at the time the poem was written) is a colorless "dot" that sits on the flat plains. Its air is too thin to nourish one's body, and its trees are "reedy." The nearest body of water is nothing but a "creek," though people describe it as a "river." The speaker seems to have little interest in and no affection for the place where she is living, which drives her to ask, "why here?" She seems to want to trace the series of events that brought her to this place.

Her thoughts on the issue send her mind back to her grandfather's time, and the detailed physical description of the area around Denver serves as a way to recall the proverbial Wild West of when her grandfather was working on the railroad. Although the US transcontinental railroad did not originally travel through Colorado, Song's description of her neighborhood shows echoes of past western life, such as the rattling train speeding by, falling-apart fences, and barking dogs. Song even mentions gunfights in the alley, bringing to mind gunslingers of the old days.

The speaker does not state precisely where the grandfather worked on the railroad. Perhaps Song felt that such detail was not important, since the hard labor and dangerous conditions were much the same throughout the long route. Alternatively, perhaps it is a purposeful omission. In explaining where the grandfather was from, the speaker is specific about the geography: in line 24, the speaker names Guangzhou, a city in the Chinese province of Guangdong. Because of the proximity of the port of Hong Kong, railroad companies recruited many workers from Guang-dong Province. This gives enriching historical detail to the poem, and in such a way that the exactness of naming her grandfather's hometown but not even naming the state where he worked while in the United States seems significant. No political place names are given in reference to the American locations; Song does not list state or city names, and the place names that do appear are more generalized, such as "the Rockies." The Rocky Mountains are a huge chain, so mentioning them by name is far more vague than naming a specific city.

The other place name used to refer to America is "Gold Mountain." This phrase is a translation of Gum San, which was a Chinese name for post–gold rush California that came to represent all of the western United States, where in spite of the prejudice they faced, Chinese laborers could find work and opportunity. By referring to America in vague or even mythic terms, Song universalizes her grandfather's experience: he was one of thousands of laborers from China who worked on the railroad, and he can also be seen as one of millions of immigrants who came to America hoping to improve their lot.

Rather than offering a rosy view of the American dream, however, Song's descriptions do not make America seem like a very inviting place. Much like in the earlier description of Denver, Gold Mountain is cold and windy. The word "landlocked" might have a connotation of feeling trapped, and the image of haunted or deserted towns is decidedly melancholy, conveying a hint of failure. The speaker's grandfather dies "dispossessed" of his homeland, and she wonders when it was that he realized he would never go home to China. Indeed, she seems uncertain that he truly made a decision to stay. Perhaps she thinks he simply waited too long to go back.

The sense of place is so central to the poem that Song even translates abstract concepts into places. When the idea of returning is discussed, the speaker explains that the desire to go back to China has passed over her mother and herself and skipped to her son. This urge to return is described in line 53 as both a garden and a grave without a marker, waiting to be unearthed. The use of the word "grave" is another choice by Song that brings in a negative connotation, and yet the overall tone of the poem is not melancholy or negative. It is interesting to consider how a poem filled with bleak descriptions and words with negative connotations manages to not leave the reader feeling sad or hopeless.

The speaker's son, in talking about heaven, does not seem to think about it as an abstract place. He imagines it as the very real if distant country of China. It is important that the speaker clearly states that she has never been to China, and it seems she never had any serious interest in going. This could be seen as a reluctance to examine her own past, or that of her family. Perhaps it is the speaker's relatively new role as a mother that makes her think more of returning to China. Many people become more interested in revisiting their homeland and getting to know more about their heritage once they have children, because it all seems more important with children to share it with.

In "Heaven," places come to represent family history and the evolution of the speaker's family as American. Perhaps Song means to suggest that it actually does not matter so much where we are or whether we have any particular affection for the place. Things are not perfect here—on the earth or specifically in America, as Song's somewhat grim descriptions of her hometown and Gold Mountain show. But "Heaven" suggests that the afterlife can be better. If the little boy is right, heaven is a place where everyone looks the same, and in a child's mind that could mean they *are* the same—or at least equal. In an idealized sense, he could mean a place where everyone is equal. In his mind, heaven is a colorful flower across the ocean that we can reach if we stretch out our hands. Through her son's imaginative wish to see all the way to heaven—or travel all the way to China—the speaker recognizes that we can embrace our family history, wherever our ancestors are from, and still belong in the here and now, uniquely ourselves and uniquely American.

Source: Kristen Sarlin Greenberg, Critical Essay on "Heaven," in *Poetry for Students*, Gale, Cengage Learning, 2016.

Susan R. Van Dyne
In the following excerpt, Van Dyne discusses why Song, as an Asian American poet, has been popular with mainstream audiences.

The ethnic text that becomes a crossover success—by that I mean a text produced by an ethnic writer that gains mainstream critical attention and proves commercially appealing to a wide national audience—marks one of the

The tall, thin aspens of the Rockies are compared to China's bamboo. (© *Jim David | Shutterstock.com*)

most significant boundaries in the mapping of literary traditions. In borrowing a term from popular music for tunes that sell simultaneously in ethnic and mainstream markets, I want to suggest that the "crossover hit" in poetry likewise signals a commodified success and hints at a betrayal of roots, that it demonstrates, in short, what is most urgently contested about how ethnicity is represented. To the ethnic critic, the crossover writer might be distrusted as a political defector; to the mainstream reader, on the other hand, she may seem a reliable native informant. How such a writer is read, by both groups, I want to argue, enables us to trace the critical methods of an emerging Asian American tradition being refined and consolidated. An emerging literary tradition allows us to analyze what is true of any literary tradition, that it is made, constructed retrospectively by critical practice as much as by some natural evolutionary sequence of writers. Or put another way, there are many poets writing who are possible participants in a tradition, but the terms in which its trajectory is charted make some writers seem less central, or less "authentic." The tensions arising

over the crossover phenomenon for the ethnic critic also demonstrate that the construction of an ethnic literary tradition is always relational, a negotiation between the minority and majority cultures about the representation and interpretation of ethnicity. The anxious ambivalence that has marked the critical attempts to define Asian American literary history over the last three decades suggests the project's twin goals have sometimes been politically polarizing and may seem, to some, inherently paradoxical. The urge to identify the distinctive voices, stances, and themes of Asian American literature responds to a need to recover the repressed histories and cultural practices of ethnic communities. Constructing a distinctive literary history has meant arguing for difference, an oppositional difference imbued with the politics of resistance to a teleology of assimilation. At the same time, the critical project's history has included a revisionary strategy to "claim Americanness," to insist on the significance of these writers' contribution to any definition of American literature as it is construed through mainstream reviews and perpetuated on college syllabi.

> WHETHER OR NOT HUGO HAS MISHEARD SONG'S VOICE, HE'S CERTAINLY LISTENED TO HER THROUGH PRECONCEPTIONS OF ASIAN FEMININITY: SHE'S CHILDLIKE RATHER THAN FULLY SEXUAL (DESPITE THE PERSISTENT THEME OF REPRODUCTION IN THE VOLUME), PASSIVE AND RECEPTIVE RATHER THAN ASSERTIVE OR EVEN SPECULATIVE…IN HER RESPONSE TO HER SUBJECTS."

Cathy Song, whose first volume, *Picture Bride*, won the Yale Younger Poets prize in 1982 and whose later volumes were published by Norton and the Pitt Poetry series in 1988 and 1994, is such a crossover hit. She's included in blockbuster mainstream literary anthologies like Norton, and Heath, as well as Asian American collections such as Joseph Bruchac's *Breaking Silence* (1983), the anthology of women artists, *Forbidden Stitch* (1989), and Garrett Hongo's *Open Boat* (1993). Song herself co-edited an anthology of Hawai'i women writers, *Sister Stew* (1991). Although it is unclear why and by whom the original title of Song's first book was changed from the title under which she submitted her collection, *From the White Place* (a tribute to the inspiration Song found in Georgia O'Keeffe) to the more ethnically marked *Picture Bride* (the title under which Yale published it in 1983), the anecdote is understood among Asian American critics as evidence that mainstream recognition brought by the Yale prize was conditional on highlighting the ethnicity of Song's subject position. Instead of announcing Song's meditations on art, the second title forefronts her reflections on history, particularly her family history of Korean immigration to Hawai'i. *Picture Bride* promises not only exotic ethnography from this poet born and raised in Hawai'i but female autobiography, an even more marketable commodity among American women readers. The impression is further underscored by the cover design in which a framed and illuminated portrait of a woman stands out from among partially obscured yet generically Asian images of other family members, as if she is both one of these historically removed subjects and the narrative eye/I for this family album.

The reasons that, since Kingston and Tan, certain versions of Asian American women's literature sell well are certainly multiple and clearly include more than their considerable artistic merits. Mainstream audiences are apt to regard ethnic texts as sources of cultural interpretation of the unfamiliar other. First-person texts, such as Song's lyric poems or Kingston's *Woman Warrior*, are probably read by the non-ethnic reader as autobiographical testimony more often than they are recognized as self-conscious fictions. If the mainstream audience expects some sort of transparent witness to ethnic experience, the autoethnography of the minority subject, as Rey Chow and Trinh Minh-ha have shown us, is never impervious to the dominant and colonizing discourse through which and against which such ethnographies are articulated. In fact, we may read with most pleasure, Sau-ling Wong contends, those fictions that produce an "Oriental effect," that is, those that best confirm our preconceptions of what the Asian American subject or experience is or ought to be ("Sugar Sisterhood" 187). Given the inevitable marking of the ethnic text by the dominant discourse and the touristic tendency to read "Asian difference" in order to shore up convictions of "American" centrality and homogeneity, Asian American critics are understandably skeptical of any writer's commercial success in a mainstream market, and have been wary, from the first, of texts that might be misappropriated and misread to reinforce stereotypes. I might argue that the error lies with the reader rather than the ethnic writer; that is, the problem is not "posing" as ethnographer but being "taken for" one. Nonetheless, some very popular writers' works have been faulted for being disloyal to a cultural collective project or unhelpful in realizing its political goals. Chin's castigation of Kingston's bestseller status as cultural treachery may seem primitive and outdated, yet the same distrust motivates, I think, Sau-ling Wong's recent sophisticated critique of Amy Tan in *The Ethnic Canon*. While the charge that a text perpetuates certain stereotypes can no longer be a sufficient basis for critical judgments, a persistent gesture among definitions of the Asian American literary tradition has nonetheless been trying to draw the line between exoticizing, prejudicial misrepresentations and authenticating ethnic details of truly "representative" texts or more lately, those that are praised as unapologetically "local" texts by Asian American writers.

What I want to point to here is the uneasy awareness among Asian American critics that the texts out of which they will construct a tradition are not their own, or at least not entirely. From the mid-1970s to the present moment, whether writers or texts are perceived as voluntarily defecting or being coopted, a residue of suspicion marks the critics' formulations, as in JanMohamed and Lloyd's *Nature and Context of Minority Discourse*: "Attending to minority cultural forms requires...a double vigilance, both with respect to their availability for hegemonic recuperation and to their strategies of resistance." The border skirmishes along this line suggest the reasons that articulating an Asian American literary tradition can never be an entirely self-defined critical task but is always deeply enmeshed with the dominant culture's perception of ethnicity. Although I've called these critical gestures anxious, uneasy, suspicious, this feature may not be entirely a liability, since a significant value of a minority text is the way it functions in relation to the dominant culture. If as JanMohamed and Lloyd argue, the minority subject position is constructed relationally through the dominant culture operating in multiple forms on minority cultures, then the texts that these minority subjects produce will always reveal important information about the processes of domination and negotiation between cultures. The poetic text can be read as an art form that confesses individual and collective histories forged through the exercise of power. As Lisa Lowe defines Asian American literature, it is an "esthetic product that cannot repress the material inequalities of its conditions of production."

Yet authorizing some meanings of a minority text is surely one of the forms of hegemonic power, as Cathy Song's case demonstrates. The late poet Richard Hugo was a judge for the Yale Younger Poets prize and wrote the foreword to *Picture Bride* in 1983. These avuncular presentations of the next-generation poet by the older-generation sponsor effectively frame the reader's sense of her stylistic signature, and Hugo's terms strikingly reappear in mainstream reviews of Song. To Richard Hugo, Song's poems are marked by "quietude"; "her senses are lucky to have remained childlike." He sees O'Keeffe's extravagant blooms transformed in Song's hands: "her poems are flowers...offered almost shyly," and he repeatedly refers to her distinctive sensibility as "passive" and "receptive." Although he notes her sympathetic portrayals of

female rebels, an American critique of old world constraints, he persistently credits her poetic strengths to her hereditary Asianness, "a patience that is centuries old, ancestral, tribal, a gift passed down." Whether or not Hugo has misheard Song's voice, he's certainly listened to her through preconceptions of Asian femininity: she's childlike rather than fully sexual (despite the persistent theme of reproduction in the volume), passive and receptive rather than assertive or even speculative...in her response to her subjects. For those readers whose only regular exposure to poetry is in the pages of the *New Yorker* and who wouldn't be likely to read *Breaking Silence*, an anthology of fifty contemporary Asian American poets also published in 1983, the Yale prize and Hugo's introduction typed Song's talent paradoxically as generically Asian and yet exceptional. In entering the mainstream literary marketplace as the winner of the Yale Younger Poets prize, she seemed the only young Asian American poet worthy of publication rather than part of a cohort of at least fifty who are recognized in Bruchac's anthology.

In a special issue of *Contact/II* devoted to Asian American poetry and criticism, Stephen Sumida tries to define Song's contribution to the tradition, yet his defensive tone suggests he expects ethnic readers are suspicious of her prize and her prominence in the mainstream press: "The title 'Picture Bride' is not an opportunistic adoption of a catchy historical symbol.... the poems themselves do not treat Hawaii's people and Asian Americans as exotics" ("Pictures"). Sumida's readings attempt to wrest Song's meanings back from Hugo's magisterial misreadings by uncovering their deeply layered allusions, available only to a knowledgeable cultural insider. For example, both comment on Song's concluding image of "a thousand cranes" that fly up unexpectedly at the end of "Youngest Daughter." Hugo sees the image as the freedom available to the daughter through visual imagination; Sumida supplies the image's sedimented history as an evocation of longevity and marital happiness, resonances that make his reading of the ending, in which the daughter chafes against a lifetime of intimate companionship with her aging mother, more ironic than optimistic. Sumida's correction to Hugo is part of his advocacy of culturally informed reading strategies and his critique [of] the shortcomings of merely aesthetic or formalist responses. Sumida's larger critical project is to reconstruct a distinctive, historically inflected literary tradition of "Asian/Pacific American" writing in Hawai'i, beginning before colonization; so he deeply distrusts a "touristic" approach to Hawaii's landscape or peoples (see "Sense of Place"). In championing the "local" in Song's poetry, he is understandably uncomfortable with the prominence of Georgia O'Keeffe in the volume, especially a long dramatic monologue spoken in her voice. Sumida's solution is to argue that rather than adopting or endorsing O'Keeffe's point of view, Song actually critiques the "artist who is a sojourner or merely a visitor," and presents O'Keeffe as "wasting away in a solipsism, a dream landscape of her own making." He recognizes that the "crossover" poet risks being misunderstood by both audiences: "whatever subversive qualities these poems may have, elements that undermine cliches, they are very subtle, and oddly, are too easily mistaken in some ways for the simply conventional, and worse, the stereotypical."

Whatever the extent to which Sumida's oppositional rereadings might restore Song's reputation among Asian American readers, his essay will never gain the currency of Hugo's introduction. Indeed, Sumida's response to Hugo is a telling example of the "belated discourse" that Shirley Lim describes as a particular disadvantage of minority scholars and their limited and often marginalized opportunities to publish. The special issue of *Contact/II* was "in the final stages prior to publication" in 1983, but did not, in fact, appear until 1986. As Lim observes, "the delayed appearance of such ethnic-related criticism creates the false appearance of belatedness," robs minority critics of the opportunity to make a timely and relevant critique and represents their thinking arrested at a stage they have most likely already revised. Meanwhile, majority scholars with access to multiple and more immediate publication resources may appropriate minority discourse from conferences and, by making "more intellectual property," further confirm their dominant position in the academy ("Ambivalent"). Not surprisingly, the brief headnote to the selection of Song's poetry in the second edition of the *Norton Anthology of Modern Poetry*, which appeared in 1988, two years after Sumida's rejoinder, reproduces without qualification Hugo's definition of her "passive/receptive sensibility." ....

Source: Susan R. Van Dyne, "Snapshots in History: Rereading Ethnic Subjects in Cathy Song," in *Replacing America: Conversations and Contestations*, edited by

> WHILE IT IS TRUE THAT LIFE CANNOT TURN BACK, MEMORY AND IMAGINATION CAN. AND IT IS ALSO TRUE THAT THROUGH THE IMAGINATION OF THE POET WE THE READERS CAN DERIVE A MEANING FROM THAT PAST THAT ILLUMINATES THIS PRESENT, A PARTICULAR SUBSTANCE THAT FAR TRANSCENDS NOSTALGIA."

Ruth Hsu, Cynthia Franklin, and Suzanne Kosanke, University of Hawai'i, 2000, pp. 181–85.

S. E. Solberg

In the following essay, Solberg examines the importance of Song's Asian heritage in her work.

Cathy Song, the poet, was born in Honolulu in 1955 where she makes her permanent home with her husband and two children. Her first book of poetry, *Picture Bride*, won the Yale Series of Younger Poets Award in 1982, one of the most prestigious literary awards for young poets in the United States. Published by Yale University Press in 1983 the book was nominated for a National Book Circle Award that same year. Her second book of poetry, *Frameless Windows, Squares of Light* (W.W. Norton) was published in 1988.

Song, who is of Chinese and Korean American descent, was a published poet by the time she was 20 years old and was one of the first Asian American poets from Hawaii to write explicitly of an Asian American heritage. In her Korean grandmother she found the subject and object of the title poem of her first collection, *Picture Bride*. The grandmother was one of those intrepid women who, in the early years of this century, left home and family for an unknown future in Hawaii with men they did not know.

> *"She was a year younger than I,*
> *twenty-three when she left Korea.*
> *Did she simply close*
> *the door of her father's house*
> *and walk away?"*

It is true that in the wonder of that single, isolated event from which stemmed her own father's side of the family, this third-generation (samse) lady celebrates her Korean roots, but, as she would be the first to point out, it is not all that simple. If her poems are grown out of her experience and knowledge to the extent that she is Korean American, her poetry will be Korean American. But there is no easy scale upon which we weigh the "Korean-ness" or "Korean American-ness" of a poem. Attractive as ethnic labels and categories might be at first glance, they tell us more about the insecurities of the labeler than about the poem itself.

Cathy Song disdains labels. She would tell you, as she did a Seattle interviewer a few years back, that she is a poet who only happens to be Asian. The poetry comes first as it should and must with anyone who aspires to the title of poet. It is, after all, the poet's experience and felt knowledge of her world that determines the subject of her poetry. A contrived book or wish-generated ethnicity can only result in contrived poems.

Yet today's new wave of immigrant Korean Americans and their offspring are subject to a nagging curiosity, a constant questioning of the terms of their relationship to their new country, of the nature of their ties to the Korea they have recently left. And on occasion, in bemused appraisal of their forerunners, those descendants of that small first wave who have been here three generations or more, the Cathy Songs, with whom they seem to hold so little in common, continue to ask: Is there anything we share beyond the Korean label? What is the nature of this "Korean-ness" we are said to share? When does being a Korean in America change to being a Korean American? What specific Korean values or traits are passed on to following American generations?

These are questions sociologists ponder, parents agonize over, and, perhaps, only poets can answer. Cathy Song writes: "I have never been to Korea. I do not speak the language. And I know that if I were to go there, I would not feel as though I were coming home, returning to a long lost place. My link to Korea is through my paternal grandparents. It is a fragile link; my grandparents have been dead for almost 20 years. I have missed them all my adult life.

"My grandfather left Korea to work in the sugarcane fields of Hawaii. It was 1903. He was 18 years old. It was not until 1921 that my grandmother arrived as a picture bride. She was 23. Once she arrived and they married and had children, the link to Korea was essentially broken. They rarely spoke, if at all, of their respective families, their former lives. It was as if they had developed a kind of necessary amnesia; remembering what they had given up was probably too painful. So much remains a mystery; photographs of my grandmother's mother, a stern-looking matriarch surrounded by figures no one in my family, least of all my father, can identify."

If the measure of "Korean-ness" is to be found in identification with the homeland and homeland ways from food and family to custom and culture, it is clear that the first wave and the new wave exist in different worlds. The terms of their "exile," the very physical condition of their relation to the "motherland," are different. Distances that were once measured in weeks and months are now measured in hours; trips "home" that once represented years of desperately accumulated savings are now a matter of putting aside a few weeks' pay. The day's headline story is the same on the streets of Los Angeles, Seattle, or New York as in Seoul and in the same language. The homeland pops up on the television news as well as in the endless miles of Korean-made video tapes, soap operas to high dramas that are reeled out in countless Korean American apartments, family rooms, and bedrooms to assuage the pain of daily confrontation with a society too often hostile and alienating.

What then of the American bred or born from among this new wave? And their children? Will America have its way with them as well, despite the wonders of communication and the transportability of so many of these artifacts of the surface culture? In the end will it be only the poets among this new first generation's grandchildren who are able to reach out with sympathy and imagination to capture the actuality of their parents' and grandparents' lives? Will this greater physical accessibility of the homeland and its products be paralleled by a greater spiritual affinity with Korea? A bonding with an ancestral home that is near at hand in fact as well as memory?

Though we press for answers now, they remain for the future. But perhaps the record of the past as seen in the lives of that first wave and its descendants may suggest both how natural the "becoming American," as the phrase has it, was and is, and yet, paradoxically, how powerful are the sense of origins, of family, class, and nation.

The poet's voice is a rare and precious thing that should not be called upon to answer questions other than those of its own choosing. Yet in the intensity and honesty of Cathy Song's poetic quest for the meaning of her past and present we may perhaps gain some sense of what a future "samse" poet might choose to find looking back at the struggles of this current new wave of Koreans becoming Americans through their children. But that is the sociology, not the poetry of it.

In her poem, "Picture Bride" Cathy Song reflects on the human center of her grandmother's life; in the prose selection that follows she reflects, not only on the genesis of that poem, but also on the passing of generations and what being "Korean" might mean for her and her children in today's (and tomorrow's) complex and confusing world.

> When I wrote the poem "Picture Bride," I was thinking of my grandmother and the distance she had to travel. She was about my age at the time I wrote the poem. I was recently out of college, homesick in New England, far from my family, Hawaii, my place of birth. But the loneliness was an illusion; I could always return. Once my grandmother left (Korea), it was forever. She could never go back. I find that incomprehensible, that she could leave willingly, forfeit all that was familiar for a place she had never seen, to marry a man she had never met. And there were thousands like her. They died never seeing their families again.
>
> They started new families, made new attachments; their children became their surrogate country. By the next generation, the bloodline, the link to the other life, was further diluted; my father married my mother, a second-generation Chinese, in 1949. Thirty years later, I married a man from New Mexico of Scottish-English descent. If my grandparents were to see my son, their great-grandson, they would be mortified. He is incongruously blond. He knows he is Korean, but he thinks everyone is Korean, including his very blond father. When his Chinese grandmother gives him good luck money, wrapped in shiny red paper on Chinese New Year, he thanks her politely for the "Japanese money." And he says with certainty that when we die we will go to China. His idea of Heaven.
>
> It's as though I—and others like myself, third-generation Asian Americans, descendants of migration and displacement—have little sense of our cultural heritage. We may eat certain foods, observe certain customs, but for the most part, we go through the motions; the gestures are haphazard and meaningless, however well-intended. We do not speak the language. Neither do our parents. They were too busy learning to be model citizens, eager to leave behind the accents and odors of the old country. Our grandparents, in turn, were actually paving the way for a better life. Perhaps it's better this way; to know no boundaries, to dispense with the restrictions of remote allegiances.
>
> I do not think of myself as being simply Korean. The world has become more complicated than that. I prefer to think that I belong, as we all do, to the human dwelling. When I look at my son, my link to the future, I wonder what the world will be like for him. Maybe the blond hair framing the Asian face is a sign of what the world is gradually becoming: a blending, a mixture; capable of a great generosity.

That evaluation of the weight of the poet's return to and recreation of the past may be taking the whole enterprise a bit too lightly; the true modesty of an accomplished artist.

While it is true that life cannot turn back, memory and imagination can. And it is also true that through the imagination of the poet we the readers can derive a meaning from that past that illuminates this present, a particular substance that far transcends nostalgia.

Cathy Song has demonstrated that informing power of the poet in two substantial collections of poetry published within a decade; a time in which she has also created her own family, a new generation in present space and time plus a poetic family of four generations in her poetry; she is one of those chosen few for whom poetry is the vocation around which life is organized, or, perhaps better, by which life is given meaning.

The subjects of the poems in *Picture Bride* range far afield, from contemplations of paintings by Georgia O'Keeffe and ukiyo-e prints of Utemoro, to brothers and parents and grandparents, family present and past. It is a remarkable achievement for a first book, yet, almost paradoxically, the narrower scope of *Frameless Windows, Squares of Light* centering more and more around motherhood and family, open out more, tap deeper themes, carry a greater load of passion. In a poem titled "The Binding," Song offers a meditation upon a mother's love for her son in light of the Virgin Mary's bargain; to be the consort of God only that her son might be well-known.

> We love them more than life, these children
> who are born to us. How did Mary endure it?
> It was more than she bargained for that this son

destined for sacrifice, was destined in his "greatest hour" to love her not more, not less than he loved the soldier who wept at his feet. It was cruel to ask that of her...

This is the cry of the universal mother; there are no direct evocations of Korea or Korean-ness in *Frameless Windows, Squares of Light* where the fourth-generation of Song's poetic family (the children of the speaker of the poems) begins to dominate. Ethnically and specifically we are led only to the "Chinese" heaven of the blond 4-year-old in a poem called simply, "Heaven." In the poem "Living Near the Water," we join the poetic family at the death of the grandfather whose "young man's eyes had scanned / the cargo the brides / who bowed before the grim life held out to them..." and where, in the time and place of the poem, "Those of us assembled on that day had descended from that moment of regret; my grandmother stepping forward to acknowledge her own face was the last to give herself away."

We are again back to origins that are Korean in this reference to the meeting of picture bride and sugarcane-worker husband, references obscure enough to lead a serious reader of the later book back to the first and the Korean picture bride that gave it its title. Then once the source of this luminous four-generation poetic family has been established, there comes a realization that in poetry as in life, there neither is nor can there be a constant minute by minute reference to origins. Life is where you are as well as where you come from; the poetry speaks to wider concerns as well. *Frameless Windows, Squares of Light* could be read without any reference to things Korean. But how much richer the poems or the Korean American life become by that awareness.

Source: S. E. Solberg, "Cathy Song and the Korean American Experience in Poetry: Peering through 'Frameless Windows, Squares of Light,'" in *The Asian Pacific American Heritage: A Companion to Literature and Arts*, edited by George J. Leonard, Garland Publishing, 1999, pp. 541–46.

Alison Townsend
In the following excerpt, Townsend describes Song's style as "elegantly modulated."

...Cathy song's third book, *School Figures*, is an intensely lyrical, elegantly modulated collection. I read it almost as a series of pictures describing the speaker's transition from girlhood

to motherhood to early middle age, all of it filtered through the complex, frequently fractured lens of her Asian American experience.

Song's poems freeze the moment like a photograph, capturing the "light of the picture / the one I've been looking at all my life," preserving it for retrieval in the present. This gives her work a circling, obsessive quality at times that serves her especially well when she writes about her family and her past. She continues to develop her precise and delicate imagery, a hallmark of bet previous work. A voice is a "fist that wants to open its pearl and sing"; the body "is a temple we worship / secretly in the traveling revivalist tent of our clothes"; scissors have a "crisp clever bite... parting like silver fish in a river of calico."

Song puts this strength to excellent use, locating the coordinates of her emotional geography in a specific time and place. Much of this process involves a complicated shuttling hack and forth between the past and present, examining her family's history, her childhood and that of her own children. "It was like falling through a mirror," she says in "Points of Reference":

> into someone else's story, the years when the children were small. Your mother's story perhaps of falling into a lake at the edge of summer when you were still in the stars, waiting to be borne across the water...

Part of what grounds Song's work is her ability to locate detail in the world of the body. Whether noting the "small dark seed" of herself growing in her daughter's "dark and fertile fire" and wondering how this will come back to haunt her, watching how her nursing son's fingers "twist and turn / the little knob of nipple / as if it were a radio dial," or describing the "skin stretched taut // like laundered sheets, clean and fragrant, / fitting the knock-kneed / corners of schoolgirl bones," Song's lyrics take on a tactile Lushness.

Not that the view of the body in this book is entirely celebratory. In "The Body's Faith" the addressee binds her milky breasts "to wean the last / drop of it from you / the overwhelming fecundity of it all." In "Sunworshippers" Song tells us, "We were not allowed to love ourselves too much." She can present difficult feelings about the body with an utter lack of self-pity, though there are times when I wish she would risk a bit more, let the pain in some of these poems be a little more raw, less polished. Nonetheless, the pulsing and, for the most part, deliciously sensual world of the body is present everywhere, "endlessly resourceful," giving the poems substance and weight.

Song's careful, painterly eye makes her the mistress of small moments of perception that, strung together, expand into a larger, frequently numinous understanding. In "The Grammar of Silk" she understands that her mother "was determined that I should sew / as if she knew what she herself was missing, / a moment when she could have come up for air." "All day I hear him," she says in "Journey," about her father's dying. And later: "Night whittles a sled of the moon. Shavings of wood / drift to the far / comers of the room."

Song writes so well about family that some of the other poems in the book (a series remembering friends from high school and beyond, several pieces about her husband's family) suffer by comparison. The writing here is slacker, more prosy, less taut, lacking the clarity and focus of the earlier visions of childhood and family. She regains her stride, however, in the last section of the book, where she writes of her husband and children with great beauty. "The years are tender, fluid like water, / when we can say we have always known each other," she says. And: "All you have ever wanted is here, / asleep. / It is all you can do to find your way home." At their very best, these luminous, musical poems provide a borne that, like the "school figures" in the title, preserve "the black and white of it"—what lasts, and what vanishes....

Source: Alison Townsend, Review of *School Figures*, in *Women's Review of Books*, Vol. 13, Nos. 10–11, July 1996, p. 40.

SOURCES

"Asian Americans Growing Faster Than Any Other Group in the U.S.," NBC News website, June 26, 2014, http://www.nbcnews.com/news/asian-america/asian-americans-growing-faster-any-other-group-u-s-n141991 (accessed May 25, 2015).

Bauer, Grace, Review of *Frameless Windows, Squares of Light*, in *Library Journal*, Vol. 113, No. 11, June 15, 1988, p. 61.

"Cathy Song," Poetry Foundation website, http://www.poetryfoundation.org/bio/cathy-song (accessed May 25, 2015).

Chang, Leslie, Review of *Cloud Moving Hands*, in *Southern Review*, Vol. 44, No. 2, Spring 2008, pp. 384–85.

"China, India Replace Mexico as Top U.S. Immigrant Origin Nations," NBC News website, May 4, 2015, http://www.nbcnews.com/news/asian-america/china-india-replace-mexico-top-u-s-immigrant-origin-nations-n353256 (accessed May 25, 2015).

"China: Travel & Transportation," U.S. Passports & International Travel, U.S. Department of State website, http://travel.state.gov/content/passports/english/country/china.html (accessed May 25, 2015).

"Chinese Immigration and the Chinese Exclusion Acts," Office of the Historian, U.S. Department of State website, https://history.state.gov/milestones/1866-1898/chinese-immigration (accessed May 25, 2015).

Cohn, D'Vera, "Census History: Counting Hispanics," Pew Research Center website, March 3, 2010, http://www.pewsocialtrends.org/2010/03/03/census-history-counting-hispanics-2/ (accessed May 25, 2015).

Dougan, Mark, *A Political Economy Analysis of China's Civil Aviation Industry*, Routledge, 2002, p. 153.

"FAQs," Chinese Railroad Workers in North America Project, Stanford University website, http://web.stanford.edu/group/chineserailroad/cgi-bin/wordpress/faqs/ (accessed May 25, 2015).

Fennelly, Katherine, "U.S. Immigration: A Historical Perspective," in *National Voter*, January 2007, http://www.hhh.umn.edu/people/kfennelly/pdf/immigration_historical_perspective.pdf (accessed May 25, 2015).

Hooper, Kate, and Jeanne Batalova, "Chinese Immigrants in the United States," Migration Policy Institute website, January 28, 2015, http://www.migrationpolicy.org/article/chinese-immigrants-united-states (accessed May 25, 2015).

"Immigration, Railroads, and the West," in *Aspiration, Acculturation, and Impact: Immigration to the United States, 1789–1930*, Harvard University Library Open Collections Program website, http://ocp.hul.harvard.edu/immigration/railroads.html (accessed July 6, 2015).

Krogstad, Jen Manuel, and D'Vera Cohn, "U.S. Census Looking at Big Changes in How It Asks about Race and Ethnicity," Pew Research Center website, March 14, 2014, http://www.pewresearch.org/fact-tank/2014/03/14/u-s-census-looking-at-big-changes-in-how-it-asks-about-race-and-ethnicity/ (accessed May 25, 2015).

Lew, Alan A., Lawrence Yu, John Ap, and Zhang Guangrui, *Tourism in China*, Routledge, 2002, p. 170.

Nomaguchi, Debbie Murakami, "Cathy Song: I'm a Poet Who Happens to Be Asian American," in *International Examiner*, May 2, 1984, p. 9; quoted in "Biography: Cathy Song, b. 1955," Poetry Foundation website, http://www.poetryfoundation.org/bio/cathy-song (accessed May 25, 2015).

Ratner, Rochelle, Review of *The Land of Bliss*, in *Library Journal*, Vol. 126, No. 20, December 2001, pp. 130–31.

Sato, Gayle K., "Cathy Song (1955–)," in *Asian-American Poets: A Bio-bibliographical Critical Sourcebook*, edited by Guiyou Huang, Greenwood Press, 2002, pp. 275–76.

Song, Cathy, "Heaven," in *Frameless Windows, Squares of Light: Poems*, W. W. Norton, 1988, pp. 77–79.

Terrazas, Aaron, and Jeanne Batalova, "Chinese Immigrants in the United States," Migration Policy Institute website, May 6, 2010, http://www.migrationpolicy.org/article/chinese-immigrants-united-states-0 (accessed May 25, 2015).

Townsend, Alison, Review of *School Figures*, in *Women's Review of Books*, Vol. 13, Nos. 10–11, July 1996, p. 40.

Song, Cathy, *School Figures*, University of Pittsburgh Press, 1994.
This is Song's third poetry collection. The title refers to the exercises of an ice skater—Song compares the skates' etching lines on the ice with the pen of a writer making lines on blank paper.

Tan, Shaun, *The Arrival*, Lothian Books, 2006.
Critics rave about Tan's wordless graphic novel, which perfectly illustrates the fascination and alienation felt by an immigrant in his new home.

FURTHER READING

Foyt, Victoria, *Revealing Eden*, Sand Dollar Press, 2012.
This novel is the first part of Foyt's Save the Pearls series, which offers an interesting take on race in a futuristic dystopian world.

Gaskins, Pearl Fuyo, ed., *What Are You? Voices of Mixed-Race Young People*, Henry Holt, 1999.
For this volume, Gaskins spent two years conducting interviews with mixed-race youths from all over the United States. They discuss issues such as family, dating, and prejudice.

SUGGESTED SEARCH TERMS

Cathy Song AND "Heaven"

Cathy Song AND Frameless Windows, Squares of Light

Cathy Song AND review

Cathy Song AND Yale Younger Poets Competition

Asian American poets

Chinese immigration

Chinese Exclusion Act

Chinese railroad workers AND nineteenth century

He Seems to Be a God

SAPPHO
c. 620 BC

"He Seems to Be a God" is a lyric poem written by the ancient Greek poet Sappho. It is available in a translation by Guy Davenport in *7 Greeks*, published in 1995. Little is known about Sappho's life, and because most of her poetry has been lost or survives only in fragments, it is impossible to know with any precision when the poem was written. Sappho was born on the isle of Lesbos, in the Aegean Sea, sometime around 612 BCE and lived to about the age of thirty, so it can be surmised that she wrote the poem sometime in the early sixth century BCE.

Sappho's poems do not have conventional titles. Generally, the poem's first line is used as the title, so the poem for Greek readers is titled "Phainetai moi." When the poems are translated from the original Archaic Greek to English or any other language, however, that first line differs depending on the translation. "He Seems to Be a God" is the rendering provided by the American poet and translator Guy Davenport. Elsewhere, the poem is titled "He Is Changed to a God Who Looks on Her," "That Man Is Peer of the Gods," "Like the Very Gods," "I Set That Man among the Gods and Heroes," "In My Eyes He Matches the Gods," and numerous others—variances that suggest the difficulties, and opportunities, of translating the poetry of a writer like Sappho. Scholars who focus more on the fragmentary nature of the poetry refer to "He Seems to Be a God" as fragment 31, following a numerical cataloging of the surviving poems and fragments adopted by scholars.

Sappho *(© Faraways | Shutterstock.com)*

Some of the fragments, found on scraps of ancient papyrus, on pottery, and wrapped around mummies, consist of isolated words and phrases. "He Seems to Be a God" is one of the few Sappho poems that appears to exist almost in its entirety—the final line has had to be reconstructed, and some scholars posit a missing final stanza. The poem is indicative of Sappho's lyricism, her interest in romantic love, and her deep appreciation of beauty in others, particularly women. She has survived as one of the most important poets of antiquity, the earliest woman writer in any Indo-European language, and a poet whose work has served as a model for numerous poets throughout the ages. Because of her close relationships with women, Sappho is further associated with the modern concept of lesbianism, a word derived from *Lesbos*, and sometimes the word *sapphic* is used as a synonym for *lesbian*.

AUTHOR BIOGRAPHY

What little is known about Sappho's life comes from two sources. One is hints and clues in her own writings, although that information is fragmentary and may not always be reliable. The other is the works of other writers in antiquity, which date from a few hundred to a thousand years after her lifetime. These writers passed on biographical information that may or may not have been based on authentic traditions. Complicating matters is that playwrights often used Sappho as a stock comic character, and the fictional and unflattering stories they invented about her morality entered the biographical stream as if they were true. Thus, much of what can be said about Sappho's life is speculative, and in many cases a reflection of the biases and outlook of each generation of biographers.

Sappho's parents were aristocrats. Sappho was born sometime between about 630 and 612 BCE at Eresos, a town on the Aegean island of Lesbos. Scholars lean toward the later date. Her father was Scamandronymus, although some sources give the name as Scamand; her mother was Cleis (or Kleis). She had three brothers: Erigyius, Larichus, and Charaxus, a wine merchant. Sometime during her childhood, between about 604 and 595 BCE, Sappho was taken to exile in Sicily because of political turmoil. After she returned to Lesbos, she spent most of her life at Mytilene, her mother's native city. She probably married, and she had a daughter she named Cleis after her mother. One of her contemporaries on Lesbos was the poet Alcaeus, and the two poets may have been close friends and colleagues.

According to the Roman poet Ovid, writing hundreds of years later, Sappho was short and had a dark complexion. The tenth-century *Suda*, a Byzantine encyclopedia, noted that she had three companions—Atthis, Telesippa, and Megara—with whom she was at the time believed to have been intimate. It seems clear from her poetry, including "He Seems to Be a God" (ca. 600 BCE), that she had intense feelings for members of her own sex.

Sappho was able to read and write, accomplishments that were rare among women of the time, and it is believed that as a central figure in a literary circle, she may have passed her abilities on to other young women, preparing them for adulthood and marriage. She likely performed religious rituals, including worship of Aphrodite, the goddess of love. Her poems were accompanied by dance and music; the word *lyric* is derived from the word *lyre*, referring to the stringed musical instrument. The hymns she wrote for public performance would have been performed by aristocratic *parthenoi*, or girls between the ages of puberty and marriage (perhaps twelve to sixteen years old). Sappho composed hymns sung at weddings (a subgenre of poetry called the epithalamium), and "He Seems to Be a God" may have been composed in connection with a wedding ceremony, although this is speculative.

Sappho died in about 580 BCE. The legend surrounding her death, promulgated through the comic playwright Menander and the epistles of the Roman poet Ovid, is that she fell in love with a boatman named Phaon. When he rejected her, she threw herself into the sea from a cliff. The story is almost certainly a fabrication, but it survived through later poetry and plays.

POEM TEXT

He seems to be a god, that man
Facing you, who leans to be close,
Smiles, and, alert and glad, listens
To your mellow voice

And quickens in love at your laughter   5
That stings my breasts, jolts my heart
If I dare the shock of a glance.
I cannot speak,

My tongue sticks to my dry mouth,
Thin fire spreads beneath my skin,   10
My eyes cannot see and my aching ears
Roar in their labyrinths.

Chill sweat slides down my body,
I shake, I turn greener than grass.
I am neither living nor dead and cry   15
From the narrow between.
But endure, even this grief of love.

POEM SUMMARY

The text used for this summary is from *7 Greeks*, translated by Guy Davenport, New Directions, 1995, pp. 74–75.

"He Seems to Be a God" consists of four four-line stanzas and a final single line. The poet appears to be speaking in her own voice to *you*, that is, a woman for whom the poet has intense feelings, although she is apostrophizing the woman (that is, the woman is not listening and does not hear). In stanza 1, the speaker begins by comparing a man speaking to the woman to a

MEDIA ADAPTATIONS

- The three-act opera *Sapho* by the French composer Charles Gounod premiered in 1851. It is available on audio CD from Gala Records (2003).
- *Sappho* is the last grand opera by the Australian composer Peggy Glanville-Hicks. It is available as an audio CD from Toccata (2012).

god—a fairly conventional comparison in an age that valued the heroic figure. The man is facing the woman, leaning toward her to be close. He smiles, and he appears to be both alert and glad as he listens to the woman's mellow voice.

Stanza 2 continues from the first without a break as the speaker senses that the man's love quickens, or grows, as he hears the woman's laughter. The scene between the man and the woman is an intimate, playful, perhaps flirtatious conversation. The speaker then begins to record the woman's reactions to the scene she is witnessing—specifically, to record her physical responses. The woman's laughter stings the speaker's breasts and shakes her heart if she dares to glance at the woman. The stanza concludes with the speaker's saying that she is unable to speak.

Stanza 3 continues the thought that ended the second. The speaker says that her tongue sticks to the roof of her dry mouth, fire spreads beneath her skin, she is unable to see, and a roaring causes the labyrinths of her ears to ache.

In stanza 4, the speaker indicates that sweat is running down her body, that she is shaking, and that she is turning greener than grass. This image suggests that the speaker is turning pale or perhaps green with envy: the poem can be read as an expression of the speaker's jealousy that the godlike man appears to have won the heart of the woman the speaker loves. The speaker goes on to indicate that she is crying out from a narrow space between living and dead, suggesting that her emotions are so intense that she does not know whether she is alive or dead.

The final single line is an expression of resignation. The speaker notes that she must endure the grief that her love is causing her. Some Greek scholars point out that *endure* could also be translated as something more like *dare*, suggesting that the speaker may dare to sustain her love, perhaps even pursue it, even in the face of a rival.

THEMES

Jealousy

From one point of view, "He Seems to Be a God" can be read as a poem expressing jealousy. The speaker of the poem has intense feelings for the woman she is apostrophizing as *you* (although the *you* of the poem does not hear the speaker). The man who appears in the first line seems to have won the heart and affections of the woman. And for him to have won such a valuable prize, he has to be godlike in his features and bearing. The speaker grows agitated and jealous while she watches the man and woman in intimate, playful conversation. The woman's mellow voice and laughter evoke a wide range of physical symptoms in the speaker: her heart is jolted, she cannot speak, her tongue sticks to the roof of her mouth, a burning sensation spreads through her body, she is unable to see, her ears buzz, and a chill sweat runs down her body as she shakes and turns green. The use of the word *green* has been a challenge for translators and interpreters. The word could refer to feeling sick, to turning pale, to experiencing great fear, or to returning to youthfulness and fresh innocence.

Romantic Love

Sappho provides a catalog of the physical symptoms of love. In both high culture and popular culture, these manifestations of love have become conventional. Sappho can be regarded as the inventor of the language of romantic and sexual desire, and her images have been used throughout history down to the present day to capture the intense feelings of romantic love. Furthermore, the poem is important because it relies on the concept of the love triangle, which has become commonplace in Western culture. Sappho is looking at and desiring a woman who is unavailable, either because she favors the man with whom she is

conversing or because the man is her husband or fiancé (and the two causes are not mutually exclusive). Because the object of Sappho's desire prefers the man, the man seems to Sappho to be godlike; he would have to be to attract the woman's regard. In the past, some translators have tried to convert Sappho into a poet of heterosexual love. One way to do so is to make the speaker of the poem a man, which is what Catullus did in his translation and imitation of the poem in a work conventionally identified as Catullus 51. The original Greek grammar, however, with its use of feminine endings, makes clear that the speaker is a woman.

Lesbianism

In antiquity, the term *lesbian*—derived from Lesbos, the Greek island on which Sappho lived most of her life—described a woman who had an unusual and excessive interest in heterosexual sex. The character Sappho in ancient Greek comedy was a lesbian in this sense. During much of the nineteenth century, *lesbian* referred to anything especially elegant and artful, a compliment paid to the beauty of the poetry of Sappho and her fellow Lesbian, Alcaeus. But as the gay movement emerged in the last decades of the nineteenth century, the term came to describe erotic desire between women. This usage was adopted because of the forthright way that Sappho describes her own desire for other women. Sappho cannot be taken as an archetype of the modern gay identity, however, because she is equally sensible to desire between the sexes, and she herself was undoubtedly married and had at least one child. In this regard, it is worth noting that the very term *homosexuality* was not coined until the late nineteenth century, by the German psychologist, Karoly Maria Benkert.

Some scholars have suggested that the poem may not be purely an expression of sexual desire for another woman. In its cultural context, the poem may be an epithalamium, that is, a wedding poem, composed to be sung at the celebration of a marriage. It is known that Sappho wrote many such poems to celebrate weddings. From this standpoint, the poem is more of an elaborate compliment to the bridegroom, recognizing that he has acquired a desirable and beautiful bride.

TOPICS FOR FURTHER STUDY

- *The Laughter of Aphrodite: A Novel about Sappho of Lesbos* (1993), by Peter Green, is a fictional re-creation of the life of Sappho. Read the novel, then prepare an oral report for your classmates in which you discuss how the author depicts Sappho.

- Locate a map of ancient Greece and the Aegean Sea. Identify places associated with Sappho, including the places where Sappho's Aeolic dialect was spoken. Share your map with your classmates using a technological tool such as EDpuzzle.

- If you have ability as a musician or dancer, prepare a performance of "He Seems to Be a God" (or another Sappho poem) that incorporates and integrates the performance arts as you imagine they may have been incorporated during Sappho's lifetime. You may want to recruit classmates for an interpretive dance. Perform the poem for your classmates.

- Search the Internet for books with terms like *Sappho*, *sapphic*, and *lesbian* by decade. For example, limit the search first to the 1860s then the 1870s and so on until 1920. Describe how the word was used in each decade and how usage changed over time. Using PowerPoint or another presentation application, describe your method, your findings, and your conclusion.

- India's earliest collection of lyric poetry is titled the *Sattasai* ("Seven Hundred"). Peter Khoroche and Herman Tieken have translated the poems in *Poems on Life and Love in Ancient India* (State University of New York Press, 2009). As the title suggests, the poems deal with the many aspects of love. Most of the poems are narrated by women, and they depict the world of local Indian village life sometime between the third and fifth centuries. Select one or more of the brief poems and interpret it orally for your classmates. Invite them to comment on any comparisons they see with "He Seems to Be a God."

- Gary Soto is the author of *Partly Cloudy: Poems of Love and Longing* (2012). The book consists of poems narrated by girls and boys of varying ethnic backgrounds who fall in love for the first time, dwell on crushes, and agonize over broken hearts. Read a selection of poems in the collection and write a review of the collection as you imagine Sappho and her circle of friends would have responded to it.

- Browse through Linda Honan's *Spend the Day in Ancient Greece: Projects and Activities That Bring the Past to Life* (1998). Select one or more of the activities Honan suggests and, with your classmates, conduct the activity.

- The ancient Roman poet Catullus admired Sappho. His poem, conventionally identified as Catullus 51, is a translation and adaptation of "He Seems to Be a God." The poem can be found in Douglas Thomson's *Catullus: Edited with a Textual and Interpretative Commentary* (University of Toronto Press, 1997) and on the Internet. Read the poem (translated from Latin into English) and prepare a written report comparing Catullus's version with the Davenport translation.

- Use a website such as puzzle-maker.com or atozteacherstuff.com to create a crossword puzzle with the individual words of a brief lyric poem of your choosing as answers to the clues you provide. Challenge your classmates to complete the puzzle and reassemble the answers back into the poem, giving them a taste of the process of reconstructing a Sappho poem from fragments.

Sappho was born on the Greek isle of Lesbos. (© *Salparadis | Shutterstock.com*)

STYLE

Stanza

Although formal meter has to a large degree been abandoned by contemporary poets, traditional English poetry from Shakespeare to Tennyson used the same system, alternating stressed and unstressed syllables in various patterns. The ancient Greek poets used a different system. In Sappho's time, Greeks used pitch accents, and their poetry had the same singsong quality (to Western ears) as modern Chinese. The stress of the syllables did not matter in comparison with the length of time it took to pronounce each syllable. Syllables with long vowels were pronounced for a longer period of time. (English has long and short vowels, but the practice of drawing out long vowels has disappeared.) So Greek prosody depended on patterns of alternating long and short vowels rather than patterns of stressed and unstressed syllables, which are more characteristic of the modern Germanic languages, including English.

This meter is often referred to as hendecasyllabic, because the first three lines of each stanza had eleven syllables. Each line was arranged as follows (˘ indicating a short syllable, - a long one, and | a syllable that could be short or long):

- ˘ - | - ˘˘ - ˘ - -

The fourth and final line of the stanza was shorter and had the following pattern:

- ˘˘ - ˘

Some ancient sources suggest that Sappho invented this meter, but it is more generally believed to have been traditional in Lesbian poetry, because the same meter is also often used by Alcaeus. Sappho's meter is remarkably regular (compared, for example, with Homer's). This is one of many lines of evidence that indicate that her poems were fully sung rather than merely recited or chanted. Because of Sappho's prominence, hendecasyllabic meter was widely imitated in antiquity by Greek and Latin poets. It is possible to use hendecasyllabic meter in English, substituting stressed for long syllables, as in Algernon Swinburne's poem "Sapphics."

A translator is faced with a difficult task in rendering the metrical quality of a poem such as "He Seems to Be a God." Davenport's translation does not use hendecasyllabic meter. Rather, most of the longer lines (lines 1–3 in each stanza) are composed of eight syllables, with variations of seven and nine. The final short line in each stanza is made up or five syllables, with variations of four and six. Overall, the translation captures the essence of the sapphic metrical style without relying on its particulars.

Apostrophe

"He Seems to Be a God" makes use of the literary device of apostrophe. An apostrophe in this instance is not a mark of punctuation. It refers to a literary device by which a poet addresses an absent person or a person who is either not listening or unable to hear, perhaps because of distance. Poets also use apostrophe to address abstract qualities, such as liberty and death, or to address an object (as when Shakespeare's Macbeth addresses the imaginary dagger he sees before his eyes). In Sappho's poem, the speaker apostrophizes the woman she loves, who is engaged in intimate conversation with a man. The result is that the poem captures a scene, a moment in time, giving it greater dramatic impact. The reader is made to feel the poet's emotions as they arise, not as they are described after contemplation and the passage of time.

Diction

Students of Sappho's poetry note that the diction of her poems is never literary or formal. She relies on simple, straightforward, colloquial diction. Davenport's translation of "He Seems to Be a God" captures this style. Most of the words consist of a single syllable, and most of the two-syllable words are everyday words or words that acquire a second syllable because they are inflected (for example, *ache* and *aching*). Perhaps the only complex word in Davenport's translation is *labyrinth*. Otherwise, the images the poet uses to describe her physical reaction to the scene she is witnessing are elemental, expressed in terms of stings, shocks, dryness, fire, chill, sweat, and the like. This simplicity of style was admired and imitated by poets throughout the ages.

HISTORICAL CONTEXT

Sappho's poems were originally sung. They were produced in domestic circumstances among her coterie of followers, almost all young, aristocratic women who were receiving training in the arts and being groomed for marriage. It is believed that many of the poems were epithalamia—that is, poems written for marriage celebrations. Although no manuscript copies of the poems survive from Sappho's lifetime, it is known that they were written down relatively soon after her death, and only a small portion of her poetry survives. By about the beginning of the sixth century BCE, there was an active market among the wealthy to accumulate manuscript materials for private libraries. One of the authors whose work was collected was Sappho, whose poems were written on long papyrus scrolls, which were then wrapped around rollers and read by feeding the papyrus from one roller to the other.

Sappho's poetry provides the modern reader with a lesson in the preservation, transmission, and restoration of very early literary works—in this case, poetry written some two millennia before the invention of the printing press. In the early part of the third century BCE, a library and museum was founded in the Egyptian city of Alexandria. Sappho's poetry was housed in this library. It is known that her poetry ran to what were called the Nine Books, and Sappho was enshrined as one of the great lyric poets. One of the nine books contained her epithalamia. Another book is known to have contained more than thirteen hundred lines.

The surviving fragments of Sappho's work number just over two hundred. The question arises: Why did the poems disappear? One traditional answer is that the library at Alexandria was sacked and ultimately destroyed by the Romans. Another, more likely answer is that literary tastes changed. As long as Sappho's poetry was held in high esteem, as it was by later Greeks and especially by Roman poets such as Horace and Catullus, it was worthwhile for dealers and collectors to engage in the laborious process of transcribing it. But in time, the poet's Aeolic dialect (the dialect of Lesbos, some Greek colonies, and central Greece) came to be regarded as backward and provincial, to be replaced by the more prestigious Attic dialect of Athens. Furthermore, as the book trade switched from papyrus to parchment (typically made of goat, sheep, or calf skin), Sappho became associated with bygone times and tastes. (A modern analogy may be the evolution from the transistor radios of the 1950s to devices such as smart phones.) Over time, the Nine Books

COMPARE
&
CONTRAST

- **500s BCE:** Poetry is recorded by hand, usually on papyrus (a paper-like material made from plants) or in many cases inscribed on pottery.

  Today: Although poetry can appear anywhere, it typically is published in book form, usually by small presses that specialize in literary productions. Individual poems often appear in magazines and literary journals.

- **500s BCE:** The primary form of public poetry is newly composed hymns. All poetry is sung.

  Today: Poetry is primarily an academic discipline, and many poets hold university positions. Poetry is rarely liturgical or meant to be performed as song, although some song lyrics have literary properties.

- **500s BCE:** A primary creative outlet among women, particularly aristocratic women and the well born, consists of informal domestic societies whose members spend their days in refined pleasures such as the composition and recitation of poetry.

  Today: Women are free to express their creativity in careers and social connections outside the home and through the arts.

simply faded out of existence. Most of what survives from Sappho's corpus consists of papyri fragments that date to the second and third centuries CE. These transcriptions were made centuries after the poet's death, so they are quotations, in some cases memories of memories of her poetry. Many of the fragments were torn into strips to use as wrappings for mummies, and others were recycled as papyrus.

Sappho's work was revitalized in Renaissance Europe. At universities such as Oxford and Cambridge, the core of the curriculum was the study of Greek and Latin literary greats. Sappho's work, which had survived largely in the form of quotations by later writers, enjoyed a resurgence of popularity, which persisted through the nineteenth century. A major event in the retrieval of Sappho's work occurred toward the end of the nineteenth century, when farmers in Egypt began to plow new fields and in the process turned up pieces of papyrus. As word of these finds spread to Europe, excavators flocked to the area. In 1882, the Egyptian Exploration Society was formed with the purpose of locating, crating, and transporting these fragments—many of them found in ancient garbage dumps—back to England, where the process of sifting and sorting them continues. Among the reams of bills, IOUs, laundry lists, receipts, and other detritus, researchers have found fragments of Sappho's poems.

CRITICAL OVERVIEW

Sappho and her poetry were held in high esteem by ancient Greek and Latin writers. Longinus, in *On the Sublime* (written in about 100 CE by an author whose identity remains in dispute), makes this remark about the poem:

> Is it not wonderful how at the same moment soul, body, ears, tongue, eyes, colour, all fail her, and are lost to her as completely as if they were not her own? Observe too how her sensations contradict one another—she freezes, she burns, she raves, she reasons, and all at the same instant. And this description is designed to show that she is assailed, not by any particular emotion, but by a tumult of different emotions. All these tokens belong to the passion of love; but it is in the choice, as I said, of the most striking features, and in the combination of them into one picture, that the perfection of this Ode of Sappho's lies.

The Roman poet Catullus composed a translation and adaptation of "He Seems to Be a God" (conventionally referred to as Catullus 51), and in

The speaker is heartbroken by the intimacy she sees between the couple. (© Alexander Tihonov / Shutterstock.com)

an epigram quoted by Margaret Reynolds, Plato praises Sappho as a tenth muse: "Some say that there are nine Muses . . . but how careless, look again, . . . Sappho of Lesbos is the tenth."

In his introduction to *7 Greeks*, an anthology of his translations of Archaic Greek poetry, including the poetry of Sappho, Guy Davenport highlights the abiding appeal of Sappho:

> Sappho spoke with . . . terseness and authority of the encounters of the loving heart, the infatuated eye's engagement with flowing hair, suave bodies, moonlight on flowers. . . . Her imagery is as stark and patterned as the vase painting of her time. . . . Her words are simple and piercing in their sincerity, her lines melodically keen, a music for girls' voices and dancing. Never has poetry been this clear and bright. "Beautiful Sappho," said Socrates.

With regard to biographical interpretations of the poem, Mary R. Lefkowitz, in "Critical Stereotypes and the Poetry of Sappho," points out the conventional view of the poem, at the same time rejecting the notion that the poem expresses sexual jealousy:

> The girl is one of Sappho's students, and the poem concerns the man and schoolmistress

Sappho's jealousy of him. This interpretation transposes the poem to the realm of sexual normality: there is no evidence at all in the text that "that man" is a husband, or the girl Sappho's pupil, or that Sappho ran a girl's school.

Lefkowitz also quotes Denys L. Page, who takes a different position in *Sappho and Alcaeus*:

> But we must not forget that the *man* was the principal subject of the whole first stanza; and we shall not be content with any explanation of the poem which gives no satisfactory account of his presence and his prominence in it. If Sappho wishes to describe nothing more than the symptoms of her passion for the girl, what motive could she have for connecting that description thus closely with an occasion when the girl is engaged in merry conversation with a man? . . . To maintain that Sappho feels no jealousy of the man would be to ignore the certain response of human nature to a situation of the type described, and to deprive the introduction of the man, and his relation to the girl, of all significance.

Marguerite Johnson, in *Sappho*, weighs in on the dispute:

Open to various interpretations, ...*fragment 31 may* be seen as the poet writing from personal experience and describing a passionate, virtually unbearable response to the sight of a desirable woman who sits beside a man.... Alternatively, scholars today tend to stress the non-personal or non-autobiographical nature of Sappho's songs, arguing instead for the primacy of her role as a lyric poet who dramatised situations for performance.

Later in the essay, Johnson observes:

The hyperbole characteristic of many of Sappho's other songs ... is given its most dramatic rendering in this piece. Sappho evokes a situation, sparsely described but nevertheless meticulously vivid, of a scene involving a man and two women.

She then notes:

The brilliance of the poem results in part from the grandiose and highly charged drama of the narrator's responses. Sappho—or, reading the piece less subjectively—the poetic raconteur, is aflame with a series of powerful psychosomatic symptoms that place her, in her deluded opinion, on the brink of death.

Franco Ferrari, in *Sappho's Gift: The Poet and Her Community*, describes the social context in which fragment 31 might have arisen: "The intimacy evoked by man and woman sitting in front of each other is ... consistent with a context of courtship." Ferrari cites several examples from classical literature in which "wooing generally takes place with the space of a sanctuary during a religious festival." He noted that this context was one of the few places, given the strictures of Greek society, in which initial courtship overtures and proposals can occur. Thus, "it is exactly within such a context that Sappho could express the feelings described in the poem."

Thomas McEvilley, in his book *Sappho*, sees the poem not as an outpouring of personal feeling but as a conventional performance written in celebration of a marriage:

Sappho's description of her passionate reaction to the girl, then, is praise of the bride, typically indirect or reflected through a witness. It prefigures the erotic delights the groom is to have. It is not an expression of jealousy, as in Catullus's version. We expect, at the end (i.e., in a fifth stanza) a farewell to the bridal pair, or an invitation to the maidens to sing the hymenaion [wedding song], or something of that sort.

CRITICISM

Michael J. O'Neal

O'Neal holds a PhD in English. In the following essay, he examines "He Seems to Be a God" in the context of Sappho's life.

One common justification for reading works of literature from different times and different places is that doing so enables the reader to reach out to people from different times and different places and recognize not only how other lives might have been different from one's own life but also how they may have been the same. Knowing, for example, that a woman from the Archaic period of Greece, who lived two and a half millennia ago, experienced emotions modern people recognize perhaps can make the world and a less lonely, less immense place. A reader can touch the words of a woman who lived half a world away and perhaps have her heart touched as well.

Sappho is among the earliest poets whose work—at least a portion of it—survives. A considerable amount of literature survives from much earlier periods, much of it written by ancient Egyptians, Sumerians, and Akkadians, along with literature written in Sanskrit and Hebrew. Many of these documents are not literature as the term is understood in the early twenty-first century. Most were legal codes, genealogies of the gods, divine hymns, scriptural literature (such as the Hebrew Bible), and the like. It was not until the eighth century BCE that works of literature in the Western tradition came to be composed. The earliest examples include the Homeric epics.

In the seventh century BCE, a tradition of lyric and elegiac poetry began to emerge in ancient Greece. Later, at the library at Alexandria, nine ancient Greek lyric poets were identified who were regarded as worthy of critical study. These poets were truly lyric poets in that their poems were performed to the accompaniment of a lyre. Poetry performed to the accompaniment of a flute, for example, was not lyric poetry. The lyric poets included such unfamiliar names as Alcman, Anacreon, Stesichorus, Ibycus, Simonides, Bacchylides, Pindar, and two from the backwater Aegean island of Lesbos: Alcaeus and Sappho.

The poetry of Sappho seems long ago and far away. It is probable that few people could find Lesbos on a map or even know that such a

WHAT DO I READ NEXT?

- One of Sappho's most widely read poems, and the only one to have survived in its entirety, is often given the title "Ode to Aphrodite" or "Hymn to Aphrodite," but scholars refer to it as fragment 1. A 1997 translation by Elizabeth Vandiver is available at http://www.stoa.org/diotima/anthology/vandiver.shtml on the *Diotima* website. Numerous earlier translations of the poem are also available.

- Jane Snyder's *The Woman and the Lyre: Women Writers in Classical Greece and Rome* (1989) is a survey of all known women writers from classical antiquity, including Sappho.

- "Sappho of Green Springs," a short story first published in 1891 by Bret Harte (*Sappho of Green Springs and Other Stories*, Hardpress, 2013) is a classic frequently found on young-adult reading lists. It concerns a talented female poet living in rural California. The name Sappho refers only to her abilities as a poet without reference to modern associations of Sappho and lesbianism.

- Readers interested in the history and culture of Archaic Greece might start with *The Cambridge Companion to Archaic Greece* (2007), by H. Alan Shapiro.

- Readers interested more specifically in the evolution of the visual arts in Archaic Greece would do well to start with Robin Osborne's *Archaic and Classical Greek Art* (1998).

- *God Loves Hair* (Arsenal Pulp Press, 2nd ed., 2014), by Vivek Shraya and illustrated by Juliana Neufeld, is a collection of twenty-one short stories for teens that take readers on the emotional voyage of a boy from a Hindu Indian family living in Canada as he discovers and develops a gender identity.

- *The Key to Everything: Classic Lesbian Love Poems* (1994), edited by Gerry G. Pearlberg, is a collection of forty-four classic love poems with lesbian themes.

- Readers interested in the intersections between Sappho's stanzaic style, Greek music during the Archaic period, and dance will take interest in *The Sapphic Stanza: A Tentative Study in Greek Metrical, Tonal and Dancing Art*. This brief book, written by Joseph Salathiel Tunison, was first published in 1896, but it was reissued by the Cornell University Library in 2009. Tunison emphasizes that although Sappho's poetry could have been spoken or declaimed, it was also probably performed to the accompaniment of music and dancing.

---

time as the Archaic period in Greece existed. It is equally likely, however, that many readers reading a poem by Sappho without knowing its authorship would find it (depending on the translation) modern. They would be able to share the poet's emotions. The language would seem familiar. The images would resonate. The poem would reach across the centuries to create a bond of humanity between this aristocratic young woman and the modern reader.

The dramatic situation of the poem is familiar to any high school student and probably to the student's parents as well. The situation is easily pictured. Perhaps the speaker, the woman she loves, and the man that woman loves, or at least favors, are taking part in a social gathering. In the twenty-first century, one may imagine a dance or party, a wedding reception, a school function.

The speaker of the poem apostrophizes the woman she loves; that is, she addresses the woman, but the woman is not listening because she is engaged in intimate, playful conversation with the man. The speaker's first response is to

> IT SEEMS CLEAR TO MANY READERS THAT 'HE SEEMS TO BE A GOD' IS AN AUTOBIOGRAPHICAL STATEMENT—THAT SAPPHO IS RECORDING THE INTENSITY OF HER FEELINGS FOR A WOMAN WHOSE IDENTITY HAS LONG BEEN DUST."

the man, whom she sees as godlike. He has to be: if he were not godlike, there is no way he could have attracted the attention of the beautiful and graceful woman the speaker covets. As the speaker watches, perhaps furtively, out of the corner of her eye, she becomes increasingly agitated. She hears the soft, creamy voice of the person she loves. She then hears a trill of laughter. The young man wooing her has touched her emotions in some way; he has a sense of humor that the woman finds appealing. The two are clearly connecting, and the speaker is excluded.

The speaker can hardly contain herself. She begins to experience the physical symptoms of intense love with an admixture of sexual jealousy. The physical symptoms will be familiar to the modern reader. Her mouth goes dry. She cannot talk. There is a buzzing in her ears, and she cannot see anything. She feels fire beneath her skin, yet she also feels a chill sweat. She shakes. She turns green. She tries to turn away, but she is forced to glance at the woman, and she comes to feel such a welter of contradictory emotions that she cannot tell whether she is alive or dead. Recognizing the futility of her love, she is resolved to endure. Her love has become a source of grief for her. Across time and generations, all have known the grief of unrequited love.

One question that arises in connection with "He Seems to Be a God" is whether and to what extent the poem is autobiographical. At a distance of twenty-five hundred years, it is impossible to be certain. Some scholars insist that the poem is autobiographical. They observe that it is impossible to separate the poetry from the circumstances of Sappho's life. Born of aristocratic parents, she acquired an education at a time when few women could read or write. In time, she became the leader of a circle of aristocratic

women who were interested in the arts and in the composition of poetry. A modern equivalent may be a book club or a chapter of a social club. Without having to labor for a living or knowing the drudgery of domestic chores, these women likely spent a great deal of time together in artistic pursuits. It seems clear from much of Sappho's surviving poetry that she often could feel intense attraction to any one of these women—although her attraction could be based just as much on the person's beauty and elegance as on sexual desire, though these sources of attraction were intertwined in complex ways. It seems clear to many readers that "He Seems to Be a God" is an autobiographical statement—that Sappho is recording the intensity of her feelings for a woman whose identity has long been dust.

Other readers may disagree. They may point out that the emphasis on biographical approaches to a work of literature reflects an outmoded historicism in literary studies. In former generations, a work of literature was explicated as a reflection of events in the author's life or perhaps social and cultural events of which the author was a part. Literary criticism was biographical criticism. This approach to literature has come to be called the biographical fallacy—a fallacy because in the view of many modern critics, a work of literature exists independently of the author and his or her life. The emphasis of these critics is on how the poem works rather than on what it may or may not tell the reader about the author and her life.

From the point of view of how the poem works, the emphasis in critical interpretation of "He Seems to Be a God" would fall on the poem's genre, which may or may not be an epithalamium. The word *epithalamium* itself is Greek. It is formed from *epi*, meaning "on" or "upon," and *thalamus*, meaning "room" or, more specifically, "bridal chamber." An epithalamium was a nuptial song or poem written in honor of a bride and bridegroom on the occasion of their wedding. The singing of such songs was a traditional way of wishing good fortune on the marriage. Sometimes the songs involved ribaldry. Although the song may have been sung in the marriage chamber, in practice it was sung during the wedding procession. The earliest epithalamia were those of Sappho, but the form was practiced by Catullus and other Roman poets and by various poets from the Renaissance through the nineteenth century.

If "He Seems to Be a God" is an epithalamium—and there is no firm basis for a conclusion about this question either way—it would not be a spontaneous outpouring of intense emotion on the part of Sappho. It would be a conventional poem that tells the reader nothing in particular about the author's life. The poem stands or falls on its own merits and is not autobiography. Ultimately, the modern reader sees in the poem an expression of love and high regard, and perhaps of jealousy, that links men and women, gay and straight, across the generations, centuries, and even millennia. For this reason the poetry of Sappho survives and continues to win new admirers.

Source: Michael J. O'Neal, Critical Essay on "He Seems to Be a God," in *Poetry for Students*, Gale, Cengage Learning, 2016.

Daniel Mendelsohn

In the following excerpt, Mendelsohn describes the difficulty of studying Sappho when so little of her work survives.

. . . One day not long after New Year's, 2012, an antiquities collector approached an eminent Oxford scholar for his opinion about some brownish, tattered scraps of writing. The collector's identity has never been revealed, but the scholar was Dirk Obbink, a MacArthur-winning classicist whose specialty is the study of texts written on papyrus—the material, made of plant fibres, that was the paper of the ancient world. When pieced together, the scraps that the collector showed Obbink formed a fragment about seven inches long and four inches wide: a little larger than a woman's hand. Densely covered with lines of black Greek characters, they had been extracted from a piece of desiccated cartonnage, a papier-mâché-like plaster that the Egyptians and Greeks used for everything from mummy cases to bookbindings. After acquiring the cartonnage at a Christie's auction, the collector soaked it in a warm water solution to free up the precious bits of papyrus.

Judging from the style of the handwriting, Obbink estimated that it dated to around 200 A.D. But, as he looked at the curious pattern of the lines—repeated sequences of three long lines followed by a short fourth—he saw that the text, a poem whose beginning had disappeared but of which five stanzas were still intact, had to be older.

> THE COMMON THEME OF MOST ANCIENT RESPONSES TO SAPPHO'S WORK IS RAPTUROUS ADMIRATION FOR HER EXQUISITE STYLE OR FOR HER SEARING CONTENT, OR BOTH."

Much older: about a thousand years more ancient than the papyrus itself. The dialect, diction, and metre of these Greek verses were all typical of the work of Sappho, the seventh-century-B.C. lyric genius whose sometimes playful, sometimes anguished songs about her susceptibility to the graces of younger women bequeathed us the adjectives "sapphic" and "lesbian" (from the island of Lesbos, where she lived). The four-line stanzas were in fact part of a schema she is said to have invented, called the "sapphic stanza." To clinch the identification, two names mentioned in the poem were ones that several ancient sources attribute to Sappho's brothers. The text is now known as the "Brothers Poem."

Remarkably enough, this was the second major Sappho find in a decade: another nearly complete poem, about the deprivations of old age, came to light in 2004. The new additions to the extant corpus of antiquity's greatest female artist were reported in papers around the world, leaving scholars gratified and a bit dazzled. "Papyrological finds," as one classicist put it, "ordinarily do not make international headlines."

But then Sappho is no ordinary poet. For the better part of three millennia, she has been the subject of furious controversies—about her work, her family life, and, above all, her sexuality. In antiquity, literary critics praised her "sublime" style, even as comic playwrights ridiculed her allegedly loose morals. Legend has it that the early Church burned her works. ("A sex-crazed whore who sings of her own wantonness," one theologian wrote, just as a scribe was meticulously copying out the lines that Obbink deciphered.) A millennium passed, and Byzantine grammarians were regretting that so little of her poetry had survived. Seven centuries later, Victorian scholars were doing their best to explain away her erotic predilections, while their literary contemporaries, the Decadents and the Aesthetes, seized on her verses for inspiration. Even today, experts can't agree on whether the poems were performed in private or in public, by soloists or by choruses, or, indeed, whether they were meant to celebrate or to subvert the conventions of love and marriage. The last is a particularly loaded issue, given that, for many readers and scholars, Sappho has been a feminist heroine or a gay role model, or both. "As far as I knew, there was only me and a woman called Sappho," the critic Judith Butler once remarked.

Now the first English translation of Sappho's works to include the recent finds has appeared: *Sappho: A New Translation of the Complete Works* (Cambridge), with renderings by Diane J. Rayor and a thoroughgoing introduction by Andre Lardinois, a Sappho specialist who teaches in the Netherlands. (Publication of the book was delayed by several months to accommodate the "Brothers Poem.") It will come as no surprise to those who have followed the Sappho wars that the new poems have created new controversies.

The greatest problem for Sappho studies is that there's so little Sappho to study. It would be hard to think of another poet whose status is so disproportionate to the size of her surviving body of work.

We don't even know how much of her poetry Sappho actually wrote down. The ancients referred to her works as *melè*, "songs." Composed to be sung to the accompaniment of a lyre—this is what "lyric" poetry meant for the Greeks—they may well have been passed down from memory by her admirers and other poets before being committed at last to paper. (Or whatever. One fragment, in which the poet calls on Aphrodite, the goddess of love, to come into a charming shrine "where cold water ripples through apple branches, the whole place shadowed in roses," was scribbled onto a broken clay pot.) Like other great poets of the time, she would have been a musician and a performer as well as a lyricist. She was credited with having invented a certain kind of lyre and the plectrum.

Four centuries after her death, scholars at the Library of Alexandria catalogued nine "books"—papyrus scrolls—of Sappho's poems, organized primarily by metre. Book 1, for instance, gathered all the poems that had been composed in the sapphic stanza—the verse form

Obbink recognized in the "Brothers Poem." This book alone reportedly contained thirteen hundred and twenty lines of verse; the contents of all nine volumes may have amounted to some ten thousand lines. So much of Sappho was circulating in antiquity that one Greek author, writing three centuries after her death, confidently predicted that "the white columns of Sappho's lovely song endure / and will endure, speaking out loud . . . as long as ships sail from the Nile."

By the Middle Ages, nearly everything had disappeared. As with much of classical literature, texts of her work existed in relatively few copies, all painstakingly transcribed by hand. Over time, fire, flood, neglect, and bookworms—to say nothing of disapproving Church Fathers—took their devastating toll. Market forces were also at work: as the centuries passed, fewer readers—and fewer scribes—understood Aeolic, the dialect in which Sappho composed, and so demand for new copies diminished. A twelfth-century Byzantine scholar who had hoped to write about Sappho grumbled that "both Sappho and her works, the lyrics and the songs, have been trashed by time."

Until a hundred years ago or so, when papyrus fragments of her poems started turning up, all that remained of those "white columns of Sappho's song" was a handful of lines quoted in the works of later Greek and Roman authors. Some of these writers were interested in Lesbos's most famous daughter for reasons that can strike us as comically arcane: the only poem that has survived in its entirety—a playful hymn to Aphrodite in which the poet calls upon the goddess to be her "comrade in arms" in an erotic escapade—was saved for posterity because the author of a first-century-B.C. treatise called "On the Arrangement of Words" admired her handling of vowels. At present, scholars have catalogued around two hundred and fifty fragments, of which fewer than seventy contain complete lines. A great many consist of just a few words; some, of a single word.

The common theme of most ancient responses to Sappho's work is rapturous admiration for her exquisite style or for her searing content, or both. An anecdote from a later classical author about the Athenian legislator Solon, a contemporary of Sappho's and one of the Seven Sages of Greece, is typical:

> Solon of Athens, son of Execestides, after hearing his nephew singing a song of Sappho's over

the wine, liked the song so much that he told the boy to teach it to him. When someone asked him why he was so eager, he replied, "so that I may learn it and then die."

Plato, whose attitude toward literature was, to say the least, vexed—he thought most poetry had no place in the ideal state—is said to have called her the "Tenth Muse." The scholars at the Library of Alexandria enshrined her in their canon of nine lyric geniuses—the only woman to be included. At least two towns on Lesbos vied for the distinction of being her birthplace; Aristotle reports that she "was honored although she was a woman." . . .

Source: Daniel Mendelsohn, "Girl, Interrupted," in *New Yorker*, Vol. 91, No. 4, March 16, 2015, p. 70.

SOURCES

Davenport, Guy, Introduction to *7 Greeks*, translated by Guy Davenport, New Directions, 1995, p. 5.

Dover, Kenneth J., *Greek Homosexuality*, updated ed., Harvard University Press, 1989, pp. 171–84.

Egypt Exploration Society website, http://www.ees.ac.uk (accessed April 27, 2015).

Ferrari, Franco, *Sappho's Gift: The Poet and Her Community*, Michigan Classical Press, 2010, pp. 184–85.

Johnson, Marguerite, *Sappho*, Bristol Classical Press, 2007, pp. 29, 80–81.

Lefkowitz, Mary R., "Critical Stereotypes and the Poetry of Sappho," in *Reading Sappho: Contemporary Approaches*, edited by Ellen Greene, University of California Press, 1996, pp. 29–30.

Longinus, *On the Sublime*, translated by H. J. Havell, Macmillan, 1890, p. 23.

McEvilley, Thomas, *Sappho*, Spring Publications, 2008, p. 127.

Page, Denys L., *Sappho and Alcaeus: An Introduction to the Study of Ancient Lesbian Poetry*, Oxford University Press, 1955, p. 28; quoted by Mary R. Lefkowitz, "Critical Stereotypes and the Poetry of Sappho," in *Reading Sappho: Contemporary Approaches*, edited by Ellen Greene, University of California Press, 1996, p. 30.

Pickett, Brent, "Homosexuality," in *Stanford Encyclopedia of Philosophy*, 2011, http://plato.stanford.edu/entries/homosexuality (accessed April 26, 2015).

Reynolds, Margaret, ed., *The Sappho Companion*, Palgrave, 2000, pp. 17–22, 70.

Sappho, "He Seems to Be a God," in *7 Greeks*, translated by Guy Davenport, New Directions, 1995, pp. 74–75.

"Sappho," History of Art website, http://www.all-art.org/world_literature/sappho1.htm (accessed April 21, 2015).

"Sappho," in *Merriam-Webster's Encyclopedia of Literature*, Merriam-Webster, 1995, p. 992.

"Sappho," Poetry Foundation website, http://www.poetryfoundation.org/bio/sappho (accessed April 21, 2015).

Steele, Timothy, *All the Fun's in How You Say a Thing: An Explanation of Meter and Versification*, Ohio University Press, 1999, pp. 269–70.

FURTHER READING

Greene, Ellen, and Marilyn Skinner, eds., *The New Sappho on Old Age*, Center for Hellenic Studies, Harvard University, 2009.

> In 1922, a scrap of papyrus from the garbage dump of an ancient Egyptian city was discovered. On it had been written a long poem by Sappho about old age and the approach of death. The poem had been torn in half lengthwise, so only the right-hand half of the lines was preserved. In 2004, a piece of papyrus used in the wrapping of a mummy owned by the University of Cologne was a different copy, of the left side. The combination of the two fragments yielded the text of one of only two complete poems by Sappho available in the twenty-first century. The essays in this volume deal with the poem and the process of discovering, reconstructing, and editing it.

Hubbard, Thomas K., *Homosexuality in Greece and Rome: A Sourcebook of Basic Documents*, University of California Press, 2003.

> Hubbard's volume is an anthology of excerpts from a wide range of writers from classical antiquity, including Sappho, that deal with the theme of same-sex love. Hubbard notes that the ancients did not have a catch-all term such as *homosexuality* that is common in modern life. Rather, the ancients tended to be accepting of a wide range of same-sex relationships, and many authors tended to regard these preferences as inborn and natural.

Lonsdale, Steven H., *Dance and Ritual Play in Greek Religion*, Johns Hopkins University Press, 2000.

> In both private and in public life, the ancient Greeks expressed divine adoration and human festivity through dance at feasts and choral competitions, at weddings and funerals, and to observe the cycles of nature and human existence. Lonsdale's book examines the role of dance in ancient Greek culture.

Nagy, Gregory, *The Best of the Achaeans: Concepts of the Hero in Archaic Greek Poetry*, revised edition, Johns Hopkins University Press, 1998.

Although Sappho is a central figure in the development of the lyric poem in Archaic Greece, the period also produced major epic works of literature, most notably the *Iliad* and the *Odyssey* by Homer. Readers interested in how the Greeks conceived of heroes during this time will find Nagy's volume a thought-provoking and controversial contribution to the topic.

West, M. L., *Greek Lyric Poetry*, Oxford University Press, 2008.

West's anthology of ancient Greek lyric poetry includes a wide range of authors. Among the earliest are Archilochus and Semonides in the seventh century BCE, Sappho and her contemporaries and near contemporaries, and several poets from the fifth century BCE.

SUGGESTED SEARCH TERMS

Archaic Greece

Archaic Greek lyric poetry

Catullus 51

epithalamia

Lesbos AND Greek island

lyric poetry

Sapphic stanza

Sappho

Sappho AND fragment 31

Sappho translations

Identity Card

MAHMOUD DARWISH
1964

Mahmoud Darwish rose to prominence as the national poet of Palestine after publishing "Identity Card" in 1964. This poem, a fiery declaration of selfhood in which the Palestinian Arab speaker speaks directly to his Israeli oppressor, became a Palestinian rallying cry, an Arab nationalist anthem, and elevated Darwish to the status of champion of the displaced and suffering Palestinian people. In the poem, the speaker demands that the Israeli official who has asked for his identification write down not the mundane numbers one would find on an identity card but the brutal reality of his life as a Palestinian Arab living inside the state of Israel. The poem's language is as simple as it is forceful, exemplifying Darwish's appeal as a popular poet of the people. First collected in *Awraq al-zeitoun* ("Leaves of Olives") as "Bitaqat Hawiyyah" in 1964, "Identity Card" remains Darwish's most popular poem both among Palestinians living in Israel and among his global community of readers, though Darwish refused to read it in public while in exile, finding that the poem lost its meaning when read aloud outside the context of the state of Israel. Darwish was labeled an "internal refugee" within his homeland throughout his childhood, and he read his poetry before audiences numbering in the thousands at the height of his career. The Palestinian poet gave voice to a voiceless people with the speaker's proud declaration: "I am an Arab!" The poem's simmering anger and

Mahmoud Darwish (© *Jamal Nasrallah | epa | Corbis*)

sparkling moments of humanity make it a timeless achievement of self-expression.

AUTHOR BIOGRAPHY

Darwish was born March 13, 1941, in al-Birwa,
a small village in Galilee, Palestine. In 1948,
when Darwish was seven years old, the Israeli
army occupied and destroyed al-Birwa, as
Darwish and his family escaped to the safety of
Lebanon. They returned to their homeland the
next year, entering the country illegally. Because
they had missed the Israeli census during their
absence, they were called "present-absent aliens"
or "internal refugees," meaning they neither
belonged in the country nor were permitted to
leave, as they lacked the official paperwork.

Throughout his school years, Darwish would
be hidden away during state inspections because of
his illegal status. He eventually gained an identity
card by claiming to have lived with one of the
northern Bedouin tribes during the census of Palestinian Arabs. He earned his General Secondary
Certificate before moving to Haifa, where he
became politically active. He wrote the poem

"Identity Card" in 1964, after enduring an experience similar to that depicted in the poem, arguing
with an Israeli government employee over his documentation. The poem was an instant sensation in
the Arab world both inside and outside the Israeli
borders. It was turned into an enduringly popular
protest song, and Darwish was put under house
arrest. He was frequently detained and imprisoned
by the Israeli government: in 1961, 1965, twice in
1967, and in 1969, each time either for traveling
within the country without a permit or for his
poetry. Darwish belonged to the third generation
of Palestinian poets who wrote outspoken political
works in response to the escalating conflict
between Palestine and Israel, but the popularity
of "Identity Card" set him apart from his contemporaries and led to his being called the national
poet of Palestine. In 1970, he was allowed to leave
Israel to attend university in Moscow. The following year, he decided to live in exile rather than
return to his homeland. After joining the Palestinian Liberation Front in 1973, he was officially
banned from returning to Israel.

He served as editor of *Shu'un Filastiniyyah*
(*Palestinian Affairs*) magazine and was a member
of the executive committee of the Palestinian Liberation Organization, as chairman of the Supreme
Council for Culture, Education and Heritage. He
lived in Cairo, Beirut (where he witnessed the Israeli siege of the city, an experience that he recorded
in *Memory of Forgetfulness*), Paris, Cyprus,
Amman, and Ramallah. In 1984 and 1987, he
was elected president of the union of Palestinian
writers and journalists. Author of more than thirty
collections of poetry, as well as the 1988 Palestinian
Declaration of Independence, Darwish has been
awarded the Lotus Prize (1969), Lenin Peace
Prize (1983), Knight of the Order of Arts and
Letters (1993), the Lannan Foundation Cultural
Freedom Prize (2001), and the Golden Wreath of
Sturga Poetry Evenings (2007). In 2008, the Mahmoud Darwish Foundation was established, along
with the Mahmoud Darwish Award for Creativity.
He died in Houston, Texas, on August 9, 2008, of
complications during heart surgery.

POEM TEXT

Write it down!
I am an Arab
and my identity card is number fifty thousand.
I have eight children
and the ninth is due after summer.   5

Does this anger you?
Write it down!
I am an Arab
employed with fellow workers at a quarry.
I have eight children.   10
I earn their bread,
clothes and books
out of these rocks.
I do not beg for charity at your doors.
Nor do I kneel   15
on your marble floor.
So does this anger you?
Write it down!
I am an Arab.
I am a name without a title,   20
patient in a country
where people live on furor or rage.
My roots
were entrenched before the birth of time
and before the opening of the eras,   25
before the pines and the olive trees
and before the grasses grew.
My father comes from the family of the plow
not from a privileged clan.
And my grandfather, a farmer,   30
not well-bred nor well-born,
taught me to be proud
before he taught me how to read.
And my house is like a watchman's hut
made of branches and cane.   35
Are you satisfied with my status?
I am without a title, just a name!
Write it down!
I am an Arab,
hair color, black as coal,   40
eyes brown.
Features:
an 'iqal on my head tied around a kaffiyah,
a hand solid as a stone
that scratches whoever touches it.   45
And my address:
a weaponless village, forgotten,
its streets too without names,
all its men are in the quarry or the fields.
Does this anger you?   50
Write it down!
I am an Arab.
You have stolen my ancestors' orchards,
the land I farmed
with my children.   55
You left us nothing
except for these rocks.
Will your State take them too
as it's been said?!
So Now!   60
Record at the top of the first page:
I do not hate people
nor do I steal.
But if I become hungry
I will eat my robber's flesh.   65
Beware then, beware of my hunger
and my anger!

POEM SUMMARY

The text used for this summary is from *Mahmoud Darwish: The Poet's Art and His Nation*, translated by Khaled Mattawa, Syracuse University Press, 2014, pp. 7–9.

"Identity Card" begins with the speaker ordering an Israeli official (addressed as "you" in the poem) to write down the fact that the speaker is an Arab. Five of the poem's six stanzas begin with this same command. His identity card number is fifty thousand. He is the father of eight children with a ninth on the way, due after summer. The speaker asks whether this angers his hearer.

The speaker orders the official to write down the fact that he is an Arab who works in a rock quarry, where he earns money to pay for his children's food, clothes, and books. He does not beg for charity or kneel on the floor to ask for help. The speakers asks again if this makes his hearer angry.

The speaker repeats again the command to write down that he is an Arab. He has a name but no title. He is patient and forbearing, where others are angry. He says that his background in this country goes back a very long time, before history and before agriculture.

The next passage gives the speaker's family background. He is from a farming family, not a privileged or wealthy background. His grandfather, also a farmer, taught the speaker to be proud even before he taught him to read. The speaker lives in a simple hut. Again he addresses the official and asks if that person is satisfied with his simple status.

Write it down, the speaker demands again. He now describes himself physically: he is an Arab with deep black hair and brown eyes. His clothing includes an 'iqal, or rope, which he wears on his head around his kaffiyah (a scarf headdress traditionally worn by Arabs). His hand is strong, like the stone in the quarry and will scratch whoever attempts to touch it. His home address is a forgotten village without weapons or names for its streets. All the men who once lived there now work in the quarry or the fields. He asks if this angers his hearer.

Write it down, the speaker says. He is an Arab. The farmland that supported his ancestors, that he would have worked with his children, has been stolen from him by the state, so that he now works in the rock quarry. He wonders if the government will take the rocks away, too, as is rumored.

At last, the speaker gives another command for the official to record an essential fact about him: he is not a thief and does not hate people. However, if he is hungry, he will rebel against those who have robbed him. The state should therefore be cautious.

THEMES

Humanity

Darwish emphasizes his speaker's humanity in "Identity Card" through providing background information about his life. Though the speaker is irate at the official, he is a family man at home, father of eight. The everyday details of his life, children, home, and job have each been touched by the force of Israeli occupation, yet he has not lost his faith in humanity, nor has he given in to hopelessness. Proud of his family's history, though they have always been poor farmers, he refuses to beg for necessities. He is a man standing tall in the face of harsh times, showing resilience, patience, and courage. He has not allowed the theft of his land to poison his mind against his enemy—in fact, he is careful to make it clear that despite his rage, he does not hate people. The root of the speaker's anger lies in the fact that despite his efforts to retain his humanity in the face of such oppression, despite his mindfulness of the humanity of his enemies, he is not being treated as a human in return. Instead, he is only a series of numbers on an identity card in the eyes of the Israeli official. Every piece of personal information he shouts at the official aims to humanize him, to show that he is not to be checked off, filed away, and forgotten but acknowledged as a person with feelings, a family, a history before the war. An identity card cannot express his anger, disappointment, and heartbreak. An identity card cannot illustrate how he toils in the quarry to feed his children. Through his display of emotion, the speaker makes it clear that he, as a human, cannot be reduced to only the facts and numbers that interest his enemy. His life is shaped by the Israeli occupation, and he will not let that fact go unrecorded or unnoticed, nor will he stand quietly by while his humanity is ignored.

Identity

The speaker, asked to identify himself by an Israeli government employee, responds with more than the information listed neatly on his identity card. He provides the messy, human account of his life under the occupation, listing the ways in which the state of Israel has altered his identity as a Palestinian. The first and most important is his new identity not as a Palestinian (a national identity) but as an Arab (an ethnic identity). There is no longer a Palestine to belong to, forcing him to reclaim the title "Arab," applied to him by his enemies, as his own, as a piece of his identity of which he is proud. With the loss of his country and nationality came the loss of his farmland and village, which lies forgotten. Who he once was—a Palestinian farmer from a small village—has been totally erased. He is left with only his name. Yet he has not lost hope. He builds a new identity from the rubble: an Arab, a father, a man who works in the quarry, his father's son, proud but without a title or riches, who neither hates people nor begs for charity. This angry, new man, the speaker warns, created by adversity, stripped of all he once knew, will be dangerous if starved of his humanity for too long.

Injustice

The speaker gives several examples of injustices against him: the loss of his village, his ancestor's orchards, and his farm. He implies many other losses: his title, his birthright, and his nationality. He is suspected of being a beggar or a thief, treated as less than human by the occupying army. He is forced to carry an identity card issued to him by his oppressors, who see him as a number rather than a man who has been pushed to his limit. Through it all, he has held his head high, refusing to beg or steal and refusing to hate those who have stolen from him. The state of Israel should recognize, the poem suggests, what it has created: the furious man, the Arab. The speaker is determined not to lose his humanity in the face of such degradation—though he will never farm his fields alongside his children or walk through the orchards of his ancestors, though he lives in a simple hut and even the rock quarry where he works may be taken soon by the state. He asks whether his situation in life—his status as an Arab, his family, his history—angers the Israeli, despite the fact that it is an Israeli-created life, lived under Israeli rule. The speaker feels that his anger

TOPICS FOR FURTHER STUDY

- What does the speaker's identity card symbolize in "Identity Card?" What information about himself does he provide to the official that would not be listed on an identity card? Consider your own identity card (driver's license, school ID, or other identifying documents). What information about you is shown there and why? What does the identity card say about you, and what about your identity is left unsaid? Answer these questions in a personal essay in which you put yourself in the shoes of the frustrated speaker in "Identity Card."

- How does the speaker's use of "you" affect the tone of "Identity Card?" How do you, as a reader, respond? Do you feel any anger at the speaker, as he repeatedly suggests? Explore your emotional response to the poem in a short essay concerning the speaker's direct address of the Israeli official.

- Create a time line of important events in Palestinian history. It should have at least eight entries, including the Nakba (the 1948 Palestinian exodus after the formation of Israel) and Darwish's publication of "Identity

Card." Use online tools to arrange the information in a meaningful graphic way. (For instance, free infographics are available at http://www.easel.ly.)

- Write a poetic rendition of a memorable argument you have experienced in your life. You may choose to include both sides of the conversation or, like "Identity Card," only one side. Consider the effect produced by your choice.

- Read *I Am a Little Moslem* (2007) by Mennah I. Bakkar, a children's book for Muslims. How does Bakkar's assertion of Arab identity differ from Darwish's in "Identity Card?" How are they alike? Compare and contrast the two works in small groups.

- How far back in history does the Palestinian-Israeli conflict extend? What are the most recent developments in this conflict? Use world news sites to learn about the conflict in the Middle East today and its historical roots. Write a brief summary of the conflict's long past and the current state of affairs. Include a list of your online sources.

---

toward the Israeli is justified, and he does not think the Israeli has a right to be angry with him. They have taken everything from him, even identity. All he has left is his anger and his patience.

STYLE

Polemic

A polemic is a work of literature that takes a firm stance on a controversial subject. "Identity Card" is in every way pro-Palestinian. The speaker (who symbolizes Palestine) warns the Israeli official (and thus all of Israel) to beware of his anger: a starving man may eat the flesh of those who starve him. The speaker presents the

case for his own humanity: his personal history, the grievances against him, the theft of his land, and the oppression of his people. No answering voice from the official contradicts his word or questions his statements, making the poem a one-sided proclamation of Palestinian pride and suffering. A polemic is confrontational and challenges well-entrenched opinion. Darwish's polemic helped foster the creation of a unified Palestinian identity and voice in the aftermath of the trauma of the Nakba, and it provided a battle cry to his people.

Zeitgeist

Zeitgeist means the cultural, social, and intellectual spirit of the times. A literary work may

The speaker's grandfather was a farmer of a humble family, but proud nonetheless. (© *Ryan Rodrick Beiler | Shutterstock.com*)

capture the zeitgeist of its time and place. For example, *The Great Gatsby*, by F. Scott Fitzgerald, reflects the zeitgeist of the American Roaring Twenties: the decadence, the emptiness, and the fragility of human connection. "Identity Card" expresses the zeitgeist of Palestinians in the early 1960s. A people without a country, without a name (for the state of Israel did not recognize the legitimacy of the descriptor "Palestinian"), and without hope of regaining their lives before Israel, Palestinians had nothing binding them to their land but their anger over losing it. Darwish tapped in to these feelings of anger and loss, of homelessness and hopelessness, patience and frustration. The speaker, who demands to be seen as a human by the Israeli official examining his documentation, becomes the nation of Palestine, shouting for recognition. So successful was Darwish in expressing the zeitgeist of his people that the poem was made into a popular anthem of Arab pride and Palestinian identity.

HISTORICAL CONTEXT

Nakba

On May 14, 1948, the British withdrew from Palestine, ending their administrative control of the country, a power that they had held since 1917. In response, Zionists (those advocating the creation of a Jewish state) living in Palestine announced the creation of the state of Israel. Palestinian Arabs, rejecting this announcement and seeing the land as rightfully theirs, went to war against them in the 1948 Arab-Israeli War. The Israelis won, increasing the size of their land claim by more than 50 percent compared with the plan put forth by the United Nations.

As a result, more than seven hundred thousand Palestinians were forced to flee their land by occupying forces (for example, seven-year-old Darwish and his family, whose village was destroyed) in a mass evacuation known as the Nakba, the Arabic word for "catastrophe." Over five hundred towns, villages, and cities were left empty as the Palestinian refugees sought asylum

COMPARE
&
CONTRAST

- **1964:** Palestinians living within Israel's borders are called Arabs, as the words *Palestinian* and *Palestine* are taboo. Those living outside Israel are known as Palestinian refugees. Palestinians struggle for recognition and to find an identity of their own across the harsh divide of the Israeli border.

  Today: The contested areas of Palestine/Israel are separated into the state of Israel and the Palestinian Territories. Many countries recognize the Palestinian Territories, which include the West Bank and the Gaza Strip, as the state of Palestine, though these territories are occupied by Israel.

- **1964:** Palestinian literature written from within Israel is nearly wiped out following the Nakba, and those few writers writing from within Israeli borders are cut off from those outside.

  Today: The *al-adab al multazim* literary movement popularizes Arabic literature, bringing global attention to the Palestinian plight. Palestinian literature is classified in three groups: those writing from within Israel, those writing from within the Palestinian Territories, and those in exile writing from elsewhere in the world.

- **1964:** The Palestinian Liberation Organization (PLO) is founded with the aim of liberating Palestine from Israel through armed conflict. The Palestinian National Council, its legislative body, elects its eighteen-member executive committee.

  Today: Both the Arab League and the United Nations acknowledge the PLO as the representative of Palestine. In the United Nations, Palestine holds permanent observer status and is actively seeking full membership. Darwish served as an executive committee member from 1987 to 1993.

---

in the surrounding countries and the few remaining Palestinian territories, such as the West Bank. Some, like Darwish, returned to what had once been their home to join the hundred and fifty thousand Palestinian Arabs who remained under Israeli rule inside Israel. These undocumented Arabs were known as "internal refugees"; they could not leave the country or travel within it without a permit. In 1954, the passage of the Prevention of Infiltration Law prevented Palestinians from returning to their homes within Israel.

Al-adab al-Multazim *Literature*
Following the Nakba, the Palestinian Arab population was scattered, their communities disrupted, and lives forever altered. For the first chaotic decade following the Nakba, Palestinians living within Israeli borders did not produce much literature. Beginning in the 1950s, though, the *al-adab al-multazim*, or "literature of commitment," began to emerge in the Arabic world both inside and outside Israel. A literary response to the displacement of their people, Arab writers who wrote in this style focused on realistic portrayals of their struggles as Arabs in accessible language so as to appeal to the largest audience of readers. In this way, the largely ignored Palestinian cause could gain political ground worldwide.

Inside Israel's borders, there was a ban on all Arab publications; there were no libraries in Arab villages, and no Arabic culture or literature was taught in schools, which were conducted in Hebrew rather than Arabic whenever possible. Additionally, the trade embargo firmly in place between Israel and the surrounding Arab countries unintentionally isolated Palestinian Arabs still living inside Israel from news of the outside Arab world. The literature of these Palestinians,

Rather than making something grow like his grandfather, the speaker works in a quarry, mining for stone. *(© Jaromir Chalabala | Shutterstock.com)*

when it began to emerge from within Israel's borders, was intensely political. What sparse news there was of the poetic trends in other Arab countries inspired poets within Israel to adopt more modern techniques, such as short lines and simply understood images. These techniques, along with their growing mastery of both the Hebrew and Arabic languages, allowed a broader audience to appreciate their work. Darwish was a devotee of commitment literature, which emphasizes the power of a community identity, with "Identity Card" a near-perfect example of the activist style.

CRITICAL OVERVIEW

The effect of "Identity Card" on the Palestinian population both inside and outside the contested borders of Palestine and Israel cannot be overstated. Edward W. Said summarizes the poem's impact in *The Question of Palestine*: "The curious power of this little poem is...it did not *represent* as much as *embody* the Palestinian,

whose political identity in the world had been pretty much reduced to a name on an identity card."

When Darwish first read the poem aloud at a reading hosted in a movie theater, the enraptured crowd asked him to repeat it six times. Its emotional appeal to Palestinians, Almog Behar explains in "Mahmoud Darwish: Poetry's State of Siege," lies in the speaker's outspoken frustration: "The poem is representative of Darwish's early writing, in which the bravery that is not always expressed in reality finds expression in poetry." Called "the most recognized Palestinian poet in the world," in his BBC News obituary, Darwish read his poetry for crowds numbering in the thousands. Mohammad Shaheen writes of his unique place in world literature in his introduction to *Almond Blossoms and Beyond*: "He wrote genuinely popular poetry, at a time when Arabic poetry and its readership were both in decline; he preserved the spirit and values of poetry, while renewing and refining them."

Darwish is a rare poet in that his work is inseparable from the Palestinian identity. Khaled

Mattawa describes this marriage between art and life in *Mahmoud Darwish: The Poet's Art and His Nation*: "His poems express Palestinians' suffering as an occupied people, their longing for peace, the particularities of their relationship to the land and to one another...and their endurance through a history filled with disappointments."

In 2000, the Israeli education minister suggested that Darwish should become a part of the curriculum in schools, an extraordinary acknowledgment of his importance in the history of Palestine and Israel. The prime minister of Israel, Ehud Barak, rejected the proposal, claiming that Israel was not ready.

CRITICISM

Amy L. Miller

Miller is a graduate of the University of Cincinnati, and she currently resides in New Orleans. In the following essay, she examines how the angry Palestinian speaker and silent Israeli official become representative of their people in Darwish's "Identity Card."

Darwish's "Identity Card" came to represent Palestinian identity in a time in which Palestinians had little to hold them together as a community and nothing but unpromising uncertainty looming on the horizon. Darwish himself was adrift in the state of Israel, living as a "present-absent alien" in what was once his home—unwelcome yet, paradoxically, unable to leave as he lacked the proper official identification papers. Palestinians inside Israel were called Arabs, Palestinians who had left during the Nakba were known as refugees, what was once Palestine was now the state of Israel, and nothing was as it had been before the war. Mattawa sets the stage onto which Darwish appeared: "Between 1948 and 1967, Palestinians in Israel...faced a daunting future where they saw their identity denigrated and where they were a poor minority in their native land in a state where they were unwanted." Darwish's speaker burst onto this daunting scene in "Identity Card" with an unapologetic shout that claimed his identity as an Arab. The exclamation is particularly remarkable for its repurposing of an epithet used by Israelis to demoralize Palestinian Arabs still living in Israel. Without Palestine, the Palestinians were insultingly called "Arabs," but Darwish permanently stole back

> USING PLAIN, ACCESSIBLE LANGUAGE AND THE POWER OF RAW EMOTION, DARWISH INSPIRED NOT ONLY PALESTINIAN ARABS BUT ALSO THE WIDER ARAB WORLD WITH HIS SPEAKER'S PROUD ANNOUNCEMENT OF HIS IDENTITY."

the respectability of the name on the day he first read "Identity Card" to an audience of Palestinians who so instantly embraced the poem that they had him repeat it six times. The powerful poem handed Palestinians an identity, a moral code, a rallying cry, a shared history, and a source of pride. In return, Palestinians handed Darwish their hearts. He became a symbol of the Palestinian, and his poetry became a metaphor for Palestine itself.

Darwish taps into the collective rage of his people from the very first line of "Identity Card" by setting up the poem as a fantasy of Palestinian confrontation: an angry Palestinian man holding nothing back as he rages against a silent Israeli official who has asked him for his identification. The Israeli may be silent in the text of the poem, but he is far from a passive figure. He represents all the injustice, the cruelty, the death and destruction of the conquering Israeli state. He is the force that overpowered the Palestinians, removed them from their land, and stripped them of their identities. This fact makes up a significant portion of the speaker's anger—the irony of being asked for his identity by the representation of Israel, which took away his identity as a Palestinian. The Israeli exists only as "you" in the poem, a disrespectful tone to answer the Israel's label of "Arab." The phrasing also serves to accuse the reader as sharing guilt in the speaker's downfall. Where fellow Palestinians might hear the sharp, accusatory tone and imagine themselves confronting the Israeli guard, readers outside the Arab world can feel the finger pointed squarely at their chest when the speaker asks if "you" are angered by what little he has in his new life as an Arab, a life he has been forced to assume if he means to survive. Behar writes: "The Israeli official is the poet's adversary and interlocutor and the poet

WHAT DO I READ NEXT?

- In Elizabeth Laird's young-adult novel *A Little Piece of Ground* (2006), a young Palestinian boy living under Israeli military rule in Ramallah meets a new friend from the nearby refugee camp and finds a perfect spot to play soccer. Before he can organize a game, however, advancing Israeli tanks threaten to tear his small world to pieces.

- Jean Zaru's nonfiction account of life as a Palestinian woman, *Occupied with Nonviolence: A Palestinian Woman Speaks* (2008), offers an alternative to the violence and destruction of the Palestinian–Israeli conflict: that of nonviolence, tolerance of all religions, and acknowledgment of the shared humanity between men and women, Palestinians and Israelis.

- Darwish's *Memory for Forgetfulness: August, Beirut, 1982* (1995) is a prose poem describing the Israeli siege of Beirut, which Darwish witnessed firsthand. Set on August 6 (the day on which, in 1945, the United States dropped an atomic bomb on Hiroshima, Japan), the work becomes increasingly erratic as the poet observes the violence of bombs dropping, fighter jets passing above, and the rubble-strewn streets.

- Egyptian novelist Naguib Mahfouz's *Midaq Alley* (1974) follows the residents of a destitute back alley in Cairo. Winner of the Nobel Peace Prize, Mahfouz was a personal friend of Darwish's. He is known as the Charles Dickens of Arabic literature for his vibrant characters and unforgettable settings.

- Ghassan Kanafani's short-story collection *Men in the Sun* (1999) tells Palestinian stories from before, during, and after the Nakba in the unflinchingly honest narrative voice of one of Palestine's most beloved authors.

- In Jabra Ibrahim Jabra's novel *In Search of Walid Masoud* (1978), a group of Baghdad intellectuals go in search of their missing colleague and friend, Walid, a priest educated in Italy who gives up city life to return to his homeland of Palestine just before the outbreak of the 1948 war.

- *Songs from Bialik: Selected Poems of Hayim Nahman Bialik* (2000) collects the work of Darwish's cultural rival, the Israeli poet Hayim Bialik, considered one of the best Hebrew poets in modern history. Bialik's work on the Jewish diaspora is particularly popular with his audiences.

- *Modern Arabic Poetry* (1991), edited by Salma Khadra Jayyusi, features the work of ninety poets from all corners of the Arab world, some translated into English for the first time.

- Emile Habiby's *The Secret Life of Saeed: The Pessoptimist* (1974) captures the absurdity of the conflict in the Middle East through the eyes of Saeed, a bumbling Palestinian who will do anything to survive. After remaining in the state of Israel following the Nakba, he turns spy for the Israelis before escaping to the safety of outer space in this tragicomic satire of politics, religion, and war.

- *I Saw Ramallah* (2003), by Mourid Barghouti, is a memoir of the poet's thirty-year exile from his homeland and the changes both external and internal—emotional, physical, mental, and spiritual—he discovers when he enters Ramallah for the first time since the 1967 Six-Day War.

- *Arabian Love Poems* (1999) collects the work of the great Damascus poet Nizar Qabbani, whose decadent lyrics have been beloved by generations of Arabic readers. A courageous defender of Arabic freedom and women's rights, Qabbani was a treasure to the Arab world.

raises his Palestinian voice in an attempt to intimidate." Each cry of "Arab," each accusatory "you," each clipped, angry sentence and shouted command lands like a blow against the monolithic, unresponsive figure of the official, who is the symbol of Israeli power.

The intended audience of "Identity Card" is not Israelis but Palestinians, both those living inside the state of Israel and those far flung in the diaspora that followed the Nakba, clinging to their hope of a better life, choking down the bile of their anger in an attempt to make it through the day. Mattawa writes: "Darwish turned private anguish into a public testament, evoking a collective feeling that broke down barriers between I and We and between the poet and his audience." By focusing on his own people rather than their enemy, Darwish built up his scattered community. The "you" of the Israeli is not nearly as important as the story of the Palestinian Arab's difficult life. Having lost his farm, his land, and his village, he must resign himself to a life under Israeli rule, in which even the rock quarry where he makes his living could be snatched away by the state. The life he lives is what he has chosen over the alternatives: to die or to leave his homeland, never to return. Mattawa writes: "He has suffered patiently and remained proud despite the cruel hand the occupation has brought upon him. But now he draws a red line: he will not beg from the one who stole his land." A man at his limit, the speaker will not supplicate himself to feed eight children, preferring hard labor in the quarry to easy, shameful money that represents the pity of his enemy for his sorry state.

Commitment literature, with its focus on broad appeal, realistic imagery, and simple language, was Darwish's favored style of writing in his early career as an embattled poet embedded in the state of Israel. This style is easily observed in the text of "Identity Card": short sentences, basic vocabulary, and few literary devices such as figurative language keep the poem uncomplicated and easy to read. Darwish designed the poem to be accessible to a wide audience of Palestinians, not just those who had been as lucky as Darwish in their access to education. Shaheen writes, "Darwish creates his language from a broad contemplation of life, which gives his poetry a spacious vividness." Using this simplified style, he could reduce complex political theories into manageable, attention-grabbing poetic lines. For example, the complicated cultural minutia of a Palestinian Arab inside Israel shouting, "I am an Arab!" is less important to the poem than the emotional forward thrust of the statement. Likewise, the broad strokes of the speaker's life (based loosely on the life of Darwish's father) make him more easily adaptable to the role of Arab everyman: a farmer without land but with deep, mythically ancient roots connecting him to his homeland. Commitment literature's goal was to create something defining and binding from the void that existed in Palestinian letters immediately following the Nakba. "Identity Card" is a remarkable triumph of the movement in its success in uniting not only Palestinians but also those from the wider Arab word in national pride, in bringing happiness and a sense of selfhood to a suffering community in the case of Palestinians both inside and outside Israel, and in its establishment of an exclusively Palestinian viewpoint in a world that had, at the time, largely forgotten the Palestinian plight. In addition, "Identity Card" was successful in making the literature of Palestinians known to Israelis through the newly minted battle cry "I am an Arab!" Though the Israeli in the poem does not respond to the speaker's shouts, "Identity Card" made Palestinian identity a reality once more inside the State of Israel, an identity that the authorities would have no choice but to acknowledge.

"Identity Card," though it is loud, is not abusive: the speaker is not a misanthrope, nor does he survive on his anger alone. He is a good man, an average man, who has been through too much, lost too much, and felt too much heartbreak but who remains resilient. Thus, in redefining what it means to be a Palestinian without Palestine, Darwish steeps the new identity in righteous anger, anger that strengthens the will to survive, rather than violent or obsessive anger that can consume a man's soul. The Arab speaker is proud, strong, unafraid of his oppressor and charges into confrontation rather than balking at the challenge. Tempered in the fires of war and loss, the new Arab is confident in his connection to the land itself, on a deeply spiritual plain of existence. In the poem's most lyrical and mythological stanza, the speaker claims to have been a part of Palestine since before the grass or the pines. He even predates the olive trees, a natural connection to the land unaffected by petty surface politics. The speaker becomes Palestine itself, a name without a title (a country without land), rough as stone, unbending though defeated, its villages empty, its orchards stolen, displaced and in flux between identities. Though this weakened nation without a claim to land hurls its anger at its conqueror, Israel is unresponsive to its outburst. A perk of victory is to have no need to explain oneself, as history gravitates toward the champion's side. Although Israel listens unmoved to the Palestinian plight, the speaker warns the official against growing comfortable in his power. As Said notes, the Israeli official "must be reminded that the card's language doesn't do full justice to the reality it supposedly contains." The greatest shows of strength occur when an opponent is cornered and all but defeated. If Palestine grows hungry, the speaker warns, it will take its meal from the flesh of Israel—an undisguised threat to those who would attempt, like the official, to ignore the legitimate anger of the Palestinians, or forget their capability to wait with patience until the time is right. Said writes: "The poem ends with what will become the standard motif in much literature by and about Palestinians during the seventies: the Palestinian emergence."

Darwish successfully resuscitated the spirit of his nearly broken people after the lost decades following the Nakba had left the Palestinian community without direction or hope for recognition. Using plain, accessible language and the power of raw emotion, Darwish inspired not only Palestinian Arabs but also the wider Arab world with his speaker's proud announcement of his identity. The poem, chanted, sung, and memorized with care, is a national treasure of Palestine. Shaheen praises Darwish not only for his political achievement but also for his skill as a poet, lauding his "linguistic aesthetics that combine surface simplicity and amazing intensity.... This produces a multilayered text that belongs at the same time to the reader and to great poetry." The poem is at once intensely personal and keenly political—a literary accomplishment as well as a historical landmark in the reemergence of Palestinian identity following the Nakba.

Source: Amy L. Miller, Critical Essay on "Identity Card," in *Poetry for Students*, Gale, Cengage Learning, 2016.

Khalled Mattawa

In the following excerpt, Mattawa describes Darwish as a "spokesman for the Palestinian people."

...During the 1990s, several literary critics in the Arab world celebrated Darwish's success in extricating himself from the details of the Palestinian problems. Critic Fakhri Saleh delights in the fact that "Darwish has been able to draw lyric condensation that addresses the universal existential tensions of our postmodern times from the specifics of his experiences" (Saleh 1999, 49). Salma Khadra Jayyusi (1992), the leading canon-maker of Palestinian literature, judges Darwish's success mainly on his ability to transcend the political expediency of his earlier work and by his submersion into aesthetic experiments while remaining dedicated to the Palestinian cause (61–65). By the time Darwish published *Sareer al-Ghariba* (1996) and *Jidariya* (2000), he had been firmly established as the national poet of Palestine for three decades. The Palestinian political situation during the brief Oslo Accord years allowed for experimentation, and he, as a poet tied to the mission of national spokesmanship, felt he had a longer leash, permitting him to explore more freely. Several critics noted that Darwish had earned this phase of personal expression having given his Palestinian, and indeed all Arab, audiences so much over the decades (Bayūn 1999; al-'Usṭā 2001; and 'Abdulmutalib 1998).

One of the early gifts Darwish offered his Arab and Palestinian audience is the 1964 poem "Identity Card," which closes the volume *Awraq al-zeitoun* (*Olive Leaves*), in which the poem "To the Reader" also appeared. "Biṭaqat hawiyah" ("Identity Card") has been a fan favorite throughout the Arab world, one that audiences frequently asked Darwish to read before thousands of listeners at his recitations. The poem was made into a popular song and has been an unofficial Arab nationalist anthem for decades. Yet it is one that Darwish never read in public after leaving Israel/Palestine in 1971....

Nothing in this poem diverges from Darwish's consistent message as a poet and spokesman for the Palestinian people. The poem's speaker, whose life details bear a remarkable resemblance to Darwish's own father, was expelled from his village, lost his farm, ended up working in a quarry, and fathered eight children. The angry speaker tells his story under occupation, how he has suffered patiently and remained proud despite the cruel hand the occupation has brought upon him. But now he draws a red line: he will not beg from the one who stole

The image of the stolen orchard echoes the Palestinians' lost homeland. *(© sripfoto / Shutterstock.com)*

his land, and he will fight his usurper to fend off hunger; indeed, he will turn into a cannibal if need be. The speaker's last words, "Beware of my hunger / and my anger," irrevocably intertwined these two conditions. This poem provides a rational basis for the speaker's rage that resonates effectively with the references to anger in "To the Reader."

Why then has Darwish refused to recite the poem in public since he left Palestine/Israel, when it still encompasses his political stance and audiences around the Arab world plea for it? During one packed recitation in Beirut, a member of the audience kept saying "Write it down, / I am an Arab," asking that Darwish read the poem. Fed up with the repeated request, Darwish shot back at the listener, "Write it down yourself!" and went on to read a different poem (al-Sayyid 2008, 7). According to Darwish, the circumstances sparking the poem occurred when he was placed under partial house arrest in Haifa in the mid-1960s. He had been tried in court for a poem he published in 1965 (Snir 2008). The judge placed him under probation with the stipulation that Darwish could not leave his residence after

sunset and that he sign in at the police station every day (al-Naqqāsh 1971).

"'Write it down: I am Arab!' I said that to a government official," Darwish explained. "I said it in Hebrew to provoke him, but when I said it in Arabic (in the poem) the Arab audience in Nazareth was electrified" (Darwish 2007a, 180). The poem, a dramatic monologue addressed to Darwish's detainers, continues as a translation of what Darwish would have said to the Israeli policemen in Hebrew. The audience was electrified because the poem succeeded in expressing in Arabic a private conversation that each humiliated Palestinian had experienced while facing Israeli officials and soldiers. Darwish turned private anguish into a public testament, evoking a collective feeling that broke down the barriers between I and We and between the poet and his audience.

"Identity Card" was written within the first decade of the state of Israel, a time when the Israelis did not recognize the Palestinians as a nationality and the words *Palestine* and *Palestinian* were never mentioned in public. Palestinians who lived within the border of the state of Israel were merely Arabs. Darwish's translation and placement of expressions uttered in Hebrew into a poem written in Arabic made the private moment public and turned humiliation on its head. Palestinians living in Israel, beginning with the audience in Nazareth who asked to hear the poem repeated six times, identified with this reversal as a way to turn *Arab* from a derogatory term into a declaration of dignified humanity before the Israelis, who confiscated their lands and officially designated them third-class citizens.

Outside of Palestine/Israel, the refrain of the poem—"Write it down, / I am an Arab"—took on a different resonance, devoid of the specific context in which Darwish wrote the poem. "Write it down, / I am an Arab!" became a battle cry throughout the Arab world, and the poem became an anthem expressing Arab national pride and even chauvinism, as opposed to the defiance of subjugation and racism that the poet had meant it to be. Darwish explains, "the Jews call the Palestinian an Arab, and so I shouted in my torturer's face 'Write it down, I am an Arab!' Does it make sense then for me to stand before a hundred million Arabs saying 'I am an Arab'? I'll not read the poem" (al-Qaissī 2008, 13).

I bring up the history of Darwish's relation to "Identity Card" and his Arab audiences' claim upon it to point out his awareness of the contingent circumstances surrounding his poems. As opposed to his desire for "universal" non-contingent poems, here we see him insist that poems do target different audiences and serve as specific rhetorical gestures or even as political messages that should not be taken out of their historical context. In other words, poems do not necessarily have "universal" messages, because they emerge during different contingencies with different interlocutors.

To understand Darwish's career as a major search for poetic agency, this study outlines the evolution of Darwish's poetry, keeping in mind these two contending forces, or rather these two definitions of the role of poetry as a means toward agency, while operating within it. And though it is difficult to accept the polarities Darwish sets between engagement and private contemplation, love and political struggle, the expedient and the enduring, the relative and the absolute, what is remarkable is the degree to which Darwish managed to remain present as a discourse-maker in the Palestinian context,

building bridges between these polarities for maximal agency. Darwish's discourse-making efforts manifest themselves in essays, interviews, and poetry.

The evolution of Darwish's poetry constitutes a struggle to preserve the poet's presence within political deliberations and to maintain and develop the aesthetic pursuit that grants the poet the degree of independence upon which his relevance as a discourse-maker depends. Darwish's poetry kept up with his various personal displacements and political affiliations. He redefined his role as a poet through his compositional practice, and his attempts to bridge the tension "between ethics and esthetics" (Darwish 1999a, 19) have helped shape the Palestinian national discourse and define the parameters and priorities of Palestinian identity formation.

Source: Khalled Mattawa, "Introduction: Perennial Tensions," in *Mahmoud Darwish: The Poet's Art and His Nation*, Syracuse University Press, 2014, pp. 6–13.

Angelika Neuwirth

In the following excerpt, Neuwirth highlights how politics and religion influence Darwish's work.

. . . Against the backdrop of the Palestinian-Israeli conflict, it is to be expected that a non-religious, Arabic reading of the Bible—a body of text that had long been politically instrumentalized by Zionists—might generate a new Arabic counter-tradition, one enabling Palestinians to confront the politicized canon of the "others" with a subversive reading of their own. In his early creative period, Darwish produced such a counter-text, a Palestinian Genesis and Exodus. However, in his later reading of the Bible, his goal is far beyond this: to resolve the antagonism between other and self and localize both in a shared world, albeit one that is in the *ghurba* (outland); the specific *conditio humana* to which the title of the collection *The Bed of the Stranger* (*ghariba*) alludes. It is little wonder then that prominent figures of exile from world literature find their way into the context constructed by Darwish in his later poetry, among them the Jewish poet Paul Celan, who with his idiosyncratic reading of the Hebraic Bible appears as Darwish's principal witness for the existential sensibility of exile.

Mahmoud Darwish is—together with Adonis—considered the most prominent Arab poet of his age. Darwish was born in 1942 in Birwa, a

" IT IS NO EXAGGERATION TO CLAIM THAT THE RELEVANCE OF HIS POETRY AND THE IMPACT IT HAS EXERTED ON THE MEMORY OF THE PALESTINIAN CATASTROPHE ARE NO LESS THAN THAT OF SUCH INTERNATIONALLY CHERISHED MANIFESTATIONS OF JEWISH MEMORY LIKE COMMEMORATION RITUALS AND—MORE LATTERLY—HOLOCAUST MEMORIALS."

Galilean village near Acre that was razed to the ground in 1948; his family, who took refuge in Lebanon only to sneak back a year later, lived as refugees in their own country, farmers who had become day-laborers. Yet Darwish enjoyed a solid education, growing up with both Arabic and Hebrew. He took to writing poetry with overtly political overtones at a very early stage. In his obituary, his friend Elias Khoury tells us:

> . . . the 12-year-old poet was called on to recite a verse at school, and wrote a poem about a child who lost his house to strangers who conquered the land. He did not know then that the poem was to be recited in memory of the *Nakba*, which over there they call Independence Day. The next day, he was summoned to the headquarters of the military governor, where they threatened to ban his father from working, "Then I understood that poetry was more serious than I thought," he said, "and I had to choose between resuming this game or giving it up. Thus oppression taught me that poetry could be a weapon."

Several years later, Darwish joined the editorial staff of the Communist literary journal *al-Jadid* (*The New*), before working for the journal *al-Ittihad* (*The Union*) in Haifa, which was closely affiliated with the Israeli Communist Party. Both press organs supported efforts to establish a transnational culture. Here he worked closely with the novelist, journalist, and politician Emile Habibi.

Written in 1966, his first long poem would mark his emergence as the voice of his society. "A Lover from Palestine" is a work in which "the Palestinian poetic project took the shape of a new language, a means to retrieve the land with words." The poet reflects on the existential

experience of a poetic "land appropriation," which he has clad in prose language in his approximately contemporaneous memoir *Diary of Daily Sadness*:

> Suddenly you remember that Palestine is your land. The lost name leads you to lost times, and on the coast of the Mediterranean lies the land like a sleeping woman, who awakes suddenly when you call her by her beautiful name. They have forbidden you to sing the old songs, to recite the poems of your youth and to read the histories of the rebels and poets who have sung of this old Palestine. The old name returns, finally it returns from the void, you open her map as if you opened the buttons of your first love's dress for the first time.

What has been forcibly expunged from the speaker's consciousness returns in a kind of vision, and its erotic radiance restores reality in its full dimension. Darwish was twenty-four at the time.

As he became more prominent, he was subjected to increasingly tighter controls by the Israeli authorities, including several spells in prison, where in fact he wrote "A Lover from Palestine." Shortly after the publication of this poem, the famous Palestinian publicist and prose writer Ghassan Kanafani, working in Beirut, came across the work of Darwish and several other young poets from Israel's Arab enclave. Suitably impressed, he managed to have a number of their poems smuggled to Beirut, presenting them to a broader Arab public as "resistance poetry"—a label that Darwish would later vehemently reject.

Increasing political pressure forced Darwish to leave the country and after a short stay in Cairo he joined the Arab intelligentsia in Beirut in 1971. It was during these years of exile in Beirut that he wrote some of his most impressive poems, creating the *fida'i* (self-sacrificing fighter), or *shahid* (martyr), as an alter ego. When the Israeli Army expelled the Palestinian resistance movement from Lebanon in 1982, Darwish was again forced to leave, moving to Paris. In exile there, he wrote his war memoir *A Memory for Forgetfulness* and embarked on a collection of new poetry, this time distinctively personal in tone. As far as the wider public was concerned, he remained the "voice of Palestine," the congenial translator of the innermost longings of Palestinians, which could only be expressed poetically, in myths and symbols. Although Darwish had begun to "re-write" his past poetically in the 1990s, reappraising it from the perspective of the "estranged" exile, it was nonetheless a surprise for readers when in 2002, six years after returning to the Arab world, he,— "Palestine's poet" for over thirty years, able to attract thousands of listeners to readings and reaching countless readers throughout the Arab world—explicitly cast off this mantle and called into question an essential part of his own mythical production in the volume *State of Siege*.

PALESTINE: A LAND INSCRIBED WITH THE BIBLICAL TEXT

An observation by Thorsten Valk about German Romantic poetry seems also to describe a hallmark of modern Arab poetry:

> Since poetry is credited with a world-transforming and time-sublating dimension, reflections about poetry often touch eschatological horizons. The poet [in Novalis' work] bears the traits of the ancient poet Orpheus. Like Orpheus, he appears as a powerful magician who suspends the laws of space and time, connects the remotest realms of reality with one another, and allows all creatures to enter into a comprehensive dialogue. (. . .) The poet occupies a preeminent position, for he possesses an almost mythical access to the Golden Age. He is capable of tangibly experiencing the unity of the ideal primordial spheres even in the most disparate phenomena of the current world. Endowed with the exclusive gift of the analogical gaze, he can grasp the connective elements in the seemingly unrelated phenomena of the empirical realm. He is able to divine and decipher those enigmatic signs, which are inscribed into everything earthly.

Although it is difficult to identify a universally accepted Golden Age in Arab secular culture, post-colonial poetry of the Near East is nonetheless nostalgic. Poets endeavor to transform reality and recover the vision of a pre-colonial paradisiacal state of their living space beyond its real, politically distorted appearance.

This applies to Palestinian poetry in particular, for its whole self-understanding is predicated by, as Richard van Leeuwen has stressed, the premise that land is the structuring principle to organize individual and collective perceptions of life:

> There are various versions of history inscribed on the land, both by the occupier and by the Palestinians. The relations of power, however, imply that the Israeli version is dominant and that the Palestinian "textual" homeland is threatened by elimination. What remains for the Palestinians is not so much "history," as "memory" consisting of recollections of childhood and of

the exodus, emotions symbolizing the attachment to the land and the natural right of the Palestinians to the land.

But these issues remain dispersed, lacking binding power, as long as no aesthetic catalyst is available to re-structure them. This is the function that poetry comes to fulfill.

It must be remembered that for a long time the Palestinian collective did not possess any relevant medium to express their experience of the *Nakba* trauma of 1948; during this period poetry was the only form of public expression left to the traumatized remnants of the population. The poet thus came to be celebrated as the speaker of the collective, a position that made him extremely vulnerable to all kinds of oppression exerted by the authorities and in several cases led to exile and loss of this public role. In spite of exile, Mahmoud Darwish's fame as the voice of Palestine survived such a crisis, thus accumulating even greater symbolic significance. It is no exaggeration to claim that the relevance of his poetry and the impact it has exerted on the memory of the Palestinian catastrophe are no less than that of such internationally cherished manifestations of Jewish memory like commemoration rituals and— more latterly—Holocaust memorials. Darwish's poetry—in his own mind—is a response to a powerful pre-existing writing that is inscribed on the land and serves to ascertain and anchor the legitimacy of the dominance of the "others": the Hebrew Bible.

Zionist inscribing of the land had not come first. A century before, American Protestants had perceived the land as oscillating between sacred ground and Biblical text, or, to quote Hilton Obenzinger, "as a female land inscribed with the male pen of the divine" waiting to be read by the heirs of the Biblical heritage. It is obvious that this vision, which would reemerge in secular form in Zionism, had and has no place for identities, which are not intrinsic to the Bible. Educated in both Arabic and Hebrew, Darwish soon became aware of the inseparable entanglement of text and land in the minds of the dominant Jewish society in his country. In his view, the mission of poetry "is essentially to strive to rewrite or to create its own Book of Genesis, to search for beginnings and to interpret myths of creation. It is through these myths that the poet can return to his origins." The master narrative of the Jewish "natural, historically preordained presence"—and of course its implication of preordained Palestinian absence and exile—had to be de-narrated.

The Palestinian-Israeli struggle is a struggle over a land claimed as the Jewish homeland; a concept that in Zionism is taken to reflect not historical contingency, but an ontological reality, as the reversal of the negative concept of *galut* (exile). This is in contradiction to traditional Jewish thought, where exile was regarded primarily not as territorial, but as spiritual, the Jews being the most obvious witnesses and evidence of a universal state of exile that—when the destruction of the Second Temple left the land devoid of the divine immanence—had affected the world as such. Yet this did not mean the dissolution of the Jews as a people; as the German-Jewish philosopher Franz Rosenzweig held: "unlike other nations, the Jewish nation was able to exist without a common land and a common language because from its very beginning as a people it did not make the peoplehood of Israel dependent on these external factors." *Zikkaron* (memory) thus played a pivotal role in preserving the past and paving the way for *ge'ula* (redemption) by keeping alive the hope for the return of the divine presence.

Zionism, which came to secularize the religious notions of Judaism, replaced the basic binarism of exile/redemption with that of exile/homecoming or homeland. This binarism is central to Zionism: indeed it is the *shelilat hagalut* (negation of exile) that provides the conceptual basis for the Zionist territorial claim to the land. Since Zionism—modifying the Christian view of the Jews as being excluded from the "History of Grace"—understood Jewish exile as an absence from history, that is, from historical time, the return to the land was perceived as a return to history. This notion, unique in its ideological dimension, turned the discourse of exile into a primarily Jewish discourse, which for a long time was then considered to be exclusively Jewish.

In modern history it is the plight of the Palestinians that comes closest in its dimensions to the Jewish exile experience, which had long stood as absolutely unique. With the concomitant loss of a political entity, the Palestinian situation evolved into a kind of replica of earlier Jewish exile, entailing a double absence: the absence of the majority from their homeland and the absence of those who had remained from political and cultural participation. It is impossible not to see both "exiles," the Jewish and the Palestinian, as related to and indeed intertwined with each other. The fateful relationship—the ending of one exile producing another, while two mutually exclusive memories coexist—has been poignantly expressed by Darwish, who wondered: "Should the Palestinian have to wait for two thousand years until Jewish memory will permit him to remember?" . . .

Source: Angelika Neuwirth, "Hebrew Bible and Arabic Poetry: Reclaiming Palestine as a Homeland Made of Words: Mahmoud Darwish," in *Arabic Literature: Postmodern Perspectives*, edited by Angelika Neuwirth, Andreas Pflitsch, and Barbara Winckler, Saqi, 2010, pp. 173–77.

SOURCES

Alkhateeb, Firas, "The Nakba: The Palestinian Catastrophe of 1948," in *Lost Islamic History*, April 23, 2013, http://lostislamichistory.com/the-nakba-the-palestinian-catastrophe-of-1948/ (accessed May 3, 2015).

"Al-Nakba," Al Jazeera website, May 29, 2013, http://www.aljazeera.com/programmes/specialseries/2013/05/20135612348774619.html (accessed May 3, 2015).

Ammous, Saifedean, "Mahmoud Darwish: Palestine's Prophet of Humanism," in *Electronic Intifada*, August 12, 2008, http://electronicintifada.net/content/mahmoud-darwish-palestines-prophet-humanism/7665 (accessed May 4, 2015).

Behar, Almog, "Mahmoud Darwish: Poetry's State of Siege," in *Journal of Levantine Studies*, No. 1, Summer 2011, pp. 189–99.

Darwish, Mahmoud, "Identity Card," in *Mahmoud Darwish: The Poet's Art and His Nation*, translated by Khaled Mattawa, Syracuse University Press, 2014, pp. 7–9.

"Introduction: I Am Not Mine," Mahmoud Darwish website, http://www.mahmouddarwish.com/english/introduction.htm (accessed May 5, 2015).

Krajeski, Jenna, "Mahmoud Darwish," in *New Yorker*, August 12, 2008, http://www.newyorker.com/books/page-turner/mahmoud-darwish (accessed May 5, 2015).

"Mamoud Darwish," Poetry Foundation website, http://www.poetryfoundation.org/bio/mahmoud-darwish (accessed May 4, 2015).

Mattawa, Khaled, *Mahmoud Darwish: The Poet's Art and His Nation*, Syracuse University Press, 2014, pp. ix–xiii, 1–61.

Muhawi, Ibrahim, Introduction to *Memory for Forgetfulness*, by Mahmoud Darwish, University of California Press, 1995, xi–xxx.

"Palestinian 'National Poet' Dies," BBC News website, August 9, 2008, http://news.bbc.co.uk/2/hi/middle_east/7551918.stm (accessed May 4, 2015).

Said, Edward W., "The Emergence of a Palestinian Consciousness," in *The Question of Palestine*, Vintage Books, 1992, pp. 155–57.

Shaheen, Mohammad, Introduction to *Almond Blossoms and Beyond*, by Mahmoud Darwish, Interlink Books, 2009, vii–xi.

FURTHER READING

Bunton, Martin, *The Palestinian-Israeli Conflict: A Very Short Introduction*, Oxford University Press, 2013.
Bunton provides the basic facts of the conflict between Israel and Palestine in this primer to the crisis in the Middle East, dividing the long history into twenty-year sections for easy reference.

Darwish, Mahmoud, *Unfortunately, It Was Paradise: Selected Poems*, University of California Press, 2013.
This collection of Darwish's poetry spans his four-decade career as the voice of Palestine, both when he lived in Israel and during his exile spent traveling the world, with a forward by Fady Joudah.

Gelvin, James L., *The Palestine-Israel Conflict: One Hundred Years of War*, Cambridge University Press, 2014.
This updated introductory history of the Palestine-Israel conflict attempts an objective presentation of both sides of the unending dispute in the Middle East.

Hoke, Mateo, and Cate Malek, *Palestine Speaks: Narratives of Life under Occupation*, McSweeney's, 2014.
Palestinians from all walks of life recite their stories of life under Israeli occupation in Hoke and Malek's collection. The firsthand accounts paint a portrait of lives shaped by the violence of the ongoing conflict between Palestine and Israel.

SUGGESTED SEARCH TERMS

Mahmoud Darwish

Mahmoud Darwish AND "Identity Card"

"Identity Card" AND "Leaves of Olives"

Mahmoud Darwish AND "Leaves of Olives"

Mahmoud Darwish AND Palestinian poetry

"Leaves of Olives" AND 1964

Bitaqat Hawiyyah

Mahmoud Darwish AND Bitaqat Hawiyyah

Mahmoud Darwish AND Awraq al-zeitoun

Bitaqat Hawiyyah AND Awraq al-zeitoun

"Identity Card" AND Palestinian poetry

Loose Woman

SANDRA CISNEROS
1994

Sandra Cisneros's poem "Loose Woman" (1994) is written in the voice of a Chicana woman speaking out against the forces of racist and sexist oppression that attempt to control her life in American culture and in Mexican American culture. The speaker wants to control her own sex life, but the society around her wants to force her into the role of a submissive, virginal good girl. The culture shames her by calling her names that highlight her sexual freedom, and it sees her as a dangerous threat to the stability of society if she transgresses the rules that are set for her. But the "loose woman" welcomes the insults; she takes back each slur and turns it into a badge that empowers her resistance. She proudly proclaims that she is dangerous, anarchic, and destructive, directing her energy back at the forces that oppress her. If the patriarchy wants to beat her down, she is happy to destroy the patriarchy. "Loose Woman" is part of a discourse of resistance widespread in twentieth-century American literature, especially among writers from marginalized groups, such as women, racial minorities, and gay people. The poem is in the collection *Loose Woman*, published by Alfred A. Knopf (1994).

AUTHOR BIOGRAPHY

Cisneros was born in Chicago, Illinois, on December 20, 1954. Although Cisneros relates

Sandra Cisneros (© *David Livingston | Getty Images*)

many fanciful family tales about her ancestry, more reliable knowledge begins only with her parents. Although the influx and movement of Mexican farmworkers in US border states were tightly controlled, Mexican workers prior to the 1960s generally had free access to the United States; there was little concept that their presence in the country was illegal. In these circumstances, Cisneros's father, Alfredo, traveled around the United States and eventually settled in Chicago, where he married Elvira, a woman from a Mexican immigrant family. Alfredo supported the family by manual labor and constantly moved Cisneros and her six surviving brothers (many other siblings died in infancy) back and forth between Mexico and Chicago on an almost annual basis. By the time Cisneros was in high school, the family settled in Chicago, since they were finally able to buy a house. They lived in Humboldt Park, a largely Puerto Rican area of Chicago, which would become the setting of Cisneros's novel *The House on Mango Street* (1984). Cisneros always viewed herself as an outsider in her own family, imagining herself as the princess in the Grimms' fairy tale "The Six Swans" and her brothers as the swans (*Cisneros*

means "swan-keeper"). She was guided toward reading by her mother, who had intellectual interests that she herself could not pursue in her social situation.

Cisneros began writing as an undergraduate at Loyola University in Chicago, where she graduated in 1976, and then earned a master of fine arts degree from the University of Iowa through the Iowa Writers' Workshop (1978). Cisneros had to teach high school and take other jobs on the fringes of academia until *The House on Mango Street* was published. This novel became the first book by a Chicana to be published by a major press (Vintage) in the United States. After its publication, she was able to work as a writer in residence at major universities, such as the University of California, Berkeley, and the University of Michigan at Dearborn. She published a collection of short stories, *Woman Hollering Creek*, in 1991, and a poetry collection, *Loose Woman*, in 1994. In 1995, she was awarded a MacArthur Fellowship. She worked for many years at Our Lady of the Lake University in San Antonio, Texas.

Cisneros now lives in the cultural center of San Miguel de Allende in Mexico, whose Baroque church is a World Heritage Site. Cisneros moved from Chicago to distance herself from her family and promote the isolation she needs for writing. She has similarly avoided marriage and children. She considers her literary works to be her offspring. Cisneros has founded two institutions that fund young writers: the Alfredo Cisneros del Moral Foundation (named after her father), which was founded in 2000 and supports writers born in or living in Texas, and the Macondo Foundation (named after a town in Gabriel García Márquez's novel *One Hundred Years of Solitude*), which was founded in 2006 and fosters writers whose work supports community building and peaceful social change.

POEM SUMMARY

The text used for this summary is from *Loose Woman*, Alfred A. Knopf, 1994, pp. 112–15. A version of the poem can be found at the following web page: http://dwwproject2012.weebly.com/loose-woman.html.

"Loose Woman" is divided into lines of varying length and into stanzas (sections) of unequal numbers of lines. The speaker of the poem refers to herself as "I" and is the loose woman referred to in the title.

Stanza 1 (lines 1–3)
This section works toward defining what a woman is. The loose woman's opponents, from the perspective of patriarchal society (that is, a society that benefits men and is controlled by men), say that she is an animal. In a way, of course, this is true, since all human beings are animals. But her opponents mean it as a slur and take pleasure in calling her names.

Stanza 2 (lines 4–6)
The loose woman's opponents make two new accusations against her, that she is a "bitch" and practices witchcraft. The first accusation repeats the claim that she is animal but in more specified form, since the word properly means "a female dog." However, it is also the most commonly applied slur against women, used to attack them by likening them not only to an animal (the implication being that women are irrational and need to be controlled for their own good) but to an animal that is thought of as being sexually indiscriminate, considered a bad trait in patriarchal society. The insult also contains a hint of fear, though: dogs can bite. The accusation of witchcraft also contains both insult and fear: the witch has power and could use magic to attack men. In many traditional societies, the penalty for witchcraft is death. The speaker says that she has made precisely the same claims for herself without regret.

Stanza 3 (lines 7–12)
This section has a much longer list of accusations from the loose woman's critics. The first is that the loose woman is a "*macha*," a coinage based on the Spanish word *macho*. It seems to suggest that she has abandoned her social role as a woman by taking on masculine attributes.

Next she is said to be "hell on wheels." Although this phrase today is obscure and might be used to describe a swiftly running athlete or a race car driver, it has a different origin, which Cisneros seems to be invoking. In the nineteenth century, a place where one went for the express purpose of sinning—going against social norms—such as a casino or a brothel, was called a hell. A hell on wheels was a mobile establishment that served the camps of the workers building the first transcontinental railroads in the United States in the mid-nineteenth

century, following along on the newly laid track in rail cars. They typically offered drink, gambling, and prostitution to the workers. The phrase is used here as a slur, with the implication that the speaker willfully transgresses social norms.

The next slur portrays the loose woman as excessively devoted to sex. It uses the Spanish word *viva*, the equivalent of "long live" in the archaic English phrase "long live the king" (that is, "may the king live long"). In Spanish, the construction is quite current, indicating the speaker's support, especially ideological or political support, for *viva*'s direct object.

A *fire and brimstone preacher* is one whose rhetoric is considered especially effective and who preaches about a traditional vision of hell. Here the epithet probably means that the loose woman is too forceful, in contrast to the modest and quiet ideal of femininity.

Next, the loose woman is accused of hating men. In traditional patriarchal culture, women are meant to be subservient to men and to exist for their convenience, so this would be a grave fault. In the same line, she is said to lay waste to, presumably, men, a nuanced description of her transgressive sexual aggression.

The last taunt in this stanza makes the loose woman out to be a female equivalent of the boogeyman, a childish term that suggests how primal the opponent's fear of women is. She is seen as this kind of primitive, devouring monster because she is gay. In traditional society, a woman's only role was as a wife to a man, and obviously a gay woman would be completely unsuitable for that role.

In the last lines of this section, the loose woman admits that some of the epithets may be accurate, while others are not, but she thanks her critics for the slurs, which she characterizes as complimentary.

Stanza 4 (lines 13–16)
Words seem to have failed to control the loose woman, so now the opposing mob attacks her with the intention of stoning her to death. In some respects, this passage seems to trivialize its subject matter, referring to the "sticks and stones" of a children's nursery rhyme. But stoning is indeed the traditional punishment for a transgressive woman, prescribed, for example in the biblical book of Deuteronomy (22:20–21). The loose woman counterattacks with her

own words, her own rhetoric. What she says—and the reader can only assume that this is her own shocking acceptance of the charges against her, her regarding them as compliments—takes the strength away from the mob of her opponents, leaving them staggering on weakened knees as if they were drunk on gin.

Stanza 5 (lines 17–20)
This stanza specifies the character of the loose woman's rhetoric. She says that, depending on her mood, either gems fall from her tongue, or vile animals like toads and snakes. On one level, the statement means that she can speak either persuasively or with anger. On another level, it is a reference to one of Charles Perrault's Mother Goose stories, a fairy tale that is translated under various titles: "Diamonds and Toads," "Toads and Diamonds," or "The Fairy." The story is about a widow with two daughters: a proud and haughty favorite, and a sweet and demure younger girl. The good daughter goes to a fountain to get water for the household and is met by a fairy disguised as a poor old woman, whom she treats kindly. As a reward, the fairy casts a spell that makes either a diamond or a pearl fall out of mouth every time she speaks. When the mother finds this out, she sends her favorite daughter to the well, hoping she will gain the same gift and ordering her to be kind to the old woman. The fairy reappears, but this time disguised as a noblewoman. The favorite daughter acts haughtily to her and is punished by having toads or snakes fall out of mouth each time she speaks. The younger daughter is further rewarded by marrying a prince, while the elder runs off into the woods, never to be seen again. The message of the story is clear: demure, submissive behavior in women will be rewarded by traditional society with a good marriage (all a woman can hope for), while independence is characterized as sinful behavior and punished. The loose woman realizes that the attitudes of both haughtiness and submission are rhetorical postures and therefore she can use either one that she finds useful; neither one has the inherent goodness or wickedness implied in the fairy tale.

Stanza 6 (lines 21–23)
The loose woman reflects on the effects of her rhetoric on the mob of her opponents. She has a bad reputation and is the subject of rumors. She metaphorically compares the sound of the rumors spoken about her to crinoline, meaning the petticoats or slips worn under a dress. The rumors obviously concern her sexual freedom contrary to society's expectations. Precisely because she is sexually transgressive, she causes sexual desire (described as an itch, a common euphemism). Since her opponents are men, they are free of the social control of their sexuality, even as they condemn the loose woman for sharing in their freedom.

Stanza 7 (lines 24–28)
This section begins a new direction in the poem. From now on, the loose woman will no longer react to her opponents but will begin to boast of her own attributes.

The loose woman claims that she is both a figure of myth and the subjects of lies; she herself is author of some of the lies. She has worked carefully to cultivate her own image. She describes her image in terms that both indicate her bad reputation in society and suggest and claim for herself the title of prostitute, identifying herself with the women most transgressive of traditional culture and the ones pushed farthest to the margins of society.

Stanza 8 (lines 29–33)
The loose woman describes her manner of life. She lives according to her emotions and desires. This fits in precisely with the traditional view of women as incapable of controlling their emotions in contrast to disciplined, unemotional men. The loose woman breaks all of the rules set for her and aims only at her own pleasure. This is her sin against society, since she is acting without regard for the controls placed on her. At the same time, it is the core of her identity and gives her the strength to resist social control. Her cultivation of the self is, she admits, an excessive indulgence.

Stanza 9 (lines 34–42)
The loose woman paints herself as an outlaw. She is dangerous to society; she is a female Pancho Villa (a Mexican revolutionary against whom the United States once waged war). She not only breaks human laws but also attacks the natural order. She causes anguish to the pope, the representative of the Catholic Church, the most traditional institution in society. It is interesting that she also makes fathers cry. One might typically expect this boast of a *macho*, meaning that he seduces young women and casts them aside. The fathers cry because their daughters

are now, in their view, ruined, made useless in the traditional marriage exchange by which families extend the control of their children. The threat, then, must be that the loose woman will turn other women into beings like herself, which she does not consider a bad thing. The loose woman stands beyond the law and is therefore an outlaw (another word Cisneros casts in Spanish). Cisneros evokes popular culture images from old westerns, with the outlaw's faces posted on the walls of sheriff's offices. But the point is that the outlaw is someone completely beyond human culture.

Stanza 10 (lines 43–47)
The loose woman reveals that the men in patriarchal society hate her because they fear her, although she is unconcerned about either feeling. In the most difficult section of the poem, she implicates Christianity, a widely respected institution that is often seen as liberating, with the powers of social control and domination, enforced by racism and sexism. The loose woman embodies the opposite: anarchy or lawlessness. If the law is oppressive, then only the outlaw is free.

Stanza 11 (lines 48–58)
The loose woman represents herself as a threat to patriarchal society. She is proficient in the use of firearms and so represents a literal threat of revolutionary resistance, a threat symbolized by a series of terms describing her sharpness. These are balanced by terms of her looseness, referring to her freedom.

Stanza 12 (lines 59–62)
The final stanza repeats the ideas that have already been introduced, this time without a mention of society's views; the speaker has fully claimed the labels for herself.

THEMES

Feminism
The speaker of "Loose Woman" deals with and transforms several slurs that are often directed against women. The obvious questions to ask are how she became the victim of these slurs and why the qualities they describe have a negative connotation that she has to transform into a positive one. The answer that Cisneros offers in this poem uses feminist ideas. Feminists view society as patriarchal, that is, run by and for men. Women in a patriarchal society have little power to make their own decisions and direct their own lives; their actions are largely determined by their fathers and husbands. (Until relatively recently, historically speaking, marriages were usually arranged by the couples' parents rather than by the young people themselves.) This is reflected in law codes that, even in the most advanced Western countries, gave women an inferior status until late in the twentieth century and in even more restrictive social conventions imposed on women. "Loose Woman" makes the feminist argument that no one but women themselves should be in control of their lives.

An interesting aspect of Cisneros's feminism is revealed in her use of the word *macha*. This word, of feminine gender in Spanish, is a neologism (a new word) formed from the masculine word *macho*. A man who is macho exemplifies the ideals of *machismo*, supporting stereotypical masculine behavior, which includes positive characteristics like self-control but also less desirable ones, such as the propensity to enforce one's will through violence while at the same denigrating the feminine to a second-class or objectified status. The term *macha* might either mean the reverse, valuing the feminine at the expense of the masculine, or mean a woman who adopts masculine traits. With the emphasis on violence throughout the poem, Cisneros seems to lean toward the second of those options, a radical position that says that violence, real or metaphorical, is necessary for feminist self-defense.

Reappropriation
Reappropriation is the process by which a marginalized community, subject to oppression and discrimination, takes control of (appropriates) the language used to insult it. It gives those same insults and slurs a positive value, so that they become proud terms of self-identification. This phenomenon seems to have occurred first in the homosexual community, as Michel Foucault suggests, in the first volume of his *History of Sexuality*:

> There is no question that the appearance in nineteenth-century psychiatry, jurisprudence, and literature of a whole series of discourses on the species and subspecies of homosexuality, inversion, pederasty, and "psychic hermaphrodism" made possible a strong advance

TOPICS FOR FURTHER STUDY

- Students reading *Beowulf* or other epic literature are often given an assignment to write their own boast poems, and many of them can be found online (for example, at http://www.teenink.com/search_google.php?q=boast&x=0&y=0). Imitating "Loose Woman," write your own boast poem, but write from the perspective of social structures that you find personally restrictive or oppressive, taking ownership and transforming any language that you feel is directed against you. Post the poem on a blog and allow your classmates to comment.

- *The House on Mango Street* (1984), often considered young-adult literature, is Cisneros's best-known work. This novel is set among a group of Chicana girls growing up in Chicago. Write a paper comparing its themes with those of "Loose Woman." The young characters in the novel grow up to eventually find themselves in the position of the loose woman, though they do not necessarily find her bravado and resources for dealing with the situation.

- Magic realism is a device commonly used by Latin American authors. It shows the magical or mythological themes and events penetrating into everyday reality. Cisneros's "Loose Woman" certainly has qualities of

magic realism—in her characterization as a witch but more especially in her seemingly cosmic power to overturn society into a state of anarchy. It is as if she thinks fundamental change can come about only through a miracle (although perhaps the miracle is merely realizing that change is possible). Write a paper exploring this idea.

- In "Loose Woman," Cisneros takes over, or appropriates, the linguistic tools of social control that are meant to shame her into conformity. This technique has a long history in American cultural politics and has nowhere been more successful than in the gay community's reappropriation of the terms *gay* and *queer*. A major step in reappropriating the word *queer* came with the publication of the anonymous pamphlet "Queers Read This," originally circulated in June 1990 at the New York Gay Pride Parade. Copies of the pamphlet are easily found online (e.g., http://www.qrd.org/qrd/misc/text/queers.read.this). This text is far more radical than Cisneros's poem, but it shows an example of politically and theoretically justified reappropriation. Using this theoretical foundation, write an essay justifying the kind of feminist reappropriation suggested by Cisneros in "Loose Woman."

of social controls into this area of "perversity"; but it also made possible the formation of a "reverse" discourse: homosexuality began to speak in its own behalf, to demand that its legitimacy or "naturality" be acknowledged, often in the same vocabulary, using the same categories by which it was medically disqualified.

As new terms such as *gay* and *queer* were invented in the nineteenth century to marginalize homosexuality, the homosexual community began to use them as self-identifiers, as if to say, *Yes, I'm gay, what could possibly be wrong with that?* Today, *gay* is the standard way of referring to homosexual people in English, and

the term *homosexual* itself is beginning to seem antiquated and derogatory. The term *queer* is especially favored by the academic community (for example, in the terms *queer theory* and *queer studies*). Cisneros does the same thing for terms used in the social control of sexually transgressive women. The poem's speaker singles out terms such as *loose woman*, *bitch*, and *man-hating* that are flung at her as insults meant to shame her into obedience and considers them compliments, proudly using them of herself. As with the term *gay*, her use of language tends to praise and value sexual transgression.

The speaker's words are compared both to gems and to reptiles, giving both positive and negative connotations. *(© iLight photo | Shutterstock.com)*

A related example of reappropriation occurred in 2011. A student at the University of California released a YouTube video making a racist attack against Asian students, using derogatory terms. (She was also evidently unable to distinguish Chinese students from Japanese students and mocked them as a group for calling to check on the safety of their families after a tsunami hit Japan.) The video went viral, and most viewers were appalled at the display of racism. The slur that she used was reappropriated and used on a T-shirt whose sales funded relief aid for victims of the tsunami.

STYLE

Boasting Poetry

Throughout "Loose Woman," Cisneros's poetic narrator boasts of her dangerous qualities: she is terrifying and threatening to men, a public enemy, the embodiment of anarchy. This kind of self-praise has a long history in poetry. It originates with the boasts of heroes in epic poems

such as *Beowulf* and the *Odyssey*. In the *Odyssey* (book 8), when Odysseus comes to the court of the Phaeacians, he gives a long list of his accomplishments in war and his athletic feats and gives evidence of them by recounting his adventures. Similarly in *Beowulf*, when the hero comes to the mead hall of King Hrothgar, he boasts of his heroic excellence. The ability to boast is itself, as Odysseus says, a skill with great currency in a preliterate, heroic society. The warriors establish their reputation by the recitation of their deeds. But it is dangerous to boast about what one will do, rather than what one has already done. If a warrior's actions fall short of their words, he will be dishonored. Of course, anyone who boasts is only a step away from being ridiculed, and epic poetry has its share of taunters.

As society evolved, the heroic ideal itself came to seem somewhat ridiculous, and medieval works such as *Sir Gawain and the Green Knight* start to verge on comedy in the ridiculous boasts made by their characters. Arthur's vow never to dine until he has seen something adventurous is childish, and Gawain's boasts are so bound by modesty that he paints himself as the world's greatest weakling and fool. Later poetry rejects the entire heroic style that gives the boasting poem meaning. In William Shakespeare's Sonnet XXV, for instance, the speaker realizes that a soldier who can boast of a thousand victories will have his reputation destroyed by a single defeat, so the simple speaker of the poem is better off in his simple domestic life than the hero.

Cisneros, however, takes a fresh approach to boasting poetry, attacking the patriarchal society that produced this tradition. She takes the dishonorable curses and insults that are aimed at her, and instead of denying them or taking them as "fighting words" that would inspire a duel, she accepts them and turns them into her own boasts. In doing this, she turns the framework of archaic patriarchal society on its head.

Poetics

In the nineteenth century, poets began to experiment with free verse. This is a style of poetry that does not rely on traditional forms and meters (strict patterns of syllables) but rather on more important defining elements of poetry, such as figurative language and especially the pointed, complex control of ideas as well as words. "Loose Woman" is written in free verse. Large portions of it would sound indistinguishable from prose. One of the most notable poetic techniques used in "Loose Woman" is the poet's use of well-worn phrases, such as *hell on wheels* or the term *loose woman* itself. Cisneros chose phrases with negative connotations in the reader's mind and transforms the reader's expectations by giving them a positive value. Cisneros frequently recalls traditional poetic form, however, through the use of internal rhyme. In this case, there is no rhyme between the ends of adjacent lines, but between a word at the end of a line and another word inside a line.

Multilingualism

Cisneros, who is a Chicana, occasionally uses Spanish words in the poem. They are for the most part words that are likely to be known or at least comprehensible to educated English speakers but which may also have a particular nuance in Spanish. *Wáchale*, for instance, can mean both "look out, danger!" and "here's something worth seeing!," a combination not available in a single English word. Perhaps the main reason for her to use Spanish, however, is that it is likely to trigger a negative response from Americans who are bigoted against Latinos.

Cisneros is, after all, making an attack against sexism and racism and intends to provoke them. An interesting example of this triggering effect came early in 2015, when the state of Vermont proposed on its website adopting a new state motto in Latin. The message board of the announcement lit up with outspoken racist attacks against Latinos from people who misunderstood and thought the motto was in Spanish.

HISTORICAL CONTEXT

Racism

Although the oppressive social structures that "Loose Woman" targets are mostly directed to women, the poem also deals with racism. Its frequent use of Spanish suggests a valuing of Chicano culture and is a response to the anti-Chicano bigotry commonly faced in the United States. In particular, the speaker of the poem identifies herself with the well-known Pancho Villa. Villa was a revolutionary general fighting against the corrupt Mexican government in the first decades of the twentieth century. He fought for progressive liberal reform of the Mexican government and society. He is well known in the United States because, after several years of supporting Villa, the US army conducted a military raid into Mexico against him in 1916, favoring stability in Mexico over freedom as the US entry into World War I loomed. Villa, then, is a symbol of Chicano resistance to American racism and imperialism.

The poem's main statement against racism, though, is quite different and more enigmatic. This comes in the difficult line 45 of the poem, which uses a mocking imitation of Chinese language as heard by an English speaker, implying not just incomprehension but a terror of any culture perceived as different. The phrase is used in the United States as a slur against ethnic Chinese, as well as against anyone who is misperceived as being Chinese. In John Steinbeck's Depression-era novel *Cannery Row*, for example, a white boy uses it in a mocking chant against an old Chinese man: "Ching-Chong Chinaman sitting on a rail—'Long came a white man an' chopped off his tail." This kind of mockery is also to be heard during racist physical attacks against Chinese. The same phrase continues to be used occasionally in public discourse, by prominent media figures like Rosie

COMPARE
&
CONTRAST

- **1990s:** Latino immigration to the United States is not an important political issue; conflicts about immigration were temporarily defused in the 1980s by President Ronald Reagan's amnesty for illegal immigrants.

  Today: Latino immigration to the United States is one of the most controversial issues in American politics.

- **1990s:** Sexual relations between persons of the same sex are illegal in many states; gay marriage is illegal in all states.

Today: The Supreme Court decision *Lawrence v. Texas* (which came only in 2003) decriminalized homosexuality, and same-sex marriage is now legal throughout the United States.

- **1990s:** Cisneros is the first Chicana author to break through to a wider American audience.

  Today: Many Chicana authors, such as Cristina García and Laura Esquivel, are published by mainstream presses.

O'Donnell and Rush Limbaugh, though it is increasingly likely to be condemned. The line in which Cisneros uses the phrase herself is hard to decipher. None of the line is in English, and it is punctuated with exclamation points at the beginning and end of the line, after the Spanish fashion. The first three words are Spanish. They translate as "Where are you going?" Especially in its Latin form. *Quo vadis?*, this is a key phrase in Western literature and history. It has traditionally been used within Christian discourse to indicate an individual's moral choice: Will you continue on your sinful, self-destructive path or accept the authority of the Church and take the path of living righteously? The next two words are a French phrase commonly used in English to mean "in the fashion of." The final three words are the anti-Chinese slur. The implication seems to be that by living according to a socially imposed authoritarian construct (Christianity), the individual will be led to racial and other forms of bigotry. Interestingly, only someone deeply implicated in Western culture and its traditions could have written the line. The interpretation offered here seems to be confirmed by the next two lines. Line 46 confirms that the acceptance of Christianity is the socially expected answer to the issue raised. But in line 47, the speaker proudly identifies herself with anarchy, the breaking down of all social constructs

including Christianity. Resistance to racism, then, means the rejection of traditional culture and the constructs that have fostered it. Conservative social forces often cite the breakdown of religion as a modern social evil, but Cisneros views it instead as liberation, something to be proud of.

CRITICAL OVERVIEW

Owing to her status as perhaps the most important breakthrough Chicana writer, Cisneros has received a good deal of scholarly attention. Robin Ganz, in her largely biographical *MELUS* article on Cisneros (written just before the collection *Loose Woman* was published), gives an assessment of her whole body of work: "For readers and writers of Chicana literature, the 1980s signalled the emergence of voices of powers and pain which many previous decades of racism, poverty and gender marginalization had suppressed." Susan Smith Nash reviewed *Loose Woman* when it was published in 1994. She finds that the work is "squarely within the realm of American feminist poets and artists who privilege the role of experience in recentering and validating women's perspectives and ways of knowing." Nash finds that the result

Cisneros compares the sound of whispered rumors to the rustling of a skirt made of crinoline.
(© Tracey Patterson / Shutterstock.com)

seems to be realistic. However, Cisneros presents a psychologically charged perspective on apparent reality: she "probes the extremes of perceptions and negotiates the boundary regions that define the self and systems of knowledge required in constructing a notion of identity." While Nash does not single out the poem "Loose Woman" for comment, her conclusions about the book as a whole are certainly relevant to the title poem: "Cisneros appropriates (or reappropriates) icons of masculinity and engenders them female. The result is anarchic, funny, earthy, and absolutely affirming to all notions of female creative energy."

Suzanne Chávez-Silverman, in "Chicanas in Love," gives the most extensive criticism of the poem "Loose Woman" itself. From her postmodern feminist perspective, Chávez-Silverman observes that "the speaker re-codes her identity as powerful and dangerous by conceding to an unnamed (but obviously patriarchal) third person plural ('They') the truth in their naming of her." But in her assessment of the poem, Chávez-Silverman asks, "Has [Cisneros], in fact really 'broken' anything?" She answers in the negative. She finds that Cisneros has correctly identified that patriarchal society has imposed a scale of values on Chicanas between looseness or wickedness and virginity. But to merely idealize the loose woman is only to reverse the existing structure; it "repeats stereotypes of wantonness overdetermined for Chicanas in the dominant Anglo culture as well. To reverse the valency without problematizing the underpinning structure is to risk inevitable containment." In other words, accepting and enacting the role of the loose woman is still yielding to the patriarchal culture which created the stereotype.

Interestingly, Julia Alvarez, in her article "Ground Zero," has made the suggestion that some ideas in Cisneros's novel *The House on Mango Street* have thematic similarities with the Gospel of Thomas, the best known of the Nag Hammadi Gnostic texts. These documents represent alternative versions of Christianity, including some that promote ideas like gender equality. But because they were the subject of persecution by the official Church, they were lost until a cache of hidden Gnostic texts was discovered at Nag Hammadi in Egypt in the middle of the twentieth century.

CRITICISM

Bradley A. Skeen

Skeen is a classicist. In the following essay, he places Cisneros's "Loose Woman" in the context of thematically similar poems: Anne Sexton's "Her Kind" and the ancient poem "The Thunder: Perfect Mind."

Cisneros's "Loose Woman" is meant to challenge the patriarchal character of both Mexican and American society. Patriarchal society attempts to control women by shaming behavior, especially sexual behavior, that it considers transgressive. Women are to be prevented from making decisions about their own sexual lives by the threat of marginalization and rejection. "Loose Woman" portrays a woman taking control of her own sexual life and identity, something forbidden in traditional culture. Until quite recently in historical terms, the social

WHAT DO I READ NEXT?

- The only book-length biography of Cisneros is *Border Crossings and Beyond: The Life and Works of Sandra Cisneros* (2009), by Carmen Haydée Rivera. The work focuses on Cisneros's dual role as writer and activist within the Chicano community.

- *Wáchale!: Poetry and Prose about Growing Up Latino* (2001), edited by Ilan Stavans, is a collection of texts for young adults about the Latino experience in America. The texts, including poetry about the difficulties of overcoming racism, are printed in Spanish with facing English translations.

- *My Wicked, Wicked Ways* (1997) is Cisneros's first collection of poetry. It treats mainly the same themes as *Loose Woman*, the struggle for sexual freedom and gender equality within a patriarchal culture.

- *The Thunder: Perfect Mind: A New Translation and Introduction* (2010), by Hal Taussig and a large number of specialist collaborators, is the longest sustained treatment of the ancient poem "The Thunder: Perfect Mind"; it is meant to be accessible

to the general reading audience. It concentrates on literary analysis of the work rather than carrying out a full philosophical, theological, or historical investigation of the poem.

- Lorna Dee Cervantes's *Emplumada* (1981) is considered one of the most important volumes of poetry by a Latina author. The poems in the collection work together to tell a coming-of-age story based on the author's own life.

- The *House of the Spirits* (published in Spanish in 1982), by Isabel Allende, is a magic realist novel critical of the fascist regimes that ruled Chile and other South American countries during the period of its writing. Like "Loose Woman," it addresses the role of women in patriarchal Latin American culture. Its two protagonists are a father who must settle down from his sexually wild youth to enter a traditional marriage, and his daughter, who triumphs despite her sexual transgressive nature.

---

control exerted on women was still more severe. Husbands would be chosen by a girl's parents, and any attempt for a woman to find sexual expression and identity outside of marriage could be met with death as a penalty. Men, on the other hand, were able to choose any sexual partners they wished; in theory they were limited to their wives, but in practice they had a wide latitude of freedom. Cisneros is keenly interested in the stereotypes that were used to enforce social control, both positive stereotypes that women were supposed to follow, such as the chaste woman or the virgin, and negative stereotypes used to shame transgressive women. The latter type included stereotypes of the "loose woman" variety, stigmatizing women who made their own sexual decisions, or threatening stereotypes that embodied male fear of women's

sexuality, such as the witch. In "Loose Woman," Cisneros rejects the power of patriarchal society to decide for her which actions are good or bad. She embraces the negative stereotypes used for social control and proclaims them to be positive attributes. They then become powerful tools of resistance against patriarchy, since the stereotypes themselves are created from male fear.

Cisneros was not the first author to use poetry to analyze the patriarchal control of women. For a generation before her, this subject had been of great interest to feminist poets who emerged as the feminist movement developed in the 1950s. Anne Sexton's 1960 poem "Her Kind," for example, shares many themes with "Loose Woman." The title is semantically identical: "Her Kind" refers to a woman who transgresses the sexual boundaries of patriarchal

"'LOOSE WOMAN' PORTRAYS A WOMAN TAKING CONTROL OF HER OWN SEXUAL LIFE AND IDENTITY, SOMETHING FORBIDDEN IN TRADITIONAL CULTURE."

culture. In the narrative of the poem, its speaker is presented as a witch who is burned at the stake. She is really being punished for forsaking her domestic role and becoming a sexual predator. The witch's night flight is a thin veil for promiscuity. She directly attacks domestic virtues, dismissing children as so many whining worms. But the speaker of the poem is proud to be that kind of woman. Like Cisneros, she reappropriates the shameful negative stereotypes heaped upon her as self-defining acts of resistance to social control. Cisneros uses the same technique in "Loose Woman," but the accusation of being a witch is only one of the many verbal attacks that her patriarchal opponents make against her. In both poems, the speakers redefine themselves as indeed standing outside of patriarchal norms, but in a position of strength and independence rather than exile. The second-wave feminism of the 1950s and 1960s, together with closely aligned social movements like the new phase of the civil rights struggle, had to invent a new conception of social roles and norms, moving from the tight social control of women's lives to a new balance based on maximizing personal freedom, a value on which the United States was founded in opposition to medieval and ancient traditions of elite and social control of society.

Another poem that comes much closer to "Loose Woman" in both form and content is interesting because its relationship to Cisneros's work is enigmatic. There can be little doubt, given the conventions of her education, that Cisneros was thoroughly familiar with Sexton's work, although she purposefully rejected Anglo models for her poetry in her attempt to create a Chicana literature. The second poem in question, however, is "The Thunder: Perfect Mind," which was written by an unknown author almost two thousand years ago. The work was scarcely known in antiquity (it is not mentioned by any other surviving text) and was preserved only because a single copy of it was placed in a collection of mostly Gnostic (heretical Christian)

books that was buried in the mountains above the monastery of Nag Hammadi during a period of persecution of Gnostics among the Egyptian clergy in the fifth century. It was discovered and brought to the attention of scholars in 1948. "The Thunder: Perfect Mind" is, despite its obscurity, one of the most original and creative pieces of literature written in antiquity, and it is all the more important because, whatever its social setting (and the poem is probably not Gnostic or even Christian), it is surely not representative of the mainstream elite culture whose products dominate surviving ancient literature.

Any work of literature composed in an oppressive society would be able to use the technique of reappropriation in its struggle for freedom. Even in ordinary Christian literature, the poor, for instance, are raised up by the reappropriation of dismissive elite language, as in the quotation "Blessed are the meek: for they shall inherit the earth" (Matthew 5:5, KJV). The Greek word underlying "meek" (*praeis*) properly describes animals like horses that have been broken for domestic use. Applying the word to people would be to classify them as subhuman, yet Jesus reappropriates it as a blessing. So it is certainly possible, even likely, that the similarities between "The Thunder: Perfect Mind" and "Loose Woman" were shaped out of their common response to patriarchal oppression.

An intriguing possibility is that Cisneros was directly influenced by reading "The Thunder: Perfect Mind" in an English translation. In the 1998 network television show *Millennium* (in an episode titled "*Amnesis*," which is Greek for "recollection"), a high school girl starts reciting lines (in English) from "The Thunder: Perfect Mind" and the Gnostic Gospel of Mary Magdalene. Investigators are baffled and conclude that the girl must be inspired to recreate these ancient texts by some supernatural agency. They overlook the possibility that she had simply read the English translation of the Nag Hammadi texts prepared under the direction of James M. Robinson for a popular audience that had been available in any sizable library or bookstore since 1977. Scholars often react the same way when they see a piece of modern literature that contains Gnostic ideas, as if the modern author could never have read any Gnostic literature. Any critic studying Cisneros's work would take it for granted that she had read Sexton, but they do not tend to imagine any influence by the

Gnostic poem, even though Cisneros's poem has more in common with the ancient text. Although Gnostic themes are often identified in modern authors by critics, little thought is given to the possibility that the author in question has simply read an ancient book in translation and has been directly influenced in this way. It is certainly possible that Cisneros read "The Thunder: Perfect Mind" in English (though not in Spanish, since a comparable Spanish translation was not available until 2003). Whether or not Cisneros is familiar with it (she seems never to have mentioned Gnosticism in any public utterance), "The Thunder: Perfect Mind" is an important work that deserves to be better known. The fact that these two poems, two thousand years apart, can approach each other so closely is evidence of the endurance of the patriarchal traditions they both oppose.

"Loose Woman" also participates in the tradition of *boasting poetry*, a style that is found in ancient Greek and Roman epic poems. There, it developed into the *aretalogy*: the utterance of a god or goddess, such as Isis, stating her own praises. "The Thunder: Perfect Mind" is such an aretalogy. The speaker is a messenger of the highest god (that is, thunder), who is also *mind*, a very high level of divinity itself in Greek philosophy. Her utterances generally take the form of pairs of paradoxes (contradictory statements), some familiar from other religious texts. For example, Thunder says she is honored and scorned, and the first and the last. More relevant to Cisneros, Thunder describes herself as a prostitute and as holy. She is also a wife and a virgin. This very distinction recognizes the patriarchal judgment according to which women are either condemned or accepted. Cisneros does the same, and she chooses to declare herself to be the disfavored member of the pair, defiantly throwing her identity back in the face of patriarchy. The approach of "The Thunder: Perfect Mind" seems more subtle. The ancient poem resolves the contradictory pairs into single unified terms that participate in both identities at once. It actually denies the applicability of the categorization in the first place. The message is that human culture seeks to impose judgmental categories on women (and elsewhere in the poem on human beings generally), but divine wisdom does not recognize such human-created categories: "prostitute" and "holy one" can be the same thing, because neither term has any real meaning in the message Thunder delivers. Thunder also points

Another metaphor compares the way the speaker moves through her life, letting her heart carry her like a sail moves a boat through the water. (© cdrin / Shutterstock.com)

out the hypocrisy of the men who hate her. At the same time they try to shame her as sexually transgressive, they desire women who are sexually transgressive. But she cannot be shamed, because she is both shameless and ashamed. Cisneros's loose woman is similarly meant to be ashamed of the judgments patriarchal culture makes against her, but she is not, because she too is shameless.

Cisneros, Sexton, and the author of "The Thunder: Perfect Mind" all reject the patriarchal structure of their societies, which has persisted from antiquity down to America in the 1950s and even the 1990s. They all use similar strategies of naming themselves by the slurs their cultures would use to shame them, taking pride in their transgressive identities. By embracing the punishments and shame that the patriarchy heaps upon them, they render it powerless.

"TO CREATE SOMETHING IS TO STAVE OFF YOUR DEATH, IT IS TO STAVE OFF THE DYING OF YOUR SPIRIT. WHETHER YOU MAKE A POEM OR A JOKE OR A PIE OR A SONG, IT'S TO KEEP YOUR SPIRIT ALIVE, TO NOURISH IT."

Source: Bradley A. Skeen, Critical Essay on "Loose Woman," in *Poetry for Students*, Gale, Cengage Learning, 2016.

Nancy Sullivan and Sandra Cisneros

In the following interview excerpt, Cisneros gives advice to those who want to become writers.

...NS: Could you tell us more about the Macondo Writers' workshop that you founded?

SC: It's a very inclusive place. For me creation isn't separate from spirituality; it's the same, and so to not mention it is a little weird. It's not based on a hierarchy as are patriarchal workshops in the academy; it's a very egalitarian collective. We have a board, but we've been making the decisions on how we grow collectively, and all the writers are invited. They are humbled and put their egos aside; they're people that are writing with a sense of service to the community. We have people that are as young as twenty-three or twenty-four, all the way to professors emeritus in universities. One of the things I learned from organizing the MacArthur "Genius" Grant is that if you mix things up by age and by disciplines, it makes for wonderful creative solutions you wouldn't normally think about. That's another nice thing about Macondo that differentiates us from academic workshops. We might have a performance artist sitting next to an anthropologist sitting next to a screen-writer sitting next to a professor of history. We are only slowly opening the door because it would be a floodgate if we accepted everybody. So we're having to do things on a volunteer basis where everybody pays back. There's no fee except for registration, and that was only recent. Because we are doing things as volunteers, we can only take on so much without the quality going amuck. We want to keep that quality, so we are keeping it small. You have to be invited by another member to come into Macondo. So it

really becomes a community—about eighty people come in the summer, and that's a lot for a group of volunteers to work with. We don't have anyone that's full-time yet. That is part of the reason we don't accept open applications. The first job is the writing, and we don't want to be full-time administrators. We would just be overwhelmed, especially since we just had an article in this month's *Poets and Writers*. There's a photo too. The scary thing in the photo is me in costume. I'm in character as Viva Ozuna. I performed Viva's piece about shoplifting from *Caramelo*. Jump Start Theatre creates a whole theme around a guest artist. Last year it was Luis Rodriguez, and his theme was low riders. So we did a whole show with some hip-hop dancers and some low rider cars in front of the theater, but the star was Luis who read his stuff. It was called *Suavecito*, the low rider show from the early seventies.

So I thought, well, what am *I* going to do? I was wearing a Catholic girls' uniform so I wasn't one of those bad girls. It came to me when I was backstage that I was going to wear what I used to wear and be Lala's character with her friend Viva. But this is theater, and backstage is like a Fellini movie, which is one of the reasons I like doing this even though it's crazy to do it on the last night when I've been teaching. The theater hires a professional man, John McBurney, who comes and transforms us. He does theater, he does television, he does movie stars. He lives here in town and travels all over. Backstage you tell him what you want. So I say, "Okay I want to be a chola. I want a ponytail down to there." So he added a big ol' hairpiece, and he did my makeup on down til there [points to neck], blue eye shadow like a painting of John Valdez's. He did the whole number on me, and I turned into Viva Ozuna and realized I am not Lala—I am going to have to do the part from Viva Ozuna!

So they take a picture of me in *Poets and Writers* hugging Angela Kariotis, a Greek writer and a performance artist from New York. Nobody explained to me that they were going to use this photo. I mean I am in character! You look at this photo and I look like a real chola girl. I thought, "Oh my god!"

NS: It keeps other people guessing about you.

SC: There is a mythology about me, and I think I've created it. I am part of authoring the bullshit. The persona you create really isn't you when you're a poet or in a performance or a story. It's part of you, but it's parts of everybody,

everybody who comes into contact with you. You are like flypaper—you take a little bit of this woman who dances on the table and that one where you know that if you go out with her your clothes will be ruined. You put it together in an "I" voice and people expect that that's you. All of those voices are me to some degree, and none of them are. So this becomes the mythology. Then you start reading biographies about yourself and you go. "Oh no no no." So now this photo is going to come out in *Poets and Writers*, and people are going to go, "So you see she was a really tough street chick," but that's not me at all. I was the girl with the Catholic uniform.

NS: And the story grows from there!

SC: Exactly. It becomes part of the mythology. I make my living going through those truths, and it's wonderful if I fool them, but there's this part of me that people don't realize: that I like to play. I like playacting and dressing up.

NS: How can people read your work and not know that you like to play? It's in your books.

SC: I have no idea how they read that and not get it. People who know me know that I am *muy payasa*, very much a clown. I dress up and play. So sometimes when others see this kind of tough girl stance, they think that's not really me, but that's me playing the tough girl, or me pretending to be the ranchera. But it's not me.

EMJ: Perhaps this desire for play accounts for the humor in your work? How do you manage to keep up the humor in your writing, Caramelo, *for instance, when there is all this tragedy, all these losses, all these terrible things happening to the family?*

SC: I think humor is a weapon or an antidote to tragedy. If you don't laugh when things are the worst, then you die. You must laugh or else you die. To create something is to stave off your death, it is to stave off the dying of your spirit. Whether you make a poem or a joke or a pie or a song, it's to keep your spirit alive, to nourish it. It's at those times when I am writing from a very dark place that something absurd happens in the writing. I laugh, and then I realize that I'm going to live. If you can laugh, you can survive that day. You have vanquished your foe. It's like wrestling with the angel. You wrestle with the angel when you're going through those deaths or near-deaths, and you are resurrected when you laugh. But I don't set out intending to

laugh or say, "Now I am going to write and vanquish that angel of death." No, no, you just really feel terrible, but you have to keep writing, or you've got a deadline, or life goes on, and so you create something that day, and invariably it will take you to some place you didn't imagine. It astonishes you and makes you laugh. The pieces that are the most tragic parts of the book happened through the most tragic parts of my life in writing the book. Humor comes out in those blackest moments of our lives; the blackest moments in history are when people are most humorous because humor is a form of vanquishing death. Don't you think?

EMJ: That makes perfect sense.

SC: I don't *think* this, I just feel things very deeply. When you feel things very deeply, when you're in the lion's den, there is some absurdity to the moment. You have to draw yourself out and look at yourself as a viewer; you're split between it happening to you and viewing yourself, and it's very funny. When you see it from that point of view, you have to laugh because who could imagine you'd be in that situation?

EMJ: Writing, then, is a performance as well.

SC: You know, I really am lucky because I have Jump Start literally in my backyard, on the other side of the river. We performed one chapter of *Caramelo* here. See, every year we do a theme depending on who the famoso is. When it was my year, we did a Cabaret de Caramelo, and it was set in a 1950s Mexico City cabaret, and they did all of these performances. So you came into a nightclub—you had to dress in that era if you wanted to—and the actors played bartenders and cigarette girls and emcees, and there was a live band. The company actors did the performances, there was a crooner, Tongolele came out and danced in the spotlight in a tigress bikini, and I came out in this wonderful fifties ball gown that—fortunately you didn't see the back—didn't close. I had long Maria Callas opera-length gloves and my hair done up.

NS: Another picture for Poets and Writers!

SC: Yes. This is another persona. I came out like this diva. I did Maria Callas, and I read the chapter that Aunty Light Skin reads about the man whose name no one is allowed to mention [imitates loud music]. I would read a little bit, then there would be a caesura, and another act would come out. Then I would come back [imitates Aunty Light Skin's voice], "And so I was telling you..." That's how we did the show. It was great.

...NS: When you think about Chicana identity and Chicana writing in the twenty-first century are there certain expectations tied to that, a certain radicalism, for instance?

SC: We are all different types of Chicanas; we have very different experiences. We all come from different parts geographically. I don't know Pat [Mora] that well. I know Denise [Chávez] really well, and we can sit down and talk with each other. I know Ruth Behar, the Cuban writer. There are other writers that I am close to. We all do different things. It happened very early on when I was a young writer that I wasn't Chicana enough. People felt that I wasn't writing Chicano poetry because I was writing about love. I wasn't writing Chicano themes. But I always have dealt with my own themes, and I am a Chicana writer and that *is* who I am. I don't have any questions about what I am doing or why I am doing it. It's not an issue. I know who I am. There's always somebody who wants you to be their way of being a Chicana writer. But they don't know me and what I am doing. I do think that the women are very polite and supportive of each other. If we have differences or things that we don't like, we don't say it to each other's faces, unless you happen to be in a workshop. We figure there is enough violence out there that we don't need to. Even if we don't know each other well, there is still a respect and camaraderie.

EMJ: You said in your disclaimer in Caramelo *that writing is asking questions. What kinds of questions are you working on now? Can you talk about your most recent projects?*

SC: I'm still adding to this essay about color and race and my father and secrets. I just came back from Buenos Aires and I still haven't put down on paper all of my notes of that trip. I don't know what I feel about that trip. There is a lot floating around that doesn't have language until I write it down. I have a children's book I need to work on. I have poetry that I've been looking to tweak and finish. I have some new things and I have essays that I am working on. So some of these answers, talking about Chicago and its emotions, are the germs for an essay that I can present when I go to Chicago, attitudes about Chicago, possibly for that new introduction [to the anniversary edition of *The House on Mango Street*]. Talking to people will lead to writing essays because I will say something and

go, "Well that's right," and then I will go and sit down and then I've got an essay. I've got two different essay projects and several little kettles.

EMJ: Do you have time to write set aside? Are you very disciplined in terms of your writing?

SC: No. No, whenever I cannot put on my shoes and leave the house is a good thing. That's when I can do it.

NS: Can you work in small blocks of time? Or do you need four or five hours?

SC: Well, I need a block. But I try to do what I can. I've been gone, and you know how it is when you go. I still have two suitcases on the floor and a bag full of receipts and my whole desk is covered.

NS: Do you have some advice for a student of mine who wants to be a writer? She's thirty years old, the first in her family to go to a university and her parents are pressuring her, expecting her to get married, which she is resisting. What can she do to get on her path to being a writer?

SC: I kept putting off children and a marriage because I had other, bigger plans. For a long time in my forties I thought I had to get married to fulfill my father's wish. But when I turned fifty, I realized that I didn't have to get my father's approval anymore. Even though he was spirit, I didn't have to do that. When I was walking down the street a couple of years ago in Havana, a very very dark man with white hair was walking down the street talking to two very dark women with white hair, and he was saying, "No, no es mi novia," she's not my girlfriend, "es l'amor de mi vida."

They giggled, and I giggled too, and I was so glad I happened to be walking down the street at that moment because I realized that's what I want. I don't want a husband; I want a "l'amor de mi vida." So I decided that I was going to have a "l'amor de mi vida" ceremony when I'm fifty-five. The reason why I wanted to get married wasn't that I want to get *married*, I wanted a party and a dress. That's what women want, so why don't we create something where you don't have to get married and can have a big party and the dress and the gifts. So I am going to reinvent it, and I'm going to have a "l'amor de mi vida" ceremony. It's going to be just splendid, all the women that come will dress as "the one" and create their own headdresses, and the men are part of the party. It will be like a circus. It would be like my dream of a Busby Berkeley. I always wanted to jump out of a cake; maybe I'll do this. This is like the whole big party that I never got for my birthday, only better. I asked my partner if he would not marry me, and he said no. And I said, now ask me, and I said no, I won't marry you, so we both agreed that we are going to have this ceremony. It will be a lot of fun.

NS: And some advice to my student?

SC: Well, first she has to hang around with writers. You can't become a writer just alone. You must *write* alone. But you've got to have a community. Sometimes that community is on the Internet, and sometimes that community is in the library, in books on the shelf. You have to hang around with writers, whether they are on paper or over cyberspace or in a workshop you go to once in a while, because even though writing is done in solitude, editing is done with your friends. That's how you grow. So you need to keep company with writers in the library, or in the books that are going to lead you to books, or through teachers that will lead you to the books. Also, it's important to have an independent means of income. That means a college degree or several, but it doesn't mean that you have to do your degree in that field, writing. But if you can, do it in some field where it'll support you, where you won't be homeless, where you will have health insurance. You have to understand that you're always going to have two jobs, and you have to remind yourself that your first job is your writing. The second one is your day job.

NS: When did you get rid of your day job?

SC: Some writers are very good and never get rid of their day jobs. You should never aspire. If it happens, you are grateful, but you shouldn't wait for it to happen because it never may in your lifetime. That is just the way it is. I mean, me tocó, it was just my luck. There are people who are better writers, and they never lose their day jobs. One percent of writers make their money from their writing. One percent! But for some reason, maybe because my first book [*The House on Mango Street*] is the one that has blurred across borders as to who it's for, it's allowed me to continue writing and to do wonderful things with that book—it's been an amazing journey that first book has taken me to. I meant it for all ages, so it has endured.

Your student just needs to understand that she'll have two jobs and that maybe those two jobs won't allow for children or a partner. They may, but it might be a rather unsympathetic partner who won't like that you have two jobs. And you know what? Get in contact with other writers because she needs to find her spiritual family. Her spiritual family will be who will lead her forward and give her support. That's what Macondo does. We are spiritual families. We are writers who are homeless or whose families don't understand them. You have to find your community, and that's called becoming an adult. It leads you forward and understands you. It is like being gay. You know your family is not going to help you with that, but other gay people will. Writing is like that too, you've got to find your community.

Source: Nancy Sullivan and Sandra Cisneros, "'Muy Payada': Conversation with Sandra Cisneros," in *Conversations with Mexican American Writers: Languages and Literatures in the Borderlands,* edited by Elisabeth Mermann-Jozwiak and Nancy Sullivan, University Press of Mississippi, 2009, pp. 64–67, 74–78.

Elizabeth Coonrod Martinez
In the following essay, Martinez gives an overview of Cisneros's career.

Little did she realize when she crafted a series of brief, poetic narratives about growing up in an inner city barrio that her accounts would forever mark the inception of women's participation in Chicano literature. At the time, the narratives were not accepted as part of her master's thesis, as the objective was poetry, so she put them aside. A few years later, Sandra Cisneros offered them up when an acquaintance sought material for publication. And a few more years later, that collection of narratives turned into her widely acclaimed first novel, *The House on Mango Street,* which has now sold over five million copies. It is now being re-issued in celebration of its 25th anniversary, with a special foreword by the author.

Cisneros did not require an entourage, a prestigious academic appointment, or a Pulitzer to become the iconic writer of Chicano literature. In fact, she continues to live humbly in a town far from the glamour and city lights connected with most big-name writers. But big she is. "If only I could have the Sandra-luck," is the refrain of many young writers. Sandra's appearance at venues in any city guarantees packed audiences and star-struck fans, and academic articles about her work easily quadruple those on other Chicano writers. Her books have been

COMPOSED DURING HER 30S, THESE POEMS SHOW HER LITERARY INFLUENCES AND HER GROWTH AS A WOMAN."

translated into sixteen languages including the unusual Thai, Croatian, Iranian, and Turkish.

One Hundred Years of Solitude by Gabriel Garcia Marquez is often thought of as the book that launched intrinsically Latin American literature onto the world stage. In a similar way, *The House on Mango Street* marked the emergence of literature written by Chicanos, that segment of people of Mexican heritage who grow up in the United States and primarily function in English. As Garcia Marquez's characters were born out of Colombian history, so the characters of Cisneros' first novel emerged from her own Chicago barrio.

The House on Mango Street continues to inspire interest and sales. The novel is often selected by public and community libraries as an annual "read"; it is found on college and high school reading lists; and it is even used by leaders of groups like the Girl Scouts to encourage female role models. Its ability to provide multiple levels of understanding surely contributes to its sales. The novel is recognized for its symbolic interpretations and for instilling ethnic awareness in young readers. Readers know she won't shy away from such difficult issues as rape, racism, poverty, and community ostracism, or realities like women being locked into their apartments by their husbands when they leave for work. Librarians and community leaders suggest this novel because they understand that it taps into a spiritual and cultural understanding of women's lives.

Long before her novel garnered attention, Cisneros published her first book of poetry, *Bad Boys*, in 1980; a second, *The Rodrigo Poems*, in 1985; and a third, *My Wicked, Wicked Ways*, in 1987. *The House on Mango Street* did not have notable sales until after its second release in 1989. During the 1990s, she burst on the scene.

Born in Chicago in 1954, Cisneros grew up "very aware of poverty" in inner city neighborhoods alongside Puerto Ricans and African

Americans. Her father instilled in her a "strong self-esteem," and her mother introduced her to libraries and museums. The only daughter among six children, Cisneros was independent, a bookworm who started writing poems at age eleven. She determined her own path, entering college right after high school and then pursuing a masters degree in creative writing at the University of Iowa Writer's Workshop. She returned to Chicago in 1978.

When Cisneros received the first fellowship she applied form—a National Endowment for the Arts (NEA) grant—in 1982, she traveled to Europe and continued writing stories. Before she left, the founder of the Arte Publico Press, Nicolas Kanellos, asked her for some stories. Cisneros gave him the accounts she had written in Iowa, what would later be recognized as the first three chapters of *The House on Mango Street*. "I would have given them to someone else, but he asked first, so he got them," she says. When he wanted more, she complied. Kanellos wanted to publish them in a book. "That was November 1982. I didn't know better, so I gave him control." Unfortunately, "he decided to copy-edit it; he would add verbs, add objects. He had made a lot of interpolations, changes."

Her poetic reasons had been lost. "I always thought my work was very good. I was doing him a favor." She wanted to stop publication, but a first edition went out. Kanellos stated he could not find her (she was traveling in Europe), and for that reason he went ahead with his corrections. The Arte Publico arrangement was not a lucrative endeavor. "I got paid maybe 500 dollars total, and I would receive it in chorritos (spurts)." Cisneros struggled for years to regain control of her rights as an artist.

In 1987, while surviving on a part-time teacher's salary in northern California, "an independent book seller gave me [literary agent] Susan Bergholz's number, saying 'she's looking for you.'" But Cisneros only tucked the piece of paper into her files. She was feeling despair over her immediate future and drove home for a holiday break with her parents. Her mother told her there was a letter for her from Washington, DC. "It was my second NEA grant. I had forgotten I had applied for it." Now more optimistic, she returned to California, where "Gary Soto got me a writer-in-residence semester in Berkeley." Cisneros launched into finalizing what would comprise her collection of short stories, *Woman Hollering Creek*, published in 1991.

But first, she contacted Bergholz, who arranged the buyout of her rights for *House*. Its re-release was followed by *Woman Hollering Creek*, which received the PEN Center West award for Best Fiction of the year and three additional literary awards. It was also selected as book of the year by several major newspapers. Bergholz asked her, "What else do you have?" and Cisneros responded, "Well, some nasty poetry that no one wants to publish. And she said, 'send it to me.'" Her poems have caused a bit of a scandal from time to time as well as avid praise.

"I think we censor ourselves so much, *Loose Woman* was peligroso. I like writing from that place that's taboo because as women we always [revert] to the place that's good and correct." The title "was not intended to be scandalous but artistic. It carne from having read and greatly enjoyed the Poemas sueltas by Jaime Sabines." Composed during her 30s, these poems show her literary influences and her growth as a woman. Cisneros states: "I was coming from reading the Boom writers and poets like Parra and Borges. I wanted to cross-pollinate. I liked the short-shorts that were in vogue. Even now I don't think people know about experimental fiction."

Loose Woman, published by New York giant Knopf in 1994, Sold a very respectable 70,000 copies. She published a children's book, *Pelitos*, that same year, and in 1995 was given a MacArthur Foundation Fellowship—dubbed the "genius grant." This financial stability supported the creation of her extensive second novel, *Caramelo*, published in 2002. It has received remarkable critical attention and has sold 250,000 copies. In a surprising twist, it has been a big hit in Spain. In a nation that is now greatly influenced by immigrants (some 1.5 million according to Spain's 2003 census), this immigrant's story (based on the life of Cisneros' father) seems to have struck a chord and symbolized the journey of many families. The novel also highlights textiles, songs, cuisine, and historic locations, details that evoke a sense of nostalgia and longing for one's roots.

Built around the story of a shawl of unique caramel color, the 450 page novel took some ten years to write. Now in her 50s, Cisneros says, "I don't think I want to write a novel again. It was

so hard, took so long. I didn't want to write a traditional novel, beginning, middle, end. No! That's not how I write. A story cannot be conventional." The novel itself was a personal journey.

"I am North American, but I was never colonized. My mother grew up with an inferiority complex, clumsy about emotions. I felt the great culture of Mexico through my father. His family was high-level; he always held his head high, told us about his family's prestige. In Mexico he never felt second-class like the Mexicans in Chicago were treated. But my mother gave me the freedom to break rules. If I had had only one of them, I could not be a writer."

Cisneros wanted to "give back to the community, right an inequity, and donate time to helping other writers." Many years ago she established the Macondo Foundation to help new writers. In 2003, the state of Texas honored Cisneros with its annual Medal of the Arts, the same year *Vintage Cisneros*, a compilation of her works, was published.

Cisneros' advice for new writers is not to give in. "I tell stories. I still feel we [Latinos] have great stories to tell. I see other writers, especially women, who don't give first importance to their work. They give away their time to others.... You have to tap into what you like, what you're passionate about. That way research will be fun."

Source: Elizabeth Coonrod Martinez, "Humble Creator of an Iconic Novel," in *Americas*, Vol. 61, No. 3, May–June 2009, p. 62.

Raul Nino

In the following review, Nino praises Cisneros's "singular voice."

Alegria is Spanish for joy, and joy is the prevailing emotion in these poems. Being a woman is better than being a man, and there's more to ponder in the relation between life and the task of living it—these themes run through Cisneros' fiery new poems. Cisneros basks in her womanhood, taking time to point out the delicate antique French lace on her bed, then exposing the grittier fabric of passion and the lust of wanting. The whole collection reflects a nervy turning of decorum's heavy stones exposing the rich soil of a woman's singular voice. These poems are not so much a self-discovery as they are a reaffirmation of the self. Cisneros teases the imagination, then leaves little for it to do; she lets loose with a punch, and then it's a cuff that makes you laugh with empathy more than pain.

Source: Raul Nino, Review of *Loose Woman*, in *Booklist*, Vol. 90, No. 17, May 1, 1994, p. 1576.

Publishers Weekly
In the following review, the anonymous reviewer points out some faults in Cisneros's poems but describes others as "excellent."

This collection reveals the same affinity for distilled phrasing and surprise, both in language and dramatic development, found in Cisneros's volumes of short stories, *Woman Hollering Creek* and *The House on Mango Street*. For a glimpse of it, see the poem "Josie Bliss": "a tropical dream / of Wednesdays / a bitter sorrow / like the salt / between the breasts." Of the book's four parts, the first two immerse the reader in the Chicana homefront, including the poet's own place in it, presumably the San Antonio familiar from her prose work. The remaining two parts leave the barrio behind, as the author's world becomes more cosmopolitan and still more personal. Here Cisneros reflects on herself and her men, on how she treats them and they her. Although some poems in the last sections are excellent—"No Mercy," with its air of a prosecutors brief, is splendid—as a love poet, Cisneros attitudinizes too much and uses her tight style more to ration her candor than to impel images. Even so, a disconcerting degree of sentimentality somehow gets through ("I forget the reasons, but I loved you once, / remember?"), along with some enervated deadpan humor: "I've leaned two things. / To let go / clean as kite string. / And to never wash a man's clothes. / These are my rules."

Source: Review of *My Wicked Wicked Ways*, in *Publishers Weekly*, Vol. 239, No. 49, November 9, 1992, p. 78.

SOURCES

Alvarez, Julia, "Ground Zero," in *To Mend the World: Women Reflect on 9/11*, edited by Marjorie Agosín and Betty Jean Craige, White Pine, 2001, pp. 21–24.

Chávez-Silverman, Suzanne, "Chicanas in Love: Sandra Cisneros Talking Back and Alicia Gaspar De Alba 'Giving Back the Wor(l)d,'" in *Chasqui: revista de literatura Latinoamericana*, Vol. 27, No. 1, 1998, pp. 33–46.

Cisneros, Sandra, "Loose Woman," in *Loose Woman*, Alfred A. Knopf, 1994, pp. 112–15.

Einarrsson, Stefán, "Old English *Beot* and Old Icelandic *Heitstrenging*," in the *Proceedings of the Modern Language Association*, Vol. 49, No. 4, 1934, pp. 975–93.

Foucault, Michel, *The History of Sexuality*, Vol. 1: *An Introduction*, translated by Robert Hurley, Vintage, 1990, p. 101.

Ganz, Robin, "Sandra Cisneros: Border Crossings and Beyond," in *MELUS*, Vol. 19, No. 1, 1994, pp. 19–29.

Gram, David, "Confused Critics Blast Latin Motto Plan," in *Burlington Free Press*, February 6, 2015, http://www.burlingtonfreepress.com/story/news/local/2015/02/06/confused-critics-blast-latin-motto-plan/23012921/ (accessed April 23, 2015).

Homer, *The Odyssey of Homer*, translated by Richmond Lattimore, Harper & Row, 1965, pp. 121–36.

MacRae, George W., translator, "The Thunder: Perfect Mind," in *The Nag Hammadi Library in English*, 3rd ed., edited by James M. Robinson, Harper & Row, 1988. pp. 295–303.

Nash, Susan Smith, Review of *Loose Woman*, in *World Literature Today*, Vol. 69, No. 1, 1995, pp. 145–46.

Perrault, Charles, "The Fairy," in *The Tales of Mother Goose*, translated by Charles Welsh, D. C. Heath, 1901, pp. 75–79.

Sexton, Anne, "Her Kind," in *The Complete Poems*, Houghton Mifflin, 1981, pp. 15–16.

Steinbeck, John, *Cannery Row*, Penguin, 2002, p. 21.

FURTHER READING

Cisneros, Sandra, *Caramelo*, translated by Liliana Valenzuela, Knopf, 2002.

Like *The House on Mango Street*, *Caramelo* is a largely autobiographical coming-of-age story. It is based on the earliest period of Cisneros's life, when her family restlessly moved between Chicago and Mexico City. It is Cisneros's only major work originally written in Spanish.

———, *Woman Hollering Creek and Other Stories*, Random House,1991.

In this collection of short stories, widely noted for their poetic language, Cisneros layers a critique of the alienating forces of society acting on Mexican Americans on top of her more deeply felt resistance to the forces exerted against women.

Madsen, Deborah L., *Understanding Contemporary Chicana Literature*, University of South Carolina Press, 2000.

In this survey, Madsen devotes a chapter to Cisneros, giving a general introduction and focusing on the gender politics in her work.

Villanueva, Alma Luz, *Gracias: New Poems*, Wings, 2015.

Gracias is the latest collection of poetry by Villanueva, perhaps the most important Chicana poet of the generation before Cisneros's. These poems represent a spiritual migration from the United States back to Central America. This reflects in part her recent move to the artists' community of San Miguel Allende in Mexico, where Cisneros also now lives.

SUGGESTED SEARCH TERMS

Sandra Cisneros

"Loose Woman" AND Cisneros

Chicana

patriarchy

Toads and Diamonds

feminism

"The Thunder: Perfect Mind"

reappropriation

Mid-Term Break

SEAMUS HEANEY

1966

"Mid-Term Break" is a lyric poem about the death of Seamus Heaney's younger brother Christopher, who was killed by a car while Heaney was away at school. First published in *Death of a Naturalist* in 1966, the poem is an example of Heaney's early work in that he shares his personal experiences. Heaney uses realistic descriptions to create emotional responses in his readers. This honest account of grief explores the themes of family, death, and tragedy that were so relevant to the people of Northern Ireland at the time. "Mid-Term Break" was republished in Heaney's *Opened Ground: Selected Poems, 1966–1996*, published in 1998, and can also be found in *The Wadsworth Anthology of Poetry* (2005) and the anthology *The Death of a Child* (2011).

AUTHOR BIOGRAPHY

The oldest of nine children, Seamus Justin Heaney was born on April 13, 1939, in Castledawson, County Londonderry, in Northern Ireland. Heaney was raised in a Catholic family in Protestant-dominated Northern Ireland when discrimination against Catholics was commonplace. Heaney earned a scholarship to the boarding school St. Columb's College when he was twelve. His four-year-old brother Christopher was killed in a traffic accident in 1953, while Heaney was away at school.

Seamus Heaney (© Colin McPherson / Corbis)

Heaney went on to study literature, Irish, and Latin at Queen's University Belfast, where he graduated in 1961. He earned a teaching certificate from St. Joseph's College, also in Belfast, and he briefly worked as a teacher. Heaney returned to St. Joseph's College as a lecturer before taking a position as lecturer at Queen's University. He married fellow poet Marie Devlin, and the couple had three children together. The *New Statesman* published three of Heaney's poems in 1964, drawing attention to his talent. His first volume of poetry, *Death of a Naturalist*, was released in 1966 and contains the poem "Mid-Term Break." *Door into the Dark* followed in 1969. Heaney's work is part of Ireland's Northern School of poetry, often addressing the violent conflicts that occurred in Northern Ireland throughout his life. Heaney and his family moved away from Belfast in 1972, when he left Queen's University, and they migrated to the Republic of Ireland. From 1976 to 1981 Heaney served as the head of the English Department at Carysfort Teachers' Training College in Dublin.

Over the years, he spent periods teaching at other universities, including Berkeley, Harvard, and Oxford.

Along with his poetry, Heaney authored lectures, literary criticism, plays, and translations. He was awarded the Nobel Prize in Literature in 1995 "for works of lyrical beauty and ethical depth, which exalt everyday miracles and the living past." Heaney's most famous translation is *Beowulf: A New Verse Translation*, which became a *New York Times* best-selling book after its publication in 2000. Heaney served as director of the Field Day Theatre Company, which performed many of the plays he adapted, including *The Cure at Troy: A Version of Sophocles' "Philoctetes"* (1990). He suffered a stroke in 2006, which limited his ability to travel with his work. After being hospitalized during an illness, he died on August 30, 2013, in Dublin.

POEM SUMMARY

The text used for this summary is from *Opened Ground: Selected Poems, 1966–1996*, Farrar, Straus and Giroux, 1998, p. 11. Versions of the poem can be found on the following web pages: http://www.poetryfoundation.org/poem/247816 and http://www.poemhunter.com/poem/mid-term-break/.

"Mid-Term Break" is a twenty-two-line poem divided into seven three-line stanzas and a final line set apart in its own stanza. It is a free-verse poem with no consistent rhyme scheme or metrical pattern throughout. While the meter does not follow a clear pattern, it is predominantly iambic. The lyric poem is written in the first person as the poet recalls the death of his younger brother.

Lines 1–6

The first stanza comprises two complete sentences. The poet is waiting at the school's medical facility in the first line, which creates an ominous tone. In line 2, while he waits, he keeps count of the chimes. The third word of the line connotes church bells and funerals, reinforcing the tone of the poem. Consonance appears prominently in the line, such as with the *cl-* of the fourth and sixth words. The end of the sentence signals the end of the poet's waiting. Line 3 is a complete sentence. Here, friends of the family drive the poet back to his household. The period at the end of the stanza signals the end of the drive.

MEDIA ADAPTATIONS

- *Seamus Heaney: Collected Poems* is a collection of fifteen CDs of the poet's work, including "Mid-Term Break." The collection is read by Heaney and was produced by Faber & Faber. The run time is 720 minutes.

- Heaney can be heard reading "Mid-Term Break" while a slide show of still photographs plays in the background in a video posted to YouTube, at https://www.youtube.com/watch?v = uF0U0pVK0bk.

The second stanza moves to the poet's family home. He finds his father weeping at the entrance to the home. The dash at the end of line 4 breaks with the image of the weeping father, to connect it to the poet's memory in line 5. In the last three words of line 5, the poet uses an expression revealing that his father is usually calm at wakes. Line 5 also marks the first time that the author directly says he is at a wake. The dash at the end of this line creates a pause while returning to the poet's present observations. In line 6, a mourner tells the poet that the loss is a particularly difficult one. The line's final five words foreshadow the cause of death, which is not revealed until the end of the poem. The end stop completes the poet's observation of his father.

Lines 7–15

In the third stanza the poet enters the house. Line 7 shifts the mood of the poem. Here the poet observes his infant sibling playing in the stroller, unaware of the finality and loss of death. The poet reveals that he is self-conscious in lines 8–10, when the older males at the wake shake his hand and offer their condolences. The poet uses enjambment in the lines of the third stanza; in avoiding punctuation at the ends of lines, he connects them and creates a sense of continuous thought and feeling. The comma in line 8 creates a caesura, or pause, between the poet's observation of his sibling and his personal discomfort with the mourners. The enjambment of line 9 continues the scene in the fourth stanza.

The period at the end of line 10 concludes the poet's encounter with the well-wishers who quote the standard words of comfort given to people in mourning. The poet's discomfort, however, continues in lines 11–12. He listens to people he does not know talking about him in hushed tones. They say that he is the oldest child and has been away at school. A comma in line 12 creates another caesura, which turns the readers' attention away from the people talking to the poet's mother, who holds the poet's hand. Enjambment, used again, continues the poet's observation of his mother into the fifth stanza.

In line 13, Heaney's mother is still holding his hand. She does not cry, as his father does. Rather, she exhales in anger as she holds on to her son's hand. The period at the end of the line concludes the poet's description of his mother. A medical vehicle arrives that night in line 14. Enjambment connects its arrival to line 15 and reveals that the vehicle has brought the body. The comma creates another caesura to transition to the fact that medical professionals have prepared the body. The period at the end of the line concludes the poet's observations of other people.

Lines 16–22

The sixth stanza transitions to the following day. The poet views the body in the first sentence in line 16. The placement of the period and lack of punctuation at the end of the line create another combination of caesura and enjambment. The flowers that end line 16 are symbolic of hope. In this case, they would symbolize the hope of life after death. The flowers and lighting beside the body seem soothing to the poet in line 17. Additionally, the fifth word of the sentence describes the coffin as like a bed, creating a serene scene. The semicolon creates another caesura. At the end of line 17, the poet remembers the last time that he saw his brother, and enjambment carries the idea to line 18. He saw his brother six weeks earlier. The period in line 18 is a caesura. The line ends with the first two words of the next sentence. The poet notes the paleness of the body and uses a comma to create a brief pause.

In the seventh stanza, line 19 uses metaphor to describe a flower-colored, or perhaps flower-shaped, bruise on the boy's head. The flower that the poet chooses for his description connotes death. The line ends with a comma before the description continues in line 20. The poet relates the small dimensions of the coffin, which hint at the young age of his brother. He also uses a simile to again compare the coffin to a bed. A period ends the line. The state of the body is described in line 21. The body is whole because the boy was thrown aside when the car hit him. A period ends the line and stanza.

Line 22 stands alone, but it rhymes with line 21, which connects the two. Here the poet repeats the dimensions of the box before revealing that his brother had lived for just four years when he died.

THEMES

Death

Death is the unescapable theme in "Mid-Term Break." Heaney specifically focuses on how people respond differently to the death of a loved one. In line 4, for example, the poet's father is weeping over the death of his son. Heaney explains that his father never wept at the death of loved ones before this funeral. His mother, on the other hand, does not display her emotions in the same way. She does not weep but exhales wordless rage in line 13. She does, however, demonstrate the need for connection and support when she holds on to the hand of her son. The poet's infant sibling displays the reaction of innocence to death. The child is happy and playful because there is no understanding of the finality of death.

The poem itself is Heaney's reaction to the death of his brother, sharing his personal observations and feelings. He is uncomfortable with the attention people give him in line 8 and notes the different and unexpected reactions of those around him. His face-to-face encounter with death occurs in the final seven lines of the poem, where he gives a realistic description of seeing his brother's body. The language he uses here shows his contrasting emotions. For example, the coffin is compared to a bed in line 20, giving the impression of peaceful slumber, while the deeply colored bruise and the explanation in line 19 serve as a reminder that the young boy was violently killed.

Family

Heaney addresses the importance of family in "Mid-Term Break." The poet finds his father's reaction to his brother's death unsettling, as it shows how deeply the loss of a child affects a

TOPICS FOR FURTHER STUDY

- Read *The Book Thief* (2005), by Markus Zusak. This young-adult book is set in Nazi Germany and narrated by none other than Death. In a group of three, write a one-act play in which Heaney, Death, and one other character from the novel meet. Record yourselves acting out the play, and upload it using EDpuzzle.

- Research the history of Northern Ireland's civil rights movement. Create a web page that provides an overview of significant events and individuals, and be sure to include information on Heaney.

- Read *Maya Angelou* (2013), edited by Edwin Graves Wilson as part of the Poetry for Young People series, and choose a poem to consider alongside "Mid-Term Break." Write a paper that compares and contrasts the style and themes of the two poems and present your paper in front of the class.

- Research the history of Northern Irish poetry up to the present day. Take note of influential poets along with the times in which they lived and the themes and topics they addressed. Create a graphic to display this information using Easel.ly and present your findings to the class.

- Research the different meanings and connotations of snowdrops and poppies. Write your own poem using one or both of the flowers, and post it on a blog. Include, music, pictures, or other artwork to help readers better understand your poem.

parent. Unlike at other funerals, his father is unable to conceal his grief. While his mother does not weep, her rage is clear. The loss of her son incites anger that she cannot express in words, but no words have to be spoken for the poet to understand what his mother is truly feeling.

While the family members grieve differently, they find comfort in each other. The need to be

The speaker comes home to find his father crying, though he usually is not upset by funerals. (© nando viciano
/ Shutterstock.com)

with family is clear when the poet's mother holds on to his hand; after losing one child, she clings to another. The house is filled with people, but they serve only to make the poet uncomfortable. It seems that he is unable to process the loss until the next day, when he is alone with his brother. The poet looks at his brother the same way any older sibling would: the boy looks as if he is sleeping in bed—but at this point the boy's death is far too real to deny. The poem's final four lines, in describing how the poet's brother died, convey the emotional reaction to losing a sibling and the void that it creates in a family.

Tragedy

Death is always tragic, but the death of a four-year-old boy is particularly heartbreaking. The parents far outlived their child, and the poet outlived his younger brother. The tragic moments recounted in the poem remind the reader of the weight of the poet's family's loss. Throughout the poem, Heaney presents scenes that reinforce the great personal tragedy that the family is facing.

The first tragic scene is the poet's father's acting so out of character by weeping in public. The anguish of losing a child is more than the typically stoic father can bear. The innocent and happy infant, in turn, creates a moment of normalcy in the poem. The image of a happy, playing child serves to highlight further the loss of another playful sibling.

The anger of the poet's mother is another clear moment of human suffering. She is unable to express her feelings in a roomful of people. Her physical and emotional connection to the poet when she holds his hand shows the bond between a mother and son. Showing this bond between mother and son reminds readers of the bond she lost with her younger son's death.

The poet's description of the body also serves to highlight the tragedy of his brother's death. He uses metaphor to compare the child's coffin with a child's bed, which serves as a reminder of the boy's young age. The repeated size of the coffin and the poem's final clause also reinforce the tragedy of a child's death.

STYLE

Figurative Language

"Mid-Term Break" uses figurative language, specifically simile and metaphor, to express ideas. In *A Glossary of Literary Terms*, M. H. Abrams defines *simile* as "a comparison between two distinctly different things . . . explicitly indicated by the word 'like' or 'as.'" For example, line 20 uses a simile to describe the coffin as a bed.

Line 19 shows an example of a metaphor. Abrams defines *metaphor* as "a word or expression that in literal usage denotes one kind of thing . . . applied to a distinctly different kind of thing." The discoloration on the boy's head is described as a flower without using a comparative word, making it an example of a metaphor.

Lyric Poem

According to Abrams, a lyric "is any fairly short poem, consisting of the utterance by a single speaker, who expresses a state of mind or a process of perception, thought, and feeling." "Mid-Term Break" begins with the first-person pronoun *I*, which introduces the poet's personal experience with what follows. The poet describes the death of his brother in outwardly realistic terms, but he does share his own inward feelings and observations. For example, he recalls his father's reaction to funerals in the past to contrast his reaction to the death described in the poem in line 5. He also shares how uncomfortable he is with the attention he receives at the funeral in line 8. When Heaney views the body, it is apparent that he believes that his brother's death was unjust. He repeats the size of the coffin in lines 20 and 22 to emphasize how young his brother was. While Heaney does not use emotional language in the poem, his experience is clearly conveyed and thus creates emotion in his readers.

HISTORICAL CONTEXT

The Irish Partition

The conflict in Northern Ireland between Catholics and Protestants goes back centuries. When Henry VIII attempted to spread the English Reformation throughout England, Ireland, and Scotland, Ireland resisted. The political influence of Catholics and Protestants shifted with the beliefs of different British monarchs. By the seventeenth century, many Protestant settlers from Scotland and England traveled to Ireland, where they displaced the rights and authority of the Catholic residents. Feargal Cochrane points out in *Northern Ireland: The Reluctant Peace*, "A series of 'Penal Laws' was also enacted at the end of the seventeenth century in an attempt to subjugate the Catholic population." Catholics were prohibited from voting, being educated, holding office, or bearing arms.

Irish home-rule bills, intended to grant Ireland independence from Great Britain, were introduced over the years. The third home-rule bill was introduced in 1912, when Nationalists supported Irish home rule and the bill. The Unionists, who were mainly Protestants in the northern counties, desired to remain a dominion of Great Britain. The bill was ignored during the crisis of World War I. The lengthy duration of the war, however, caused unrest in what was already a tense relationship between Ireland and England. Nationalist groups began to splinter during the war over the use of force in the fight for home rule. Violence soon broke out and continued after the war ended. British recruits joined the Royal Irish Constabulary to help control the dissent. They were called the Black and Tans because of their uniforms.

The Irish War for Independence officially began on January 21, 1919, when the Irish Republican Army (IRA) killed members of the Royal Irish Constabulary. As the IRA Nationalists and the Black and Tans fought over the years, civilians suffered. More than half of those killed during the conflict were civilians.

The British Parliament passed the Government of Ireland Act in 1920, which gave a parliament to both the Unionists and the Nationalists. Ireland was partitioned when a referendum made six Unionist counties into Northern Ireland, which remained under the dominion of Great Britain, while the rest of the counties were granted independence. Thomas Bartlett, in *Ireland: A History*, points out that it would have been sensible to include "some provision for the protection of the rights of the Catholic minority" in Northern Ireland, "but this was not done."

1960s Northern Ireland

Northern Ireland's civil rights movement began in the 1960s. Decades after the Government of Ireland Act, Catholic citizens, like Heaney's family, faced discrimination from powerful Unionists. Discrimination affected employment, housing, representation, and education. For

COMPARE
&
CONTRAST

- **1960s:** Northern Ireland is officially part of Great Britain and separate from the Republic of Ireland. While part of Great Britain, the six counties of Northern Ireland make their own laws and regulations with little interference.

  Today: Northern Ireland is still part of the United Kingdom. The Good Friday Agreement of 1998 allows for the possibility of Northern Ireland's joining Ireland if the majority of the population demands it.

- **1960s:** The Troubles officially begin on October 5, 1968, when Catholic Nationalists march in Londonderry for their civil rights and are attacked. Violence between the Unionists and Nationalists continues for the next thirty years.

Today: The Good Friday Agreement in 1998 has resulted in a decrease in violence between Catholics and Protestants. Violence between the groups, however, has not been completely eliminated.

- **1960s:** Discrimination against Catholic citizens is common in Northern Ireland. Discrimination extends to housing, representation, education, and the workplace.

  Today: Antidiscrimination laws, such as the Fair Employment Act of 1976, the Fair Employment Act of 1989, and the Fair Employment and Treatment Order of 1998, protect the rights of all citizens.

example, Cochrane points out that the Catholic city of Derry had an unemployment rate of 20 percent, compared with the national average of 8 percent. Additionally, Catholic employees were often hired for labor or service jobs but denied opportunities for advancement. In government, Cochrane notes that Unionist councils "'gerrymandered' electoral boundaries to ensure that they held onto their dominant position." The councils also limited housing for Catholics, allocating the majority of houses to Protestants, even in areas where they were the minority.

Many leaders refused to acknowledge that there was discrimination against Catholic citizens in Northern Ireland. In 1963, Terence O'Neill was the first Northern Irish prime minister to address the issue. Although he attempted to bridge the religious and political divide, both sides criticized him for his attempts at compromise, and they were unsuccessful. Much like in the American civil rights movement, civil rights leaders in Northern Ireland argued about the direction of their movement. The moderate Northern Ireland Civil Rights Association (NICRA) was created in 1967, shortly after "Mid-Term Break" was published.

In 1968, a protest march was planned through Derry. The march was forbidden, but Unionists planned a countermarch. On October 5, 1968, the Royal Ulster Constabulary (RUC) used violence against the unarmed civil rights marchers. The attack sparked riots that left more than eighty people wounded. The march was televised and, according to Cochrane, "moved the civil rights campaign into the international spotlight, and the violent reaction of the RUC strengthened NICRA." Violence spread as different Nationalist and Unionist groups clashed, and some Nationalist groups, such as the IRA, even encouraged violence. The British government sent soldiers to aid in keeping order, but they were unsuccessful in stopping the violence. Westminster took direct rule of Northern Ireland in 1972, but violence persisted until the Good Friday Agreement of 1998.

CRITICAL OVERVIEW

Heaney's career spanned decades, and both critics and readers praised his talents, making him one of the most renowned poets of his time. His first volume of poetry, *Death of a Naturalist,*

The speaker's brother is laid out for viewing with candles and flowers nearby. (© Africa Studio | Shutterstock.com)

won awards and was well received by critics. The 1966 book was given cautious praise by some critics, such as John Unterecker. He states in the *New York Times Book Review*, "Heaney writes poetry that is urbane, accomplished, predictable." He expresses hope for the poet's future work when he remarks upon "how fine a poet Heaney can be when he isn't trying to show us what a clever fellow he is." When *Door into the Dark* followed in 1969, reviewers praised its profound simplicity. Anthony Thwaite, for one, believed that the rural setting of Heaney's poetry was what attracted readers. In his review for the *New Statesman*, Thwaite relates his certainty "that the appeal of Heaney's work is of an exotic sort, to people who can't tell wheat from barley or a gudgeon from a pike."

Heaney's poetry at times reflects the violence in Northern Ireland, but not all reviewers have been pleased with the scope of his work. The Poetry Foundation's biography of Heaney notes that "some reviewers criticized Heaney for being an apologist and mythologizer." Heaney's status as the latter, at least, was particularly true after he moved away from Northern Ireland in

1972. Richard Murphy notes Heaney's view of violence in Ireland in "Poetry and Terror," stating: "His poetry traces modern terrorism back to its roots in the early Iron Age, and mysterious awe back to the 'bonehouse' of language itself."

Heaney's prose and translations have also been objects of praise. James Wood's review of *Beowulf: A New Verse Translation* in the *Guardian* claims, "Now Heaney has turned to *Beowulf*, and the result is magnificent, breathtaking." Heaney's work has continued to inspire ordinary people and reviewers alike. His final book of poetry, *Human Chain* (2010), for example, received high praise. In his review "Living Ghosts," John Banville states, "In this volume he has found a new fluidity of line, and his rhythms have a lightly skipping quality that belies the sombre themes he addresses."

CRITICISM

April Paris

Paris is a freelance writer with a degree in classical literature and a background in academic

WHAT DO I READ NEXT?

- *Modern Irish Poetry: An Anthology*, edited by Patrick Crotty and published in 1995, presents the work of forty-seven Irish poets, including some of Heaney's verse.

- Published in 2000, *Beowulf: A New Verse Translation* is Heaney's version of the classic Anglo-Saxon epic. The best-selling volume demonstrates Heaney's skill as both a translator of literature and a poet.

- *A Summer to Die*, by Lois Lowry, tells the story of Meg and her older sister, Molly. When Meg learns that her sister is ill, their lives are changed forever. Published in 1977, the novel explores the themes of family, loss, and death.

- *New Collected Poems*, by Derek Mahon, is a collection of the Irish poet's work that was published in 2011. Mahon is well respected as a contemporary of Heaney's, and the collection helps students identify common topics and themes in Irish poetry.

- Published in 2002, *Making Sense of the Troubles: The Story of the Conflict in Northern Ireland*, by David McKittrick and David McVea, examines the history of civil rights in Northern Ireland. The book provides insight into the setting of Heaney's early work.

- Michael Parker's *Seamus Heaney: The Making of the Poet* is a biographical interpretation of Heaney's work. Published in 1993, the volume provides valuable insight into the poet's early work.

- *African American Poetry*, edited by Arnold Rampersad and Marcellus Blount as part of the Poetry for Young People series in 2012, is a collection of poems from prominent African American authors. Many of the poems address the same topics and themes as Heaney's work.

writing. *In the following essay, she argues that Heaney's honest account of his brother's death in "Mid-Term Break" sheds light on the complex*

> IN 'MID-TERM BREAK,' HEANEY CAREFULLY EXAMINES THE COMPLEX WAYS IN WHICH DEATH AFFECTS INDIVIDUALS AND SOCIETY BY SHARING CONFLICTING OBSERVATIONS, IMAGES, AND REACTIONS WITHIN BOTH THE PUBLIC AND PRIVATE SPHERES OF MOURNING."

reactions that people have toward death while emotionally connecting with his audience.

Death is part of nature, a universal theme that connects with all people. The theme of death particularly resonates with the plight of Northern Ireland in the 1960s, a time when many suffered personal loss as the result of religious and political violence. In "Mid-Term Break," Heaney carefully examines the complex ways in which death affects individuals and society by sharing conflicting observations, images, and reactions within both the public and private spheres of mourning. By disclosing the personal tragedy of his brother's death to his readers, Heaney develops a profound emotional connection with them. Death and mourning become sources of commonality that link people together. Regardless of religious or political affiliation, death is inevitable and affects everyone.

Irene Gilsenan Nordin states in the essay "Seamus Heaney: From the Personal to the Universal": "Personal memories from Seamus Heaney's childhood, growing up on a farm in rural Ireland, are central to Heaney's early work. In *Death of a Naturalist* the poet's immediate family figure prominently." Heaney's memories, however, are not idealized images of rural life. He is not afraid to examine the harsh realities of his world. For example, the death of his brother, Christopher, was a tragic moment in Heaney's life, which he shares in "Mid-Term Break." Unlike in emotionally charged elegies, Heaney uses a dispassionate tone in the poem. He simply presents his observations in a clear and organized manner. Outside of his feelings of discomfort that occur when the older visitors offer their condolences, Heaney simply narrates the events that followed Christopher's death. The poem, nevertheless, does not lack emotion.

By not focusing on his emotional reaction to his brother's death, Heaney presents the first of many contrasts in this lyric poem. The realistic language and topic of the poem naturally elicit emotion from the readers. For example, the emotional reaction of the poet's parents is heartbreaking. Their grief needs no emotionally charged adjectives to be understood by the reader. The mother's wordless anger and the father's weeping are sufficient. Additionally, by including the opposing expressions of grief that his parents display, the poet can demonstrate the different and often extreme ways in which people respond to death, particularly the death of a little child.

Heaney reveals the identity and tender age of his brother gradually. He hints at the close familial relationship of the deceased in the second stanza when he reveals how unusual it is for his father to weep at a wake. It is not until the end of the poem, however, that the readers are able to put together the information provided. In the final line, Heaney reveals that his brother was four years old at the time of his death. Choosing not to disclose this information until the end of the poem is a calculated move on the part of the poet. The final line plays upon the sympathy that people feel when the young and innocent are tragically killed.

The structure of "Mid-Term Break" transitions between different locations. This structure allows Heaney to separate the act of mourning into public spheres and private spheres. Both the public and private rituals of mourning play an important role for individuals and society. The two rituals that Heaney explores in the poem would have been familiar to his readers. They are the public wake and the private viewing.

The first five stanzas of "Mid-Term Break" occur in public settings. There is no privacy for the poet or the other members of his family. The first stanza takes place at school as Heaney waits for a ride home. The second occurs at the threshold of his home, where he finds his father weeping over the death of his son. The presence of his father's friend is a reminder that the family is not alone. In this case, the family friend is supportive and understanding of the way Heaney's father mourns the death of his son. As the poet moves inside the house, older men offer their condolences on the passing of his brother, counteracting the cheerful greeting from his infant sibling. The whispers of people he does not know distract him from his mother, who holds on to him in

her anger. In the fifth stanza, his brother's body arrives. Heaney separates himself from the scene by referring to his brother as an object—not as his brother but as "the corpse"—in line 15. In this public setting, his descriptions remain impersonal and detached.

The final stanzas make the poet's experience with death personal. Heaney now refers to his brother with masculine personal pronouns. When they are alone together, his brother ceases to be a body and becomes Christopher again. In line 18, Heaney recalls seeing him just six weeks earlier, when Christopher was flush and full of life. This private moment with his brother's body creates a number of conflicting ideas and feelings, which are evident in his images and descriptions. Heaney contrasts the harsh manner of his brother's death with the serenity of the viewing room. In line 20, he uses a simile to compare the coffin to a bed, creating the idea of peaceful slumber. The peace is shattered, however, in line 21, where Heaney tells readers how a car killed his brother. The stark explanation of the poet's personal loss, again, aids in connecting him with his audience. His grief would particularly resonate with those who have lost loved ones to unexpected deaths.

According to Seamus Deane's review in the *Times Literary Supplement*, which appears in Elmer Andrews's *The Poetry of Seamus Heaney*, "Heaney has been much concerned with deaths of various kinds. His life as a writer has almost exactly coincided with the most recent period of crisis in Northern Ireland." Heaney's personal experience with death also connects his work to the suffering of the people in Northern Ireland. As Heaney's poem shows, mourning the death of a loved one is both a communal experience and a solitary one. Funerals are communal. The poet does not even know some of the people who are present at his brother's wake. As he overhears the other attendees tell complete strangers who he is, it is a reminder that the wake is a public setting where people come together to share their grief.

Much like a wake, Heaney's "Mid-Term Break" became a public forum for shared mourning when he chose to publish the poem and share his personal bereavement. The loss that he experienced mirrors the grief that many other people in Northern Ireland suffered. Death is an unavoidable part of the natural cycle. As Timothy Kearney states in "The Poetry of the North: A Post-Modernist Perspective," also quoted in Andrews, nature is not only "the provider of plenty but also the perpetrator of sacrifice, the creator of victims. And it is precisely the figure of the victim which receives most of Heaney's imaginative generosity." Although death and loss are natural and unavoidable, the poet does not minimize the profound impact that occurs when life is lost. Christopher is gone, but his influence on the world is not lost. Heaney chooses to use images from nature to memorialize his brother's life and death.

The shared tragedy of death and loss is part of the natural condition, and the floral images that Heaney uses connect his brother with the natural world. They also serve to show the dual nature of the poet's understanding. He at once has hope for life beyond the grave as well as an understanding of death's finality. The flowers in line 16 are a symbol of hope and purity in the Catholic tradition. Heaney has chosen this flower to illustrate both his brother's innocence and a hope in the afterlife. The flower metaphor in line 19, on the other hand, is a symbol of death. This symbol specifically represents violent death and sacrifice. The flower is a reminder of the soldiers who died in poppy fields during World War I. The BBC article "Why the Poppy?" notes that John McCrea popularized the image in his poem "In Flanders Fields," and "the poppy came to represent the immeasurable sacrifice made by his comrades and quickly became a lasting memorial to those who died in World War One and later conflicts."

The connection of the poet's brother's death with fallen soldiers is not merely a coincidence. Christopher is another Irish Catholic who was killed before his time, like so many others before him. This symbol links the family's personal loss with the deaths of people from the conflict in Northern Ireland. Although Heaney does not create poetry that is specifically political, he still connects with readers by drawing on the world in which he lives. Elmer Andrews addresses this in "The Gift and the Craft: An Approach to the Poetry of Seamus Heaney": "As a man like any other man, politics are a part of his life: being a poet does not separate him from the concerns of common humanity." People who have lost family members to violent and unexpected deaths share the same experience of loss and mourning. Heaney did not lose his brother to political violence, but sharing his

experience demonstrates that he is able to sympathize with those who have.

Source: April Paris, Critical Essay on "Mid-Term Break," in *Poetry for Students*, Gale, Cengage Learning, 2016.

Floyd Collins

In the following excerpt, Collins asserts that Heaney's work exemplifies the Irish struggle to define identity, both personal and national.

... The matter of identity is especially troublesome for Irish citizens, who must confront an unwieldy cultural and historical legacy that includes both their relationship with England and the reality of political and sectarian strife in their homeland. In this respect, Ireland seems an anomaly, as Elmer Andrews observes in his discussion of "Bogland," the concluding poem of Heaney's second collection, *Door into the Dark*: "Normally, millions of years would help a country to achieve and define itself. Not so in Ireland." Polly Devlin, a former Irish journalist who is also Seamus Heaney's sister-in-law, notes in *All of Us There* how a repressive, authoritarian Irish Catholic educational system affected children's sense of identity:

> In this prevailing ethos, the questions asked of children differed only in their emphasis from the genuine questions asked in other systems. But emphasis makes all the difference. "Who do you think *you* are?" asked to wound, as a reprimand, or as the amazed response to what has been been interpreted as conceit, immodesty or the dreaded boldness is very different from the genuine enquiry bent on genuine exploration: "*Who* do you think you are?"... Why should our mentors, our teachers, our guides ask the question like this? We knew nothing of our history, of the reductive process of a way of life built on deprivation and poverty, nothing of the cruelty of a religion or a political system that made self-effacement the safest way to live and which took away from a race its ability to esteem itself. . . . Effacement and quietness became equated with goodness, no new equation in Ireland, where effacement had once contributed to survival.

In *Transitions: Narratives of Modern Irish Culture* (1987), Richard Kearney observes that the cultural crisis in twentieth-century Ireland was often experienced as a conflict between the claims of tradition and modernity. Today's Irish must confront "the prevailing sense of discontinuity, the absence of a coherent identity, the breakdown of inherited ideologies and beliefs, [and] the insecurities of fragmentation."

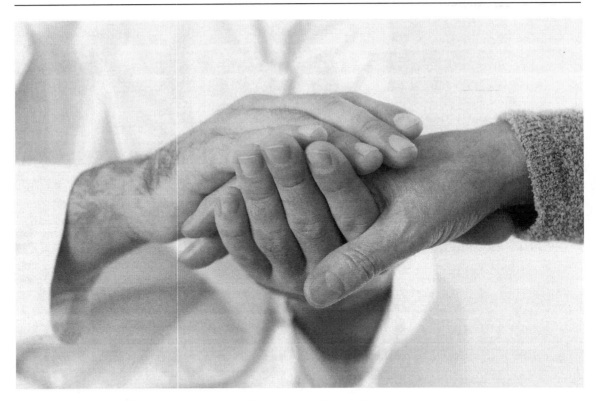

Neighbors and friends shake hands and offer comfort for the family's loss. (© LeventeGyori | Shutterstock.com)

It is not surprising, then, that identity has traditionally been a concern for Irish writers: "With no continuity, no shared history, no reliable audience, the Irish writer's experience has typically been one of exposure and alienation. His is, as Thomas Kinsella says, a divided mind." Interestingly, Erikson listed "the Irish expatriates" among those writers who have become "the artistic spokesmen and prophets of identity confusion," and notes the difficulty of identity for the creative artist who finds himself in the midst of a cultural crisis: "Artistic creation goes beyond complaint and exposure, and it includes the moral decision that a certain painful identity-consciousness may have to be tolerated in order to provide the conscience of man with a critique of conditions, with the insight and the conceptions necessary to heal himself of what most deeply divides and threatens him." Writing in the mid to late 1960s, Erikson almost seems to foretell the extent to which identity would continue to be a problem for successive generations of Irish writers. According to Kearney, the tension between revivalism and modernism has occasioned a transitional crisis in contemporary

Irish writers: "They often write as *émigrés* of the imagination, conveying the feeling of being both part and not part of their culture, of being estranged from the very traditions to which they belong, of being in exile even while at home." Here Kearney takes his cue from Heaney, who casts himself as "an inner émigré" in "Singing School" and whose speaker in "The Tollund Man" paradoxically finds himself as "lost, / Unhappy and at home" in Denmark as in Ireland. Like all contemporary Irish writers, Heaney must resolve for himself the competing claims of tradition and modernity, but he must also face the specter of self-imposed exile, a repudiation of his own identity and the community to which he belongs. As Robert Penn Warren has declared, "[N]either extreme offers a happy solution. Yet there is no simple solution of half-and-half, for the soul doesn't operate with that arithmetical tidiness." Contemporary Irish poets confront a difficult literary ancestry, as they explore the extremes of Yeats's Romanticism and Joyce's Modernism, Yeats's myth-making and Joyce's exile and expatriation, while simultaneously questioning themselves

" HEANEY'S CAPACITY TO LISTEN GENEROUSLY, ALMOST PASSIVELY, ENABLES WORLD AND WORD TO PERMEATE ONE ANOTHER SO THOROUGHLY THAT EACH BECOMES INEXTRICABLY LINKED WITH THE OTHER."

about identity. Small wonder that Elmer Andrews describes Seamus Heaney as "a skeptical, defensive, displaced poet, torn by conflicting dogma and troubled by the nightmare of history, constantly threatened with the dissolution of the self yet deeply suspicious of the more obvious forms of ideological control."

Though Heaney's identity may not have been as profoundly influenced by experiences such as the one Polly Devlin describes above, his poetry and prose express what may at best be termed a sense of dividedness. Like many postcolonial writers, he notes the presence of conflicting influences or origins: "the voices of my education," he explains, "pull in two directions, back through the political and cultural traumas of Ireland, and out towards the urgencies and experience of the world beyond it" (*Pr*). Oddly enough, an education emphasizing English literature and all things English in one respect reinforced his identity: he became more sensitive to Irish influences. In an essay on Patrick Kavanagh, which originally saw print in the *Massachusetts Review* and reappeared in his second collection of critical prose, *The Government of the Tongue* (1989), Heaney describes the startling yet intimate experience of encountering Kavanagh's poems for the first time:

> I was excited to find details of a life which I knew intimately—but which I had always considered to be below or beyond books—being presented in a book.... Potato-pits with rime on them, guttery gaps, iced-over puddles being crunched, cows being milked, a child nicking the doorpost with a pen-knife, and so on. What was being experienced was not some hygienic and self-aware pleasure of the text but a primitive delight in finding world become word. (7–8)

The encounter with Kavanagh's work marks the beginning of his own poetic identity: "I began as a poet when my roots were crossed

with my reading" (*Pr*). The obvious delight with which Heaney culls, rehearses, and savors the rich sensory detail of Kavanagh's verse is a sure indication of how indelibly the penknife reinscribes his own experience. He suddenly apprehends the emblems of life through an abrupt nick that cuts to the roots of consciousness.

"Digging," the first piece presented in Heaney's *Poems 1965–1975*, commemorates this initial encounter with "world become word" by recalling the deft precision of a rural laborer in the peat-bogs "Nicking and slicing neatly, heaving sods / Over his shoulder, going down and down / For the good turf" (*Poems*). As the man continues to negotiate this neat patchwork of ground, the turf breaks up into damp monosyllables, "the squelch and slap / Of soggy peat." Each spadeful prickles with root hairs like raw nerve endings: "the curt cuts of an edge / Through living roots awaken in my head" (*Poems*). Heaney's capacity to listen generously, almost passively, enables world and word to permeate one another so thoroughly that each becomes inextricably linked with the other. In "Digging," he cultivates an empathic mode of composition wherein words function as aural counters beautifully adapted to the phenomena described.

The most dynamic feature of the poem's dramatic situation, however, inheres not in its crisp imagery, but in simple autobiographical fact— the worker plying his spade with a sapper's single-minded aplomb is Heaney's grandfather. Earlier on in the piece, the poet recalls his father digging in the potato drills: "By God, the old man could handle a spade. / Just like his old man" (*Poems*). Raised on a farm in the townland of Mossbawn, County Derry, in Northern Ireland, Heaney must confront the crisis of identity from the very outset: "But I've no spade to follow men like them." He resolves this sense of discontinuity, eventually choosing to efface through poetry the boundaries between world and word: "Between my finger and my thumb / The squat pen rests. / I'll dig with it." Though he has called it "a big coarse-grained navvy of a poem" (*Pr*), "Digging" serves as an *ars poetica* for Heaney.

Heaney's designation of Kavanagh as an immediate literary forebear, one whose example would facilitate or resolve his own crisis of identity, is especially significant. Indeed, Blake Morrison asserts that "[i]f Kavanagh had not existed, Heaney would have had to invent him: he needed the example of an Irish poet through whom he could place himself—and Yeats would not serve." This pronouncement seems somewhat surprising, when we consider Yeats's struggle with the problem of identity. Indeed, we may see Yeats and his successors as participating in a tradition of the crisis of identity. When Yeats's artist father moved the family from Sligo to London in 1873, a Pollexfen aunt told the boy: "You are going to London. Here you are somebody. There you will be nobody at all." Perhaps as a result of this sense of his own difference, the Pre-Raphaelite dreaminess of his early poetry eulogized the bleakly beautiful countryside along the west coast of Ireland: "There midnight's all a glimmer, and noon a purple glow, / And evening full of the linnet's wings." Yeats forsook the English landscapes of Matthew Arnold, resolving the discontinuity between his identity and his locale by celebrating the waterfalls around Sligo and the ancient burial cairn on the hill of Knocknarea, all of which prompted his father to comment: "We [the Yeatses] have ideas and no passions, but by marriage with a Pollexfen we have given a tongue to the sea cliffs." The fledging Irish poet delved subsequently into the rich lore of Cuchulain and the Red Branch warriors, and immediately recognized in Celtic mythology an alternative to Tennyson's Arthurian narratives and the Icelandic sagas of the thirteenth century. Yeats's determination to recount the deeds of pre-Christian Irish heroes in "Ballad and story, rann and song" ultimately led to the revival of a national literature in Ireland. But helping to create a national consciousness for his homeland did not solve Yeats's personal crisis of identity.

Source: Floyd Collins, "The Crisis of Identity and the Development of a Poetic Consciousness," in *Seamus Heaney: The Crisis of Identity*, Rosemont Publishing and Printing Corp., 2003, pp. 17–21.

Thomas C. Foster

In the following excerpt, Foster discusses Death of a Naturalist, *which includes "Mid-Term Break."*

. . . In this first volume Heaney experiments with, and often stumbles over, tone and diction matters. Particularly troublesome is the poem "Docker," a polemic that misses its mark by several yards. This worker, sitting in the corner of the publichouse, is not man but symbol, not human but mechanical: "The cap juts like a gantry's crossbeam, / Cowling plated forehead and

sledgehead jaw. / Speech is clamped in the lips' vice" (*DN*). Not only are the metaphors based on tools, but they are particularly restrictive and violent—the vice, the sledge, the crossbeam that suggests not only a railroad gantry but a gallows. Of course, then, the man's "fist would drop a hammer on a Catholic," for this is a man made of instruments rather than flesh and blood. His "God is a foreman" who will sound the second coming with the "blare" of a "factory horn." We cannot share the poet's scorn at this figure, however real he might be, because he never rises above type; Heaney fails to breathe enough life into him to make us care about or believe in him. As so often happens with this sort of propaganda, the poem turns against the propagandist. When Heaney tells us the "only Roman collar" the Docker will tolerate "Smiles all round his sleek pint of porter," we can only ascribe to the poet the prejudice and intolerance he would place on his character. Ironically, the work proves prophetic, for the Troubles, "that kind of thing," did indeed start again, only two years after the publication of the book. Yet here accuracy loses importance to tone and attitude, and the reader finds it impossible to sympathize with a poem that is capable of so little sympathy of its own.

The chief fault of "Docker," perhaps, is that it wears its feelings too openly. Elsewhere in the volume, Heaney practices the caution, the defensiveness that will characterize much of his later verse. In "Twice Shy" he writes of the reserve that makes courting partners unwilling to speak:

Our juvenilia
Had taught us both to wait,
Not to publish feeling
And regret it all too late—
Mushroom loves already
Had puffed and burst in hate.
(*DN*)

The mushroom imagery is a delightful device in a poem that otherwise proves quite conventional, even predictable. The mushroom, spontaneous but short-lived, typically does not respond to cultivation, to time and care and nurturing. Its use here suggests an alternative vision of this romance, one more closely based on agricultural experience; the poem, however, leaves that alternative unstated, trusting to the strength of the image to embody its opposite.

His handling of grief is similarly terse and understated in "Mid-Term Break." From the opening the poem seems a recitation of fact: "I

> " THE FINAL LINE, DESPITE ITS HEAVILY ALLIT-
> ERATIVE DEBT TO ANGLO-SAXON, IS HEARTBREAK-
> INGLY SIMPLE, CONVEYING SO MUCH MORE THAN IT
> SAYS."

sat all morning in the college sick bay / Counting bells knelling classes to a close. / At two o'clock our neighbours drove me home" (*DN*). We have no idea in this first stanza why he sits in the sick bay; not until the first line of stanza 2, when we see the father crying, do we know that the trouble is external. The first and third lines of the opening are conversational and could easily appear in prose.

Throughout the poem Heaney maintains a distance between himself and his material. We can make inferences about his adult feelings only through the precision of his recollection, and the only sensations he reveals of his fourteen-year-old self are of embarrassment and self-consciousness. Indeed, it is the distance that suggests the pain of loss. The ambulance arrives not with a younger brother but with "the corpse." The young Seamus waits until the next morning to see the body, intimating the difficulty involved as well as personal or parental reluctance to open him up to that level of grief just at bedtime. The details he provides instead are of everyone else: his mother's "angry tearless sighs," old men shaking his hand and expressing sorrow, strangers whispering information, and in the midst of it all the baby, who "cooed and laughed and rocked the pram," a happy island untouched by the ocean of sadness surrounding it. Even at the end, when the young Heaney does see the body, the recitation is flat, factual, as he finds his brother "Paler now,"

> Wearing a poppy bruise on his left temple,
> He lay in the four foot box as in his cot.
> No gaudy scars, the bumper knocked him clear.
>
> A four foot box, a foot for every year.
> (*DN*)

Clearly this is an unemotional rendering of an emotional moment, and the restraint is not achieved without cost. The regularity of the end-stopped lines, as well as the caesura in the last

two lines, suggests the effort involved in suppressing the memory of grief. The verse does not flow; it falters and halts. The final line, despite its heavily alliterative debt to Anglo-Saxon, is heartbreakingly simple, conveying so much more than it says.

In its terseness it recalls a characteristic tone in contemporary British and Irish verse: defensive, tight-lipped, understated. One thinks of a similar hard edge in Jon Silkin's "Death of a Son" or any number of poems by Philip Larkin, Charles Tomlinson, Geoffrey Hill, Roy Fuller, Kavanagh, and Hughes. While the British may have learned that pose and attitude from Thomas Hardy, Edward Thomas and the Georgian poets, as well as, according to Larkin, the privations of World War II, Heaney and the Irish, the Ulster Irish especially, have learned to hold their tongues from extraliterary affairs, particularly matters of local politics, where "whatever you say, you say nothing" (*N*).

Throughout this early volume Heaney reveals his early influences: Gerard Manley Hopkins, Anglo-Saxon verse, Robert Frost, Wordsworth, Yeats, Theodore Roethke, and, of course, Ted Hughes. What he finds among them is a use of nature and farm imagery and subject matter, a readiness to employ the materials at hand, an ability to work successfully in the short lyric and in conventional forms, yet to bend those forms to suit individual vision and whim. Of Hughes's influence on *Death of a Naturalist* much has already been written. Roland Mathias sees the first third of the book, in particular, as "pretty clearly a response to the new climate in poetry initiated by Ted Hughes," a climate of nature and power and life and violence that offers a rough and tumble alternative to the stifling verse of the Movement.

At the same time, however, Mathias also sees Heaney as pulling back from the direct, fascinated gaze Hughes would direct at the natural, nonhuman world. In poems like "The Barn" or "Death of a Naturalist" Heaney shows a child recoiling from nature not because of any inherent threat but because of the overly vigorous workings of his imagination: seeing himself as an interloper from the world of humans, he imagines the nonhuman world preparing a counterattack:

> Right down the dam gross-bellied frogs were cocked
> On sods; their loose necks pulsed like sails. Some
>   hopped:

The slap and plop were obscene threats. Some sat
Poised like mud grenades, their blunt heads farting.
I sickened, turned, and ran. The great slime kings
Were gathered there for vengeance and I knew
That if I dipped my hand the spawn would clutch it.
(*DN*)

In the power of the diction, the explicit violence and sexuality of the imagery, Heaney conveys a young boy's terror at stepping out of his own element into another. Yet the terror is entirely self-manufactured; we know, as does the author, that the frogs are neither vengeful kings nor grenades. Nevertheless, we are likely to recognize (and share in the embarrassment over) the hysterical reaction to an early, direct encounter with nature. This is not a Hughesian poem in sentiment or attitude, yet it may well be in terms of subject matter, imagery, and language.

A poem more conventionally in the Hughes mode is "Trout," which Neil Corcoran identifies as largely unassimilated Hughes, from its elision of title into first line to its "almost absurd range of military metaphors." The trout is "a fat gunbarrel" that "darts like a tracer- / bullet," "A volley of cold blood / / ramrodding the current," who is "fired from the shadows" to the surface, where moths are "torpedoed" (*DN*). Corcoran is correct in asserting, later in the same passage, that in this poem and others, "trout and cow and turkeys disappear unrecognizably into pale imitation and pastiche." The military imagery is more than either the trout or the poem can bear. Throughout this book and the one to follow, Heaney deals more successfully with Hughes's influence in those poems, like "Death of a Naturalist," where he has absorbed that influence, turned it to his own purposes, and filtered it through his own voice....

Source: Thomas C. Foster, "Learning the Craft: *Death of a Naturalist* and *Door into the Dark*," in *Seamus Heaney*, Twayne Publishers, 1989, pp. 19–22.

SOURCES

Abrams, M. H., "Figurative Language" and "Lyric," in *A Glossary of Literary Terms*, 7th ed., Harcourt Brace College Publishers, 1999, pp. 97, 146.

Andrews, Elmer, "The Gift and the Craft: An Approach to the Poetry of Seamus Heaney," in *Twentieth Century Literature*, Vol. 31, No. 4, Winter 1985, pp. 368–79.

Banville, John, "Living Ghosts," in *New York Review of Books*, November 11, 2010, http://www.nybooks.com/articles/archives/2010/nov/11/living-ghosts/ (accessed May 17, 2015).

Bartlett, Thomas, *Ireland: A History*, Cambridge University Press, 2010, pp. 403–405.

Cochrane, Feargal, *Northern Ireland: The Reluctant Peace*, Yale University Press, 2013, pp. 9, 44, 49.

Corcoran, Neil, "Seamus Heaney Obituary," in *Guardian* (London, England), August 30, 2013, http://www.theguardian.com/books/2013/aug/30/seamus-heaney (accessed May 17, 2015).

Deane, Seamus, "Powers of the Earth and Visions of Air," in *The Poetry of Seamus Heaney*, edited by Elmer Andrews, Columbia University Press, 1998, p. 151.

Heaney, Seamus, "Mid-Term Break," in *Opened Ground: Selected Poems, 1966–1996*, Farrar, Straus and Giroux, 1998, p. 11.

Kearney, Timothy, "The Poetry of the North: A Post-Modernist Perspective," in *The Poetry of Seamus Heaney*, edited by Elmer Andrews, Columbia University Press, 1998, p. 65.

Murphy, Richard, "Poetry and Terror," in *New York Review of Books*, September 30, 1976, http://www.nybooks.com/articles/archives/1976/sep/30/poetry-and-terror/ (accessed May 17, 2015).

"The Nobel Prize in Literature 1995," Nobel Prize website, http://www.nobelprize.org/nobel_prizes/literature/laureates/1995/ (accessed May 17, 2015).

Nordin, Irene Gilsenan, "Seamus Heaney: From the Personal to the Universal," in *Studia Neophilologica*, Vol. 72, No. 2, 2000, pp. 174–80.

"Seamus Heaney," Poetry Foundation website, http://www.poetryfoundation.org/bio/seamus-heaney (accessed May 17, 2015).

"Seamus Heaney—Biographical," Nobel Prize website, http://www.nobelprize.org/nobel_prizes/literature/laureates/1995/heaney-bio.html (accessed May 17, 2015); originally published in *Les Prix Nobels/The Nobel Prizes, 1995*, edited by Tore Frängsmyr, Nobel Foundation, 1996.

Thwaite, Anthony, "It's Impossible to Fault Seamus Heaney's Clean Language and Sensuous Delight," in *New Statesman*, June 27, 1969, http://www.newstatesman.com/books/2013/08/27-june-1969-its-impossible-fault-seamus-heaneys-clean-language-and-sensuous-delight (accessed May 17, 2015).

Unterecker, John, Review of *Death of a Naturalist*, in *New York Times Book Review*, March 26, 1967, http://www.nytimes.com/1967/03/26/books/review/heaney-naturalist.html?_r=0 (accessed May 17, 2015).

"Why the Poppy?," BBC website, http://www.bbc.co.uk/remembrance/how/poppy.shtml (accessed May 17, 2015).

Wood, James, "Anglo-Saxon Attitude," in *Guardian* (London, England), October 16, 1999, http://www.theguardian.com/books/1999/oct/16/poetry.costabookaward (accessed May 17, 2015).

FURTHER READING

Heaney, Seamus, *Human Chain*, Farrar, Straus and Giroux, 2010.
>   *Human Chain* is the last collection of poetry published while Heaney was still alive. The book demonstrates his growth as a poet.

Hufstader, Jonathan, *Tongue of Water, Teeth of Stones: Northern Irish Poetry and Social Violence*, University Press of Kentucky, 1999.
>   Hufstader's essays examine the works of different Northern Irish poets, including Heaney, focusing on the effect of social violence in their work.

Killeen, Richard, *A Brief History of Ireland*, Running Press, 2011.
>   This nonfiction text provides a complete, concise overview of Irish history. It is a useful introductory text for anyone wanting to know more about the history of Ireland and Irish culture.

O'Donoghue, Bernard, ed., *The Cambridge Companion to Seamus Heaney*, Cambridge University Press, 2009.
>   This collection of essays provides insight into Heaney's life and work. It is a valuable resource for anyone interested in better understanding Heaney's writings.

O'Driscoll, Dennis, *Stepping Stones: Interviews with Seamus Heaney*, Farrar, Straus and Giroux, 2008.
>   This collection of interviews provides valuable insight into Heaney's own views of his work and what inspired him to write.

SUGGESTED SEARCH TERMS

Seamus Heaney

Seamus Heaney AND biography

Seamus Heaney AND "Mid-Term Break"

Northern Ireland AND civil rights movement

Northern Ireland AND history

1960s AND Northern Ireland

Seamus Heaney AND criticism

Irish poetry

Irish poetry AND Seamus Heaney

Nebraska

JACK KEROUAC
1992

Jack Kerouac's "Nebraska" was first published as part of the 1992 collection *Pomes All Sizes*, though the poem itself was written sometime around 1954. Part of the "Bus East" series of poems, "Nebraska" is one of Kerouac's early explorations of how the intersection of jazz and poetry might create a new form of expression for an age in transition. In the poem, readers can see the literary techniques and style that Kerouac shared with his fellow Beats, most notably Allen Ginsberg, and which would appear in what he called the spontaneous prose that gave life to his masterwork, *On the Road* (1957).

AUTHOR BIOGRAPHY

Jean-Louis Lebris de Kerouac, who would be called "Jack" by his American friends, was born on March 12, 1922, in Lowell, Massachusetts. His parents, Léo-Alcide Kéroack and Gabrielle-Ange Lévesque, were both French Canadians from Saint-Hubert-de-Rivière-du-Loup, in the province of Quebec. His mother was a devout Catholic who played an important role in his life; he would go so far later in life as to not only admit his devotion to his mother but also claim that she was the only woman he ever loved. He had two siblings: an older sister, Caroline, and an older brother, Gérard. When Jack was four, the family was traumatized by Gérard's death from

Jack Kerouac (© Bettmann / Corbis)

rheumatic fever. While his mother resorted to her faith to find solace, his father resorted to gambling, drinking, and smoking.

Kerouac had a promising start as an athlete. Skilled at football, he excelled as a running back for Lowell High School, which garnered him scholarship offers from Notre Dame, Boston College, and Columbia University. He chose Columbia but broke his leg in his freshman year, effectively ending his football career. During his time in New York, Kerouac lived on the Upper West Side with his girlfriend, Edie Parker, who was to later become his first wife. During this time he also met the friends who would, alongside Kerouac himself, become known as the Beat generation, including Allen Ginsberg (1926–1997), Neal Cassady (1926–1968), and William S. Burroughs (1914–1997).

Kerouac joined the US Navy in 1943 but served only eight days of active duty before being put on the sick list. The medical examiner reported that Kerouac had a poor adjustment to the military, and he was honorably discharged two days later on psychiatric grounds, with a diagnosis of "schizoid personality." Kerouac wrote his first novel, *The Sea Is My Brother*, in 1942, but it was never released during his lifetime. It was published posthumously in 2011. The same can be said of his poem "Nebraska,"

which was written around 1954 but did not appear in print until the 1992 volume *Pomes All Sizes* was released. Despite the modest start to his writing career, Kerouac would go on to publish extensively, including fifteen works of fiction and more than a handful of books of poetry. His most famous title, *On the Road* (1957), has long been considered an exemplar of Beat writing, claiming an iconic position in American literature.

Following his involvement in a 1944 murder (he helped dispose of the body), Kerouac married and divorced twice, took long trips across the United States and Mexico, and struggled perpetually with bouts of depression and extended periods of heavy drinking. By 1954 he had embarked on a study of Buddhism, in part as a means of dealing with the fame (and infamy) that came with his growing success. A chronic heavy drinker throughout his life, Kerouac died from an internal hemorrhage caused by cirrhosis on October 21, 1969. He was forty-seven years old.

POEM TEXT

April doesnt hurt here
Like it does in New England   20
The ground
Vast and brown
Surrounds dry towns
Located in the dust
Of the coming locust   25
Live for survival, not for "kicks"

Be a bangtail describer,
like of shrouded traveler
in Textile tenement &
the birds fighting in yr   30
ears—like Burroughs
exact to describe &
gettin $
The Angry Hunger
(hunger is anger)   35
who fears
the hungry
feareth
the angry)

And so I came home   40
To Golden far away
Twas on the horizon
Every blessed day
As we rolled
And we rolled   45
From Donner tragic Pass
Thru April in Nevada

And out Salt City Way
Into the dry Nebraskas
And sad Wyomings   50

Where young girls
And pretty lover boys
With Mickey Mantle eyes
Wander under moons
Sawing in lost cradle   55
And Judge O Fastera
Passes whiggling by
To ask of young love:
"Was it the same wind
Of April Plains eve   60
that ruffled the dress
Of my lost love
Louanna
In the Western
Far off night   65
Lost as the whistle
Of the passing Train
Everywhere West
Roams moaning
The deep basso   70
—Vom! Vom!
—Was it the same love
Notified my bones
As mortify yrs now
Children of the soft   75
Wyoming April night?
Couldna been!
But was! But was!"

And on the prairie
The wildflower blows   80
In the night
For bees & birds
And sleeping hidden
Animals of life.

Then Chicago   85
Spitters in the spotty street
Cheap beans, loop.
Girls made eyes at me
And I had 35
Cents in my jeans—   90

Then Toledo
Springtime starry
Lover night
Of hot rod boys
And cool girls   95
A wandering
A wandering
In search of April pain
A plash of rain
Will not dispel   100
This fumigatin hell
Of lover lane
This park of roses
Blue as bees

In former airy poses   105
In aerial O Way hoses
No tamarand
And figancine

Can the musterand
Be less kind   110
Sol—
Sol—
Bring forth yr
Ah Sunflower—
Ah me Montana   115
Phosphorescent Rose
And bridge in
fairly land
I'd understand it all—

POEM SUMMARY

The text used for this summary is from *Pomes All Sizes*, City Lights Books, 1992, pp. 3–7. Versions of the poem can be found on the following web pages: http://allpoetry.com/Nebraska, http://poemhunter.com/poem/nebraska/, https://www.poeticous.com/jack-kerouac/nebraska, and http://hellopoetry.com/poem/67391/nebraska/. None of these versions preserves the line breaks or indentations of the original, which contains 101 lines spread over six stanzas.

Lines 1–8

"Nebraska" is a free-verse poem that reads as a stream-of-consciousness accounting of a west-to-east road trip across geographies, with a strong first-person subjectivity. As the title suggests, the poem begins in Nebraska, which is defined initially by a negative comparison (that is, Nebraska is *not* like another place) before being defined in physical terms: color, size, dryness, and the perpetual threat of environmental damage.

Lines 9–15

The poet-speaker next turns from the long-perspective survey of the landscape to the industrialized texture of the town tenements, which is said to have been captured in the work of at least one other Beat writer, Burroughs.

Lines 16–21

Moving across a white space on the page, the poem moves to an internal geography of emotion that links three base emotions in sync: fear, anger, and hunger.

Lines 22–66

Crossing a white space of two lines—where a single blank line divides all the other stanzas—the poet-speaker begins a series of reflections on home, which appears as a promise on the horizon of his consciousness. The journey in the moment is heading always toward that mythic place, which cuts through a series of other places and other histories. Each of these locations brings into his field of view opportunities that are romantic, spiritual, and cultural. The Western world—in sound, space, and the presence of the train—is felt in the bones of the poet-speaker as he moves, searching, eastward.

Lines 67–72

Visiting Chicago, the landscape shifts from one of vastness to one of contained (and even compressed) romantic interactions and consumer options that leave him feeling impoverished and disconnected from his own humanity.

Lines 73–101

The poet-speaker ventures to Toledo, Ohio, where the smaller-town, industrialized experiences push him deeper into his own consciousness and subjectivity. Replacing the geography of the opening lines of the poem are closing images that emphasize emotion over physicality, foregrounding unspoken sensuality as the key to a deep yet unarticulated understanding of an experience known only to the poet himself.

THEMES

Activism

Many of the issues and themes that caught the attention of the so-called Beat generation of writers would go on to shape the more well-known counterculture of the 1960s. Predominant among these was a backlash against status quo politics, capitalism (which is linked to the expansion of the US military-industrial complex), and the rise of suburban living and middle-class consumerism. Many of the original Beat poets remained staunch supporters and activists in the antiwar movement, for instance, and were engaged in the civil rights movement throughout the 1960s.

The Beats as a loosely acknowledged group supported spiritual liberation, sexual liberation, black liberation, and counterculture activism. They worked toward ecological consciousness, most notably through the writings of such authors as Gary Snyder (b. 1930) and Michael McClure (b. 1932). Along with their openly political and sexual agenda, the Beats had a

TOPICS FOR FURTHER STUDY

- In light of Kerouac's affinity for building poems so as to emphasize sound rather than structure, produce a digital (or audio-cassette) reading of the poem that lifts the words from the page and turns them into active sound through which the audience gains understanding. Be prepared to share this recording with your class.

- Research a specific jazz musician from the 1950s to get a sense of his or her style, sound, and approach to the notes being played. Then write a well-structured and thoughtful essay in which you trace the similarities between the chosen jazz artist's music and Kerouac's use of sound and rhythm in "Nebraska."

- Kerouac was an avid sketch artist throughout his travels back and forth across America. On a poster-size sheet of paper, sketch your interpretation of "Nebraska." Feel free to incorporate words and/or symbols into your final product.

- Read Christopher Paul Curtis's youth novel *Bud, Not Buddy* (1999), and write a well-structured essay comparing Curtis's representation of 1920s jazz culture with the 1950s version that shaped Kerouac and other Beat writers.

respect for the land and indigenous peoples and cultures, which they proclaimed often in their prose writings.

Language and the freedom to write freely and openly about a full range of topics were also fundamental focuses of the Beats, who were often the target of censors. Shortly after Ginsberg's *Howl and Other Poems* was published in 1956, for instance, a movement arose to ban it for obscenity. However, the work overcame censorship trials, and "Howl" became one of the most widely read poems of the century. Ginsberg, in particular, was involved in many political

The Western landscapes Kerouac saw when traveling were very different from what he was used to growing up in New England. (© *Sharon Day* / *Shutterstock.com*)

activities, including anti–Vietnam War protests, and he openly spoke about free speech and gay rights agendas.

Beat Movement

The *Beat* movement, or generation, was a term used to describe a self-proclaimed group of writers who emerged in the post–World War II era and whose philosophies and politics challenged directly many of the norms and mores that had come to define American culture. Openly engaged in experimentation with psychedelic drugs, members of the group were anti-industry, antiwar, open about their sexual orientations (often bisexuality), and generally nonconformist in all aspects of their lives. Having met initially at Columbia University, in New York City, the group wandered the country but came to be associated most directly with San Francisco.

Although the majority of the Beats' best-known works were published in the 1950s, they remained active well into the sixties. Creatively, they privileged a number of common themes and concerns: a concentrated opposition to standard

narrative values; a belief in writing, especially of poetry, as a spiritual quest; the benefits of exploring Native American and Eastern spiritualities; and the power of the first person, as narrator, to undertake a direct and unwavering examination of the human condition.

The titles that are generally the best and most representative examples of Beat literature include Kerouac's *On the Road* (1957), Ginsberg's *Howl and Other Poems* (1956), and Burroughs's *Naked Lunch* (1959). Interestingly, two of these works, *Howl* and *Naked Lunch*, were at the center of obscenity trials that eventually did lead to liberalizing publishing in the United States.

STYLE

Language

Like many of the Beat writers, Kerouac was concerned with the limitations of traditional language to convey the depth of subjective experiences in a world that includes opportunities for transcendence through meditation, Buddhism, and even consciousness-altering drugs. In "Nebraska," for instance, he embeds symbols (including ampersands and a dollar sign), constructed words, spontaneous contractions, and even an Old English construction (with the traditional *-eth* ending). In each instance, the goal is to convey meaning—literal and poetic—that is not tied to conventional words or punctuation. Meaning floats freely across Kerouac's poem, released in sound as well as in the more familiar denotative and connotative levels of words and phrases.

Musicality

Kerouac's writing style, in both prose and verse, was heavily influenced by many of the cultural changes taking place in the 1950s, most notably the appreciation of jazz music as part of mainstream culture. He translated this musicality to poems like "Nebraska" through his almost improvisational style, or what he called spontaneous prose in his fiction writing. Approaching a kind of stream of consciousness in this poem, Kerouac generates a strong rhythm through his use of short lines (often only three or four words), a general absence of terminal punctuation (period or comma), and his use of constructed words and symbols to convey meaning.

HISTORICAL CONTEXT

The 1950s

The 1950s saw a post–World War II boom in consumerism and economic optimism that would come to define the decade, as well as create some backlash in the 1960s. In 1955, for instance, over eight million cars were sold, with 70 percent of families now owning an automobile. The first McDonald's restaurant was built in 1955 in response, in part, to the rapidly expanding middle-class market for fast food and TV dinners. The American cultural experience was increasingly being defined by an emphasis on entertainment and enhanced consumer experience. Disneyland opened in California in 1955, the same year that Coca-Cola moved to include cans alongside its trademark bottles. Music was dominated by the first wave of domestic rock and roll, with such iconic artists as Elvis Presley, Bill Haley and His Comets, Chuck Berry, and the Platters rising through the charts.

On a darker note, the US involvement in the Vietnam War began in 1955 with the arrival of the US Military Assistance Group in South Vietnam. In Montgomery, Alabama, on December 1 of that year, a young African American woman named Rosa Parks refused to obey a bus driver's demand to give up her seat to a white passenger. Parks's refusal and subsequent arrest were the catalyst needed to set the American civil rights movement in motion. In 1954 the Supreme Court ruled unanimously in *Brown v. Board of Education* that laws establishing segregated schools were unconstitutional.

As the decade progressed, living standards improved, and a specific focus on education fueled a renewed interest in postsecondary education. It is estimated that by mid-decade, 30 percent of American high-school graduates were now heading to pursue a college degree. Suburban housing was expanding dramatically, as was the attendant emphasis on a lifestyle focused on the automobile. By 1957, cars were all the rage, with bigger tail fins, larger engines, and enhanced, cosmetic lighting being the key changes to designs. As car prices rose—the average in 1957 was $2,749—so, too, did the use of credit and credit cards.

The year 1958 saw a dip in the economy, causing the United States to slip into a mild recession with a large increase in unemployment, to over 7 percent. Despite this downturn, automobiles continued to get larger, more powerful, and heavier. At the same time, the prominence of imported cars from Japan began to grow, as Datsun and Toyota made inroads into American markets.

Technologies of all types began to figure more and more prominently as the decade unfolded. Cape Canaveral saw America's first satellite launch, and Russia launched the first of its Sputnik projects. The first microchips were in development, and television, now expanding into color, made such shows as *Rawhide*, *Bonanza*, and *The Twilight Zone* extremely popular. At movie theaters, patrons were drawn to such titles as *Some Like It Hot* (1959), *Ben Hur* (1959), and *North by Northwest* (1959). Barbie dolls became popular, Fidel Castro came into power in Cuba, and (in 1960) the birth control pill was introduced widely into the American market. By the end of the 1950s, all the pieces were in place for the countercultural energies of the 1960s to find fertile soil.

COMPARE & CONTRAST

- **1950s:** The economy of the United States is relatively active, sparked in part by two periods of inflation and a swing toward increased consumerism. Following the removal of price controls after World War II, housing construction takes off, with families flocking to newly minted suburbs. The outward migration from traditional urban homes spreads through the economy both directly (through an increase in car sales) and less obviously (in a flourishing of life-insurance companies, for instance).

  Today: The United States is one of the world's largest economic engines when measured by real Gross Domestic Product (the financial value of all the finished goods and services produced by a country annually). The domestic economy has benefited from the use of natural resources as well as the productivity of its large workforce.

- **1950s:** Environmentalism is emerging as a deeply held and political belief in the responsibility of individuals to protect and improve the land for future generations. Specific issues addressed under the umbrella of the movement include pollution, protection of indigenous plant and animal life, and the concept of a minimal "footprint" of human development. Environmentalism also begins to emphasize the deep symbiotic connection between humans and the land and the need to maintain a balanced relationship between humans and the land's natural systems. By 1950, Aldo Leopold published one of the seminal environmentalist books of a generation, *A Sand County Almanac*. Immediately influential, the book articulates Leopold's philosophy that humans should have ethical respect for the environment and not hurt or harm the land in any way. Leopold's writing sparks a new awareness of environmental issues, which leads, in turn, to a surge in membership in organizations like the Sierra Club. The movement gets another boost with the publication a decade later of biologist Rachel Carson's *Silent Spring* (1962), which focuses specifically on the environmental impacts of DDT spraying. Public outcry sparked by her book culminates in the creation of the Environmental Protection Agency in 1970 and the ban of agricultural use of DDT from 1972 onward.

  Today: Environmental concerns are more significant than ever, ranging from oil spills through global warming's impacts on climate and weather patterns. Activism and science continue to focus on such issues as the extraction and consumption of fossil fuels, the growing list of extinct or endangered plant and animal species, and the dramatic rates of reduction in polar ice caps and glaciers around the world.

- **1950s:** Kerouac and fellow members of the Beat generation are openly exploratory in their sexuality and sexual activities, which leads to numerous protests and calls for censorship of their writing. In the 1950s, the terms *sex* (referring to biological determinants) and *gender* (sociocultural determinants) are commonly seen as closely related concepts. In the latter part of the decade and into the 1960s, however, this changes as increased interest in homosexuality, transsexuality, and other sexual orientations and preferences comes into focus. Although homosexuality is still illegal in many parts of the United States, attitudes and assumptions are undergoing seismic changes.

  Today: Today scientists are increasingly curious about how and why a person might develop a particular sexual orientation. Many scientists believe that it is a combination of nature and nurture, meaning it is a montage of genetic, hormonal, and interpersonal influences. However, scientists favor biologically based theories that center on what happens in the early utero environment. There is much more acceptance of alternative sexual orientation today, with awareness raised through such activities as gay pride parades, media coverage, and training around the dangers of discrimination and bullying.

The lonely sound of a train whistle captures the empty feeling of some of the West's wide-open spaces.
(© Arina P Habich | Shutterstock.com)

CRITICAL OVERVIEW

Although much has been written about Kerouac as a writer of prose and as a cultural icon, relatively little has been said about his poetry, despite its importance, and even less about the posthumous collection *Pomes All Sizes* (1992), in which "Nebraska" first appeared. As Gail Wronsky notes in the *Antioch Review*, "Kerouac's influence on American poetry is ubiquitous. Reading this book will both confirm that fact and demonstrate just how much of what he did has eluded all of his students."

"There is a delightful sly playfulness" to the poems in this collection, Wronsky relates, "moments when poetry is simultaneously pumped up and deflated. Repeatedly, the poet places bad writing ... next to exquisite, discreet, simply beautiful musical phrases." In a remark that aligns neatly with the Beat generation's own disregard for social propriety, Wronsky concludes that "this book makes you wish that Kerouac were alive ... and living with Elvis in Kalamazoo, Michigan."

Writing in *World Literature Today*, Michael Leddy is respectful and noncommittal, noting that the collection "recalls the cheerful assortments of merchandise for sale in what used to be called 'a variety store.'" Marking the volume as variegated and perhaps inconsistent, Leddy sees it "as a record of Kerouac's attempts to find a working model of a sustainable poetic form.... The best poems," he concludes, "are those in which Kerouac is able to cast out preoccupation and remorse," as well as those dedicated "to what he calls sketching."

CRITICISM

Klay Dyer

Dyer is a freelance writer specializing in topics related to literature, popular culture, and innovation.

WHAT DO I READ NEXT?

- Kerouac's own *On the Road* (1957) is a true must-read for students and fans of the Beat generation and its influence on American counterculture from the 1950s onward. Based on the travels of Kerouac and his friends across the United States, it is a story of friendship and creativity set against a vivid backdrop of jazz, poetry, and drug use.

- Henry David Thoreau's *Walden; or, Life in the Woods* (1854) is a natural predecessor to the work of Kerouac and the Beats in its discussion of the pressing forces of industrialization and consumerism on a nineteenth-century world that was, to Thoreau's view, losing focus on what is important and crucial to the future of humanity.

- The young-adult title *The Beats: A Graphic History* (2009), edited by Paul Buhle, with text contributors including Harvey Pekar and artists including Ed Piskor, combines cultural history with graphic storytelling techniques in an accessible, though at times underperforming, primer on the art and ideas of the Beat writers.

- John Tytell's *Naked Angels: The Lives & Literature of the Beat Generation* (1976) remains a seminal and eminently readable sociocultural study of Kerouac and his fellow Beat writers in the context of 1950s conservatism as well as the backlash of 1960s counterculture.

- Robert Pirsig's *Zen and the Art of Motorcycle Maintenance: An Inquiry into Values* (1974) ranks with Kerouac's novel as one of the great road books of all times.

- Any of Shel Silverstein's books of poetry, including *Falling Up* (1987), are in many ways a tame but nonetheless relevant contemporary homage to the open creativity of the Beat writers, as seen through Silverstein's blending of sketch and verse.

In the following essay, he explores the relationship between Kerouac's poem "Nebraska" and the influences of 1950s jazz culture.

> RADICAL IN VIRTUALLY EVERY ASPECT, JAZZ PROVED A NATURAL ATTRACTION FOR KEROUAC AND HIS FELLOW BEATS, ARTISTS WHO WERE THEMSELVES LOOKING TO BREAK WITH WHAT THEY SAW AS THE CONSERVATIVE LIMITATIONS OF POETIC FORM AND STRUCTURE."

The relationship between poetry and music has always been one of intimacy and mutual influence. From medieval minstrels, who set tales to the sounds of music in order to convey complex social messages, to contemporary hip-hop and rap music, the combination has been potent and enduring. At few times in American cultural history, however, has the union of music and language been more creatively catalytic than in the years following World War II, when a small group of talented, creative writers, self-proclaimed as the Beats, began experimenting with jazz rhythms and syncopations. What they produced, both on the page and in performance, would go on to change the contours (and sound) of poetry for generations to follow.

Just as the Beats were gathering at Columbia University, bebop was already going strong in New York City, where pioneers like Charlie Parker (1920–1955), Miles Davis (1926–1991), and Chet Baker (1929–1988) were already moving jazz toward a new horizon of cool. It was a horizon that would see more improvisation and experimentation, an emphasis on relaxed and fluid tempos, and a new freedom to borrow openly and creatively from classical and non-jazz antecedents. Significantly, this new coolness also allowed musicians to adopt more intimate postures in their music, turning away from the physicality of bebop to allow more expressive elements to be highlighted.

For a poet like Kerouac, the raw yet highly technical musicality of jazz was seen as a potential vehicle through which he could explore and articulate the emotion and political energies of the day. Rising out of industrialized urban centers, charged with racial overtones, and freed into improvisation in a time of formal conservatism, jazz broke with the sociocultural landscape of music with its emphasis on vocal-driven pop, traditional country and western, and the fading echoes of postwar swing. Radical in virtually every aspect, jazz proved a natural attraction for Kerouac and his fellow Beats, artists who were themselves looking to break with what they saw as the conservative limitations of poetic form and structure. Kerouac wrote often about his love of jazz and of his admiration for the legendary Charlie "Bird" Parker, for one.

What Kerouac saw in jazz music was what might best be described as a spontaneous inter-connectedness. In its purest form, the jazz music of the day was at once highly technical and intensely improvisational. Musicians were asked to play off each other with no specific direction or form, responding only to the organic flow of the notes and the directions set by the other players. This combination of spon-taneity and interdependent creativity intrigued the Beats, especially Kerouac, who aimed to write poetry that would break with all constric-tions of meter, rhyme, and imagery. As he did in writing prose, Kerouac was determined to find a way that would allow him to transform free thoughts (often raised through sessions with alcohol or drugs) into equally free writing that would capture authentically the rhythms and meanings that he felt in the moment.

What Kerouac was aiming for was by no means new. Ralph Waldo Emerson (1803–1882) speaks in his famous essay *Nature* (1836) about his desire to move poetry beyond the lim-its of metaphor, which he saw as the most elo-quent and yet obtuse literary device currently available. Such predecessors as Gertrude Stein (1874–1946), William Carlos Williams (1883–1963), and E. E. Cummings (1894–1962) experi-mented successfully with similar ideas. Indeed, such experimental works as Cummings's 1949 poem "a thrown a" proved relatively successful in conveying the goal of having meaning con-veyed through printed words that were, in the end, notations of sound. As in many of Cum-mings's poems, sound was meaning and meaning was sound.

Kerouac was determined to take this rela-tionship even further, through what he saw as the potential of poetry when combined with jazz to articulate the thought processes that drove him to write. In "Nebraska," for instance, the short, uneven, and intensely rhythmic lines that accrue in the poem are far more aligned with jazz

than with traditional poetics (of the lyric, the sonnet, the ballad) that stress metrical beats, rhyme schemes, and definable rhythms. Struc-ture and form are submerged in the stream of consciousness that drives the lines forward. Words are seemingly blurted out in vigorous bursts, at times with little, if any, obvious con-nection to what came previously other than a sound or rhythm holding them together by a perceptual thread. Punctuation is sparse, and more often than not breaks occur organically. Well-timed breathing is imperative when trying to read "Nebraska" aloud, as is allowing pauses to come organically through the poem rather than looking for the usual markers of hesitation or break (commas and periods).

"Nebraska" begins to devolve relatively quickly into the kind of linguistic improvisation that Kerouac would foreground more dramati-cally in his *Mexico City Blues* (1959) and which Ginsberg would take to new limits in "Howl" (1955). In comparison to these works, the play with language in "Nebraska" is relatively mild, most notably marked by a shift to include sym-bols, the ampersand and dollar sign, to stand as replacements for the usual terms *and* and *dollars, cash,* or *money.*

But herein lies a good example of the even-tual endgame of Kerouac's project. For while a simple, common symbol ($) can be stabilized to mean one thing (i.e., cash or money or dollars) it is never fully locked into a stable semantic rela-tionship. Put another way, the $ is never linked *only* to the concept of dollars but is free to cas-cade outward to include a plethora of synonyms and meanings: cash, wealth, power, control, and so on. The line itself thus represents a multitude of potential meanings, each of which is held in the $ symbol and open to the interpretation/improvisation of each reader. The line is about cash, to be sure, but is also about so much more than cash. It is about wealth (with its own attendant connections to influence, power, leg-acy), value, and even freedom. Like a great work of jazz, Kerouac's poem spins around this single symbol to create an impression and through that impression creates a multitude of meanings.

It was not only the improvisational aspect of jazz that appealed to Kerouac. Jazz brought with it a powerful and often rebellious sociopolitical impact that flew in the face of mainstream Amer-ican preoccupations with postwar consumerism and the perceived value of living a suburban life.

Jazz was distinctly urban, predominantly the venue of African American musicians (with trumpet player Baker and pianist Dave Brubeck being notable exceptions), and was aligned openly, though not always accurately, with a type of lifestyle. This latter truth was underscored by the fact that many of its key figures struggled openly with addictions (heroin being a favorite among some of the greatest players of the day). Not surprisingly, jazz culture was seen as intense, edgy, exponentially creative, and more than a touch dangerous. By the early 1950s, in other words, jazz already was what the Beat writers hoped to become: a groundbreaking creative movement that tossed social norms aside with fervor, embraced creativity with passion, and tested limits, both psychological and physical, with fearlessness.

Kerouac, though more tame than his friends Ginsberg and Burroughs, embraced the opportunity to challenge American ideals of the day through his poetry. His subtle reference to America's industrialized heartland as something akin to a tenement (slum) is an open challenge to the common and deeply held perception of long-term economic prosperity that took hold in the postwar boom. To the Beats, all prosperity came with a corresponding cost, and to see an almost blind faith in industrialization take hold of the country was akin in their eyes to a descent into the depths of a cultural hell.

Similarly, Kerouac's emphasis on the sexual energies of men and women, including girls that Kerouac senses he is unable to impress with a mere 35 cents in his pocket, albeit tame in comparison to what Burroughs undertook in his homoerotic *Naked Lunch* (1959), raises a clear challenge to the assumptions of middle-class Americans. If heroin was the trademark vice of 1950s jazz, sexual experimentation (along with chronic alcoholism) would become that of Kerouac. (Of course, many Beats, Kerouac included, also used heroin, a kind of tragic homage to their jazz mentors.)

As in the finest jazz improvisation, "Nebraska" spins further and faster as the poem unfolds. By the time the poet-speaker turns to peruse the westward horizon from which he has come, the poem has found its own rhythm, one still tied to words (unlike in Cummings, who slides toward phonetic representations) but at the same time alienated from their common usages. As the final line of the poem underscores, in the end it was understanding communicated through the rhythms and sounds of

> IF KEROUAC HAD TAKEN BETTER CARE OF HIMSELF, HE MIGHT BE ALIVE TODAY, GIVING TED TALKS."

language that mattered most to Kerouac. Words are simply a means to his unique and invigorating creative end.

Source: Klay Dyer, Critical Essay on "Nebraska," in *Poetry for Students*, Gale, Cengage Learning, 2016.

Alan Pell Crawford
In the following essay, Crawford speculates about possible influences on Kerouac's style.

"Never try to be something you're not, because the audience is looking for authenticity." So, in *Adweek*, says drag celebrity RuPaul, who ought to know. This pursuit of authenticity, of course, goes back a long way, to Rousseau, I understand, if not earlier. But it took on a special urgency in this country in the years following World War II when, the story goes, Republican conformity was bulldozing all the joy and spontaneity out of life.

This itch to get real has continued unabated to our own day, becoming a cliche and an obsession of the marketing business that *Adweek* celebrates. It will always be possible, evidently, to sell blue jeans not so much by evoking images of the people who actually wore them to work—everyone does now—but of those who tried to look like the people who wore them to work: Marlon Brando and James Dean. Or Jack Kerouac.

The desire for genuine experience was a central concern of the Beats, who came to public attention about the same time, and for many of the same reasons, as Brando and Dean and the rebellion against square society they expressed. It is the central concern of Kerouac's *On the Road* which, decade after decade, casts its peculiar spell over young readers. I was one of those young readers myself once, and I re-read the novel recently to see how it held up. I can't say I was disappointed, but my expectations were not high.

The speaker talks to the sun, asking it to cause flowers to bloom. (© *SJ Travel Photo and Video | Shutterstock.com*)

It's hard to imagine I was ever so young as to have found this book enchanting. Kerouac's would-be rebels strike me today as far more impressed by their own frantic grasping for genuine experience than anyone else should be. This is not news now, but they treated the women who pass in and out of their lives with about as much regard as you might expect of grown-up drunks who—as Kerouac himself did—live with and off their aging mothers. Knowing what we know today about the drug use and sexual practices of the men on whom the author based his characters, it is apparent, too, how much this fearlessly candid author in fact concealed.

I was also "tremendously amazed," as Kerouac would probably have written, at how badly he wrote. Kerouac "writes not so much about things," Alfred Kazin noticed, "as about the search for things to write about." Sal Paradise and Dean Moriarty's adventures are never as "crazy," "fantastic," "mad," "wild," or "tremendous" as Kerouac would have us believe, no matter how "crazy," "fantastic," "mad," "wild,"

or "tremendous" he tells us they were. Kerouac seemed to think that by the use of these adjectives he can move the reader as deeply as his narrator professes to be by, say, hanging around in a jazz club with real Negroes. He is mistaken.

I was awfully naive once, but never so naive as Kerouac/Paradise, who understands so little about the lives of black Americans that he wishes he "were a Negro [because] the best the white world could offer was not enough ecstasy, not enough life, joy, kicks, darkness, music, not enough night." It is passages like that—about, for instance, the "happy, true-heart ecstatic Negroes of America"—that inspired me to pull from the shelf another book that expresses much the same desire. It did so, however, with greater honesty and courage than *On the Road*. It also conveys more pleasure, in large part because it makes far fewer claims for itself.

This was *Really the Blues*, the autobiography of an endearing oddball named Milton "Mezz" Mezzrow. Born in Chicago in 1899 to Russian Jewish parents, Mezzrow fell under the spell of Bix Beiderbecke, Sidney Bechet, and other early jazz musicians. He learned to play the clarinet, recorded with many of these better known musicians, including Louis Armstrong and Fats Waller, and—here's where things get fun—decided he too wanted to be black. Mezzrow determined that he "was going to be a Negro musician, hipping the world about the blues the way only Negroes can."

Effectively renouncing his white citizenship, he married a black woman, moved to Harlem, and declared himself a "voluntary Negro." This was years before Norman Mailer wrote his 1957 essay declaring the "white Negro" a "fact of American life." Examples of this new species could then be seen from tour buses passing through Greenwich Village, among other places, where "the bohemian and the juvenile delinquent came face-to-face with the Negro," developing the hip, as opposed to square, sensibility. But this hip cat Mezzrow was way ahead of all of the Norman-come-lately's.

An only passable reed man—"Any little boy can play the clarinet of sax as good as Mezz can," Pops Foster wrote in his autobiography, "He just stands up there and goes toot-toot-toot"—Mezzrow, like so many early jazz musicians, had a day job. He sold marijuana. In his time, his name became so closely associated with the product he sold that in certain circles he became a brand; the word "mezz" became slang for marijuana. (You can hear it referred to in the old standard "If You's a Viper.")

In *Really the Blues*, Mezzrow writes with admirable honesty about his involvement with drugs, including an opium habit. It was his drug use that resulted in possibly the most memorable passage in his autobiography, and certainly the most amusing. In 1940, while trying to get into the Gay New Orleans performance space at the World's Fair in Flushing, he was arrested carrying 60 joints. He was convicted of possession with intent to distribute and sent to Riker's Island. There he told the guards he was black, hoping to be housed in the segregated unit.

"I'm colored, even if I don't look it," he said, "and I don't think I'd get along in the white blocks." The deputy "studied my features real hard. He seemed a little relieved when he saw my nappy head" and sent the felon off to live with his own kind, as Mezzrow defined it. When he had paid his debt to society, he moved back to Harlem and eventually to Paris, where in 1972 he died.

Really the Blues bears a significant and generally unacknowledged relationship to the Beat Generation and almost certainly to its literary experiments. There have been elaborate attempts to account for Kerouac's "spontaneous bop prosody," and the more elaborate they are, the drearier and more pathetic they become. The simplest explanation seems to be that Kerouac, having gorged himself on Henry Miller and Walt Whitman, attempted to mimic in prose the phrasing of jazz improvisation. That, of course, also appears to be the chief influence on Mezzrow, whose slangy hipster prose at times sounds like Kerouac's—or vice versa. Of a parade by the prison band, for example, Mezzrow writes:

> Right away the whole band stiffened up and began to sparkle, like they all got a heavy shot of thyroid extract. Travis, who was playing the lead on his horn, got carried away in the flood too and he began to swing out with a sudden husky vibrant tone, taking his breath at the natural intervals just where he felt them, and the whole band was suddenly marching and swaying to a new rhythm. And every beat Frankie pounded on his drums was in perfect time with every variation somebody picked out on my clarinet, and my clarinet and the trumpet melted together in one gigantic harmonic orgasm, and my fingers ran every whichaway, and the fellows in the Ninth Division began to grin and stomp and shout, "Blow it Mezz!" they yelled, "Yeah I hear you!" "Get away, poppa!" "Put me in the alley!"

Of course, Mezzrow never wrote any of this. The author of *Really the Blues* was in fact a minor writer of the time named Bernard Wolfe, who ghosted Mezzrow's story. Wolfe is an interesting case himself, having served as Leon Trotsky's secretary when the latter was in Mexico.

As for the book's connection to the Beats, Kerouac didn't cop to having read it, much less been influenced by it, but Allen Ginsberg remembered it well. Ginsberg, who recalled its appearance at the Columbia University bookstore, said *Really the Blues* was "for me the first signal into white culture of the underground black hip culture that pre-existed before my own generation." (Woody Allen, for what it is worth, calls *Really the Blues* one of the five books that had the greatest impact on his own life and work, even though he thinks the stories in it are "probably just a bunch of junk.")

Ginsberg says it was the mid-'40s, and he is correct: *Really the Blues* was published in 1946. The events that form the story of *On the Road* took place between 1947 and 1950. *On the Road* was not published until 1957. All of which is to say that however authentic the Beats might have thought they were, however eager they were to drench themselves in raw experience and express it in their work, *On the Road* was very likely the imitation of one white guy (Kerouac) imitating another white guy (Wolfe) imitating another white guy (Mezzrow) imitating—black people. All in the name of authenticity.

Of course, authenticity is now a kind of racket in America. Alleged experts write entire books telling "business leaders" how to fake it. Kerouac, it's my bet, could teach these imposters a few tricks they've never thought of, including not to acknowledge your sources when you steal from them. If Kerouac had taken better care of himself, he might be alive today, giving TED talks.

Source: Alan Pell Crawford, "Black like Kerouac: What the Beats Stole from an Authentically Fake Jazzman," in *American Conservative*, Vol. 14, No. 2, March–April 2015, p. 40.

Cary Nelson

In the following excerpt, Nelson points out the successes and failures of Kerouac's collected poems.

...He is universally known for his fiction, but his poetry has so far attracted only a much smaller, although devoted, audience. In fact, he wrote a great deal of poetry, some of which is compelling and some of which fails. A collected poems—unlike a selected poems—will inescapably include poetry of both sorts, given that the published books and the finished manuscripts dictate much of the contents. It is far from clear, however, that one would even want to select only his best poems, since diversity of tone, form, subject matter, and seriousness are central to Kerouac's aesthetic. In her introduction to *Book of Haikus*, a collection that adds unpublished archival poems as a supplement to Kerouac's manuscript, Regina Weinreich reports that friends said it was "best not to show Kerouac at his worst" and to "throw away the clinkers" but that she has nonetheless "chosen many against their sound counsel" (xxxix). The haiku that is meticulously crafted stands next to the haiku that is casual or flippant. We cannot understand Kerouac if we filter him through an aesthetic foreign to him.

> BUT THE EVIDENCE SUGGESTS THE RELATIONSHIP BETWEEN GENRES IN KEROUAC'S WORK IS UNUSUALLY INTERDEPENDENT. THAT IS ONLY ONE REASON WHY WE SHOULD WELCOME THE FACT THAT THE OVERALL SCHOLARLY NEGLECT OF HIS POETRY IS COMING TO AN END."

The challenges presented by the task of editing Kerouac's poetry do not, however, end there. Although he wrote and published in traditional forms, he also revised older forms and invented new ones. In the case of his blues poetry, he used the label conceptually, thematically, and attitudinally, with no reference to the formal tradition of the blues stanza. In fact Kerouac's blues are more obviously jazz-influenced. His haikus, which helped define an alternative English-language haiku practice—a practice that has since thrived in the work of other poets and shaped a new haiku tradition—abandoned the Japanese syllabic and seasonal standard and turned the haiku into a short poem of varied length on any topic. But, in truth, with Kerouac it is not always even clear what counts as a poem. Some of the *Dharma* is full of what amount to one-paragraph prose poems, as are *The Scripture of the Golden Eternity* and *Old Angel Midnight*, though there is no evidence Kerouac identified all of them as such. His work also contains many examples of what is arguably prose lineated as poetry, or constructed as what we might call shaped paragraph stanzas, as with the 54th section of *Old Angel Midnight*. His overall sensibility was so conditioned and inspired by writing over a thousand haikus that his novels are often sprinkled with haiku-like moments of observation, as in the following passage from *The Dharma Bums*: "The old tree brooded over me silently, a living thing. I heard a mouse snoring in the garden weeds. The rooftops of Berkeley looked like pitiful living meat sheltering grieving phantoms from the eternality of the heavens which they feared to face" (*Road Novels*).

The *Dharma Bums* often appeals particularly to readers of Kerouac's haikus, or, for that matter, to students of haiku poetry generally. Early on in the novel, Ray Smith has a wonderful discussion with Japhy Ryder about the challenges faced in translating T'ang Dynasty poet Han Shan's famous "cold mountain" poem from Chinese to English. Then later, Ray, Japhy, and Morley climb Matterhorn Peak in Yosemite National Park together, trading spontaneously composed haiku and discussing them with one another:

> "Look over there," sang Japhy, "yellow aspens. Just put me in the mind of a haiku... 'Talking about the literary life—the yellow aspens.'" Walking in this country you could understand the perfect gems of haikus the Oriental poets had written, never getting drunk in the mountains or anything but just going along as fresh as children writing down what they saw without literary devices or fanciness of expression. We made up haikus as we climbed, winding up and up now on the slopes of brush. "Rocks on the side of the cliff," I said, "why don't they tumble down?" "Maybe that's a haiku, maybe not, it might be a little too complicated," said Japhy. "A real haiku's gotta be as simple as porridge and yet make you see the real thing. . . ."

What is at stake here for Kerouac is not just the near-absolute economy of language desirable in haikus, a principle Pound earlier helped codify for imagist poetry, but also a certain fantasy of the possibility of unmediated representation, the possibility that poetry might give us access to the thing itself without language seeming to intervene. That fantasy would haunt him long thereafter, despite the fact that some of his inventive haikus pivot precisely on evidence of mediation, of the difference that human thought, the mind, makes in what we see and how we see. It would haunt him despite his creation of blues meditations that set aside the principle of economy. And it would haunt him despite the recognition, in his Buddhist poetry and prose, that the world we see is the one we make.

Regina Weinreich quotes another passage from *The Dharma Bums* as evidence of the stylistic conjunction of haiku and prose: "The storm went away as swiftly as it came and the late afternoon lake-sparkle blinded me. Late afternoon, my mop drying on the rock. Late afternoon, my bare back cold as I stood above the world in a snowfield digging shovelsful into a pail. Late afternoon, it was I not the void that changed" (*Book of Haikus*). Then she points out that the same passages occur as three-line haiku

in one of Kerouac's notebooks. In "Hidden Visions: Embedded Haiku in Jack Kerouac's *The Dharma Bums*," author Mark Smith goes one step further, breaking out a series of haiku from the prose of *The Dharma Bums*. As early as 1983, Gerald Nicosia finds some prose lines of *Visions of Gerard* to be "like haiku" (501).

Gerald Nicosia points out that the prose lines of *Visions of Gerard* are actually haiku and then quotes a line from a Kerouac letter to New Direction's founding editor James Laughlin: "All my books are as it were poetry sheeted in narrative steel" (501, 545). James T. Jones suggests that Kerouac is a novelist whose "fictional technique led him directly to poetry" (12).

All this is not to say that the editor of a Kerouac *Collected Poems* can meet all these challenges. No one, including Mark Smith, would expect an editor to be midwife to the birth of innumerable poems from Kerouac's prose. But the evidence suggests the relationship between genres in Kerouac's work is unusually interdependent. That is only one reason why we should welcome the fact that the overall scholarly neglect of his poetry is coming to an end. The other reason, as the *Collected Poems* at least in part shows, is that many of his poems are innovative and unforgettable. It is fitting to cite some examples.

Midway through the *Collected Poems* one comes to "Poems of the Buddhas of Old," composed of forty-five rhymed quatrains divided into five numbered groups. Its thematic, constructed as a narrative parable, centers on what—in the Western context—is the central lesson of Buddhism, here offered in Kerouac's appealing vernacular:

> Life is like a dream,
> You only think it's real
> Cause you're born a sucker
> For that kind of deal

While Kerouac's Buddhism is regularly characterized as an extremely specialized interest—and he was only focused intensely on it for a limited number of years, basically 1954–57—in fact, his Buddhist poetry is often accessible, witty, and of pointed interest to anyone willing to think about the illusions that sustain Western culture. There is no lesson more difficult for Americans to learn than that all they believe to be vitally important is actually evanescent and will pass, and that the meanings they think are linked to material reality are actually mental constructs: "only imagination makes the lilacs grow, / turn blue in July—makes the ant hurry— / the cat conceive of himself as cat" (*Some of the Dharma*). That the lilacs "turn blue," that the ant is "hurrying," that the feline species has the name of cat, all this is human cultural construction, though our resistance to coming to terms with that recognition could hardly be greater. Kerouac rings changes on just that recognition in scores of poems, no doubt in part because it offered an antidote to his own suffering. However, Kerouac's personal circumstances should not inoculate us from confronting a fundamental cultural blindness.

"Poems of the Buddhas of Old" is a poem from *Some of the Dharma* that made its way into *Pomes All Sizes* and thus into the *Collected Poems*. So is "'Sight is just dust'" reprinted here, as Phipps-Kettlewell rather uninformatively puts it, "in the form in which it appeared in the post-humous selection *Scattered Poems*" (707). That "form" represents less than a third of a triumphant longer poem, "The Perfect Love of Mind Essence," that no one is likely to discover unless they make their way to page 229 of *Some of the Dharma*. If anything, Phipps-Kettlewell discourages curiosity by characterizing that book simply as "an immense assemblage of notes on Buddhism," adding that she has not taken any poems directly from it because it "needs to be read as an organic whole." *Some of the Dharma* is an astonishing achievement in its entirety, but I cannot accept either an aesthetic or a moral requirement that it must be read on its own so its poems cannot be anthologized. Certainly it is Kerouac's most radical mixed form and rewards direct experience, but it includes some of his most important poems, without which a Kerouac canon and a Kerouac *Collected Poems* is unacceptably impoverished....

Source: Cary Nelson, Review of *Jack Kerouac: Collected Poems*, in *Journal of Beat Studies*, Vol. 2, 2013, p. 101.

Nancy M. Grace

In the following excerpt, Grace compares Kerouac's poetic style to the improvisation of jazz music.

As so much of Kerouac's private and published works attest, his pursuit of a literary life devoted to probing the metaphysical and ontological was predicated upon few if any concrete distinctions between poetry and prose. Neither

> RARELY DO THESE CHORUSES END MIDSENTENCE OR MIDTHOUGHT—THAT IS, AT SEMANTIC POINTS THAT FAIL TO BRING CLOSURE TO THE CHORUS. KEROUAC SEEMS TO HAVE DEVELOPED A FELT SENSE FOR THE FORM IMPOSED BY THE SIZE OF THE PAGE AND LEARNED HOW TO COMPRESS HIS SUBJECT INTO THAT TINY SPACE."

the debate about the nature of genre nor the consistent exercise of precise literary terminology appears to have much interested him. Consequently, the historical record presents contradictory claims on his part. As *Dharma* illustrates, he could fastidiously create and define genres or subgenres, such as haiku, blues choruses, tics, dreams, and bookmovies, some adhering to more standard generic conventions, others flagrantly violating them. Yet prose was either "an endless one-line poem," as he wrote in a poetic statement for Donald Allen's anthology *New American Poetry* (*Blonde*), or a series of poems called "paragraphs," as he told Ted Berrigan (Plimpton 114). *Mexico City Blues*, easily recognizable as free verse, he identified as blues poems, while *Old Angel Midnight*, distinctly proselike in form, he defined for Lawrence Ferlinghetti in 1958 as "not prose, it's really a long one-line poem" (*Letters* 2:98). While he identified narrative as the primary function of prose as opposed to the wide-open imaginative and confessional impulse of poetry (Plimpton 104–05), the Legend effects a critique of genre as hermetic, suggesting that all language is legitimate as long as it serves a higher purpose.

What he considered most integral to his writing was the writer's commitment to the most honest form of expression, which he persistently called "the true blue song of man" (*Blonde*) or the "eternal search for truth" (*Atop*). It is safe to say that while Kerouac never composed a systematic theory of genre, in this equation the element of song acts as a portal of human discovery. Poetry such as *Mexico City Blues*, *Old Angel Midnight*, and other poems that this chapter will address, was meant to be sung, and it could not escape its fundamental musical nature. For Kerouac, the new American poets of the 1950s represented "childlike graybeard Homers singing in the street," telling the story of America. Their new poetry was to be experienced by anyone who could sing (or swing), and within this timeless universe, Kerouac intended to rescue poetry from the rigid, elitist depersonalization or "gray faced Academic quibbling" (*Scattered Poems*, unnumbered). His practice meant to return poetry to its origins in the bardic oral tradition and, through the singing of stories, to reawaken the ancient, lyric, visionary voice of truth.

Connecting the musical concepts of the bard and the lyric, much of Kerouac's writing also attempted to create with pencil and typewriter what jazz musicians created with horns, pianos, drums, and voices. The bardic/jazz-inspired product, as he often described it, was antiformalistic, unpremeditated, and unrevised, grounded in improvisation and spontaneity. Writing to his editor Malcolm Cowley in 1955, he declared, "The requirements for prose & verse are the same, i.e. *blow*—what a man most wishes to hide, revise, and unsay, is precisely what Literature is waiting and bleeding for—Every doctor knows, every *Prophet* knows the convulsion of *truth*" (*Letters* 1 emphasis mine). Kerouac's evoking of *prophet* and *truth* in the Cowley correspondence ostensibly configures the poet as one who rejects socially contrived prescriptions and draws instead on cognitive processes to reach an essential form of consciousness rendering authenticity from which the poet as sage and sayer derives both the power to transcend human consciousness and the authority to speak that universal truth. The result is *spontaneous bop prosody* equating essentialist truth with personal honesty through free, unpremeditated flow of sound—a construct that, rightly or wrongly, still dominates definitions of Beat literature. In effect, Kerouac's composition method redefined twentieth-century poetry as a recombinant power in which the poet's relationship with the audience was that of public performer (the bard/musician) and solitary speaker (the lyric, visionary voice). The method situates him as a bridge between modernism and postmodernism, his poetry existing in dynamic tension as (1) the voice of the human soul communing with the metaphysical, recognizing the symbolic transparency of language, and (2) an "intellectual and sonic construction" privileging technique and the materiality of language (Hoover xxxv).

"E BOP SHE BAM"

Kerouac declared in the author note to *Mexico City Blues* that he wanted "to be considered a jazz poet blowing a long blues in an afternoon jam session on Sunday," Jazz, a complex form of social and individual expression with visible connections to both preliterate and literate vocal and instrumental musical production, also guided much of his thinking about his writing. The distinctions between musical and literary composition are sometimes not easy to delineate, primarily because the cultural and psychological histories of both are rooted to some degree symbiotically in the same materials and processes. Since music and literature have always drawn on many of the same devices, any discussion of jazz as a literary influence will be somewhat vexed, particularly if the goal is to separate the distinctly musical from the distinctly literary. My intent is not to identify a set of practices and forms that are uniquely jazz oriented to argue their place in Kerouac's literary and spiritual life. Rather, my discussion will explicate particular devices associated with but not necessarily unique to jazz that function as analogues for the sui generis forms of cognition on which Kerouac drew and the complicated, socially derived structures that he manipulated. Dipping into and out of jazz and literary production, he wrote *with and against* these art forms.

Like Western European music, jazz has a history of musical notation, but it was not this particular feature of jazz that captivated Kerouac. He remained uninterested in pursuing the page to score lyrics or create a poetic version of musical composition, as, for example, Anne Waldman does in "skin Meat BONES," in which the three titular words are placed on the page as notes on a scale. However, Kerouac's poems occasionally feature elements alluding to the composer's page. One sometimes encounters broken words that read as if scored to accompany notes in a song, the common pronunciation of a word distorted by the linking of phonemes and syllables with musical phrases, such as "Of o cean wave" and "Ra diance!" from "Bowery Blues" (*Blues*); "Ai la ra la / la rai la ra" and "M'e'r y o cking" from *Mexico City Blues* (8th, 26th choruses); and "A—mer—ri—kay" and "ho / o / ome" from "San Francisco Blues" (*Blues* 34th, 38th choruses). He also used large blank spaces to represent the pause or rest that a musician takes (138th Chorus *MCB*) or parenthetically included words such as *pause* (143rd Chorus *MCB*). Sometimes he worked with the standard three-line A-A-B form of the blues song, and when he wanted to leave no doubt that his poetry depicted conventional singing, he told the reader outright, as he does in the 84th Chorus of *Mexico City Blues*, which begins with "SINGING:—" directing the reader to sing the stanza, which plays with lyrics from the early twentieth-century popular ballad "By the Light of the Silvery Moon."

However, there is no heavy reliance on these devices. As heuristics, they seem to have proven somewhat inflexible for Kerouac. Instead, the jazz form that he directly acknowledged and used routinely was the set number of musical bars. Many of his most successful poems, those that he called blues choruses, loosely mimicked the twelve-bar form of blues/jazz composition. As he stated in the introduction to *Book of Blues*, his jazzlike method limited each poem, often titled a "Chorus," to the size of the page of the small breast-pocket notebook in which he wrote them. For a poet like Kerouac who relied on aleatory procedures, a lot could happen within those bars, that is, the approximately twenty lines per page, but when he came to the final bar—the end of the page, the composition was complete. This method enables the carryover of, repetition of, or the variation on themes, sounds, and images from chorus to chorus, analogous to the carryover of musical phrases from measure to measure.

For instance, choruses 79 through 84 from *Mexico City Blues* flow smoothly into one another, a movement produced primarily by the carryover of key phrases. "Goofing at the table" in the 79th Chorus becomes the opening line of the 80th, which introduces the theme of ham, bacon, and eggs. In the 81th Chorus, this trio is transformed into "Mr. Beggar and Mrs. Davy," otherwise known as "Looney and CRUNEY," which are transformed into "dem eggs & dem dem / Dere bacons, baby." Using Beat black jazz lingo, the singer then calls on a "brother" to continue the riff on eggs, bacon, and so on, only now with the sounds of his trumpet instead of the singer's spoken/written words. "Lay that down / solid [. . .]" he directs, "'Bout all dem / bacon & eggs [. . .] All that luney / & fruney," "Fracons, acons, and beggs" begin the 82nd Chorus, which concludes with "Looney & Booney / Juner and Mooner / Moon, Spoon, and June." The 83rd Chorus returns to a directive to the trumpeter to "lay it down"—the sequence ending in the 84th with "Croon— / Love— /

June—." The dominant aesthetic foregrounds continuation, or time, rather than structure, or space—in other words, how long can the jazz musician/poet spin the musical invention. The resemblance to a musical composition is fashioned by recurring rhythms, recurring phrases, and the linking of sound units from line to line and chorus to chorus. The language of this set of choruses in particular exemplifies Ginsberg's analysis that Kerouac was highly sensitive to the way "black speech influences the breath of the music which influences the breath of Kerouac's [written] speech" (Nicosia, "Interview"). The semantic links, integrating the song element into the work, suggest surrealistic metamorphosing, as a breakfast meal is transformed into a man and a woman, who through their nicknames become, ironically, the very words they sing from "By the Light of the Silvery Moon."

This structure emphasizes the performance of continuation while employing a structuralist approach to achieve that prolongation. The small notebook pages, instead of inhibiting the progression of his ideas, as one might expect, became a template for expression. For instance, in *Mexico City Blues*, a supermajority of the poems, 186, or 76 percent of the choruses, are highly similar in length, ranging from nineteen to twenty-five lines, thirty-five having twenty-two, thirty-five having twenty-four, and thirty-one having twenty-three lines. The shortest chorus is seven lines long and the longest contains thirty-one lines. This commonality makes sense if one accepts Kerouac's claim that each chorus was composed within the parameters of the breast-pocket notebook pages. Rarely do these choruses end midsentence or midthought—that is, at semantic points that fail to bring closure to the chorus. Kerouac seems to have developed a felt sense for the form imposed by the size of the page and learned how to compress his subject into that tiny space. With *Mexico City Blues*, of the 244 choruses (the 216th Chorus contains parts A, B, and C), only the 164th ends midsentence: "and suddenly there's a guy," which continues as "under the table" in the first line of the 165th. However, because the speaker is describing a dream in the 164th Chorus, the illogical introduction of "a guy" to conclude the poem fits the surreal quality of the chorus, rendering it a textual whole. Likewise, the phrase "under the table" in the subsequent chorus situates the reader in *media res*, a fairly conventional introduction for lyric verse. In this respect, each chorus, while thematically a constituent part of a whole, carries formal integrity. The notebook page, then, simultaneously provides the expansion of space necessary for the poet to improvise while arbitrarily establishing a form as tightly prescribed as for a sonnet or sestina.

Improvisation is the characteristic most often associated with jazz composition, a process that Kerouac addressed in "Essentials," stating that continual and unrestrained movement of words was imperative. In *Book of Blues* he even instructed readers to aim for "non stop ad libbing within each chorus, or the gig is shot." At one level these statements affirm a lay understanding of improvisation as naive and uninformed. They also allude to something that happens on the spot, and in this regard his method corresponds with real musical performance: in the act of performance a musician rarely has the luxury of stopping to correct a mistake or improve expression—what comes out comes out. Kerouac's practice reflected the application of this point as well. The four breast-pocket notebooks in which he penciled *Mexico City Blues*, within a week, according to his correspondence with Sterling Lord (*Letters* 1), shows that 155 of the 244 choruses were published exactly as they were originally composed. In the entire set of 244 poems, only two words appear to have been erased: the last line of the third stanza of the 26th Chorus contains a space between the words "pale light" where another word had once stood, and the second line of the 45th Chorus clearly shows erasure marks and the word *softened* written over them. Similarly, most of the published sections of *Old Angel Midnight* were composed without revision, except substituting "Old Angel" for "Lucien" and a tiny revision related to Ginsberg and Burroughs' relationship, presumably to avoid libel. This textual evidence reinforces and validates the myth that Kerouac wrote quickly and on the spot. . . .

Source: Nancy M. Grace, "Songs and Prayers: *Mexico City Blues* and Other Poems," in *Jack Kerouac and the Literary Imagination*, Palgrave, 2007, pp. 161–66.

SOURCES

Kerouac, Jack, *Pomes All Sizes*, City Lights Books, 1992, pp. 3–7.

Leddy, Michael, Review of *Pomes All Sizes*, in *World Literature Today*, Vol. 67, No. 3, Summer 1993, pp. 612–13.

Maltin, Leonard, *Classic Movie Guide: From the Silent Era Through 1965*, Plume, 2010.

Seiler, Cotten, *Republic of Drivers: A Culture of Automobility in America*, University of Chicago Press, 2008.

Wronsky, Gail, Review of *Pomes All Sizes*, in *Antioch Review*, Vol. 51, No. 3, Summer 1993, p. 469.

FURTHER READING

Holladay, Hilary, *Herbert Huncke: The Times Square Hustler Who Inspired Jack Kerouac and the Beat Generation*, Schaffner Press, 2015.

This volume offers a great look into the background of the Beat generation through the biography of a man largely dismissed from cultural history as a scam artist, junkie, and hustler despite his influences on Kerouac, Ginsberg, and Burroughs.

Jones, James T., *A Map of "Mexico City Blues": Jack Kerouac as Poet*, Southern Illinois University Press, 1992.

Jones's pioneering critical study of Kerouac's book-length poem *Mexico City Blues* (1959) argues, albeit with varying degrees of success, for his position as a prominent shaper of American poetry.

Kerouac, Jack, *Collected Poems*, edited by Marilène Phipps-Kettlewell, Library of America, 2012.

The canonical Library of America has issued a comprehensive collection of Kerouac's poems that also includes comments by writers and artists on the significant influence of his verse as well as his prose.

Morgan, Bill, and Stanford, David, eds., *Jack Kerouac and Allen Ginsberg: The Letters*, Viking, 2010.

The first published collection of letters between two of the leading figures of the Beat movement, this collection is invaluable for shedding light on the personal dynamics of a creative and spiritual friendship as well as on the ideas, arguments, and day-to-day decisions that defined a literary generation.

SUGGESTED SEARCH TERMS

Jack Kerouac

"Nebraska" AND poem

"Nebraska" AND Kerouac

"Bus East" AND Kerouac

Pomes All Sizes AND Kerouac

poetry AND 1950s

Beat poetry

Beat generation AND poetry

poetry AND jazz

poetry AND music

Poem

MURIEL RUKEYSER
1968

Muriel Rukeyser's "Poem" was published originally as part of the collection *The Speed of Darkness* in 1968. Very much a poem of its historical time, it speaks to the spirit and hope of a generation that sought to embrace a new spirituality and a new way of being in a world rife with war and death. "Poem" juxtaposes the pressures of a society increasingly fixated on news and media coverage of Vietnam with the hope of a new generation to transcend the politics and ego that brought the world to such a dramatically violent place in its history. The poem captures very eloquently the cultural collision when the culture of 1950s postwar America collides with the Age of Aquarius.

AUTHOR BIOGRAPHY

Muriel Rukeyser was born on December 15, 1913, into a middle-class Jewish family in New York City. Her father, Lawrence, was a construction engineer who had moved to the city from Wisconsin. Her mother, Myra (née Lyons), was a bookkeeper who was born in Yonkers, New York. The home was, from Rukeyser's own accounts, a place of silence, marked by an absence of books, ideas, and spirituality. Rukeyser attended the Ethical Culture Fieldston School in the Bronx before enrolling at Vassar College in Poughkeepsie, where she edited the left-wing

Muriel Rukeyser (© Oscar White / Corbis)

oppose the American presence in Vietnam. She was, in fact, arrested in Washington, DC, for protesting the Vietnam War. It was during this period, too, that she married painter Glynn Collins. She divorced him after only six weeks and months later gave birth to a son, William.

An active poet throughout her life, Rukeyser published her first volume in 1935, *Theory of Flight*, which won the Yale Series of Younger Poets competition. It was followed by more than a dozen books of poetry, including *U.S. 1: Poems* (1938), *A Turning Wind* (1939), *Wake Island* (1942), and *Beast in View* (1944). "Poem" appeared initially in her 1968 volume, *The Speed of Darkness*. She also wrote a number of illustrated books for children, numerous books of prose, four plays (including *Houdini*, 1973), three biographies, and a memoir (*The Orgy*, 1965). She was also the recipient of a number of awards throughout her career, including a Guggenheim Fellowship. Despite her unwavering and determined support for the underdog and victims of injustice, her poems are shaped more by optimism than hopelessness, choosing to focus on the interconnectedness of people and cultures.

Rukeyser died from a stroke on February 12, 1980, at the age of sixty-six. The *Journal of Narrative Theory* dedicated a special issue to a discussion of her work in 2013.

POEM SUMMARY

The text used for this summary is from *The Speed of Darkness*, Vintage Books, 1968, p. 37. Versions of the poem can be found on the following web pages: http://www.poetryfoundation.org/poem/177125 and http://www.poemhunter.com/poem/poem-58/.

"Poem" is a twenty-one-line free-verse poem that does not use consistent metrical patterns, rhyme schemes, or identifiable structural components that one might find in more formal poems. The poem opens by introducing three key elements of the composition as a whole: the focus on the experiences of a first-person poet-speaker, whose subjectivity will shape the poem; a focus on past tense, which makes this a poem of reflection and, perhaps, about a sense of loss or deeply felt changes; and a recognition from the poet-speaker that she is living in a time dominated by war and conflict. The opening line ends with a period, marking it as a clear, definitive statement.

undergraduate *Student Review*. She returned to New York in 1930 to take classes at Columbia University through 1932.

Active in progressive politics throughout her life, Rukeyser wrote for a number of political publications from her early twenties onward as a correspondent. She covered the 1932 Scottsboro trial in Alabama and the People's Olympiad in Barcelona and traveled to Gauley Bridge, West Virginia, to investigate the recurring silicosis (a lung diseases caused by the inhalation of silica dust) among the miners of the region. Her experience during this time became the fuel for what is arguably her most powerful collection: *The Book of the Dead* (1938). Rukeyser remained active throughout World War II, giving a number of passionate public lectures that were later collected in her volume *The Life of Poetry* (1949), which has been reprinted numerous times since.

She swept into the politically charged 1960s with her passion fully engaged and with a deep sense of responsibility for the gender, class, and racial inequalities she saw around her. She served as president of the PEN American Center. She was a strong feminist voice who used her words to

The poet-speaker, still working in the past tense, remembers waking each morning to a world inundated with news that does little to bring peace to the mind and does much to push one toward insanity. The poet-speaker does, however, find an odd sense of community in knowing that her friends are equally affected by the world in which they find themselves.

Moving from reflection to action, the poet-speaker reaches for her pen and paper so that she might chronicle her thoughts and the politics of her age for those in other places as well as for future generations. As she writes, she imagines people before her and in other lands who are contemplating other ways of being and living in the world.

As day turns to night, the poet-speaker and her friends gather, trying to connect with those people of other times and other lands. The connection they seek is a spiritual one rather than a political or geographic one, a connection grounded in peace and love. In discovering this connection, the poet-speaker believes that she and her community will also find their own sense of belonging in a world from which they feel disconnected and disengaged. In other words, they will connect with themselves as a result of connecting with others.

The process of connection is, as the poet-speaker goes on to suggest, an experience in transcendence, of moving beyond the experience of being in the reality of the everyday to a new level of awareness and understanding. The last few lines of the main body of the poem catalogue a series of descriptions that the poet-speaker attaches to this new sense of being: it is variously a reaching beyond the known, a letting go, and an awakening.

The final line of the poem is set off from the main body by a space. The space highlights the last line as a closing statement and also stresses the fact that the final line restates the opening line with only a single word changed. The first and last lines function as a kind of frame, providing structure to the free-verse poem.

Reminding readers that they, like the poet-speaker, live in an age of war, the final sentence resonates with meaning. Read pessimistically, the line collapses the imagining of a new world-view back into the harsh reality of present day. All the dreams in the world cannot erase the fact that the late 1960s is a time of war and inhumanity. Read more optimistically, the final line becomes an iteration of the reality that the

poet-speaker articulates in the preceding lines. It is exactly because she finds herself in an age of war that she needs poetry and, by extension, needs to explore a new way of being a part of the world.

THEMES

1960s

Rukeyser was clearly a poet who wrote for and in her time, so it is not surprising that "Poem" reflects two of the central concerns of the 1960s: the divisiveness and inhumanity of war, and the desire for a sense of being in the world that transcends ego and otherness. The poem suggests that through poetry (and other forms of expressive art), society can collectively overcome the impulses that lead to the devastation of war and awaken into a new reality that sees individuals fully realized and communities deeply connected through a new, collective consciousness.

In this sense, "Poem" captures the spirit of a decade in which dreaming of yet-unimagined values was the cultural motivation for an entire generation of young people who felt disconnected from the values of previous generations. Whereas the previous military conflicts (World War II and the Korean War) had galvanized American society around shared values and icons, the Vietnam conflict had the opposite effect, polarizing generations and creating deep social tensions. Such late-decade movies as *2001: A Space Odyssey* (1968), *Easy Rider* (1969), *Butch Cassidy and the Sundance Kid* (1969), and *Midnight Cowboy* (1969) all deal variously with the sometimes violent realities associated with a culture that was changing in profound and unprecedented ways.

Creative Process

The creative process is one by which something new and original is created (for example, an idea, poem, painting, or solution to a problem). Ideas are conceived through any number of strategies but most often are realized through some combination of the senses (sight, sound, smell, touch, and taste). Over the centuries, a multitude of theories have tried to explain or even map out the dynamics of creativity according to any number of distinct or interrelated disciplines, including psychology, education,

TOPICS FOR FURTHER STUDY

- Rukeyser often wrote about events, process, or historical figures that supported a vision of the world that allows the mysteries and incongruities to be explained by a single theory or explanation. Write a well-structured and thoughtful essay in which you argue for "Poem" as a work that either continues in this tradition or breaks away from it to promote an alternative (that is, more individualistic) worldview.

- As Virginia R. Terris notes in a profile of Rukeyser in *Contemporary Literature*, "Rukeyser has always believed that poetry is the most effective mode of communication between people." In a well-structured essay, discuss how poetry (very loosely defined) functions in your world as a tool of communication. Does the music you listen to, for instance, function similarly to poetry in the 1960s? How about the 140-character world of Twitter or other social media platforms? Do they constitute a new poetic form? If so, how?

- In a review of *A Muriel Rukeyser Reader*, Richard Gray writes, "Rukeyser was a traveller as well as a poet and a thinker, fascinated by literal geographies along with the imaginative ones." Picking up on this idea of an imaginative geography, construct a map of your school or classroom that engages a multimedia approach (print, pictures, textures, sounds) to expressing your interpretation of this specific space and geography.

- Read JonArno Lawson's young-adult graphic novel *Sidewalk Flowers* (2015), which explores a girl's inspiring ability to find beauty and color in a world that seems to be dominated by business and the pressures of life. Using Lawson's book as inspiration, create a digital representation of Rukeyser's "Poem" that blends image and word, juxtaposes black-and-white with color, and reveals the tension of the world of wars with the peacefulness and love of a unified view of the world.

philosophy, neuroscience, and even economics. Studies have also focused on the relationship between the creative process and personality type, mental health, and education and on how it relates both positively and negatively to advancements in technology.

Although there is an abundance of writing on the creative process, most of the major theories contain some variation of stages that include many of the elements referred to (directly or obliquely) in "Poem": incubation or idea generation (a temporary break from a problem to allow new insights to occur); convergent and divergent reflection (thinking from various angles about a problem); illumination (the bursting forth of a creative solution); and verification or validation (the testing of the solution in an applied context).

Given that the late 1960s was a time of particularly eclectic creativity, from Woodstock through to Truman Capote's *In Cold Blood* (1966), it is not surprising that "Poem" explores the pressures (and opportunities) facing creativity in a new age of media, consumerism, and international politics. It was a time, in short, when creativity was becoming increasingly important and valuable and when the ability to conceptualize new approaches to existing problems via right-brain (creative) thinking was valued over the ability to resolve problems wholly through left-brain (analytical) thought.

Transcendence

In the long tradition of American transcendentalists, Rukeyser explores in "Poem" the possibility of moving beyond an individual state of being (trapped in ego and fear, for instance) to awaken to the possibilities of other ways of seeing and being in the world. For the self-proclaimed visionaries of the late 1960s, the pathways to this type of enlightenment could be through new spiritual experiences (such as Buddhism or meditation), experimentation with hallucinogenic drugs (as advocated by writer and psychologist Timothy Leary), through poetry and language (as practiced by poets like Robert Creeley), or through a collective experience that blended both of these with music (Woodstock). "Poem" refers openly to the goals of this enlightened state of awareness as peace and love, which is common in Eastern philosophies as well as in 1960s counterculture.

Although the speaker lives in a time of important events, like world wars, she calls the news items in the paper "careless." (© Brian A Jackson | Shutterstock.com)

STYLE

Punctuation

Punctuation creates both rhythm and meaning in poetry, allowing lines to become distinct units of thought and sound (each ending with a period or terminal point) or allowing ideas to flow across lines in order to connect and build gradually as the poem develops (known as enjambment or run-on lines). Rukeyser uses periods and commas very carefully in "Poem" to allow some ideas to flow and unfold almost organically while others are framed as powerful, almost definitive statements of fact. The first and last lines of the poem, for instance, are not only almost identical in wording but are both firmly punctuated with a period, which sets them off as statements that frame the poem with an emphasis on the first-person ("I"), the past tense, and the defining presence of war. While the internal lines ebb and flow through periods, commas, or the absence of punctuation, the poem finds itself in a kind of tension as statements attempt to curtail the explorative nature of the framed lines. The transition between lines ten and eleven, for instance, builds across a framing pair of commas that combine to highlight the quality of bravery or valor in the face of great change.

Repetition

Repetition of a sound, word, phrase, or line is a basic and unifying device of all poetry, whether structured formally or written in free verse. Repetition connects poetry to the primitive religious chants that transcend cultures, suggesting a unified and common foundation to the use of language to communicate powerful and transformative ideas.

"Poem" includes various layers of repetition, from the regular occurrence of *p* sounds to the direct repeating of such words as "ourselves" (which suggests a collective identity) and "to" (which creates the sense of an action without tying that action to a specific subject or tense). Considered collectively, repetition works to connect distinct lines into a broader commentary on the connectedness of all ideas and all people despite the presence of line breaks (literal and metaphoric) and punctuation.

COMPARE & CONTRAST

- **1968:** Military activity in Vietnam leads to protests but also to the conscription, or drafting, of young American men into military service. Approximately one-third of the troops deployed to Vietnam and neighboring regions are drafted during the 1960s. Draft evasion, or draft dodging, becomes a common and highly contentious issue during this period.

  Today: Conscription is no longer compulsory after the draft ends in 1973, making the United States military an all-volunteer military force.

- **1968:** The Vietnam conflict marks the beginning of a new type of media coverage of both international and domestic events. Graphic footage of scenes from Vietnam, both in print and on television, provide an engaged public with unprecedented open and relatively timely access to what was happening with and to US troops. A new generation of journalists reports on events without traditional claims of objectivity and with a willingness to become part of the story through an energetic first-person (and often participatory) writing style. The works of such writers as Hunter S. Thompson and Tom Wolfe (especially *The Electric Kool-Aid Acid Test*, 1968) are seen as the exemplars of an emerging and powerful blend of fact and fiction.

  Today: Digital technologies and social media have further transformed the means

and style by which information is shared around the world. Information and opinions are shared by such varied means as blogs, social networks, video sharing, business networks, and virtual worlds. Information can be found in seconds and from anywhere that a personal cell phone can connect to the Internet. Similarly, newspapers and broadcast news can be accessed by people anywhere at almost any time.

- **1968:** The New Age movement in spirituality rises to prominence in 1968 as a hybrid combination of such earlier religious philosophies and movements as Buddhism, Hinduism, and yoga. In February of 1968, for instance, the Beatles, who are interested in transcendental meditation, travel to Rishikesh in northern India to attend a training session with the renowned Maharishi Mahesh Yogi. With their position as cultural influencers of the day, the trip sparks a surge in the West in the study and practice of Eastern philosophies and metaphysical traditions.

  Today: With secularism still on the rise, traditional pathways to spiritual awareness are broadening and becoming less formal and more popular and less institutional. Yoga and meditation, for instance, continue to gain supporters, as do the writing of self-professed spiritual guides and experts.

HISTORICAL CONTEXT

1968: A Turbulent Year

The year 1968 was one that was defined, in part, by the eruptions of conflict in various regions of the world, many of which were captured by a new type of journalist. On February 1, for instance, a graphic photograph of a North Vietnamese officer being executed by a South Vietnamese officer

made headlines around the world. This photograph, which eventually won the 1969 Pulitzer Prize, proved to be a pivotal moment in the conflict, galvanizing American antiwar sentiments. March was equally dramatic, with the battle of Lima Site 85 recording the largest single ground combat loss of American Air Force troops in the war, followed closely by the notorious My Lai massacre, which saw hundreds of unarmed

The news comes out of radios and televisions, but the speaker does not seem to pay any more attention to it than to the commercials that air. (© Marius Rudzianskas / Shutterstock.com)

civilians killed by American troops. The story did not break in the media until late 1969, leading to a full investigation into the military cover-up.

Conflict was not limited to overseas regions but was also breaking out around the civil rights movement on American soil. On February 8, a civil rights protest was held at a whites-only bowling alley in Orangeburg, South Carolina. Three college students were killed when highway police attempted to disperse the crowd. A few days later, civil rights disturbances occurred at the University of Wisconsin and the University of North Carolina at Chapel Hill.

The American sense of security at home was rocked by two assassinations in 1968. The assassination of Martin Luther King Jr. on April 4 at the Lorraine Motel in Memphis, Tennessee, sparked riots in many American cities that lasted for several days. A week later, President Lyndon B. Johnson signed the Civil Rights Act of 1968. The second assassination took place on June 5, when presidential candidate Robert F. Kennedy was shot by twenty-four-year-old Sirhan Sirhan following a speech at the Ambassador Hotel in Los Angeles. Kennedy died the next morning.

This season of violence, both at home and abroad, contributed in significant ways to what has become known in retrospect as the summer of '69, during which the Woodstock Music and Art Fair (known simply as Woodstock) took place over a rainy weekend on a dairy farm near the town of Bethel, New York. Over four hundred thousand young people joined together in what has come to be recognized as a pivotal moment in the expression of American counterculture of the 1960s. Thirty-two acts performed on the outdoor stage, including Jimi Hendrix, the Who, Janis Joplin, and the Grateful Dead.

Elsewhere in music, the Beatles released *Abbey Road*, which topped the charts in the United Kingdom and in the United States for more than twenty months while spawning one of the most iconic album covers of all times. The album was the product of the band's final studio session before breaking up and included such hits as "Here Comes the Sun," "Come Together," "Octopus's Garden," and "Maxwell's Silver Hammer."

CRITICAL OVERVIEW

Although it would be a stretch to call Rukeyser a "neglected writer," as both Richard Gray and David Seed do, it is appropriate to say that her body of work has garnered uneven and mixed attention both during her life and posthumously. This unevenness comes despite the fact, as Gray suggests, that as a poet "Rukeyser was of and from *her* time, drawn and committed to the political conflicts and spiritual obsessions that defined the forty-five years of her writing life." Writing in *College Literature*, Michele S. Ware celebrates Rukeyser's "persistent, career-long dedication to the poetry of witness, her wide-ranging intellectual curiosity, and her powerful, inclusive, and generous vision." Ware is unwavering in marking Rukeyser as "a poet of unquestionable importance and value to twentieth-century American literature."

Terris defines Rukeyser as "a writer of profound human feeling working in the mainstream of American poetry, a Whitmanian in the truest sense." What she is not, Terris continues, is "a poet of 'fashion,' nor has she ever been." It is this rejection of passing fashion that might have harmed the legacy of Rukeyser, notes Terris in a 1974 retrospective essay. "The critical hierarchy since the nineteen forties and fifties has so strongly identified her with themes of social protest," Terris argues, "that it has generally failed to notice that her greatest creative strengths have manifested themselves in her poems of intimate human relationships and myth-making." Aligning Rukeyser with the great traditions of the American transcendentalists (from Ralph Waldo Emerson to Hart Crane), Terris goes on to suggest that

> her poetry is in harmony with much that animates [her] own times. She has been published for forty years. Her canvas has encompassed a vast field—the self in many guises, America and the world in all its beauty and ugliness, and even the limitless cosmos of metaphysical speculation.

M. L. Rosenthal calls Rukeyser a "driven artistic experimenter" in the long tradition of "poet-prophets" that includes Walt Whitman, Hart Crane, and Hugh MacDiarmid. "Her intimately self-searching lyricism," the review continues, "and her identification with the world's insulted and injured have a special place in [American] poetry." According to Rosenthal, Rukeyser should be recognized as "one of [the]

country's most politically committed yet undoctrinaire poets," writing "a poetry that grows out of the rich modern history of the art and is inextricably enmeshed in the political and cultural struggles—or agonies—of its own age." "Her approach" to the cultural mythologies of both past and present, as Gray explains, "was eclectic because like so many American poets from Whitman through Ezra Pound and Hart Crane to someone like Allen Ginsberg, she encloses faiths ancient and modern in her search for truth."

David Orr picks up on the idea of Rukeyser as an experimenter to point out that 'her poems range from the sprawling to the epigrammatic," often with "a flat, documentary feel." When at its best, he argues, her poetry "can be open, energetic, and well constructed," but it equally can sometimes be described as "tedious." Orr seems particularly bothered by readers and critics who overlook what he sees as the limitations of Rukeyser's poems, noting that it is important "to recognize that history tends to view the most 'engaged' poets as those who have made art worth engaging with."

CRITICISM

Klay Dyer

Dyer is a freelance writer specializing in topics related to literature, popular culture, and innovation. In the following essay, he explores Rukeyser's "Poem" as an example of her alignment with the poetics and philosophies of the American transcendentalist movement in her own critique of an era dominated by war and conflict.

To read Muriel Rukeyser's "Poem" is, as Richard Gray suggests, to take a journey through a moment in time and more specifically through a sensitive but clear-minded "map of that elaborate circuit of power and passion which, she believed, charged and illuminated all our lives, social, sexual, and spiritual." It is not a wholly positive journey, to be sure. The opening line, for instance, asserts a sobering truth for a poet of Rukeyser's age: the world had been at war for her entire lifetime, or so it must have seemed. From the end of World War II in 1945, through the Korean War (1950–1953), and culminating in the Vietnam War (1955–1975), this was, indeed, an era unlike any other in modern history.

WHAT DO I READ NEXT?

- Rukeyser's *The Life of Poetry* (1949) is her only work of criticism and remains an important American defense of the power of poetry to shapes lives and the world. Positioning herself clearly in opposition to cultural elitism as well as what she saw as an American fear of emotion, Rukeyser creates a compelling argument that is accessible, passionate, and interdisciplinary in its scope.

- Adrienne Rich's *Poetry and Commitment* (2007) is a more contemporary complement to Rukeyser's defense. In this volume, Rich challenges assumptions that poetry is either immoral or unprofitable in today's world while arguing that it is not only an essential but necessary antidote to an increasingly divided and violent world.

- One of Rukeyser's five books for children, *Bubbles* (1967) explores the creative wonders that come with blowing soap bubbles on a warm summer day.

- Tom Wolfe's *The Electric Kool-Aid Acid Test* (1968) is a remarkable first-person account of late 1960s counterculture as well as arguably the best example of the new, or gonzo, journalism that emerged from this period. Wolfe presents a creative nonfictional recounting of life on the road with novelist Ken Kesey and his infamous band of Merry Pranksters, who traveled across the country experimenting with psychedelic drugs and searching for new levels of self-awareness and creativity.

- In *Woodstock: Three Days That Rocked the World* (2010), Mike Evans and Paul Kingsbury compile an exhaustive, day-by-day account of the event that defined a generation. The volume is full of interviews, media accounts, and a wealth of photographs.

- Sarvenaz Tash's young-adult novel *Three Day Summer* (2015) revisits Woodstock through the eyes of two graduating teenagers, one deciding what to do with his life (enlist or go to college) and the other a small-town girl who volunteers in the medical tent only to discover a world that she had not imagined could exist.

The simplicity of this opening statement about living a life in an era defined by violent conflict is the key to the weight and authority that it delivers. The line rings like a pronouncement, a clear and formal declaration of what is felt every day but is oftentimes overlooked or left unsaid. At the same time, the sentence carries with it the impact of a lament, an expression of the sorrow that is felt by the poet-speaker and her friends as they try to make sense of the insanity that is thrust upon them. This will be, the line announces powerfully, a poem that swings from a realization that approaches despair to an invigorating anger that will, one hopes, spark change.

It is important to note that both responses are valid, and both are reasonable responses from a speaker who has lived her life against a backdrop of violence and conflict. The war in Vietnam, in particular, was a crucial moment in American cultural history, bringing the horror and immediacy of the violence into living rooms across the country. The first war captured in graphic detail on television, the Vietnam War affected American culture in profound and complicated ways. This increasingly graphic and at times biased coverage brought up deep questions about truth and honesty. It raised concerns about both the politics and the morality of engagement, especially as images of body bags became part of the everyday diet of news. A growing sense that reality was being bent to fit a political agenda led, as the poet-speaker suggests, to a growing sense of being out of control and to a feeling of powerlessness.

> THROUGH THE NETWORKING OF LIKE-MINDED PEOPLE THROUGH THE WRITING OF HER POEMS, THE POET-SPEAKER WORKS DILIGENTLY AND PASSIONATELY TO OPEN LINES OF COMMUNICATION THAT COUNTERACT OR RESIST THE PRESSURES OF THE DEVICES THAT THREATEN TO OVERWHELM HUMANITY AND MAKE PEACE BUILDING IMPOSSIBLE."

As the poet-speaker reaches out to her community of friends, this madness simultaneously spreads (they, too, suffer from morning madness) and dissipates. Individual conditions are cast across a community of sufferers, giving an odd sense of belonging in a world spinning violently beyond their control.

As the poem unfolds, a sense of pending madness gives way to the creative energies of building poems. Isolation unfolds into community. The natural cycle of the day leads to evening. Put another way, the poem builds away from a single experience of a single writer (the "I" voice in the poem) toward a collective imagining of how change can happen. Significantly, change does not happen in a moment, like a flash of insight, but is built through a conscious and organized arrangement of ideas like peace, love, and reconciliation.

It is these various oscillations—depression and challenge, solitude and community, war and love—that situates Rukeyser very much in line with the American transcendentalist tradition of Ralph Waldo Emerson (1803–1882), Henry David Thoreau (1817–1862), and Walt Whitman (1819–1892). Like the transcendentalists, Rukeyser's poet-speaker believes that her own humanity (the humanity of the individual) is bound morally to the world that has been created by the broader society, which in this case is the world outside the poem.

Being bound to the morality of a world seen as insanity-making does not mean complacency. The poet-speaker of "Poem" understands that she must constantly question the values and actions of that outside world. She does not sit silently or withdraw passively. To do so would

be to give over to the madness. Rather, her program of dissent is an expression of a deep engagement, and the variety of opinions and values that reside in the poem becomes a witness to the complex issues and emotions shaping her world.

Despite the complexity of the expressions captured in "Poem," there is an underlying confidence that means that she must constantly question the values and actions of that world. Dissent is an expression of engagement, and variety (of opinion and expression) resides elegantly within the implied unity of the poem. The building blocks of peace necessarily involve individual transformation as well as changing the world more broadly. The journey toward integrating consciousness and unconsciousness (light and night commingled) is the common journey of the one (the poet-speaker) and the many (the world outside the poem). The goal of accomplishing peace both within the poem and beyond the poem is a familiar transcendentalist allegiance to the Emersonian belief that there is a powerful, organic unity to the universe, a common source from which all being springs and can reconnect through a mind that is open to a new level of awareness.

The final line of the poem, which alters the modifier of the word *wars*, does little to settle the oscillation of the poem. Although the emphasis on the past tense of *to live* does suggest survival in an age of unprecedented violence, the triumph is undercut somewhat by the continued (and continuing) presence of wars as a defining characteristic of the poet-speaker's world. The implication is subtle: the first century of war will possibly become the first in a series of centuries, each defined by growing levels of conflict that will be captured and shared on any number of yet-unimagined devices.

This is not to suggest that "Poem" ends on a lingering note of despair. On the contrary, Rukeyser's poet-speaker aligns herself neatly with the transcendentalist commitment to use their words to spread wisdom. Through the networking of like-minded people through the writing of her poems, the poet-speaker works diligently and passionately to open lines of communication that counteract or resist the pressures of the devices that threaten to overwhelm humanity and make peace building impossible.

Poetry becomes a part of the underground resistance that Rukeyser and the transcendentalists

The speaker's use of pen and paper might seem a quaint or old-fashioned way of communication compared with the various devices, but she feels connected to the world through the written word.
(© sergign / Shutterstock.com)

saw as a cornerstone of a new awareness. The poet-speaker and her friends are part of the brave movement referred to in the poem. Battling insanity, they write poems for an unseen (and even unborn) public as a kind of public record of what has been endured as well as a way to reimagine and rebuild the world for future generations. The individual and collective making of poems is her own act of creative resistance to the hardware of destruction that she sees as dominating world geography.

"Poem" extends itself, in other words, from being a poem about a particular moment in historical time to becoming a poem about the perpetually unfolding pattern of conflict, inhumanity, and violence. While the poem is a lament about a specific war (or more accurately a series of wars), it is at the same time a powerful condemnation of the very concept of war as a universal (across all places) and transhistorical (across all times) expression of ego and power.

Although the poet-speaker finds herself very clearly in an era of war, her solution is not limited to her own specific moment or event. Her

solution, and by extension the power of all poetry, is to confront directly the thinking and ambition that is made manifest in war. Her call away from arms and to a new consciousness, which is very much aligned with the late 1960s counterculture, is to provoke the world to wake up, to discover peace within oneself as a first step to building a more globalized peace. Ultimately, as the poem iterates, this growth is as much a letting go as it is an acceptance.

Source: Klay Dyer, Critical Essay on "Poem," in *Poetry for Students*, Gale, Cengage Learning, 2016.

Shira Wolosky

In the following excerpt, Wolosky investigates the influence of Rukeyser's Jewish heritage on her work.

. . . What do Jews stand for? That is: What do they represent? What are they figures for? But also: What are they committed to? What do they stand up for? And further: What do they endure, tolerate, put up with? One thing Jews stand for is standing for almost anything. Jews are a kind of universal figure, standing for what anyone wishes to project onto them. To the rich they are poor; to the poor they are rich. They are capitalists, they are Bolsheviks. They are rootless cosmopolitans, they are exclusionary nationalists. And, as has emerged especially in post-Holocaust discussions, the more Jews are figures, representing others, the less they exist as concrete persons in history. They lose their definition as an identity in terms of themselves, concrete in the concrete world. As Dominick LaCapra discusses, there is a tendency to make Jews into "scapegoats onto whom any variety of anxieties can be projected." This is to "trope" Jews "away from specificity," thus "obliterat[ing] both the specificity of the Jews as a complex historical people and the problem of their actual and formal relations to other peoples or traditions." Yet concern that making Jews into figures makes them lose their own identity, in turn raises questions as to what Jewish identity even is: what it entails, how it is constructed, and what its boundaries, or continuities, may or may not demand. Indeed, Jews stand also for this very question of identity, what constitutes it, its inclusions and exclusions. Jewish identity stands for identity as such, as it has emerged in post-war, post-modern discourses and politics as an arena of radical contention and high stakes.

Muriel Rukeyser's sonnet "To Be a Jew" was written in 1944, well before the Holocaust emerged as a topical subject in America. Included in the *Reform and Reconstructionist Prayer Books*, it is one of a number of poems by Rukeyser that engage her Jewish identity. Being Jewish, however, was only one of Rukeyser's multiple identities and commitments, residing alongside her leftist politics, her pathbreaking feminism, and her role as a poet. What are the relationships between these identities? How do or don't they confirm or contend with each other? Rukeyser's work offers an arena in which such questions of identity are enacted and to some extent investigated, specifically within the modes of representation that poetry offers. Bringing Jewishness into various relationships with other commitments, she explores how each does or does not represent the others. Each emerges, that is, as a figure within the image networks that comprise poetry, in ways that stand for and also in tension, confirmation and contention with each other.

> FOR HER, POETIC LANGUAGE WAS NOT A SELF-REFERENTIAL ENCLOSURE; IT SHARED A PERMEABLE BOUNDARY WITH OTHER KINDS OF DISCOURSES AND SOCIAL PRACTICES. HER TEXTS THUS INTERCROSS DIVERSE SPHERES AND HETEROGENEOUS MATERIALS."

In this poetic way Rukeyser affirms her Jewish identity, but also questions its status. Her work enacts a borderline where figures assert but may also efface identity, which may become dissolved into representational meanings that point beyond it in many directions rather than back concretely to itself, its own historical existence, meanings, courses and claims.

In one of the few treatments of Rukeyser as a Jewish poet, Janet Kaufman underscores the importance of Rukeyser's essay contribution to "Under Forty: A Symposium on American Literature and the Younger Generation of American Jews." Rukeyser's essay offers a cutting portrait of her contemporary Jewish milieu. Unlike many other Jewish intellectuals of her generation, Rukeyser was born (in 1913) to non-immigrant parents. She describes her typical "second generation" as "split with the parent culture, leaning backward to be 'American' at its most acceptable." Her own American-born parents had, in her account, little of Jewish or any other cultural resource. Her father, an engineer and building contractor, grew up secular "among the Western stories" in Wisconsin. Her mother joined him in her own "anti-religious reaction against [her] studious and improvident father." This left them, writes Rukeyser, with "no cultural resources to strengthen them," and her own upbringing with "no mark of Judaism," with "not a trace of Jewish culture that I could feel—no stories, no songs, no special food—but then there was not any cultural background that could make itself felt."

Rukeyser here rather understates the Jewish facts of the case.

Her secular education at the Ethical Culture School at Fieldston, New York, redefined rather than abandoned identity. The School's commitment to racial equality made it a "haven for secular Jews" whose entry elsewhere was limited by quotas, and who wished their children educated in the ethical principles they associated with Judaism—principles that could substitute for ritual or Halakhic practices. As to religious education, Rukeyser recounts in "Under Forty" that she "went to religious school automatically" and attended a Reform synagogue "every Saturday for seven years," after her mother experienced a return to religion. In Hebrew School, however, Rukeyser found only "digests and easy versions of Jewish history," while the synagogue was a scene of "pale sermons" and "muted organ." To her, these were exercises not in identity but in its evasion. She writes: "I grew up among a group of Jews who wished, more than anything else, to be invisible," to be "quiet and polite" and "never protest." They were "starving" for two crucial "phases of religion: poetry and politics.... If they had a mission as a responsible and inspired people, they did not want it."

But Rukeyser wanted what they did not: "poetry and politics," and the "struggle" missing from her parents' Jewish life, what she repeatedly calls "responsibility." Her parents may have wished a "sheltered" life of "comfort" for her, but, she writes, "it was not comfortable to me." Her own sense of mission instead led her, in the 1930s, to involvement in the Popular Front and to writing for leftist journals such as the *New Masses* and the *Daily Worker* (although she was never on record as a member of the Communist Party, she was nonetheless later investigated by the McCarthy Committee on Un-American Activities). Sent as a reporter to the 1935 anti-fascist People's Olympiad in Spain, organized to protest the upcoming Olympics in Nazi Berlin, she was evacuated with the outbreak of the Spanish Civil War. She went on to cover the Scottsboro trial of eight black men accused of raping a white woman, during which she was jailed. She then investigated the first major industrial disaster in the United States at Gauley Bridge, West Virginia, where, during tunneling and construction of a Union Carbide dam, thousands of mostly migrant workers died of silica inhalation as a consequence of unprotected mining practices. Her efforts produced both influential newspaper exposures of the disaster and her remarkable sequence of poems, *The Book of the Dead*.

Rukeyser's political activism continued through the next decades, importantly including foundational feminist writing as well as anti-war protests. Her Jewish identity, as she writes in "Under Forty," was braided into and with these other self-definitions.

> My themes and the use I have made of them depended on my life as a poet, as a woman, as an American and as a Jew. I do not know what part of that is Jewish; I know I have tried to integrate these four aspects, and to solve my work and my personality in terms of all four.... To live as poet, woman, American and Jew—this chalks in my position. If the four come together in one person, each strengthens the other.

"To live as poet, woman, American and Jew." This account in one sense confirms, but in another intensifies the questions of identity it seeks to address. Just what and how is being a Jew defined here? How do these different identities work or correlate (or not) with each other? What is the status of Jewish culture for a woman who held it as only one of a number of her identities? Are there, or need there be, priorities, displacements, assimilations?

I would like to propose that Rukeyser's poetic offers her both method and model of negotiating her different identities. It is in poetic terms that her different identifications become figures for each other, standing for and also with or against each other. Such mutual figuration itself deeply defines Rukeyser's poetic. Rukeyser emerged as a writer at the time when the New Criticism was taking hold in the American academy. Her work defied all its norms, making hers a distinctive, indeed dissident voice in American letters, as reflected in the relative lack of commentary on her work. She rejected New Criticism, and it rejected her. The New Criticism idealized a poetry chiseled and iconic in form, a self-enclosed object of language referring to itself regardless of historical context, biographical reference or cultural frame. Rukeyser instead saw her writing as a form of direct cultural, political and social activism. As she wrote: "in poetry, the relations are not formed like crystals on a lattice of words, although... the New Criticism would have us believe it so." Rather, it "is a meeting place between all the kinds of imagination." For her, poetic language was not a self-referential enclosure; it shared a permeable boundary with other kinds of discourses and social practices. Her texts thus intercross diverse spheres and heterogeneous materials. The texture, the strength, the composition and also the event of poetry inheres exactly in its power to bring to encounter and interaction multiple domains of experience.

The self that Rukeyser constructs in her work similarly departs from the closed, iconic, traditional lyric "I" that Marjorie Perloff describes as a "transcendental ego" and "authentic self," or from the "unified self" that Charles Bernstein names as the traditional "primary organizing feature of writing." Rukeyser's selfhood is instead enacted as a multiple negotiation among a variety of mutually representative, contentious, constitutive parts of the self, each situated in concrete social, political histories. This multiply embedded selfhood is both a poetic and a political commitment, at once feminist, leftist and Jewish. In each aspect, identity is not only something personally determined but also a contextual, historical identification. To be a Jew, for Rukeyser, is one such historical and communal identification that enters into and shapes personal identity....

Source: Shira Wolosky, "What Do Jews Stand For?: Muriel Rukeyser's Ethics of Identity," in *Journal of Jewish Women's Studies and Gender Issues*, Vol. 19, Spring 2010, p. 199.

SOURCES

Gray, Richard, Review of *A Muriel Rukeyser Reader*, in *Modern Language Review*, Vol. 90, No. 4, October 1995, pp. 990–91.

Herzog, Anne, "Art of the World: Muriel Rukeyser's Poetry of Witness," in *Bridges*, Vol. 9, No. 2, Fall 2002, p. 28.

Howe, Florence, "The Poetry of Life," in *The Women's Review of Books*, Vol. 12, No. 2, November 1994, pp. 12–13.

Kolodny, Annette, "Review," in *American Literature*, Vol. 53, No. 2, May 1981, pp. 320–24.

Orr, David, Review of *Muriel Rukeyser: Selected Poems*, in *Poetry*, Vol. 187, No. 3, December 2005, pp. 242–43.

Rosenthal, M. L., Review of *A Muriel Rukeyser Reader*, in *Ploughshares*, Vol. 21, No. 1, Spring 1995, pp. 198–200.

Rukeyser, Muriel, "Poem," in *The Speed of Darkness*, Random House, 1968, p. 37.

Schwartz, Michael J., "Muriel Rukeyser," in *Jewish Women's Archive*, http://jwa.org/encyclopedia/article/rukeyser-muriel (accessed May 1, 2015).

Seed, David, Review of *A Muriel Rukeyser Reader*, in *Journal of American Studies*, Vol. 29, No. 2, August 1995, pp. 285–86.

Terris, Virginia R., "Muriel Rukeyser," in *Contemporary Literature*, Vol. 23, No. 1, Winter 1982, pp. 117–19.

———, "Muriel Rukeyser: A Retrospective," in *American Poetry Review*, Vol. 3, No. 3. May/June 1974, pp. 10–15.

Ware, Michele S., Review of *The Collected Poems of Muriel Rukeyser*, in *College Literature*, Vol. 33, No. 2, Spring 2006, pp. 199–201.

FURTHER READING

Herzog, Anne, "Art of the World: Muriel Rukeyser's Poetry of Witness," in *Bridges*, Vol. 9, No. 2, Fall 2002, pp. 26–31.
    Placing Rukeyser in the long tradition of poets who see their role as bearing witness to the politics of the world in which they live and write, this article focuses on how she explores (and questions) "the cultural forces which fragment and split our world into discrete arenas, thereafter defined in oppositional terms."

Kaufman, Janet E., and Anne Herzog, *How Shall We Tell Each Other of the Poet: The Life and Writing of Muriel Rukeyser*, 1999.
    This inclusive and eclectic volume brings together in one place the voices of former friends, colleagues, editors, and students whose lives intersected with Rukeyser's. Included, too, are numerous works of critics and scholars offering new and invigorating interpretations of her work.

Kertesz, Louise, *The Poetic Vision of Muriel Rukeyser*, Louisiana State University Press, 1979.
    Still considered a seminal work, this book is one of the first to look at Rukeyser's works both individually and collectively and also in the context of the social ethos of which she spoke with such elegance. Noted feminist critic Annette Kolodny notes that this incisive volume is shaped, in part, by an "anger at the stupidity which marked many reviews of Rukeyser's work, and at the lack of generosity which marked critics' responses to Rukeyser herself."

Levi, Jan Heller, *A Muriel Rukeyser Reader*, Norton, 1994.
    Spanning 1935 to 1976, this collection intercuts images from the various decades of Rukeyser's life with a full range of her writing, from the well known to the out of print.

SUGGESTED SEARCH TERMS

Muriel Rukeyser

"Poem" AND Rukeyser

The Speed of Darkness AND Rukeyser

American poetry

metapoetic

American transcendentalism

Rukeyser AND poetry

poetry AND war

poetry AND 1960s

Reading Aloud to My Father

**JANE KENYON
1995**

"Reading Aloud to My Father" is a work of free verse by American poet Jane Kenyon. It was first published in *Poetry* magazine in February 1995 and was reprinted in Kenyon's collection *Otherwise: New and Selected Poems* in 1996, a year after her death. The poem is narrated by a woman who is looking after her dying father. She starts to read from a book, but from the content and her father's reaction, she quickly realizes that she has made the wrong choice— the passage suggests an atheistic conception of life, which does not match either the poet's belief or the way she interprets the behavior of the terminally ill. The poem is autobiographical in the sense that Kenyon is recalling her own father, Reuel Kenyon, who died of lung cancer in 1982. Along with her mother and her husband, Kenyon looked after Reuel during the last six months of his life, when he was in hospice care. "Reading Aloud to My Father" is exemplary of Kenyon's subject matter and style: she wrote often of sickness and death and frequently adopted a religious point of view, and her poems reflect careful observation and often are presented in an informal, conversational tone. "Reading Aloud to My Father" can be found in *The Best American Poetry 1996*, edited by Adrienne Rich, and *The Best of the Best American Poetry: 1988–1997*, edited by Harold Bloom, as well as Kenyon's *Collected Poems* (2005).

The first book the speaker selects is not appropriate and is rejected. (© wavebreakmedia / Shutterstock.com)

AUTHOR BIOGRAPHY

Kenyon was born on May 23, 1947, in Ann Arbor, Michigan, the daughter of a jazz musician, Reuel Kenyon, and his wife, Polly, a nightclub singer who later became a seamstress in order to be at home with her two children, Reuel and Jane. Kenyon grew up just outside Ann Arbor. She first began writing poems in junior high school. When she enrolled at the University of Michigan in 1965, she at first majored in French but eventually switched majors and received a bachelor of arts degree in English in 1970. She received a master of arts degree from the same university in 1972. While she was an undergraduate, she took an introduction to poetry course from the well-known poet Donald Hall and later enrolled in Hall's creative writing course. Kenyon and Hall, who had recently become divorced, became friends, and the relationship continued to blossom over the

next few years. They married in April 1972, despite the fact that Hall was nineteen years Kenyon's senior. For the next three years they remained in Ann Arbor, with Hall continuing as a professor of English and Kenyon working on the *New English Dictionary* project as well as developing her own poetic craft.

In 1975, Kenyon and Hall moved to a farmhouse near Wilmot, New Hampshire, to pursue their writing careers, with Hall no longer holding an academic position. Kenyon's first volume of poetry, *From Room to Room*, was published in 1978 and received favorable reviews. While living at the farm, Kenyon rediscovered the Christian faith in which she had been raised but which she had rejected in the 1960s. Her faith helped her to deal with the severe depression that dogged her on and off throughout her life. However, this did not prevent her from establishing a reputation as one of America's most promising young poets. She won several awards, including fellowships from the National Endowment for the Arts in 1981 and from the New Hampshire State Council on the Arts three years later. Having developed an interest in the Russian poetry of Anna Akhmatova, Kenyon collaborated with Vera Sandomirsky Dunham to translate some of it. The result was *Twenty Poems of Anna Akhmatova*, published in 1985. Kenyon's second collection of poetry, *The Boat of Quiet Hours*, followed one year later. *Let Evening Come* (1990) and *Constance* (1993) were the final volumes of poetry published in Kenyon's lifetime.

In 1994, Kenyon was diagnosed with leukemia, and she died fifteen months later, on April 22, 1995, at the age of forty-seven. She had been named poet laureate of New Hampshire just three months earlier, in January, a position that her husband had held from 1984 to 1989.

Kenyon's collection *Otherwise: New and Selected Poems* was published in 1996. It contains twenty poems written in the months before her death, including "Reading Aloud to My Father." A second posthumous collection, *A Hundred White Daffodils: Essays, the Akhmatova Translations, Newspaper Columns, Notes, Interviews, and One Poem*, collects some of Kenyon's prose writings and other works. Her *Collected Poems* was published in 2005.

POEM TEXT

I chose the book haphazard
from the shelf, but with Nabokov's first
sentence I knew it wasn't the thing
to read to a dying man:
The cradle rocks above an abyss, it began,   5
*and common sense tells us that our existence
is but a brief crack of light
between two eternities of darkness.*

The words disturbed both of us immediately,
and I stopped. With music it was the same—   10
Chopin's Piano Concerto—he asked me
to turn it off. He ceased eating, and drank
little, while the tumors briskly appropriated
what was left of him.

But to return to the cradle rocking. I think   15
Nabokov had it wrong. This is the abyss.
That's why babies howl at birth,
and why the dying so often reach
for something only they can apprehend.

At the end they don't want their hands   20
to be under the covers, and if you should put
your hand on theirs in a tentative gesture
of solidarity, they'll pull the hand free;
and you must honor that desire,
and let them pull it free.   25

POEM SUMMARY

The text used for this summary is from *Otherwise: New and Selected Poems*, Graywolf Press, 1996, p. 22. A version of the poem can be found on the following web page: http://www.poetryfoundation.org/poetrymagazine/browse/165/5#!/20604322.

Lines 1–8

"Reading Aloud to My Father" consists of four unrhymed stanzas varying in length between five and eight lines. In the first stanza, the speaker explains that she is reading to her father, who is dying. She has just picked out a book at random from the bookshelf. It happens to be a book by twentieth-century Russian American novelist Vladimir Nabokov (1899–1977), but as soon as she starts reading it aloud, she realizes it is a bad choice. It is not the sort of book that should be read to someone who is dying. In the second half of the stanza, lines 4–8, the speaker quotes from the book, using italics. The title of the book, though not stated in the poem, is *Conclusive Evidence: A Memoir*, published in 1951. In the sentence quoted in the poem, which is the book's

MEDIA ADAPTATIONS

- Although there is no audio recording of "Reading Aloud to My Father," Kenyon can be heard reading a number of her poems on the website of the Poetry Foundation, at http://www.poetryfoundation.org/bio/jane-kenyon#about.

- Kenyon can also be heard reading her poetry in *A Life Together: Donald Hall and Jane Kenyon*, a video profile of the couple by Bill Moyers released on December 17, 1993, and available at http://billmoyers.com/content/a-life-together-donald-hall-jane-kenyon/.

first sentence, Nabokov expresses the view that, seen in the larger context, the life of a human being represents just a brief moment of consciousness between the time that existed before that person was born and the equally endless stretch of time that will go on after he or she is dead. Nabokov uses a metaphor of light and darkness to describe this.

Lines 9–14

In the second stanza, the speaker reports that both she and her father are unsettled by Nabokov's words. She stops reading. Then she recalls a similar experience she had while looking after her father, that time not with words but with music. A piano concerto by Chopin was playing, but her father told her to turn it off. The speaker then comments, in lines 12–14, about the inevitable progress of her father's illness. He stops eating and drinks little while the cancerous tumors continue to do their work in destroying his body.

Lines 15–19

In the third stanza, the speaker returns to the Nabokov quotation cited in the first stanza, explicitly disagreeing with the opinion Nabokov expressed. She argues, beginning in line 16, that the reverse is the case. It is human life itself that is the *abyss* that Nabokov assigns to the endless period of nonexistence that surrounds, both before and after, the short span of a human life. In line 17, the speaker explains that this is why babies cry when they are born. (That is, they recognize the abyss into which they have just entered for what it is.) In lines 18–19, the speaker adds that those who are dying sense something that those caring for them are unable to perceive: they seem to be aware that they are approaching something, through death, that is quite different from an abyss, and they may even wish to physically reach out for it with their hands.

Lines 20–25

In the fourth stanza, the speaker further explores this deathbed phenomenon, speaking in general terms, not just about her father. The dying do not rest easily with their hands under the bed-covers, and if a caregiver tries to offer comfort by putting a hand on the hand of a dying person, that person will withdraw the hand; he or she does not want to be restrained in such a way. In lines 24–25, the speaker states that such a desire on the part of the dying person must be honored, and the caregiver must allow the person to withdraw the hand.

THEMES

Death

Kenyon's poem is about death, dying, and what may or may not lie beyond death. The poet cleverly takes the quotation from Nabokov and uses it as a springboard for metaphysical speculation and the suggestion of a religious view of the world and human life. She takes issue with the view expressed in the first sentence of Nabokov's memoir, that there is no life after death, only nothingness. Reversing Nabokov's argument, she sees the abyss not as the nothingness that supposedly precedes and follows human life but as human life itself. It is an abyss, one may assume, because it involves so much suffering, a fact that in the poet's view eclipses Nabokov's notion that human life is like a small light in the darkness that precedes and follows it. The speaker continues this line of thought by suggesting that the dying sense something that lies beyond the mortal realm, and it is not, one may conclude, contra Nabokov, nothingness or

TOPICS FOR FURTHER STUDY

- In an interview with David Bradt in March 1993, Kenyon said, "The poet's job is to tell the whole truth and nothing but the truth, in such a beautiful way that people cannot live without it; to put into words those feelings we all have that are so deep, so important, and yet so difficult to name." Bearing this in mind, write your own lyric poem—a short poem in which a first-person speaker gives expression to a certain emotion or feeling. What prompted that emotion to emerge? A particular event or occurrence in the speaker's life? Base the poem on something genuine about yourself.

- Read *What Have You Lost?* (2001), a collection of 140 contemporary poems, compiled by Naomi Shihab Nye, designed to appeal to young-adult readers. All the poems describe some kind of loss, including the deaths of friends and family members. With a partner, select three or four of these poems and read them aloud to your class, explaining why you picked them and what they convey to you.

- Research hospice care in the mid-2010s. What do hospices do? Who enters a hospice? What are some of the current trends in hospice care? What is the underlying philosophy behind hospice care? Find some current statistics about hospices. Then go to Easel.ly online and create an infographic that provides information at a glance about hospices in America today.

- Read some more poems by Kenyon. If a print text is not available, a selection can be found online at the Poetry Foundation. Select a few poems that you like or feel are typical of her work, and then write an essay in which you discuss these poems along with "Reading Aloud to My Father." How would you describe her style and her themes?

darkness. Lines 17–18 make clear that this is something which those who are still fully involved in the business of living are unable to

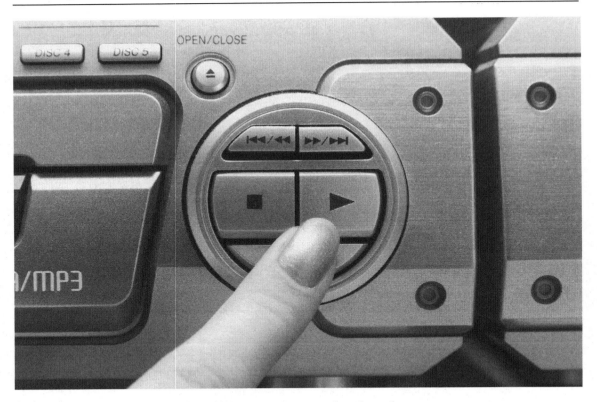

Just as some books are not acceptable, some music must be silenced. (© chaoss / Shutterstock.com)

perceive, but which the dying see or feel in some way, and this makes them want to move toward it, to sever their connection to their earthly life in the natural process of dying. They want to reach toward it, whatever it might be—and no details are supplied—which is why they resist anything that seems to pull them back, or keep them attached to their lives, even if it is the comforting hand of a loved one. It is as if they are being called elsewhere, and are aware of it.

Although the poet avoids making an explicitly religious or theological statement, it seems that she is espousing a rather Christian view of human life as a "vale of tears," the notion that sorrow and suffering are inevitable. This is shown by the reference to this world as the *abyss*, for example, and by the image of the crying infant that immediately follows it. Human life may yet give way to an afterlife in which the virtuous souls find happiness and fulfillment in the presence of God in heaven. At the very least, the speaker suggests the possibility, based on what she has observed in the dying and the metaphysical framework into which she has fitted those observations, that life may continue after death in some form or another.

Care

The poem is about death and dying, but it is also about the caregiver, the person—in this case the man's daughter—who watches over the dying person, doing her best to make him comfortable and attend to his needs. The attitude of the man to his approaching death is apprehended by the caregiver, and the poem is written from her point of view. It is a learning process for her, and she reaches some conclusions based on her own observations, both of her father and of others who have approached death in her presence. The fact that the speaker has experienced other deaths is established in the general statement about how the dying behave, in line 23. The poem is autobiographical, and Kenyon herself had taken hospice training, which likely meant that she had been at the bedsides of quite a number of dying people.

The learning process for the daughter seems to be a matter of learning from her mistakes. She picks the wrong book to read from; she knows it herself and also observes her father's discomfort at hearing the words she reads aloud. In the second stanza she records how what was presumably her effort to put on some soothing music—the Chopin concerto—was equally a mistake. In the fourth stanza, she comes to a conclusion: it is much more important to allow dying people to be the way they want to be, without trying to distract them or impose on them what the caregiver might think is something that would help. Even a hand placed on a dying person's hand could be an unwanted gesture. Meant to be comforting, it may not be received as such, in which case the caregiver must honor the reaction the dying person has, since that person may be aware of something of great spiritual importance that eludes the caregiver, as lines 18–19 convey.

STYLE

Lyric Poem

A *lyric* is a poem, often relatively short, that expresses the thoughts and emotions of a first-person speaker. Such a poem may, as in this case, involve a process of observation on the part of the speaker, as a result of which the speaker may offer certain conclusions, as this poem does. The speaker in "Reading Aloud to My Father" might even be said to reveal, right at the end, a well-meaning didactic purpose (that is, one intended to teach or instruct), advising the reader directly (*you*) about the most appropriate ways of responding to a dying person.

Free Verse

Like most contemporary American poetry, the poem is written in free verse, without rhyme or meter. The poet varies the rhythm of the poem with the placing of caesuras, pauses within lines indicated by a comma, period, or some other mark of punctuation. The caesuras are most noticeable in the second stanza, in which the middle four of the six lines contain caesuras. Some of the caesuras are made necessary by the fact that the poet frequently uses run-on lines, or *enjambment*, whereby the end of the line does not coincide with the completion of a single syntactical unit, and the reader's eyes must "run on" to the next line for that syntactical unit to be completed. In terms of language, the poem uses informal phrasing, with contractions such as *wasn't* and *that's*, and the tone is conversational, as if the speaker is talking to someone she knows.

HISTORICAL CONTEXT

Growth of Hospice Care

In the early 1980s, Kenyon trained as a hospice worker, and her father, who suffered from lung cancer, was the recipient of hospice care for the last six months of his life. He died in 1982. According to the website of the National Hospice and Palliative Care Organization (NHPCO), "the term 'hospice'...can be traced back to medieval times when it referred to a place of shelter and rest for weary or ill travelers on a long journey."

The term was first used to refer to a place offering care for the terminally ill in the 1940s. The number of hospices grew over the following decades. According to the report *NHPCO's Facts and Figures: Hospice Care in America*, hospices offer "compassionate care for people facing a life-limiting illness." This care includes "expert medical care, pain management, and emotional and spiritual support expressly tailored to the patient's needs and wishes. Support is provided to the patient's loved ones as well." Hospice, states the NHPCO report, "focuses on caring, not curing. In most cases, care is provided in the patient's home but may also be provided in freestanding hospice centers, hospitals, nursing homes, and other long-term care facilities."

In the 1980s, industry standards were developed by the Joint Commission on Accreditation of Hospitals, and hospice accreditation began in 1984. Many hospices became Medicare-certified. During the mid-1990s, the hospice movement continued to grow, and more research and funding went into improving understanding of end-of-life issues and how best to care for the terminally ill, with an emphasis on quality of life.

American Poetry in the 1990s

In 1991, poet and critic Dana Gioia published a much-discussed article in the *Atlantic Monthly* titled "Can Poetry Matter?" Gioia argued that although a large amount of poetry was published each year, poetry was no longer relevant to mainstream American cultural life. Instead, it had become a subculture, largely based within colleges and universities, consisting of professors of English and teachers of creative writing and their graduate students, as well as editors, publishers, and administrators. Poetry had become a profession, Gioia argued, with its own career

COMPARE & CONTRAST

- **1990s:** Leading American poets in this decade, as measured by the winners of the Pulitzer Prize for Poetry, include Yusef Komunyakaa, Jorie Graham, Philip Levine, Lisel Mueller, Charles Simic, Mona Van Duyn, Mark Strand, Charles Wright, Louise Glück, and James Tate. In 1996, the award goes to Graham's *The Dream of the Unified Field*, which is made up of five of Graham's previously published volumes.

  Today: Leading American poets in this decade, as measured by the winners of the Pulitzer Prize for Poetry, include Gregory Pardlo, who wins the 2015 prize for his second collection, *Digest*. Other prizewinners in the 2010s include Rae Armantrout, Kay Ryan, Tracy K. Smith, Sharon Olds, and Vijay Seshadri.

- **1990s:** According to Gallup, in 1996, 57 percent of Americans say that religion is "very important" in their lives, 28 percent say it is "fairly important," and 15 percent say it is "not very important."

- **Today:** According to Gallup as of 2013, 56 percent of Americans say that religion is "very important" in their lives, 22 percent say it is "fairly important," and 22 percent say it is "not very important." The rise in the last category over the two preceding decades is notable.

- **1990s:** In 1996, according to a Gallup poll, 56 percent of Americans identify as Protestants, 25 percent as Catholics, 3 percent as Jewish, and 6 percent as belonging to some other religion. About 7 percent do not identify with any religion.

  Today: According to a Gallup poll, 37 percent of Americans identify as Protestants, 10 percent as nonspecific Christians (a question not asked in 1996), 23 percent as Catholics, 2 percent as Jewish, and 6 percent as members of another religion. Some 16 percent do not identify with any religion. The number of those not identifying with any religion has risen markedly since 1996; also notable is the fall in the number of those identifying as Protestants.

---

track and system of recognition and rewards. Poets wrote no longer for the general reader but for other members of their profession, their fellow poets. The decline of the cultural importance of poetry could be seen in the fact that daily newspapers no longer reviewed poetry.

Gioia was not the only person to bring attention to this state of affairs in American poetry. As noted by Christopher Beach in *Poetic Culture: Contemporary American Poetry between Community and Institution*, poet Greg Kuzma and critic Joseph Epstein, among others, had complained in the 1980s about a system that they believed rewarded mediocrity rather than talent, in which attaining a powerful academic position was more important than producing excellent poetry. In 1983, Donald Hall, who had left his academic position in the mid-1970s,

published an essay in which, according to Beach, "he referred to the homogenized graduates of creative-writing programs as 'McPoets' and cited careerist ambition as the primary motivation of poets who churned out mass-produced 'McPoems' as fast as Chevrolets or disposable razors."

The publishing industry in the 1990s reflected this shift in the readership of poetry, continuing a trend that had been established over the two previous decades: the number of poetry books published by trade publishers was falling, leaving university presses and small presses (such as Graywolf Press, based in Minnesota, which published all of Kenyon's work) to produce a greater share of the poetry published in the United States. By the late 1990s, trade publishers published only between thirty and forty contemporary American

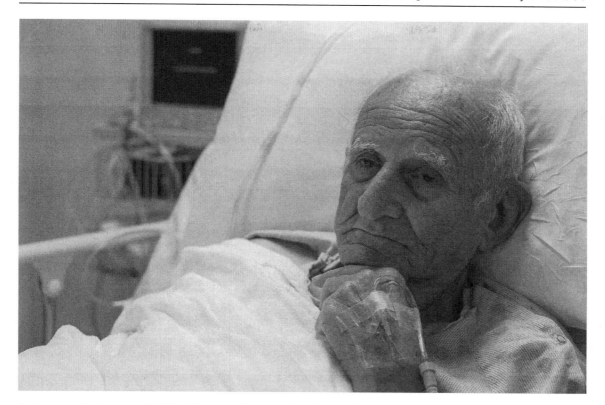

It is not until the second half of the second stanza that the speaker makes it clear that her father is dying.
(© Fotoluminate LLC / Shutterstock.com)

poetry books each year, down from more than a hundred per year in the mid-1960s, according to Beach, who also notes that the majority of poetry volumes sold only between one thousand and two thousand copies, while many sold less. In spite of the small readership, however, over one thousand new volumes of poetry were published annually in the United States, Beach notes.

In 1994, a year before the death of Kenyon, his wife, Hall wrote another essay, this one titled "Death to the Death of Poetry," in which he emphasized a different aspect of the American poetry scene. Having enjoyed nearly twenty years outside the confines of the American academy as a freelance poet and writer, Hall celebrated what he saw as a vibrant poetic culture that still had the power to appeal to ordinary people, not merely the specialists. Citing, like Beach, the impressive output of verse in the United States, Hall writes:

> More than a thousand poetry books appear in this country each year. More people write poetry in this country—publish it, hear it, and

presumably read it—than ever before. Let us quickly and loudly proclaim that no poet sells like Stephen King, that poetry is not as popular as professional wrestling, and that fewer people attend poetry readings in the United States than in Russia. Snore, snore. More people read poetry now in the United States than ever did before.

Hall goes on to say that the cultural environment for poetry in the 1990s was much better than it had been when he was growing up, noting that from the 1930s to the 1950s, poets did not often read their works aloud in public, whereas in the 1990s, based on his own experience,

> the American climate for poetry is infinitely more generous. In the mail, in the rows of listeners, even in the store down the road, I find generous response. I find it in magazines and in rows of listeners in Pocatello and Akron, in Florence, South Carolina, and in Quartz Mountain, Oklahoma. I find it in books published and in extraordinary sales for many books.

CRITICAL OVERVIEW

Right from the beginning of her career, Kenyon received positive reviews for her work. Praised for her observations of nature and her treatment of the daily routines of her life in rural New Hampshire, she has been compared to earlier American poets such as Emily Dickinson, Robert Frost, and Anne Sexton. Reviews of *Otherwise: New and Selected Poems* were uniformly appreciative. For example, Emily Gordon, in the *Nation*, notes that "Kenyon stretches the limits of her faith—religious, personal and natural. Her phrasing is playful and rhythmic, stitched together with unexpected rhymes and caesuras." For Adrian Oktenberg, in the *Women's Review of Books*, Kenyon possesses

> a unique voice, one with staying power. Kenyon's voice is the body and soul of her poetry, full of gravity and grace, characterized by a kind of simplicity which is the product of long consideration, that has great depth and resonance.

Oktenberg continues, "Her poems must have been devilishly difficult to write but they are a song to read, and they live a long time in memory."

Regarding "Reading Aloud to My Father," no less a figure than American poet Adrienne Rich selected the poem for inclusion in the annual series volume *Best American Poetry 1996*. Constance Merritt, in her review of *Otherwise* in *Prairie Schooner*, writes that in that poem, "emblematic truth and vision provide a proof against doubt and desolation where conventional faith and dogma have utterly failed." Rose Lucas, in "'Into Black Air': Darkness and Its Possibilities in the Poetry of Jane Kenyon," notes in connection with "Reading Aloud to My Father" that Kenyon "describes life, rather than death, as the period of exile which is to be endured." Lucas adds that elsewhere, Kenyon's poetry

> does not shy away from any delineations of such an abyss and is at times confronting in its depictions of the bleakness of those holes in the fabric of a life through which one can fall.

In *Jane Kenyon: A Literary Life*, John H. Timmerman classifies "Reading Aloud to My Father" as one of the "poems of personal sorrow" contained in *Otherwise*. Timmerman frames the issue raised in the poem as follows: "Is life the tenuous existence that only points to, or shadows forth, the solidity of eternal reality?"

He compares the point of view expressed by the poet to that set forth by C. S. Lewis (1898–1963), who is well known as a writer about Christianity, in books such as *Mere Christianity* (1952). According to Timmerman, Lewis's view is "that what we long for in this life is fully realized only in eternal life."

CRITICISM

Bryan Aubrey
Aubrey holds a PhD in English. In the following essay, he discusses "Reading Aloud to My Father" in terms of Kenyon's religiosity and how it finds expression in the poem.

Kenyon had a well-developed spiritual view of the world. In quite a few of her poems, she gives expression to her religious, indeed Christian, beliefs regarding the existence of a loving God and an afterlife. It is therefore somewhat ironic that, as recorded in "Reading Aloud to My Father," the book she should pull off the shelf to read to her dying father happened to be Nabokov's *Conclusive Evidence: A Memoir*, the first sentence of which expresses a view that is quite opposite to her own. (Although it might sometimes be a mistake to equate the *I* of a lyric poem with the poet herself, this is not so in the case of "Reading Aloud to My Father," which is one of several poems Kenyon wrote about her father's illness and death.) This is Nabokov's first sentence: "The cradle rocks above an abyss, and common sense tells us that our existence is but a brief crack of light between two eternities of darkness." He goes on to refer to "the two black voids, fore and aft," and the "impersonal darkness on both sides of my life." In other words, in his view, this existence, on this earth, is all a person ever has. One does not exist before one's birth and will not exist after one's death.

Kenyon, as she writes in the poem, has a fundamental disagreement with this view of human existence, and it was something to which she had given considerable thought over the course of her life. In her essay "Childhood, When You Are in It...," she writes that as a child she was heavily influenced by the strongly held religious beliefs of her grandmother, who advocated a strict obedience to the commandments of God. Everyone would be judged at the time of the Second Coming of Christ, according

WHAT DO I READ NEXT?

- Kenyon's "Otherwise," the title poem in her collection *Otherwise: New and Selected Poems* (1996), is about the inevitability of change in life. People live out their daily routines, getting thoroughly used to them, enjoying them, and expecting them to continue, but the day will dawn when that routine gets broken and something else, likely unexpected and less welcome, will take its place. This poem first appeared in Kenyon's 1993 collection *Constance*.

- Kenyon's poem "Happiness" was also published in *Otherwise: New and Selected Poems*. Kenyon often suffered from depression, but this poem is a reminder that happiness can suddenly appear in a person's life at any time, bringing with it great relief. The poem is also available in Kenyon's *Collected Poems*, published in 2005.

- "Do Not Go Gentle into That Good Night" is a famous poem by Welsh poet Dylan Thomas (1914–1953). The situation the poem describes has similarities to "Reading Aloud to My Father," since it is addressed to the poet's dying father. However, the poet's attitude toward death is quite different from that which appears in Kenyon's poem. Thomas urges his father not to accept the onset of death but to fight against it. First published in 1951, the poem can be found in Thomas's *Collected Poems: 1934–1952* (1952).

- *Simply Lasting: Writers on Jane Kenyon* (2005), edited by Joyce Peseroff, is a collection of essays, poems, and reviews that explore Kenyon's life and work. It also includes previously unpublished letters by Kenyon. Contributors include Wendell Berry, Robert Bly, Hayden Carruth, Michael Dirda, Donald Hall, Robert Hass, Marie Howe, Galway Kinnell, Peter Kramer, Maxine Kumin, Alice Mattison, Molly Peacock, Robert Pinsky, Jean Valentine, and many others.

- Kenyon has sometimes been compared to Emily Dickinson. Dickinson wrote many poems about death, and one of the best known is "Because I could not stop for Death," which expresses an optimistic view about life beyond death. The poem can be found in Dickinson's *Selected Poems* (1990), edited by Gregory C. Aaron.

- Where some of Kenyon's poems express a quiet faith in God even in the face of illness and death, seventeenth-century English poet John Donne's poem "Death, Be Not Proud" expresses a more openly triumphant attitude toward death: the belief that death will be defeated because eternal life awaits the virtuous soul. The poem, which is one of Donne's Holy Sonnets, can be found in Donne's *The Complete English Poems* (1974), edited by A. J. Smith.

- Aimed at young-adult readers, *Stopping for Death: Poems of Death and Loss* (1996), edited by British poet Carol Ann Duffy and illustrated by Trisha Rafferty, is an anthology of eighty mostly simple poems from all over the world, both classic and contemporary. The poems express a wide variety of attitudes toward and beliefs about death.

- *Japanese Death Poems: Written by Zen Monks and Haiku Poets on the Verge of Death* (1986), compiled by Yoel Hoffmann, is an unusual book, made up entirely of Japanese monks' and poets' writings about their own approaching deaths. This is a Japanese tradition called *jisai* (death poem) and has existed for many centuries, as Hoffman explains in his introduction to the place occupied by the poetry of death in the history of Japan.

> THE POEM STANDS AS A SUBTLE, QUIET
> AFFIRMATION OF FAITH THAT SOMETHING—
> UNSPECIFIED BUT NOT TO BE FEARED—AWAITS THE
> DEPARTING SOUL OTHER THAN THE 'IMPERSONAL
> DARKNESS' INVOKED BY NABOKOV."

to this view, and Kenyon grew up associating religion with fear. By the time she attended high school, she writes, she had developed a contempt for religion, although she continued to believe in the existence of God. Later, after she had moved to New Hampshire with her husband, Donald Hall, she began attending church again. The couple became regular churchgoers, and Kenyon even became church treasurer. In 1980, Kenyon had a profound mystical experience of light that changed her way of seeing the world. This experience found expression in her poem "Having It Out with Melancholy," published in her collection *Constance* in 1993. In a 1993 interview with Kenyon, Bill Moyers asked her to talk about the experience, and this was her response:

> I really had a vision of that once. It was like a waking dream. My eyes were open and I saw these rooms, this house, but in my mind's eye, or whatever language you can find to say these things, I also saw a great ribbon of light and every human life was suspended. There was no struggle. There was only this buoyant shimmering, undulating stream of light. I took my place in this stream and after that my life changed fundamentally. I relaxed into existence in a way that I never had before.

This spiritual awakening found expression in a number of the poems that Kenyon wrote in the 1980s and up until her death in 1995. In "In Memory of Jack" (which likely refers to Dr. Jack Jensen, the minister of the church that Kenyon and Hall attended in New Hampshire), she refers to the subject's death in terms of light rather than darkness. "Notes from the Other Side," a first-person report from a speaker who has died and is experiencing an afterlife, refers to the light of God, as well as his mercy. "In the Nursing Home," likely about the sickness of Hall's mother, is remarkably explicit in the religiosity

of its conclusion, under the guise of a metaphor about a dying horse. "Let Evening Come" is a serene poem of acceptance, expressing the belief that God will always offer comfort, no matter what the circumstances. The evening referred to is not only the end of each day but also the approaching end of one's life. "Looking at Stars" is a short poem about the saving power of Christ's blood. In "Having It Out with Melancholy," the poem referred to earlier, Kenyon refers to souls not yet born on earth as existing within the vision of light she describes, which is a hint that even what Nabokov called the "prenatal abyss" (the time before one was born on earth) may not, at least in Kenyon's view, be as empty as Nabokov supposed. Kenyon also experienced times of spiritual aridity that only the believer can know, as detailed for example in "Woman, Why Are You Weeping?"

In terms of religiosity, "Reading Aloud to My Father" is not explicit, but it does hint at a complete reversal of the proposition outlined by Nabokov and quoted in the poem. It is this world, not the time before and after an individual's existence, that is the abyss, and this suggests that perhaps the "brief crack of light"— Nabokov's metaphoric description of the span of a human life—might better refer, vastly expanded, to life after death, which, for the Christian believer, is to be lived in the eternal light of God. The poet does not actually say this directly, but she does make it abundantly clear that during the process of dying, something is calling the dying person away from the world of mortality and encouraging him or her to let go of earthly attachments. The strongest hint that some new reality (other than the nothingness or darkness envisioned by Nabokov) awaits the dying comes in the last two lines of the third stanza, which speak of the dying, as they turn away from the things they have known, reaching for something else, something perhaps incorporeal but nonetheless real, which is beyond the perception of the caregiver, who is still bound to the human world, with all its limitations.

Only fourteen months after "Reading Aloud to My Father" was published, Kenyon died of leukemia. Donald Hall, in two separate pieces of writing, told of her death and linked it to several of the phenomena observed by Kenyon in "Reading Aloud to My Father." In the first passage, which is quoted by editors Robert Pinsky

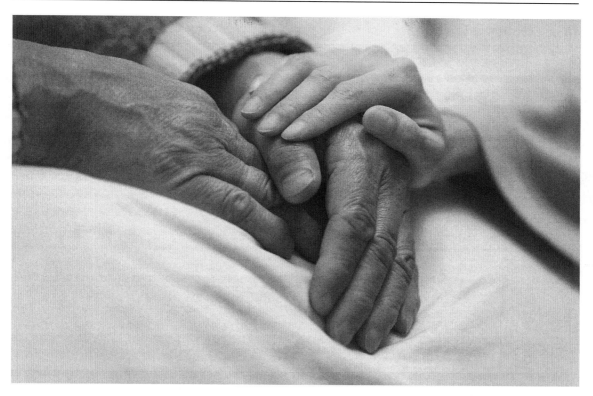

Learning to let go of her father's hand is the first step toward letting her father go emotionally. (© Arman *Zhenikeyev / Shutterstock.com*)

and David Lehman in *Best of the Best American Poetry*, Hall writes:

> Jane wrote many poems about her father's illness and death, of which "Reading Aloud to My Father" is the latest and last.... When Jane was dying I thought of this poem. Music was her passion, as it was her father's; at the end, she could not bear to hear it, because it tied her to what she had to leave. In her last twenty-four hours, her hands remained outside the bedclothes, lightly clenched. I touched them from time to time, but I did not try to hold tight.

The relevance to the poem is that the dying father also rejected music, telling his daughter to turn off the Chopin piano concerto that was playing. He also preferred to have his hands over the bedcovers, and he pulled his hands free when his daughter touched them, which is why Hall, remembering the poem, "didn't try to hold tight."

In *The Best Day the Worst Day: Life with Jane Kenyon*, Hall recalls that during his wife's final illness, many people sent her flowers, but

> flowers were a major adhesion to the world Jane was leaving. She would not look at them.

When I brought them into the bedroom, she had me take them away.... She would not look at flowers nor allow me to play her favorite CDs. These things tied her to what she had to part from.

Thus the manner of Kenyon's going echoed that which she described in her own poem, itself a recollection of her father's death some thirteen years prior. The poem stands as a subtle, quiet affirmation of faith that something—unspecified but not to be feared—awaits the departing soul other than the "impersonal darkness" invoked by Nabokov.

Source: Bryan Aubrey, Critical Essay on "Reading Aloud to My Father," in *Poetry for Students*, Gale, Cengage Learning, 2016.

Joyce Peseroff

In the following review, Peseroff explains how Kenyon's poetry was influenced by her work with other poets.

I first met Jane Kenyon in the early 1970s in Ann Arbor, where I was a young writer and visiting fellow at the University of Michigan.

> BOTH POETS ARE INTERESTED IN WHAT THINKING FEELS LIKE, BUT WHILE BISHOP QUALIFIES, BACKTRACKS, AND AMPLIFIES HER OBSERVATIONS, AS IF THINKING OUT LOUD, KENYON SEEMS TO ERASE THE BOUNDARY BETWEEN SPEAKER AND AUDIENCE."

Shortly after, Kenyon and her husband Donald Hall moved to New Hampshire, and I moved to the Boston area. I resumed a friendship that would grow to include coediting the literary magazine *Green House*; working together in the writers' cooperative Alice James Books; and, for over a decade, exchanging poems in a literary workshop together with Alice Mattison. Our workshop ended only when Jane's treatment for the leukemia that killed her in 1995 made meeting impossible. Alice, when asked by National Public Radio's Noah Adams to evaluate Kenyon's poetry on the first anniversary of her death, cut him off, saying, "Jane is great!" Like Alice, I'm in no position to be an objective critic. Instead, I'd like to take the publication of Kenyon's *Collected Poems* as an occasion to examine the distinctive qualities of her art, to consider her as a woman writer, and to place her among others—mostly American but including the Russian poet Anna Akhmatova, whom she read with love and ambition.

In a 1989 interview with Bill Moyers, Kenyon explained how she negotiated her marriage to the well-known, older Hall:

> Don is at the point in his career where he's getting to be thought of as quite a statesman of poetry, someone with a lot of answers. And he is someone with a lot of answers. He knows things nobody else knows. But I also know things nobody else knows. It's funny how everything in your life, every experience, everything in your reading, everything in your thinking, in your spiritual life—you bring it all to your work when you sit down to write. And he knows what he knows and I know what I know.

Throughout the *Collected Poems*, Kenyon connects the smallest things she knows to the largest, whether these are the noise of a hen flinging a single pebble—"Never in eternity the same sound— / a small stone falling on a red

leaf" ("Things") or grief delivered by a gravy boat with "a hard, brown / drop of gravy still / on the porcelain lip" ("What Came to Me"). Whatever the subject—the inscrutable nature of happiness ("Happiness"); moments of ecstatic joy and spiritual doubt ("Briefly It Enters and Briefly Speaks"; "Staying at Grandma's") or struggles with depression ("Having It Out with Melancholy")—Kenyon insists on the value of paying attention. Her poetics is based in what she called the "luminous particular," and her quest for it was the backbone of an art she characterized as "brief musical cries of the spirit."

The cries are expressed through a female body. In an early poem (omitted from *Otherwise: New and Selected Poems* but included here). Kenyon writes frankly about "This long struggle to be at home / in the body, this difficult friendship" ("Cages"). Several poems in her first book, *From Room to Room*, suggest a body easily displaced or effaced, a concern Kenyon continues to address in later volumes. "From Room to Room" describes a speaker "Out of my body for a while, / weightless in space" as a result of her move from Ann Arbor. Coming back to bed after seeing "the thermometer read twenty-four below," she finds "the pillows cold, as if I had not been there two minutes before" ("The Cold"). In "Full Moon in Winter," her shadow "lies down in the cold . . . / like someone tired / of living in a body, / needy and full of desire." Certainly these poems prefigure those about depression that begin to appear in *The Boat of Quiet Hours*.

What sustains Kenyon, and keeps her from joining her shadow in the snow, is a community of women she intuits in and around the space she inhabits. In "Finding a Long Gray Hair," she senses, while washing floors, the "motions of other women / who have lived in this house." When she finds physical evidence of their bodies in "a long gray hair/floating in the pail," she feels her "life added to theirs." Ancestors whose photographs appear in the first line of "From Room to Room" become intimates. In "Hanging Pictures in Nanny's Room," Kenyon decorates her study with "a poster of Mary Cassatt's 'Women Bathing'" and imagines another woman's body: "No doubt Nanny bent here summer mornings, her dress down about her waist, water dripping through her fingers." By the fifth paragraph of this prose poem, the point of view has shifted from the first person to the second, as the speaker thinks herself into details of Nanny's sexual life: "And if people weren't good enough, if your husband . . . was a philanderer, well, you could move back to the house where you were born." In *From Room to Room*'s final poem, a whippoorwill, joyous in tall grass, announces, "I belong to the Queen of Heaven!" Belonging to a female body—exemplified by a real gray hair, created through sympathetic imagination, and asserted by a symbol of the Holy Spirit—is essential to Kenyon's artistic perspective.

When Robert Bly, after reading Kenyon's poems in manuscript, suggested that she apprentice herself to a master, Kenyon said, "I cannot take a man as my master." Bly then recommended Anna Akhmatova. Not finding any translations to her liking, Kenyon began working on her own. This project would stretch any writer's vocabulary. Kenyon also learned from Akhmatova's short lyrics how to join imagery with intense emotion (something that would become Kenyon's signature): "Already the narrow canals have stopped flowing; / water freezes. / Nothing will ever happen here— / Not ever!" ("Evening").

Equally important is what this project taught her about syntax.

> Wild honey has the scent of freedom,
> dust—of a ray of sun,
> a girl's mouth—of a violet,
> and gold—has no perfume.
>
> Watery—the mignonette,
> and like an apple—love,
> but we have found out forever
> that blood smells only of blood.

Kenyon writes in her note to this poem, "It seemed important to keep the abstractions—freedom and love—in parallel positions within their stanzas. I couldn't bring myself to say "Of water smells the mignonette . . . "—that's not English. So I left out the verb and invented 'watery.'" Compare the last poem in *From Room to Room* to the first poem in *The Boat of Quiet Hours*, and you'll see the difference between:

> Fat spider by the door.
>
> Brow of hayfield, blue
> eye of pond.
> Sky at night like an open well.
>
> ("Now That We Live")

and:

> From here I see a single red cloud
> impaled on the Town Hall weathervane.

> Now the horses are back in their stalls,
> and the dogs nowhere in sight
> that made them run and buck
> in the brittle morning light.
>
> ("Evening at a Country Inn")

The strained syntax—the natural order of lines four through six would be "the dogs that made them run and buck in the brittle morning light are nowhere in sight"—mirrors the strained situation in the poem, with the speaker anxious about a companion who "laughed only once all day" while "thinking about the accident— / of picking slivered glass from his hair." The assonance of "accident" / "picking" / "slivered" / "his" combines with the hard consonants of "thinking" / "accident" / "picking" / "glass" to create the experience of a windshield splintering in the reader's ear.

Other women poets Kenyon read with care included Adrienne Rich, Elizabeth Bishop, and Emily Dickinson. She kept a picture of Rich above her desk, and several of Kenyon's poems allude to Bishop's directly: "But sometimes what looks like disaster / is disaster" ("The Pond at Dusk") answers "One Art"; and the situation provoking "The Argument"—viewing a corpse at a funeral-nods to "First Death in Nova Scotia." Both poets are interested in what thinking feels like, but while Bishop qualifies, backtracks, and amplifies her observations, as if thinking out loud, Kenyon seems to erase the boundary between speaker and audience. Poems framed by ellipses reject the sense of beginning or end, and seem lifted directly from the writer's consciousness:

> . . . a mote. A little world. Dusty. Dusty.
> The universe is dust. Who can bear it?
> Christ comes. The women bathe his feet
> with tears, bring spices, find the empty tomb,
> burst out to tell the men, are not believed . . . .
>
> ("Depression")

Like Dickinson, Kenyon often infuses spiritual longing with psychic pain, using the Bible as her lexicon. "Depression" results from 1) being a woman; 2) knowing something sacred; and 3) not being believed. She shares Dickinson's wariness toward God the father, preferring the "son / whose blood spattered / the hem of his mother's robe" ("Looking at Stars"); trying to comfort her dying father, Kenyon offers John 14: "I go to prepare a place for you":

> . . . "Fine. Good," he said.
> "But what about Matthew? 'You,
> therefore, must be perfect, as your heavenly Father

is perfect.'" And he wept.

("We Let the Boat Drift")

In her longest poem, "Having It Out with Melancholy," Kenyon turns the language of spiritual ecstasy inside out. The "unholy ghost" of depression violates her in a travesty of annunciation, "pressing / the bile of desolation into every pore." An early draft ended with "Credo," a Protestant black mass saluting "the mutilator of souls" with a line of scripture: "There is nothing I can do / against your coming. / When I awake, I am still with thee." In the finished poem, Kenyon allows her despair—assuaged by "pharmaceutical wonders"—to be lifted by love for the hermit thrush's "bright unequivocal eye"; like Dickinson, she finds solace in creation's clay despite doubts about the Creator.

In late poems like "Happiness," "Mosaic of the Nativity: Serbia, Winter 1993," "Reading Aloud to My Father," and "Woman, Why Are You Weeping?" Kenyon becomes more discursive and speculative, directing her scrupulous attention to broader details of history, politics, and philosophical inquiry. One closes the book imagining the poems that remain unwritten, the things Jane Kenyon knew that she never got to tell anyone. What she accomplished in the three decades of her writing life, now gathered finally in the *Collected Poems*, will sustain readers who crave what Kenyon called "the inside of one person speaking to the inside of another." Here is the world made palpable by a patient intelligence— honest, radiant, and rare.

Source: Joyce Peseroff, "The Luminous Particular," in *Women's Review of Books*, Vol. 23, No. 5, September– October 2006, pp. 22–23.

SOURCES

Beach, Christopher, *Poetic Culture: Contemporary American Poetry between Community and Institution*, Northwestern University Press, 1999, pp. 19–20, 218.

Cookson, Sandra, Review of *Otherwise: New and Selected Poems*, in *World Literature Today*, Vol. 71, No. 2, Spring 1997, pp. 390–91.

Gioia, Dana, "Can Poetry Matter?," in *Atlantic Monthly*, May 1991, https://www.theatlantic.com/past/docs/unbound/poetry/gioia/gioia.htm (accessed May 7, 2015).

Gordon, Emily, "'Above an Abyss,'" in *Nation*, Vol. 262, No. 17, April 29, 1996, pp. 29–30.

Hall, Donald, *The Best Day the Worst Day: Life with Jane Kenyon*, Houghton Mifflin, 2005, p. 244.

———, *Death to the Death of Poetry: Essays, Review, Notes, Interviews*, University of Michigan Press, 1994, http://www.poets.org/poetsorg/text/death-death-poetry (accessed May 7, 2015).

"History of Hospice Care," National Hospice and Palliative Care Organization website, http://www.nhpco.org/history-hospice-care (accessed May 6, 2015).

Kenyon, Jane, "Childhood, When You Are in It...," in *A Hundred White Daffodils: Essays, the Akhmatova Translations, Newspaper Columns, Notes, Interviews, and One Poem*, Graywolf Press, 1999, pp. 61–72.

———, "Having It Out with Melancholy," in *Collected Poems*, Graywolf Press, 2005, p. 231.

———, "In Memory of Jack," in *Collected Poems*, Graywolf Press, 2005, p. 251.

———, "An Interview with Bill Moyers," in *A Hundred White Daffodils: Essays, the Akhmatova Translations, Newspaper Columns, Notes, Interviews, and One Poem*, Graywolf Press, 1999, p. 160; originally published in *The Language of Life: A Festival of Poets*, edited by Bill Moyers, Doubleday, 1995.

———, "An Interview with David Bradt," in *A Hundred White Daffodils: Essays, the Akhmatova Translations, Newspaper Columns, Notes, Interviews, and One Poem*, Graywolf Press, 1999, p. 183; originally published in *Plum Review*, No. 10, September 1996, pp. 115–28.

———, "In the Nursing Home," in *Collected Poems*, Graywolf Press, 2005, p. 282.

———, "Let Evening Come," in *Collected Poems*, Graywolf Press, 2005, p. 213.

———, "Looking at Stars," in *Collected Poems*, Graywolf Press, 2005, p. 210.

———, "Notes from the Other Side," in *Collected Poems*, Graywolf Press, 2005, p. 267.

———, "Reading Aloud to My Father," in *Otherwise: New and Selected Poems*, Graywolf Press, 1996, p. 22.

———, "Woman, Why Are You Weeping?" in *Collected Poems*, Graywolf Press, 2005, p. 292.

Latimer, Robin M., "Jane Kenyon," in *Dictionary of Literary Biography*, Vol. 120, *American Poets since World War II, Third Series*, edited by R. S. Gwynn, Gale Research, 1992, pp. 172–75.

Lucas, Rose, "'Into Black Air': Darkness and Its Possibilities in the Poetry of Jane Kenyon," in *Plumwood Mountain: An Australian Journal of Ecopoetry and Ecopoetics*, Vol. 2, No. 1, http://plumwoodmountain.com/into-black-air-darkness-and-its-possibilities-in-the-poetry-of-jane-kenyon-by-rose-lucas/ (accessed April 27, 2015).

Merritt, Constance, Review of *Otherwise: New and Selected Poems*, in *Prairie Schooner*, Vol. 72, No. 1, Spring 1998, pp. 171–76.

Nabokov, Vladimir, *Conclusive Evidence: A Memoir*, Harper & Brothers, 1951, pp. 1–2.

NHPCO's Facts and Figures: Hospice Care in America, 2014 Edition, National Hospice and Palliative Care Organization, http://www.nhpco.org/sites/default/files/public/Statistics_Research/2014_Facts_Figures.pdf (accessed May 6, 2015).

"The 1996 Pulitzer Prize Winners," Pulitzer Prizes website, http://www.pulitzer.org/works/1996-Poetry (accessed May 18, 2015).

Oktenberg, Adrian, "In Solitude and Sorrow," in *Women's Review of Books*, Vol. 13, Nos. 10–11, July 1996, pp. 27–28.

Pinsky, Robert, and David Lehman, eds., *Best of the Best American Poetry*, 25th Anniversary Edition, Scribner Poetry, 2013, pp. 277–78.

"Poetry," Pulitzer Prizes website, http://www.pulitzer.org/bycat/Poetry (accessed May 4, 2015).

"Religion," Gallup website, http://www.gallup.com/poll/1690/religion.aspx (accessed May 3, 2015).

Timmerman, John H., *Jane Kenyon: A Literary Life*, William B. Eerdmans, 2002, pp. 221–22.

———, "Jane Kenyon," in *American National Biography Online*, April 2014, http://www.anb.org/articles/16/16-03898.html (accessed April 27, 2015).

FURTHER READING

Dennis, Dixie L., *Living, Dying, Grieving*, Jones and Bartlett, 2009.
This book seeks to educate people about all aspects of death. It discusses such topics as how to overcome fear of death; how to express grief; cultural and historical perspectives on death; the US health care system, including hospice care; terminal diseases and conditions; the process of dying; end-of-life issues, such as do-not-resuscitate orders; and how to deal with the death of a loved one.

Hall, Donald, *Without: Poems*, Houghton Mifflin, 1998.
This is a collection of poems that Hall, husband of Jane Kenyon and one of the most distinguished American poets of his generation, wrote about Kenyon's last days, her death, and his own grief.

Hornback, Bert G., ed., *"Bright Unequivocal Eye": Poems, Papers, and Remembrances from the First Jane Kenyon Conference*, Peter Lang, 2000.
This is a collection of essays from the First Jane Kenyon Conference, which met in April 1998. Conference attendees included Hall, Wendell Berry, Galway Kinnell, Alice Mattison, Gregory Orr, and Joyce Peseroff, whose essays are included in this volume, along with essays by many others.

Kübler-Ross, Elisabeth, ed., *Death: The Final Stage of Growth*, Prentice-Hall, 1975.
Kübler-Ross was a well-respected writer on the topics of death, dying, and grief. In this book she examines such topics as coming to terms with the inevitability of death, examining fears about death, expressing grief, and preparing for one's own death. Kübler-Ross ranges widely over different cultures in discussing such topics; she interviews ministers, nurses, doctors, and others and presents personal accounts given by people who are near to death and by family and friends who survived them.

SUGGESTED SEARCH TERMS

Jane Kenyon

Kenyon AND "Reading Aloud to My Father"

Christian faith AND death

hospice movement

American poetry AND 1990s

Donald Hall AND Jane Kenyon

caregiving AND death

poetry AND death

Saturday at the Canal

GARY SOTO
1991

"Saturday at the Canal" is a twenty-one-line free-verse poem by Gary Soto that captures both the disillusionment of youth and the visionary longing that it can lead to. Soto, a prolific American author of Mexican descent, has dozens of poetry collections, novels, young-adult novels, short-story collections, juvenile and picture books, nonfiction works, and auto-biographies to his name. He has been greatly inspired artistically by the circumstances he was raised in, among the disadvantaged minority populations of Fresno, California, especially Chicanos.

In "Saturday at the Canal," Soto draws on the sense of the greater world that youths such as he would have had back in the late 1960s, when he was in his late teens, in presenting a narrator who dreams of escaping his home environs for a far more promising place: the cultural mecca of San Francisco. Eschewing any racial or political discussion in conveying the narrator's personal reflections on his existence, "Saturday at the Canal" is a poem that many modern youths, whatever their race or record of achievement, will relate to. The poem is included in Soto's collection *Home Course in Religion: New Poems* (1991) and can also be found in the anthologies *Leaving Home: Stories* (1998), *Poems of the American West* (2002), and *Poetry 180: A Turning Back to Poetry* (2003), edited by then US poet laureate Billy Collins.

Gary Soto (© *Associated Press*)

AUTHOR BIOGRAPHY

Soto was born on April 12, 1952, in Fresno, California, in the San Joaquin Valley, where he grew up along with an older brother. His grandparents were born in Mexico but came to America to do field and factory work, and his parents were born in Fresno. His father sought to follow in his parents' footsteps but spent a fair deal of his time during Soto's young life doing labor as part of sentencing for stealing a car, along with an uncle, while drunk. When Soto was just five, his twenty-seven-year-old father had his neck broken in an industrial accident and died, an experience that emotionally hardened the young Soto.

Soto has written about the deprivation that surrounded his family environment in his earliest years in such autobiographical pieces as "The Childhood Worries; or, Why I Became a Writer." In addition to witnessing the death of his father, he watched an uncle suffering from skin cancer use the family couch as his deathbed, and he saw another uncle, a teenager, cradle and bury his dog after it got hit by a car. Of a neighbor who whiled his life away dying from cancer, Soto was inclined to observe that "he didn't seem to be getting anywhere." Of the house where his

mother dropped him and his brother off when she went to work—with a woman who had nine children of her own—Soto states, "It scared me because in its carelessness lurked disease and calamity": he once got tapeworms from eating raw bacon with them, while he also became familiar with pigeon soup. Things started to seem especially precarious when their house began slipping off its foundation, producing tilted rooms. Going over the childhood cruelties that he became wont to inflict on his peers—like bullying two orphan playmates and once fooling them into thinking the ghosts of their parents were scratching at the window—Soto, recognizes, "I was turning out bad. I was so angry from having to worry all the time that I had become violent." He once stabbed his brother's leg with a broken bottle, but his aggressive inclinations faded to an extent when, in the early 1960s, the family moved to a more agreeable suburban neighborhood.

Graduating from high school in 1970, Soto first attended Fresno City College, where he was inclined to study geography but eventually gravitated toward poetry. Moving on to California State University, Fresno, Soto studied under the accomplished poet Philip Levine and graduated magna cum laude in 1974. In the next two years he married Carolyn Oda and earned an MFA from the University of California, Irvine. With a visiting position at San Diego State University, Soto embarked on an academic career that would soon take him to Berkeley for over a decade, where he gradually shifted to part-time teaching and finally full-time writing. Through the late 1970s and 1980s he earned numerous fellowships and awards, including Guggenheim and National Endowment for the Arts fellowships and an American Book Award. His publications gained increasing critical attention from the 1990s onward, with *Home Course in Religion*, containing "Saturday at the Canal," being published in 1991, and now number in the dozens in a wide swath of genres. Soto is a household name in literature of the American Southwest, especially for younger readers.

POEM TEXT

I was hoping to be happy by seventeen.
School was a sharp check mark in the roll
  book,

An obnoxious tuba playing at noon because
    our team
Was going to win at night. The teachers were
Too close to dying to understand. The hallways   5
Stank of poor grades and unwashed hair. Thus,
A friend and I sat watching the water on
    Saturday,
Neither of us talking much, just warming
    ourselves
By hurling large rocks at the dusty ground
And feeling awful because San Francisco
    was a postcard   10
On a bedroom wall. We wanted to go there,
Hitchhike under the last migrating birds
And be with people who knew more than three
    chords
On a guitar. We didn't drink or smoke,
But our hair was shoulder length, wild when   15
The wind picked up and the shadows of
This loneliness gripped loose dirt. By bus or
    car,
By the sway of train over a long bridge,
We wanted to get out. The years froze
As we sat on the bank. Our eyes followed
    the water,   20
White-tipped but dark underneath, racing out
    of town.

POEM SUMMARY

The text used for this summary is from *Home Course in Religion: New Poems*, Chronicle Books, 1991, p. 31. Versions of the poem can be found on the following web pages: http:// writersalmanac.publicradio.org/index.php?date = 2014/11/15 and http://www.tweetspeakpoetry .com/2010/04/17/national-poetry-month-gary-soto/.

Lines 1–6

The first line of "Saturday at the Canal" presents a first-person speaker opening a meditation with an expression of emotion, namely, his desire to have found happiness by the age of seventeen. The line suggests that the poem is set when the narrator was seventeen or perhaps a year or two younger; with the poem set entirely in the past, the narrator is presumably now older. The first line also suggests, through the mention of a hope without any hint of its being fulfilled—the period ending the sentence is like a note of resignation—that the poet at this young age has not yet found that hoped-for happiness. The tone of the ensuing lines supports this inference: In line 2, the sharpness of the angular check rotely entered into an educational logbook suggests the strictness and severity of the goal-oriented

culture at school. Notably, this line does not give any indication that the narrator is struggling at school, suggesting that the culture more than the intellectual environment is what he finds burdensome. In line 3, the characterization of the tuba—likely being played at a midday pep rally at school, such as for the football team—as annoying suggests that the author feels distant from collectively glorified athletic culture and the pursuit of victory. To some extent, he may be a loner or "misfit." In lines 4–5, most likely what the teachers, who are perhaps being characterized as too far beyond youth in terms of perspective as much as of bodily age, fail to understand is the narrator's disillusionment with his teenage world. Disillusionment, it seems, is in the very air, in the real odor of insufficient hygiene—with unclean hair suggesting poverty—as well as the figurative odor of poor academic performance, as if these impoverished students are destined for failure in terms of academic achievement and the American dream's definition of success. Line 6 ends with a transitional word indicating that what follows is a consequence of what has been stated.

Lines 7–21

With the first several images referring only vaguely to any location in the school environment—the hallways are not mentioned until line 5—a firm setting does not take hold of the poem until line 7, which finally produces the locale posited by the title, with the poet and a friend sitting at a canal together. For whatever reason, they are not drawn to extensive conversation with each other, which suggests a subdued mood. They are more concerned with the activity of their bodies, it being perhaps a cool day, such that they are conscious of warming themselves through the exertion of throwing rocks around. The area is depicted as dusty and thus dry, perhaps desert-like, alongside the canal's waters. The sentence begun with the end of line 6 continues until reaching a concrete explanation for the mood of the poet and his friend in lines 10–11: they are thinking of being in what is, one readily imagines, a much more exciting and fulfilling place, San Francisco, which is actually no more to them than a picture on a postcard hung on one of their walls; it is a veritably unattainable destination.

Line 11 makes clear that San Francisco is where the two youths want to be, even if hitchhiking might be the only way to get there—an undertaking that would ally them with migratory birds that they might see along the way. Once in San Francisco, they would be able to spend time with people whose musical knowledge would dwarf that of their peers in their town—which itself may well be quite small if no one (or at least no one these youths know) can play any more than three guitar chords. This mention of music may be just an example of something that reflects the worldliness of San Francisco city folk in comparison with folks in the poet's hometown, or it may be a specific interest that the poet and his friend share, as if they have dreams of starting a band, but even they themselves thus far know only three chords.

A new sentence starts in line 14, now characterizing the poet and his friend through their behavior, specifically their refraining from drinking or smoking, habits they might be easily exposed to through their peers. The statement of their abstinence is so bare that it suggests no judgment of those who do drink or smoke; the poet and his friend are, it seems, simply not interested. That they, in fact, have sympathy for rebelliousness is suggested by their having long hair—one symbol of the counterculture of the sixties, when, based on Soto's life chronology, the poem may be presumed to take place—which imparts a wildness to their sense of themselves as it blows in the wind. Their wild images

are projected in the form of their shadows, which the poem perhaps suggests are embodiments of their loneliness, on the dusty ground of a wind-blown landscape which is, despite—or perhaps especially in juxtaposition with—the canal, relatively barren.

After the general mention of hitchhiking earlier, the poet now invokes concrete images of vehicles that could take him and his friend away to the city. The bus and car are prosaic enough, while there might be something more romantic (not affectionately but existentially) about hopping aboard a train that would rock back and forth while crossing a bridge. Whatever the vehicle, the poet and his friend simply want to leave. The passage of the years somehow slows to a stop when they sit on the bank of the canal. They look at the water as it flows onward, the vibrant surface image with its miniature crests contrasting with the dark and profound depths as the water acts precisely as the youths wish to act, rushing toward distant lands.

THEMES

Disillusionment

The overarching mood of "Saturday at the Canal" is one of disillusionment, a sentiment suggested by the opening line through the reference to hope unfulfilled, which almost by definition entails the recognition that an optimistic expectation for the world has turned out to be an illusion. This abstract sentiment is given substance in the ensuing lines, which present specific aspects of life with which youth in general are likely to find themselves disillusioned, as the poet is here. First and foremost is school, which for too many adolescents, especially ones with challenging existential circumstances to contend with—jailed fathers, overburdened mothers, urban gang domination, lack of resources at home—proves too irrelevant to their immediate circumstances to sustain their attentions. This might be especially true for minority students learning from majority-white teachers who underestimate their students' abilities, overestimate their capacity for misbehavior, or both.

This point is relevant in light of Soto's heritage and life circumstances, and yet it is worth recognizing that the poem actually makes no issue of race—perhaps as if the political

TOPICS FOR FURTHER STUDY

- Write a poem centered on a moment of longing, whether experienced individually or as shared with a friend, for another place. As in Soto's poem, set up a contrast in some fashion between the place where you were and the place where you wished you were. You might also wish to contrast how you felt at that time with how you feel now.

- Produce a graphic poem version of "Saturday at the Canal"—like a very brief graphic novel—drawing approximately one image for each line, or more if you choose, telling the story that the poem represents in visual form. The poem itself should be included in text boxes, as conventionally used for narration, in the course of your graphic poem. Alternatively, create a slide show using stylistically arranged clip art found online.

- Read the Soto poems "Saturday in Chinatown" and "Saturday under the Sky," which can both be found in his *New and Selected Poems* (1995) and then write an essay in which you separately analyze the content of these two poems; conclude by discussing whether or not Soto presents in these two poems and "Saturday at the Canal" a cohesive or disparate sense of that day of the week, citing from the poems to support your argument.

- Read Soto's poem "The Levee," also found in *Home Course in Religion*, which has a very similar focus to that of "Saturday at the Canal." Write a dual analysis in which you compare specific passages of the poem with regard to the nature of the content, pointing out how comparable passages stylistically differ. Conclude by discussing which poem you find more effective in making an impression on the reader.

- Read Langston Hughes's poem "The Negro Speaks of Rivers," which can be found in the "Poetry for Young People" volume *Langston Hughes* (2006) and which offers an interesting poetic contrast to Soto's "Saturday at the Canal." Create a dual poster-board or Prezi presentation in which each poem is adorned with commentaries on contrasting aspects of the poem as well as visual representations that bring out those contrasts.

---

implications of any racial discussion would, in differentiating individuals based on skin color, work against the capacity of the poem to evoke compassion in any and all who read it, whatever their color. Thus can all readers sympathize with the poet's indifference toward, even irritation with the competitive culture encouraged by the school, a culture that glorifies those with competitive inclinations and skills, which, of course, promotes the development of more such people, creating a culture filled with and ultimately run by such people (i.e., the 1 percent). To the sensitive poet, this competitive culture is readily seen as illusory, with people valuing and even caring about what they have accomplished more than who they actually are, a state of affairs that too often allows morality, the virtue of the conscience, to go by the

wayside; if one is not self-reflective enough to care about how one's acts define oneself, about whether one's acts are virtuous or not, then it is all too easy to allow others to be harmed (often indirectly) in the pursuit of material gain. The schoolteachers, in playing a supportive role in this culture of competition, are part of the illusion and are thus unable to understand the disillusionment of youths like the poet.

The poverty, too, can be seen as a source of disillusionment: American society's governing culture of achievement leads those with wealth to presume that the poor do not have wealth because they have not tried hard enough to get it. This reasoning ignores all kinds of barriers to poor people's attainment of wealth—including shortcomings in education in poor districts,

Whether by bus, car, or train, the speaker and his friend hope to escape. (© Leonid Andronov / Shutterstock.com)

predatory lending practices, biased attitudes toward minorities, and that very lack of wealth as a resource for securing more. Thus, the poet's recognition that American culture's governing conception of poverty is a sociological illusion also amounts to disillusionment.

Longing

While the state of disillusionment connotes looking back on a formerly held idealism or optimism with disappointment, and this state dominates the first six lines of the poem, the remaining lines are overlaid with a state of longing. At the canal, the environment is engaging enough, in several respects, to leave the poet with no inclination to look back on that school where he is so antithetic to spending time anyway; he is glad to be away and to seize the chance to look longingly ahead instead of looking back. The longing that the poet feels is more than simply a desire to have something or be somewhere; it is a powerful sensation that leaves him feeling *awful* under its influence, and it is this ache or distress that specifically suggests a state of intense yearning or longing. The word *longing* is especially appropriate because San Francisco seem such a long way away, most obviously in terms of distance but also in terms of the culture the poet expects to find and hopes to become a part of there, one in which the aesthetic values

represented by music are embraced to an extent entirely unknown in his home environs. The poet's repetition in lines 11 and 19 of the statement that he and his friend want to leave, with only slight variation between the two expressions—*go there* versus *get out*—reiterates and thus reinforces the importance of their longing, while the variation also shifts toward the theme bringing a sense of ambivalent closure to the poem, that of escape.

Escape

The poet and his friend do not just want to *go* to San Francisco, they want to *get out* of wherever it is they live—the poem never says—framing that place as one from which the poet and his friend need somewhat desperately to escape. The poet's awful feeling in thinking of San Francisco may stem as much from his desire to be there as from his desire *not* to be where he is. Indeed, the poet seems to be caught between the competitive, type A culture of the school and the poverty in which so many of his peers seem to be mired, in danger of watching his sense of self-worth dwindle to nothing if too much under the school's influence, or of feeling like giving up if caught too firmly in the grip of poverty. To evade the constraints represented by both school and poverty, then, he must literally escape, must not only break free of those constraining forces but moreover remove himself far enough away as to be outside of their gravitational pull, so to speak—all the way to the veritable paradise of San Francisco.

The descriptions of the poet and his friend in lines 14–17 are especially suggestive of the idea of escape. The poet's declaration that he and his friend do not drink or smoke may seem like little more than an offhand comment, even a self-consciously moralistic one, but it actually connotes a very mature perspective with regard to such intoxicants, which represent only the most temporary form of escape, a chemical escape that relieves tensions, but only in an illusory way—an escape that may relax the mind and body but does nothing to get to the root of the tension necessitating that sense of escape in the first place. What the poet wants, then, is not the temporary, illusory escape of intoxication but real and true escape, from a dissatisfying life to a fulfilling one through a dramatic change in his circumstances. As for the images of the youths themselves, their hair, in its wind-blown wildness, is evocative of the idea of escaping the regimentation and control of strict codes of crew-cut masculinity. Even the dirt, loosened by the wind, seems to want to escape, while the water in the canal is fortunate enough to go so far as to achieve it. Meanwhile, the poet and his friend, alas, for the time being at least, are stuck where they are.

STYLE

Free Verse

Like most of the poems in *Home Course in Religion*, "Saturday at the Canal" consists of lines roughly the length of standard sonnet lines (ten beats), with the base unit of organization being a long stanza. There is no rhyme or meter, making the poem free verse and allowing the long stanza to produce an unbroken feel of continuous flow. This sense is enhanced by Soto's tendency to use caesuras, or line breaks in the middle of grammatical sentences, instead of ending sentences at the ends of lines. The first line, the mood of which governs the rest of the poem, and the last line are the only ones that end in periods. In fact, perhaps the most interesting structural aspect of the poem is Soto's use of sentences of varying lengths. After the first self-contained, stage-setting line, there is a sentence of two and a half lines, and then—as the discussion of school is quickly

brought to a head—two sentences of little more than one line in length. From the end of line 6 onward, then, the open-ended feel of the long sentence spanning some six lines is itself like a release from the constraints and burdens of the school environment. The two sentences that follow are also longer, spanning four lines each, sustaining the more open sense of the scene at the canal. The sentences shorten as the poem draws to a close, with one being equivalent to two lines in length (lines 17–19) and the next just one line in length (lines 19–20). The rhythmic last sentence, divided by commas into three relatively even phrases, conveys the movement of the water while aptly concluding the broader movement of the poem.

Metonyms

A metonym is a figure of speech in which a part of a whole is used to represent the whole, such as in the saying "Many hands make light work," where laborers are represented by the appendage most relevant to doing manual labor. Two metonyms are explicitly formulated in lines 2–4, where school is said to be first a check marked in a logbook, then an annoying tuba playing in support of one of the school's teams. Essentializing school as such particulars powerfully associates the entire school environment with what those two things, the checkmark and the tuba, are seen to represent, specifically, one imagines, achievement and competition. The characterization of the teachers is not strictly a metonym and yet is metonymic in function, effectively saying that the teachers are, in fact, their aged and out-of-touch perspectives. Similarly, the hallways are not said to be the bad grades and dirty hair, but the characterization remains metonymic, presenting the grades and hair as the most significant, even the defining aspect of those hallways. There is one last explicit metonym, in a somewhat abstract sense. San Francisco is said to be the postcard picture of it hanging on a wall; whatever image the postcard shows certainly represents an aspect of the city, a view of it, and yet technically speaking the postcard is not a part of the city, even if it is readily seen as a material extension of the city. The distance between city and postcard, between object and representation, a distance emphasized by the metonym, contributes to the sense of San Francisco as an idyllic place, much as one can only ever see heaven through paintings representing it—until one finally arrives there, of course.

COMPARE & CONTRAST

- **1960s:** With major hydroelectric and canal projects having been undertaken to redirect water from the Sacramento River in the north of California to the drier San Joaquin Valley during the Great Depression, in the mid-twentieth century the San Joaquin Valley enjoys an abundance of water that allows for Fresno County's agricultural output to be tops in the nation.

  1990s: During the booming US economy overseen by President Bill Clinton, California enjoys its status as the premiere destination in the continental United States, a land of surf and sunshine with no limits to consumption in sight.

  Today: Owing to changes in climate patterns recognized by environmental scientists to be attributable to human-caused global warming and altered atmospheric currents, California endures through the 2010s one of the worst droughts in the state's recorded history, with water levels dropping and plans implemented to ration and conserve water in the driest regions.

- **1960s:** While television has recently made images of distant places available to any home with an antenna and receiver, programming is highly limited in variety and largely contained within studio productions. A postcard, then, featuring an image that a person can perhaps find nowhere else, can hold great significance for providing a vision of a place only dreamed of.

  1990s: Using newer, more portable technologies in television production equipment, cable stations, which have multiplied, have greatly expanded their programming, with such

  outlets as the Public Broadcasting Service, the Discovery Channel, and, later, the National Geographic Channel offering explorations of far-reaching corners of the earth, from the Antarctic to Fiji to the Serengeti.

  Today: Postcards can still have sentimental value, depending on the identity of the sender and the location sent from, but, in light of the availability of images of virtually every corner of the planet through GoogleEarth and multitudes of uploaded photographs, a postcard's image in itself can have little value.

- **1960s:** While short hair remains the norm among men in mainstream society, longer hair, such as worn by the likes of famous rock guitarists (Jimi Hendrix) and genre-defining bands (the Grateful Dead), is in style within the hippie counterculture and part of its broader cultural rebellion.

  1990s: While pockets of hippie culture linger around the country, long hair is just as likely to be seen on members of alternative music cultures ranging from punk (the Ramones) to heavy metal (Metallica) to grunge (Nirvana).

  Today: With mainstream youths being more image conscious than ever thanks to social media platforms like Facebook and Instagram, many are less likely to take risks such as growing their hair long. On the other hand, alternative cultures are as diverse as ever, with tattoos and piercings proliferating to such an extent that long hair, worn sometimes by some famous musicians (Foo Fighters) but not others (Fall Out Boy), is often only a minor statement.

HISTORICAL CONTEXT

San Francisco and Fresno in Mid-Twentieth-Century California

"Saturday at the Canal" is a curious poem as far as setting is concerned, in that the city where the

poem takes place goes unstated, while the city of San Francisco gets a starring role through no more than mention of a postcard. By the 1960s, as stated by James Brook in his "Remarks on the Poetic Transformation of San Francisco," the city had become such a dominant cultural center

The school hallways make the speaker feel depressed and trapped. (© Monkey Business Images / Shutterstock.com)

that it was dubbed "the Paris of the Pacific." Perhaps no moment was more iconic in terms of poetics and the city than Allen Ginsberg's electrifying first public reading of "Howl" at the Six Gallery on October 7, 1955. Ginsberg's collection *Howl and Other Poems* (1956), published by Lawrence Ferlinghetti's City Lights bookstore and imprint, was initially banned for obscenity but then emerged victorious from censorship trials in a landmark decision in favor of free speech. Ginsberg's best-known companion was Jack Kerouac, who wrote some poetry but is far better known for *On the Road* (1957) and other autobiographical novels in which he changed his own name—to Jack Duluoz—as well as the names of friends like Ginsberg. Also active in the San Francisco poetry scene in this era were Kenneth Rexroth, Gary Snyder, and William Carlos Williams. Ginsberg and Kerouac especially, headliners of the Beat generation, helped popularize the sort of greater existential awareness represented by Eastern mysticism, and Soto, who even as a teenager expressed a belief in reincarnation, is readily seen as one of the multitude of heirs to the Beats' philosophical tradition.

Soto himself, as it happened, never quite made it to San Francisco—at least not to stay—while otherwise making a tour of key California cities in the course of his education and early employment, progressing from Fresno to universities in Irvine, San Diego, and Berkeley. Indeed, more relevant to the poem is Soto's life in Fresno, California, in the late 1960s. As the urban hub of the fertile San Joaquin Valley, Fresno has long been a home to various immigrant populations arriving to work on the surrounding farmlands. By the mid-twentieth century, Chinese railroad workers, among the area's earliest immigrants, had been joined by Scandinavians, Germans, Japanese, Armenians, and especially Mexicans and other Hispanic populations coming from Latin America.

Soto offers anecdotes and details of life in Fresno in his episodic autobiographical volume *A Summer Life* (1990). The vignette "The Canal" makes clear that Soto wrote "Saturday at the Canal" based on experience. "The canal raced out of town before us, green sparkling water," Soto begins, relating how he and his best friend would drive out to the canal, sit on the bank, and ruminate on such topics as the attractiveness of girls (as well as a certain teacher, Mrs. Tuttle), the seeming sadism of their phys-ed teacher, and the comparative merits of Jimi Hendrix and the far less well-known musicians T. Rex. Soto states in a later vignette that the scene was less than ideal, with the canal composed of "sand, reeds, and feeble fish stunted by the chemicals from agricultural runoff." Yet he explains in "The Canal" that the watercourse remained meaningful to them in a natural sense in the absence of other waterways: "We didn't know rivers or lakes, and the sea was a postcard that came our way now and then"—such as on a San Francisco postcard, one posits. Soto pensively concludes the vignette much as he concludes his correlative poem: "We could go only so far in our car but, while we sat, the canal water got the hell out of town."

Soto mentions the canal in other vignettes as well, such as "The River," the book's last, about a visit to the vast but dried-up Los Angeles River. His description of their arrival in Los Angeles helps set the historical scene (while also providing a bit of relevant psychological insight vis-à-vis his poem): "Because we were seventeen, something had to happen. There were mobs of young people in leather vests, bell-bottoms, beads, Jesus thongs, tie-dyed T-shirts, and crowns of flowers." The scent pervading the air, he adds, was one of patchouli oil, sweat, cigarette smoke, wine, and incense. Perhaps Soto's most poignant look at the canal is presented at the end of "The Wrestler," the volume's penultimate vignette:

> The water in the canal was quick as a wind-blown cloud. The 1960s were coming to an end, and the first of the great rock stars were beginning to die. We were dying to leave home, by car, thumb or on water racing west to where the sun went down.

CRITICAL OVERVIEW

Although Soto had already published over a dozen volumes, with both regional and major publishers, by the early 1990s, he was not yet being widely reviewed. In a *Publishers Weekly* review, Penny Kaganoff calls *Home Course in Religion* (1991) a "wry, meditative collection" dealing with both "physical and metaphysical identity" and "transcendent reality." Kaganoff

concludes that Soto's verse is "sweetly nostalgic, but never sentimental; his ruminations are full of unusual imagery that is both amusing and ingenuous." Of Soto's *New and Selected Poems* (1995), a *Publishers Weekly* reviewer finds "a youth of gritty determination" insightfully conveyed. Soto's poems are said to "gather an impressive force with their quick rhythms and recurrent images."

In *Chicano Writers, First Series* (volume 82 of the *Dictionary of Literary Biography*), Héctor Avalos Torres hails Soto's "remarkable ability to write poetry that captures some existential common denominator," with prominent themes including assimilation and its inverse, alienation. Torres quotes Arthur Ramírez as calling Soto "a leading Chicano writer"; Christopher Buckley as stating, after reading Soto's debut collection, *The Elements of San Joaquin*, "Soto has something *human* and important to say, and this makes the craft worthwhile, and sets these poems above many"; and Alan Williamson as affirming, "At his frequent best, Soto may be the most exciting poet of poverty in America."

Pamela Shelton, in *Twentieth-Century Young Adult Writers*, quotes *New York Times* reviewer Alan Cheuse as calling Soto "one of the finest natural talents" among contemporary Chicano writers. Shelton herself declares,

> Soto's ability to tell a story, to recreate moments of his own past in a manner that transcends the boundaries of race or age, to transport his reader to the world of his own childhood is felt within each of his written works.... But it is his joyful outlook, strong enough to transcend the poverty of the barrio, that makes his work so popular.

In *Contemporary Poets*, noted Native American author Joseph Bruchac gives Soto high praise, especially for his ability to portray characters from the disadvantaged world he grew out of—characters

> whose visions of America are those of ones looking up from the bottom, not out over wide expanses of possibility.... Despite their poverty, their despair, and the ugliness of their surroundings, his characters inhabit a world which is precisely visioned, full of a fierce love for life.

Regarding technique, Bruchac observers that "Soto's diction is classically spare, his images exact"; his poems are marked by "an aggressive imagination" and "the careful description, the exactness, the somatic nature of the simile."

While Soto is seen to at times approach the sort of sentimentality that can compromise verse, he "avoids the traps of rhetoric and overstatement," and "he also avoids appearing grandiose by concentrating...his images on small incidents, on individuals rather than world-shaking events." Bruchac declares that at the heart of Soto's poetics is "the vision of the ordinary and oppressed." Torres concludes, "Soto's consistent attention to the craft of writing and his sensitivity to his subject matter have earned him an undisputable place in American and Chicano literature."

CRITICISM

Michael Allen Holmes

Holmes is a writer with existential interests. In the following essay, he examines how Soto's "Saturday at the Canal" derives power from playing with time.

The closing lines of Soto's poem "Saturday at the Canal" make clear that time is of the essence in the poem, with the years said to be frozen, or not moving—a noteworthy description of something that in truth never stops going forward. Metaphorical as it may be, the poem's suggestion of the sudden stoppage of time produces a palpable sense of stasis weighing down the passing youth of the poet and his friend. On closer examination, one sees that Soto has been playing with senses of time from the poem's first line, building toward, and lending that much more power to, the explicit revelation of the theme in the closing lines.

Line 1 of the poem has a straightforward connection to time, in the poet's desire to be contented by the age of seventeen. This certainly makes seventeen a benchmark age as far as the poem is concerned, and yet the line is entirely unclear about the poet's age at the time of the action as well as at the time of narration. The poet as a youth, as a character in his poem, might be exactly seventeen, meaning he has reached the age when he realizes he ought to be happy and yet is not. Alternatively, he might easily be younger or older than seventeen—a sixteen-year-old all too conscious of the likelihood of being jaded in the near future or an eighteen-year-old as jaded as can be. Thus, the language Soto uses leaves entirely open the actual age of the poet in the period of youth described. The second ambiguity

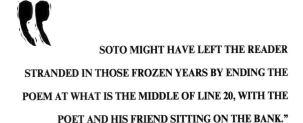

SOTO MIGHT HAVE LEFT THE READER STRANDED IN THOSE FROZEN YEARS BY ENDING THE POEM AT WHAT IS THE MIDDLE OF LINE 20, WITH THE POET AND HIS FRIEND SITTING ON THE BANK."

is the age of the poet as he narrates the poem. One might simply suggest that the narrator is the age of Soto when he wrote it, which was approximately thirty-eight or thirty-nine, and this squares well enough with the poem, phrased as it is strictly in the past tense. And yet any poet can adopt a persona not his or her own, and many do, such that this poem demands consideration as potentially displaced from Soto's own experience. The narrator could be approaching forty, or he could be thirty and mired in the same oppressive circumstances as always (in a job now rather than school), or he could be twenty and living happily in San Francisco already (perhaps the least likely possibility based on the tone). The paired ambiguities of the age of the poet both within and without the poem, so to speak, might be said to leave the reader dangling in a doubly indefinite frame existing outside ordinary time.

Line 2 hints at the passage of time, if one imagines the logbook gradually filling up with checkmarks over the course of a year, but more compelling is the malleability of time in lines 3–4. In one sense, the tuba can be seen to serve as a metonym for an entire band—only the sound of the tuba is specifically invoked, but one likely does not imagine that the tuba is playing alone in support of the school's athletic team. (*Team* might be imagined to refer to a nonathletic team, like a chess or debate team, but unfortunately for the participants in such worthy competitions, schools rarely seek to throw support behind intellectual teams through pep rallies with the school band, for various reasons. One can easily imagine a Wes Anderson film featuring a pep rally for a chess team, ill attended, and indeed with naught but a tuba playing, but this only supports the notion that it could hardly happen in reality.) The mention of the tuba alone perhaps suggests that its particular low reverberations are what the poet happens to be attuned to, or maybe the poet is inclined to skip

WHAT DO I READ NEXT?

- If one is drawn to Soto's poetry for the quality of the verse, one might turn next to his highly regarded debut collection, *The Elements of San Joaquin* (1977), or his second collection, *The Tale of Sunlight* (1978), which was nominated for the Pulitzer Prize.

- If one is drawn to the life story behind poems like "Saturday at the Canal," one might next read one of his autobiographical volumes, such as *Living up the Street: Narrative Recollections* (1985), *Small Faces* (1986), *Lesser Evils: Ten Quartets* (1988), or the more recent compendium *The Effects of Knut Hamsun on a Fresno Boy: Recollections and Short Essays* (2001).

- While Soto flirted with deviant behavior as a youth, Chicano poet Jimmy Santiago Baca's exploits landed him in jail—which is where he finally became functionally literate, solidified his education, and discovered his poetic voice. A sense of alienation is prevalent in his collection *Immigrants in Our Own Land and Selected Early Poems* (1990), including in the poem "Who Understands Me but Me," a masterstroke of defiance of limitations and confinement.

- Poet Philip Levine was a major influence on Soto as one of his creative writing instructors at California State University, Fresno. Soto, cited by Torres, called Levine "a constant master of the nuts and bolts of how to read a poem—how to analyze and how to critique a poem." Levine won the Pulitzer Prize in 1995 for *The Simple Truth: Poems* (1994)

- One particular poem that opened Soto's eyes to the possibilities inherent in verse was Edward Field's "Unwanted," which to Soto represented a universal expression of alienation from society. Field, a New York–born poet of Russian and Polish Jewish ancestry, included the poem in his debut collection *Stand Up, Friend, with Me* (1963).

- Ohio poet James Wright is, like Soto, greatly respected for his odes of impoverished environments and peoples. He won the Yale Series of Younger Poets award for *The Green Wall* (1957), and he won the Pulitzer Prize for his *Collected Poems* (1971).

- A Chicana poet who, like Soto, has made a point of producing collections of poetry expressly for juvenile as well as teen audiences, is Pat Mora. Her young-adult collection *My Own True Name* (2000) presents existential considerations centered on the metaphorical motif of the cactus plant.

---

the pep rallies and sit in the library, only to hear the sound of the tuba echoing through the halls and preventing him from focusing on his studies. Regardless, when one thinks of an annoying tuba, one likely imagines a highly repetitive cycle of huffed and puffed notes that over time grate on the nerves, especially if one prefers quiet (a tendency among poets).

Aside from suggesting the key concept of cyclicity, lines 3–4 tweak time in that the poet suggests that the tuba is playing *because* the team will win at night. This is, of course, a curious statement of causal relation, since something cannot really happen *because* something else

will happen in the future when that particular outcome is by no means certain. It would be more appropriate to say that the tuba is playing *to help* the team win that night, by boosting morale, or *in the hope that* the team will win. The use of the word *because*, then, hints at a skewed conception in the minds of those people supporting the team. The assertion "We're going to win!" is indeed extremely common among sports players, despite the fact that such an assertion can never justifiably be made before a contest has begun. Many a defeated athlete has eaten those precise words in retrospect. The skewed causal relation in the poem thus speaks

---

to the temporal disorientation brought about by the hypercompetitive culture that encourages such declarations of future success. Through no more than verb tense, Soto manages to seem to ask, Why not just play games without feeling a self-inflating need to blur the lines of verbal integrity?—which integrity is, of course, the pride of the poet. Moreover, he seems to suggest that those who are conditioned to mindlessly support a certain faction (there are political implications here, of course) experience the breaking down of chronological rationale—they are being shifted outside normal passing time.

In speaking of teachers being close to dying, lines 4–5 once again incorporate temporal ambiguity. This may well mean that the teachers are literally old, approaching senility and death, or it may simply mean that the teachers' mind-set is reflective of their having given up on the ideals of youth, like ambition, hope, and personal dreams. Thus, while seeming to locate the teachers at a certain point along a time line of ages, the sentence rather takes a quantity that was unknown to begin with—the teachers' ages—and secures its indeterminacy, ensuring that the reader can have no concrete conception of how old the teachers are. The last sentence on the school environment, in lines 5–6, seems at last to bring a solid image that the reader can pin to a temporal setting, and yet Soto defies this possibility through the metaphorical reference to the odor of bad grades. It is true that the smell of unwashed hair can be inhaled in a mere moment in time (though for one to declare that an entire hallway smells as such, one may need to be walking down it), but the smell of bad grades would seem to need far longer to coalesce in the air. Soto is likely trying to evoke not the day when students all get their report cards and fret or fume over the results, but the overall mood as resulting from the indifference, resistance, and disillusionment that both cause and are caused by poor grades, which do not necessarily reflect poor intelligence. Such an aroma would need a fair deal of time to ripen—and thus the image spans a far greater portion of time than seems at first to be the case.

Finally, with line 7 the poem deposits the reader, along with the poet and his friend, at a specific point in time, a Saturday spent at the canal. This may be a ritual that the boys share, visiting the canal, but henceforth the poem does carry the sense of relating the experience of a single occasion. And yet the images continue to express uncertainty, malleability, or especially cyclicity of time. The lack of conversation is something that de-emphasizes the passage of time. A conversation, of course, can only keep moving forward, regardless of how one person responds to the other—one cannot pretend that what has been said has not been said. Thus, when it comes to losing oneself in the moment, so to speak—such as in a meditative or Zen sense—there is nothing more conducive than silence. The mind slips away from its act-and-react protocol and drifts into a more holistic awareness of the surroundings and one's sense of self. One's thoughts do often proceed like a one-sided conversation, that is to say, continuously progressing forward, and yet in an ideal meditative state, that is, Buddhism's nirvana, one's sense of time is completely obliterated. In light of the Beat generation's exploration of expansive mentalities through the 1950s, Buddhism was very much in the air in 1960s San Francisco and thereabouts.

While the poet and his friend's lack of conversation might contribute to a certain stillness of time, their actions return to the concept of cyclicity, as throwing rocks at the ground is an activity that accomplishes nothing and could be repeated indefinitely—like bailing water out of a scuttled boat or like Sisyphus pushing his boulder up the same hill day after day for eternity. Meanwhile, stillness is again invoked in the depiction of San Francisco not as a bustling city but as a picture postcard, an image that is frozen in time, and which thus prefigures and mirrors the freezing of time at the poem's end.

Ensuing images return to various types of cycles. Migrating North American birds follow the same cyclical routes year in and year out as they head south for the winter and north for the summer. While this is a cycle of life that at least gets the birds somewhere, the mention of people who can play only three chords on a guitar suggests—not unlike the image of the tuba—repetitive playing that before long grates on one's nerves, instilling in the listener a powerful desire to escape the severely limited and thus oppressive patterns. The images of lines 16–17 suggest dirt blowing around the wind, a potentially cyclical pattern not unlike the action of youths throwing rocks at the ground.

There is finally some forward direction to the images in lines 17–18, as the poet envisions

The boys long to see San Francisco, but so far it is only an image in a postcard to them. *(© Mike Flippo /
Shutterstock.com)*

the modes of transportation that could take him
and his friend to San Francisco. The image of a
train swaying as it passes over a long bridge is at
once both cyclical—in the swaying back and
forth as the train gradually crosses—and progressive, since the bridge must be crossed in the
end, suggesting an advance beyond cyclicity to
forward motion. These images come close to
implying that these means of escape are within
the poet's grasp, but the mention of the freezing
of time in this key location whisks away any
suggestion of escape—at least for the time
being. There is no forward progress for the
poet and his friend; the years are going nowhere,
are not moving at all, however much the youths
might wish otherwise. Indeed, even their youth
itself is not going anywhere, as suggested by their
declining to either drink or smoke, which are
age-appropriate decisions that serve to maintain
their youthful innocence.

Soto might have left the reader stranded in
those frozen years by ending the poem at what is
the middle of line 20, with the poet and his friend
sitting on the bank. Such an ending would have
perhaps even more strongly connoted the lam-
entable lack of forward progress in the lives of
the poet and his friend. But perhaps such an
ending would also have been too prosaic and
bleak. After all, however much the years may
have felt frozen to the poet back when he sat

with his friend at the canal, they must have
unfrozen eventually. The poet, with his polished
verse, surely finished high school, and however
much throwing rocks at the canal may have felt
satisfying—or rather like the perfect embodiment of his dissatisfaction—at the time, he
surely went on to find more productive ways to
spend his time. The poem might be seen to hint at
this resolution of the frozen state of his youth
with the last line and a half, which shift from the
boys' longing stasis to the ever-rushing water, its
depths, like the boys', more profound than meets
the eye, its destination, like the poet's—and perhaps like his friend's—beyond the town's borders, somewhere out there in the greater world.

Source: Michael Allen Holmes, Critical Essay on "Saturday at the Canal," in *Poetry for Students*, Gale, Cengage
Learning, 2016.

Nina Lindsay

*In the following review, Lindsay points out how
Soto's humor shines through his poems.*

Soto is well known for his range, but here's a
first for him: seventy-seven original poems all
about teenage love. Divided into two sections,
"A Girl's Tears, Her Songs" and "A Boy's
Body, His Words," the free-verse poems all somehow ring true: appropriately corny, rich with
image, accessible and believable. They describe a
range of emotions and experience, from "Not

Yet" ("I a small tree, / You a taller, bending / Tree. The sun / Will roll over us, / And if a cloud / Of worry throws lightning, / Let's remember our fear") to "Imagination" ("Mr. Fried, you're a nice man, / But, please, you pick up the book / And float on an iceberg to Norway! / . . . I don't want to read / About love, but feel love–/ Her hand in mine, / Her hair against my throat, / And the pink bud of her tongue . . . "). Humor, devastation, tenderness, jealousy . . . if any theme seems to repeat, it's Soto's soft spot for the date that can't afford the date, like the guy who orders a strawberry milkshake (her favorite) and only pretends to sip his half. Inevitably, readers will be drawn more to some poems than to others, but the simple, open design encourages browsing, and readers flipping through are bound to find the right words when they need them.

Source: Nina Lindsay, Review of *Partly Cloudy: Poems of Love and Longing*, in *Horn Book*, Vol. 85, No. 2, March–April 2009, p. 211.

Gary Soto

In the following interview, Soto discusses where he finds inspiration for his writing.

TEACHINGBOOKS: If someone who doesn't know you asks what you do for a living, what do you say?

GARY SOTO: I answer, "I'm retired." Usually, the person will nod his head and say, "Lucky fellow." I never mention that I'm a writer, unless it's clearly in a situation where people assume I must act like a poet and writer, meaning sort of witty or dotty, depending upon the moment. Yesterday, in fact, while I was warming up for a game of tennis, someone asked "What do you do?" I sent the ball over the net and answered in a winded way, "Oh, not a whole lot." I like to go incognito and play up the retired image. I get into movies for half the price playing retired.

TEACHINGBOOKS: When did you begin to describe yourself as a poet?

GARY SOTO: I was twenty-one, a senior at Fresno State, and hung out with other poets who were not ashamed, worried or conceited in proclaiming themselves poets. It seemed natural. We were writing poetry and so, by a logical conclusion, we were poets. We even acted like poets, a little off-the-wall. Plus sometimes very moody, as if we had swallowed a storm cloud.

> EVEN THOUGH I HAVE SOME STATURE IN THE WORLD (A POET! A WRITER!), I TELL STUDENTS THAT I'M NOT UNLIKE THEM, THAT MY OWN CHILDHOOD WAS FILLED WITH BASEBALL, KICKBALL, PLAYGROUND ANTICS."

TEACHINGBOOKS: Were you writing and/ or reading poems when you were a boy?

GARY SOTO: No, I didn't write when I was a child, though in high school I kept a journal of my daily thoughts. I recall that journal—it was striped like a candy cane and, I suppose, had a lot of sweet words inside it. However, I did read while I was in elementary school, but which titles I don't recall. I then stopped reading for the longest time—shame on me—and didn't pick up this wonderful activity again until I was in high school. Then it was Hemingway, Steinbeck, Edgar Lee Masters, Robert Frost, etc.

TEACHINGBOOKS: Can you share what it means to you to be a poet for children?

GARY SOTO: It means handling words and images in an interesting way. All of us use words daily, unless of course we are the silent type. Everyday we say simple things like, "Gee, look at this tan of mine." Or: "I feel sort of sad." But say you wrote something like: "Our faces were the color of pennies," *and* "Our souls are broken like jars." The language becomes interesting and perks up our spirits and imagination. This is what poetry means—language that surprises and keeps us on our toes.

TEACHINGBOOKS: Your poems are rarely in rhyme and meter.

GARY SOTO: How true. I depend upon rhythm, not rhyme and meter, for a poetry cadence that will attract the musically conscious reader. Young readers—and older ones—should look for strong images. Images can be so satisfying and breathtaking.

TEACHINGBOOKS: The subjects of your poems feel so realistic. How do you do this?

GARY SOTO: By interest and training, I'm what they refer to as an Imagist. I try to appeal to the sense of seeing—and sometimes hearing, as in the cadence of a poem—as I believe that poems should convey a realism, even if that realism is a fiction. I find that poems that depend on easy description are often sloppily written.

TEACHINGBOOKS: I'm curious how you, as a poet, reflect on the common assignment of memorizing poems. Do you memorize your own poems?

GARY SOTO: Poems written in rhyme and meter can be easily memorized, even longish poems. However, because I write in free verse, my lines are probably more difficult to take in, to absorb, to memorize. But I'm not seeking any students to memorize my poetry—heck, I don't even know my poems. I'm hoping for a sentiment that will linger in the reader's mind. Sentiment, or feeling, is so important to the reader. One of my most popular poems is "Oranges," which is about first love. Very few have memorized this poem, but they do remember the feeling. In some regards, this is a memorization, that is, the feeling one takes away from a poem after reading it.

TEACHINGBOOKS: Poems and short stories are sometimes seen as more accessible than novels because they are shorter. Is that your perception?

GARY SOTO: I would say that novels are more accessible than poetry and short stories. With novels you have a narrative—story, in other words—and with poetry and short stories you have to work for the *meaning*. In fact, there's a classic complaint that poems are obscure; sometimes this is true, and it's the fault of the poet. Other times it's the laziness of the reader and his or her willingness to try to understand a poem's meaning. Some smart person said that poetry is an act of attention. How true—"an act of attention." It's the same with short stories. Of course, short stories are narratives, but the endings sometimes can be elusive, almost tricky. Let's use the word subtle here. Short stories often end with subtleties that require the reader to reflect.

TEACHINGBOOKS: Can you share a bit about Baseball in April, *one of your most popular books?*

GARY SOTO: This was a book that almost didn't get published. It went around to different publishers, who liked what they read but were mystified that it featured Mexican American characters and, in turn, was a book composed of short stories (literary history tells us that most publishers avoid short stories because they aren't commercial enough). At the time (1987–88), I was an essayist and poet, and *Baseball in April* was the first venture into writing for young people. Finally, it was accepted by Harcourt Inc., published, and went on to make a lot of young people (and parents and teachers) happy. I think what caught people off guard was its realism when most readers were looking for fantasy. It also featured a real place—Fresno, my hometown. Children's literature usually invents these places that are not real. But not me! Fresno is all over my work.

TEACHINGBOOKS: Your novel Off and Running *touches on political activism and the election process. Were you conscious of writing such a positive book about activist children?*

GARY SOTO: No, not really. In my mind this novel features a spunky girl named Miata and her sidekick, Ana, plus two happy-go-lucky boys Rudy and Alex. It's in some ways a girl vs. boy novel, and comic, of course. It's about school politics, or, perhaps, a popularity contest. In the adult world, we have politics and usually a stodgy group of candidates speaking the most vapid clichés imaginable, and we're supposed to like them because they prop up smiles. But the smiles in *Off and Running* are real. Here we have real kids seeking positions that will offer classmates more ice cream. Even as an adult, I would side with more ice cream.

TEACHINGBOOKS: The life of farmers and laborers appear to be very important to you, often appearing in your writing. You're also the Young People Ambassador for California Rural Legal Assistance and the United Farm Workers of America, and wrote an inspiration biography of Cesar Chavez. Can you please share your feelings about this topic?

GARY SOTO: Cesar Chavez, the great labor leader, evoked a great spirit for change, and his call for the cause—*la causa*—is difficult to fathom unless you were present during the labor strife of the 1960s and 1970s. If you were Mexican American, you felt his presence and rooted for farm laborers up and down the San Joaquin Valley. His chant of *Sí se puede/You can do it* became something that I lived by. I'm a writer who overcame a lot of obstacles—including prejudice—in order to become a writer. I think my best YA novel is *Jesse* that portrays two young men, both part-time farm workers. It's something

I think of daily, that is, farm workers and the people who advocate for them, including José Padilla of California Rural Legal Assistance and Arturo Rodriguez, the president of the United Farm Workers of America. They are giant souls. I encourage young people to view the film *A Fight in the Fields* and to register for information on farm workers by going to www.ufw.org.

TEACHINGBOOKS: What inspired you to write the Chato books [Chato's Kitchen, Chato & the Party Animals, and Chato Goes Cruisin']?

GARY SOTO: I love Chato, that low-riding ese vato cat from East Los Angeles! I forget what inspired me, but I've done these three books, plus another that didn't get published. But the cat lives. He has nine lives and hasn't used up one yet! It would make me immensely happy if Chato could become a cartoon character. Heck, I would sit in my pajamas on Saturday to watch him kick around *el barrio.*

TEACHINGBOOKS: In almost all of your books and writings you employ Spanish words and phrases among the English, and include a glossary of Spanish words at the end. Why do you do this?

GARY SOTO: Often my characters—a Jesus, a Hector, a Gloria—will be bilingual, or if not bilingual at least know enough Spanish to throw words and phrases into conversation. As a writer, I'm trying to capture the voice of my characters, who sometimes will speak in Spanglish. I'll give you an example: "Hay te watcho," is poor academic Spanish but clearly understandable to those who know street Spanish. You can translate this simple sentence as "Better watch out."

TEACHINGBOOKS: Too Many Tamales *is so often used in schools. Tell us about it.*

GARY SOTO: After I wrote *Baseball in April* and *Taking Sides*, my agent suggested that I write a picture book. I had to ask her, "What's a picture book?" She explained, and off I went writing a little story about a girl fascinated by her mother's wedding ring. It's not unusual for girls—and boys—to wear things that belong to their parents. They like the idea of "dressing up" or pretending to be older. How many have seen a boy wearing his father's shoes, or a girl's mouth smeared with a mother's lipstick? But in the story I wanted the complication of little Maria losing the ring, or thinking she's lost the ring. I think this one of the fears of all children, that is, losing something—anything!

TEACHINGBOOKS: Please describe your typical workday.

GARY SOTO: If I'm writing a novel, I begin just after a breakfast of Wheaties (as I will need strength). I work from about 8:30 until noon, and then a couple of hours after lunch. Usually I'm drained by 3:30 and have to go outside to get a breath of fresh air. Writing is exhausting, even though it doesn't appear that I'm doing a whole lot: just sitting in a chair, typing, staring at a screen.

TEACHINGBOOKS: What do you do when you get stuck?

GARY SOTO: I seldom have what folks call "writer's block." I'm always working on a book, or if not a book, then random poems and stories.

TEACHINGBOOKS: Can you please share a bit about the writing process?

GARY SOTO: If it's a poem, I will share it immediately with my wife, Carolyn, who will mark it up. Later I will send it to my poet friend, Christopher Buckley, for a final opinion. He's pretty brutal and won't tolerate bad writing. If it's prose, I will share it first with Carolyn and then later my friend José Novoa. No one works alone. Everyone has an editor, and I have mine.

TEACHINGBOOKS: What do you like to tell students when you speak with them?

GARY SOTO: Even though I have some stature in the world (a poet! a writer!), I tell students that I'm not unlike them, that my own childhood was filled with baseball, kickball, playground antics. Yes, I tell them, I was no good at spelling, was haunted by a bully named Frankie T., fell in and out of love, loved lunch, loved dinner, ate candy bars by the fistful, got into fights (lost most of them), and loved to read despite no family encouragement to read. I want young people to make the best decisions for their lives, so I'll say to some, "Hey, don't mess up." They know what I'm talking about.

TEACHINGBOOKS: What do you like to tell teachers?

GARY SOTO: I tell them on the sly, "Stay strong." Teachers work so hard and give so much of themselves that I sit in awe of them. I know I couldn't do what they do. They have to work with the policy of "No Child Left Behind," and from what I gather with speaking with them, they are not very happy with all this testing. Granted, we should have standards, but I've assessed from speaking with hundred of teachers that standards should be local, not national.

Source: Gary Soto, "Gary Soto: In-depth Written Interview," in *TeachingBooks.net*, August 29, 2007.

Fred L. Dings

In the following review, Dings points out some faults in the second part of Soto's collection One Kind of Faith.

The three-part volume *One Kind of Faith* is characteristically Gary Soto in its first and third parts. Part one includes poems averaging a page in length with hallmark Soto qualities: humor ("two non-paying flies" riding in a cab, dogs sitting in cars reading the *Wall Street Journal*) and insouciance mixed with an undercurrent of seriousness, the "points" not too seriously made, left on the table to be picked up by the reader or not. Here we have an array of children, Latino workers, dogs, and dog days. The poems in the perspective of children are (as usual for Soto) completely persuasive, though sometimes a little "light" in their effect. The poems featuring workers do so through deft, succinct descriptions suffused with humor rather than studied, grim depictions that weigh down the poems; the workers themselves are also sometimes comical and always humanly flawed, not cutout proletarians pressed into service for a political cause. For this reason, his workers are more sympathetic and his poems more affecting than they otherwise might be.

The most satisfying example of such portraiture is the eighteen-page poem "Gil Mendez and the Metaphysics of a Blimp," which comprises the entire third section. Here, the character of an old man, Gil Mendez, is affectingly developed as he moves through his days, unable to find work, in a low-income Latino neighborhood. He still mourns the death of his son, whose rake once touched a power line as he playfully extended it toward a blimp in the sky. At the end of the poem, the old man sees another blimp in the sky, a blimp "the size of God's fist," a God that seems determined to keep Gil Mendez from love, youth, an irretrievable past, and his son.

Part 2 of the collection contains some problematic work. It is subtitled "Film Treatments for David Lynch," but some of the poems seem more the literary equivalents of *Pulp Fiction* with their grotesque dismemberments ("an arm and foot in a zipped-up gym bag") robbed of horror

through bored, distanced humor and flat effect. Not all poems in this section, however, are like this. In fact, one of the best short lyrics in the book, "An Old Man's Belief," poignantly draws the portrait of an old man bitterly disaffected with the world and the notion of God. Overall, Soto fans will not be disappointed.

Source: Fred L. Dings, Review of *One Kind of Faith*, in *World Literature Today*, Vol. 78, Nos. 3–4, September–December 2004, pp. 102–103.

Rafael Perez-Torres

In the following essay, Perez-Torres presents an overview of critical reception to Soto's work.

One of the most celebrated contemporary Chicano poets is Gary Soto. He has received recognition from outside Chicano circles and this is partially reflected in his many awards, among them the Academy of American Poets Prize in 1975. . . .

Soto's poetry differs markedly from that of the Movement poets . . . for it does not call its readers to action, nor is it declamatory. It also eschews the often idealized elements of home, and *carnalismo* found in so much Chicano poetry. But it does reflect a Chicano consciousness of racial identity and the despair that can come from poverty and alienation. Many critics have discussed his skill as an artificer of language.

Gary Soto was born in . . . Fresno, California, which is located in the San Joaquin Valley, a fertile and productive agricultural area. This geographic background thoroughly informs his first collection of poems, *The Elements of San Joaquin* (1977). The volume's three divisions include powerful vignettes of Fresno, fieldwork, and private visions of humans in an often meaningless landscape. . . .

Jose Varela-Ibarra has commented that Soto's *San Joaquin* poems are essentially rural and urban landscapes while his second collection of poetry, *The Tale of Sunlight* (1978), treats inner space. Soto does explore the inner world of the emotions as well as memory here, and the mood is not as bleak as in *San Joaquin*; indeed, events are at times even magical. . . .

Black Hair (1985) is a departure in mood from previous collections of Soto's poetry. The economical, acute images are still present, but the desolate feelings so often described in previous poems are usually replaced by more hopeful ones.... *Black Hair* chronicles a life, from the boy of eight through adolescence, young manhood, and fatherhood. Humor untouched by sadness is allowed more space here.

... Gary Soto is the epitome of a new trend within Chicano literature. While the ethnic element is not missing from his work, he writes more for a general public than for solely Chicanos. His poetry is well within the mainstream of United States poetic style; concise metaphors, elimination of prosaic or narrative elements, brief illuminations of emotions, conversational tone. He publishes predominantly in mainstream magazines rather than in Chicano outlets.

Also, Soto is the first major Chicano writer trained by a major U.S. poet, Philip Levine. Not only has Soto entered the mainstream, but he was groomed for it by someone who could open doors previously closed to many Chicano writers. Young Chicano writers more and more often would like to follow Soto's example.

... A ... sense of subjectivity and agency is evident in Gary Soto's "Between Words," the closing poem of *Black Hair*.... Animal needs form, ultimately, the essential basis of existence, since, as the poetic voice soon makes clear, all life ends in the gaping smile of death. The poem thus seems to rely on a very traditional theme of lyric poetry: carpe diem....

Certainly this sense of movement between birth and death fits thematically with Soto's collection as a whole. *Black Hair* opens, after all, with the title poem, a celebration of identity and community that has at its center the recollection by a child of his father's death. That first poem places death at the center of life. This final poem places the passage through life at the center of death. A sense of inversion and closure is therefore achieved in Soto's closing lyric expression.

Yet the language and images of "Between Worlds" suggest conflict. There is a tension evoked as this crossing between, which suggests a linear movement of never arriving, is described as being "the point." Just as a line indicates continuity and a point fixity, so the act of "never arriving" becomes a form of arriving. The only "arriving" evoked in the poem, however, is that moment at which the ants "Climb our faces to undo the smiles." So Soto's work probes the border between placement and placelessness,

both evoking and undoing an endlessly transient notion of arrival....

The language of the poem celebrates silence and so, too, is caught between the desire to express and the consciousness that it is unable to do so....

By assuming a quintessentially European genre—a genre that at once seems most alien to and yet offers great ground for the Chicano poet to traverse, scrutinize, and mark (a mode of poetic expression that may indeed be "dead" to the world that first mapped and circumscribed it)—Chicano lyric poetry negotiates the difficult terrain between the voice, the subject, and the world. It also calls into question the traditional generic boundaries of the lyric form. The mutual interpenetration of subject and object explored by Chicano lyric poetry stands in contradistinction to the traditional lyric as a meditation premised upon the very separation between self and other. The mutually traversing agents and objects suggest a radical reconfiguration of subjectivity, a subjectivity whose artistic expression lives vigorously and productively crossing the border between genres, between languages, between cultures. The terrain marked by the terms modernism and postmodernism, colonial and postcolonial, represent only part of the cultural landscape across which Chicano poetry migrates.

Source: Rafael Perez-Torres, "Soto, Gary (1952–)," in *Modern American Literature*, 1999, pp. 213–14.

Penny Kaganoff

In the following review, Kaganoff praises Soto's creative use of imagery.

The first half of this wry, meditative collection brings us through Soto's boyhood and teenage years and his tentatively evolving spiritual and sensual awareness. There is the usual kid's stuff here—shoplifting candy bars, "walking with Pepsi cans smashed onto my shoes"—but Soto was no ordinary kid, pondering the nature of the soul, God's intrusive omniscience and the absurdity of Catholic ritual. Soto (*Who Will Know Us?*) was also possessed of a keen imagination that sought to elaborate upon the fairly ordinary circumstances of his youth. In his teens, he began to question his physical and metaphysical identity: "I had these feelings / I was Chinese, that I had lived before." In the latter half of the book, the poet searches the practical aspects of his adult life—his marriage, job, hobbies—for signs of a transcendent reality. In the end, sadly enough, he is sure of only our material status: "We invent misery for our bodies, / Then our minds, and then, having nothing else to do, / Look for ways to make it stop." Soto's language is sweetly nostalgic, but never sentimental; his ruminations are full of unusual imagery that is both amusing and ingenuous.

Source: Penny Kaganoff, Review of *Home Course in Religion*, in *Publishers Weekly*, Vol. 238, No. 18, April 19, 1991, pp. 62–63.

SOURCES

"Allen Ginsberg," Poets.org, Academy of American Poets, http://www.poets.org/poetsorg/poet/allen-ginsberg (accessed May 14, 2015).

Brook, James, "Remarks on the Poetic Transformation of San Francisco," in *Reclaiming San Francisco: History, Politics, Culture*, edited by James Brook, Chris Carlsson, and Nancy J. Peters, City Lights Books, 1998, pp. 123–36.

Bruchac, Joseph, "Gary Soto: Overview," in *Contemporary Poets*, 6th ed., edited by Thomas Riggs, St. James Press, 1996.

"History of Fresno," City of Fresno website, http://www.fresno.gov/Government/DepartmentDirectory/DARM/HistoricPreservation/History.htm (accessed May 15, 2015).

Kaganoff, Penny, Review of *Home Course in Religion*, in *Publishers Weekly*, Vol. 238, No. 18, April 19, 1991, pp. 62–63.

Lavender, David, *California: Land of New Beginnings*, Harper & Row, 1972, pp. 392, 400–401.

Review of *New and Selected Poems*, in *Publishers Weekly*, Vol. 242, No. 13, March 27, 1995, p. 79.

Shelton, Pamela L., "Gary Soto: Overview," in *Twentieth-Century Young Adult Writers*, edited by Laura Standley Berger, St. James Press, 1994.

Soto, Gary, "The Childhood Worries; or, Why I Became a Writer," in *Iowa Review*, Vol. 25, No. 2, Spring–Summer 1995, pp. 105–15.

———, "Saturday at the Canal," in *Home Course in Religion: New Poems*, Chronicle Books, 1991, p. 31.

———, *A Summer Life*, University Press of New England, 1990, pp. 92–94, 109–15.

Torres, Héctor Avalos, "Gary Soto," in *Dictionary of Literary Biography*, Vol. 82, *Chicano Writers, First Series*, edited by Francisco A. Lomeli and Carl R. Shirley, Gale Research, 1989, pp. 246–52.

FURTHER READING

Buckley, Christopher, David Oliviera, and M. L. Williams, eds., *How Much Earth: The Fresno Poets*, Roundhouse Press, 2001.
    Book 8 in the California Poetry series, this volume features a number of authors connected in some way to the city or county of Fresno, including Soto and his poem "Saturday at the Canal," among others.

Espada, Martín, ed., *El Coro: A Chorus of Latino and Latina Poetry*, University of Massachusetts Press, 1997.
    Included in this anthology are poems by such notable writers as Sandra Cisneros, Ana Castillo, Luis Rodriguez, and Soto.

García Márquez, Gabriel, *One Hundred Years of Solitude*, translated by Gregory Rabassa, Harper & Row, 1970.
    Colombian Novel Prize winner García Márquez, best known for his poetically styled magical realist novels, is one of Soto's favorite writers. Torres cites Soto as calling García Márquez's generational masterpiece *Cien años de soledad* (1967)—Rabassa's original translation remains the critical standard—"one of the greatest books of our time."

Hoskyns, Barney, *Beneath the Diamond Sky: Haight-Ashbury, 1965–1970*, Simon & Schuster, 1997.
    Hoskyns provides a photographic exploration of the countercultural nexus in the heart of San Francisco in the era of Soto's teenage years in this lively volume. Had Soto ever stationed himself in San Francisco, he might have ended up leading a more colorful bohemian life.

Kherdian, David, ed., *Beat Voices: An Anthology of Beat Poetry*, Greenwillow Books, 1996.
    With Soto recognizable as an heir to the existential awareness of the Beat generation—as suggested in part by the implied idealization of the artistic culture in San Francisco in "Saturday at the Canal"—this volume, published for young adults, gives an age-appropriate taste of the Beats' California-flavored tradition.

SUGGESTED SEARCH TERMS

Gary Soto AND "Saturday at the Canal"

Gary Soto AND Home Course in Religion

Gary Soto AND juvenile OR young adult

Gary Soto AND Fresno

Fresno AND agriculture AND Hispanics

Gary Soto AND San Francisco

San Francisco AND 1960s counterculture

California AND canals OR dams

California AND water shortage

Sonnet 60

WILLIAM SHAKESPEARE
1609

William Shakespeare's sonnets, first published in 1609 under the title *Shake-speares Sonnets*, are one of the greatest works of world literature. In English, the sonnets are considered the very model of love poetry, but if indeed they are erotic in character, they chronicle a love between men, whose complexities escape any easy interpretation that does not take into account the vast cultural differences between the seventeenth and twenty-first centuries. Sonnet 60 is a meditation on the war of death against humanity, whose first casualty is beauty. It is a beautiful Baroque image of the inexorable grinding down of life by time, beginning with the Ovidian image of pebbles tossed by the waves and reaching a strident climax in a depiction of the grim reaper. The only way out, Shakespeare concludes, is through art, whose worth, inspired by the human beauty it transforms into language, alone can endure the destructive effect of the passing ages. Sonnet 60 appears in *The New Oxford Book of English Verse*, edited by Helen Gardner, Oxford University Press (1972).

AUTHOR BIOGRAPHY

William Shakespeare was baptized on April 26, 1564, in Stratford-on-Avon, England. He was presumably born only a few days earlier. His father was a successful glove manufacturer. In

William Shakespeare (© *Georgios Kollidas /*
Shutterstock.com)

1582, Shakespeare married Anne Hathaway, and shortly thereafter she gave birth to their first child, Susana, and later twins, Hamnet and Judith. After 1585, Shakespeare moved to London, maintaining his family in their residence in Stratford. He began to act in a theater company known after their patrons as the Lord Chamberlain's Men and later as the King's Men. Shakespeare was soon the chief playwright for the company and wrote thirty-eight plays (though as many as six of them may have been collaborations) In addition, Shakespeare published the volume containing his 154 sonnets (including Sonnet 60) in 1609. He wrote a few other poems, including *The Rape of Lucrece* (1594) and *Venus and Adonis* (1593). These make up an incomparable body of work that establishes Shakespeare as the greatest writer in English and perhaps the single greatest literary figure in any language. Plays like *Hamlet* (ca. 1602), *Romeo and Juliet* (ca. 1596), *Othello* (ca. 1603), *Macbeth* (ca. 1603), *King Lear* (ca. 1608), *A Midsummer Night's Dream* (ca. 1595), and *The Tempest* (ca. 1611) are without parallel in their popularity and in their critical reputation. The plays were performed in public theaters in London (such as the Globe, Blackfriars, or the Rose) leased by the company and sometimes in command performances before King James at various palaces in London.

In 1611, Shakespeare retired back to Avon with a fortune of several hundred pounds, enough to sustain a middle-class family. He thereafter visited London frequently, and many of his collaborative plays are thought to date from this period. He died on April 23, 1616, aged only fifty-two. There is no knowledge of the cause of his death. He left a will dividing part of his property between his daughters. (Hamnet died in childhood; both daughters had several children, but none of Shakespeare's grandchildren survived to adulthood.) By law, a third of his estate went to his widow, but Shakespeare also specified in the will that she was to receive his second-best bed, an obscure detail that has attracted endless speculation. Almost all of Shakespeare's plays, as well as being performed, were published in various books during his lifetime, but a comprehensive edition, known as the First Folio, was not published until 1623 (and with a much better text) by John Hemings and Henry Condell, colleagues of Shakespeare's from the King's Men.

Despite its brevity, this account contains most of what is known of Shakespeare's life. Early biographers, beginning with Nicholas Rowe, filled out more extensive pictures partly with rumor that may reflect fact to some degree and partly with invention. It is possible, for instance, that before beginning to act, Shakespeare worked as a tutor or schoolteacher. Shakespeare's biography is very slight in proportion to his fame and accomplishment. It is understandable that people impressed by the poetry would want the life of the poet to be grander than it is. This has generated an entire scholarly industry trying to construct a biography for him out of the text of his writings, but such a procedure is little more than speculation. Although Shakespeare's authorship of his works is perfectly well attested in his publication and in the written testimony of his contemporaries, and despite the fact that no one in his lifetime suggested that Shakespeare was not the author of the plays, sonnets, and other works, the world's first conspiracy theory became organized around the idea that someone, anyone other than Shakespeare, wrote Shakespeare's works. Beginning about two hundred years after Shakespeare's death, Anti-Stratfordians, as they are called, from Mark Twain to Sigmund Freud to the contemporary Shakespearian actor Derek Jacobi, have all denied Shakespeare's authorship. Candidates to replace Shakespeare range from Edward de Vere, seventeenth Earl of Oxford (who as a nobleman would supposedly have been ashamed to be known as a playwright), to the well-known contemporary playwright Christopher Marlowe (who died in 1593 before most of the plays were written). The dubious evidence typically adduced for such identifications is a perceived parallel between the biography of the candidate and the plot of one of the plays or a supposed acrostic discovered in the sonnets.

POEM SUMMARY

The text used for this summary is from *The New Oxford Book of English Verse*, edited by Helen Gardner, Oxford University Press, 1972, p. 147. A version of the poem can be found at the following web page: http://www.poetryfoundation.org/poem/174362.

Sonnet 60 can be divided into three quatrains, or stanzas of four lines, and a final couplet. The poetic voice of the poem addresses the fair youth (as do the first 126 of Shakespeare's sonnets) whose eventual aging is lamented in the poem even as his beauty becomes the inspiration of the poet's immortality.

First Quatrain

Shakespeare evokes the image of the tides to illustrate the passage of time. Just as the regular alternation of day and night is a natural process that marks time going by, so does the regular alternation of the tides going in and out. He shows the reader the image of pebbles being washed up the beach by the waves as the tide rises. The pebbles being brought in by each wave leapfrog from the bottom of the beach to the high-water mark of the wave, above the last group of pebbles that rolled in. He explicitly indicates that the waves show the passage of time. "Our" is a pun on *hour* to reinforce this theme. Moreover, since the quanta of time belong to the poet and the reader, that is to human beings, the end that they are approaching is the limit of human life, or death.

Second Quatrain

The maritime imagery is continued in the second quatrain in that "main" means the *high seas*. The

MEDIA ADAPTATIONS

- Sonnet 60 has been set as a lieder by Joseph Summer. A recording of the piece was released on the album *What a Piece of Work Is Man* from Albany Records in 2005. The run time is five minutes, twenty-one seconds. In addition, there were several settings throughout the nineteenth and twentieth centuries, but none have been recorded.

term is applied metaphorically here to refer to the plane of the ecliptic as the "main" of the heavens, where the Milky Way and the zodiacal constellations are concentrated. "Nativity" is an astrological term and denotes the time of birth; in this case it metonymically (using the part to stand for the whole) means infancy. Astrology is a pseudo-science that was widely believed in during the seventeenth century and to which Shakespeare often refers (in at least some cases skeptically). Astrology began in ancient Babylon before 500 BCE. Ancient peoples believed that their gods spoke to them about what was going to happen in the future and to tell them what they should or should not do (compare the concept of prophecy in the Hebrew Bible).

The kings of Babylon employed highly trained scholars (specialists in what today would be termed pseudo-sciences) to constantly monitor the natural world for signs that might be divinity trying to communicate its will to the state. One of the most obvious places to look for this kind of communication was the sky. Their observations produced the science of astronomy, which reliably predicted the motions of the heavenly bodies and also the inseparable (to them) pseudo-science of astrology. After a huge catalog of observations was compiled with a record of following events (e.g., a planetary conjunction was observed on a given date, and a plague broke out a certain number of days later), they came to believe that they could make predictions about the future based on the movements of the stars and planets alone. Refining the process, they thought that they could make predictions about individuals. Specifically, a nativity was a record of the location of the planets at any given time, from which information predictions could be made. The nativity of a person's birth would enable general predictions to be made about the entire course of the subject's life. In practice, astrology is simply metaphor: the planet Mars, for instance, is said to be associated with war and the constellation Libra with justice, so a king born while Mars is in Libra would be just in war and so on. A well-written horoscope seems to apply to any person reading it, since it is usually a list of virtues that anyone would wish to imagine they possess. Astrology was enthusiastically taken up by Greek and Roman culture after Alexander's conquest of Babylon and remained important in European culture until the eighteenth century.

Time again in this quatrain is measured by the predictable progression of natural phenomenon; in this case eclipses. Unlike the tides, eclipses in traditional culture are seen to have an ominous or threatening value, so this characterization is part of the poem's progressively dire presentation of time.

Human beings pass through what is known as the three ages of man: infancy, mature life, and old age. In this way, time destroys what it first gave, that is, life. These three time periods are typically called the three ages of man and have a literary history going back to the myth of Oedipus in ancient Greece. According to the story, the city of Thebes was being oppressed by a monster called the Sphinx ("strangler"), who would kill anyone who tried to enter or leave the city unless they answered her riddle: What goes on four legs at dawn, two legs at noon, and three legs at sunset? When Oedipus was traveling by Thebes and was asked the riddle, he realized what it was metaphorically describing: a man. When human beings are infants (dawn), they crawl on all fours. When they are mature (noon), they walk on two legs. In old age (sunset) they walk with the aid of a cane, that is, a third limb. Her riddle solved, the Sphinx threw herself over a cliff, and the grateful Thebans made Oedipus their king (their former king Laius having been murdered by someone in the confusion of the crisis). Shakespeare references the story by describing the crawling of the infant and the limping gait of an old man using a cane.

Third Quatrain

Time becomes the subject of the sentence in the fourth quatrain. Time again is shown by the progress of natural phenomena, in this case of human aging. The effects of aging are highlighted by their attack on what the poet cherishes most: the fair youth's beauty. The flower of his beauty begins to fade, his brow becomes wrinkled, and the exceptional qualities of his body are worn away. Time is revealed as the traditional figure of death: the god Saturn in skeletal form wielding a scythe with which he mows down everything that lives.

Final Couplet

The final couplet for the first time in the poem directly addresses the fair youth in the second person. The poet laments his aging and the passing of his beauty. Time destroys everything, but one thing may be able to endure into the future: the poet's verse may have the strength to resist time and death because it has been inspired by the fair youth's beauty.

THEMES

Time

The main theme of Sonnet 60 is the passage of time and its destructive effect on human life. The misfortune is raised to the level of tragedy because what is being destroyed is the beauty of the fair youth, the object almost of veneration by the poet. The passage of time is symbolized by the inexorable forces of nature: the clock of the heavens, which keeps perfect time and is responsible for the progression of the tides and the cycle of eclipses as much as for the passage of day and night. The ages of human life from birth to death are another kind of marker for time. In the final quatrain of the poem, time is personified by the traditional figure of death: the god Saturn, a skeleton, mowing down everything that lives with a scythe as a farmer mows down the wheat when the plants have completed their life cycle of growth, maturity and aging, and death. Death is too strong even for beauty to resist, but one thing can endure. The poet's verse itself may last because it has been inspired by the fair youth's beauty and not even time and death can destroy that inspiration. The conceit comes from the Roman poet Horace, who in his *Odes* declared that his poetry was a monument more lasting than a bronze statue.

Art

The art of the seventeenth century is typically called Baroque, whether it is literature, music, or the pictorial arts. Its vocabulary is still the neoclassicism of the Renaissance (itself based on ancient art), but its style of expression is more

TOPICS FOR FURTHER STUDY

- Sonnet 60 and Sonnet 18 both treat the theme of the poet's work becoming an immortal monument, derived from Ode 3.30 of the Roman poet Horace. Write an essay comparing how the theme is developed in the three poems.

- Wanka poetry is one of the oldest poetic forms in Japanese. It was revived around 1900, with the modern pronunciation tanka. One use of tanka was in exchanges between lovers in place of prose letters, but it was also used between poets, leaving considerable ambiguity of addressee in the form. *The Seasons of Time: Tanka Poetry of Ancient Japan* (1968), edited by Virginia Olsen Baron, is a collection of tanka poems in translation that deal with the passage of time. Using these as a model, write a poem that transforms Sonnet 60 into the new form, as Shakespeare transformed lines from Ovid's epic poetry into a sonnet. Similar to haiku, the tanka form can be approximated in English with lines containing 5/7/5/7/7 syllables. Tanka poems are almost as popular as haiku, and many examples can be seen at the *American Tanka* magazine website (http://www.americantanka.com/). Post your poem on a blog and allow your classmates to comment.

- James Thurber's *The 13 Clocks* (1950) is a modern fairy tale about a duke who is obsessed with time. Although the text is printed as prose, its metrical structure renders it much closer to blank verse. Rewrite Sonnet 60 as a short story using Thurber's as a model.

- Sonnet 60 forms a closely bound pair with the preceding Sonnet 59. Write an essay explaining how themes of eternity and endurance link the two poems.

---

dynamic and brooding. It seeks excitement rather than stateliness. Sonnet 60 is typical of the Baroque style. Its vivid evocation of the motion of the waves finds a parallel in Baroque sculptures, which often include tons of marble shaped into the chaotic forms of clouds or draperies—not hanging in good neoclassical order, but violently pulled aside and flying through the air. The interest in the third quatrain in time's attack not merely on youth but also on the intimate signifiers of youthful beauty is typical of the intricacy of the Baroque. In fact, the theme of the poem is quite reminiscent of a Baroque sculpture that the Italian artist and architect Gian Lorenzo Bernini would begin in the 1640s but never finish: *Truth Unveiled by Time*. The work was meant to show a beautiful young nude (a woman in this case, and her figure is the only part of the sculpture that was completed) with a drapery being pulled off her by the personified figure of Time. The figure of Time was to be shown as a golden skeleton holding an hourglass or a scythe. As in the Shakespeare sonnet, the viewer would understand that the beauty of the figure was to be inevitably degraded and destroyed by the passage of time.

Seafaring

While the first quatrain of Sonnet 60 is closely based on a passage of Ovid's *Metamorphoses* (15.200–205), one of the transformations that Shakespeare works on his source material is to transfer the imagery of the waves from a river to the ocean. This is in keeping with Britain's identity as a seafaring nation, which was being established at this time. Britain owed its very existence to its navy, which had defeated Spanish invasions twice in the last generation and gained its wealth through its expanding maritime trade. The maritime British Empire had begun in 1584 with the planting of the first (albeit initially unsuccessful) colony in Virginia.

STYLE

Sonnet

Shakespeare's sonnets are the defining works of the form in English, but the sonnet has a long history before entering English. The sonnet (which means "little song") is a metrical form that was developed at the brilliant court of the Holy Roman Emperor Frederick II in Sicily during the second quarter of the thirteenth century. It was originally a type of song and was spread by traveling performers known as troubadours, who wandered through the graduations of

The waves in the first image of the poem represent the never-ending march of time. (© Maryna Pleshkun / Shutterstock.com)

romance languages from Sicily through Italy and southern France to the Catalan-speaking region of Spain. The sonnet became a form for written poetry (as opposed to sung performance) with the fourteenth-century Florentines Petrarch and Dante. The first English sonnets were written in the early sixteenth century, a generation before Shakespeare, and were translations of Petrarch and of French sonnets.

A defining feature of the sonnet across languages is its fourteen-line structure and distinctive rhyme schemes. However, the details of the sonnet's meter and form vary from language to language. In English, sonnets are written in iambic pentameter, the meter used in most English poetry. Each line consists of five iambs, a metrical foot that consists of an unstressed followed by a stressed syllable. Some resolutions and substitutions are allowed in the meter. Petrarch's and Dante's sonnets are divided into two large sections: the Italian sonnet with the first eight lines, or octave, and the following six lines, or sestet. Most of Shakespeare's sonnets, including

Sonnet 60, however, follow a different pattern, known as the English or Spenserian form, which was worked out in the sonnet collections that Edmund Spenser and Sir Philip Sydney published in the decade before Shakespeare wrote his sonnets. The poem is organized into three four-line-long units called quatrains, followed by a final couplet. This division is reflected in the poem's rhyme scheme (*abab cdcd efef gg*) as well as in its grammar, since each quatrain and the couplet are an independent sentence and, logically, since each grouping expresses a different (though related) idea. Hence Sonnet 60 is a *perfect* sonnet.

From its beginning and in Shakespeare's immediate English predecessors the sonnet was principally used to write about love. Sonnet 60 is part of a cycle of sonnets (1–126) addressed to an anonymous young man. There is certainly a strong bond between the speaker of the poems and the youth. In Sonnet 60, the youth is told that it is only because it takes his beauty as its subject that the work of the poet will endure through the ages. Whether the relationship should be taken as sexual is unclear. Sonnet 20 is the most explicit poem in the cycle, but it would seem to suggest that a same-sex romance between them is impossible. In any case, it would be a mistake to project conceptions of sexuality and modern social roles onto people, or even characters, of the seventeenth century.

Translation

Given the exceptional volume of Shakespeare's poetic output, it should not be surprising that much of his writing follows older models, sometimes quite closely. The source text can be described as being *Shakespearized*, since his transformation of the text is certainly a valid work of art on its own. Sonnet 60 has long been recognized as relying on Ovid's *Metamorphoses* (a favorite book of Shakespeare's) at book 15, lines 200–205. Katherine Duncan-Jones, like many commentators, prints the 1567 translation by Arthur Golding as the probable source. There can be no doubt that Ovid stands behind the text of the sonnet; the parallels are far too close to allow any other conclusion. If Golding's translation was indeed Shakespeare's proximate source, then what Shakespeare did with the text stands somewhere between translation and plagiarism. Still, there seems to be no way not to describe Shakespeare's text as wholly original. On the other hand, some commentators, such as J. B. Leishman, prefer to compare the text with the original Latin, which Shakespeare would have been well able to read. Even in that case the result is not close enough to be termed translation. It is no small gift to be able to see where the works of others can be improved by transforming it into a new creation.

HISTORICAL CONTEXT

The Business of Writing in the Seventeenth Century

Shakespeare made a middle-class income from his writing. The theater was popular enough in Tudor and Jacobean London to support several playwrights. His contemporaries Christopher Marlowe and Ben Jonson are first-class dramatists themselves, however overshadowed they are by Shakespeare. The bulk of Shakespeare's income would have come from his association with his playing company, the Lord Chamberlain's Men (later the King's Men). The group was patronized by Henry Carey, the Lord Chamberlain, who was responsible for providing entertainment at the royal court; later James I himself became their patron. While they did sometimes perform at court, the bulk of their performances were for the general public in leased theaters. Shakespeare was their chief playwright and a secondary actor. (It is not known what roles he played or how often he performed.) The company was owned by eight men designated as sharers because they received an equal share of the profits; they were all actors. Shakespeare may have been invited to take over one of these positions in 1594 on the basis of his performances with other companies. Other actors and other staff, such as stagehands, were employees of the company. If Shakespeare did not make more money out of the theater than others did, for example, the company's lead actor, Richard Burbage (who profited by acting with other companies, as indeed did Shakespeare himself), he was far wiser in his management of his income, supporting his early retirement.

The other way to profit from writing is through book publication. Most of Shakespeare's plays were published in his lifetime, but it is not clear that these were authorized publications (and hence whether or not he would have been paid for them). The case is different with Shakespeare's nondramatic poetry. His narrative poems *Venus and Adonis* and *The Rape of Lucrece* were published in very well-made editions by Shakespeare's friend and fellow Stratford man Richard Field. These were published in 1593–1594. At the time, the theaters were closed by government order because of an outbreak of plague in London. It seems, then, that Shakespeare composed and published these poems as an alternative means of income. Both books were dedicated to Henry Wriothesley, third Earl of Southampton. This means that Southampton very likely acted as Shakespeare's patron, paying him to provide leisure for the composition of the poems. This may have been the source of the money Shakespeare apparently used to buy his share of the Lord Chamberlain's Men. The volume of sonnets in 1609 originated in the same way, during a period when the plague caused the closure of the theaters. Whether the unknown Mr. W. H.

COMPARE
&
CONTRAST

- **1600–1610:** Astrology, though sometimes the subject of skepticism, is also widely accepted and believed in.

  Today: Astrology is recognized by the scientific community as a pseudo-science with no predictive power, no possible basis in science, and no relationship to reality, although some people still believe in the power of horoscopes and some even make a living casting them.

- **1600–1610:** Homosexual acts are conceptualized under the legal category of sodomy and are not recognized as the basis for a personal identity.

Today: Homosexuality is conceived of under the category of the gay identity, a generalized social role.

- **1600–1610:** Poets are often supported by the personal gifts of wealthy patrons.

  Today: Writers can obtain grant money from government offices and from private foundations; money from these institutions is eagerly competed for and usually dispensed by a panel of critical experts rather than on the basis of personal connection.

to whom the sonnets are dedicated also acted as Shakespeare's patron is unknown.

CRITICAL OVERVIEW

The sexuality expressed in Shakespeare's sonnets is one of the chief concerns of recent critics. Margreta de Grazia, in her seminal article, "The Scandal of Shakespeare's Sonnets" (1993), uses Michel Foucault's reconstruction of the history of sexuality to argue that while the apparent homoerotic content of the fair youth sonnets has been considered scandalous in modern times, in the seventeenth century, it was the dark lady sonnets that were scandalous because of the adultery and the transgression across racial boundaries they imply. Sexual conventions between the two periods can hardly be compared, since in the seventeenth century sex was a social category, while in the twentieth it is a personal concern. Robert Matz, in "The Scandals of Shakespeare's Sonnets" (2010), builds on de Grazia's foundation to investigate the reception history of the fair youth sonnets. A traditional form of scholarship on the sonnets is a text of the poems with a sonnet accompanying each sonnet. The commentary was given new life by

the prominent critic Helen Vendler's *The Art of Shakespeare's Sonnets* (1997). She prints a facsimile of the 1609 first-edition text followed by a second text with modernized spelling. Vendler follows the traditional assumption that the texts of the various sonnets interact with each other and that the 1609 order of the sonnets was chosen by Shakespeare to enhance the cohesiveness of the sonnets as a whole, which not all modern critics do. In her reading, the three quatrains offer three separate models of human life. The first is an orderly progression that reminds her of religious preaching and ritual. The second is chaotic, with time marked by the ominous signs of eclipses rather than the normal measurements of time. In the third quatrain, time becomes a destructive agent working to gradually eat away life. The only power that can resist time, as revealed in the final couplet, is poetry. Further, she sees the reading in the third quatrain as analytic or philosophical rather than the simple chronological schemes of the first two.

David West's commentary (2007) appends a prose summary of the sonnet and concentrates on an explanation of the figurative language in the poem. West is very good at explaining how Shakespeare transformed his textual starting point in Ovid. The wave imagery of the original

A scythe is a tool for cutting grasses, but it also calls to mind the grim reaper, an image of death.
(© Auhustsinovich / Shutterstock.com)

is translated to the sea, more appropriate to the maritime nature of British society and giving a more cosmic scope to the poem. Rare among recent commentators, he thinks that Shakespeare was working from the original Latin, echoing Ovid's *sequuntur* with *sequent*, rather than Arthur Golding's translation, which some scholars suggest Shakespeare may have consulted. Carl D. Atkins' *Shakespeare'sSonnets: With Three Hundred Years of Commentary* (2007) draws heavily and pointedly on the earlier extensive commentary literature, although his interpretation is ultimately dependent on Vendler. The Arden Shakespeare volume of the sonnets (2010) has a basic commentary by Katherine Duncan-Jones. Like many commentators, Don Paterson, in his *Reading Shakespeare's Sonnets: A New Commentary* (2010), points out that the placement of this sonnet as no. 60 in the collection is not an accident but was intended by Shakespeare to pun on the poem's theme of time and call attention to the further pun in the second line with hours and minutes—in that there are sixty minutes in an hour and

sixty seconds in a minute—but he uniquely points out the same trick had been pulled with Edmund Spenser's sixtieth sonnet. Paterson's commentary is rather abrupt and postmodern in feel, though not in content.

CRITICISM

Rita M. Brown

Brown is an English professor. In the following essay, she examines the context of Sonnet 60 in light of the sexual roles available in Jacobean England.

We know shockingly little about Shakespeare in proportion to his fame and talent. This has led to an insatiable curiosity about the facts of his life, which simply cannot be recovered. With little or no evidence available, even scholars who ought to have known better have often turned to his literary work to seek answers for their questions. This is hardly unique. The biographies of ancient Greek poets, often

WHAT DO I READ NEXT?

- *Shakespeare* (1970) is a biography of Shakespeare by the novelist and critic Anthony Burgess. Deeply embedded in the scholarly controversies of its time, Burgess's account is uniquely readable because it is informed by his matchless creative imagination.

- *The Goldengate* (1986), by Indian poet Vikram Seth, is a novel composed from 690 sonnets.

- Bruce R. Smith's *Homosexual Desire in Shakespeare's England: A Cultural Poetics* (1994) is a favored interpretation of the period among students of queer studies. Smith privileges Elizabethan drama over nonliterary sources and attempts to create an understanding of the era's sexualities out of the literature itself.

- Robert Matz's *The World of Shakespeare's Sonnets* (2008) is an introduction to the sonnets aimed at students.

- Marilyn Nelson's *A Wreath for Emmett Till* (2009) is an award-winning book for young adults. It uses a cycle of fifteen sonnets to tell the story of Emmett Till, a young black man lynched in 1955 and whose murderers were acquitted by an all-white jury, a key event in the civil rights movement.

- *The Cambridge Introduction to Shakespeare's Poetry* (2010) is an introductory volume that devotes a chapter to the theme of time in the sonnets, which naturally results in an extended discussion of Sonnet 60.

composed two thousand years after their deaths in the Byzantine Empire, can be little more than fiction based on their writings. Because of its central role in human life, Shakespeare's sexuality has been among the most sought-after details of his lost life. Shakespeare's sonnets have been mined to prove that he was a homosexual or an adulterer, and just as often to prove the opposite. Sonnet 60 may seem an unlikely poem to be used

> "SHAKESPEARE'S SONNETS HAVE BEEN MINED TO PROVE THAT HE WAS A HOMOSEXUAL OR AN ADULTERER, AND JUST AS OFTEN TO PROVE THE OPPOSITE."

for this purpose, but as one of the sonnets addressed to the fair youth, it bears on the theme of love between men. The poem's basic message is that if the sonnets endure through the ages, it will be because they were inspired by the fair youth's beauty. This is certainly extraordinary praise and something that might be romantic flattery.

It is not hard to summarize what is known about Shakespeare's romantic life. Shakespeare married Anne Hathaway when he was eighteen years old and she was twenty-six, as unusual an age relationship in the sixteenth century as now. To judge from the fact that their first child was born six months after the marriage, the relationship must have been built on genuine ardor. Three years later the couple had twins. The only other evidence relating to Shakespeare's sexuality is a joke written down in 1602 by John Manningham:

> Upon a time when Burbage played Richard III there was a citizen grew so far in liking with him that before she went from the play she appointed him to come that night unto her by the name of Richard the Third. Shakespeare, overhearing their conclusion, went before, was entertained, and at his game ere Burbage came. Then message being brought that Richard the Third was at the door, Shakespeare caused return to be made that William the Conqueror was before Richard the Third.

Richard Burbage was the lead actor in the King's Men and played Richard III in the original production. As with any joke, it would be unwise to consider it a factual account, but it does indicate that Manningham expected his audience to believe that Shakespeare was inclined to having an extramarital affair with a woman.

Some critics, however, are willing to find evidence for Shakespeare's sexual life in the sonnets, as if the poems were a straightforward account of Shakespeare's private life. Poetry does not provide that kind of evidence. It is as likely to deal with fantasy or desire as it is with the hard facts of the poet's life. In Sonnets 127–152, for example, the poet addresses the dark lady, who is obviously his lover. In the absence of other evidence—and there is none—this cannot become the basis for a supposition that Shakespeare had such an affair. The affairs between Romeo and Juliet or between Miranda and Orlando are created entirely out of Shakespeare's imagination, and the mere existence of the dark lady sonnets offers no evidence that that affair was not equally fictional. The same is true of the fair youth sonnets (1–126), including Sonnet 60. Rather than assuming that the fair youth must have been a real person and trying to guess who he was, one could only substantiate a relationship of the sonnets to an objective reality if there was independent evidence of such a relationship. Although it is often assumed that the fair youth is identical to the addressee of the original published volume of the sonnets (presumably Shakespeare's patron, called only by his initials, W. H.), this too is nothing more than an assumption: it is not impossible, but there is no evidence for it either.

If the sonnets tell us nothing about Shakespeare's personal sexuality, they certainly provide a picture of a Jacobean relationship that can be examined in its historical context. It must be noted at the beginning of such an investigation that sexual roles and sexual identities are not fixed and unchanging throughout time and across cultures. Marriage, for instance, is not one thing in every time and place. In classical Athens, for instance, marriage was principally a reassignment of property between families meant to cement social and political ties; the children produced by the marriage would serve the same purpose. The bride and groom were picked by family elders and in many cases would never have seen each other before the wedding. While it would be unusual for a girl to be married at an age older than fourteen or fifteen, the groom would be at least a few years older and could well be middle-aged or older. By law, the wife was confined to her husband for a sexual partner, but the husband was free to have relations with anyone he wished, except women married to other Athenian citizens: this would include slaves, prostitutes, and young men. One can see how, far from being part of the some unchanging tradition of marriage, this arrangement is hardly recognizable compared with the form marriage takes today. The form of marriage in Elizabethan England was intermediate. Shakespeare's marriage obviously grew out of the mutual attraction between him and his wife, which led them to private meetings that would have been forbidden (even if expected) by their society; his father certainly had no wealth that needed to be protected or transferred through marriage. On the other hand, Shakespeare lived most of his adult life in isolation from his wife, so it would hardly be surprising if he took other sexual partners. In Jacobean England, some married men certainly had sex with other men, including the king, James I. As a private matter, it would usually be ignored unless some third party had a grievance and brought the matter to the authorities. The crime in this case was legally categorized as sodomy and could potentially carry the death penalty, although prosecutions were rare.

The relationship described in the fair youth sonnets seems so intense, and so based on the poet's admiration of the youth's beauty, that many modern readers consider that it must have had a sexual component. On the other hand, in Sonnet 20, although he describes the youth as being as beautiful as a woman, the poet specifically denies homoerotic desire for the fair youth (which may be mere teasing) and concedes that he is fated to be a lover of women. It is often suggested that friendship between men existed in Elizabethan England on a spectrum that reached homoerotic desire at one extreme and that seemingly sexualized compliments. Even physical affection could be exchanged between men who were not lovers, making the relationship in the sonnets more understandable. Still, there is little evidence outside the sonnets themselves for this kind of relationship. There was a discussion around the relationship between Jesus and the "beloved disciple" in the Gospel of John that might support such relationships, but it never occurs in consideration of relationships that were not homoerotic in nature. If sexual relationships between men were sometimes ignored or condoned in the seventeenth century, they could also be occasions for embarrassment. In the second edition of the sonnets, published in 1640, the gender of the pronouns relating to the fair youth were switched by the publisher from masculine to feminine, making it appear as though the poet was praising a beautiful woman. The original readings were not restored until the 1780s.

Even if one accepted every claim made on the basis of the sonnets—that Shakespeare and some young man were lovers—that would not mean Shakespeare was gay, precisely because of the evolution of sexual roles over time. In the seventeenth century, sexual acts between men were understood as just that: discrete acts that any man might or might not engage in. They were conceptualized under the legal definition of sodomy. The philosopher Michel Foucault and the classicist David M. Halperin show how this situation changed in the late nineteenth century. As the medical profession began to study homosexuality, the state reacted by proscribing not individual homosexual acts but the homosexual identity. Words like *homosexual* or *gay* that principally identified individuals by their sexual orientation emerged for the first time. Sodomy is something you do; gay is something you are. It is impossible to import the later ideas into the earlier period.

Shakespeare's sonnets had a role to play in this social transformation. Oscar Wilde, who may be thought of as the first gay man in the modern sense, had suggested in his trial for homosexuality that the sonnets show a gay relationship between Shakespeare and the fair youth, an idea worked out in more detail in his 1889 short story, "The Portrait of Mr. W. H." Wilde offered this reading of the sonnets as justification and as a model for his own letters of extravagant praise to Lord Alfred Douglas, which were put into evidence against him. After Wilde's conviction, there was a rush among Shakespeare scholars to deny any homoerotic content in the sonnets at all. At the same time, the opinion of so perceptive a critic as Wilde could hardly be ignored. As fashions changed throughout the twentieth century, critical opinion about Shakespeare's homosexuality and the apparent homosexuality in the sonnets was alternately attacked and defended. The fact that there is no real evidence in the matter often fueled the fires of speculation that it ought better to have been put out.

Source: Rita M. Brown, Critical Essay on "Sonnet 60," in *Poetry for Students*, Gale, Cengage Learning, 2016.

William Baker

In the following excerpt, Baker provides an overview of Shakespeare's sonnets.

. . . First published in their entirety in 1609, the sonnets have a curious dedication. This

Time passes quickly, and beautiful youths age.
(© Kuzma / Shutterstock.com)

reads, "To the onlie begetter of these ensuing sonnets Mr. W. H. all happinesse and that eternite promised by our ever-living poet wisheth the well-wishing adventurer in setting forth. T.T." (Thomas Thorpe [active 1584–1625], the printer, "the well-wishing adventurer"). Whether or not the initials "W. H." are Henry Wriothesley (the Earl of Southampton) in reverse or a printer's error has been the subject of much speculation.

The dating of the 154 sonnets, too, has been the subject of much debate. Francis Meres in his *Palladus Tamia* of 1598, observes, "The sweet witty soul of Ovid lies in mellifluous and honey-tongued Shakespeare, witness his *Venice and Adonis*, his *Lucrece*, his sugared sonnets among his private friends, &c." In the same year, the poet Richard Barnfield (1574–1627) in his *Lady Pecunia* praises the "honey flowing vein" of Shakespeare's sonnets. Barnfield wrote two distinct homoerotic verse collections, *The Affectionate Shepherd* (1594) and a year later, *Cynthia* (1595). So although not published in

> "MANY OF SHAKESPEARE'S SONNETS ARE REGARDED AS AMONG HIS VERY FINEST WORK AND THEY HAVE STOOD THE TEST OF TIME."

their entirety until 1609, Shakespeare's sonnets were extolled at least a decade before their publication. Two sonnets, 138 and 144, are printed in the second edition of a collection of 20 brief poems attributed to Shakespeare, *The Passionate Pilgrim*, published in 1599 by William Jaggard (1591–1623). Jaggard, subsequently with his son Isaac (d. 1627), was to print the *First Folio*. *The Passionate Pilgrim* also includes three extracts from *Love's Labour's Lost* in addition to poems by others. In terms of subject matter, there appears to be a critical consensus that Sonnets 1–126 are an account of the speaker's complicated relationship or love for an effeminate, attractive, aristocratic young man. The initial 17 sonnets are addressed to the "Fair Youth" and urge him to get married and produce an heir. Sonnets 78–80 and 82–86 reveal a poetic competitor for his affections, and there is a love triangle revealed in Sonnets 40–42. Sonnets 87–90 are laments: "Farewell, thou are too dear for my possessing" (87), regrets that the poet has been forgotten, "When thou shalt be dispos'd to set me light" (88). However, Sonnets 91–96 indicate some kind of restoration in the relationship, and 117–120 suggest infidelity on the poet's part: "So I return rebuk'd to my content" (119).

Sonnets 127–152 are regarded as the bitter sonnets preoccupied with "black beauty's successive heir" (127), the dark non-aristocratic lady: "Thou art as tyrannous, so as thou art" (131). Sonnet 126, with its opening "O thou, my lovely boy, who in thy power ‖ Dost hold Time's fickle glass, his sickle, hour," a 12-line rather than 14-line sonnet, is perceived as a transition mark, as the final poem addressed to the aristocratic young man. The second line contains the admonishment that the boy, too, will be subject to time. Indeed, time, mutability, is one of the great repetitive motifs in the sonnets and throughout Shakespeare's work. It does, however, lead the poet to moments of hubris. For instance, in Sonnet 18

beginning, "Shall I compare thee to a Summers day?" utilizing imagery drawn from nature, the "rough winds," "the darling buds of May," legal imagery so common in Shakespeare's work, "summer's lease hath all to short a date," he tells the addressee, the subject of the poem that he/she will live on as long as the poem does: "Nor shall Death brag thou wand'rest in his shade, ‖ When in eternal lines to time thou grow'st."

Many of Shakespeare's sonnets are regarded as among his very finest work and they have stood the test of time. Throughout the centuries, they have meant many things to a great many people, different people from diverse backgrounds. For instance, the great nineteenth-century English novelist George Eliot (Marian Evans, 1819–1880) wrote out lines from the powerful Sonnet 29, "When, in disgrace with Fortune and men's eyes, ‖ I all alone beweep my outcast state," on the manuscript of her final completed novel *Daniel Deronda* (1875–1876), dedicated to the man she lived with since the mid-1850s, George Henry Lewes (1819–1878). The poem speaks of social isolation and a state of personal self-pity, of the need for assurance. It speaks of a non-comprehending, unsympathetic god: "And trouble deaf heaven with my bootless cries, ‖ And look upon myself and curse my fate." The sonnet speaks of total personal lack of confidence and personal jealousy, of "Wishing me like to one more rich in hope, ‖ Featur'd like him, like him with friends possess'd." Yet in the final couplet, the final turn of the Sonnet, all is redeemed through personal love: "For thy sweet love rememb'red such wealth brings ‖ That then I scorn to change my state with kings."

There are several sonnets that appear different structurally or in other ways from the others. Sonnet 145, beginning "Those lips that Love's own hand did make," is not in iambic pentameter, unlike most of the others, but consists of eight-syllable (iambic tetrameter) lines. The next sonnet in the sequence, 146, with its opening line, "Poor soul, the centre of my sinful earth," appears to be more Christian in its sentiments and preoccupied with the saving of the soul, rather than with the body and the obsession with time and mortality that pervades the other sonnets. The final two (153 and 154) focus upon Cupid and seem to draw upon fifth century Greek epigrams. Sonnet 153 opens, "Cupid laid by his brand [firebrand or flaming torch] and fell asleep; || A maid of Dian's [Diana, the goddess of chastity] this advantage found."

Sex, desire and lust, dominate many of the sonnets. Sonnet 129, "Th' expense of spirit in a waste of shame," for instance, is a fine illustration of the play of puns, lexical complications and psychological contradictions in the Sonnets, expressed at times in legal, hunting and fishing metaphors. In the first of the four divisions of the poem, lust is shown as the "expenditure of vital power (mind and semen) in a wasting of shame (chastity and genitalia), and until action" (Jakobson and Jones: 14), "lust || is perjur'd, mur-d'rous, bloody, full of blame, || Savage, extreme, rude [harsh], cruel, not to trust." In the second division of the sonnet, lust is "Past reason hunted, and no sooner had, || Past reason hated, as a swallowed bait." This "bait" has been "On pur-pose laid to make the taker mad." So, in the third quatrain, that which has been so madly pursued and as soon as had, regretted, is "A bliss in proof and prov'd, [a] very woe"—a wonderfully contra-dictory line playing upon the language of "proof" and "proved" of a will or contract and the very human emotions of "bliss" and "woe." In the final couplet, again there is a paradox. Human beings know all this, are aware of them but still lust: "All this the world well knows, yet none knows well || To shun the heaven that leads men to this hell."

There are various contenders for the young man and the Dark Lady with whom the poet seems obsessed. The young man has been iden-tified with the Earl of Southampton. The other leading male contender, given the dedication in the 1609 Quarto to "The Onlie Begetter of These . . . Sonnets. Mr. W.H.", is William Her-bert (1580–1630), Third Earl of Pembroke. Cer-tainly a patron of Shakespeare's and with his younger brother Philip (1584–1650, the 4th Earl) a co-dedicatee of the *First Folio*. Pem-broke, the elder, was a patron to among other dramatists Ben Jonson, Philip Massinger (1583–1640), and Inigo Jones (1573–1652), the architect and designer of court masques. In 1601, he was briefly thrown into prison following an affair with Mary Fitton, one of Queen Elizabeth I's maids of honour, whom he had made pregnant. In common with the Earl of Southampton, he, too, became connected with the Virginia Company.

A. L. Rowse (1903–1997), a leading if some-what idiosyncratic and controversial English scholar, conjectures in, for instance, *Discovering Shakespeare* (1989) that Emilia Lanier is without question the Dark Lady of the sonnets although there are other candidates too. Probably of Sephardic Jewish origin, the daughter of a court musician, at the age of 20 she became mistress of the Lord Chamberlain and patron of Shakespeare's theatrical company, Henry Carey, the First Lord Hunsdon. In 1593, follow-ing her marriage to another court musician, she gave birth to Carey's son. She also consulted in 1597 the influential astrologer and physician Simon Forman (1552–1611), whose notes form the earliest extant descriptions of performances of *Macbeth*, *The Winter's Tale* and *Cymbeline*, Lanier became the first Englishwoman to have published a substantial volume of her own poems with the appearance in 1611 of her *Salve Deus Rex Judaeorum* (Hail, God, King of the Jews). Rowse introduced in 1978 an edition of this under the title *The Poems of Shakespeare's Dark Lady*. . . .

Source: William Baker, "The Poems and Sonnets," in *William Shakespeare*, Continuum, 2009, pp. 26–30.

SOURCES

Atkins, Carl D., *Shakespeare's Sonnets: With Three Hun-dred Years of Commentary*, Fairleigh Dickinson Univer-sity Press, 2007, pp. 165–67.

Duncan-Jones, Katherine, ed., *Shakespeare's Sonnets*, Methuen, 2010, pp. 31–33, 230–31.

Foucault, Michel, *The History of Sexuality*, Vol. 1, trans-lated by Robert Hurley, Vintage, 1990, pp. 1–50.

Grazia, Margreta de, "The Scandal of Shakespeare's Son-nets," in *Shakespeare Survey*, Vol. 46, 1993, pp. 35–49.

Halperin, David M., *One Hundred Years of Homosexual-ity*, Routledge, 1990, pp. 15–74.

Leishman, J. B., *Themes and Variations in Shakespeare's Sonnets*, Hutchinson, 1961, pp. 134–48.

Matz, Robert, "The Scandals of Shakespeare's Sonnets," in *English Language History*, Vol. 77, No. 2, 2010, pp. 477–508.

Paterson, Don, *Reading Shakespeare's Sonnets: A New Commentary*, Faber and Faber, 2010, pp. 175–77.

Shakespeare, William, "Sonnet 60," in *The New Oxford Book of English Verse*, edited by Helen Gardner, Oxford University Press, 1972, p. 147.

———, *The Tragedy of King Richard III*, edited by John Jowett, Oxford University Press, 2000, p. 74.

Vendler, Helen, *The Art of Shakespeare's Sonnets*, Bel-knap, 1997, pp. 283–86.

West, David, *Shakespeare's Sonnets with a New Commentary*, Duckworth, 2007, pp. 194–96.

Wilde, Oscar, "The Portrait of Mr. W. H.," in *Lord Arthur Savile's Crime, The Portrait of Mr. W. H., and Other Stories*, Methuen, 1908, pp. 145–96.

FURTHER READING

Burgess, Anthony, *Nothing like the Sun*, Heinemann, 1964.
Taking its title from one of the dark lady sonnets (130), this is a novelistic exploration of Shakespeare's sexuality by one the most important novelists of the twentieth century.

Gajowski, Evelyn, ed., *Presentism, Gender and Sexuality in Shakespeare*, Palgrave, 2009.
Presentism is the critical analysis of works of the past according to modern perspectives or moral standards. Generally considered a fallacy, preventing the understanding of literary works in their own context, postmodernism has brought the practice into fashion. Exemplified by the essays in this volume, many of the authors collected read the sonnets as indicative of Shakespeare's participation in a modern gay relationship.

Parr, Johnstone, *Tamburlaine's Malady and Other Essays on Astrology in Elizabethan Drama*, University of Alabama Press, 1953.
Parr provides a survey of references to astrology in Shakespeare and his contemporaries and also includes a bibliography of sixteenth- and seventeenth-century technical books on astrology.

Wells, Stanley, *Shakespeare, Sex, and Love*, Oxford University Press, 2010.
Wells's book is a general study of sexuality in Shakespeare's works that also concerns itself with his life. He concludes that the sonnets do not contain much in the way of autobiographical material about Shakespeare and that there is no reason to suppose a real relationship between the historical poet and any fair youth.

SUGGESTED SEARCH TERMS

William Shakespeare

Shakespeare AND sexuality

Sonnet 60 AND Shakespeare

sonnets

Ovid

time

Oedipus

astrology

So, We'll Go No More a Roving

LORD BYRON

1830

Lord Byron was an English poet associated with the romantic movement, an artistic movement of the late eighteenth and early to mid-nineteenth century characterized by a focus on the individual, nature, and the imagination. Bryon is known for his lyric poetry—poetry that explores emotions from an individual's perspective—and his 1817 poem "So, We'll Go No More a Roving" exemplifies Bryon's romantic lyricism.

The brief, three-stanza poem is about an ending of sorts, although Bryon does not specify what is ending. Some interpretations suggest it is simply a night out that has come to a close, but such readings ignore the weight of the poem's metaphors and the larger literary context of romantic lyrics, which made heavy use of figurative language. Read with respect to this tradition, the poem may be regarded as a lyric that contemplates the ending of a relationship or the ending of a man's youth. In addition to the use of metaphor within the poem, Byron additionally employs other strategies associated with the romantic lyric, including rhyme and meter. Byron's language and imagery, the poem's structure, and the use of metaphor all combine to lend the poem an overall serious and melancholy tone. The poem appears in *Byron: Poetical Works* (1970)

AUTHOR BIOGRAPHY

Byron was born George Gordon Byron on January 22, 1788, in London, to Scottish heiress

Lord Byron (© Georgios Kollidas / Shutterstock.com)

Catherine Gordon of Gight and Captain John Byron, also known as "Mad Jack." John Byron was an English fortune hunter with a daughter, Augusta, from a previous relationship. Shortly after Byron's birth, in 1789, Catherine and her son returned to Scotland, and Byron's father, having relieved Catherine of her inheritance, died two years later.

Byron began attending Aberdeen Grammar School when he was six years old. In 1798, when Bryon was ten, he inherited the title of baron upon the death of his great-uncle, the fifth Lord Byron. Byron then became sixth Baron Byron of Rochdale, and the heir to Newstead Abbey in Nottinghamshire in England. Despite the fact that the estate was in serious disrepair, Catherine rented it out to help pay for renovations, as well as Byron's schooling at Harrow, which he attended from 1801 through 1805. He then went on to Trinity College in Cambridge, earning a master's degree in 1808.

In 1806, Byron privately printed *Fugitive Pieces*, a collection of poetry he had worked on through college. Byron later revised the collection and published it as *Hours of Idleness* in 1807. It was panned by the esteemed *Edinburgh Review*, but Byron's satirical response to the *Review*, titled *English Bards and Scottish Reviewers*, published in 1809, met with critical acclaim. For the next two years, Bryon wrote and toured Europe. He returned to England in 1811 when his mother died. Byron published the first two cantos of his famous *Childe Harold's Pilgrimage* in 1812. The poem was wildly successful, and Byron suddenly found himself famous.

Over the next several years, Byron had a string of prominent relationships. He courted Anne Isabelle (also known as Anabella) Milbanke, whom he married in 1815. The couple had a daughter, Augusta Ada, but the marriage fell apart in 1816 when Byron's wife accused him of having an incestuous relationship with his half-sister, Augusta. With the marriage ended and the public speculation becoming intolerable for Byron, he left England in 1816 and would never return.

He traveled with fellow poet Percy Shelley and his wife, author Mary Shelley, and continued to write, completing *Childe Harold's Pilgrimage* as well as his other lengthy poem, *Don Juan*. In 1817, while staying in Venice, he wrote "So, We'll Go No More a Roving" in a letter to his friend Thomas Moore. The poem was not published until 1830, when it appeared in a collection of his private writings, *Letters and Journals of Lord Byron, with Notices of His Life, by Thomas Moore*, in 1830. In Venice, Byron became increasingly involved in Venetian politics. He also became intensely interested in the struggle of neighboring Greece for independence from Turkey. In 1823, Bryon traveled to Greece to support the cause. The next year, he succumbed to fever and died in Mesolonghi, Greece, on April 19, 1824.

POEM TEXT

I

So, we'll go no more a roving
So late into the night,
Though the heart be still as loving,
And the moon be still as bright.

II

For the sword outwears its sheath,   5
And the soul wears out the breast,
And the heart must pause to breathe,
And love itself have rest.

III

> Though the night was made for loving,
> And the day returns too soon,   10
> Yet we'll go no more a roving
> By the light of the moon.

POEM SUMMARY

The text used for this summary is from *Byron: Poetical Works*, edited by Frederick Page, new ed. revised by John Jump, Oxford University Press, 1970, p. 101. Versions of the poem can be found at the following web pages: http://www.poetryfoundation.org/poem/173101 and http://www.poets.org/poetsorg/poem/so-well-go-no-more-roving.

"So, We'll Go No More a Roving" is a poem composed of three four-line stanzas, or quatrains. As a lyric, the poem is about a mood or a feeling; it is not a narrative that describes events or tells a story. In the first stanza, the speaker announces that the time of roving—which could mean adventuring, pleasure-seeking, companionable exploring, or romantic exploits—is over. He uses the first person pronoun "we" as if speaking with another person about how they will not continue to share these nocturnal encounters. The speaker emphasizes his desire to continue to do so, his heart remaining as loving as it has ever been, while the moon shines brightly, illuminating the evening.

In the second stanza, the speaker provides something of a reason for the ending he has described in the first stanza. Byron uses the image of sword and a sheath and the parallel composition of the soul and the body to emphasize the notion of fatigue. The physical self becomes worn and tired with exertion and age, and an exhausted heart continues to experience love and longing. Byron contrasts the ideas of feelings and intentions with the self's ability to act on those desires and emotions. He seems to be suggesting that one can love very fervently but must pause and rest to avoid exhaustion.

The poem's final stanza repeats phrases and ideas from the previous stanzas. The idea that the night is an ideal one for love recurs, building on the idea in the first stanza that the brightness of the moon created a perfect night for love. Here though, the speaker draws attention to the impending dawn, emphasizing closure and the ending of the night, either the ending of a

MEDIA ADAPTATIONS

- "So, We'll Go No More a Roving" was set to music as part of John Webster's album *Lord Byron and the Greek War*, which is available as an MP3 audio file performed by Brindabani. The album was originally released by Pathfinder Audio in 2002 and re-released in 2006. The song has a running time of about three minutes.

- Byron's poem is available as an MP3 file on the album *Listen to Britain*, released by Classic Home Entertainment in 2007. The audio file for the poem has a running time of twenty-eight seconds.

night of love or the ending of a relationship hinted at through the metaphor of the night. Notably the morning is arriving—according to the speaker's perspective, prematurely. This underscores how unprepared he is to say goodbye to his lover. As the poem closes, Byron refers back to the first stanza, once again reiterating the poem's title as well as the imagery of the moon.

THEMES

Aging

Throughout "So, We'll Go No More a Roving," Byron makes references to time, ending, and fatigue or exhaustion. The restless and youthful desires—roving, loving—are contrasted with the speaker's inability to continue pursuing these desires. The poem's first stanza focuses on the continued existence of the intention to live life to the fullest, to fill it with love and exploration, and to enjoy a night brightly lit by the moon. In the second stanza, however, the speaker hints at why his time of roving is coming to an end.

He speaks of a sword, wearing out the sheath that protects it, and in the next line, of a soul wearing out the body in the same manner.

TOPICS FOR FURTHER STUDY

- Byron was not extremely wealthy but inherited the title of baron and an estate that helped provide for his education. Research the class system in Britain as it existed in the nineteenth century. Consider the factors that contributed to one's social standing and the advantages that were increasingly available to members of higher social classes. Seek out statistics on various elements of the class system: what percentage of British society were nobles, for example? Were there higher mortality rates for one segment over another? What percentage of middle-class citizens graduated from college? Create a visual presentation, such as a PowerPoint or an online presentation, that enables you to share your findings.

- N. T. Gore's collection *Poetry of Thoughts: Poems by and for Young Adults*, published in 2013, explores such themes as love and identity. With a small group, read the collection. Select poems that speak to some of the themes of "So, We'll Go No More a Roving," such as love, growing older, or loss. Compare these works to each other and to Bryon's poem. In what ways do the poems use similar methods to treat their themes? Do the poets use sound and rhyme to achieve their ends? What types of images are common? Which of the poems are your favorites? Why? Create an online blog that you use as a forum to discuss these and other ideas pertinent to the works.

- In *Early Indian Poetry in English: An Anthology: 1829–47*, editor Eunice de Souza explores the experiments of Indian poets with style, language, formal elements, and theme. The editor additionally provides detailed information about each poet. The collection includes poetry written not long after Byron's death, but from a different part of the world. The British had an economic stake in India, which became a British colony in the mid-nineteenth century. Scan this collection, published in 2005, and select a poem that you will analyze. Study the poem's formal elements, including rhyme and meter, and consider as well the themes and tone of the poem. Does the editor's introduction provide any insights into the poet and his or her career that informs your reading? Write an analytical essay on the poem of your choosing.

- Byron wrote his poem during the time period in Venice when Carnival is celebrated, just prior to the Christian Lenten season. Research the history of Carnival in Venice. What is the religious background of the celebration? How long does it last? What are the traditional customs centered on this season? Prepare a presentation or a research paper in which you discuss or display your findings. Be sure to cite your sources.

These references suggest a spiritual vitality that continues despite the diminished physical capacity of the vessel that contains this energy. Next Byron refers to the heart wearing out as well, needing to pause and breathe.

In all these ways, Bryon alludes to the physical slowing down of the body that seems to come with age. The spirit is just as vigorous, but the body finds it cannot keep up anymore. At the time Byron wrote the poem, he was twenty-nine years old. By modern standards, this seems a young age to be contemplating aging, but the average life expectancy in England at the time was roughly thirty-eight years.

Love

In "So, We'll Go No More a Roving," the speaker laments a love lost. In each stanza, love is referred to. Byron states in the first stanza that the heart continues to love, despite the lateness of the hour. In the second stanza, he speaks of love needing to rest. In the final stanza, he insists

The bright moon has allowed the speaker to venture outdoors late at night. (© M. Pellinni / Shutterstock.com)

that the night is one designed for love, as if it is the perfect night, as it may have been the night in Venice when the poem was composed. In the poem, the speaker desires to continue loving or to continue being in love or pursuing love. However, love needs to pause, the speaker insists. The heart must take a moment to breathe, love must rest. Interwoven between the messages about love is the sense of fatigue that Bryon brings to the poem by referring to things being worn and used. Love, then, as depicted here, is something vulnerable. It is not impervious to time.

Byron does not specify what type of love he is referring to. It may be an ongoing romantic relationship or simply an amorous night out. Scholars have suggested both possibilities. The fact that Bryon composed the poem while in Venice during a time of festivity, as he discusses in the letter to his friend Thomas Moore, suggests to some that Byron was simply exhausted by consecutive nights of drinking and passion. At the same time, Byron refers to the notion of one's heart twice in the poem. He does not speak specifically in this poem, as he does in other poems, of sexual desire by referring to the female anatomy or by alluding to illicit affairs with specific women. Given this, the love he contemplates in

"So, We'll Go No More a Roving" may concern a sustained romantic relationship that is ending.

STYLE

Rhyme and Meter

Poets use meter and rhyme in a poem as means of providing structure to support the emotion or narrative they are trying to convey. The nineteenth-century romantic poets created lyrics designed to portray the workings of their imagination as well as the emotions of an individual. "So, We'll Go No More a Roving" is written with a clear rhyme scheme and a mixed metrical pattern.

A rhyme scheme is the pattern in which the ending sounds of the lines of the verse are repeated. In Bryon's poem, there are three quartets, or three four-line stanzas. Each stanza follows an *abab* rhyme scheme, which means that the ending of the first and third lines rhyme, as do the endings of the second and fourth lines. Byron, however, features a few off-rhymes, also known as near-rhymes. The word pairs share the same structure, but the vowel sounds are slightly different, making it an imperfect rhyme.

Also imperfect is the metrical scheme Byron employs. Meter is a pattern of unstressed and stressed syllables in a line of poetry. Each set of unstressed and stressed syllables is called a foot. The number of feet per line determines the poem's meter. For example, a line of poetry that employs iambic pentameter has five units in each of which there is an unstressed syllable followed by a stressed syllable—or an iamb (as in the word *hello*).

Most of Byron's poem employs iambic trimeter: three iambs per line. Some of the lines in the poem follow this pattern, though in a number of lines, the opening foot actually has two unaccented syllables, followed by an accented syllable. This is known as an anapest. Byron incorporates the anapestic feet into the iambic flow of the poem. By using the combination of opening anapestic feet with an iambic trimeter structure, Byron creates a soft, contemplative quality within a musical, rhythmic structure.

Romantic Lyric Imagery

Romantic lyric poets made heavy use of imagery in their poetry. They particularly employed images related to nature. In Byron's brief poem, he focuses on one natural image: the moon. The image is introduced in the first stanza and repeated again in the third. The moon's brightness is referred to as a constant, it remains bright, although the roving referred to in the title and first line is coming to an end. The lateness of the night is also emphasized and underscores the passage of time—the hour is late. Yet the poem is confined to the night.

Though the moon shines brightly, Byron uses this image as one of contrast. It is a symbol with some vibrancy, whereas the speaker in the poem is full of melancholy. There is a sense of desire, in the first stanza, to continue the adventures previously enjoyed, to rove, and to love. The heart still wishes to do these things, and yet, as the second stanza explains, the time for such exploits is over.

Byron uses other imagery here, a sword and its sheath. There is a sense that time and overuse have dulled the blade and worn out the sheath as well. Similarly, Byron refers to the soul wearing itself free of one's breast—an image that suggests death, the release of the soul after the body dies. In the final stanza, Byron repeats the moon imagery, reiterating the sentiments of the first stanza. Again, the bright moon stands in contrast to the diminished ability or opportunity the speaker has to continue as he has before, loving and living.

HISTORICAL CONTEXT

British Romantic Poetry

The romantic movement was a cultural and artistic development that began in Europe in the closing decade of the eighteenth century and carried over into the nineteenth century. There were a number of factors that influenced the development of the romantic period in British poetry at the end of the eighteenth century and into the nineteenth century. In some ways, the romantic period was a reaction against the previously held cultural and artistic standards embodied in the Enlightenment period.

Enlightenment writers were influenced by classic Greek and Roman philosophers and emphasized rationality and reason. Their work focused on society as a whole. In contrast, romantic writers rebelled against these conventions. They focused on the imagination over reason, and the individual, rather than society, became the focus of artistic works. In part, this

intellectual rebellion was sparked by the French Revolution. The upheaval in French society, the fight by the poor for political and economic freedom, and the subsequent sense of despair and disillusionment that followed an ultimately unsuccessful rebellion all contributed to generating in neighboring England an artistic movement away from the Enlightenment ideals that initially inspired the revolution in France in the 1780s. M. H. Abrams, in his essay "English Romanticism: The Spirit of the Age," refers to work by nineteenth-century poet William Hazlitt and his view on the importance of the French Revolution to the poetry of the time period. Abrams states that

> from [Hazlitt's] essays emerges plainly his view that the crucial occurrence for his generation had been the French Revolution. In that event and its repercussions, political, intellectual, and imaginative, and in the resulting waves of hope and gloom, revolutionary loyalty and recreancy, he saw both the promise and the failures of his violent and contradictory era.

The Industrial Revolution and Social Class in Nineteenth-Century British Society

Byron inherited his title, Lord Byron, sixth Baron of Rochdale, at the death of his great-uncle in 1798. As a member of this line of nobility, Byron inherited the title and land of his ancestors. Britain during this time period was divided into several social classes: the working class, the new burgeoning middle and upper classes, and the nobility.

The Industrial Revolution, which began in the late eighteenth century and continued into the nineteenth century, was a period during which new inventions and technologies mechanized various industries, allowing for the mass production of goods and for tasks formerly completed by hand to be accomplished with machinery. These advancements created new wealth and transformed formerly rural areas into larger cities. It further created more class distinctions, as individuals were now able to gain wealth—and the benefits associated with it—formerly unavailable to them.

Despite the fact that the working class could now aspire to gain middle- and upper-class status, the noble class remained elite, a class an individual could only be born into. Only individuals with inherited titles could serve in the House of Lords in Parliament, and individuals within this class typically

COMPARE
&
CONTRAST

- **1817:** The romantic movement is a prominent artistic movement in England and is characterized, in poetry, by an emphasis on the individual, on the imagination and subjective experience, and on nature.

  Today: Modern poetry in England takes a variety of forms. Like poetry in America, it follows two major strains, either the free-verse poetry that became prominent in the mid-twentieth century or the formalist poetry that adheres to traditional conventions of form such as meter and rhyme scheme.

- **1817:** Society in England at this time is divided into distinct classes based on both wealth and ancestry. Industrialization has created new wealth, as well as new social classes resulting from this wealth. Advantages such as higher education can now be accessed by an entirely new segment of the population. Nevertheless, inherited wealth and titles also maintain the traditions and high social standing of the noble class, a class standing that one cannot buy into.

  Today: According to a recent study, British society remains stratified in terms of social class. The study indicates the existence of seven social classes in the countries that make up the United Kingdom (England,

Scotland, Wales, and Northern Ireland). The study measured economic resources and cultural interests and activities and revealed that British society can be divided into the following classes: elite (the most privileged sector of society), established middle class, technical middle class (a prosperous group but one in which cultural activities and interests are low), new affluent workers (a young sector with middle incomes and high levels of social and cultural interests), traditional working class, emergent service workers (a group that is relatively poor economically but that scores high in social and cultural capital), and the proletariat (the poorest class with low scores in culture and social interests).

- **1817:** Many young British artists and writers tour Europe for extensive periods of time while pursuing their craft. Byron's social circle included other writers—among them, Percy and Mary Shelley—who traveled with him abroad as they wrote and published their novels and poetry.

  Today: Many British citizens—including artists and college students—opt to live and work abroad, in Europe and around the world. Among the current hot spots are Germany, Ireland, and Romania.

enjoyed great wealth and property amassed by ancestors. Members of this class, including Byron and many of his contemporaries, partook in such luxuries as higher education and travel abroad, and these individuals often lived for significant stretches of time in locations throughout Europe. Such advantages were unattainable for the working and middle classes in England. Many romantic poets, including Byron and his friend Percy Shelley, were noblemen who traveled abroad as they pursued their paths as poets.

CRITICAL OVERVIEW

"So, We'll Go No More a Roving" was first published in a collection of letters and journals. Though it is a favorite, well-known, much anthologized lyric, it is not considered a major poem, like his longer poems, such as *Childe Harold's Pilgrimage* or *Don Juan*. Yet it has been reviewed favorably. In general, in the nineteenth century, Bryon was considered a popular poet, though as Matthew Arnold observes in a preface to an 1881 collection published after Byron's

Dawn comes too soon for the night wanderer. (© Maxim Khytra | Shutterstock.com)

death (*Poetry of Byron*), he was not taken as seriously as he should have been. Arnold states, "In spite of his prodigious vogue, Byron has never yet, perhaps, had the serious admiration he deserves."

Modern critics have found much to praise in Byron's short poem, "So, We'll Go No More a Roving." J. R. Watson, in *English Poetry of the Romantic Period: 1789–1830*, notes that while the poem "trembles on the edge of banality," it nevertheless "succeeds in remaining moving and even serious." Watson discusses the "melancholic" tone of the poem and the way it seems

to end with a mood of contentment. He attributes this to the "spare economy of the stanzas," the "evenly-paced lines," and the imagery that is "suggestive, atmospheric, but firmly controlled."

Fiona Stafford, in *Reading Romantic Poetry*, likewise notes the origins of the poem and Byron's exhaustion from a "string of parties excessive even by his own standards," which he discusses in the letter to Thomas Moore in which the poem is included. Yet Stafford additionally observes that

> the poem seems to embrace far more than the waning of erotic energy. It seems rather a

wistful expression of involuntary but unavoidable ending. . . . The "we" has an inclusiveness that takes the words beyond the individual moment, beyond the private conversation of friends or lovers, opening the feeling to anyone who cares to listen.

Stafford further praises "the satisfying nature of the rhythm" in the poem.

CRITICISM

Catherine DiMercurio

DiMercurio is a novelist and a freelance writer and editor. In the following essay, she studies the way Byron, in "So, We'll Go No More a Roving," combines the effects of sounds within each syllable of the poem with other formal elements to produce the poem's melancholy tone.

Bryon's "So, We'll Go No More a Roving" is a poem in which a few key ideas and images are repeated in three short quatrains. The poet's letter to Thomas Moore, in which the poem was included, suggests that Byron was fatigued by the festivities in Venice during the pre-Lenten celebration of Carnival. In the footnotes to the poem, in the collection *The Broadview Anthology of British Literature: One-Volume Compact Edition*, Byron's letter to Thomas Moore is quoted, with Bryon noting that Carnival is over and that Lent has begun. The festivities closed, Byron notes, "with a masked ball . . . and, though I did not dissipate much upon the whole, yet I find 'the sword wearing out the scabbard,' though I have just turned the corner of twenty-nine."

Some scholars, such as Martin Garrett, in *Venice: A Cultural and Literary Companion*, dismiss the poem as something dashed off in a moment of sadness at the exhaustion felt after too much celebration. Garrett states, of the poem and other works by Bryon, "After-the-party melancholy often tinges writing in or about Venice." Byron also had a reputation for being something of a womanizer. His alleged romantic relationship with his half-sister, Augusta, was only one of the affairs that led to Byron's infamy in this area. One of his lovers, Lady Caroline Lamb, once called him "mad—bad—and dangerous to know." Given this reputation, it may be easy to see why Garrett and other scholars, perhaps even Byron's correspondent and friend Thomas Moore, may have not regarded his stanzas in

WHAT DO I READ NEXT?

- Byron's *Childe Harold's Pilgrimage* is one of his best-known works, and it brought him instant fame. Published over a period of several years, between 1812 and 1818, it describes the travels of a young man. It is available today in many collections, including *Lord Byron: The Major Works*, published by Oxford University Press in 2008.

- *Byron's Letters and Journals: A New Selection*, edited by Richard Lansdown and published in 2015, is a new selection of his informal writings that are annotated and introduced to provide the historical and biographical context within which Byron's words may be better understood.

- The young-adult collection *Death Poetry: Death, Be Not Proud*, is an anthology that features American and English poets through the twentieth century whose work examines such topics as aging and death. The collection, edited by Stephanie Buckwalter, was published in 2014 by Enslow Publishers.

- Juan Filipe Herrara, is a Mexican American poet and the son of migrant farmworkers. His young-adult novel-in-verse *CrashBoomLove*, published by the University of New Mexico Press in 1999, uses poetry to explore issues of personal and cultural identity, love and desire, and growing older.

- *English Romantic Poetry: An Anthology*, published in 1996 by Dover Publications, includes selections from Byron and his contemporaries and offers an introduction into the variety of work being produced during this time period.

- Prominent scholar and critic Harold Bloom's *The Visionary Company: A Reading of English Romantic Poetry*, published by Cornell University Press in 1971, offers a critical examination of the works of the major romantic poets.

"So, We'll Go No More a Roving" as particularly serious or emotionally weighty.

Yet Byron's language and imagery, and the patterns of repetition, all suggest that the lament of the poem is rooted in something deeper than mere temporary physical fatigue. Some critics, such as J. R. Watson, in *English Poetry of the Romantic Period: 1789–1830*, have recognized this. Watson discusses a few of the technical elements of the poem that underscore the poet's skill and the poem's more serious tone and themes. In the poem, Bryon achieves a tone of melancholy that girds its theme of the loss of youth. Critics have highlighted the way Bryon's imagery and the poem's rhythm help achieve this effect. Additionally, though, Byron pays close attention to such minute details as sound and the impact of each syllable on the overall tone of the poem. These aural effects are seldom examined. These elements, however, combined with the intimate nature of the poem, hinted at through the repetition of the word *so* and the use of the first-person plural pronoun *we*, all contribute to the hushed, melancholic, private nature of the work.

From the first word of the title, Byron creates an expectation in the poem. By beginning the poem (note that the first line is the same as the title) with the word *so*, Byron establishes that this, in a way, is a conversation. The reader enters into an in-progress conversation. The next word of the title and first line confirms this: "we'll." This contributes to the notion that we as readers have entered into an ongoing exchange between the speaker and an unspecified companion. As the poem proceeds, it is clear that something—a night out, a relationship—is over and that there is a consequent sense of loss. Byron seems to suggest that he/the speaker is ruminating to himself, that the conversation the reader is overhearing is in actuality an imagined

one. The speaker seems to be thinking about his relationship to the understood "other" party.

It is easy to imagine a conversation that occurred between the speaker and a lover prior to the poem's start, perhaps about the relationship being terminated. The speaker then moves on, alone, and thinks to himself, as if he is still speaking to his lover, answering her, "So, we'll go no more a roving," even though he wishes they still could, even though the heart still loves. In this hinted-at scenario and in the internal dialogue the poem seems to represent, Byron establishes a sense of intimacy. He reveals the speaker's reaction and response to the loss of a lover, and the reader is privy to this deeply personal thought process.

This intimacy, as well as the melancholy the speaker seems to feel at his sense of loss, is deepened by the hushed tones of the poem. There are no loud, percussive, harsh sounds in the poem. It sounds, when read aloud, almost like a whisper, or a sigh. The *s* sound is repeated four times at the beginning of words in the first stanza ("so" and "still") and twice as an end sound ("as"). Byron also makes use of internal rhyme—a repeated sound within a line or within multiple lines—throughout the poem. In the first stanza, the long *o* sound, as in "so" is repeated multiple times—four times within the title itself ("so," "go," "no," and "RO-ving"), five if one counts the off-rhyme of "more." It is the sound of surprise, or dismay, like a soft exclamation, "oh."

In the second stanza, the soft sound of *s* is repeated both at the beginning of words like "sword" and within words, like "breast" and "itself" and "rest." These last three examples are also instances of Byron's continued employment of internal rhyme, this time with the quietness of the *eh* sound. Additionally in the second stanza, Byron makes use of other soft beginning sounds like *sh* in sheath and *p* in "pause."

In the poem's final stanza, Byron repeats the *s* sound throughout the stanza, both at the beginning and at the end of words, as in "soon" and "was." As he did in the previous stanzas, he makes use of internal rhyme, linking the lines together with quiet repetition, as in the soft, awestruck vowel sound of *oo* in "too," "soon," and "moon." In this stanza, however, Byron does make use of several beginning consonant sounds that provide more of a clash or clatter within the poem as well as some louder vowel sounds that are more strident than the soft *oh*,

The soul is compared to a sword in its sheath, suggesting that it will not wear out for a long time.
(© Ana Martinez de Mingo / Shutterstock.com)

eh, and *oo* that have to this point been repeated. "Day" begins with a forceful consonant sound, though it is one of few words in the poem to do so. The long *a* sounds in "day" and "made" are just a bit more urgent than the softer, whispery vowel sounds the reader has heard so far. The use of these sounds work together to emphasize that with the impending arrival of the day, the night of loving—whether it is indeed a night, or a metaphor for the relationship between the lovers, or more likely both—will be finally at an end.

Additionally, the repetition of consonant sounds and the repeated use of internal rhyme links the individual lines of a stanza with the other lines in the stanza. These technical elements also serve the function of linking the stanzas themselves together in a way that supports the structure established by the poem's rhyme scheme and use of imagery. It becomes a tightly knit work in which all of the elements work together to achieve the same effects, creating mood and tone as well as conveying the poem's themes. The bright moon—an image repeated in the first and third stanzas—frames the poem and in this way helps to unify the stanzas as well.

The *abab* rhyme scheme functions in a similar manner. The rhyme scheme works together effortlessly with the metrical pattern of the poem. Byron employs iambic trimeter, or three feet per line consisting of an unstressed syllable followed by a stressed syllable. At the same time, Byron incorporates anapestic feet as the opening feet in many of the lines. Anapestic feet, in that they are composed of two unstressed syllables followed by a stressed syllable, contribute to the softness of the sound produced.

These elements work together to establish the poem's rhythm, which reads as natural, everyday speech. This rhythm is soft, undulating, and relatively uninterrupted by sounds that jar or clash. The rhythm, rhyme, and sound patterns establish and support the poem's intimacy, its melancholy tone, and its themes of love and loss.

Source: Catherine DiMercurio, Critical Essay on "So, We'll Go No More a Roving," in *Poetry for Students*, Gale, Cengage Learning, 2016.

James Soderholm

In the following excerpt, Soderholm speculates about the influence of William Wordsworth's poetry on Byron.

The idea of the Romantic lyric as a confessional and sincere effusion overheard by a sympathetic auditor was most influentially presented in M.H. Abrams's "Structure and Style in the Greater Romantic Lyric." In this essay, Abrams traced the genealogy of the internal colloquies one often finds in Wordsworth's and Coleridge's poems. But Abrams does not mention Byron. Still the odd man out in many discussions of Romantic poetry, Byron would not seem to merit the serious treatment critics lavish on the lyrics of Wordsworth. Perhaps this neglect is partly a legacy of Wordsworth's own judgments of Byron's poetry, which he thought dishonest, insincere, and perverse. Are we still constrained by this judgment, silently ratified by Abrams's failure to account for Byron's distinctive achievement in the lyric? Why to this day are Byron's lyrics relatively ignored?

Let me begin by suggesting that Byron's lyrics have been ignored because they do not fit any of the modes of the lyric, from "the greater Romantic lyric" Abrams identified in his famous essay in 1965 to the observations on the lyric offered by W.R. Johnson in *The Idea of Lyric* in 1982. Johnson's book also contains no mention of Byron. Discussing ancient and modern lyric forms, he claims that the ancients were far more concerned with audience than are their modern counterparts, that the public forum for delivering one's poems made poets especially conscious of the presence of listeners, and that this setting produced a dramatic intimacy modern lyric poets have lost. Johnson has percentages to back up his claim. Eighty-seven percent of Horace's lyrics are what Johnson calls "I-You" poems, and only nine percent are "meditative." For Mallarmé's lyrics, however, the percentage of "I-You" poems has dropped to twenty-five, and the percentage of meditative poems has swelled to seventy. Leaving aside for the moment the question of how to distinguish between "I-You" and meditative poems, Johnson's analysis is clearly biased in favor of Greek and Latin lyrics. Of classical lyrics, Johnson writes:

> The specific context, the fiction of I and You and their situation of discourse, concretizes the universal, makes it perceptible and makes it

> " RELUCTANT TO THINK OF HIS OWN LYRICS AS HAVING A RHETORIC OF SENSIBILITY, WORDSWORTH WAS EAGER TO SEE THIS RHETORIC IN BYRON, WHOM HE THOUGHT PROFOUNDLY DISHONEST."

singable.... Complex thoughts and feelings that have no name find perceptible re-creations and patterns in the sung story that the singer and his audience shared.

For Johnson, the shift from the "I-You" pronominal form to the meditative form roughly parallels the decline of the West, its loss of faith in universals, its spiral into soliloquy, solipsism, disintegration, and decadence. Interestingly enough, Johnson cites the different versions of Wordsworth's *Prelude* as "[a] precise adumbration of this process." Johnson recounts growing up with the 1850 edition, but rejoicing in the later publication of the 1805 original version, which he regards as "very possibly the freshest, the greatest lyric poem in the language." Johnson writes:

> I don't suggest that it is the weakening of the pronominal form in the course of revisions that accounts for what I regard as the final ruin of the poem...it is not Wordsworth's growing failure to speak his poem to Coleridge that causes the poem to disintegrate—Wordsworth murders his poem with insipid philosophizing and destructive moralism and demented religiosity.

Having made this judgment, Johnson goes on to depict the deterioration of the lyric as a fall from pronominal grace.

But one cannot help but feel that the destruction of the pronominal form (Wordsworth no longer addressing his poem to Coleridge, as if to thee alone) is symptomatic of the larger ruin of this poem's initial transparencies and unique exultations. The later versions of *The Prelude* are meditative poems with a vengeance—and they contain, in microcosm, much of the later lyric catastrophe.

The "I-You" lyric has, for Johnson, the status of Buber's Ich und Du. Meditative lyrics, by contrast, smell of isolation and impotence; they enact the catastrophe of privacy, the extinction of zoon politikon. This Straussian narrative serves the interests of those who wish to see the ancients as having understood the true nature of the lyric and the community it so richly harmonizes.

Abrams likewise describes the kind of poem he has in mind:

> They present a determinate speaker in a particularized, and usually a localized, outdoor setting, whom we overhear as he carries on, in a fluent vernacular which rises easily to a more formal speech, a sustained colloquy, sometimes with himself or with the outer scene, but more frequently with a silent human auditor, present or absent.

For Abrams, Coleridge's "Frost at Midnight" and Wordsworth's "Tintern Abbey" perfectly illustrate this paradigm. This "present or absent" auditor is of little consequence for the quality of the lyric. For Johnson, on the other hand, the presence or the absence of a human auditor makes all the difference.

Since poets like Horace usually read or rather performed their poems for an audience, Johnson's "I-You" model works perfectly well. But its usefulness would seem to be limited to the highly specific "situation of discourse" Johnson celebrates. How well does this model work for later lyric poets and poems and audiences? One is forced to consider the relative presence of what one might call the implied audience or auditor. It is not clear what Johnson would do with a poem such as Coleridge's "The Eolian Harp," which seems to be a meditative lyric until one considers that it began as a verse letter to Sara Flicker and still contains notices of her reproving presence.

Must a lyric be—to use John Stuart Mill's famous distinction—overheard rather than heard to qualify as a Romantic lyric? Coleridge spoke "Frost at Midnight" to the infant Hartley, though it was Wordsworth who listened closely to it and responded with his own blank-verse meditation, "Tintern Abbey." In Wordsworth's poem, a more grown-up but equally silent auditor reposes with her brother "under [the] dark sycamore" a few miles from Tintern Abbey (line 10). At the end of the poem, the self-absorbed poet turns to his listener and speaks directly to her. Is this an "I-You" or a meditative lyric? Is Dorothy an implied or actual auditor? Geoffrey Hartman sees the address to William's sister as "a vow, a prayer, an inscription for Dorothy's heart." Marjorie Levinson, on the other hand, calls this turn to Dorothy "a decidedly feeble

gesture toward externality." But many lyric poets, Romantic and otherwise, float in and out of an explicit consciousness of an auditor, even as the lyric "I" fantastically pieces itself together. Like Mill's distinction between overheard and heard poetry, Johnson's distinction between "I-You" and meditative lyrics ignores the interplay of voice, context, and auditor in a given poem, an interplay that defies arithmetic.

Unlike Johnson, Abrams sees the greater Romantic lyric as something truly great, as a stunning achievement, not as a moment in the decay of the genre. Abrams writes that "Only Byron, among the major poets, did not write in this mode at all." Before I consider the justice of this observation, let me cite Abrams's other dismissal of Byron's works. In the preface to *Natural Supernaturalism*, Abrams writes: "Byron I omit altogether; not because I think him a lesser poet than the others but because in his greatest work he speaks with an ironic counter-voice and deliberately opens up a satirical perspective on the vatic stance of his Romantic contemporaries."

I am not alone in seeing this vatic stance as one Abrams himself assumes in order to treat Romantic poetry as the best kind of spilt religion, a testimony to the essential truths of human being, and so forth. Yet this dismissal contains an important insight about the changes Byron works in the type of lyric Abrams admires and sees as exemplary. The poem I have in mind can be thought of as a weird sister poem to "Tintern Abbey," an unwanted companion piece to that famous Romantic lyric. Byron's answer to this lyric appears as a sequence of stanzas in *Childe Harold's Pilgrimage*, canto 3.

The following stanza is often cited to show Byron's giving over to nature worship:

> I live not in myself, but I become Portion of that around me; and to me, High mountains are a feeling, but the hum Of human cities torture: I can see Nothing to loathe in nature, save to be A link reluctant in a fleshly chain, Class'd among creatures, when the soul can flee, And with the sky, the peak, the heaving plain Of ocean, or the stars, mingle, and not in vain.

Most of us have been trained to respond to this stanza not as Wordsworth responded to it but as later critics, most of them Blakeans or Wordsworthians, have responded to it. Harold Bloom, for example, refers to canto 3 as a poem "in the confessional mode of Rousseau and Wordsworth...[that] marks Byron's first imaginative maturity." Leaving aside the fact that the confessional modes of Rousseau and Wordsworth vastly differ, this judgment traffics in an all-too-common, all-too-Wordsworthian set of directions for reading poetry composed between 1798 and 1832. According to these ideological directions, we must read poems as anthems of sincerity, of confessional autobiography, of personal mythology, and, especially, of the redemptive power of the Human Imagination. It leads readers along a garden path where the meanest flower blows and gives thoughts too deep for tears. Such thoughts indicate the final imaginative maturity toward which Byron's canto 3, heavy-laden (one imagines) with nature piety, gravitates.

But what are we to make of the fact that canto 3 piqued Wordsworth? In a letter to Henry Taylor, Wordsworth wrote:

> I have not, nor ever had, a single poem of Lord Byron's by me, except the Lara, given me by Mr Rogers, and therefore could not quote anything illustrative of his poetical obligations to me: as far I am acquainted with his works, they are most apparent in the 3rd canto of *Childe Harold*; not so much in particular expressions, tho' there is no want of these, as in the tone (assumed rather than natural) of enthusiastic admiration of Nature, and a sensibility to her influences. Of my writings you need not read more than the blank verse poem of the river Wye to be convinced of this.

Wordsworth saw something Bloom missed: that even in Byron's most "feeling" meditations one can detect artifice, or as Wordsworth put it, "assumed rather than natural" feelings. Reluctant to think of his own lyrics as having a rhetoric of sensibility, Wordsworth was eager to see this rhetoric in Byron, whom he thought profoundly dishonest. In canto 3 Wordsworth saw the resemblance to his own poems, particularly to "Tintern Abbey," but, unlike Bloom, Wordsworth thought Byron more a damned plagiarist than an imaginatively mature lyricist. It is only because we have been trained to read Byron's works in the context of Coleridge's and Wordsworth's lyrics, celebrated by later critics as Romantic lyrics par excellence, that his poems have become more or less confessional, sincere, or mature. But Wordsworth himself was angered by appreciations of canto 3. Byron's unacknowledged imitation was, for Wordsworth, the insincerest form of flattery....

Source: James Soderholm, "Byron's Ludic Lyrics," in *Studies in English Literature, 1500–1900*, Vol. 34, No. 4, Fall 1994, p. 739.

Kurt Heinzelman

In the following excerpt, Heinzelman examines the struggle Byron felt between his art and the need to earn a living.

... The first paragraph of Byron's Preface to his first published book, *Hours of Idleness* (1807), reveals how ambivalent Byron was: "In submitting to the public eye the following collection, I have not only to combat the difficulties that writers of verse generally encounter, but may incur the charge of presumption for obtruding myself on the world when, without doubt, I might be, at my age, more usefully employed." For Pound, the *agon* of character building occurs in respect to two audiences: (1) the "little public" that reads poetry at all and (2) the audience of Diogenes and Sophocles, the great dead. From the former the neophyte will find little if any economic reward, only a kind of impatient curiosity; from the latter he will learn if his poetic name is a true one. But Byron attempts to sever the question of mastering artistic discipline from the question of "poetical character." While acknowledging the "difficulties" of the first, he belittles the seriousness and utility of the second. His aristocratic disdain for "the public eye" derives from his "situation" as a lord, and this disdain is exacerbated by just such a (public) declaration of this "reputation and feelings." Byron concludes: "It is highly improbable, from my situation and pursuits hereafter, that I should ever obtrude myself a second time on the public" (Preface, 1807). This gesture declares a Poundian apprenticeship supererogatory, for Byron is saying that he will produce one book and *gladly* die of it. And yet, quoting "the opinion of Dr. Johnson on the Poems of a noble relation of mine, 'That when a man of rank appeared in the character of an author, he deserved to have his merit handsomely allowed'" (Preface, 1807), Byron reveals that he wants public approbation, too, and that he wants it for *this* work.

For Dr. Johnson, the lives of the poets may or may not determine the life of their poetry, but in his criticism, poets' lives do precede discussion of their work. Such biographical precedence (still a prominent concern in Byron scholarship) both reassured and distressed Byron himself. In his youthful work especially, he appealed alternatively to his biographical character as "a man of rank" and to his aesthetic character as a poet, depending upon which kind of emotional support

> AS A PATRICIAN, HIS POETIC EMPLOYMENT WAS A LABOR TO PASS THE TIME; BUT WHATEVER HIS DOUBTS ABOUT THE MERIT OF THE VOLUME, HE IS NOT CONTENT TO DROP THE ECONOMIC METAPHOR."

he needed. According to Jerome J. McGann, the "conflicted aspects" of Byron's characterization of himself did not contradict his persistent "concern for public recognition as a validating condition of achievement." But how would this validation occur? Byron's Preface belittles his own poetical character for having no character—for being useless, idle, and trifling, for having no significant "rank." At the same time, as "a man of rank" he sees his authorial self as an indiscreet problem. Byron's conventional deprecation of his own public authority leads here to a dilemma of aesthetic valorization: How can he both earn public approbation for the labor of his poetry and at the same time devalue the public personage that created the poems? Denying his own "character" as an author, can he still claim authority for his work?

Byron's "first" volume of poems actually comprises four separate editions issued over two years. Some aesthetic permutations occurred in that time, but the most important change is the mode of self-advertisement. The first of the four volumes, *Fugitive Pieces* (1806), was a lark; "never intended to meet the public eye," it was privately produced for the "amusement or approbation" of friends (dedication page). In that stock phrase, the "or" has the rhetorical force of "and therefore," as if approbation and amusement were interchangeable modes of credit. When one of those friends objected to a poem as being "rather too warmly drawn," the poem was suppressed and the volume withdrawn. But early in the next year (1807), a slightly altered version of the same volume [including the dedication] appeared under the title *Poems on Various Occasions*. The next version, *Hours of Idleness*, appeared later that year and continued to draw upon the earlier volumes for its content and even for its formal layout ("Fugitive Pieces" was one of the section subheads). *Hours of Idleness* was, however, a more august and "finished" product.

It sported a "literary" title, supplied by the publisher, John Ridge of Newark; it came in full public dress, parading a subtitle, mottos, epigraphs, and the soon-to-be infamous preface, all supplied by the poet himself, who for the first time identified himself by name, rank, and age ("A Minor") on the title page. For Byron, this public act of self-identification was also susceptible of more private irony. To his friends (such as Edward Noel Long), he merely said: "you will behold an 'Old friend with a new face.'"

This trying on of faces, which became a trying out of selves as well as a testing of one's audience, is precisely the luxury that such seriatim production made possible. If, in the beginning, his audience was his friends, then in *Hours of Idleness* the elaborately naive "character" of the poet-as-minor was needed to avoid being held publicly accountable for that original intention. But in his fourth version of this same first volume, Byron's pose will be less evident, as we shall see. In his private correspondence, Byron will express a more overtly professional curiosity about the production of *Poems Original and Translated* (1808). While still maintaining a putative disinterest in the commercial aspects of publishing a "second edition," Byron will also evidence a greater self-understanding of the *quality* of that disinterestedness.

Through this process of nominating one authorial self, finding it unacceptable, and then discarding it for another, Byron evolved a kind of aesthetic stratagem which he explored more fully *as* a stratagem in *Don Juan*. It is a stratagem based on the idea of speculation in the economic sense, a risking of an immediate investment on future prospects in hopes of a disproportionately large return. Psychologically, this velleity is a form of play that banks the psychic resources of the present on an imaginary projection of what the future might hold. Economically, we must remember, Byron was doing something similar during the period leading up to his majority in 1808. As is well documented, the Byron estate at this time was in financial disarray, and Byron's mother needed to concoct elaborate loans to get her and her son through. Partly because of his prodigious expenses at Cambridge and partly because of his largesse to friends as economically strapped as himself, Byron increased his loans, sometimes resorting to the complicated fiscal maneuvering described by Doris L. Moore:

The consequence [of Byron's profligacy as a minor] was that he could not produce the interest on the loans his mother had raised for him, and he was borrowing afresh. To run up debts while still a minor was a costly and intricate operation. One of Byron's ways of doing it was to undertake to pay annuities, when he came of age, to persons whose capital was secured by an insurance on his life effected by some other part at his expense. The premiums fell due relentlessly at moments of greatest inconvenience.

While a minor, therefore, Byron was not living in debt so much as he was living on credit, the collateral for which was literally himself and his future prospects, and his creditors were often the very "friends" who nominally comprised the original audience for his poetry. To image himself as a public author would be tantamount to attaining a more mature and unencumbered sense of economic identity for himself. He never put it this crudely. By the time he was prepared to put it directly at all, his directness had the rich burden of self-irony. That irony has, as Byron may have wished, distracted his readers, even scholarly ones, from considering seriously the economic basis of his "poetical character."

The issue of self-authorization is manifested in the early poems as a concern with nominating the self to an authentic "name." In a poem of 1803, originally untitled when it appeared in the privately printed and anonymous volume *Fugitive Pieces* (1806), Byron asserts:

> My *epitaph* shall be my name alone:
> If *that* with honour fail to crown my clay,
> Oh! may no other fame my deeds repay!
> *That*, only *that*, shall single out the spot;
> By that remember'd, or with that forgot.

In the poem's first publication, the thrice-repeated "that" lacks the very antecedent—a specific name—which its repetitions affirm. Only when reprinted as "A Fragment" in *Hours of Idleness* is Byron's name given. But even so, the "other fame," which in the poem probably means "ill repute," is, according to the Preface to *Hours of Idleness*, poetic fame itself. The author's "deeds" *as a poet* remain not merely unnamed but analogically related to ignominy.

In "Elegy on Newstead Abbey," a poem that recounts the political history of Byron's ancestral home, the speaker identifies himself as "The last and youngest of a noble line" who "holds thy mouldering turrets in his sway." Here Byron nominates himself as a nobleman, albeit a lord of ruins, but the poem curiously refuses to name

a poetic self at the same time. It is curious because the passage quoted above could easily accommodate such a nomination. In this poem Byron himself is writing in (and using the clichés of) "a noble line" of country-house poetry, and the double meaning of "line" could be used to reconcile empirical self and poetic vocation. In fact, the next line reads: "Deserted now, he scans thy gray worn towers"—where again "scans" could have become a weighted word. Instead, the peculiar grammar that makes the "he" rather than the "towers" sound "deserted now" merely shows us Byron's own self-desertion of the poetical character.

Naming becomes a most perilous act when the nominating vehicle, poetry itself, is divested of any intrinsic authority. The ironies in the last stanza of "The Tear," one of only two poems that Byron signed with his name in the otherwise anonymous *Fugitive Pieces* (and one of seventeen poems from that volume that he reprinted as late as 1808), exhaust Byron's capacity to harmonize them:

> May no marble bestow
> The splendour of woe,
> Which the children of Vanity rear;
> No fiction of fame
> Shall blazon my name
> All I ask, all I wish, is a *Tear*.
> (Byron, 26 October 1806)

The "fiction" he rejects here—literally an epitaph—is linked to what he calls earlier in the poem "a fanciful wreath / In Glory's romantic career"—that is, military fame. But it is linked also to the fiction-making career of poetry, and so, both ways to fame—that of romantic public action and that of equally romantic poetic fancy—are rejected in favor of the "Truth" (1, 3) of the heart's affection, symbolized by a tear. When friendship's tears have such authority, then the whole idea of an honorable name is stripped of any public consequence. And yet the inscriptive force of this very stanza belies its own renunciations. The last line of this lugubriously affirmative stanza, which is stamped with Byron's name and the date like an epitaph, does not reject *fame* as a fiction; indeed, it specifies just what kind of temporal approbation is required and from whom.

At the end of the 1807 Preface, Byron claims that he does not want to "triumph in honours granted solely to a title"—that is, merely to a name. At the same time, he agrees with Dr. Johnson in admiring Carlisle, whose "works have long received the meed of public applause to which, by their intrinsic worth, they are well entitled." To what intrinsic worth does Byron's (titled) name entitle *him*?—that question provides the subtext of "The Tear." The Preface seeks to discriminate between the "intrinsic worth" of Byron's poems and the intrinsic worthlessness of their author's "character," a discrimination that makes the act of naming oneself either pathetic or self-aggrandizing. "The Tear" tries to hold a middle ground, countering pathos with a putative disdain for fame. Rejecting all aggrandizing fictions, however, the speaker's name becomes blazoned here with its own act of self-effacement, a brilliant sentimentalizing of that private "Vanity" which is publicly being deprecated.

The poems in *Hours of Idleness* and the Preface to them are not working at cross-purposes, then. They speak to the same burden of identifying the author's "character" as an author but without appearing to understand how and why this becomes a dilemma. The root of the dilemma is that Byron's rather conventional descriptions of (and special pleadings for) himself as author did not satisfactorily reflect the enthusiasms expressed in his verse nor did they authentically represent the ("vulgar") pride he took in making his verse accomplished. So, on the one hand, he invokes the modesty topos to his Cambridge acquaintance, William Bankes: "in fact I never looked beyond the Moment of Composition, & published merely at the Request of my Friends.— Notwithstanding so much has been said concerning the Genus irritabile Vatum' we shall never quarrel on the Subject, poetic fame is by no means the 'acme' of my Wishes" (6 March 1807). One sees that this modesty is both sincere *and* a topos when one recognizes how Byron's language echoes what Thomas Moore said as "editor" of *The Poetical Works of the Late Thomas Little, Esq.*—indeed, how Byron quotes Moore almost verbatim. In a follow-up letter to Bankes, this topos has acquired the name of action: "Contrary to my former Intention, I am now preparing a volume for the Public at large, ... This is a hazardous experiment, but want of better employment, the encouragement I have met with, & my own Vanity, induce me to stand the Test" (*Letters*, p. 112). A mock heroism colors the tone of certain phrases here, but when Byron speaks of hazard, he is also serious. The recipient of this letter was not one of those who gave Byron unqualified encouragement.

In 1807 Byron had no clear sense of how to hold the mirror up to his own social status, and the economic tropes in the following May 14 letter (to E. N. Long) show the consequent strain of representing himself as a poet: "I am tired of versifying, & am irrevocably determined to rhyme no more, an employment I merely adopted '*pour passer le Temps*' when this work [*Hours of Idleness*] is accomplished, I shall have obtained all the *Eclat* I desire at present, when it shall be said that I published before I was 20; the merit of the contents is of little Consequence, provided they are not absolutely execrable, the novelty of the *Deed* (which though not unprecedented, is at least uncommon, particularly amongst *Patricians*) will secure some share of Credit" (14 May 1807). This ingeniously ingenuous passage says not only that he will rhyme no more but also that he will avoid writing more rhymes like Moore. As a patrician, his poetic employment was a labor to pass the time; but whatever his doubts about the merit of the volume, he is not content to drop the economic metaphor. His work becomes a deed, a proprietary contract, signifying not only the prodigality of its author (who is not even old enough to hold deeds) but also the incremental value of that prodigality (it secures some share of credit). Byron borrows the social connotations of this common economic metaphor to show that his work is "uncommon" (i.e., more than common, baronial) even among patricians. By means of wit, he is claiming proprietary rights of authorship *in spite of* the actual poems he produced, and, he is grounding that claim in an elaborate economic trope: his "employment" is more prodigious, of *greater* "Consequence" perhaps, precisely because his work is accomplished with the nonutilitarian genius of youth....

Source: Kurt Heinzelman, "Byron's Poetry of Politics: The Economic Basis of the 'Poetical Character,'" in *Critical Essays on Lord Byron*, edited by Robert F. Gleckner, G.K. Hall, 1991, pp. 135–41.

SOURCES

Abrams, M. H., "English Romanticism: The Spirit of the Age," in *Romanticism: Points of View*, 2nd ed., edited by Robert F. Gleckner and Gerald E. Enscoe, Prentice-Hall, 1974, pp. 314–30.

Arnold, Matthew, Preface to *Poetry of Byron*, Macmillan, 1885, pp. vii–xxxi.

Byron, Lord George Gordon, "So, We'll Go No More a Roving," in *Byron: Poetical Works*, edited by Frederick Page, new ed. revised by John Jump, Oxford University Press, 1970, p. 101.

Garrett, Martin, "Byron's Fairy City of the Heart," in *Venice: A Cultural and Literary Companion*, Interlink Books, 2001, pp. 195–97.

"Huge Survey Reveals Seven Social Classes in UK," BBC website, April 3, 2013, http://www.bbc.com/news/uk-22007058 (accessed May 19, 2015).

Jones, Harvey, "A UK Expat's Guide to Ireland," in *Guardian*, November 28, 2012, http://www.theguardian.com/money/2012/nov/28/uk-expat-guide-ireland (accessed May 19, 2015).

"Lord Byron," Poetry Foundation website, http://www.poetryfoundation.org/bio/lord-byron (accessed May 19, 2015).

Rosner, Max, "Life Expectancy," Our World in Data website, http://ourworldindata.org/data/population-growth-vital-statistics/life-expectancy/ (accessed May 19, 2015).

"So, We'll Go No More a Roving," in *The Broadview Anthology of British Literature: One-Volume Compact Edition*, 2015, p. 1333.

Stafford, Fiona, "The Pleasures of Poetry," in *Reading Romantic Poetry*, Wiley-Blackwell, 2012, pp. 1–33.

Taylor, Jerome, "British Expats in Romania: They Come Over Here, Taking Our Jobs," in *Independent*, February 12, 2013, http://www.independent.co.uk/news/world/europe/british-expats-in-romania-they-come-over-here-taking-our-jobs-8492393.html (accessed May 19, 2015).

Watson, J. R. "Byron," in *English Poetry of the Romantic Period, 1789–1830*, Addison Wesley Longman, 1985, pp. 260–98.

Wilson, Josh, "So, You Want to Live in Berlin? An Expat's Guide," The Skinny website, Jan. 3, 2013, http://www.theskinny.co.uk/travel/features/so-you-want-to-live-in-berlin-an-expats-guide (accessed May 19, 2015).

FURTHER READING

Abrams, M. H., *Natural Supernaturalism: Tradition and Revolution in Romantic Literature*, W. W. Norton, 1971.
Abrams's book is considered a seminal work in the study of the British romantic movement.

He explores the influences—cultural, historical, political, philosophical, and literary—on the romantic poets and analyzes the commonalities among their themes, methods of expression, and style.

Hay, Daisy, *Young Romantics: The Tangled Lives of English Poetry's Greatest Generation*, Farrar, Straus, and Giroux, 2010.
Hay's volume studies the intertwined lives of the young romantic era poets and explores their mutual influence on one another, in terms of their personal lives, their literary work, their artistic philosophy, and their political leanings.

McCarthy, Fiona, *Byron: Life and Legend*, Farrar, Straus and Giroux, 2002.
McCarthy's acclaimed and comprehensive biography examines Byron's life and career as well as his influence on later writers. She further assesses the cultish following Byron developed after his death.

Ruwe, Donelle, *British Children's Poetry in the Romantic Era*, Palgrave Macmillan, 2014.
Ruwe's study explores the history and development of children's poetry during the years of the romantic movement, giving students of Byron's work a glimpse into the ways in which poetry written for young-adult audiences was similar to and different from the work of the major Romantic poets.

SUGGESTED SEARCH TERMS

Byron AND "So, We'll Go No More a Roving"

Byron and romantic movement

British romantic movement

British romantic movement AND French Revolution

British expatriate writers AND nineteenth century

nineteenth-century Venice AND Byron

Byron AND Greek revolution

Byron AND Shelley

Byron AND lyricism

British romanticism AND lyric poetry

They Called Them "Blue"

KATIA KAPOVICH

2003

"They Called Them 'Blue'" is a work of free verse by Moldovan American poet Katia Kapovich that explores the milieu of a marginalized gay couple in the poet's home city of Chişinău—a city formerly known through its Russian appellation and referred to in the poem as Kishinev. Moldova, a small European nation located between Ukraine and Romania just northwest of the Black Sea, was a Soviet Socialist Republic until the dissolution of the USSR in 1991. Kapovich's biography suggests that her poem is set in the 1970s, when the region was fully under Soviet Communist rule. Kapovich, herself suppressed as a dissident while living and working in Moldova and Russia, left the dissolving Soviet Union first for Jerusalem and then for the United States. She published two English-language poetry collections in addition to eight Russian collections through the mid-2010s.

The poem's consideration of the couple in question—the ones referred to as "blue"—is conducted through a visit to their home undertaken by the poet, as escorted there by a schoolmate from the same bohemian neighborhood. The visit demonstrates the plain, upstanding humanity of the two men who constitute the couple, encouraging sympathetic reflections on their circumstances on the part of the reader. "They Called Them 'Blue'" was published online in *Jacket*, No. 23, August 2003, and in print in Kapovich's 2004 collection *Gogol in Rome*.

Sergey is hospitable, making Turkish coffee for his unexpected guests. (© Levent Konuk / Shutterstock.com)

AUTHOR BIOGRAPHY

Kapovich was born in Kishinev (now Chişinău), Moldavian Soviet Socialist Republic, in 1960. She has been writing poetry since she was seven years old. In her Soviet schooling, she was memorizing long works of verse by age eleven. Her father was an architect who worked illicitly to help build facilities to support underserved populations. As a result, he was arrested in the late 1970s and sentenced to eight years in prison and labor camps.

A turning point in Kapovich's life came when she met Evgenii Khorvat in 1978, when she was eighteen. In an *Open Letters Monthly* interview with Mark Vincenz, Kapovich described Khorvat as "a year younger but ages older as a poet." While he inspired her to adopt a dissident outlook on life, their rebellion was at first restricted to little more than drinking and wandering around; they were "free from the inside and disobedient on the outside," she related. For a brief spell, after being arrested for fighting with a policeman, she was obligated to take sedatives while confined in a mental institution. In January 1980, while in Leningrad,

Kapovich and Khorvat were recruited to help circulate an underground anti-Soviet manifesto at the city's ten universities. At the Academy of Arts, they were arrested but seemed to escape arraignment; however, they were being followed by the KGB.

On Khorvat's insistence, Kapovich returned to Chişinău, while he stayed in Leningrad trying to stabilize their circumstances. Three days later he was arrested, and shortly after, he was exiled to Petrozavodsk, the Russian city hundreds of miles to the north where his mother and sister were staying. Kapovich visited him three times; she was escorted back to Chişinău by the KGB the final time. Then Khorvat left for the West in 1981. Kapovich herself remained in the Soviet Union, with her education culminating in a dissertation on Nikolai Gogol, but she had great difficulty publishing owing to Soviet condemnation of the underground samizdat literary circle she belonged to.

Kapovich finally left the Soviet Union in 1990, on the cusp of the union's breakup, moving to Jerusalem, home to a substantial Russian émigré community. After a couple of years there, during which time she published her first Russian collection and edited a Russian magazine, she moved to the United States, settling in Boston. After producing a couple of Russian collections in the 1990s, she increased her output to nearly a book a year through the following decade, including half a dozen more Russian volumes and her two English collections, *Gogol in Rome* (2004)—which includes "They Called Them 'Blue'"—and *Cossacks and Bandits* (2008).

In 2001, Kapovich was selected by US poet laureate Billy Collins to be a Witter Bynner Fellow in Poetry with the Library of Congress. Kapovich once held the position of poet in residence at Amherst College in Massachusetts, and she has lived in Cambridge for over a decade. She has a daughter who was born in the 1990s, and she is married to Russian American poet Philip Nikolayev, who also writes bilingually. Together, they coedit the literary journal *Fulcrum: An Annual of Poetry and Aesthetics*. Kapovich's English poems have appeared in anthologies that include *Poet for Poet* (1998); *Poetry 180: A Turning Back to Poetry* (2003), which was edited by Collins; and *New European Poets* (2008).

POEM SUMMARY

The text used for this summary is from *Gogol in Rome*, Salt, 2004, p. 16. A version of the poem can be found on the following web page: http://jacketmagazine.com/23/kapo.html.

Lines 1–8

"They Called Them 'Blue'" begins with a restatement of the title, adding that the subjective *they* are inclined to discuss the objective *them* at a level no louder than a whisper. For only a moment, the reader might imagine that these are whispers of respect or even reverence. However, line 2 at once explains that the whispering suggests that the subjective *they* think of the objective *them* as a mysteriously isolated, ill-intentioned, and evil group.

The second stanza quickly illuminates the identity of the poem's objective *them*—or at least the identity of two people belonging to this greater *them*. Line 3 focuses on a couple, and this couple thus shifts from being the object to the implied subject of the poem. That is to say, whoever the *they* of the first stanza might be, they make no further appearance in the poem. The couple in question now assumes priority of focus with regard to actions and intentions.

The nature of the neighborhood in which the couple lives is the first indication of their individual identities, with the terms used connoting an impoverished district serving as a refuge for artists and other freethinkers. Most relevantly as far as this poem is concerned, as line 4 indicates, the partners being referred to are gay, living in the European state of Moldova. Even if one is unaware of the arc of Kapovich's life, the poem's combination of whispering, suspicions, and implied oppression strongly suggests that it takes place when Moldova was living under the Soviet Union's Communist rule.

In line 5, the poet acknowledges that she had never been to the slum in question, until a first visit was arranged and managed by an acquaintance from school. Presumably the word *schoolmate* is intended to suggest a peer from primary, intermediate, or secondary school, as opposed to a college or university, since the word would rarely if ever be used as such in American English. The acquaintance is understood to be familiar with the district from living within it. The setting of the poem at last takes definitive shape with line 7, where the poet is shown to be

visiting the couple living in the slum. Having arrived at the couple's home, the poet and her acquaintance extinguish their cigarettes and ascend the stairs to the highest floor of what is presumably a standard apartment building.

Lines 9–21

An older man opens the door of the apartment; therefore the couple in question may be inferred to consist of two men. The man's appearance resembles that of a monk, or someone accustomed to solitary living, wearing not the ordinary Western clothes favored for daily interactions—pants, shirt, etc.—but a robe. There is something fairly magnificent about this man's robe; perhaps it is lined with fur or has ornate embroidery or makes a monument of itself in some other way. An oriental sort of ambience is further achieved with the mention of Turkish coffee in line 11. (Moldova is not far from Turkey, which lies south of the Black Sea.) The "tonsure" that the man scratches is the bald spot on his head. Although the bald spot is presumably a natural one rather than an intentionally shaved one as monks sometimes wear, the word choice enhances the figurative description of the man as being monk-like. Someone asks, presumably with regard to the coffee, where it ought to be put. This could be the host indirectly acknowledging that the guests may have to hold their cups while standing or sitting on the floor, since there is no furniture aside from a bookcase; it could also be either the poet or her acquaintance uncertainly asking for help in figuring out where to safely place a hot cup that might leave a ring wherever it is left.

The fourth stanza, beginning with line 14, more formally introduces the man they have met, whose name is Sergey. By occupation he binds books, at times restoring noteworthy old books in compromised conditions. His place of employment is a local history archive. He gained the education and skills needed to practice his trade while incarcerated for the so-called crime of homosexual activity. That books are all Sergey has suggests that the process of being incarcerated served to strip him of all his possessions, whether they were auctioned off to pay fines or fees or were simply looted from his home, perhaps by the authorities themselves, in his absence.

The large window in line 17 offers an admirable view of the impoverished districts of the city named in line 18, Kishinev, the Russian name of what is now known globally as Chişinău, capital of the Republic of Moldova. In Sergey's kitchen, a tape recorder is playing continuously, reproducing the sounds of a guitar and violin playing together as if dueling or competing. Before the poet gets a chance to ask about the music, Sergey, as if reading her mind, explains that the music is jazz from Czechoslovakia, a nation that was aligned with the Soviet Union under the Warsaw Pact (and is now two separate countries).

Lines 22–30

The fifth stanza marks the arrival of a younger man said to be Sergey's friend. As befits the bohemian slum, this man is an artist working to some extent within the underground, suggesting the hidden community of resisters to Soviet rule. At this moment, the young man is carrying an especially large watermelon. By his own aggravated report, he has had to wait in line for an hour in order to receive or purchase the watermelon, an experience that has left him testy; he declares that if the watermelon is not ripe to be eaten, he will be inclined to dispose of it by ejecting it out of their apartment window, which, being on the top floor, would result in the fruit's destruction.

The sixth stanza reports that the watermelon proved to be green on the inside. Certain species of watermelon are said to have green flesh, but the reader may assume that this watermelon is, after all, not yet ripe. Regardless, the

two men, who are presumably the couple from line 3, and the poet and her companion all share the watermelon. Meanwhile, they listen to the Czech jazz, which the poet affirms she finds enjoyable. The poet indicates that a fair deal of time has passed since the experience of the poem occurred, in reporting that she still—despite the passage of time—recalls the watery taste of the melon and the large quantity of seeds that remained after the consumption of the melon's green flesh.

THEMES

Communism

Kapovich's poem contains several veiled references to Communism. The first such reference is the mention in the title and first line of a group of people, a *they*, who whisper about the perfectly dignified, ordinary couple in the poem as if they represent some threat to society. Although unspecified oppressive *they*s are often meant to represent figures of authority, such is not necessarily the case here: the authorities, after all, can speak openly about whatever they wish to speak about. However, it is possible that homosexuality is seen by the Communist authorities as so taboo that even as officials they are reluctant to speak about it—as if to do so in regular tones of voice would suggest some degree of sympathy for gay people.

Even so, *they* in the poem's title seems to more strongly suggest mainstream society under the severe influence of Communism. Obligating neighbors to spy on one another was one way the Soviet regime historically identified individuals with even the slightest inclinations toward dissidence so as to silence them, whether by expulsion to Siberia or straightforward death sentences. The urgent importance of remaining on the safe side of any whispers was one reason why individuals such as homosexuals remained persecuted or at least marginalized well beyond Joseph Stalin's midcentury reign of terror. A final indication that the poem is set in a Communist environment is the circumstance of the young man's waiting in line for an hour merely to get a potentially unripe watermelon; long lines for inadequate goods were one reason for the popular upsurge against Communism that eventually broke the USSR apart.

TOPICS FOR FURTHER STUDY

- Write a poetic vignette about a recalled visit to the home of someone you had never met before—or, if you cannot recall such a circumstance, of someone you already knew. Include as much physical detail as you can recall, but also feel free to invent detail if you think it will improve the poem. The poem need not contain a momentous event but should aptly convey the feel of the visit from your perspective. Post your poem on a classroom blog to share with your classmates. Allow your classmates to comment.

- Paint or draw a picture in which you represent as much of "They Called Them 'Blue'" as possible in a single coherent scene.

- Read "A Paper Plane to Nowhere," one of Kapovich's most admired poems, which can also be found in *Gogol in Rome*. Write an explication of this poem, addressing its content, themes, and style, and conclude by discussing what this poem may have that "They Called Them 'Blue'" may lack.

- Select a poem from *Bend, Don't Shatter: Poets on the Beginning of Desire* (2004), edited by T. Cole Rachel and Rita D. Costello. Most of the poems in this young-adult anthology treat first-person adolescent experiences related to sexual identity. Write an essay in which you analyze the poem you selected with regard to themes, tone, and verse style, and also compare this poem with "They Called Them 'Blue'," discussing the differences in their effects.

- Write a research paper about the experiences of homosexuals in the Soviet Union, with whatever narrower focus you choose, drawing from at least five reputable online sources, which must be cited.

Homosexuality

In giving narrative priority to the gay couple who live in the Moldovan slum that the poet

visits, "They Called Them 'Blue'" highlights the circumstances of homosexual individuals in a Soviet republic in the later twentieth century. Interestingly, however, beyond the identification of the poem's couple as gay, few if any narrative details suggest any singularly "homosexual" aspects to the couple's lifestyle.

Sergey's lounging around the house in a robe—especially one marked by a certain monumentality—faintly suggests laziness or dissipation, but the detail should not be taken too far. The time of day, which is not specified, may make the wearing of a robe perfectly reasonable, even with visitors in the house; moreover, many a heterosexual man might be depicted as lounging in a robe at any given hour (à la Hugh Hefner). Sergey is something of a craftsman with respect for literature, a book binder, while the young man is only vaguely referred to as an artist; neither of these occupations stereotypically suggests homosexual status.

With all of these details portraying Sergey and his friend not so much as a homosexual couple but simply as a couple, the poem suggests that a rational perspective must acknowledge that homosexual couples function within society almost identically to the way heterosexual couples function, which is to say that there is nothing sinister or cultish about them. Through the universality of their daily activities, and in contrast to the mainstream Soviet perception of them as an ideological threat, the men making up the couple in Kapovich's poem are perfectly humanized.

Marginalization

The poem says very little about how Sergey and his friend might be persecuted by the Soviet state apparatus. The fact that Sergey was imprisoned for his sexual orientation alone amounts to persecution, but the poem shies away from addressing the specifics of that incarceration—whether Sergey was publicly shamed through his arrest, whether he was treated harshly or even tortured, or how long he was incarcerated for. Rather, the poem deals more directly with the aftermath of the persecution, the effective marginalization of Sergey and his friend.

Whatever art the young friend practices, he must do so underground, on the margins of society; presumably this is the only way that he can express himself freely. Sergey may have had a well-paying job before being jailed, but

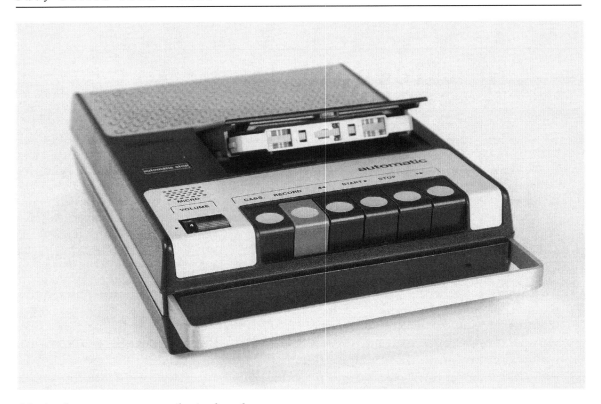

Music plays on a tape recorder in the other room. (© photocritical / Shutterstock.com)

presumably his being a convicted criminal and outcast has precluded the possibility of his holding a vast number of forms of employment in Soviet Moldova. He has been relegated to a job that, one hopes, he at least finds personally rewarding, the preservation of books.

People who meet with marginalization at the hands of their peers are often more likely to turn to books, not only to escape the unpleasantness of a marginalized reality but also often to find a sympathetic perspective that cannot be found among one's contemporary society. Of course, Sergey may not get his hands on many dissidence-oriented books if he is working through the auspices of the Soviet government, as he was trained through them. Still, many intellectuals hold sacred the idea of preservation of the written word, and Sergey himself, marginalized perhaps like a rare book, might even see in his employment a symbol for the preservation of his own life and dignity.

Perseverance

While evoking various disadvantages that Sergey and his friend must face in their marginalized lives, the governing mood of the poem is one of perseverance. They may live in a dilapidated, impoverished section of the city, but this does not prevent Sergey from being comfortable in his home; his lounging about in a fabulous robe is like the act of thumbing his nose at the forces of oppression. The apparent absence of chairs or tables in their apartment does not prevent Sergey from enjoying the ritual of drinking Turkish coffee and serving it to his guests. The sound of the guitar and violin playing nonstop, meanwhile, serves as a symbol of perseverance.

The concept of perseverance is highlighted with the tale of the watermelon. The young man spends an entire valuable hour of his day waiting in line in order to bring home a bounty of watermelon for Sergey and their guests. This can hardly be considered as important as waiting in line for an hour for rice, flour, vegetables, or meat—watermelon being, of course, mostly water and thus not exactly a bounty of nutrition. Rather it is a bounty of taste, of enjoyment of life. Even if the watermelon is hardly ripe, this does not stop the couple and their guests from appreciating the juicy fruit, from persevering in their appreciation of life itself.

STYLE

Free Verse

"They Called Them 'Blue'" is effectively free verse at its freest. The stanzaic structure is irregular, with stanzas ranging from two to eight lines in length with no apparent broader design to the arrangement. Rather, the senses and contexts of the particular lines seem to govern the spacing. The first stanza, for example, standing out as a signification of external judgment of the bohemian couple, isolates just two lines as a stanza, giving minimal attention to the negativity of that judgment before shifting attention decidedly to the couple and their milieu.

Within the stanzas, there is no meter and no noteworthy rhyme, even internally. There are small words and syllables that amount to assonance/consonance (repeated vowel/consonant sounds) or near rhymes: *out our* in line 7, *monk* and *monumental* in line 10, *Turkish* and *tonsure* in line 11, *violin* and *vying* in lines 19 and 20. However, only a couple of these instances suggest themselves as intentional in terms of aural effects; in this poem, at least, rhyme was not one of Kapovich's priorities. In fact, she has expressed that she naturally favors English when she is inclined to write free verse, while her Russian poetry is more apt to feature the rhyme and meter of a classical form.

Vignette

Kapovich's poem amounts to a vignette as much about the bohemian couple who ostensibly constitute the primary subjects of the poem as about the experience of the poet's visit to the couple's home. After a few lines of background information, the poet deposits the reader alongside her as she visits the couple on the day in question. The poem thus includes the sorts of details of ordinary experience that mark the visit—the extinguishing of cigarettes, the host's attire and coffee service, the music they listen to—alongside more factual reporting of the circumstances in which Sergey and his friend find themselves. These facts may have been stated by Sergey himself during their chat over coffee, or they may be facts reported at a different time by the poet's acquaintance, who presumably has some degree of familiarity not just with the neighborhood but with Sergey himself as well as his friend.

The term *vignette* is often used to discuss not merely a short episode but one that features only a modest occurrence or revelation. Part of this poem's intent thus seems to accord with the sense of a vignette, namely, the intent to normalize the experiences of a homosexual couple, indirectly equating them with the experiences of any romantic couple. Any extraordinary occurrence, of course, would do the opposite and would potentially estrange the heteronormative reader from the couple's unfamiliar experiences.

HISTORICAL CONTEXT

The Moldavian SSR and Literary Dissidence

While many of the constituent republics of the Soviet Union were carved out of Russia, the land of what is now called the Republic of Moldova has a slightly more complex history. The northeastern sliver on the bank of the Dniester River was formerly a part of Ukraine, while the remaining bulk of the country was a Romanian territory called Bessarabia. The Soviet Union first claimed the region to be called the Moldovian Soviet Socialist Republic in 1940, briefly lost it back to Romania, and then secured it for good in 1944. The population of the republic is some two-thirds ethnic Romanians, an eighth Ukrainian, an eighth Russian, and the remainder other ethnicities.

Kapovich has not made her ethnicity clear in interviews, but given that she shows native mastery of Russian, her primary literary language, and has not mentioned any other linguistic roots, one may presume that she was at least educated in Russian from her earliest years of schooling in the Soviet system in Chişinău. In a 2002 volume, Alla Skvortsova records that as of the 1980s, three-quarters of Moldovans in Chişinău were fluent in Russian, including 12 percent who considered themselves native Russian speakers.

Moldova is known for lying in a fertile region that made up one of the key breadbaskets of the Soviet Union, and it also has a flourishing wine industry. This largely accounts for the USSR's desire to seize the region. Generally speaking, not much has been published in English about the history of small countries like Moldova during their time under the Soviet sphere, because at the time dissemination of news was highly controlled by state authorities, and then, once records became available after

COMPARE
&
CONTRAST

- **1970s:** The Moldavian Soviet Socialist Republic has a population of some 3.75 million, including 418,000 in the capital of Kishinev.

  Today: The independent Republic of Moldova's population is approximately 4.44 million—it is the most densely populated of the former Soviet Socialist Republics—with Chişinău home to about 700,000 people.

- **1970s:** Political and literary dissidents in the Soviet Union are liable to be branded as treasonous, blacklisted, exiled internally, expelled, imprisoned, and/or institutionalized—all without broader public knowledge of the suppression taking place.

  Today: Vladimir Putin's Russia is gaining a reputation for bringing back Soviet-style autocracy and suppression through new freedom-stifling laws as well as darker means. Notable cases have included the 2009 death in prison of whistle-blowing tax lawyer Sergei Magnitsky, who uncovered widespread government extortion, and assassination of human rights lawyer Stanislav Markelov. Musicians from the West voiced support for the temporarily imprisoned members of female punk band Pussy Riot, who in 2012 were convicted of hooliganism for a guerrilla performance of lines from their protest song "Virgin Mary, Get Putin Out" in the form of punk prayer in a Russian Orthodox cathedral.

- **1970s:** With audio technology having advanced from the record to the cassette tape, it is possible to use a commercially available tape recorder to make a live recording of a musical performance. The quality will be fuzzy in comparison with studio-recorded albums.

  Today: With most people in developed nations carrying phones with recording capacities, people can create MP3s of live sound at a moment's notice. However, most people seeking recordings of music, including in such out-of-the-way nations as Moldova, will turn to the Internet, where MP3s—of only slightly lesser quality than purchasable CDs—can be downloaded for fees or, usually illicitly, for free.

---

the fall of the Soviet Union, study of the defunct union was no longer a pressing academic concern. In many respects, Moldova remains, as phrased by Skvortsova, "hardly known to the outside world."

A Soviet historical topic that has gained more attention in the West is the activity of dissidents, especially literary dissidents, the most famous of whom is Alexander Solzhenitsyn, author of *One Day in the Life of Ivan Denisovich* and *The Gulag Archipelago*. Other dissident writers of note include Andrei Sakharov and Yevgenia Ginzburg. As well known as such writers became in the West, their influence within the USSR was marginal, again because of strict Soviet control of means of publication and dissemination. That Soviet influence dictated the will of the Writers Union is attested to by the fact that when Solzhenitsyn was nominated for expulsion owing to his dissidence, only eight of almost seven thousand union members voted in his favor. Handwritten or typed underground publications, called samizdat, did proliferate, but much of the fiction and poetry published in samizdat was not so much anti-Soviet as simply too un-Soviet to merit sanctioned publication as works of "Socialist Realism"—that is, works depicting and hailing socialist values and the communist system as exemplified in daily life.

There remained among the common public criticism of the Soviet system, including, as

Sergey's apartment has a large window, but it looks out over the city's slums. (© Fototaras / Shutterstock.com)

recorded by Leo Hecht in his 1978 volume *The USSR Today: Facts and Interpretations*, "complaints about the lack of consumer items, about the inadequacy of housing, about the slow service given by civil servants, about the unfairness of plant officials, labor union leaders or Party and government functionaries." Such criticism was not entirely forbidden, and local newspapers did print letters of complaint—though editors would restrict published letters to those regarding concerns that the Soviet system would see fit to remedy. This was one means of keeping the populace confident that their needs were being addressed. Still, for those who became too problematic, there were a number of means of silencing them. As Hecht relates,

> Some, like Solzhenitsyn, may be expelled to the West and therefore branded as treasonous defectors. Others may lose their jobs and be barred from living in major population centers.... Still others, especially those who engage in anti-Soviet activities or overt propaganda, may be sentenced to prison for up to ten years or may be exiled to remote areas. Those dissidents who persist in attacking the system no matter what the personal consequences may

be, are obviously mad and are confined to mental institutions.

Between her father's, her friends', and her own experiences, Kapovich was familiar with all of these means of suppression of liberal thought.

CRITICAL OVERVIEW

Although Kapovich's sparse English-language output has limited her critical exposure, those who have approached her work have shared favorable impressions. Library of Congress representative Grace Cavalieri, who saw a draft of the manuscript for *Gogol in Rome* in 2002, readily declared, "This will be in hardcover before very long, I predict this." Cavalieri called Kapovich's career "a meteor just starting up in America," describing her poetry as "distinctive," "masterful," and among the "freshest" verse she had seen. Cavalieri also affirmed that Kapovich demonstrates that she knows "what the human heart can endure in an alien climate." Vincenz, writing after the publication of Kapovich's 2004 and 2008 English collections, was similarly enthusiastic about her verse, finding that she deftly "wrestles with the trauma of dissident life." He states,

> Katia Kapovich sees herself as deeply flawed, and perhaps this is precisely where the strength of her poems [is] embedded. Miniature—at times marginalized—narratives reflect loss, trauma, heartache, but embrace a slightly watered-down version of the American dream.

Vincenz admiringly compares Kapovich to the most esteemed Russian predecessors in terms of language and style—namely Vladimir Nabokov and Anton Chekhov—calling her "a late English-language poet who teases the unexpected out of her adopted tongue" and who is "adept at crystallizing minute detail, human flaws, ticks and wrinkles; capable of delivering great quivering moments of flux."

Tim Kindseth extended *Gogol in Rome* a closely considered assessment for the *Harvard Review*. While he judges that the less inspiring poems should have been left out, he declares,

> The poems in Kapovich's impressive English-language debut are gripping more often than tepid, particularly when she produces photographic, vibrantly visualized scenes by zooming in on small images and magnifying their resonance with a solid, cogent metaphor.

Kindseth also compares her with renowned authors writing in English as an adopted language, Nabokov and Joseph Conrad, though less favorably, stating that she lacks their "pure control." He adds that "some unnatural phrases inevitably surface. Not abrasive, they instead disorient subtly, like flavored cigarettes." Of the tone of the collection, he notes that "a lonesome chill blows through her poems"; there are some warmer poems, but here "Kapovich tends to lapse into heart-string sentimentality." Of the style, Kindseth states that while "the level of imagination is high," often "her rhythms and declarative tone approximate documentary newsprint." Kindseth concludes that Kapovich's "eerie, frosty first collection of English-language verse is...arresting, commanding, and fluid." Don Share, writing on behalf of the Netherlands' Poetry International Rotterdam festival, states of Kapovich,

> Her poems, with a wry sense of humour, address and meditate on the lives of those who have survived—or have tried to endure—war, terror, loss, injustice, trauma, displacement and marginalisation....Yet her work fights off despair at every turn.

CRITICISM

Michael Allen Holmes

Holmes is a writer with existential interests. In the following essay, he contends that "They Called Them 'Blue'" fails to rise above the status of a remembrance recorded as a poem.

Upon reading Kapovich's free-verse poem "They Called Them 'Blue,'" one likely concludes that it is, at the very least, a *nice* poem. The reader is transported, to a fair extent, to the apartment of Sergey and his friend, where the poet finds a domestic situation not unlike that of any loyal, innocent, well-meaning couple. Despite Sergey's being labeled a criminal, he and his friend appear to be perfectly well-adjusted, to intend no harm toward anyone, and to be willing to welcome a stranger with open arms—even if in general they might not be accorded the same treatment owing to their sexual identity. The reader likely concludes, even with such limited exposure to their lives, that they are *good* people. And if the poem's intent is to put their goodness on display, to inspire the reader to agree that their situation merits public recognition as a legitimate relationship, then it must be said to succeed. However, upon a second or third reading, one may find that in a certain sense, the poem is somewhat frustrating. The poem seems to bristle with potential that, in the end, is never quite fulfilled.

The concept of potential energy as applied in the field of physics seems especially apt in discussing this poem. Most often one refers to an object as having potential energy if it is placed in an elevated location, such that all that is needed is some initial action to overcome the inertia of stillness and bring the object sliding, rolling, or plummeting downward—like the push given to a child on a sled at the top of a hill. Potential energy can be conceived with respect not only to gravitational force but to other forces as well. For example, a loaded gun represents a great deal of potential energy, requiring only the trigger to release that potential in the form of the kinetic energy of the bullet.

Anton Chekhov—with whom Kapovich is sometimes compared—famously declared, specifically with respect to the theater, that if a loaded gun is hanging on the stage, at some point in the play, it must go off. This speaks to the inevitable disappointment brought about when a source of potential energy is displayed

WHAT DO I READ NEXT?

- Kapovich's second English-language collection is *Cossacks and Bandits: Poems, 2003–2006* (2008). As with her earlier collection, many of these poems address people's responses to loss, injustice, marginalization, and other trying or traumatic experiences and circumstances.

- Joseph Brodsky was a Russian writer who spent a year and a half in a labor camp before being expelled from the Soviet Union in 1972 and settling in America. He went on to win the Nobel Prize in Literature in 1987 and to serve as US poet laureate from 1991 to 1992. His US verse publications culminated in *Collected Poems in English* (2000), edited by Ann Kjellberg and including poems both written in and translated into English.

- Anna Akhmatova is perhaps the most highly regarded poetess in Russian history. Her work represents a sharp contrast to Kapovich's in that she remained under Soviet censure throughout her life, declining to leave even when she had the chance, and was thus obligated to encode her dissidence in complex, highly symbolic poems. An accessible modern collection is *The Word That Causes Death's Defeat: Poems of Memory* (2004), translated by Nancy K. Anderson and featuring biographical, critical, and annotative contributions.

- As do many Russian authors, Kapovich cites Aleksandr Pushkin as the primary originator of Russian verse, with his historical role akin to that of Shakespeare for the English language. Pushkin's lyrical dramatization of life in a marginalized community is presented in *The Gypsies & Other Narrative Poems*. A 2006 edition, translated by Antony Wood, is readily available.

- *An Anthology of Contemporary Russian Women Poets* (2005), edited by Valentina Polukhina and Daniel Weissbort, presents translations of Russian-language verse by some eighty poets living both within and without Russia. Two of Kapovich's poems are included.

- Kapovich's poem only grazes the surface of the topic of liberated sexuality. *The Full Spectrum: A New Generation of Writing about Gay, Lesbian, Bisexual, Transgender, Questioning, and Other Identities* (2006), includes poems, stories, and essays by young adults about past experiences related to sexual identity.

- *Mariposas: A Modern Anthology of Queer Latino Poetry* (2008), edited by Emanuel Xavier, presents verse reflections from a modern community in which homosexuality is largely still seen as cause for marginalization. Some of the poems feature mixed English and Spanish usage, while others appear in translation.

- The control exerted by the Soviet Union is placed in a fantasy context in the young-adult novel *Sekret* (2014), set in the 1960s, in which seventeen-year-old Yulia is forced by the KGB to use her psychic powers to help the Soviet government against her will.

---

before the reader but never released. The feeling of unreleased potential energy is precisely that of frustration. Arguably there are other things that can be done with a loaded gun onstage—for example, the play might lead up to a confrontation in which two people threaten each other and even wrestle over the gun, only for a third person to step in, seize the gun, and dramatically unload it. This would seem to be a legitimate circumvention of Chekhov's maxim, but without a doubt the real or figurative loaded gun in a work of literature must be attended to. It must be dealt with for the work to leave the reader satisfied.

THE FACT OF AN EXPERIENCE ALONE DOES

NOT NECESSARILY MAKE IT FIT FOR POETRY."

Turning back to Kapovich's poem, one finds from the very beginning sources of potential energy that are never released or satisfactorily defused. The first such source would be the *they* of the title. Given the placement of this group as the first word in the title, they would seem to have a great deal of significance in the poem. Thus it is curious that this group goes unidentified throughout the poem, indeed is never even mentioned after the first line. There is surely a point and value to this: Kapovich does not, in fact, want to focus on this oppressive *they* any more than to set the stage for the reader by making clear that the people she meets in this poem are pariahs or outcasts. One might even say that Kapovich's declining to identify the *they* lends extra dignity to the couple; the *they* merit so little attention that the poem has no interest in making clear just who they are, while Sergey and his friend are fleshed out with voices and identities. This, then, is a good example of a source of unrealized potential energy, a significant contextual uncertainty that yet serves the poem through an implied statement of values.

The same cannot be said for some of the other poem's unrealized potentials. Proceeding with the title, for example, one comes across the word *blue*, the word reportedly applied to the couple to identify them as gay. This may strike the American reader as a curious, even a harmless slur, if a slur all the same. The color blue can hardly be said to have standout negative connotations and in fact more often carries the positive connotations of blue skies, refreshing waters, and perhaps sparkling eyes. American English slurs for homosexual people, to the contrary, typically connote some perceived negative aspect of their identity. None of them are worth elaborating in this context. But in the poem, the use of the color blue as a slur seems to demand extra attention. Where did the term's apparently derogatory use come from? Could Kapovich have included some usage of the term that would demonstrate how hurtful it presumably is?

One might suggest that a poem is no place for contextual explanations spoon-fed to the reader, and yet in other poems Kapovich does not shy away from such clarification; for example, in her poem "Moscow—Berlin," she opens with three lines describing a train being lifted and resettled on a new set of wheels, then uses the fourth line to deliver in parentheses the factual remark that the width of railway tracks is different in Russia and in Europe. Whether this utterly unsentimental remark improves that poem is up in the air, but there can be little doubt that "They Called Them 'Blue'" would have been improved if the poem had lent greater depth to the crux of the title, the word *blue*, which is otherwise lent no contextual significance whatsoever.

There is not a single blue object in the poem, symbolic or otherwise, whether to parallel or reinforce or to oppose the sense implied by the title. The only merit in the term, it would seem, is the presumed fact that it is truth, that the word was indeed used as a slur as Kapovich suggests. Yet factual truth is rarely the sole reason for the inclusion of a word or idea in a poem. The word *blue*, then, represents a source of potential energy that is simply left unreleased—like an object sitting high up on a storage shelf that will simply go on meaninglessly sitting there, untouched, with the tension of the potential energy rendered irrelevant.

Moving into the poem, another problem that surfaces is the simple declaration, not description, of locales and actions. The neighborhood itself is described with only two significant words, *slum* (twice) and *bohemian*. Neither of these words is especially descriptive, simply calling to mind whatever preconceived notions the reader may have. What the buildings, cars, streets, shops, signs, or passersby in that neighborhood are like goes entirely unstated. Even when the poet steps up to Sergey's top-floor window to take in the view, all the reader learns is that the *view* itself was *majestic*—though what exactly the poet is looking at is not at all clear.

What is so majestic about the view? Is it the height, the expanse of buildings, the clouds hanging overhead, the sun piercing through, the people moving about in their daily patterns below? In fact, given that the poet is looking at the slum, a description of the view of it as being *majestic* is easily seen as condescending—like a Western tourist flying over Kibera, the wasteland tin-shack slum of Nairobi, rife with crime, disease, and death owing to the deplorable living conditions, and muttering to his seatmate as she sips from her first-class complimentary champagne, "What a *majestic* view this is!" In the circumstances, the word is both condescending and insulting, reflecting not the slightest bit of compassion for the people who endure life in the compromised circumstances of the area, likely through little to no fault of their own. Kapovich's use is not much better.

The slum itself, then—the word might be called a *loaded* term—is a source of potential, a place with broad implications attached to it that may or may not hold in the circumstances in which it is being used. The slum offers great potential for poignant description, but Kapovich passes this potential by, offering no independently constructed description of the neighborhood at all. What she offers instead, in line 7, is mention of how, upon arriving at the apartment, she and her companion put out their cigarettes. Perhaps she was too busy paying attention to herself smoking—indeed the habit promotes a sustained inward focus, perhaps even self-absorption—to actually notice what the neighborhood was like.

That line, as it happens, also contains another potentially irritating feature: the indistinct use of the phrase *check them out*. This may be one of those instances where Kapovich's relative lack of familiarity with the English language does her no favor. It would be reasonable enough to be checking the *slum* out, to be looking it over in an evaluative way. But the slum is an *it*; *them* might be seen to refer to the *rooms* of line 4, and yet the use of the term in that line was nonspecific, referring to all the cheap rooms in the district, and surely the poet cannot be said to be going to check out the *rooms* as she has used the term.

That leaves the only possible referent as *this couple*, from line 3. Frankly, this is a rude way of referring to a trip to the home of strangers. You can politely *visit* people, or go to *meet* them, or *get acquainted* with them, but to go *check* people *out* implies going to simply look at them as objects, to observe and assess them, much as one would *check out* a sporting event, or the scene at a party, or perhaps an attractive woman walking down the street, which is to say objectify her by assessing her based strictly on her appearance. The use of the phrase *check them out* may be just a clumsy use of colloquial

language by an adoptive speaker, but it nonetheless connotes a lack of interpersonal integrity on the part of the poet.

Littered throughout the rest of the poem are problematic references and unfulfilling descriptions. The poem never reveals anything about the poet's acquaintance. Surely this acquaintance is not the point of the poem, but to fail to even identify the schoolmate as male or female means that the reader is that much less able to actually imagine or visualize the scene being painted by the poet. Even a single adjective to describe the schoolmate—*hip*, or *outgoing*, or *lonesome*, perhaps—could have contributed significantly to the feel of the poem. As it is, the reader does not even get a sense for the degree of closeness between the poet and this person referred to only as a *schoolmate*—not as a friend, or companion, or object of affection, but simply as someone who attends the same school as the poet. As a descriptor for a relationship, the term is strictly factual. The schoolmate, then, as a character in the poem, represents another source of potential, for description, emotion, or action, that goes unrealized.

With regard to Sergey, the reader at least learns that he has gray hair and a bald spot. Meanwhile, he might be tall or short, heavy or thin—or perhaps he is simply nondescript. The characterization of Sergey as a monk-like person with a monumental bathrobe is another curious one; if the term *monk* is only meant to connote a person who is relaxed and spends time at home, then the description is passable. And yet the term also connotes a spiritual strictness and antipathy to materiality. Sergey may *look* like a monk, but a *monumental* bathrobe would seem ill fitting for a true monk, given the grandiosity that the term *monument* connotes; a monk's robe would be, first and foremost, simple and functional. Nor would a monk be likely to serve coffee as Sergey does; tea, maybe, but Turkish coffee, no. Thus, the potential represented by the metaphorical use of the word *monk* is effectively negated by the description that follows.

Sergey's occupation, too, represents potential, since it invites the possibility of describing him as he works—the steadiness of his hands, the focus of his eyes, the contented or resigned or tired look on his face—but Kapovich offers no such description. She does not *show* the reader Sergey at work but simply *tells* the reader what he does. This may accord with how she learned of Sergey's trade in real life, but again, the fact of an experience alone does not necessarily make it fit for poetry.

Of course, Sergey at least gets a profession; his *friend* meanwhile, is only an artist of the most generic sort. Perhaps in real life Kapovich could not recall what sort of artist this friend was, or perhaps she never even learned, but she does the poem no favors by leaving the characterization as generic as it was in her mind, however truthful it might be. If Sergey and the young artist are meant to be a couple, why is he being called only a friend? If part of the poem's intent is to normalize the idea of a romantic homosexual relationship, calling Sergey's partner a *friend* works against this intent, taking a linguistic step back from the idea of homosexual romance. Many choices of descriptors for the young artist's relation to Sergey would have been far bolder and more poetically intriguing.

The music being played in Sergey's kitchen represents another source of potential energy, since there is the chance for the poet to describe the music—which she does in minimalist fashion—as well as for Sergey to explain when and where the music was recorded. Yet the poet cannot even phrase a comment or question about the music, as Sergey preemptively, and quite dryly, informs her that the music is Czech jazz. Does this mean he recorded the music himself while in Czechoslovakia, or is it an underground recording that was smuggled into Moldova, or did his favorite Czech group happen to play in Chişinău recently? The poet might have asked a question to elicit a discussion about the recording, but apparently she is satisfied with the simple fact of Sergey's classification. In this case, instead of an object with potential energy being left sitting on a shelf, it has simply been picked up and unceremoniously placed in a corner on the floor, rather than being, say, passed around, handled, and examined or pushed off the shelf to crash to the floor. The potential has been lost, but nothing has been gained.

The poem's final stanza is the pinnacle of the poet's failure to bring out the life of the scene that she is purportedly inhabiting. As far as the music goes, the poet has nothing to say other than that she *liked* it. Such a declaration is unfortunately no more poetic than clicking on the "Like" button on a social media page to express the blandest possible form of support for a given event or achievement. As for the

bounty of sweet (but possibly unripe) fruit shared by Sergey, his nondescript friend, the poet, and her nondescript schoolmate, how did it taste? The poet *still remembers* that the watermelon tasted *watery* and had lots of seeds.

If there is a hidden symbolic meaning to this watermelon, it is as elusive as can be. Should an unripe, watery, seed-filled melon be seen to represent Sergey and his friend, or their relationship, or life in Communist Chişinău, or perhaps the poet's sense of compassion? It is difficult, if not impossible, to say. In fact, one likely comes to the conclusion that there is no profounder meaning to be found in the watermelon—it must simply have been what the poet truly ate when she truly visited Sergey and his friend.

One is thus left to draw a broader conclusion about "They Called Them 'Blue'": it is not so much a poem through and through as a remembrance recorded in the form of a poem. By the evidence of its contents, it appears to have been written not directly from experience, that is, literally in the moment or at least soon after, but from distant memory. If the event indeed took place when Kapovich was of school age in the 1970s and was written not long before its initial 2003 publication, then a good quarter century would have elapsed between the event and the poem. Indeed the poem suggests such a great temporal distance. The poet, it seems, can remember certain facts and details about the day, but, in truth, not that many.

There is much to be said for compression in a poem, but if a poem sets out to tell a story, even the minimalist sort of story represented by a vignette, then it must adequately function as a story as far as details and character are concerned. It is not clear that Kapovich's poem functions adequately as such. She has apparently remembered only the sorts of things a naturally self-interested, which is to say, for the time being, self-centered, teenager would notice about such a visit, which is to say, not much. Some readers will be satisfied by such a poem as this, but some will not.

Source: Michael Allen Holmes, Critical Essay on "They Called Them 'Blue'," in *Poetry for Students*, Gale, Cengage Learning, 2016.

Tim Kindseth
In the following review, Kindseth describes Kapovich's first collection in English as "impressive."

They eat the watermelon with spoons, even though it is not ripe. (© *AnirutKhattirat* | *Shutterstock.com*)

Few non-native writers have mastered the mongrel English tongue. Conrad immediately jumps to mind, as does Nabokov. While Katia Kapovich, who emigrated to the United States from Moldova in 1990 and writes in both English and her native Russian, lacks Conrad's and Nabokov's pure control—she alludes to the latter's work frequently and with palpable admiration in her poems—her eerie, frosty first collection of English-language verse is nonetheless arresting, commanding, and fluid.

Some unnatural phrases inevitably surface. Not abrasive, they instead disorient subtly, like flavored cigarettes. For instance, in the titular "Gogol in Rome," a crisp sketch of the Russian author's shuddersome descent into a madness and death, she labels the painter Alexander Ge as Gogol's "bosom friend." The phrase is rather musty and expired; it belongs to different century. (Melville uses it to head the tenth chapter of *Moby Dick*.)

Referring to Russian writers, Dostoevsky supposedly once said, "We all crawled out from under Gogol's 'Overcoat.'" If the statement is hyperbolic, Gogol is nevertheless an obvious and admitted guiding spirit in Kapovich's work. As in Gogol's glum and gloomy life and fiction, a lonesome chill blows through her poems, which, despite their formal architecture, with cut and stacked lines, are closer in flow and spirit to the prose-poetry of Baudelaire; a handful of the pieces have clunky, mechanical end-rhymes, but her rhythms and declarative tone approximate documentary newsprint.

Frigid weather and harsh, dreary landscapes dominate: an ominous "gray winter sun" looms in "Silhouette"; and "Kishinev chimneys/were coughing up their first smoke into the winter air," Kapovich writes in "Golden Fleece," a poem, like "Moscow—Berlin," about smuggling contraband goods (Bulgarian sheepkins in the former, banned books from West Berlin in the latter) into the merciless, ironfisted Soviet Union, where, as she dryly recalls in "Blacklisted Titles," "Lolita,/Mandelstahm's Voronezh Notebooks,/ let alone a Solzhenitsyn, could earn you/a couple of years in jail."

Kapovich was arrested once for assaulting a policeman; spared prison, she was thrown into an asylum. "A Paper Plane to Nowhere" recounts her time there and introduces us to Carmen, a "little ugly angel" whose "flesh was older than her mind," and who resembles the simple girl from Wordsworth's macabre "We Are Seven." Kapovich offered Carmen a coffin folded from gray paper. Carmen "seemed happy." Yet Kapovich stared into Carmen's eyes and found the opposite. She writes, in a memorable couplet, "I looked in them and saw an abyss of sadness,/the asylum of our mutual madness."

Kapovich's poems teem with portraits of dispossessed, dead souls: a bibulous marine, a vituperative beggar, deracinated Russian expatriates, and an obese woman who commits suicide. The sheen of death also shrouds "Silhouette" and "Privacy," but the horridness peaks in "Tanya," whose eponymous protagonist is found in Central Park "on an unusually cold March morning,/frozen to death." With deceptively simple language and acute attention to detail, Kapovich masterfully imagines Tanya's haunting final moments:

> She simply sat on a wooden bench,
> an open pad in her lap,
> drawing the naked trees
> glistening white after an ice storm,
> a dead fountain under a crust of snow,
> black crows on staircase banisters.
> She must have warmed herself from time to time
> with gulps of brandy
> (she had developed a drinking problem
> when working at the hospital).
> So she sat for hours, oblivious to the snow
> and the arriving darkness,
> as the temperature kept falling and falling.

Not all of her poems are so funereal and gelid. When her poems do warm, however, Kapovich tends to lapse into heart-string sentimentality. A group of teens, for example, skinny-dip in "Anna-Maria and the Others," and Kapovitch calls them "water-shaking cherubim" and exhorts that "hoary Neptune bless its sparkling spawn!"

Any collection close to one hundred pages is bound to have its duller moments, and many of these poems should have been omitted for the sake of a sturdier book. However, the poems in Kapovich's impressive English-language debut are gripping more often than tepid, particularly when she produces photographic, vibrantly visualized scenes by zooming in on small images and magnifying their resonance with a solid, cogent metaphor. Describing women laundering clothes in a frozen lake, she writes, "Their red hands fall like roses/in the narrow ice-holes

with linen shirts." The temperature may be ungodly low, but the level of imagination is high.

Source: Tim Kindseth, Review of *Gogol in Rome*, in *Harvard Review*, No. 30, June 2006, pp. 181–82.

SOURCES

Cavalieri, Grace, "Interview with Katia Kapovich," Library of Congress website, April 3, 2002, http://www.loc.gov/today/cyberlc/feature_wdesc.php?rec=3292 (accessed May 25, 2015).

"Chisinau—the Capital of Moldova," in *World of Moldova*, http://worldofmoldova.com/en/cities-of-moldova/chisinau/ (accessed May 27, 2015).

Denber, Rachel, "Pussy Riot and Russia's Surreal 'Justice,'" CNN website, August 17, 2012, http://www.cnn.com/2012/08/17/opinion/denber-pussy-riot-verdict (accessed May 27, 2015).

Hecht, Leo, *The USSR Today: Facts and Interpretations*, "Scholasticus" Publishing, 1978, pp. 16–17, 105–107, 161–66.

Helsinki Watch, *Human Rights in Moldova: The Turbulent Dniester*, Human Rights Watch, March 1993, pp. v–vii.

Kapovich, Katia, "Moscow–Berlin" and "They Called Them 'Blue,'" in *Gogol in Rome*, Salt, 2004, pp. 8–9, 16.

"Katia Kapovich," Poetry Foundation website, http://www.poetryfoundation.org/bio/katia-kapovich (accessed May 25, 2015).

Kindseth, Tim, Review of *Gogol in Rome*, in *Harvard Review*, No. 30, 2006, pp. 181–82.

"Population of the Republic of Moldova," World of Moldova, http://worldofmoldova.com/en/moldova-general-information/people-of-moldova/ (accessed May 27, 2015).

Share, Don, "Katia Kapovich," Poetry International Rotterdam website, June 1, 2010, http://www.poetryinternationalweb.net/pi/site/poet/item/15895/9421/Katia-Kapovich (accessed May 26, 2015).

Skvortsova, Alla, "The Cultural and Social Makeup of Moldova: A Bipolar or Dispersed Society?," in *National Integration and Violent Conflict in Post-Soviet Societies: The Cases of Estonia and Moldova*, edited by Pål Kolstø, Rowman & Littlefield, 2002, pp. 159, 170–71.

Vincenz, Mark, "A Cloud of Voices: A Conversation and Twenty Cigarettes with Katia Kapovich," in *Open Letters Monthly*, July 1, 2010, http://www.openlettersmonthly.com/voices-before-and-after-the-storm/ (accessed May 25, 2015).

FURTHER READING

Gogol, Nikolai, *Collected Tales of Nikolai Gogol*, translated by Richard Pevear and Larissa Volokhonsky, Pantheon Books, 1998.

> In the United States, Gogol is known for depictions of madness—the subject of Kapovich's dissertation—reminiscent of the writing of Edgar Allan Poe. He also wrote fantastic tales deemed accessible to children by Soviet authorities in charge of education, and he was one of the first and most powerful literary influences in Kapovich's life.

Goldman, Amy, *Melons: For the Passionate Grower*, Artisan Books, 2002.

> In this volume, Goldman, who has been featured on television by Martha Stewart, presents a bounty of photographs and profiles of over one hundred different types of melons. She also offers growing and harvesting tips and explains how to preserve seeds.

McKane, Richard, ed., *Ten Russian Poets: Surviving the Twentieth Century*, Anvil Press Poetry, 2003.

> This volume edited by a prominent translator of Kapovich's Russian poetry zeros in on a topic significant to both her life and her verse: survival in the face of Soviet/Russian oppression. Kapovich is one of the featured poets.

Moss, Kevin, ed., *Out of the Blue: Russia's Hidden Gay Literature; An Anthology*, Gay Sunshine Press, 1997.

> Noting the historical absence of attention to gay characters, culture, and themes in Russian literature, Moss has collected fiction by authors ranging from Pushkin and Mikhail Lermontov in the nineteenth century to more recent authors who forthrightly approach gay issues.

SUGGESTED SEARCH TERMS

Katia Kapovich AND Gogol in Rome

Katia Kapovich AND Cossacks and Bandits

Katia Kapovich AND poetry

Katia Kapovice AND "They Call Them 'Blue'"

Russian American poetry

Russian poetry AND translation

Moldova OR Moldavia AND Soviet Union

Moldova AND history OR news

Soviet Union AND homosexuality

Russian homosexuals AND blue

To the Sun

INGEBORG BACHMANN
1956

"An die Sonne," translated into English as "To the Sun," is one of the poems in the second, and sadly last, collection by revered mid-twentieth-century Austrian writer Ingeborg Bachmann. After her 1953 debut collection was awarded the annual prize given by the influential post–World War II German-language literary circle known as Gruppe 47, Bachmann was thrust into the spotlight. She published her second collection three years later, but then, for whatever reasons— she tended to dance around the question in interviews—her inclination to write poetry rapidly waned. She went on to write a great number of radio plays, lectures, librettos, and short stories, as well as a few individual poems, but never another collection of verse.

Bachmann wrote "To the Sun" while living in Italy, which became a second home nation to her—she had been raised in a corner of southern Austria only an hour away from the two nations' border, and Italian was spoken in her home. The Mediterranean environs are certainly reflected in the landscape, or perhaps image-scape, of the poem, which fairly shimmers with the beauty discerned in and illuminated by the sun's rays. In the end, the poem is as much about love as about nature. First published in 1956 in *Anrufung des großen Bären* (Invocation of the Great Bear) and first translated for New York's *Encounter* by Michael Hamburger in April 1964, "To the Sun" can be found as translated

Ingeborg Bachmann (© Buhs / Remmler / ullstein bild via Getty Images)

by Mark Anderson in *In the Storm of Roses: Selected Poems by Ingeborg Bachmann* (1986) and as translated by Peter Filkins in the first and follow-up editions of her collected poems, *Songs in Flight* (1994) and *Darkness Spoken* (2006).

AUTHOR BIOGRAPHY

Bachmann was born on June 25, 1926, in Klagenfurt, Austria, located in a valley in the south-central province of Carinthia, half an hour from Slovenia and an hour, over the mountains, from Italy. Her father was a high school teacher, and she had two younger siblings. By the time she was old enough to be reading the Grimms' fairy tales, she began writing. She reports in a poetic biographical note,

> I liked to lie beside the railroad embankment and send my thoughts on journeys to foreign cities and countries and to that unknown sea which, somewhere, merges with the sky to complete the globe. It was always of seas, sand, and ships that I dreamed.

A pivotal moment in her youth was her witnessing, at the age of twelve, the triumphant march of Adolf Hitler and his troops into the city, where, despite their aggressive intentions, they were enthusiastically welcomed by a willingly subjugated populace. Under Nazi rule, Bachmann studied at a girls' school until graduation in 1944. Upon the war's end she proceeded with studies at the universities in Innsbruck, Graz, and finally Vienna, where she earned a doctorate with her thesis on Martin Heidegger's existential philosophy in 1950.

At this point Bachmann's life became fairly itinerant. For several years she alternated time working for Radio Rot-Weisz-Rot in Vienna and for Bavarian television in Munich, and it was in 1952 that she read for Gruppe 47 in Germany. Her appearance coincided with that of poet Paul Celan, whom she had met in Vienna and became romantically involved with. Regarding that first public appearance, in the words of Filkins in his introduction to *Songs in Flight: The Collected Poems of Ingeborg Bachmann*, "the German literary world was immediately swept away by the young blond-haired poet reading her poems in a near whisper." She soon won the Gruppe 47 Prize for her debut collection, was featured on the cover of *Der Spiegel*, and was inundated with requests for writings and appearances. From 1953 to 1957 she lived in Italy, splitting time between Rome, Naples, and the island of Ischia. In 1954 she published her second poetry collection, *Anrufung des großen Bären*, which includes "An die Sonne," later translated as "To the Sun." She visited the United States in 1955 at the invitation of Harvard University.

In ensuing years Bachmann lived in Munich, West Berlin, and Zurich, Switzerland, but eventually resided mostly in Rome. She lived with composer Hans Werner Henze for several years and, later, with Swiss writer Max Frisch for another several. Her breakup with Frisch in 1962 led to an emotional breakdown and eventual dependence on alcohol, painkillers, and sleeping pills. Through the later 1950s and 1960s, Bachmann was especially well known for her radio plays. She was chosen as the inaugural chair of poetry at the University of Frankfurt in 1959 and in that capacity delivered a series of lectures titled Problems of Contemporary Poetry. She did write a great deal of long-unpublished poetry in the mid-1960s. Meanwhile she issued an award-winning volume of short stories in 1961, and the first of what was to be a series of three novels was published in 1971. But in September 1973 in Rome, Bachmann fell asleep while smoking a cigarette in bed and upon awaking was engulfed in flames. She died a month later, on October 17, 1973, from the burns as well as from convulsions brought on by withdrawal from a substance doctors could not identify.

POEM SUMMARY

The text used for this summary is from *In the Storm of Roses*, translated and edited by Mark Anderson, Princeton University Press, 1986, pp. 132–35. Versions of the poem can be found on the following web pages: http://www.unz.org/Pub/Encounter-1964apr-00032 and http://allpoetry.com/To-The-Sun.

As properly reproduced in translation from the original, "To the Sun" is broken up into nine stanzas of steadily descending and then ascending length, going from five lines to four, to three, and so on down to one and then back up to five. Through the first half of the poem, each stanza comprises a single sentence; in the second half, while an internal period and exclamation point break up two of the stanzas into two sentences each—and, depending on the translation, one stanza's sentence continues into the next—otherwise the pattern holds.

Lines 1–5

The poem begins by apparently describing the entity to which the poem is dedicated, the sun (which is made clear in line 5), pointing out that its beauty surpasses that of several other celestial objects. These include the moon, however esteemed, worthy, or worshipped its light may be; the stars, however renowned they may be and however much they may order, decorate, or be the pride of the night; and the comet, despite its fiery or explosive appearance. Line 4 iterates that no other star or planet in the sky is endowed with as much significance and beauty as the sun, which is a result, according to line 5, of the fact that the lives of the poet and a *you* who seems to be the poet's human companion depend on it.

Lines 6–9

The beauty of the sun as it rises is stated plainly to open the second stanza, along with a suggestion

MEDIA ADAPTATIONS

- Bachmann can be seen and heard reading "An die Sonne" in the original German (with Dutch subtitles) in 1961 in a clip found on YouTube, at https://www.youtube.com/watch?v=J8e0Xj7cdBM, or on Vimeo, at https://vimeo.com/98724803.

that the sun, upon appearing, goes straight to his daily work, which he duly completes. At the top of the list of the sun's chores might be providing the sunlight that is essential to the growth of plant life on earth, not to mention warming and nourishing (with vitamin D) humans and other living creatures. The suggestion of work being completed is followed up with a mention of how the sun is fairest in the summer—perhaps after the chores are done—when a day can veritably steam off of what one imagines to be a tropical or subtropical coast, or at least a very hot one. On such a day, without anyone's needing to act on intentions, images of sails pass over the eye of the poem's addressee, the *you*, until that person is led by fatigue to cut the image of the last sail short—that is, one imagines, to blink, such that the image of the sail does not complete the crossing of the person's eye. Perhaps the two people are sitting very close to the shore as a well-rigged sailboat passes by, with the poet positioned between the addressee and the boat.

Lines 10–12

The third stanza evokes, for the first time, imagery in which the sun is absent, whether it should be understood to have set for the night or to be simply disappeared for the sake of these images. Without light, art can no longer be perceived; it is said to replace the veil that was formerly removed from its surface. With art representing a broad category of what can be seen—even of what is important to see—the poet proceeds to specify other entities that will go unseen in the sun's absence, including foremost the poet's companion, as well as, with the setting of the sunlit coast persisting, the sea and sand. These panoramic aspects of the natural world are said to gain shelter under the poet's eyelids, as if their bright, sweeping images were imprinted on the poet's brain when the sun was shining.

Lines 13–14

The poem grows more effusive, perhaps sentimental, in the fourth stanza, where the beauty of the sun is once more reiterated, now specifically in the context of keeping the poet and another warm, as well as providing essential energy and loving support. The *us* of line 13 could potentially refer to many people but seems intended to represent only the poet and the companion. The sense of the sun's return in this stanza is emphasized when the poet praises being once more able to see, and specifically able to see the companion.

Line 15

The one-line fifth stanza represents the midpoint—perhaps axis or fulcrum—of the poem. The line might be said to contain the poem's foundational thematic statement, declaring that there is nothing more beautiful than the state of simply *being* beneath and thus lit by the sun. The ellipsis ending the line sustains this ambient image longer than other punctuation marks (comma, period, etc.) would allow.

Lines 16–17

Line 16 amplifies the significance of line 15 by opening with the same phrasing, declaring that nothing is more beautiful than what the poet describes—here, the sight of a rod or stick in the water, perhaps a fallen branch, and of a bird which, flying through the air above, is considering its current state. Line 17 brings the reader's gaze back down to the water by referring to fish collectively swimming about.

Lines 18–20

The verbs in adjectival form that open the seventh stanza are most readily understood to refer to the fish of the preceding stanza. (In fact, while Anderson ends the sixth stanza with a period—perhaps to match all the other stanzas—making the referent of "colored" and "shaped" unclear, Hamburger preserves the comma that ends the sixth stanza in the original and thus makes clear the grammatical continuation of that stanza's sentence.) The reflectively shiny fish, being not apparently significant in and of themselves, are thus suggested as emblematic of all things with color and shape. The verbal image of a "mission of light" suggests that the fish have been endowed with the raison d'être of the sun itself. The sun is also what allows the poet to see, in line 19, the geometrical aspects of a field, with the terms suggesting the distance from center to edge, the area, and the overall shape and the different perspectives of it. The poet turns in line 20 back to the companion, who has put on a dress, indicating for the first time that the companion is female. The beauty of the dress—or perhaps rather of the companion in her dress—is emphasized with the echo within line 20, with the dress said, upon the second mention, to be puffing outward as if from an intake of air, while its color is blue.

Lines 21–24

The dress's color becomes paramount in the eighth stanza, where now that color itself is said to be beautiful. It is the color of peacocks walking about and bowing, as if politely acknowledging each other, as well as of open skies that reveal great distances. In these distances are regions of happiness—though perhaps they are not all under blue skies, since the weather is said to suit the entire range of the poet's moods; surely some of those skies, and moods, are cloudy. Perhaps owing to the existential open-endedness that a blue sky represents, blue is even seen to be the color of chance, of luck or fortune. The appearance of this image embodying fortune on the horizon inspires the poet to exclaim upon its presence. The poet's eyes, in their excitement, seem to widen and take in too much light, leading to blinking and a burning soreness.

Lines 25–29

Following on the image of the overexposed eyes, the poet returns in the first two words of the final stanza to a bare statement of the sun's beauty. The statement that even dust offers superlative admiration to the sun is perhaps inspired by the sight of a shaft of sunlight in which motes of dust seem to intently gather to bask in the glow. The poet's concluding formulation is drawn out in a way that produces suspense over what is being said: It is not for the sake of the sight of the moon or stars, or the ostentatious comets with which the night tries to dazzle the poet, but for the sake of the companion that the poet will—soon in an unending, all-absorbing sense—mourn the inevitable loss of the ability to see.

THEMES

Nature

As much as any poem—or so it first appears—"To the Sun" revolves around (appropriately enough) an aspect of nature, the one named in the title. The focus of the poet's admiration for the sun is nominally its aesthetic value, its beauty, although there is more to the poet's concept of beauty than meets the eye. Through the first stanza, the sun is glorified through comparison with several other similar aspects of nature, namely, other celestial bodies: the moon, the stars, and for good measure a comet. Through these comparisons, the sun is valued expressly for its active role in the lives of the poet and the female companion, indeed their dependence on it. Nature is not simply something to be looked at but something to be lived in, and first and foremost in humankind's dependency on nature is the sun, that original stimulator of the earth's primordial soup. In a word, people *need* the sun. In the course of the poem the sun is presented not strictly in isolation but also in conjunction with such other natural elements as the sea and the sand, the birds on high and fish down low, and, above all, blue skies. It is not hard to imagine that not only does the poem take place entirely out of doors—even in the sun's absence in the third stanza, the sea and sand linger in the mind's eye—but it was quite likely written out of doors as well; it seems as if the poet's inspiration must have been directly channeled from the experience of sunshine to words on paper.

Beauty

The most conventional definition of beauty regards it as the visual appeal of something, beauty being in the *eye* of the beholder. Bachmann leans on this sense of beauty to an extent in the first stanza, where the comparison of the sun's beauty with that of other celestial objects implies a comparison of their appearances to the eye. Yet in this sense the comparison is curious, since, of course, one cannot actually look directly at the sun without suffering damage to the eyes (a fact alluded to in line 24). And of course, even if and when a person can look briefly at the sun—such as at sunrise or sunset, or perhaps through a perfectly proportioned layer of clouds—one may not be apt to describe it as *beautiful* per se, since it is no more than a glowing circle of light. Part of the moon's beauty, in contrast, lies in the details like craters

TOPICS FOR FURTHER STUDY

- Write a poem in the style of "To the Sun," juxtaposing a praiseworthy element of nature with a person who is an object of affection, whether romantic, friendly, or familial. Also mimic the stanzaic structure of Bachmann's poem as part of an effort to suggest the mirroring of the poem's dual subjects.

- Read Shakespeare's Sonnet 18, "Shall I compare thee to a summer's day?," which can be found in the Poetry for Young People series volume *William Shakespeare* (2000). Write an essay in which you explicate this poem as fully as possible—acknowledging any sources used—and compare and contrast it with Bachmann's "To the Sun."

- Explore print collections or online resources to find a poem by a lesbian poet—such as Audre Lorde, Amy Lowell, or Gertrude Stein—in which a female beloved is being addressed. Then write an essay in which you analyze this poem individually and also consider it alongside "To the Sun," discussing such topics as the author's openness with regard to her sexuality, the importance of her sexuality within the poem, and whether or not the poems encourage readers to draw any conclusions about the author's sexuality.

- Create a website that serves as a tribute to the sun, using appropriate photographs and graphics, scientific facts, informative text, links to other relevant sites, and key quotations from Bachmann's poem.

that can be perceived with the naked eye, with the subtle texture of the sight allowing the brain to begin to calculate the great distance between moon and beholder. This may partly explain why the moon has been, as the poem acknowledges, venerated (i.e., as a deity) and enshrined as noble, flush with the stature and pride of royalty. The sun, too, has been venerated, by most cultures, and yet from sight one can form little sense of the details of its visual appearance or of its profound distance from the viewer.

It would seem fitting, then, that in combination the first stanza's comparisons serve to shift attention away from visual beauty. The first line suggests that part of the moon's beauty, perhaps even the foundation of its beauty, is its strength of character. In turn, the description of stars as *orders* (or *medals*) of the night can be seen to allude to what the nighttime sky enables humans to accomplish, namely the navigating of long voyages, the ordering of their direction. That is, part of the stars' beauty lies in their functionality, their use—once irreplaceable—as a system whereby, with the proper instruments and knowledge, one can determine one's location anywhere on earth. The sun is perhaps *much* more beautiful, in turn, than the comet because the comet, unlike moon or stars, serves no significant spiritual or practical function. Functionality is explicitly framed as essential in line 5, where the sun is said to be more beautiful than the other celestial bodies precisely because of humans' functional dependence on it.

Throughout the remainder of the poem, beauty is repeatedly contextualized and recontextualized in ways that de-emphasize the sense of visual appearance. In lines 6–7, it is the sun's ability to accomplish work, to get things done—to make things grow—that makes it beautiful. The superlative beauty attributed to the sun on a steamy summer day, as linked with images of apparent indolence on a beach, may seem to undermine any emphasis on functionality, but the placement of this commentary just after the mention of chores suggests that the sense of the work of a day, or of a season, having been completed is yet accountable for the beauty. In line 13, the functionality of the sun for humans is brought up once more, with the poet shifting to a focus on the sun's enabling the poet to see things. This, too, is a source of its beauty—and by line 15, the sense of beauty expands into an overarching sense that encompasses existence itself: what is superlatively beautiful is simply *being* out in the sun. The existentiality of this line makes it a fitting central line, isolated from any other description and thus bearing both the most pure and the most universal connotations.

Vision

While the visual aspect of beauty is de-emphasized by the poem's iterations of the sun's practical value, one of the things said to be beautiful is vision itself. In line 16, *seeing* is what is beautiful, with the specific objects of the bird and fish seeming less relevant for what they are than for their signifying the act of looking up as well as down, encompassing as much in one's vision as possible. The importance of vision is reinforced when the poem highlights the characteristics of color and shape; though line 18 seems to refer to the fish, it does not detail their specific appearances, suggesting that color and shape in general are really what is being presented for consideration. The mentions of the mathematical or geometric properties of a field, meanwhile, emphasize the crucial role that vision plays in both getting around the world and determining what can or should be claimed for oneself, what is significant in one's own life. The consideration of vision inevitably turns to the poet's companion, with a focus on the color and shape of her dress. Thus, the poet does return to a visual sense of beauty—and yet, in mentioning only the dress the companion wears, and not her facial features or the color of her hair or the shape of her body, the poet seems to suggest that whatever physical attractiveness the woman may have is not the essence of her beauty. Indeed, the poet never calls the woman herself beautiful. Rather, it is the capacity for vision, the ability to see and thus commune with the other—to read her expression and body language, to register the impact of one's own words and gestures on her—that is so essential to the poet's life. The poet's eyes or sight will be lost eventually—whether from old age and infirmity or death in any form—and the inability to *see* the companion is what will be the source of angst of an endless, all-encompassing sort.

STYLE

Poetry in Translation

As with any translated poem, the reader approaching "To the Sun" in English is well advised to keep in mind that the precise wording does not necessarily—and often cannot—reflect Bachmann's precise verbal intentions. Bachmann herself addressed the issue of translated poetry in the second of her five lectures given at the University of Frankfurt in 1959–1960. As encapsulated by Karen Achberger in the

The poem describes an idyllic day by the sea. (© Ron Kacmarcik / Shutterstock.com)

Dictionary of Literary Biography, Bachmann argued "that each poem has a new and unique grasp on reality and that this uniqueness is inherent in the idiom in which it is written"; in other words, the connotations of a given arrangement of words change, sometimes dramatically, when those words are translated, because language usage is rarely strictly schematic or formulaic in definitional terms; rather, people use words in *idiomatic* or colloquial, acquired ways. For example, one can say "I haven't the foggiest idea" in English and be understood by most anyone, but translated directly into another language, such a saying may baffle listeners. Bachmann concludes, in Achberger's words, that "a poem cannot, therefore, be translated without losing some of its power to capture reality." There are, moreover, the problems of rhyme and meter, which, like idioms, can be reconstituted only using more or less different words in a different language.

Anderson's 1986 translation in *In the Storm of Roses* merits comparison with Hamburger's, which became the first published English translation in 1964. Between the two, many of the lines vary in phrasing while conveying identical meanings—such as "puts its veil back on" versus "takes the veil again"—while other variations amount to more significant differences. For example, in line 2, for the German "Orden," Hamburger uses "medals," Anderson "orders"; the former connotes a sense of achievement, the latter a sense of patterning. Generally, Hamburger tends to offer a more direct translation, while Anderson is more willing to alter phrasing to produce what is judged a better sound or feel in English. For example, in line 3, Hamburger's reference to the comet's "entrance" is closer to the German "Auftritt" than Anderson's more melodramatic "burst," which might be seen to (inaccurately) insert the suggestion of an explosion. In line 5, Hamburger accurately reproduces the German with "his work not forgotten," whereas Anderson alters the perspective with "remembers his chores." In line 19, Hamburger's "thousand angles" reflects more accurately than Anderson's "geometry" the German term "Tausendeck." In line 25, Hamburger's "great admiration" directly translates "größte Bewundrung," while there are simply no grounds for Anderson's license-taking insertion of the fantastic term "infinitely." Identifying other minor differences between the poems may help the reader perceive how daunting, given the arrays of options, the task of doing a poem full justice in translation can be.

Personification

Bachmann makes widespread use of personification in "To the Sun"—though, keeping the act of translation in mind, it is not always possible to distinguish *its* from *his* or *her* in certain languages. As such, specific pronoun usage should perhaps not be given excess weight. Regardless, human characteristics are attributed to nonhuman entities throughout the poem. The moon's light is said to be noble, thus attributing nobility, a moral quality, to the moon itself by extension. Art is said to put on a veil, like a reserved maiden, when the sun disappears. The images of sea and sand take shelter, as if they are vulnerable dependents who need protection from the shadows. The night flaunts her comets as if to lure the poet to unfaithfulness. Above all the sun itself is rendered human, in that he is seen to not just warm but take care of people, perhaps even to have a mission to do so.

Ambiguity

"To the Sun" contains a few ambiguities in terms of the identities of images and correspondences between phrasings. The wording in the second stanza is especially indeterminate as far as what exactly is occurring. Whatever other contextual ambiguity might be identified can be chalked up as the sort of modernist or surrealist positioning that lets some images float freely while contributing nonetheless to the overall sense of the poem. That is, the reader must simply take the images as they come.

More specific to Bachmann's work is the ambiguity of the identity of the narrator. Anderson, in his introduction to *In the Storm of Roses*, points out that this is well-trodden ground in critical studies, as her poetry, along with her later fiction, at times explicitly allows for a psychic duality of gender in the narrator. Some critics have taken the combination of an apparently female beloved with the presumably female narrator in poems such as "To the Sun" as evidence of what Anderson cites as a "lesbian aesthetics." But Bachmann suggested in a 1971 interview that the ambiguity or duality is more complex than a classification of sexuality. As

quoted by Anderson, she stated—not without ambiguity—

> One of my oldest memories...is that I can narrate only from a masculine position. But I have often asked myself: why is that? I didn't understand, not even in my short stories, why I had to adopt the masculine "I" so often....It was as if I had found my own person, that is, had not denied this feminine "I" and still placed emphasis on the masculine "I."

Anderson seems to throw up his hands in confusion in committing to simply referring to the poet as female, but he acknowledges that this is a "pragmatic decision," not "a resolution of the problem." English does not have a gender-neutral personal pronoun in popular usage—*one* and *one's* having their limits in terms of ready comprehensibility and accepted usage—such that some circles have been led to provide neologisms—such as *zhe* and *zher*—allowing for nongendered terms of reference to individuals. Given Bachmann's own statement, it would be hard to argue that the usage of any particular singular personal pronoun to refer to her poetic narrator would be incorrect.

HISTORICAL CONTEXT

Twentieth-Century Austria and a National Literature

The modern nation of Austria came into existence in the wake of World War I. First designated a duchy in the twelfth century, the region was under the rule of the royal Hapsburgs from the thirteenth century up to the twentieth, growing into a modest empire eventually ruled as the dual monarchy of Austria-Hungary. The German language is spoken in Austria, with variations and dialects in provincial regions. One of the Central powers during World War I, Austria-Hungary endured great human losses in defeat and, in the reconstruction of the region, saw the empire dissolved into separate nations; forbidden from even expressing alliance with Germany by naming itself "German-Austria," the nation settled for "Austria."

The interwar era was politically divisive, with rural conservative Catholics and progressive Social Democrats centered in Vienna sustaining a delicate balance, one that was disturbed by a Catholic paramilitary shooting of a Socialist man and boy during a confrontation in 1927. Meanwhile, Germany's special

COMPARE & CONTRAST

- **1950s:** Following the defeat of Germany as well as coerced but cooperative Austria in World War II, Austria is forbidden to form any political alliance or affiliation with Germany. After four-part occupation at the hands of France, Britain, the United States, and Russia, Austria finally regains status as an independent republic with the Austrian State Treaty of 1955.

  Today: Austria and Germany have very close ties as mutually most important trading partners, sources of tourists, and diplomatic allies, in addition to the requited cultural enrichments made possible by the shared language.

- **1950s:** Regarding the identity of (German-language) Austrian literature, Bachmann is inclined to pragmatically state in 1955 that, as paraphrased by Katrin Kohl and Ritchie Robertson, "Austrian writers should be considered part of German literature, since 'provincial' and 'regional' literary products had no chance of long-term survival."

  Today: Austrian literature in the twenty-first century retains the distinct identity notably attributed to it in the 1970s. Bachmann in 1973, compared Austria's German to the difference between British and American English, affirming that the difference in language amounts to a difference in thinking. In the late 1970s, scholar Herbert Zeman produced a history of Austrian literature intended to identify the unique cultural perspective that Austrian works represent.

- **1950s:** The Preis de Gruppe 47 is one of the most prestigious German literary awards in the postwar era. German-speaking Austrian writers largely aspire to such German awards.

  Today: Since 1977 the Ingeborg-Bachmann-Preis has been awarded in Klagenfurt, Austria, while the nation's Tage der Deutschsprachigen Literatur, or "Days of Literature in German," is a festival that attracts local as well as German and Swiss writers and offers courses, prizes, and international media exposure.

---

brand of National Socialism—Nazism—was on the rise, and Adolf Hitler, who was in fact a native of Branau am Inn, Austria, gained control of the Austrian Nazi Party in 1926. Electoral support for Nazi politicians in Austria rose steadily over the following decade. Conservative Catholics eventually held power in the person of Chancellor Engelbert Dollfuss, who sought to shut out Nazi influence—through 1934 some five thousand Nazis were arrested for political and other criminal offenses—as well as shut down restless Socialists: the Socialist paramilitary was disbanded, and when insurrection was briefly undertaken, leaving hundreds dead, the Social Democratic party was banned.

Unfortunately for Austria, Dollfuss's actions left the divided nation that much more vulnerable to Nazi takeover. Dollfuss was assassinated in 1934. Hitler told the succeeding chancellor in 1938 that Nazis were to be permitted to run the show, and when that chancellor sought to stage a referendum potentially deciding against any union with Germany, Hitler simply marched his army into Austria, in March 1938, to preempt such an undertaking. At this point, the majority of the populace was ready to welcome their native son with open arms. Union with Germany, the Anschluss, was rapidly carried out through official annexation into the Reich. Austria proved more than willing to participate in World War II on the side of Germany, with Austrians accounting for disproportionate numbers of death-camp staffs and Schutzstaffel (SS) officers. After the defeat of the Axis powers, Austria was occupied and rehabilitated and at last reconstituted as the Second Republic in 1955. Despite the dispensation of justice through postwar trials, some former Nazis surreptitiously gained and remained in positions of influence and power in Austria for decades.

Austria's political history in the twentieth century is highly relevant to a consideration of Bachmann's life and work for two reasons. To begin with, as a teenager, she herself experienced and was greatly distressed by the Nazi takeover of Austria, and the postwar recovery left her no less disillusioned about the integrity of her home nation. As expressed in her debut 1953 volume of poems, she saw the continuing influence of Germany as a cloud hanging over Austria. Yet she could not help but continue to be an Austrian writing and publishing in German. This inherent contradiction in perspectives in part accounts for her gravitating to and eventually settling in Italy, which as a land of light and warmth in her verse dramatically contrasts with the land of cold and darkness that Austria largely figures as.

The second point of relevance is that the linguistic and cultural alliance with Germany left the matter of "Austrian literature" in doubt, Austrian works generally being considered a part of broader German—that is, German-language—literature. The German literary master Thomas Mann (1875–1955), for one, sought to recognize an Austrian aesthetic but could only vaguely gesture toward one; as translated by Katrin Kohl and Ritchie Robertson in *A History of Austrian Literature, 1918–2000*, he responded to a 1936 survey on the matter by remarking, "The specific particularity of Austrian literature is not easy to define, but everyone perceives it." In his essay "Austrian Literature: A Concept," Klaus Zeyringer observes that the question became more urgent following the Austrian State Treaty of 1955. Leaders of the new republic were intent on fostering "Austrian national self-consciousness" and "the concept of a 'cultural nation.'" Thus, as Zeyringer relates, "in the fifties and sixties a clear connection evolved between the idea of Austria and the concept of an Austrian literature; it became a component in the construction of a national identity." The substantial role that Bachmann played in this construction stemmed more from her prose than from her two collections of poetry, though the originality of her poetry especially made her one of Austria's earliest and most prominent modernists.

A school of fish is one of the many things Bachmann lists that are dependent on the sun for life. (© Vilainecrevette / Shutterstock.com)

In the present day, Bachmann's name is mentioned often alongside those of other key contributors to the concept and body of Austrian literature, including Robert Musil, Hermann Broch, Peter Handke, Thomas Bernhard, Erich Fried, and Elfriede Jelinek.

CRITICAL OVERVIEW

Karen R. Achberger, in the *Dictionary of Literary Biography*, declares that Bachmann "was and is a legend" for her writings as well as for her public persona. The scholar points out that during Bachmann's lifetime and even more after her sensational death, the German-language press was highly interested in her personality and appearance. Bachmann was seen as "the blond, fairy-tale princess from Austria, fragile and girlish in appearance yet proud and wise, the shy, awkward, 'great' poet." Still, in *Understanding Ingeborg Bachmann*, Achberger asserts that Bachmann's poems "were received with almost unanimous praise and recognition, just as her decision to stop writing poetry was met with regret and sadness over the tremendous loss."

Anderson, in his introduction to *In the Storm of Roses*, observes that from the beginning Bachmann's poetry was recognized as so original that as far as literary classification goes, "she had created her own categories. Part of this originality was her characteristic fusion of abstract language with powerfully concrete images, or what was termed a 'philosophical language of images.';" While Bachmann's two volumes of poetry have not been published separately as such in the United States, Anderson says of her second collection, "Critics have generally concurred that it marks a strengthening of her poetic voice. The images are calmer and yet more powerfully direct." Anderson states that alongside the several "justly celebrated" poems that open *Anrufung des Großen Bären*, "To the Sun" is an "equally fine hymn of praise." Katrin Kohl similarly remarks, in "Austrian Poetry, 1918–2000," that "To the Sun" is a "hymnic celebration" which exemplifies the "powerful rhythms and richly evocative imagery" of Bachmann's verse. Anderson suggests that her later poems are "luminous, but suffused with a light that knows itself close to extinction."

A *Publishers Weekly* reviewer states that the poems in the first collected Bachmann edition in English, *Songs in Flight*, feature "profoundly striking" images and "forceful" entreaties to the reader. The reviewer suggests that, despite the tangible cold war context, Bachmann's verse is "transhistorical," a comment elaborated by Sara Lennox in the *Women's Review of Books* when she points out that *Darkness Spoken: Collected Poems of Ingeborg Bachmann* "allows English-speaking readers to understand how this brilliant writer grappled with a destructive era not entirely different from our own." In a comment suggestive of "To the Sun," Lennox writes, "In opposition to images of danger and destruction, this volume also powerfully invokes a utopian alternative, figured as fairy tale, erotic love, or a natural world of Mediterranean light and warmth."

In the *Harvard Review*, Brian Hanrahan praises the "passionate vituperation" with which Bachmann approaches political topics; he is just as impressed with how her "political and philosophical seriousness comes in a strikingly personal voice, a voice palpably confident in its poetic gifts, relishing its own formal and imaginative flair, at times profoundly and

shockingly intimate." He goes on to describe her as "a persistent and vividly imaginative explorer" of "the liminal spaces of the mind"—"moments of departure, doubt or change" that signify "the temporal and emotional complexity of what lies between people and between states." Hanrahan acknowledges the particular difficulty of translating Bachmann (calling Peter Filkins's work "patchy"; Lennox similarly notes of Filkins that "it's not always clear that his German is up to the task"). The difficulty, according to Hanrahan, lies in Bachmann's singular use of

> a language which is both dense and light, filled with historical and literary allusion, philosophical while concrete to the point of being visceral, a language whose rhythms are at times almost skip-along childish, but the very opposite of banal.

In the *Dictionary of Literary Biography*, Achberger affirms that Bachmann is "one of the most distinguished Austrian prose writers of the twentieth century" and "the most prominent German-language lyrical voice of the early post–World War II period." Hanrahan simply calls her "one of the most important of postwar European poets." In "On the Border of Speech," Filkins considers Bachmann "not only the most celebrated writer of the post-war generation, but also...the most important German poet" of her day.

CRITICISM

Michael Allen Holmes

Holmes is a writer with existential interests. In the following essay, he considers how "To the Sun" creates a shimmering sunlit realm in which the ideas of the sun and the companion mirror and merge into each other.

As a representative poem of Bachmann's, "To the Sun" well demonstrates the interest her work holds. Her diction is at once often very simple—she effectively states and restates that the sun is beautiful more than half a dozen times—and yet complex enough to render intriguing what might otherwise be ordinary formulations, such as with the suggestion, at the end of the second stanza, that the poet's companion "cuts short the last." Even if one rationally concludes that this must be a reference to the sails reflected in the companion's eyes, until at last she blinks, the link between language and actuality is

WHAT DO I READ NEXT?

- Having gained exposure to Bachmann's collected poetry, one might next turn to the lyrical, imagistic, reflective stories in her first short-fiction collection, *Das dreißigste Jahr* (1961), translated by Michael Bullock as *The Thirtieth Year* (1964).

- Paul Celan gave a stirring reading at the same Gruppe 47 meeting where Bachmann first appeared; she was the one to secure his presence there (though some sources indicate vice versa). Hailing from a Jewish family in a part of Romania now in Ukraine, Celan survived the Holocaust—though family members including his parents did not—and became one of German-language literature's most prominent poetic voices. A recent English edition of his verse is *Corona: Selected Poems of Paul Celan* (2013), translated by Susan H. Gillespie.

- The relationship between Celan and Bachmann is brought to light in *Correspondence: Ingeborg Bachmann and Paul Celan; With the Correspondences between Paul Celan and Max Frisch and between Paul Celan and Gisèle Celan-Lestrange* (2010), edited by Bertrand Badiou and translated by Wieland Hoban.

- The one writer from within the borders of modern-day Austria to be awarded the Nobel Prize in Literature is 2004 winner Elfried Jelinek (1946–), known for her exuberant voice and verbal ambition. Her novel *Die Ausgespertten* (1980), translated by Michael Hulse as *Wonderful, Wonderful Times* (1990), is set in postwar Vienna in the 1950s, the era of Bachmann's rise to fame.

- Rainer Maria Rilke, who was born in Prague when it was part of Austria-Hungary, is one of the most significant German-language poets in history. A recent bilingual English-German edition is *The Inner Sky: Poems, Notes, Dreams* (2010), selected and translated by Damion Searls.

- While readers may not be familiar with the works discussed in Margarete Lamb-Faffelberger's collection *Out from the Shadows: Essays on Contemporary Austrian Women Writers and Filmmakers* (1997), the book serves to introduce Austrian women who have contributed to the nation's culture, including popular culture. One essay considers Bachmann alongside Jelinek in terms of their fictional acts of resistance.

- Nature plays a prominent role in many of the existential considerations presented in *The Whispering Wind: Poetry by Young American Indians* (1972), written by students at the Institute of American Indian Arts and edited by Terry D. Allen.

---

tenuous enough that the reader likely lingers on the phrase awhile, as if it may yet hold some additional secret. The phrase might be seen to suggest the inevitable closing of the companion's eyes for good, in death, or perhaps the companion's closing her eyes to exclude the vision of the poet, once their relationship has come to an end, or something else entirely. The ambiguity of the phrasing allows for the words to work themselves into the reader's mind until some further conclusion is subconsciously or consciously reached.

Among such ambiguities of content in "To the Son," the ambiguity of the poet's relation to the companion is at the top of the list. The poem reads in many senses like a classic love poem, expressing a love so great that it verges on the painful, as when the poet imagines the angst to be brought about when one day the companion can no longer be seen. That both Bachmann and the companion in the poem are women by no means precludes a romantic scenario, and indeed some critics are inclined to expressly read such poems

> CALLING THE FIFTH STANZA, THE FIFTEENTH LINE, A FULCRUM—LIKE THE PIVOT POINT OF A SEESAW—ACCURATELY CONNOTES THE SHIFTING OF THE BALANCE OF THE POEM, BUT IT MAY BE MORE FITTING TO THINK OF THE LINE AS A SORT OF EXISTENTIAL MIRROR AT THE POEM'S CENTER."

as this one as embodying a lesbian perspective. Interestingly, though, Bachmann herself was demonstrably invested in several long-term heterosexual relationships that marked eras in her adult life, with no publicly known experimentation with homosexuality. The downward spiral of substance dependence that followed the dissipation of her relationship with Max Frisch suggests that she may even have been too invested in that relationship. Whether or not "To the Sun" speaks to the enlightening possibility of same-sex romance, it does appear to foreshadow the painful possibility of overdependence on another, a foreshadowing achieved through the subtle interplay of words and images regarding the sun and the companion.

That something curious may be going on is suggested as soon as one delves into the poem, which, according to the title, takes the form of an *apostrophe*, meaning a poem (or other verbal form) that directly addresses either a person or some typically personified thing. This poem was ostensibly written *to* the sun, which connotes not just praising it but singing its praises *to* it. In such a case, the sun would naturally be addressed in the second person, as *you*. By line 5 a certain *you* does appear, yet in such a formulation that the *you* would certainly seem to be someone other than the sun, since it would be redundant and misleading to surreptitiously state that the sun's life depends on the sun, which goes without saying. The *you* must surely be someone else. But this means that the poem is not an apostrophe after all, or at least not one to the sun—it is an apostrophe to the companion, despite what the title declares. Perhaps the title should have been "On the Sun" or "Of the Sun"; the discrepancy, in fact, may simply be attributable to the translation, and perhaps Bachmann really did intend

the sense of one of these titles. Still, the fact remains that the sun is the object of worship named in the title, but as the poem plays out, the poet's worship is directed not toward the sun but toward the companion. Already by the end of the first stanza, the juxtaposition of the mentions of poet and companion—their lives are placed side by side—suggests that even as the poet praises the beauty of the sun, the companion is the one the poet is looking toward. Or perhaps the poet is glancing back and forth from one to the other.

The second stanza, similarly, begins with unmistakable praise of the sun, now especially for its work ethic, but at length, here almost imperceptibly, shifts attention to the companion. The setting of the coast may initially serve as a framework for the hanging sun, but it soon becomes clear that the setting is more important as a framework for the poet and the companion, who are perhaps lying on a sandy beach. When the key word "mirrored" appears in line 8, the reader likely at first expects this word to relate to the sun, which is perhaps being mirrored off a shiny surface. But by the end of the line it is clear that the mirroring in question has little to do with the sun, as rather the sails are being mirrored in the eyes of the companion—which now the poet is quite plainly looking into. And yet that initial floating, unanchored sense of the word "mirrored" lingers in the reader's mind—as if there is perhaps more mirroring going on within the poem.

The same pattern recurs in the third, fourth, and sixth/seventh stanzas: the beauty of the sun in a certain sense is extolled, but the poetic focus inevitably shifts from the sun to the companion. The central fifth stanza functions aptly as a turning point in the poem, since the preceding stanzas contextualize the sun's beauty as stemming from its various traits—the sun is arguably the primary focus—while in the ensuing stanzas the role of the sun is dramatically reduced, as the poet boils the sun's virtue down to its illumination of other things for the poet to see, especially the companion. Calling the fifth stanza, the fifteenth line, a fulcrum—like the pivot point of a seesaw—accurately connotes the shifting of the balance of the poem, but it may be more fitting to think of the line as a sort of existential mirror at the poem's center. From one side the poet, standing in juxtaposition with the sun, looks in and sees the image of the companion; from the other side the poet, standing alongside the companion, looks in and sees the image of the sun. (Which side is which would be hard to say.) It as if the sun is the reflection of the companion, the companion the reflection of the sun. Veritably the poet cannot see one without seeing the other; their images and senses alike have become intertwined.

Considering the poem in this way, one realizes that the conflation of sun and companion has been taking place since the beginning. On the one hand it is easy enough to read all of the poem's *you*s as referring to the companion, not the sun, however the poem's title may be addressed. And yet the precise language referring to those *you*s by and large allows for the alternate conclusion that the *you* is also the sun—that the sun is being referred to sometimes in the third person, sometimes in the second. If the "your" in line 5 means "the sun's," this would indeed make for an unnecessary statement, that the sun's life depends on itself, but it is at least a true statement. In the second stanza, it may indeed be the companion's eye over which the sails are gliding, but the sun itself is readily conceived as an eye, allowing for lines 8–9 to suggest sails passing in front of a setting sun, until at last the sun closes its eye—that is, it sets—cutting short the image of the last sail in letting darkness overtake it. The identification of the sun with the "you" does make sense if the reader notes that the sun is the one completing chores in line 6, leading to the "you" being tired in line 9. Again in the third stanza, there would be redundancy if the "you" of line 11 is the sun—the poem would be stating in consecutive lines that the sun has disappeared—but redundancy is at least truthful in its consistency.

The flip side of the "you" potentially referring to the sun is the "sun" potentially referring to the companion. There does appear to be one significant verbal obstacle to this latter potentiality, since the companion, wearing a dress, is apparently female, while the sun, in line 6, is characterized as male. Yet inconsistency in translation may be accountable for this obstacle: the original German uses the term "ihr," conventionally translated as "her," in line 6 as well as line 5, but this is translated as "his" and "it," respectively, in these lines by both Hamburger and Anderson. It is possible that the translators have knowledge of German that suggests that the alternate translations are more suitable, but

it is also possible that they feared that referring to the sun as female would be confusing, since the companion is also female and the references to the two would thus be easily conflated. And yet Bachmann may have precisely intended for the references to be confusing and conflated—as if the poet herself or himself has conflated the senses of the sun and of the companion.

By the seventh stanza, the poem indeed makes the most sense if one conceives of the sun and the companion as conflated in the poet's mind. The poem's rapidly turning from a consideration of the land that belongs to the poet ("my land") to the image of the dress worn by the companion suggests a certain possessiveness on the part of the poet, as if the poet is jealously, perilously attached to the idea of being with, of possessing the companion. Meanwhile, that the companion wears a dress of billowing blue may not simply be meant to lead into a consideration of the blue sky; this may be a direct metaphorical description of the sun as, surrounded by a blue sky, wearing a billowing blue dress. In the eighth stanza the poet gets veritably lost in the blue of the companion's dress, or of the sun's sky, or of both. This stanza is especially notable for having no direct reference to the sun or any aspect of it, such as its light. Instead, the idea of inclement weather is evoked—perhaps a storm is on the horizon, as if this is what the poet must face in turning away from the companion/sun, while if the poet looks back directly at the companion/sun, the poet's mesmerized eyes are left burning and sore.

The poet, it appears, may not be able to hold on to the image of the sun-like companion much longer. There is a dependence on the sun/companion, as the poet acknowledges in the first and final stanzas, and yet a separation is inevitable, in death if not before. This, indeed, is the thrust of the final stanza. The poet revisits in lines 26–27 the celestial bodies brought up for comparison in the first stanza, closing up the poem's symmetric/circular pattern, but the crux of the stanza is line 28, where the poet at last leaves no question about the extent to which she or he is invested in the relationship with the companion. The loss of the poet's eyes figured in line 29 is likely not meant to connote death, since even afterward the poet will go on (consciously) lamenting this loss without end, as if this loss were the only thing to matter in the (living) world. It stands to reason that if the poet were

The speaker feels that the moon, the stars, and even comets cannot compare with the beauty of the sun. (© Bildagentur Zoonar GmbH | Shutterstock.com)

to at least retain the *presence* of the companion, the loss of the *image* of the companion would not be so devastating. Why would the lost sight of the companion be the *only* thing that mattered to the poet if the feel of the companion's presence remained? In the course of the final stanza, the poet clarifies that the inevitable loss of vision will be lamented not for the sake of the moon, or the stars, or the nighttime comets—but the poet does not go so far as to say that the loss will not be lamented for the sake of the sun. If the companion is really being enshrined as the most important thing in the poet's world, as the last stanza suggests, it would seem natural for the poet to go so far as to compare the companion to the sun. But such a comparison cannot make sense if the companion *is* the sun, or at least is the *poet's* sun—if, one way or another, the companion and sun are one. In the end, in the poet's mind, it seems that they are, and the loss of the poet's eyes is equivalent to the loss of the sun as well as to the loss of the companion, a doubly tragic loss indeed.

Source: Michael Allen Holmes, Critical Essay on "To the Sun," in *Poetry for Students*, Gale, Cengage Learning, 2016.

John Taylor
In the following excerpt, Taylor characterizes Bachmann as a distinctly Austrian poet.

Now and then someone reminds us that the Austrian poet, playwright, short-story writer, and novelist Ingeborg Bachmann (1926–1973) is too little known in English-speaking countries. May I myself take on this challenge? For once, the problem does not really derive from a lack of translations. In the late 1980s, Mark Anderson rendered an important selection of poems (*In the Storm of Roses*), while Mary Fran Gilbert and Michael Bullock, respectively, translated Bachmann's two short-story collections, *Three Paths to the Lake* (1972) and *The Thirtieth Year* (1961). These books were crowned in 1990 by Philip Boehm's version of *Malina* (1971), one of the most absorbing and complex European modernist novels.

Yet whereas the first translation mentioned is out of print and the three others sleep on a backlist, I can stroll up the rue du Pressoir, hop on Bus No. 3, drop by my provincial French bookstore, and find on the shelves a cheap paperback copy of Philippe Jaccottet's French version of *Malina*, which dates to 1973. Jaccottet's own reputation may somewhat keep the novel in the public eye in France, though I notice that his name is not on the front cover.

Shouldn't we be lending our ears to a poet capable of writing such perpetually thought-provoking aphorisms as "What separates you, is you," as Peter Filkins renders "Was dich trennt, bist du" in an important new American edition of Bachmann's collected poems? Or to a poet who meditates relentlessly on "the one / and only world," all the while admitting: "to know / just whose world is forbidden to me"?

Bachmann indeed explores the fundamental, though—for her—not always unbridgeable opposition of the "I" and the World (or the Other). Her writing is tensely, if obliquely, autobiographical, all the while drawing on German romanticism, biblical symbolism, folklore, fairy-tales, Viennese psychoanalysis, and the philosophy of language. She engages with multifaceted aspects of personal identity, yet never neglects the responsibilities of literature after the Shoah, the treacheries of her homeland, the destruction of nature, the battle of the sexes, the ambiguities of gender, as well as exiles and imprisonments of all kinds. "One must rush . . . ," she writes, "from one land / into another, beneath the rainbow, / the compass points stuck in the heart / and night the radius." Time and again, she evokes estrangement in a devastated contemporary world in which the impact of the past on individuals nonetheless seems decisive. "A sled brocaded with history," she remarks in "Curriculum Vitae," "sweeps over me (I cannot stop it)." Elsewhere, a six-line poem pessimistically ends: "Our godhead, / history, has ordered for us a grave / from which there is no resurrection." Despite or because of this determinism, felt by so many other Europeans after the war and even today, Bachmann also constantly ponders the possibilities of liberation.

. . . Filkins's edition refutes the critical myth that Bachmann gave up verse for fiction and play writing after her second collection, *Invocation of the Great Bear* (1956). Even if she chose not to publish other poems, Bachmann wrote verse until about 1967, when the *Death Styles* project took up all her energy. She always worked in various literary genres, sometimes simultaneously, a creative flexibility that can be perceived par excellence in *Malina* and even in single long poems.

The best example is "A Monologue of Prince Myshkin," a "ballet pantomime" that was set to music by Bachmann's lifelong friend, the composer Hans Werner Henze. This dramatic poem concludes *Borrowed Time* (1953), a first collection published to acclaim only one year after the event that made her famous overnight: a reading in Munich with Paul Celan—another poet with whom she had an unhappy love affair—and members of the Gruppe 47, a postwar association of major German writers. According to Filkins, "the German literary world was immediately swept away by the young blonde-haired poet reading her poems in a near whisper." (Take up the hint: read her poems in a whisper.)

Filkins's introduction is insightful. At the onset, he offers a deep-probing summary of Bachmann's originality, implicitly formulating

reasons why engrained Anglo-American realism and empiricism have so much conceptual trouble accommodating her poetics:

> Bridging the poetry of experience and the poetry of ideas, Bachmann's vision is one continually fixed upon the terror she perceived within the quotidian, as well as the need to elicit the unspoken, primeval truth that lies just beyond the pale of the "unspeakable." In following this trajectory, Bachmann's poems conduct a journey *in* thought *towards* feeling, for hers is not a poetry of recollected experience, nor a poetry of ideas about experience, but rather a poetry that enacts *the experience of ideas* in order to evoke the nature of true feeling, despite the impediments that exist in cognitive speech.

Darkness Spoken can be accompanied by *Last Living Words: The Ingeborg Bachmann Reader* (Green Integer). Translated by Lilian M. Friedberg, the volume gathers eight key stories and fourteen of the best-known poems. As English poems, Friedberg's versions are occasionally livelier than Filkins's. When Bachmann evokes, in the all-important "Great Landscape Near Vienna," a "Lächeln Ja" and the "Lächeln Nein," literally a "smile of Yes and the smile of No" (Filkins), Friedberg interestingly construes the words as a "smirking yes and the smirking no." But in the distich introducing this image, Bachmann writes "unter den Pappeln am Römerstein grab ich / nach dem Schauplatz vielvölkriger Trauer." Filkins accurately translates the lines as "under the poplars I dig by a Roman stone, / searching for the theater of many peopled grief," whereas Friedberg characteristically interprets: "beneath the poplars at the Roman obelisk, I dig / for the buried arena of multi-national tragedy." Extrapolations like "multinational" are debatable: Bachmann usually bases multiple meanings on a relatively concrete, physical, image ("peoples" as opposed to the more abstract "nations"); and these images are habitually expressed in phrasal contexts somewhat removed from immediate colloquial patterns. Moreover, I have difficulties imagining an "obelisk" beneath poplars, as opposed to the comparatively much smaller Roman steles, landmarks or engraved "stones," as Bachmann literally writes, that are frequently found in Europe.

Always closer to the German, Filkins is more attentive to the rhymes and meters of the original; and his English is surer. In "Night Flight," Friedberg renders "Nenn's den Status der Einsamen, / in dem sich das Stauen vollzieht" ungrammatically as "Call it the status of solitaries / where astonishment occurs." Filkins rightly proceeds: "Call it the status of the lonely / in whom wonder still occurs." And in "Wood and Shavings," Filkins correctly offers "But in wood, / as long as it is still green, and with bile, / as long as it is still bitter, I am / willing to write what happened at the start!", while Friedberg more ambiguously and incompletely proposes "But / as long as it is still green, and bitter gall, / I would write into the wood / what was in the beginning!" However, Friedberg's phrase "what was in the beginning" echoes biblical phraseology, which is often conjured up in Bachmann's verse, not to mention in *Malina*. I cannot untangle why the latter translator begins "Great Landscape Near Vienna" with a quatrain that Filkins publishes separately (and correctly, I think) as "In the Storm of Roses." As to the reliable versions of *Darkness Spoken*, an oversight occurs in "The Tightened Lip," dedicated to the poet Nelly Sachs (1891–1970), who despite her 1966 Nobel Prize also remains mostly unknown to English readers. Filkins oddly renders "und wie du schweigst, wenn du mündig bist" by "and how silent one becomes when you come of age" instead of "and how silent you become."

With *The Night Begins with a Question*, Carcanet and the Scottish Poetry Library have co-published a pleasant anthology of twenty-five Austrian poems, written by as many poets. Memorable are an atmospheric prose text by Ilse Aichinger (b. 1921), which gives the title to the book, and a sensitive love poem by Evelyn Schlag (b. 1952). Schlag charts the progress of a privileged moment of self-awareness as she feels—but this we learn only at the end—"the resonance / Of your casual words / That I had been thinking over." The diction may appear simplistic, but it convincingly stages not only this delicate mental meeting of the woman and her seeming lover, but also an apperception, in the sense that Kant, Leibniz, and Maine de Biran gave to the term. After the poet puts her "fingers to the shadows / under [her] eyes," her mind becomes aware of its own movements. It is as if the self also became an "other" during the kind of border-crossing experience that Bachmann also described. "My fingers belonged to a being / From a world with different measures," admits Schlag, "It was an often-performed / Gesture but relieved of its weight / Capable only of the echo of a pressure." The anthology also comprises pieces by three of Bachmann's contemporaries

whose work is familiar to American "language poets": Friederike Mayröcker (b. 1924), Ernst Jandl (1925–2000), and H. C. Artmann (1921–2000). Austrian literature has long been marked not only by philosophical quests, but also by linguistic experimentation. Bachmann, however, was concerned less with language as a medium that could be boldly manipulated, than with the psychological and ontological implications of speech.

The anthology opens with her "Bohemia, a Country by the Sea." Iain Bamforth's version captures Bachmann's poetic music, which is forthright here, as well as its meanings. His translation reminds us that the lyric factor in her work must never be underestimated. Here, she wittily and also sadly evokes her exile from Austria, symbolically merged with her relentless poetic task of pushing language beyond limits:

> If I'm not the one, then someone else will do just as
> well.
> If a word here lies beside me, it'll be my borderline.
> If Bohemia's still a country by the sea, I can believe
> in the sea again.
> the sea, I can hope for land.
> (. . .)
> Still I border on a word and on another country,
> verging more closely, if never very much, on what
> exists,
> a penniless Bohemian, a vagabond without ties,
> my sole talent to be at sea at the sight of my chosen
> land.

In his introduction, Iain Galbraith recalls a discussion, in 1967, between Bachmann and the exiled Austrian poet Erich Fried (1921–1998), whose claustrophobic portrait of Georg Trakl is also included in *The Night Begins with a Question*. Fried wondered about the "Austrian elisions" that Bachmann had employed in this poem, in contrast to the standard German in which she usually wrote. Some two decades later, Thomas Bernhard (1931–1989) had the main character of his novel *Extinction* (1986) define this same poem as "so Austrian, but at the same time so permeated by the whole world, and by the world surrounding this world." As you take Ingeborg Bachmann's complex and compelling poems in hand, remember this clue as well.

Source: John Taylor, "Ingeborg Bachmann: Complex and Compelling," in *Antioch Review*, Vol. 65, No. 4, Fall 2007, pp. 758–65.

Karen R. Achberger

In the following excerpt, Achberger gives an overview of the themes in the collection that includes "To the Sun."

The approaching night of the earlier collection has now arrived, leaving the constellations in the heavens to arouse the imagination and fantasy. As if in the face of the undeniable signs of restoration in postwar Germany, the only recourse appeared to be flight into the world of magic and myth. Bachmann's own flight to Italy, like that of many German intellectuals after the war, offered another world, where the creative imagination could feed on a culture rich in ancient myths and customs. Her second and final volume of poetry. *Anrufung des Großen Bären*, which appeared in 1956. three years after the first, focuses on the mythological and metaphysical in the context of the largely Mediterranean landscape. These are her poems of Italy, written between 1953 and 1956 while she was living with Henze in her "firstborn land."

The night theme is a central one in this volume, as is the dark side of the world for Bachmann's later writing. The constellation Ursa Major, referred to in the title *Anrufung des Großen Bären*, is visible only at night, and one of the poems in this collection, "Curriculum Vitae," makes it explicit: "Always the night. And no day." In the face of this night, Bachmann offers a mythical layer of meaning, a second level of reference in which other truths can be told. In turning here to mythical images, Bachmann has taken a direction that becomes more prominent in her prose writing, where she often counters a hopeless "reality" with a utopian world of mythic fantasy.

The end of all illusions is clearly announced in the opening poem. "Das Spiel ist aus" ("The Game Is Over"). While ship and water metaphors continue to prevail, the message they carry has changed significantly over the previous volume. While the adult reader was called to social positions and actions in the earlier poems, "The Game Is Over" offers an imaginary conversation of a child talking to her little brother in an intimate family setting. The moral call to vigilance and upright posture in "Leaving Port" is now the invitation to go to bed: "We must go to bed, dearest, the game is over." The socially responsible adult is now the child playing in the private world of family and fantasy. The journey itself has now become a voyage into the world of dreams and illusion, an imaginary trip "down the sky." The hope implicit in the earlier collection has yielded here to explicit resignation: "we will sink and die." In

> WITH THE SIMPLICITY OF A FIVE-NOTE SCALE DESCENDING TO AND THEN ASCENDING FROM THE TONIC KEYNOTE (5-4-3-2-1-2-3-4-5), WITH THE CURVE OF AN ORBIT OR AN HOURGLASS, THE POEM COUNTERS THE DESTRUCTION OF THE GREAT BEAR ON THE NIGHT SIDE OF THE EARTH WITH AN APPRECIATION OF LIFE'S BEAUTY UNDER THE SUN."

its regression into the private world of the child's imagination, this poem is typical of the volume as a whole and of the spirit of the times. At the same moment that the poet is retreating into the inner world, she is reaching out into the cosmos, to the Great Bear, whose mention in the title also underscores the animal and folktale motifs common to these poems.

Although departure and flight are key themes in the second collection, the poems also introduce metaphysical themes which become increasingly important in Bachmann's later writing: death and destruction, opposing parts of the self, the painful dualism of thinking and sensuality, consciousness and undivided oneness with nature. The title poem of the volume opens with an exchange between shepherds on earth and the Great Bear in the sky. The humans challenge the bear to come down to earth and appear before them. The bear answers that they, as humans, are of no significance, likening them to the scales of a pine cone which the bear hunts, snorts on, and tests with its muzzle. In the ancient symbol of the celestial Great Bear—that "zottige Nacht" (shaggy night). as the shepherds call it—rests the threat of destruction and the consciousness of downfall, a fear of that distant and uncanny supernatural force whose teeth and claws are indifferent toward humans at the same time that they break gratuitously into human lives. All human striving, as the final two stanzas of the poem seem to suggest, is of no consequence in effecting, or in comprehending, the bear's actions.

The threatening darkness of the night sky has its counterpart in the Mediterranean landscape flooded with the light of the southern sun, just as the poem "An die Sonne" ("To the Sun") constitutes a counterpart to the title poem of the collection. In contrast to the destruction and threats of the Great Bear on the dark side of the earth, the hymn in praise of the sun celebrates an elemental existence without alienation or repression, centered around the one sentence, which itself is almost circular: "Nothing more beautiful under the sun than to be under the sun . . . ." The twenty-nine lines of the poem are structured symmetrically around this central line with four sentences on each side, the first and last sentence with five lines, the second and penultimate with four, then three, and then two lines each. With the simplicity of a five-note scale descending to and then ascending from the tonic keynote (5-4-3-2-1-2-3-4-5), with the curve of an orbit or an hourglass, the poem counters the destruction of the Great Bear on the night side of the earth with an appreciation of life's beauty under the sun. It is not only the sun itself but a simple existence for its own sake that the poem celebrates, just as it laments the end of all that beauty in the final line as "the unavoidable loss of my eyes."

The danger of consumerism is addressed in the poem "Reklame" ("Advertisement"), a concern already voiced in "Autumn Maneuver" from the earlier volume. In the earlier poem, the materialism of modern consumer society is exposed as repressing or distracting from "the throb of guilt" in the human heart. Bargain tours to sunny islands leave the poet again and again "in the cellar of my heart, sleepless." In the later poem, the theme is intensified to the point where the really important questions about human existence and death are subdued by repeated fragments of advertising slogans offering pat answers and easy solutions to all of life's problems. The poem has a contrapuntal structure in which two voices are interwoven: a questioning voice, and a mollifying voice continually repeating and varying slogans in italics. The narcoticizing, brainwashing effect of the advertisement is named explicitly in the poem's longest line: "*in the dream laundry you haven't a care, not a care.*" The voice of the advertising clichés is ultimately brought to silence, leaving a blank penultimate line and the questioning voice wondering in unaccompanied solo what happens "when dead silence / sets in."

The poem "Advertisement" shares important aspects with other works by Bachmann that appear to have been written either shortly before or after this same period: her last two radio plays and her novel, *Malina*. The most obvious visual aspect is the use of italics to separate part of the text and remove it to another level of the poem. After attempts in her poetry to indicate another voice or level of speaking orthographically through the use of parentheses. Bachmann employed italics as a separating device most extensively in *Malina*, where the "beautiful book" the narrator attempts to write throughout the novel is set off from the rest of the narrative, as a countertext of sorts. As in "Advertisement" the "normal" text in *Malina* survives the italicized countertext: the novel's passage in italics cannot be sustained and its final section is explicitly revoked by the narrator in the normal text.

"Advertisement" also calls to mind the contrapuntal voice leading a year earlier in the radio play *Die Zikaden* between the soothing voice of Antonio and the unsettling questions of the island inhabitants. Like the intoxicating tones of Antonio's voice, the narcotizing effect of the advertising voice is associated with music. The poem's slogans repeat three times the phrase "*with music,*" expanded to "*merrily and with music,*" also in the variation "*merrily . . . with music*" to underscore the inebriating potential of music. Like the advertisements, Antonio is ultimately unable to respond to the islanders' questions and must simply withdraw from their needs.

In Bachmann's last radio play, *The Good God of Manhattan*, first broadcast two years after "Advertisement" appeared, a chorus of the city's public "Voices" cite a litany of advertising slogans and clichés in endless repetition and variation. Throughout the play, the lovers are bombarded with commands and slogans, boldly printed in the text in all capital letters: "THINK ABOUT IT WHILE THERE IS TIME / GIVE GOD A CHANCE / BRIGHTEN UP YOUR LIFE. . . ." Like the italics in "Advertisement," the all-capital letters in *The Good God of Manhattan* serve to set off the text of the city's "voices" from the remainder of the play's dialogue. Both the radio play and the poem stem from the period immediately following Bachmann's visit to New York City in July 1955. Her first encounter with a technologically advanced, capitalist society seems to have left her shocked at the constant bombardment with indoctrinating slogans in the mass media.

The influence of Bachmann's close friendship and collaboration with Hans Werner Henze is obvious in both volumes of her poetry and in her second radio play. Just as the "Myschkin" monologue for Henze's ballet pantomime had appeared at the end of the first volume of poetry in 1953, so her cycle of fifteen poems. "Lieder auf der Flucht" ("Songs in Flight"), comprised the fourth and final section of her second collection of poems three years later. While he did not set these poems to music, the personal background to the song cycle seems to have been Bachmann's painful realization of the impossibility of a marriage relationship with Henze, a homosexual with whom she enjoyed a long and productive friendship. The cycle is informed by a tension between ecstatic, utopian love and the lonely reality of the relationship between man and woman. This, together with the cycle's extensive subtextual quotations and allusions to other literary works, anticipates the "Death Styles" cycle she was to begin writing a decade later. The five *Lieder von einer Insel* (Songs from an Island) in the third section of the same volume were set to music by Henze in 1964 under the title *Chorphantasie* (Choral Fantasy). He also composed the music for her second radio play, *Die Zikaden*, which warns of the dangers of aestheticism and of living on islands.

A central theme of Bachmann's writing after 1956 is the impotence of language, the impossibility of using words to express the truths of human existence. More than a resounding of that specifically Austrian remorse at linguistic shortcomings in general, associated most frequently with Hofmannsthal's "Chandos crisis" and Wittgenstein's "language skepticism," Bachmann's emphasis is directed specifically at the illegitimacy of the poetic word in the face of the horrors of historical reality. When she insists in her Frankfurt Lectures on the need for art to be a force for change, one can see this aesthetic in the context of her own false reception. One can also appreciate her turn from poetry to prose at this time in the context of the reception her poetry was given. To convey her perceptions of the times, she needed a different genre, one that was less ambiguous and less artistic. It was not her personal suffering and painful insights about the world that she wanted to serve up in beautiful form, but the connections between that suffering and the insensitivity of both pre- and postwar German society—suffering, decay, death, destruction, those recurrent themes in her work, not in a timeless, vague world, but in their concrete, historical and social context, a context she may have felt she could better convey in prose genres. . . .

Source: Karen R. Achberger, "The Poems," in *Understanding Ingeborg Bachmann*, University of South Carolina Press, 1995, pp. 16–20.

SOURCES

Achberger, Karen, "Ingeborg Bachmann," in *Dictionary of Literary Biography*, Vol. 85, *Austrian Fiction Writers after 1914*, edited by James Hardin and Donald G. Daviau, Gale Research, 1989, pp. 24–39.

———, "The Poems," in *Understanding Ingeborg Bachmann*, University of South Carolina Press, 1995, pp. 12–30.

Anderson, Mark, ed. and trans., "Introduction: Poet on the Border," in *In the Storm of Roses: Selected Poems by Ingeborg Bachmann*, Princeton University Press, 1986, pp. 3–23.

Bachmann, Ingeborg, "An die Sonne/To the Sun," in *In the Storm of Roses: Selected Poems by Ingeborg Bachmann*, edited and translated by Mark Anderson, Princeton University Press, 1986, pp. 132–35.

———, "Biographical Note," in *In the Storm of Roses: Selected Poems by Ingeborg Bachmann*, edited and translated by Mark Anderson, Princeton University Press, 1986, pp. 193–94.

Boyers, Robert, "Many Types of Ambiguity: The Enigma of Ingeborg Bachmann," in *Harper's*, Vol. 310, No. 1859, April 2005, pp. 92–97.

Filkins, Peter, ed. and trans., "On the Border of Speech," in *Songs in Flight: The Collected Poems of Ingeborg Bachmann*, Marsilio Publishers, 1994, pp. xv–xxxiii.

Hanrahan, Brian, Review of *Darkness Spoken: Collected Poems of Ingeborg Bachmann*, in *Harvard Review*, No. 32, June 2007, pp. 162–64.

Kohl, Katrin, "Austrian Poetry, 1918–2000," in *A History of Austrian Literature, 1918–2000*, edited by Katrin Kohl and Ritchie Robertson, Camden House, 2006, pp. 146–47.

Kohl, Katrin, and Ritchie Robertson, eds., Introduction to *A History of Austrian Literature, 1918–2000*, Camden House, 2006, pp. 1–20.

Lennox, Sara, "Harder Days Are Coming," in *Women's Review of Books*, Vol. 24, No. 5, September–October 2007, pp. 26–28.

Review of *Songs in Flight: The Collected Poems of Ingeborg Bachmann*, in *Publishers Weekly*, Vol. 241, No. 44, October 31, 1994, p. 54.

"Waldner: 'Relations between Germany and Austria Are Based on Close Friendship and Cooperation,'" Federal Ministry for European and International Affairs, Republic of Austria website, May 17, 2011, http://www.bmeia.gv.at/en/the-ministry/press/announcements/2011/waldner-relations-between-germany-and-austria-are-based-on-close-friendship-and-cooperation/ (accessed May 24, 2015).

Zeyringer, Klaus, "Austrian Literature: A Concept," in *Shadows of the Past: Austrian Literature of the Twentieth Century*, edited by Hans Schulte and Gerald Chapple, Peter Lang, 2009, pp. 1–33.

FURTHER READING

Bjorklund, Beth, ed., *Contemporary Austrian Poetry: An Anthology*, Fairleigh Dickinson University Press, 1986.
    The fact that this collection is dated means that, despite its title, the poems included extend as far back as 1945, covering all of Bachmann's output. She and Celan are cited as the era's two most important poets.

Hanlin, Todd C., *Beyond Vienna: Contemporary Literature from the Austrian Provinces*, Ariadne Press, 2008.
    This collection focuses on nine twenty-first-century authors who, like Bachmann, hail from provincial Austria, rather than urban Vienna, and whose worldviews and writings reflect their distance from the nation's cultural center.

Heaton, John, *Wittgenstein for Beginners*, illustrated by Judy Groves, Icon Books, 1994.
    The greatest philosophical influence on Bachmann was her Vienna-based contemporary Ludwig Wittgenstein, especially for his considerations of the limits of language. Heaton's two-hundred-page text is designed to be accessible to those with even the most limited philosophical background.

Koch, Kenneth, and Kate Farrell, eds., *Talking to the Sun: An Illustrated Anthology of Poems for Young People*, Macmillan, 1985.
    This volume, produced on behalf of the Metropolitan Museum of Art, contains traditional hymns and songs as well as representative works from nearly every famous English-language poet in history, including Shakespeare, Dickinson, Blake, Tennyson, Frost, Whitman, Hughes, and Ashbery, along with a few international names, such as Rilke, Lorca, Neruda, and Breton.

SUGGESTED SEARCH TERMS

Ingeborg Bachmann AND "To the Sun"

Ingeborg Bachmann AND Collected Poems OR Selected Poems

Ingeborg Bachmann AND Austrian poetry

Ingeborg Bachmann AND German literature

Austria AND German literature

Austrian culture AND Second Republic

Ingeborg Bachmann AND Italy

Ingeborg Bachmann AND Max Frisch

Glossary of Literary Terms

A

Abstract: Used as a noun, the term refers to a short summary or outline of a longer work. As an adjective applied to writing or literary works, abstract refers to words or phrases that name things not knowable through the five senses.

Accent: The emphasis or stress placed on a syllable in poetry. Traditional poetry commonly uses patterns of accented and unaccented syllables (known as feet) that create distinct rhythms. Much modern poetry uses less formal arrangements that create a sense of freedom and spontaneity.

Aestheticism: A literary and artistic movement of the nineteenth century. Followers of the movement believed that art should not be mixed with social, political, or moral teaching. The statement "art for art's sake" is a good summary of aestheticism. The movement had its roots in France, but it gained widespread importance in England in the last half of the nineteenth century, where it helped change the Victorian practice of including moral lessons in literature.

Affective Fallacy: An error in judging the merits or faults of a work of literature. The "error" results from stressing the importance of the work's effect upon the reader—that is, how it makes a reader "feel" emotionally, what it does as a literary work—instead of stressing its inner qualities as a created object, or what it "is."

Age of Johnson: The period in English literature between 1750 and 1798, named after the most prominent literary figure of the age, Samuel Johnson. Works written during this time are noted for their emphasis on "sensibility," or emotional quality. These works formed a transition between the rational works of the Age of Reason, or Neoclassical period, and the emphasis on individual feelings and responses of the Romantic period.

Age of Reason: See *Neoclassicism*

Age of Sensibility: See *Age of Johnson*

Agrarians: A group of Southern American writers of the 1930s and 1940s who fostered an economic and cultural program for the South based on agriculture, in opposition to the industrial society of the North. The term can refer to any group that promotes the value of farm life and agricultural society.

Alexandrine Meter: See *Meter*

Allegory: A narrative technique in which characters representing things or abstract ideas are used to convey a message or teach a lesson. Allegory is typically used to teach moral, ethical, or religious lessons but is sometimes used for satiric or political purposes.

Alliteration: A poetic device where the first consonant sounds or any vowel sounds in words or syllables are repeated.

Allusion: A reference to a familiar literary or historical person or event, used to make an idea more easily understood.

Amerind Literature: The writing and oral traditions of Native Americans. Native American literature was originally passed on by word of mouth, so it consisted largely of stories and events that were easily memorized. Amerind prose is often rhythmic like poetry because it was recited to the beat of a ceremonial drum.

Analogy: A comparison of two things made to explain something unfamiliar through its similarities to something familiar, or to prove one point based on the acceptedness of another. Similes and metaphors are types of analogies.

Anapest: See *Foot*

Angry Young Men: A group of British writers of the 1950s whose work expressed bitterness and disillusionment with society. Common to their work is an anti-hero who rebels against a corrupt social order and strives for personal integrity.

Anthropomorphism: The presentation of animals or objects in human shape or with human characteristics. The term is derived from the Greek word for "human form."

Antimasque: See *Masque*

Antithesis: The antithesis of something is its direct opposite. In literature, the use of antithesis as a figure of speech results in two statements that show a contrast through the balancing of two opposite ideas. Technically, it is the second portion of the statement that is defined as the "antithesis"; the first portion is the "thesis."

Apocrypha: Writings tentatively attributed to an author but not proven or universally accepted to be their works. The term was originally applied to certain books of the Bible that were not considered inspired and so were not included in the "sacred canon."

Apollonian and Dionysian: The two impulses believed to guide authors of dramatic tragedy. The Apollonian impulse is named after Apollo, the Greek god of light and beauty and the symbol of intellectual order. The Dionysian impulse is named after Dionysus, the Greek god of wine and the symbol of the unrestrained forces of nature. The Apollonian impulse is to create a rational, harmonious world, while the Dionysian is to express the irrational forces of personality.

Apostrophe: A statement, question, or request addressed to an inanimate object or concept or to a nonexistent or absent person.

Archetype: The word archetype is commonly used to describe an original pattern or model from which all other things of the same kind are made. This term was introduced to literary criticism from the psychology of Carl Jung. It expresses Jung's theory that behind every person's "unconscious," or repressed memories of the past, lies the "collective unconscious" of the human race: memories of the countless typical experiences of our ancestors. These memories are said to prompt illogical associations that trigger powerful emotions in the reader. Often, the emotional process is primitive, even primordial. Archetypes are the literary images that grow out of the "collective unconscious." They appear in literature as incidents and plots that repeat basic patterns of life. They may also appear as stereotyped characters.

Argument: The argument of a work is the author's subject matter or principal idea.

Art for Art's Sake: See *Aestheticism*

Assonance: The repetition of similar vowel sounds in poetry.

Audience: The people for whom a piece of literature is written. Authors usually write with a certain audience in mind, for example, children, members of a religious or ethnic group, or colleagues in a professional field. The term "audience" also applies to the people who gather to see or hear any performance, including plays, poetry readings, speeches, and concerts.

Automatic Writing: Writing carried out without a preconceived plan in an effort to capture every random thought. Authors who engage in automatic writing typically do not revise their work, preferring instead to preserve the revealed truth and beauty of spontaneous expression.

Avant-garde: A French term meaning "vanguard." It is used in literary criticism to describe new writing that rejects traditional approaches to literature in favor of innovations in style or content.

B

Ballad: A short poem that tells a simple story and has a repeated refrain. Ballads were originally intended to be sung. Early ballads, known as folk ballads, were passed down through generations, so their authors are often unknown. Later ballads composed by known authors are called literary ballads.

Baroque: A term used in literary criticism to describe literature that is complex or ornate in style or diction. Baroque works typically express tension, anxiety, and violent emotion. The term "Baroque Age" designates a period in Western European literature beginning in the late sixteenth century and ending about one hundred years later. Works of this period often mirror the qualities of works more generally associated with the label "baroque" and sometimes feature elaborate conceits.

Baroque Age: See *Baroque*

Baroque Period: See *Baroque*

Beat Generation: See *Beat Movement*

Beat Movement: A period featuring a group of American poets and novelists of the 1950s and 1960s—including Jack Kerouac, Allen Ginsberg, Gregory Corso, William S. Burroughs, and Lawrence Ferlinghetti—who rejected established social and literary values. Using such techniques as stream of consciousness writing and jazz-influenced free verse and focusing on unusual or abnormal states of mind—generated by religious ecstasy or the use of drugs—the Beat writers aimed to create works that were unconventional in both form and subject matter.

Beat Poets: See *Beat Movement*

Beats, The: See *Beat Movement*

Belles-lettres: A French term meaning "fine letters" or "beautiful writing." It is often used as a synonym for literature, typically referring to imaginative and artistic rather than scientific or expository writing. Current usage sometimes restricts the meaning to light or humorous writing and appreciative essays about literature.

Black Aesthetic Movement: A period of artistic and literary development among African Americans in the 1960s and early 1970s. This was the first major African-American artistic movement since the Harlem Renaissance and was closely paralleled by the civil rights and black power movements. The black aesthetic writers attempted to produce works of art that would be meaningful to the black masses. Key figures in black aesthetics included one of its founders, poet and playwright Amiri Baraka, formerly known as LeRoi Jones; poet and essayist Haki R. Madhubuti, formerly Don L. Lee; poet and playwright Sonia Sanchez; and dramatist Ed Bullins.

Black Arts Movement: See *Black Aesthetic Movement*

Black Comedy: See *Black Humor*

Black Humor: Writing that places grotesque elements side by side with humorous ones in an attempt to shock the reader, forcing him or her to laugh at the horrifying reality of a disordered world.

Black Mountain School: Black Mountain College and three of its instructors—Robert Creeley, Robert Duncan, and Charles Olson—were all influential in projective verse, so poets working in projective verse are now referred as members of the Black Mountain school.

Blank Verse: Loosely, any unrhymed poetry, but more generally, unrhymed iambic pentameter verse (composed of lines of five two-syllable feet with the first syllable accented, the second unaccented). Blank verse has been used by poets since the Renaissance for its flexibility and its graceful, dignified tone.

Bloomsbury Group: A group of English writers, artists, and intellectuals who held informal artistic and philosophical discussions in Bloomsbury, a district of London, from around 1907 to the early 1930s. The Bloomsbury Group held no uniform philosophical beliefs but did commonly express an aversion to moral prudery and a desire for greater social tolerance.

Bon Mot: A French term meaning "good word." A *bon mot* is a witty remark or clever observation.

Breath Verse: See *Projective Verse*

Burlesque: Any literary work that uses exaggeration to make its subject appear ridiculous, either by treating a trivial subject with profound seriousness or by treating a dignified subject frivolously. The word "burlesque" may also be used as an adjective, as in "burlesque show," to mean "striptease act."

C

Cadence: The natural rhythm of language caused by the alternation of accented and unaccented syllables. Much modern poetry—notably free verse—deliberately manipulates cadence to create complex rhythmic effects.

Caesura: A pause in a line of poetry, usually occurring near the middle. It typically corresponds to a break in the natural rhythm or sense of the line but is sometimes shifted to create special meanings or rhythmic effects.

Canzone: A short Italian or Provencal lyric poem, commonly about love and often set to music. The *canzone* has no set form but typically contains five or six stanzas made up of seven to twenty lines of eleven syllables each. A shorter, five- to ten-line "envoy," or concluding stanza, completes the poem.

Carpe Diem: A Latin term meaning "seize the day." This is a traditional theme of poetry, especially lyrics. A *carpe diem* poem advises the reader or the person it addresses to live for today and enjoy the pleasures of the moment.

Catharsis: The release or purging of unwanted emotions—specifically fear and pity—brought about by exposure to art. The term was first used by the Greek philosopher Aristotle in his *Poetics* to refer to the desired effect of tragedy on spectators.

Celtic Renaissance: A period of Irish literary and cultural history at the end of the nineteenth century. Followers of the movement aimed to create a romantic vision of Celtic myth and legend. The most significant works of the Celtic Renaissance typically present a dreamy, unreal world, usually in reaction against the reality of contemporary problems.

Celtic Twilight: See *Celtic Renaissance*

Character: Broadly speaking, a person in a literary work. The actions of characters are what constitute the plot of a story, novel, or poem. There are numerous types of characters, ranging from simple, stereotypical figures to intricate, multifaceted ones. In the techniques of anthropomorphism and personification, animals—and even places or things—can assume aspects of character. "Characterization" is the process by which an author creates vivid, believable characters in a work of art. This may be done in a variety of ways, including (1) direct description of the character by the narrator; (2) the direct presentation of the speech, thoughts, or actions of the character; and (3) the responses of other characters to the character. The term "character" also refers to a form originated by the ancient Greek writer Theophrastus that later became popular in the seventeenth and eighteenth centuries. It is a short essay or sketch of a person who prominently displays a specific attribute or quality, such as miserliness or ambition.

Characterization: See *Character*

Classical: In its strictest definition in literary criticism, classicism refers to works of ancient Greek or Roman literature. The term may also be used to describe a literary work of recognized importance (a "classic") from any time period or literature that exhibits the traits of classicism.

Classicism: A term used in literary criticism to describe critical doctrines that have their roots in ancient Greek and Roman literature, philosophy, and art. Works associated with classicism typically exhibit restraint on the part of the author, unity of design and purpose, clarity, simplicity, logical organization, and respect for tradition.

Colloquialism: A word, phrase, or form of pronunciation that is acceptable in casual conversation but not in formal, written communication. It is considered more acceptable than slang.

Complaint: A lyric poem, popular in the Renaissance, in which the speaker expresses sorrow about his or her condition. Typically, the speaker's sadness is caused by an unresponsive lover, but some complaints cite other sources of unhappiness, such as poverty or fate.

Conceit: A clever and fanciful metaphor, usually expressed through elaborate and extended comparison, that presents a striking parallel between two seemingly dissimilar things— for example, elaborately comparing a beautiful woman to an object like a garden or the sun. The conceit was a popular device throughout the Elizabethan Age and Baroque Age and was the principal technique of the seventeenth-century English metaphysical poets. This usage of the word conceit is unrelated to the best-known definition of conceit as an arrogant attitude or behavior.

Concrete: Concrete is the opposite of abstract, and refers to a thing that actually exists or a description that allows the reader to experience an object or concept with the senses.

Concrete Poetry: Poetry in which visual elements play a large part in the poetic effect. Punctuation marks, letters, or words are arranged on a page to form a visual design: a cross, for example, or a bumblebee.

Confessional Poetry: A form of poetry in which the poet reveals very personal, intimate, sometimes shocking information about himself or herself.

Connotation: The impression that a word gives beyond its defined meaning. Connotations may be universally understood or may be significant only to a certain group.

Consonance: Consonance occurs in poetry when words appearing at the ends of two or more verses have similar final consonant sounds but have final vowel sounds that differ, as with "stuff" and "off."

Convention: Any widely accepted literary device, style, or form.

Corrido: A Mexican ballad.

Couplet: Two lines of poetry with the same rhyme and meter, often expressing a complete and self-contained thought.

Criticism: The systematic study and evaluation of literary works, usually based on a specific method or set of principles. An important part of literary studies since ancient times, the practice of criticism has given rise to numerous theories, methods, and "schools," sometimes producing conflicting, even contradictory, interpretations of literature in general as well as of individual works. Even such basic issues as what constitutes a poem or a novel have been the subject of much criticism over the centuries.

D

Dactyl: See *Foot*

Dadaism: A protest movement in art and literature founded by Tristan Tzara in 1916. Followers of the movement expressed their outrage at the destruction brought about by World War I by revolting against numerous forms of social convention. The Dadaists presented works marked by calculated madness and flamboyant nonsense. They stressed total freedom of expression, commonly through primitive displays of emotion and illogical, often senseless, poetry. The movement ended shortly after the war, when it was replaced by surrealism.

Decadent: See *Decadents*

Decadents: The followers of a nineteenth-century literary movement that had its beginnings in French aestheticism. Decadent literature displays a fascination with perverse and morbid states; a search for novelty and sensation—the "new thrill"; a preoccupation with mysticism; and a belief in the senselessness of human existence. The movement is closely associated with the doctrine Art for Art's Sake. The term "decadence" is sometimes used to denote a decline in the quality of art or literature following a period of greatness.

Deconstruction: A method of literary criticism developed by Jacques Derrida and characterized by multiple conflicting interpretations of a given work. Deconstructionists consider the impact of the language of a work and suggest that the true meaning of the work is not necessarily the meaning that the author intended.

Deduction: The process of reaching a conclusion through reasoning from general premises to a specific premise.

Denotation: The definition of a word, apart from the impressions or feelings it creates in the reader.

Diction: The selection and arrangement of words in a literary work. Either or both may vary depending on the desired effect. There are four general types of diction: "formal," used in scholarly or lofty writing; "informal," used in relaxed but educated conversation; "colloquial," used in everyday speech; and "slang," containing newly coined words and other terms not accepted in formal usage.

Didactic: A term used to describe works of literature that aim to teach some moral, religious, political, or practical lesson. Although didactic elements are often found in artistically pleasing works, the term "didactic" usually refers to literature in which the message is more important than the form. The term may also be used to criticize a work that the critic finds "overly didactic," that is, heavy-handed in its delivery of a lesson.

Dimeter: See *Meter*

Dionysian: See *Apollonian and Dionysian*

Discordia concours: A Latin phrase meaning "discord in harmony." The term was coined by the eighteenth-century English writer Samuel Johnson to describe "a combination of dissimilar images or discovery of occult resemblances in things apparently unlike." Johnson created the expression by reversing a phrase by the Latin poet Horace.

Dissonance: A combination of harsh or jarring sounds, especially in poetry. Although such combinations may be accidental, poets sometimes intentionally make them to achieve particular effects. Dissonance is also sometimes used to refer to close but not identical rhymes. When this is the case, the word functions as a synonym for consonance.

Double Entendre: A corruption of a French phrase meaning "double meaning." The term is used to indicate a word or phrase that is deliberately ambiguous, especially when one of the meanings is risque or improper.

Draft: Any preliminary version of a written work. An author may write dozens of drafts which are revised to form the final work, or he or she may write only one, with few or no revisions.

Dramatic Monologue: See *Monologue*

Dramatic Poetry: Any lyric work that employs elements of drama such as dialogue, conflict, or characterization, but excluding works that are intended for stage presentation.

Dream Allegory: See *Dream Vision*

Dream Vision: A literary convention, chiefly of the Middle Ages. In a dream vision a story is presented as a literal dream of the narrator. This device was commonly used to teach moral and religious lessons.

E

Eclogue: In classical literature, a poem featuring rural themes and structured as a dialogue among shepherds. Eclogues often took specific poetic forms, such as elegies or love poems. Some were written as the soliloquy of a shepherd. In later centuries, "eclogue" came to refer to any poem that was in the pastoral tradition or that had a dialogue or monologue structure.

Edwardian: Describes cultural conventions identified with the period of the reign of Edward VII of England (1901-1910). Writers of the Edwardian Age typically displayed a strong reaction against the propriety and conservatism of the Victorian Age. Their work often exhibits distrust of authority in religion, politics, and art and expresses strong doubts about the soundness of conventional values.

Edwardian Age: See *Edwardian*

Electra Complex: A daughter's amorous obsession with her father.

Elegy: A lyric poem that laments the death of a person or the eventual death of all people. In a conventional elegy, set in a classical world, the poet and subject are spoken of as shepherds. In modern criticism, the word elegy is often used to refer to a poem that is melancholy or mournfully contemplative.

Elizabethan Age: A period of great economic growth, religious controversy, and nationalism closely associated with the reign of Elizabeth I of England (1558-1603). The Elizabethan Age is considered a part of the general renaissance—that is, the flowering of arts and literature—that took place in Europe during the fourteenth through sixteenth centuries. The era is considered the golden age of English literature. The most important dramas in English and a great deal of lyric poetry were produced during this period, and modern English criticism began around this time.

Empathy: A sense of shared experience, including emotional and physical feelings, with someone or something other than oneself. Empathy is often used to describe the response of a reader to a literary character.

English Sonnet: See *Sonnet*

Enjambment: The running over of the sense and structure of a line of verse or a couplet into the following verse or couplet.

Enlightenment, The: An eighteenth-century philosophical movement. It began in France but had a wide impact throughout Europe and America. Thinkers of the Enlightenment valued reason and believed that both the individual and society could achieve a state of perfection. Corresponding to this essentially humanist vision was a resistance to religious authority.

Epic: A long narrative poem about the adventures of a hero of great historic or legendary importance. The setting is vast and the action is often given cosmic significance through the intervention of supernatural forces such as gods, angels, or demons. Epics are typically written in a classical style of grand simplicity with elaborate metaphors and allusions that enhance the symbolic importance of a hero's adventures.

Epic Simile: See *Homeric Simile*

Epigram: A saying that makes the speaker's point quickly and concisely.

Epilogue: A concluding statement or section of a literary work. In dramas, particularly those of the seventeenth and eighteenth centuries, the epilogue is a closing speech, often in verse, delivered by an actor at the end of a play and spoken directly to the audience.

Epiphany: A sudden revelation of truth inspired by a seemingly trivial incident.

Epitaph: An inscription on a tomb or tombstone, or a verse written on the occasion of a person's death. Epitaphs may be serious or humorous.

Epithalamion: A song or poem written to honor and commemorate a marriage ceremony.

Epithalamium: See *Epithalamion*

Epithet: A word or phrase, often disparaging or abusive, that expresses a character trait of someone or something.

Erziehungsroman: See *Bildungsroman*

Essay: A prose composition with a focused subject of discussion. The term was coined by Michel de Montaigne to describe his 1580 collection of brief, informal reflections on himself and on various topics relating to human nature. An essay can also be a long, systematic discourse.

Existentialism: A predominantly twentieth-century philosophy concerned with the nature and perception of human existence. There are two major strains of existentialist thought: atheistic and Christian. Followers of atheistic existentialism believe that the individual is alone in a godless universe and that the basic human condition is one of suffering and loneliness. Nevertheless, because there are no fixed values, individuals can create their own characters—indeed, they can shape themselves—through the exercise of free will. The atheistic strain culminates in and is popularly associated with the works of Jean-Paul Sartre. The Christian existentialists, on the other hand, believe that only in God may people find freedom from life's anguish. The two strains hold certain beliefs in common: that existence cannot be fully understood or described through empirical effort; that anguish is a universal element of life; that individuals must bear responsibility for their actions; and that there is no common standard of behavior or perception for religious and ethical matters.

Expatriates: See *Expatriatism*

Expatriatism: The practice of leaving one's country to live for an extended period in another country.

Exposition: Writing intended to explain the nature of an idea, thing, or theme. Expository writing is often combined with description, narration, or argument. In dramatic writing, the exposition is the introductory material which presents the characters, setting, and tone of the play.

Expressionism: An indistinct literary term, originally used to describe an early twentieth-century school of German painting. The term applies to almost any mode of unconventional, highly subjective writing that distorts reality in some way.

Extended Monologue: See *Monologue*

F

Feet: See *Foot*

Feminine Rhyme: See *Rhyme*

Fiction: Any story that is the product of imagination rather than a documentation of fact. Characters and events in such narratives may be based in real life but their ultimate form and configuration is a creation of the author.

Figurative Language: A technique in writing in which the author temporarily interrupts the order, construction, or meaning of the writing for a particular effect. This interruption takes the form of one or more figures of speech such as hyperbole, irony, or simile. Figurative language is the opposite of literal language, in which every word is truthful, accurate, and free of exaggeration or embellishment.

Figures of Speech: Writing that differs from customary conventions for construction, meaning, order, or significance for the purpose of a special meaning or effect. There are two major types of figures of speech: rhetorical figures, which do not make changes in the meaning of the words, and tropes, which do.

Fin de siecle: A French term meaning "end of the century." The term is used to denote the last decade of the nineteenth century, a transition period when writers and other artists abandoned old conventions and looked for new techniques and objectives.

First Person: See *Point of View*

Folk Ballad: See *Ballad*

Folklore: Traditions and myths preserved in a culture or group of people. Typically, these are passed on by word of mouth in various forms—such as legends, songs, and proverbs—or preserved in customs and ceremonies. This term was first used by W. J. Thoms in 1846.

Folktale: A story originating in oral tradition. Folktales fall into a variety of categories, including legends, ghost stories, fairy tales, fables, and anecdotes based on historical figures and events.

Foot: The smallest unit of rhythm in a line of poetry. In English-language poetry, a foot is typically one accented syllable combined with one or two unaccented syllables.

Form: The pattern or construction of a work which identifies its genre and distinguishes it from other genres.

Formalism: In literary criticism, the belief that literature should follow prescribed rules of construction, such as those that govern the sonnet form.

Fourteener Meter: See *Meter*

Free Verse: Poetry that lacks regular metrical and rhyme patterns but that tries to capture the cadences of everyday speech. The form allows a poet to exploit a variety of rhythmical effects within a single poem.

Futurism: A flamboyant literary and artistic movement that developed in France, Italy, and Russia from 1908 through the 1920s. Futurist theater and poetry abandoned traditional literary forms. In their place, followers of the movement attempted to achieve total freedom of expression through bizarre imagery and deformed or newly invented words. The Futurists were self-consciously modern artists who attempted to incorporate the appearances and sounds of modern life into their work.

G

Genre: A category of literary work. In critical theory, genre may refer to both the content of a given work—tragedy, comedy, pastoral—and to its form, such as poetry, novel, or drama.

Genteel Tradition: A term coined by critic George Santayana to describe the literary practice of certain late nineteenth-century American writers, especially New Englanders. Followers of the Genteel Tradition emphasized conventionality in social, religious, moral, and literary standards.

Georgian Age: See *Georgian Poets*

Georgian Period: See *Georgian Poets*

Georgian Poets: A loose grouping of English poets during the years 1912-1922. The Georgians reacted against certain literary schools and practices, especially Victorian wordiness, turn-of-the-century aestheticism, and contemporary urban realism. In their place, the Georgians embraced the nineteenth-century poetic practices of William Wordsworth and the other Lake Poets.

Georgic: A poem about farming and the farmer's way of life, named from Virgil's *Georgics*.

Gilded Age: A period in American history during the 1870s characterized by political corruption and materialism. A number of important novels of social and political criticism were written during this time.

Gothic: See *Gothicism*

Gothicism: In literary criticism, works characterized by a taste for the medieval or morbidly attractive. A gothic novel prominently features elements of horror, the supernatural, gloom, and violence: clanking chains, terror, charnel houses, ghosts, medieval castles, and mysteriously slamming doors. The term "gothic novel" is also applied to novels that lack elements of the traditional Gothic setting but that create a similar atmosphere of terror or dread.

Graveyard School: A group of eighteenth-century English poets who wrote long, picturesque meditations on death. Their works were designed to cause the reader to ponder immortality.

Great Chain of Being: The belief that all things and creatures in nature are organized in a hierarchy from inanimate objects at the bottom to God at the top. This system of belief was popular in the seventeenth and eighteenth centuries.

Grotesque: In literary criticism, the subject matter of a work or a style of expression characterized by exaggeration, deformity, freakishness, and disorder. The grotesque often includes an element of comic absurdity.

H

Haiku: The shortest form of Japanese poetry, constructed in three lines of five, seven, and five syllables respectively. The message of a *haiku* poem usually centers on some aspect of spirituality and provokes an emotional response in the reader.

Half Rhyme: See *Consonance*

Harlem Renaissance: The Harlem Renaissance of the 1920s is generally considered the first significant movement of black writers and artists in the United States. During this period, new and established black writers published more fiction and poetry than ever before, the first influential black literary journals were established, and black authors and artists received their first widespread recognition and serious critical appraisal. Among the major writers associated with this period are Claude McKay, Jean Toomer, Countee Cullen, Langston Hughes, Arna Bontemps, Nella Larsen, and Zora Neale Hurston.

Hellenism: Imitation of ancient Greek thought or styles. Also, an approach to life that focuses on the growth and development of the intellect. "Hellenism" is sometimes used to refer to the belief that reason can be applied to examine all human experience.

Heptameter: See *Meter*

Hero/Heroine: The principal sympathetic character (male or female) in a literary work. Heroes and heroines typically exhibit admirable traits: idealism, courage, and integrity, for example.

Heroic Couplet: A rhyming couplet written in iambic pentameter (a verse with five iambic feet).

Heroic Line: The meter and length of a line of verse in epic or heroic poetry. This varies by language and time period.

Heroine: See *Hero/Heroine*

Hexameter: See *Meter*

Historical Criticism: The study of a work based on its impact on the world of the time period in which it was written.

Hokku: See *Haiku*

Holocaust: See *Holocaust Literature*

Holocaust Literature: Literature influenced by or written about the Holocaust of World War II. Such literature includes true stories of survival in concentration camps, escape, and life after the war, as well as fictional works and poetry.

Homeric Simile: An elaborate, detailed comparison written as a simile many lines in length.

Horatian Satire: See *Satire*

Humanism: A philosophy that places faith in the dignity of humankind and rejects the medieval perception of the individual as a weak, fallen creature. "Humanists" typically believe in the perfectibility of human nature and view reason and education as the means to that end.

Humors: Mentions of the humors refer to the ancient Greek theory that a person's health and personality were determined by the balance of four basic fluids in the body: blood, phlegm, yellow bile, and black bile. A dominance of any fluid would cause extremes in behavior. An excess of blood created a sanguine person who was joyful, aggressive, and passionate; a phlegmatic person was shy, fearful, and sluggish; too much yellow bile led to a choleric temperament characterized by impatience, anger, bitterness, and stubbornness; and excessive black bile created melancholy, a state of laziness, gluttony, and lack of motivation.

Humours: See *Humors*

Hyperbole: In literary criticism, deliberate exaggeration used to achieve an effect.

I

Iamb: See *Foot*

Idiom: A word construction or verbal expression closely associated with a given language.

Image: A concrete representation of an object or sensory experience. Typically, such a representation helps evoke the feelings associated with the object or experience itself. Images are either "literal" or "figurative." Literal images are especially concrete and involve little or no extension of the obvious meaning of the words used to express them. Figurative images do not follow the literal meaning of the words exactly. Images in literature are usually visual, but the term "image" can also refer to the representation of any sensory experience.

Imagery: The array of images in a literary work. Also, figurative language.

Imagism: An English and American poetry movement that flourished between 1908 and 1917. The Imagists used precise, clearly presented images in their works. They also used common, everyday speech and aimed for conciseness, concrete imagery, and the creation of new rhythms.

In medias res: A Latin term meaning "in the middle of things." It refers to the technique of beginning a story at its midpoint and then using various flashback devices to reveal previous action.

Induction: The process of reaching a conclusion by reasoning from specific premises to form a general premise. Also, an introductory portion of a work of literature, especially a play.

Intentional Fallacy: The belief that judgments of a literary work based solely on an author's stated or implied intentions are false and misleading. Critics who believe in the concept of the intentional fallacy typically argue that the work itself is sufficient matter for interpretation, even though they may concede that an author's statement of purpose can be useful.

Interior Monologue: A narrative technique in which characters' thoughts are revealed in a way that appears to be uncontrolled by the author. The interior monologue typically aims to reveal the inner self of a character. It portrays emotional experiences as they occur at both a conscious and unconscious level. Images are often used to represent sensations or emotions.

Internal Rhyme: Rhyme that occurs within a single line of verse.

Irish Literary Renaissance: A late nineteenth- and early twentieth-century movement in Irish literature. Members of the movement aimed to reduce the influence of British culture in Ireland and create an Irish national literature.

Irony: In literary criticism, the effect of language in which the intended meaning is the opposite of what is stated.

Italian Sonnet: See *Sonnet*

J

Jacobean Age: The period of the reign of James I of England (1603-1625). The early literature of this period reflected the worldview of the Elizabethan Age, but a darker, more cynical attitude steadily grew in the art and literature of the Jacobean Age. This was an important time for English drama and poetry.

Jargon: Language that is used or understood only by a select group of people. Jargon may refer to terminology used in a certain profession, such as computer jargon, or it may refer to any nonsensical language that is not understood by most people.

Journalism: Writing intended for publication in a newspaper or magazine, or for broadcast on a radio or television program featuring news, sports, entertainment, or other timely material.

K

Knickerbocker Group: A somewhat indistinct group of New York writers of the first half of the nineteenth century. Members of the group were linked only by location and a common theme: New York life.

Kunstlerroman: See *Bildungsroman*

L

Lais: See *Lay*

Lake Poets: See *Lake School*

Lake School: These poets all lived in the Lake District of England at the turn of the nineteenth century. As a group, they followed no single "school" of thought or literary practice, although their works were uniformly disparaged by the *Edinburgh Review*.

Lay: A song or simple narrative poem. The form originated in medieval France. Early French *lais* were often based on the Celtic legends and other tales sung by Breton minstrels—thus the name of the "Breton lay." In fourteenth-century England, the term "lay" was used to describe short narratives written in imitation of the Breton lays.

Leitmotiv: See *Motif*

Literal Language: An author uses literal language when he or she writes without exaggerating or embellishing the subject matter and without any tools of figurative language.

Literary Ballad: See *Ballad*

Literature: Literature is broadly defined as any written or spoken material, but the term most often refers to creative works.

Lost Generation: A term first used by Gertrude Stein to describe the post-World War I generation of American writers: men and women haunted by a sense of betrayal and emptiness brought about by the destructiveness of the war.

Lyric Poetry: A poem expressing the subjective feelings and personal emotions of the poet. Such poetry is melodic, since it was originally accompanied by a lyre in recitals. Most Western poetry in the twentieth century may be classified as lyrical.

M

Mannerism: Exaggerated, artificial adherence to a literary manner or style. Also, a popular style of the visual arts of late sixteenth-century Europe that was marked by elongation of the human form and by intentional spatial distortion. Literary works that are self-consciously high-toned and artistic are often said to be "mannered."

Masculine Rhyme: See *Rhyme*

Measure: The foot, verse, or time sequence used in a literary work, especially a poem. Measure is often used somewhat incorrectly as a synonym for meter.

Metaphor: A figure of speech that expresses an idea through the image of another object. Metaphors suggest the essence of the first object by identifying it with certain qualities of the second object.

Metaphysical Conceit: See *Conceit*

Metaphysical Poetry: The body of poetry produced by a group of seventeenth-century English writers called the "Metaphysical Poets." The group includes John Donne and Andrew Marvell. The Metaphysical Poets made use of everyday speech, intellectual analysis, and unique imagery. They aimed to portray the ordinary conflicts and contradictions of life. Their poems often took the form of an argument, and many of them emphasize physical and religious love as well as the fleeting nature of life. Elaborate conceits are typical in metaphysical poetry.

Metaphysical Poets: See *Metaphysical Poetry*

Meter: In literary criticism, the repetition of sound patterns that creates a rhythm in poetry. The patterns are based on the number of syllables and the presence and absence of accents. The unit of rhythm in a line is called a foot. Types of meter are classified according to the number of feet in a line. These are the standard English lines: Monometer, one foot; Dimeter, two feet; Trimeter, three feet; Tetrameter, four feet; Pentameter, five feet; Hexameter, six feet (also called the Alexandrine); Heptameter, seven feet (also called the "Fourteener" when the feet are iambic).

Modernism: Modern literary practices. Also, the principles of a literary school that lasted from roughly the beginning of the twentieth century until the end of World War II. Modernism is defined by its rejection of the literary conventions of the nineteenth century and by its opposition to conventional morality, taste, traditions, and economic values.

Monologue: A composition, written or oral, by a single individual. More specifically, a speech given by a single individual in a drama or other public entertainment. It has no set length, although it is usually several or more lines long.

Monometer: See *Meter*

Mood: The prevailing emotions of a work or of the author in his or her creation of the work. The mood of a work is not always what might be expected based on its subject matter.

Motif: A theme, character type, image, metaphor, or other verbal element that recurs throughout a single work of literature or occurs in a number of different works over a period of time.

Motiv: See *Motif*

Muckrakers: An early twentieth-century group of American writers. Typically, their works exposed the wrongdoings of big business and government in the United States.

Muses: Nine Greek mythological goddesses, the daughters of Zeus and Mnemosyne (Memory). Each muse patronized a specific area of the liberal arts and sciences. Calliope presided over epic poetry, Clio over history, Erato over love poetry, Euterpe over music or lyric poetry, Melpomene over tragedy, Polyhymnia over hymns to the gods, Terpsichore over dance, Thalia over comedy, and Urania over astronomy. Poets and writers traditionally made appeals to the Muses for inspiration in their work.

Myth: An anonymous tale emerging from the traditional beliefs of a culture or social unit. Myths use supernatural explanations for natural phenomena. They may also explain cosmic issues like creation and death. Collections of myths, known as mythologies, are common to all cultures and nations, but the best-known myths belong to the Norse, Roman, and Greek mythologies.

N

Narration: The telling of a series of events, real or invented. A narration may be either a simple narrative, in which the events are recounted chronologically, or a narrative with a plot, in which the account is given in a style reflecting the author's artistic concept of the story. Narration is sometimes used as a synonym for "storyline."

Narrative: A verse or prose accounting of an event or sequence of events, real or invented. The term is also used as an adjective in the sense "method of narration." For example, in literary criticism, the expression "narrative technique" usually refers to the way the author structures and presents his or her story.

Narrative Poetry: A nondramatic poem in which the author tells a story. Such poems may be of any length or level of complexity.

Narrator: The teller of a story. The narrator may be the author or a character in the story through whom the author speaks.

Naturalism: A literary movement of the late nineteenth and early twentieth centuries. The movement's major theorist, French novelist Emile Zola, envisioned a type of fiction that would examine human life with the objectivity of scientific inquiry. The Naturalists typically viewed human beings as either the products of "biological determinism," ruled by hereditary instincts and engaged in an endless struggle for survival, or as the products of "socioeconomic determinism," ruled by social and economic forces beyond their control. In their works, the Naturalists generally ignored the highest levels of society and focused on degradation: poverty, alcoholism, prostitution, insanity, and disease.

Negritude: A literary movement based on the concept of a shared cultural bond on the part of black Africans, wherever they may be in the world. It traces its origins to the former French colonies of Africa and the Caribbean. Negritude poets, novelists, and essayists generally stress four points in their writings: One, black alienation from traditional African culture can lead to feelings of inferiority. Two, European colonialism and Western education should be resisted. Three, black Africans should seek to affirm and define their own identity. Four, African culture can and should be reclaimed. Many Negritude writers also claim that blacks can make unique contributions to the world, based on a heightened appreciation of nature, rhythm, and human emotions—aspects of life they say are not so highly valued in the materialistic and rationalistic West.

Negro Renaissance: See *Harlem Renaissance*

Neoclassical Period: See *Neoclassicism*

Neoclassicism: In literary criticism, this term refers to the revival of the attitudes and styles of expression of classical literature. It is generally used to describe a period in European history beginning in the late seventeenth century and lasting until about 1800. In its purest form, Neoclassicism marked a return to order, proportion, restraint, logic, accuracy, and decorum. In England, where Neoclassicism perhaps was most popular, it reflected the influence of seventeenth-century French writers, especially dramatists. Neoclassical writers typically reacted against the intensity and enthusiasm of the Renaissance period. They wrote works that appealed to the intellect, using elevated language and classical literary forms such as satire and the ode. Neoclassical works were often governed by the classical goal of instruction.

Neoclassicists: See *Neoclassicism*

New Criticism: A movement in literary criticism, dating from the late 1920s, that stressed close textual analysis in the interpretation of works of literature. The New Critics saw little merit in historical and biographical analysis. Rather, they aimed to examine the text alone, free from the question of how external events—biographical or otherwise—may have helped shape it.

New Journalism: A type of writing in which the journalist presents factual information in a form usually used in fiction. New journalism emphasizes description, narration, and character development to bring readers closer to the human element of the story, and is often used in personality profiles and in-depth feature articles. It is not compatible with "straight" or "hard" newswriting, which is generally composed in a brief, fact-based style.

New Journalists: See *New Journalism*

New Negro Movement: See *Harlem Renaissance*

Noble Savage: The idea that primitive man is noble and good but becomes evil and corrupted as he becomes civilized. The concept of the noble savage originated in the Renaissance period but is more closely identified with such later writers as Jean-Jacques Rousseau and Aphra Behn.

O

Objective Correlative: An outward set of objects, a situation, or a chain of events corresponding to an inward experience and evoking this experience in the reader. The term frequently appears in modern criticism in discussions of authors' intended effects on the emotional responses of readers.

Objectivity: A quality in writing characterized by the absence of the author's opinion or feeling about the subject matter. Objectivity is an important factor in criticism.

Occasional Verse: Poetry written on the occasion of a significant historical or personal event. *Vers de societe* is sometimes called occasional verse although it is of a less serious nature.

Octave: A poem or stanza composed of eight lines. The term octave most often represents the first eight lines of a Petrarchan sonnet.

Ode: Name given to an extended lyric poem characterized by exalted emotion and dignified style. An ode usually concerns a single, serious theme. Most odes, but not all, are addressed to an object or individual. Odes are distinguished from other lyric poetic forms by their complex rhythmic and stanzaic patterns.

Oedipus Complex: A son's amorous obsession with his mother. The phrase is derived from the story of the ancient Theban hero Oedipus, who unknowingly killed his father and married his mother.

Omniscience: See *Point of View*

Onomatopoeia: The use of words whose sounds express or suggest their meaning. In its simplest sense, onomatopoeia may be represented by words that mimic the sounds they denote such as "hiss" or "meow." At a more subtle level, the pattern and rhythm of sounds and rhymes of a line or poem may be onomatopoeic.

Oral Tradition: See *Oral Transmission*

Oral Transmission: A process by which songs, ballads, folklore, and other material are transmitted by word of mouth. The tradition of oral transmission predates the written record systems of literate society. Oral transmission preserves material sometimes over generations, although often with variations. Memory plays a large part in the recitation and preservation of orally transmitted material.

Ottava Rima: An eight-line stanza of poetry composed in iambic pentameter (a five-foot line in which each foot consists of an unaccented syllable followed by an accented syllable), following the ababacc rhyme scheme.

Oxymoron: A phrase combining two contradictory terms. Oxymorons may be intentional or unintentional.

P

Pantheism: The idea that all things are both a manifestation or revelation of God and a part of God at the same time. Pantheism was a common attitude in the early societies of Egypt, India, and Greece—the term derives from the Greek *pan* meaning "all" and *theos* meaning "deity." It later became a significant part of the Christian faith.

Parable: A story intended to teach a moral lesson or answer an ethical question.

Paradox: A statement that appears illogical or contradictory at first, but may actually point to an underlying truth.

Parallelism: A method of comparison of two ideas in which each is developed in the same grammatical structure.

Parnassianism: A mid nineteenth-century movement in French literature. Followers of the movement stressed adherence to well-defined artistic forms as a reaction against the often chaotic expression of the artist's ego that dominated the work of the Romantics. The Parnassians also rejected the moral, ethical, and social themes exhibited in the works of French Romantics such as Victor Hugo. The aesthetic doctrines of the Parnassians strongly influenced the later symbolist and decadent movements.

Parody: In literary criticism, this term refers to an imitation of a serious literary work or the signature style of a particular author in a ridiculous manner. A typical parody adopts the style of the original and applies it to an inappropriate subject for humorous effect. Parody is a form of satire and could be considered the literary equivalent of a caricature or cartoon.

Pastoral: A term derived from the Latin word "pastor," meaning shepherd. A pastoral is a literary composition on a rural theme. The conventions of the pastoral were originated by the third-century Greek poet Theocritus, who wrote about the experiences, love affairs, and pastimes of Sicilian shepherds. In a pastoral, characters and language of a courtly nature are often placed in a simple setting. The term pastoral is also used to classify dramas, elegies, and lyrics that exhibit the use of country settings and shepherd characters.

Pathetic Fallacy: A term coined by English critic John Ruskin to identify writing that falsely endows nonhuman things with human intentions and feelings, such as "angry clouds" and "sad trees."

Pen Name: See *Pseudonym*

Pentameter: See *Meter*

Persona: A Latin term meaning "mask." *Personae* are the characters in a fictional work of literature. The *persona* generally functions as a mask through which the author tells a story in a voice other than his or her own. A *persona* is usually either a character in a story who acts as a narrator or an "implied author," a voice created by the author to act as the narrator for himself or herself.

Personae: See *Persona*

Personal Point of View: See *Point of View*

Personification: A figure of speech that gives human qualities to abstract ideas, animals, and inanimate objects.

Petrarchan Sonnet: See *Sonnet*

Phenomenology: A method of literary criticism based on the belief that things have no existence outside of human consciousness or awareness. Proponents of this theory believe that art is a process that takes place in the mind of the observer as he or she contemplates an object rather than a quality of the object itself.

Plagiarism: Claiming another person's written material as one's own. Plagiarism can take the form of direct, word-for-word copying or the theft of the substance or idea of the work.

Platonic Criticism: A form of criticism that stresses an artistic work's usefulness as an agent of social engineering rather than any quality or value of the work itself.

Platonism: The embracing of the doctrines of the philosopher Plato, popular among the poets of the Renaissance and the Romantic period. Platonism is more flexible than Aristotelian Criticism and places more emphasis on the supernatural and unknown aspects of life.

Plot: In literary criticism, this term refers to the pattern of events in a narrative or drama. In its simplest sense, the plot guides the author in composing the work and helps the reader follow the work. Typically, plots exhibit causality and unity and have a beginning, a middle, and an end. Sometimes, however, a plot may consist of a series of disconnected events, in which case it is known as an "episodic plot."

Poem: In its broadest sense, a composition utilizing rhyme, meter, concrete detail, and expressive language to create a literary experience with emotional and aesthetic appeal.

Poet: An author who writes poetry or verse. The term is also used to refer to an artist or writer who has an exceptional gift for expression, imagination, and energy in the making of art in any form.

Poete maudit: A term derived from Paul Verlaine's *Les poetes maudits* (*The Accursed Poets*), a collection of essays on the French symbolist writers Stephane Mallarme, Arthur Rimbaud, and Tristan Corbiere. In the sense intended by Verlaine, the poet is "accursed" for choosing to explore extremes of human experience outside of middle-class society.

Poetic Fallacy: See *Pathetic Fallacy*

Poetic Justice: An outcome in a literary work, not necessarily a poem, in which the good are rewarded and the evil are punished, especially in ways that particularly fit their virtues or crimes.

Poetic License: Distortions of fact and literary convention made by a writer—not always a poet—for the sake of the effect gained. Poetic license is closely related to the concept of "artistic freedom."

Poetics: This term has two closely related meanings. It denotes (1) an aesthetic theory in literary criticism about the essence of poetry or (2) rules prescribing the proper methods, content, style, or diction of poetry. The term poetics may also refer to theories about literature in general, not just poetry.

Poetry: In its broadest sense, writing that aims to present ideas and evoke an emotional experience in the reader through the use of meter, imagery, connotative and concrete words, and a carefully constructed structure based on rhythmic patterns. Poetry typically relies on words and expressions that have several layers of meaning. It also makes use of the effects of regular rhythm on the ear and may make a strong appeal to the senses through the use of imagery.

Point of View: The narrative perspective from which a literary work is presented to the reader. There are four traditional points of view. The "third person omniscient" gives the reader a "godlike" perspective, unrestricted by time or place, from which to see actions and look into the minds of characters. This allows the author to comment openly on characters and events in the work. The "third person" point of view presents the events of the story from outside of any single character's perception, much like the omniscient point of view, but the reader must understand the action as it takes place and without any special insight into characters' minds or motivations. The "first person" or "personal" point of view relates events as they are perceived by a single character. The main character "tells" the story and may offer opinions about the action and characters which differ from those of the author. Much less common than omniscient, third person, and first person is the "second person" point of view, wherein the author tells the story as if it is happening to the reader.

Polemic: A work in which the author takes a stand on a controversial subject, such as abortion or religion. Such works are often extremely argumentative or provocative.

Pornography: Writing intended to provoke feelings of lust in the reader. Such works are often condemned by critics and teachers, but those which can be shown to have literary value are viewed less harshly.

Post-Aesthetic Movement: An artistic response made by African Americans to the black aesthetic movement of the 1960s and early '70s. Writers since that time have adopted a somewhat different tone in their work, with less emphasis placed on the disparity between black and white in the United States. In the words of post-aesthetic authors such as Toni Morrison, John Edgar Wideman, and Kristin Hunter, African Americans are portrayed as looking inward for answers to their own questions, rather than always looking to the outside world.

Postmodernism: Writing from the 1960s forward characterized by experimentation and continuing to apply some of the fundamentals of modernism, which included existentialism and alienation. Postmodernists have gone a step further in the rejection of tradition begun with the modernists by also rejecting traditional forms, preferring the anti-novel over the novel and the anti-hero over the hero.

Pre-Raphaelites: A circle of writers and artists in mid nineteenth-century England. Valuing the pre-Renaissance artistic qualities of religious symbolism, lavish pictorialism, and natural sensuousness, the Pre-Raphaelites cultivated a sense of mystery and melancholy that influenced later writers associated with the Symbolist and Decadent movements.

Primitivism: The belief that primitive peoples were nobler and less flawed than civilized peoples because they had not been subjected to the tainting influence of society.

Projective Verse: A form of free verse in which the poet's breathing pattern determines the lines of the poem. Poets who advocate projective verse are against all formal structures in writing, including meter and form.

Prologue: An introductory section of a literary work. It often contains information establishing the situation of the characters or presents information about the setting, time period, or action. In drama, the prologue is spoken by a chorus or by one of the principal characters.

Prose: A literary medium that attempts to mirror the language of everyday speech. It is distinguished from poetry by its use of unmetered, unrhymed language consisting of logically related sentences. Prose is usually grouped into paragraphs that form a cohesive whole such as an essay or a novel.

Prosopopoeia: See *Personification*

Protagonist: The central character of a story who serves as a focus for its themes and incidents and as the principal rationale for its development. The protagonist is sometimes referred to in discussions of modern literature as the hero or anti-hero.

Proverb: A brief, sage saying that expresses a truth about life in a striking manner.

Pseudonym: A name assumed by a writer, most often intended to prevent his or her identification as the author of a work. Two or more authors may work together under one pseudonym, or an author may use a different name for each genre he or she publishes in. Some publishing companies maintain "house pseudonyms," under which any number of authors may write installations in a series. Some authors also choose a pseudonym over their real names the way an actor may use a stage name.

Pun: A play on words that have similar sounds but different meanings.

Pure Poetry: Poetry written without instructional intent or moral purpose that aims only to please a reader by its imagery or musical flow. The term pure poetry is used as the antonym of the term "didacticism."

Q

Quatrain: A four-line stanza of a poem or an entire poem consisting of four lines.

R

Realism: A nineteenth-century European literary movement that sought to portray familiar characters, situations, and settings in a realistic manner. This was done primarily by using an objective narrative point of view and through the buildup of accurate detail. The standard for success of any realistic work depends on how faithfully it transfers common experience into fictional forms. The realistic method may be altered or extended, as in stream of consciousness writing, to record highly subjective experience.

Refrain: A phrase repeated at intervals throughout a poem. A refrain may appear at the end of each stanza or at less regular intervals. It may be altered slightly at each appearance.

Renaissance: The period in European history that marked the end of the Middle Ages. It began in Italy in the late fourteenth century. In broad terms, it is usually seen as spanning the fourteenth, fifteenth, and sixteenth centuries, although it did not reach Great Britain, for example, until the 1480s or so. The Renaissance saw an awakening in almost every sphere of human activity, especially science, philosophy, and the arts. The period is best defined by the emergence of a general philosophy that emphasized the importance of the intellect, the individual, and world affairs. It contrasts strongly with the medieval worldview, characterized by the dominant concerns of faith, the social collective, and spiritual salvation.

Repartee: Conversation featuring snappy retorts and witticisms.

Restoration: See *Restoration Age*

Restoration Age: A period in English literature beginning with the crowning of Charles II in 1660 and running to about 1700. The era, which was characterized by a reaction against Puritanism, was the first great age of the comedy of manners. The finest literature of the era is typically witty and urbane, and often lewd.

Rhetoric: In literary criticism, this term denotes the art of ethical persuasion. In its strictest sense, rhetoric adheres to various principles developed since classical times for arranging facts and ideas in a clear, persuasive, appealing manner. The term is also used to refer to effective prose in general and theories of or methods for composing effective prose.

Rhetorical Question: A question intended to provoke thought, but not an expressed answer, in the reader. It is most commonly used in oratory and other persuasive genres.

Rhyme: When used as a noun in literary criticism, this term generally refers to a poem in which words sound identical or very similar and appear in parallel positions in two or more lines. Rhymes are classified into different types according to where they fall in a line or stanza or according to the degree of similarity they exhibit in their spellings and sounds. Some major types of rhyme are "masculine" rhyme, "feminine" rhyme, and "triple" rhyme. In a masculine rhyme, the rhyming sound falls in a single accented syllable, as with "heat" and "eat." Feminine rhyme is a rhyme of two syllables, one

stressed and one unstressed, as with "merry" and "tarry." Triple rhyme matches the sound of the accented syllable and the two unaccented syllables that follow: "narrative" and "declarative."

Rhyme Royal: A stanza of seven lines composed in iambic pentameter and rhymed *ababbcc*. The name is said to be a tribute to King James I of Scotland, who made much use of the form in his poetry.

Rhyme Scheme: See *Rhyme*

Rhythm: A regular pattern of sound, time intervals, or events occurring in writing, most often and most discernably in poetry. Regular, reliable rhythm is known to be soothing to humans, while interrupted, unpredictable, or rapidly changing rhythm is disturbing. These effects are known to authors, who use them to produce a desired reaction in the reader.

Rococo: A style of European architecture that flourished in the eighteenth century, especially in France. The most notable features of *rococo* are its extensive use of ornamentation and its themes of lightness, gaiety, and intimacy. In literary criticism, the term is often used disparagingly to refer to a decadent or over-ornamental style.

Romance: A broad term, usually denoting a narrative with exotic, exaggerated, often idealized characters, scenes, and themes.

Romantic Age: See *Romanticism*

Romanticism: This term has two widely accepted meanings. In historical criticism, it refers to a European intellectual and artistic movement of the late eighteenth and early nineteenth centuries that sought greater freedom of personal expression than that allowed by the strict rules of literary form and logic of the eighteenth-century neoclassicists. The Romantics preferred emotional and imaginative expression to rational analysis. They considered the individual to be at the center of all experience and so placed him or her at the center of their art. The Romantics believed that the creative imagination reveals nobler truths—unique feelings and attitudes—than those that could be discovered by logic or by scientific examination. Both the natural world and the state of childhood were important sources for revelations of "eternal truths." "Romanticism" is also used as a general term to refer to a type of sensibility found in all periods of literary history and usually considered to be in opposition to the principles of classicism. In this sense, Romanticism signifies any work or philosophy in which the exotic or dreamlike figure strongly, or that is devoted to individualistic expression, self-analysis, or a pursuit of a higher realm of knowledge than can be discovered by human reason.

Romantics: See *Romanticism*

Russian Symbolism: A Russian poetic movement, derived from French symbolism, that flourished between 1894 and 1910. While some Russian Symbolists continued in the French tradition, stressing aestheticism and the importance of suggestion above didactic intent, others saw their craft as a form of mystical worship, and themselves as mediators between the supernatural and the mundane.

S

Satire: A work that uses ridicule, humor, and wit to criticize and provoke change in human nature and institutions. There are two major types of satire: "formal" or "direct" satire speaks directly to the reader or to a character in the work; "indirect" satire relies upon the ridiculous behavior of its characters to make its point. Formal satire is further divided into two manners: the "Horatian," which ridicules gently, and the "Juvenalian," which derides its subjects harshly and bitterly.

Scansion: The analysis or "scanning" of a poem to determine its meter and often its rhyme scheme. The most common system of scansion uses accents (slanted lines drawn above syllables) to show stressed syllables, breves (curved lines drawn above syllables) to show unstressed syllables, and vertical lines to separate each foot.

Second Person: See *Point of View*

Semiotics: The study of how literary forms and conventions affect the meaning of language.

Sestet: Any six-line poem or stanza.

Setting: The time, place, and culture in which the action of a narrative takes place. The elements of setting may include geographic location, characters' physical and mental environments, prevailing cultural attitudes, or the historical time in which the action takes place.

Shakespearean Sonnet: See *Sonnet*

Signifying Monkey: A popular trickster figure in black folklore, with hundreds of tales about this character documented since the 19th century.

Simile: A comparison, usually using "like" or "as," of two essentially dissimilar things, as in "coffee as cold as ice" or "He sounded like a broken record."

Slang: A type of informal verbal communication that is generally unacceptable for formal writing. Slang words and phrases are often colorful exaggerations used to emphasize the speaker's point; they may also be shortened versions of an often-used word or phrase.

Slant Rhyme: See *Consonance*

Slave Narrative: Autobiographical accounts of American slave life as told by escaped slaves. These works first appeared during the abolition movement of the 1830s through the 1850s.

Social Realism: See *Socialist Realism*

Socialist Realism: The Socialist Realism school of literary theory was proposed by Maxim Gorky and established as a dogma by the first Soviet Congress of Writers. It demanded adherence to a communist worldview in works of literature. Its doctrines required an objective viewpoint comprehensible to the working classes and themes of social struggle featuring strong proletarian heroes.

Soliloquy: A monologue in a drama used to give the audience information and to develop the speaker's character. It is typically a projection of the speaker's innermost thoughts. Usually delivered while the speaker is alone on stage, a soliloquy is intended to present an illusion of unspoken reflection.

Sonnet: A fourteen-line poem, usually composed in iambic pentameter, employing one of several rhyme schemes. There are three major types of sonnets, upon which all other variations of the form are based: the "Petrarchan" or "Italian" sonnet, the "Shakespearean" or "English" sonnet, and the "Spenserian" sonnet. A Petrarchan sonnet consists of an octave rhymed *abbaabba* and a "sestet" rhymed either *cdecde, cdccdc,* or *cdedce*. The octave poses a question or problem, relates a narrative, or puts forth a proposition; the sestet presents a solution to the problem, comments upon the narrative, or applies the proposition put forth in the octave. The Shakespearean sonnet is divided into three quatrains and a couplet rhymed *abab cdcd efef gg.* The couplet provides an epigrammatic comment on the narrative or problem put forth in the quatrains. The Spenserian sonnet uses three quatrains and a couplet like the Shakespearean, but links their three rhyme schemes in this way: *abab bcbc cdcd ee.* The Spenserian sonnet develops its theme in two parts like the Petrarchan, its final six lines resolving a problem, analyzing a narrative, or applying a proposition put forth in its first eight lines.

Spenserian Sonnet: See *Sonnet*

Spenserian Stanza: A nine-line stanza having eight verses in iambic pentameter, its ninth verse in iambic hexameter, and the rhyme scheme ababbcbcc.

Spondee: In poetry meter, a foot consisting of two long or stressed syllables occurring together. This form is quite rare in English verse, and is usually composed of two monosyllabic words.

Sprung Rhythm: Versification using a specific number of accented syllables per line but disregarding the number of unaccented syllables that fall in each line, producing an irregular rhythm in the poem.

Stanza: A subdivision of a poem consisting of lines grouped together, often in recurring patterns of rhyme, line length, and meter. Stanzas may also serve as units of thought in a poem much like paragraphs in prose.

Stereotype: A stereotype was originally the name for a duplication made during the printing process; this led to its modern definition as a person or thing that is (or is assumed to be) the same as all others of its type.

Stream of Consciousness: A narrative technique for rendering the inward experience of a character. This technique is designed to give the impression of an ever-changing series of thoughts, emotions, images, and memories in the spontaneous and seemingly illogical order that they occur in life.

Structuralism: A twentieth-century movement in literary criticism that examines how literary texts arrive at their meanings, rather than the meanings themselves. There are two major types of structuralist analysis: one examines the way patterns of linguistic structures unify a specific text and emphasize certain elements of that text, and the other interprets the way literary forms and conventions affect the meaning of language itself.

Structure: The form taken by a piece of literature. The structure may be made obvious for ease of understanding, as in nonfiction works, or may obscured for artistic purposes, as in some poetry or seemingly "unstructured" prose.

Sturm und Drang: A German term meaning "storm and stress." It refers to a German literary movement of the 1770s and 1780s that reacted against the order and rationalism of the enlightenment, focusing instead on the intense experience of extraordinary individuals.

Style: A writer's distinctive manner of arranging words to suit his or her ideas and purpose in writing. The unique imprint of the author's personality upon his or her writing, style is the product of an author's way of arranging ideas and his or her use of diction, different sentence structures, rhythm, figures of speech, rhetorical principles, and other elements of composition.

Subject: The person, event, or theme at the center of a work of literature. A work may have one or more subjects of each type, with shorter works tending to have fewer and longer works tending to have more.

Subjectivity: Writing that expresses the author's personal feelings about his subject, and which may or may not include factual information about the subject.

Surrealism: A term introduced to criticism by Guillaume Apollinaire and later adopted by Andre Breton. It refers to a French literary and artistic movement founded in the 1920s. The Surrealists sought to express unconscious thoughts and feelings in their works. The best-known technique used for achieving this aim was automatic writing—transcriptions of spontaneous outpourings from the unconscious. The Surrealists proposed to unify the contrary levels of conscious and unconscious, dream and reality, objectivity and subjectivity into a new level of "super-realism."

Suspense: A literary device in which the author maintains the audience's attention through the buildup of events, the outcome of which will soon be revealed.

Syllogism: A method of presenting a logical argument. In its most basic form, the syllogism consists of a major premise, a minor premise, and a conclusion.

Symbol: Something that suggests or stands for something else without losing its original identity. In literature, symbols combine their literal meaning with the suggestion of an abstract concept. Literary symbols are of two types: those that carry complex associations of meaning no matter what their contexts, and those that derive their suggestive meaning from their functions in specific literary works.

Symbolism: This term has two widely accepted meanings. In historical criticism, it denotes an early modernist literary movement initiated in France during the nineteenth century that reacted against the prevailing standards of realism. Writers in this movement aimed to evoke, indirectly and symbolically, an order of being beyond the material world of the five senses. Poetic expression of personal emotion figured strongly in the movement, typically by means of a private set of symbols uniquely identifiable with the individual poet. The principal aim of the Symbolists was to express in words the highly complex feelings that grew out of everyday contact with the world. In a broader sense, the term "symbolism" refers to the use of one object to represent another.

Symbolist: See *Symbolism*

Symbolist Movement: See *Symbolism*

Sympathetic Fallacy: See *Affective Fallacy*

T

Tanka: A form of Japanese poetry similar to *haiku*. A *tanka* is five lines long, with the lines containing five, seven, five, seven, and seven syllables respectively.

Terza Rima: A three-line stanza form in poetry in which the rhymes are made on the last word of each line in the following manner: the first and third lines of the first stanza, then the second line of the first stanza and the first and third lines of the second stanza, and so on with the middle line of any stanza rhyming with the first and third lines of the following stanza.

Tetrameter: See *Meter*

Textual Criticism: A branch of literary criticism that seeks to establish the authoritative text of a literary work. Textual critics typically compare all known manuscripts or printings of a single work in order to assess the meanings of differences and revisions. This procedure allows them to arrive at a definitive version that (supposedly) corresponds to the author's original intention.

Theme: The main point of a work of literature. The term is used interchangeably with thesis.

Thesis: A thesis is both an essay and the point argued in the essay. Thesis novels and thesis plays share the quality of containing a thesis which is supported through the action of the story.

Third Person: See *Point of View*

Tone: The author's attitude toward his or her audience may be deduced from the tone of the work. A formal tone may create distance or convey politeness, while an informal tone may encourage a friendly, intimate, or intrusive feeling in the reader. The author's attitude toward his or her subject matter may also be deduced from the tone of the words he or she uses in discussing it.

Tragedy: A drama in prose or poetry about a noble, courageous hero of excellent character who, because of some tragic character flaw or *hamartia*, brings ruin upon him- or herself. Tragedy treats its subjects in a dignified and serious manner, using poetic language to help evoke pity and fear and bring about catharsis, a purging of these emotions. The tragic form was practiced extensively by the ancient Greeks. In the Middle Ages, when classical works were virtually unknown, tragedy came to denote any works about the fall of persons from exalted to low conditions due to any reason: fate, vice, weakness, etc. According to the classical definition of tragedy, such works present the "pathetic"—that which evokes pity—rather than the tragic. The classical form of tragedy was revived in the sixteenth century; it flourished especially on the Elizabethan stage. In modern times, dramatists have attempted to adapt the form to the needs of modern society by drawing their heroes from the ranks of ordinary men and women and defining the nobility of these heroes in terms of spirit rather than exalted social standing.

Tragic Flaw: In a tragedy, the quality within the hero or heroine which leads to his or her downfall.

Transcendentalism: An American philosophical and religious movement, based in New England from around 1835 until the Civil War. Transcendentalism was a form of American romanticism that had its roots abroad in the works of Thomas Carlyle, Samuel Coleridge, and Johann Wolfgang von Goethe. The Transcendentalists stressed the importance of intuition and subjective experience in communication with God. They rejected religious dogma and texts in favor of mysticism and scientific naturalism. They pursued truths that lie beyond the "colorless" realms perceived by reason and the senses and were active social reformers in public education, women's rights, and the abolition of slavery.

Trickster: A character or figure common in Native American and African literature who uses his ingenuity to defeat enemies and escape difficult situations. Tricksters are most often animals, such as the spider, hare, or coyote, although they may take the form of humans as well.

Trimeter: See *Meter*

Triple Rhyme: See *Rhyme*

Trochee: See *Foot*

U

Understatement: See *Irony*

Unities: Strict rules of dramatic structure, formulated by Italian and French critics of the Renaissance and based loosely on the principles of drama discussed by Aristotle in his *Poetics*. Foremost among these rules were the three unities of action, time, and place that compelled a dramatist to: (1) construct a single plot with a beginning, middle, and end that details the causal relationships of action and character; (2) restrict the action to the events of a single day; and (3) limit the scene to a single place or city. The unities were observed faithfully by continental European writers until the Romantic Age, but they were never regularly observed in English drama. Modern dramatists are typically more concerned with a unity of impression or emotional effect than with any of the classical unities.

Urban Realism: A branch of realist writing that attempts to accurately reflect the often harsh facts of modern urban existence.

Utopia: A fictional perfect place, such as "paradise" or "heaven."

Utopian: See *Utopia*

Utopianism: See *Utopia*

V

Verisimilitude: Literally, the appearance of truth. In literary criticism, the term refers to aspects of a work of literature that seem true to the reader.

Vers de societe: See *Occasional Verse*

Vers libre: See *Free Verse*

Verse: A line of metered language, a line of a poem, or any work written in verse.

Versification: The writing of verse. Versification may also refer to the meter, rhyme, and other mechanical components of a poem.

Victorian: Refers broadly to the reign of Queen Victoria of England (1837-1901) and to anything with qualities typical of that era. For example, the qualities of smug narrowmindedness, bourgeois materialism, faith in social progress, and priggish morality are often considered Victorian. This stereotype is contradicted by such dramatic intellectual developments as the theories of Charles Darwin, Karl Marx, and Sigmund Freud (which stirred strong debates in England) and the critical attitudes of serious Victorian writers like Charles Dickens and George Eliot. In literature, the Victorian Period was the great age of the English novel, and the latter part of the era saw the rise of movements such as decadence and symbolism.

Victorian Age: See *Victorian*

Victorian Period: See *Victorian*

W

Weltanschauung: A German term referring to a person's worldview or philosophy.

Weltschmerz: A German term meaning "world pain." It describes a sense of anguish about the nature of existence, usually associated with a melancholy, pessimistic attitude.

Z

Zarzuela: A type of Spanish operetta.

Zeitgeist: A German term meaning "spirit of the time." It refers to the moral and intellectual trends of a given era.

Cumulative Author/Title Index

Dunbar, Paul Laurence
  A Golden Day: V49
  Sympathy: V33
  We Wear the Mask: V40
Duncan, Robert
  An African Elegy: V13
Dunn, Stephen
  The Reverse Side: V21
Duration (Paz): V18

E

The Eagle (Tennyson): V11
Early in the Morning (Lee): V17
Earth Tremors Felt in Missouri (Van
  Duyn): V48
Easter 1916 (Yeats): V5
Easter Wings (Herbert): V43
Eating Poetry (Strand): V9
Ego-Tripping (Giovanni): V28
*Elegy for My Father, Who is Not
  Dead* (Hudgins): V14
*Elegy Written in a Country
  Churchyard* (Gray): V9
*An Elementary School Classroom in a
  Slum* (Spender): V23
Elena (Mora): V33
Eliot, T. S.
  The Hollow Men: V33
  Journey of the Magi: V7
  *The Love Song of J. Alfred
    Prufrock:* V1
  The Waste Land: V20
Emerson, Claudia
  *My Grandmother's Plot in the
    Family Cemetery:* V27
Emerson, Ralph Waldo
  Concord Hymn: V4
  The Rhodora: V17
  The Snow-Storm: V34
The Emigrant Irish (Boland): V47
The Emperor of Ice-Cream (Stevens):
  V49
The End and the Beginning
  (Szymborska): V41
Enlightenment (Trethewey): V52
Erdrich, Louise
  Bidwell Ghost: V14
  *Indian Boarding School: The
    Runaways:* V43
The Erlking (Goethe): V48
Espada, Martín
  Colibrí: V16
  My Father as a Guitar: V43
  We Live by What We See at Night:
    V13
*The Esquimos Have No Word for
  "War"* (Oliver): V45
Ethics (Pastan): V8
Evans, Mari
  When In Rome: V36

Everything is Plundered
  (Akhmatova): V32
The Exhibit (Mueller): V9
Exile (Alvarez): V39
The Explorer (Brooks): V32

F

Fable (Paz): V49
Fable for When There's No Way Out
  (Dao): V38
Facing It (Komunyakaa): V5
Fading Light (Creeley): V21
Falling Upon Earth (Bashō): V2
A Far Cry from Africa (Walcott): V6
A Farewell to English (Hartnett): V10
Farrokhzaad, Faroogh
  A Rebirth: V21
Fear (Mistral): V37
A Felicitous Life (Miłosz): V49
Fenton, James
  The Milkfish Gatherers: V11
Ferlinghetti, Lawrence
  Christ Climbed Down: V28
  Constantly Risking Absurdity: V41
Fern Hill (Thomas): V3
Fiddler Crab (Jacobsen): V23
Fifteen (Stafford): V2
Filling Station (Bishop): V12
Finch, Anne
  A Nocturnal Reverie: V30
Fire and Ice (Frost): V7
First Thought (Cervantes): V51
The Fish (Bishop): V31
The Fish (Moore): V14
The Floral Apron (Chin): V41
Flounder (Trethewey): V39
The Fly (Blake): V34
Fog (Sandburg): V50
Follower (Heaney): V30
*For a New Citizen of These United
  States* (Lee): V15
For An Assyrian Frieze (Viereck):
  V9
*For Jean Vincent D'abbadie, Baron
  St.-Castin* (Nowlan): V12
For Jennifer, 6, on the Teton (Hugo):
  V17
For the Sake of Strangers (Laux):
  V24
For the Union Dead (Lowell): V7
*For the White poets who would be
  Indian* (Rose): V13
For the Young Who Want To
  (Piercy): V40
*The Force That Through the Green
  Fuse Drives the Flower*
  (Thomas): V8
Forché, Carolyn
  The Colonel: V43
  The Garden Shukkei-en: V18
The Forest (Stewart): V22

The Forge (Heaney): V41
400-Meter Freestyle (Kumin): V38
Four Mountain Wolves (Silko): V9
Fragment 2 (Sappho): V31
Fragment 16 (Sappho): V38
Fragment 34 (Sappho): V44
Francis, Robert
  Catch: V50
  The Base Stealer: V12
Fraser, Kathleen
  *Poem in Which My Legs Are
    Accepted:* V29
Freeway 280 (Cervantes): V30
From the Rising of the Sun (Miłosz):
  V29
Frost at Midnight (Coleridge): V39
Frost, Robert
  Acquainted with the Night: V35
  After Apple Picking: V32
  Birches: V13
  The Death of the Hired Man: V4
  Fire and Ice: V7
  Home Burial: V41
  Mending Wall: V5
  Nothing Gold Can Stay: V3
  Once by the Pacific: V47
  Out, Out—: V10
  The Road Not Taken: V2
  *Stopping by Woods on a Snowy
    Evening:* V1
  The Wood-Pile: V6
Fu, Tu
  Jade Flower Palace: V32
Fully Empowered (Neruda): V33
Fulton, Alice
  Art Thou the Thing I Wanted:
    V25
Funeral Blues (Auden): V10

G

Gacela of the Dark Death (García
  Lorca): V20
Gallagher, Tess
  I Stop Writing the Poem: V16
García Lorca, Federico
  Gacela of the Dark Death: V20
  The Guitar: V38
  *Lament for Ignacio Sánchez
    Mejías:* V31
  Romance sonámbulo: V50
The Garden Shukkei-en (Forché):
  V18
Geometry (Dove): V15
Ghazal (Spires): V21
Ghost of a Chance (Rich): V39
Gibran, Kahlil
  Defeat: V51
The Gift (Lee): V37
Ginsberg, Allen
  Howl: V29
  A Supermarket in California: V5

Cumulative Nationality/Ethnicity Index

Cumulative Nationality/Ethnicity Index

Cumulative Nationality/Ethnicity Index

Subject/Theme Index

Cumulative
Index of First Lines

Cumulative Index of Last Lines

and clothes, tobacco crumbs, vases and fringes (The Bean Eaters) V2:16

as we crossed the field, I told her. (The Centaur) V30:20

As what he loves may never like too much. (On My First Son) V33:166

at home in the fish's fallen heaven (Birch Canoe) V5:31

away, pedaling hard, rocket and pilot. (His Speed and Strength) V19:96

B

back towards me. (The Cord) V51:34–35)

Back to the play of constant give and change (The Missing) V9:158

Beautiful & dangerous. (Slam, Dunk, & Hook) V30:176–177

Before God's last *Put out the Light* was spoken. (Once by the Pacific) V47:195–196

Before it was quite unsheathed from reality (Hurt Hawks) V3:138

Before they started, he and she, to play. (The Guitarist Tunes Up) V48:115

before we're even able to name them. (Station) V21:226–227

behind us and all our shining ambivalent love airborne there before us. (Our Side) V24:177

Bi-laterally. (Legal Alien) V40:125

Black like me. (Dream Variations) V15:42

Bless me (Hunger in New York City) V4:79

bombs scandalizing the sanctity of night. (While I Was Gone a War Began) V21:253–254

But a dream within a dream? (A Dream within a Dream) V42:80

But, baby, where are you?" (Ballad of Birmingham) V5:17

But be (Ars Poetica) V5:3

But endure, even this grief of love. (He Seems to Be a God) V52:76

But for centuries we have longed for it. (Everything Is Plundered) V32:34

but it works every time (Siren Song) V7:196

but the truth is, it is, lost to us now. (The Forest) V22:36–37

But there is no joy in Mudville— mighty Casey has "Struck Out." (Casey at the Bat) V5:58

But we hold our course, and the wind is with us. (On Freedom's Ground) V12:187

by a beeswax candle pooling beside their dinnerware. (Portrait of a Couple at Century's End) V24:214–215

by good fortune (The Horizons of Rooms) V15:80

By the light of the moon. (So We'll Go No More a Roving) V52:232–233

C

Calls through the valleys of Hall. (Song of the Chattahoochee) V14:284

cherry blossoms (A Beautiful Girl Combs Her Hair) V48:20

chickens (The Red Wheelbarrow) V1:219

clear water dashes (Onomatopoeia) V6:133

clenched in his stranger's fever. (Ah Mah) V46:19

Columbia. (Kindness) V24:84–85

Come, my *Corinna*, come, let's goe a Maying. (Corinna's Going A-Maying) V39:6

come to life and burn? (Bidwell Ghost) V14:2

comfortless, so let evening come. (Let Evening Come) V39:116

Comin' for to carry me home (Swing Low Sweet Chariot) V1:284

coming out. All right? Mama might worry. (To My Brother Miguel) V48:225

cool as from underground springs and pure enough to drink. (The Man-Moth) V27:135

crossed the water. (All It Takes) V23:15

D

Dare frame thy fearful symmetry? (The Tyger) V2:263

"Dead," was all he answered (The Death of the Hired Man) V4:44

deep in the deepest one, tributaries burn. (For Jennifer, 6, on the Teton) V17:86

Delicate, delicate, delicate, delicate—now! (The Base Stealer) V12:30

delicate old injuries, the spines of names and leaves. (Indian Boarding School: The Runaways) V43:102

designed to make the enemy nod off. (The History Teacher) V42:101

Die soon (We Real Cool) V6:242

dispossessed people. We have seen it. (Grace) V44:68

Do what you are going to do, I will tell about it. (I go Back to May 1937) V17:113

Does thy life destroy. (The Sick Rose) V47:211

down from the sky (Russian Letter) V26:181

Down in the flood of remembrance, I weep like a child for the past (Piano) V6:145

Downward to darkness, on extended wings. (Sunday Morning) V16:190

drinking all night in the kitchen. (The Dead) V35:69

Driving around, I will waste more time. (Driving to Town Late to Mail a Letter) V17:63

dry wells that fill so easily now (The Exhibit) V9:107

dust rises in many myriads of grains. (Not like a Cypress) V24:135

dusty as miners, into the restored volumes. (Bonnard's Garden) V25:33

E

endless worlds is the great meeting of children. (60) V18:3

Enjoy such liberty. (To Althea, From Prison) V34:255

Eternal, unchanging creator of earth. Amen (The Seafarer) V8:178

Eternity of your arms around my neck. (Death Sentences) V22:23

even as it renders us other to each other. (Enlightenment) V52:35

even as it vanishes—were not our life. (The Litany) V24:101–102

ever finds anything more of immortality. (Jade Flower Palace) V32:145

every branch traced with the ghost writing of snow. (The Afterlife) V18:39

F

fall upon us, the dwellers in shadow (In the Land of Shinar) V7:84

Fallen cold and dead (O Captain! My Captain!) V2:147

False, ere I come, to two, or three. (Song) V35:237

father. (Grape Sherbet) V37:110

filled, never. (The Greatest Grandeur) V18:119

Firewood, iron-ware, and cheap tin trays (Cargoes) V5:44

Fled is that music:—Do I wake or sleep? (Ode to a Nightingale) V3:229

In ghostlier demarcations, keener sounds. (The Idea of Order at Key West) V13:164

In hearts at peace, under an English heaven (The Soldier) V7:218

In her tomb by the side of the sea (Annabel Lee) V9:14

in the family of things. (Wild Geese) V15:208

in the grit gray light of day. (Daylights) V13:102

In the rear-view mirrors of the passing cars (The War Against the Trees) V11:216

In these Chicago avenues. (A Thirst Against) V20:205

in this bastion of culture. (To an Unknown Poet) V18:221

in winter. (Ode to My Socks) V47:173–174

in your unsteady, opening hand. (What the Poets Could Have Been) V26:262

Inns are not residences. (Silence) V47:231

iness (l(a) V1:85

Into blossom (A Blessing) V7:24

Is breaking in despair. (The Slave Mother) V44:213

Is Come, my love is come to me. (A Birthday) V10:34

is love—that's all. (Two Poems for T.) V20:218

is safe is what you said. (Practice) V23:240

is going too fast; your hands sweat. (Another Feeling) V40:3

is still warm (Lament for the Dorsets) V5:191

It asked a crumb—of Me ("Hope" Is the Thing with Feathers) V3:123

It had no mirrors. I no longer needed mirrors. (I, I, I) V26:97

It hasn't let up all morning. (The Cucumber) V41:81

It is always brimming May. (A Golden Day) V49:129

It is Margaret you mourn for. (Spring and Fall: To a Young Girl) V40:236

It is our god. (Fiddler Crab) V23:111–112

it is the bell to awaken God that we've heard ringing. (The Garden Shukkei-en) V18:107

it over my face and mouth. (An Anthem) V26:34

It rains as I write this. Mad heart, be brave. (The Country Without a Post Office) V18:64

It takes life to love life. (Lucinda Matlock) V37:172

It was your resting place." (Ah, Are You Digging on My Grave?) V4:2

it's always ourselves we find in the sea (maggie & milly & molly & may) V12:150

its bright, unequivocal eye. (Having it Out with Melancholy) V17:99

It's funny how things blow loose like that. (Snapping Beans) V50:244–245

It's the fall through wind lifting white leaves. (Rapture) V21:181

its youth. The sea grows old in it. (The Fish) V14:172

J

Judge tenderly—of Me (This Is My Letter to the World) V4:233

Just imagine it (Inventors) V7:97

K

kisses you (Grandmother) V34:95

L

Laughing the stormy, husky, brawling laughter of Youth, half-naked, sweating, proud to be Hog Butcher, Tool Maker, Stacker of Wheat, Player with Railroads and Freight Handler to the Nation (Chicago) V3:61

Learn to labor and to wait (A Psalm of Life) V7:165

Leashed in my throat (Midnight) V2:131

Leaving thine outgrown shell by life's un-resting sea (The Chambered Nautilus) V24:52–53

Let my people go (Go Down, Moses) V11:43

Let the water come. (America, America) V29:4

life, our life and its forgetting. (For a New Citizen of These United States) V15:55

Life to Victory (Always) V24:15

like a bird in the sky ... (Ego-Tripping) V28:113

like a shadow or a friend. *Colombia.* (Kindness) V24:84–85

like it better than being loved. (For the Young Who Want To) V40:50

Like nothing else in Tennessee. (Anecdote of the Jar) V41:3

Like Stone— (The Soul Selects Her Own Society) V1:259

like the evening prayer. (My Father in the Navy) V46:87

Little Lamb, God bless thee. (The Lamb) V12:135

Look'd up in perfect silence at the stars. (When I Heard the Learn'd Astronomer) V22:244

love (The Toni Morrison Dreams) V22:202–203

Love is best! (Love Among the Ruins) V41:248

Loved I not Honour more. (To Lucasta, Going to the Wars) V32:291

Luck was rid of its clover. (Yet we insist that life is full of happy chance) V27:292

M

'Make a wish, Tom, make a wish.' (Drifters) V10: 98

make it seem to change (The Moon Glows the Same) V7:152

May be refined, and join the angelic train. (On Being Brought from Africa to America) V29:223

may your mercy be near. (Two Eclipses) V33:221

midnight-oiled in the metric laws? (A Farewell to English) V10:126

Monkey business (Business) V16:2

More dear, both for themselves and for thy sake! (Tintern Abbey) V2:250

More simple and more full of pride. (I Am Not One of Those Who Left the Land) V36:91

must always think good thoughts. (Letter to My Wife) V38:115

My foe outstretchd beneath the tree. (A Poison Tree) V24:195–196

My love shall in my verse ever live young (Sonnet 19) V9:211

My skin alive with the pitch. (Annunciation Overheard from the Kitchen) V49:24

My soul has grown deep like the rivers. (The Negro Speaks of Rivers) V10:198

My soul I'll pour into thee. (The Night Piece: To Julia) V29:206

N

never to waken in that world again (Starlight) V8:213

newness comes into the world (Daughter-Mother-Maya-Seeta) V25:83

Nirvana is here, nine times out of ten. (Spring-Watching Pavilion) V18:198

the knife at the throat, the death in the metronome (Music Lessons) V8:117

The Lady of Shalott." (The Lady of Shalott) V15:97

The lightning and the gale! (Old Ironsides) V9:172

The lone and level sands stretch far away. (Ozymandias) V27:173

the long, perfect loveliness of sow (Saint Francis and the Sow) V9:222

The Lord survives the rainbow of His will (The Quaker Graveyard in Nantucket) V6:159

The man I was when I was part of it (Beware of Ruins) V8:43

the quilts sing on (My Mother Pieced Quilts) V12:169

The red rose and the brier (Barbara Allan) V7:11

The sea whisper'd me. (Out of the Cradle Endlessly Rocking) V46:125

The self-same Power that brought me there brought you. (The Rhodora) V17:191

The shaft we raise to them and thee (Concord Hymn) V4:30

the skin of another, what I have made is a curse. (Curse) V26:75

The sky became a still and woven blue. (Merlin Enthralled) V16:73

The song of the Lorelei. (The Lorelei) V37:146

The spirit of this place (To a Child Running With Outstretched Arms in Canyon de Chelly) V11:173

The town again, trailing your legs and crying! (Wild Swans) V17:221

the unremitting space of your rebellion (Lost Sister) V5:217

The wide spaces between us. (Poem about People) V44:175

The woman won (Oysters) V4:91

The world should listen then—as I am listening now. (To a Sky-Lark) V32:252

their dinnerware. (Portrait of a Couple at Century's End) V24:214–215

their guts or their brains? (Southbound on the Freeway) V16:158

Then chiefly lives. (Virtue) V25:263

There are blows in life, so hard ... I just don't know! (The Black Heralds) V26:47

There in the fragrant pines and the cedars dusk and dim. (When Lilacs Last In the Dooryard Bloom'd) V51:265–269

There is the trap that catches noblest spirits, that caught— they say— God, when he walked on earth (Shine, Perishing Republic) V4:162

there was light (Vancouver Lights) V8:246

They also serve who only stand and wait." ([On His Blindness] Sonnet 16) V3:262

They also serve who only stand and wait." (When I Consider (Sonnet XIX)) V37:302

They are going to some point true and unproven. (Geometry) V15:68

They are the watchful eyes of future generations. (The Answer) V52:3

They have not sown, and feed on bitter fruit. (A Black Man Talks of Reaping) V32:21

They rise, they walk again (The Heaven of Animals) V6:76

They say a child with two mouths is no good. (Pantoun for Chinese Women) V29:242

They think I lost. I think I won (Harlem Hopscotch) V2:93

they *touch* you. They fill you like music. (What Are Friends For) V41:305

They'd eaten every one." (The Walrus and the Carpenter) V30:258–259

This bed thy centre is, these walls thy sphere. (The Sun Rising) V47:247

this is a beautiful way) (who are you,little i) V47:283

This is my page for English B (Theme for English B) V6:194

This Love (In Memory of Radio) V9:145

Tho' it were ten thousand mile! (A Red, Red Rose) V8:152

Thou mayst love on, through love's eternity. (If Thou Must Love Me) V46:72

Though I sang in my chains like the sea (Fern Hill) V3:92

Through the narrow aisles of pain. (Solitude) V49:256

Thus mayest thou ever, evermore rejoice. (Dejection: An Ode) V51:68–69)

Till human voices wake us, and we drown (The Love Song of J. Alfred Prufrock) V1:99

Till Love and Fame to nothingness do sink (When I Have Fears that I May Cease to Be) V2:295

Till the gossamer thread you fling catch somewhere, O my soul. (A Noiseless Patient Spider) V31:190–91

To an admiring Bog! (I'm Nobody! Who Are You?) V35:83

To be a queen! (Fear) V37:71

To beat real iron out, to work the bellows. (The Forge) V41:158

To every woman a happy ending (Barbie Doll) V9:33

To find they have flown away? (The Wild Swans at Coole) V42:287

To find out what it really means. (Introduction to Poetry) V50:167

to float in the space between. (The Idea of Ancestry) V36:138

to glow at midnight. (The Blue Rim of Memory) V17:39

to its owner or what horror has befallen the other shoe (A Piéd) V3:16

To live with thee and be thy love. (The Nymph's Reply to the Shepherd) V14:241

To mock the riddled corpses round Bapaume. ("Blighters") V28:3

To see the cherry hung with snow. (Loveliest of Trees, the Cherry Now) V40:160

To strengthen whilst one stands." (Goblin Market) V27:96

To strive, to seek, to find, and not to yield (Ulysses) V2:279

To the moaning and the groaning of the bells (The Bells) V3:47

To the temple, singing. (In the Suburbs) V14:201

To wound myself upon the sharp edges of the night? (The Taxi) V30:211–212

too. (Birdfoot's Grampa) V36:21

torn from a wedding brocade. (My Mother Combs My Hair) V34:133

Tread softly because you tread on my dreams. (He Wishes for the Cloths of Heaven) V51:125–126

Turned to that dirt from whence he sprung. (A Satirical Elegy on the Death of a Late Famous General) V27:216

U

Undeniable selves, into your days, and beyond. (The Continuous Life) V18:51